Contract Law in Lithuania

Contract Law in Lithuania

Second Edition

Laurynas Didžiulis

This book was originally published as a monograph in the International Encyclopaedia of Laws/Contracts.

Founding Editor: Roger Blanpain
General Editor: Frank Hendrickx
Volume Editor: Jacques Herbots

Wolters Kluwer

Published by:
Kluwer Law International B.V.
PO Box 316
2400 AH Alphen aan den Rijn
The Netherlands
E-mail: lrs-sales@wolterskluwer.com
Website: www.wolterskluwer.com/en/solutions/kluwerlawinternational

Sold and distributed by:
Wolters Kluwer Legal & Regulatory U.S.
920 Links Avenue
Landisville, PA 17538
United States of America
E-mail: customer.service@wolterskluwer.com

ISBN 978-94-035-2886-1

e-Book: ISBN 978-94-035-3066-6
web-PDF: ISBN 978-94-035-3076-5

The Author

Dr Laurynas Didžiulis is an active figure in Lithuanian civil law theory and practice. As a legal scholar, Dr Laurynas Didžiulis holds PhD in Private Enforcement of EU Financial Regulation, is an associate professor at Vilnius University and a member of the Institute of Comparative Private Law. He was a visiting scholar at Ghent University and has delivered lectures at various European universities. Dr Laurynas Didžiulis is an author of several books and a number of articles on various problems of civil patrimonial law with particular focus on its intersections with financial regulation. In 2016, Dr Laurynas Didžiulis was recognised by Vilnius University Law Faculty Alumni Society as an exceptional junior scholar. As a legal practitioner, Dr L. Didžiulis is an advocate of civil law, member of Lithuanian Bar and founder of Confidence Law Office. In his legal practice, Dr L. Didžiulis is mostly dealing with contract, property and financial cases. He has almost six years of experience in the Staff of Supreme Court of Lithuania and is a recommended arbitrator at the Vilnius Court of Commercial Arbitration. Dr Laurynas Didžiulis was also a member of the Consumers and Banks Board at the Bank of Lithuania.

The Author

Table of Contents

Table of Contents

List of Abbreviations

BGB	German Civil Code
BW	Dutch Civil Code
CRD	Consumer Rights Directive
CSD	Central Securities Depository
CCP	Lithuanian Code of Civil Procedure
CISG	The United Nations Convention on Contracts for the International Sale of Goods
CMR	Convention on the Contract for the International Carriage of Goods by Road
CCD	Consumer Credit Directive
DvP	Delivery versus Payment
DCD	Digital Content Directive
DCFR	Draft Common Frame of Reference
ECHR	European Court of Human Rights
EMIR	European Market Infrastructure Regulation
ECJ	European Union Court of Justice
EU	European Union
LME	Liberal Market Economy
LVAT	
LCC	Lithuanian Civil Code
MiFID II	Directive 2014/65/EU of the European Parliament and of the Council on markets in financial instruments
NATO	North Atlantic Treaty Organization
MCD	Mortgage Credit Directive
UNIDROIT PICC	UNIDROIT Principles of International Commercial Contracts
UK	United Kingdom of Great Britain and Northern Ireland
UNCITRAL	The United Nations Commission on International Trade Law
UNIDROIT	International Institute for the Unification of Private Law
USSR	Union of Soviet Socialist Republics

List of Abbreviations

US	United States of America
ГК	Russian Civil Code
SGD	Sale of Goods
SPV	Special Purpose Vehicle

General Introduction

§1. The General Background of the Country

I. Geography

1. Territory of the Republic of Lithuania lies on the eastern coast of the Baltic Sea and is the southernmost, largest and most populous Baltic State. The country is predominantly flat, with a few low hills in the western uplands and eastern highlands. Forests cover just over 30% of the country.[1] The total area of the country covers 65,300 km^2, and neighbours are Latvia, Russia, Poland and Belarus. Climate in Lithuania is oceanic/continental with an average temperature of +17°C in July, of –4.9°C in January. However, temperatures can soar up to +30°C in summer, and drop down to –30°C in winter.[2]

II. History

2. Lithuanian lands were united under Grand Duke Mindaugas in 1236, who afterwards became the first and the only Lithuanian King. Over the next century, through alliances and conquest, Lithuania extended its territory to include most of present-day Belarus, Ukraine and Western Russia. By the end of the fourteenth century, Lithuania was the largest state in Europe, ruled by Vytautas the Great. An alliance with Poland in 1386 led the two countries into a personal union with a common ruler. In 1569, Lithuania and Poland formally united into a single dual state, the Polish-Lithuanian Commonwealth. This entity was not sustainable, eventually degraded and survived until 1795 when its remnants were partitioned by surrounding countries. Lithuania regained its independence following World War I but was annexed by the Union of Soviet Socialist Republics (USSR) in 1940 – an action never recognised by the Western countries. On 11 March 1990, Lithuania became the first of the Soviet republics to declare its independence, but Moscow did not recognise this proclamation until September 1991 (following the abortive coup in Moscow). The last Russian troops withdrew in 1993. Lithuania subsequently restructured its economy for integration into Western European institutions; it joined both North Atlantic Treaty Organization (NATO) and the EU in the spring of 2004.

1. *See* http://europa.eu/european-union/about-eu/countries/member-countries/lithuania_en.
2. *See* http://www.lithuania.travel/en-gb/lithuania/common-information-for-tourists/about-the-country/17102.

In January 2014, Lithuania assumed a non-permanent seat on the UN Security Council for the 2014–2015 term; in January 2015, Lithuania joined the eurozone.[3]

III. Political System

3. Lithuania is a unitary semi-presidential constitutional democratic republic, led by the President, who is a general leader and face of the nation, deciding on the strategic issues and leading foreign policy. Lithuania is a member of NATO, EU and Schengen area. Day-to-day management of the national economy is exercised by the Government consisting of Ministers and chaired by the Prime Minister, who usually is the most influential person in State economic policy. The Parliament of Lithuania ('Seimas') is a very important institution, since it has the exclusive delegated authority to issue statutory acts – 'laws' ('*įstatymai*') and 'constitutional laws' ('*konstituciniai įstatymai*') – to whom all other legal acts, single exception being only the Constitution, should be subordinated. Also, Lithuania has Constitutional Court and judicial system consisting of general competence courts and administrative courts, which enforce laws and provide justice.

IV. Economy

4. After the country has declared independence from the Soviet Union in 1990, Lithuania faced an initial dislocation that is typical during transitions from a planned economy to a free market economy. Macroeconomic stabilisation policies, including privatisation of most state-owned enterprises, and a strong commitment to a currency board arrangement led to an open and rapidly growing economy and rising consumer demand. Foreign investment and EU funding aided in the transition. Lithuania joined the World Trade Organization (WTO) in May 2001, the EU in May 2004, and the Eurozone in January 2015 and in May 2018 was invited to join the OECD. The Lithuanian economy was severely hit by the 2008–2009 global financial crisis, but it has rebounded and become one of the fastest growing in the EU. Increases in exports, investment and wage growth that supported consumption helped the economy grow by 3.6% in 2017. In 2015, Russia was Lithuania's largest trading partner, followed by Poland, Germany and Latvia; goods and services trade between the United States (US) and Lithuania totalled USD 2.2 billion. Lithuania's ongoing recovery hinges on improving the business environment, especially by liberalising labour laws, and improving competitiveness and export growth, the latter of which has been hampered by economic slowdowns in the EU and Russia. In addition, a steady outflow of young and highly educated people is causing a shortage of skilled labour. Lithuania opened a self-financed liquefied natural gas terminal in January 2015, providing the first non-Russian supply of natural gas to the Baltic States and reducing Lithuania's dependence on Russian gas from 100% to approximately 30% in 2016.[4]

---

3. *See* https://www.cia.gov/the-world-factbook/countries/lithuania/
4. *Ibid.*

5. Lithuanian financial system is based on bank financing and clearly follows continental ('Rhenish') European model with the particularity that although capital markets are nominally secondary source of finance, in fact, they are tiny in size and poorly developed. This is a shortcoming, but at the same time an unexploited financial business opportunity, taking into account that real economy which could potentially be serviced by the financial markets in Lithuania is much more developed and bigger. Possible transformation of financial system was expected to be catalysed also by the recent Government policy, which focused on attracting FinTech start-ups to establish businesses in Lithuania. However, since it tends to attract risky (sometimes even 'toxic') businesses, the policy now is shifted back to stricter supervision.

6. Having said that about the Lithuanian financial system, one can be surprised that, under the terms of 'Varieties of Capitalism' (first proposed by political economists Peter A. Hall and David Soskice),[5] in general, Lithuanian economy is usually classified as being closer not to the coordinated market economy (CME), but to the liberal market economy (LME) of Central and Eastern Europe.[6] Social institutions, characteristic to LME, playing a substantial role in Lithuania are: the predominance of shareholder interests in corporate governance bodies, competition of prices in the product market, hierarchical corporate leadership, high employee mobility, flexible, informal institutional practices of industrial relations, flexible wage determination (with the exception of the minimum monthly wage) and general skills-oriented higher education. On the other side, Lithuania did not yet achieve all the attributes of a mature LME, which functions in Anglo-Saxon countries. Despite possibilities given by law, in practice, Lithuanian economy still lacks contemporary corporate governance, dispersed corporate ownership, developed capital market and liberal formal institutional rules of industrial relations. It should be noted that recently an important part of the political agenda has become 'orientation to the North' or 'northward', which is one of the recent examples of such a discourse on the political economy of Lithuania. However, this approach was disputed in Lithuanian scholarship on the ground that objective institutional terms for approaching this type of capitalism are unfavourable and still are more favourable for the development of institutions characteristic to the LME.[7]

---

5. P.A. Hall, D. Soskice. *Varieties of Capitalism: The Institutional Foundations of Comparative Advantage*. Oxford: Oxford Scholarship Online, 2003.
6. Ralph M. Wrobel. *From Independence to the Euro Introduction: Varieties of Capitalism in the Baltic States*. *In.* Central and Eastern European Journal of Management and Economics. Vol. 3, No. 1, 2015, p. 9–38; and Zenonas Norkus. *Lietuva tarp Estijos ir Slovėnijos: dėl pokomunistinio kapitalizmo tipologinės diferenciacijos*. *In.* Politologija, Nr. 1 (49), p. 75.
7. Marius Kalanta. *Kapitalizmo Lietuvoje tipologinė analizė institucinės kaitos diskurso aspektu*. Doctoral Dissertation. Social sciences, Sociology (05 S). Vytautas Magnus University. Kaunas, 2015, p. 82, 231–233.

V. Demography

7. Several significant waves of emigration – the first one which has started after accession to the EU internal market and the second one in line with depreciated economic terms during the global financial crisis of 2008 – recently decreased Lithuanian population below 3,000,000. Ethnicity of Lithuanian habitants now consists of 83.5% of Lithuanians, 6.7% of Poles, 6.3% of Russians, 1.2% of Belarusians and 2.3% of other ethnical groups. Despite the fact that religion in Lithuania is predominantly Roman Catholic (approximately 80% of the total population), Lithuania was always a religiously tolerant country, and there are a variety of other religious communities, such as Orthodox, Old Believers, Lutheran, Reformat, Jewish, Sunni and Karaite.[8]

VI. Business Manners

8. Regarding Lithuanian business etiquette, it is worth knowing that in many ways this is still a hierarchical culture, so showing respect and deference to people of authority is recommended. Although they are industrious and hardworking, most Lithuanians are very modest. People who brag are deemed arrogant. The most common greeting there is a handshake, with direct eye contact, and a smile. Table manners are quite relaxed, but business meetings are formal. Lithuanians prefer face-to-face meetings, as they need to build relationships of mutual understanding and even prefer to turn business relationships into friendships. Once a friendship has developed, Lithuanians are willing to discuss business. Meetings often conclude with a summary of the discussion and a toast to future dealings. Business moves slowly due to the bureaucratic nature of society. However, it is important not to display anger, even if frustrated by the excessive bureaucracy. Lithuanians will not be rushed into making a deal. They must think it is in their best interest before agreeing.[9]

§2. Legal Tradition and Hierarchy of Sources

9. Transition of Lithuanian economy from Soviet-style communism to Western-style capitalism was naturally followed by the fundamental legal reforms and recodification of private law, necessarily transforming the legal system from Soviet socialist to democratic Western tradition. However, description of Lithuanian jurisdiction as democratic and Western is too general and tells only about the *ideology*,

8. *See* http://www.lithuania.travel/en-gb/lithuania/common-information-for-tourists/about-the-country/17102.
9. *See* http://www.commisceo-global.com/country-guides/lithuania-guide.

which is in fact common to all democratic countries. Therefore, we should consider not only ideology but also all classic comparative criteria for the classification of legal systems.[10]

10. Historically, Lithuania has always been, even in the Soviet period, civil law jurisdiction.

11. Hierarchy of legal sources in Lithuanian law is continental, although not very typical and crystal clear. Primary and most important sources of national law in Lithuania are statutes: first and foremost, written Constitution; second, parliamentary promulgated constitutional laws and ordinary laws; and third, lower regulation adopted by Government and other public agencies within the boundaries fixed by higher legislation (laws). Since Lithuanian courts do not have constitutional legitimacy to create law, at least in theory, case law plays only a secondary role and generally has interpretive, not lawmaking, character.[11] In legal practice, however, it is a much more significant legal source, especially practice of Constitutional Court which from time to time declares disputed acts of Parliament or Government as anticonstitutional and not applicable afterwards. Case law of ordinary courts is less dramatic as it just shapes the content of statutory rules or establishes new lines in legal interpretation, but not to the extent reachable for the Constitutional Court. *Contra legem* decisions of ordinary courts, stemming not from legal error,[12] but based on open stance against statute,[13] are extremely rare. Nevertheless, one of the most notable examples is surprise introduction of administrative contract law solely by the case law of administrative courts and without any statutory ground.[14] Having this in mind, it is highly advised to check the relevant case law before concluding any significant transaction or taking legal action in Lithuania.

10. *See* Konrad Zweigert; Hein Kötz. *An Introduction to Comparative Law.* Clarendon Press, 1998, p. 63–73.
11. *See* Valentinas Mikelenas, *et al. Civilinė teisė. Bendroji dalis.* Justitia, 2009, p. 47. Interestingly, limitation on court's power to create rules was imposed by Court of Justice of European Union (ECJ) in Joined Cases C-688/15 and C-109/16, regarding Snoras securities. ECJ in judgment of 22 Mar. 2018 has ruled that in a situation where claims fall within both the deposit-guarantee schemes provided for by Directive 94/19/EC of the European Parliament and of the Council of 30 May 1994 on deposit-guarantee schemes and the investor-compensation schemes provided for by Directive 97/9/EC of the European Parliament and of the Council of 3 Mar. 1997 on investor-compensation schemes, and the national legislature has not directed such claims to a scheme under one or other of those directives, *the court dealing with the case may not decide itself*, on the basis of that provision, which scheme the holders of those claims may benefit from. On the contrary, in such a situation it falls to the holders of the claims to choose to be compensated by one or other of the schemes laid down *in* national *law* to implement those two directives. Thus, it goes from above, that in eyes of ECJ, court judgments are not part of law.
12. For instance, Lithuanian Supreme Court in several cases has been reluctant to characterise retail investors as consumers, despite approval of consumers status for retail investors (which, of course, fall into the concept of consumer) in EU legislation and even *expressis verbis* characterisation in ECJ judgment of 28 Jan. 2015 in case *Kolassa v. Barclays Bank* (C-375/13) of retail investor as a consumer. *See* Judgments of the Lithuanian Supreme Court of 29 Sep. 2014 in the civil case No 3K-3-446/2014 and of 15 May 2015 in the civil case No 3K-7-168-687/2015.
13. Judgment of the Lithuanian Supreme Court of 5 Jan. 1998 m. in the civil case No 3K-1/1998.
14. Judgment of the Senior Administrative Court of Lithuania of 25 Nov. 2005 in the administrative case A-14-1479-05.

12. Predominant legal thought in Lithuanian law has been also a continental one. In particular, Lithuanian legal thinking operates in the environment of highly sophisticated and systematic legal codes, which include such broad notions as reasonableness, good faith and abuse of rights. No need to say that in order to properly apply the law, judges and lawyers need to learn and use abstract systemic thinking. Despite this, one can notice slight influences from common law, stemming, first, from comparative jurisprudence, which affects the process of modern legislation and, second, from legal practice because leading business law firms in Lithuania are highly Westernised and usually follow trends from UK and US legal industries.

13. In terms of distinctive legal institutions, fundamental structures of Lithuanian civil law can be characterised as having attributes close to the French legal family. Lithuanian Civil Code (LCC) and other sources of law acknowledge: very broad scope of property law objects, including intangible property; unitary concept of ownership; a general theory of obligations based on the multiple sources of obligations; a general rule on tortious liability, enabling recovery of pure economic loss; the principle of non-concurrence of contractual and tortious liability; a general concept of quasi-contracts; the judicial recognition of *contrats administratifs*; the division of unjustified enrichment remedy in two separate claims (*condictio indebiti* and *actio de in rem verso*), the concept of real obligations, strict application of force majeure, prohibition of insolvency set-off, etc. Significant Germanic legal influences also are evident: whole LCC, following the German pandectist approach, is divided into the General part (Book I – General Notions, Book II – Persons) and the Special part (Book III – Family Law, Book IV – Property Law, Book V – Inheritance Law, Book VI – Law of Obligations); intellectual property law is systemically independent from the general property law; all unilateral, bilateral and multilateral lawful acts, which give rise to the civil legal relations, are covered by the single concept of 'transaction' or 'deal' (*sandoris*) in LCC Article 1.63; the formation of contract normally does not require *causa* or consideration; the reformed civil procedure is based on the Austrian 'social model' of civil procedure,[15] which emphasises promptness in legal proceedings, role of active court and, untypically for Lithuanian model of capitalism, very assertive protection of public interest (and in effect – state intervention) in civil matters. Moreover, the reception of prominent common law concepts in Lithuanian law is also present. For example, LCC provides for a possibility of a floating charge (LCC Article 4.177, 4.202), regulates restitution independently from unjustified enrichment law (Article 6.145), gives equitable discretion to the judge in the law of remedies (Article 6.145(2), Article 6.233(4), 6.251(2)), enables disgorgement on the basis of damages (Article 6.249(2)), case law acknowledges the concepts of fiduciary duties[16] and Lithuanian Code of Civil Procedure (CCP) Article 441^3 gives possibility for the group of plaintiffs to submit their contractual remedies in the 'opt in' style class action.

15. Valentinas Mikelėnas, Vytautas Nekrošius, Egidijus Laužikas. *Civilinio proceso teisė. T. 1.* Justitia, 2003, p. 31.
16. *See* Judgment of the Lithuanian Supreme Court of 19 Nov. 2001 in the civil case No 3K-3-1010/2001; Judgment of the Lithuanian Supreme Court of 1 Feb. 2012 in the civil case No 3K-3-19/2012; etc.

14. Overall, Lithuanian legal system can be characterised as civil (continental) law jurisdiction, which in the province of patrimonial law is closest to the style of Romanistic (French) legal family.

§3. Internal Structure and Branches of Lithuanian Law

15. Internal structure of Lithuanian law is best described by using the distinctions of *public law v. private law* and *substantive law v. procedural law*, both of which are recognised in Lithuanian legal doctrine and play an important role in the application and interpretation of law.[17]

I. Private and Public Law

16. According to the type of interest served, whole Lithuanian law is divisible into public law and private law. Public law serves public interest by framing internal structure and organisation of the State, also governs vertical, i.e., based on public authority, relations between the State and private persons. Branches of Lithuanian public law are constitutional law, criminal law, administrative law, social security law and procedural law. A huge amount of economic activities, such as energy, construction and trade in financial markets, today is regulated by the public economic law. Disputes arising from administrative law are adjudicated in the special subsystem of administrative courts (Law on Courts Article 12(4)) and do not belong to the jurisdiction of the general competence courts.

17. Whole private law is substantive in nature and serves private interests by regulating horizontal, i.e., parity based, relations between autonomous private persons (including State acting not as public authority, but as property rights holder or private counterparty). Lithuanian private law branches are civil law, labour law and private international law. Civil law is the core body of private law, which is based on the ideas of good faith, substantial justice, reasonableness, equality of persons' rights, inviolability of property, freedom of contract, non-interference in private relations, legal certainty, proportionality, and legitimate expectations, prohibition of abuse of subjective right, as well as the principles of comprehensive judicial protection of civil rights (LCC Article 1.2, 1.5). Civil law is residual in the sense that other branches of private law are derived from it. It has the general part encompassing very abstract rules common to all private relations, such as legal principles, limitations, transactions, remedies, persons, and special part, which consists of patrimonial law (property law and law of obligations), family law and inheritance law. Law of obligations, again, has general part and special part – contract law, tort

17. For instance, in judgment of 21 Feb. 2001 in the civil case No 3K-3-201/2001, the Lithuanian Supreme Court has ruled that bankruptcy law is part of private law, which supposes disposition (freedom) of parties to opt for civil remedies expressly unprescribed in insolvency law. In judgment of 16 Nov. 2009 in the civil case No 3K-3-500/2009, the Lithuanian Supreme Court has ruled that the bailiff during the execution procedure cannot decide on substantive law issues (in this case on modification of contract), only on procedural issues.

law, law on quasi-contracts and law of statutory civil obligations. As can be noticed, in Lithuania, contract law – one of the core branches of private law – systemically belongs to the law of obligations since contract is bilateral or multilateral legal act which gives rise to the obligations (LCC Article 6.2, 6.154).

18. Characterisation of legal relations is extremely important because the main legal act of Lithuanian private law – LCC – primarily governs only civil relationships, i.e., private economic relationships and related personal relationships, as well as family relationships. In the cases provided for by laws, other personal non-economic relationships shall likewise be regulated by LCC (LCC Article 1.1(1)). However, the provisions established by LCC shall apply to economic relationships based on the legal subordination of persons to state institutions and directly resultant from their exercise of functions of state power (realisation of subordination), or from the performance of persons' obligations established by laws towards the state, or from the infliction of administrative or criminal sanctions established by laws, including relationships in the field of taxation and other obligatory payments or dues to the state or to its institutions, also in the field of the state budget, as well as to any other relationships governed by the provisions of public law to the extent that these relationships are not regulated by the relevant laws, also in the cases when it is expressly prescribed by LCC (LCC Article 1.1(2)). Despite labour relationships are regulated by the Labour Code, LCC Article 1.1(3) prescribes that the provisions of LCC apply to labour relations to the extent that they are not regulated by special laws, i.e., Labour Code.

II. Substantial and Procedural Law

19. Another important classification of Lithuanian law is the division between substantive law and procedural law. Substantive law covers direct regulation of State status and affairs, public order, status of private persons as well as their economic and social relations, while the whole purpose for existence of procedural law is to enforce rights and duties stemming from substantive law. Procedural law replaces individual self-help with State institutions and in effect makes application of substantive law more efficient and uniform. As a rule, all branches of Lithuanian law are substantive in nature, except law of civil procedure, law of administrative procedure, law of criminal procedure and law of constitutional adjudication in Constitutional Court.

§4. Commercial Contracts

20. In contrast with law of core continental jurisdictions – France and Germany, civil law in Lithuania is monistic: LCC encompasses both – rules on general civil relationships and calibrated rules which govern commercial relationships. This legislative decision stands on the proposition that separation between civil law and commercial law, reflected in the title of EU Brussels I bis Regulation,[18] is highly superficial. Modern trend in recent codifications, such as in the Netherlands or Canadian province of Quebec, is to abandon this division and regulate all private economic relationships in one code. Thus, commercial contracts (B2B) in Lithuanian law are type of civil contracts next to consumer contracts (B2C) and general civil contracts (C2C).

21. Nevertheless, the division of contracts into the commercial contracts and other civil contracts remains important. For example, parties for the commercial contracts, unlike those of consumer contracts, are permitted to submit their dispute for arbitration in advance (Law on Commercial Arbitration Article 12(2)), only commercial parties may conclude a contract for financial leasing (LCC Article 6.567), only debtors in commercial contract by default should pay enhanced interest rate for late payment, compared to rate set for other contracts in LCC (Law on the Prevention of Late Payment in Commercial Transactions Article 2(5)), etc.

§5. Administrative Contracts

22. Administrative contract is another borderline, but much more controversial, category in Lithuanian law. As the reader may well know, there is no general acceptance of the *contrats administratifs* concept throughout the world. For example, such notable, from the comparative law standpoint, civil law jurisdictions as France, Germany, the Netherlands and Quebec do recognise a separate category of administrative contracts, while in Italy, UK and US, this category is treated as unnecessary and officially inexistent.[19] The latter position, i.e., unitary for all national contracts, was also initially chosen by the drafters of the new LCC, obviously seeking to avoid excessive sophistication and over complication of the new Lithuanian contract law. For this reason, according to LCC Article 6.155, general rules of contract law provided for in LCC shall apply to all contracts taking regard of their nature. Special rules for certain contracts may also be established by other laws of the Republic of Lithuania.

23. Since rules in LCC have laid down only minimal standards of public interest protection in cases when public authority concludes contracts, Lithuanian Senior Administrative Court (LVAT) decided to push the protection of public interest in contractual matters forward. Accordingly, case law of administrative courts, having no direct ground in statutory law and without any national doctrinal background,

18. Regulation (EU) No 1215/2012 of the European Parliament and of the Council of 12 Dec. 2012 on jurisdiction and the recognition and enforcement of judgments in civil and commercial matters.

19. *See* Colin C. Turpin. *International Encyclopedia of Comparative Law.* Vol. VII, ch. 4, 1982, Tübingen: Mohr (Siebeck), The Hague: Nijhoff, p. 27–32; Benedicte Fauvarque-Cosson, Hugh Beale, Jacobien Rutgers, Denis Tallon, Stefan Vogenauer. *Cases, Materials and Text on Contract Law.* 2nd ed., Hart Publishing, 2010, p. 160–168; P. Garant and J. Garant. *Droit administratif.* 6th ed., 2010, p. 349.

surprisingly introduced a new concept in Lithuania, but well known to other civil law jurisdictions – the notion of administrative contract (*administracinė sutartis*).[20]

24. Although the concept of administrative contract as bilateral administrative act, which is used in Lithuanian case law,[21] resembles French model of administrative contract,[22] at least currently the list of administrative contracts in Lithuania is much narrower and in fact closer to the German model. Courts qualify the contract as administrative when the contract is concluded under the mandatory rules of public law, which lay down terms for the performance and the end of the contract, create administrative relationships and seek to fulfil a public interest,[23] in other words, when contract concerns agreement on the realisation of *acta iure imperii*. Under the case law, such contracts are, for example, the contract of general guarantee between the custom and guarantee association,[24] contract for the delegation of right to organise land zoning,[25] tripartite contract between unemployed, employment public agency and private company for the training and employment of unemployed,[26] contract for subsidising the prescribed drugs in drugstores and hospitals from the public funds[27] and contract for the financing from EU structural funds.[28] Other clear candidates for the status of administrative contracts are agreement with tax authority on tax loan, i.e., postponement and allotment of tax obligations (Law on Tax administration Article 2(19)), agreement on exploitation of underground resources, which are exclusive property of State (The Underground Law Article 12), and settlement agreement in administrative litigation (Law on Litigation in Administrative Cases Article 51). In contrast with French law, public procurement contracts,[29] concession contracts, public-private partnerships and contracts concerning state property are not characterised as administrative by Lithuanian courts, thus falling under

20. *In a landmark case, decided just several years after the adoption of new LCC, Lithuanian Senior Administrative Court declared that 'the contract of general guarantee between the custom and guarantee association is not civil contract and relationship stemming from it is domain of public, not civil law. This type of relationship between public agency and private person, where public agency concludes contracts with private persons in pursuit of its statutory functions and in a need to satisfy a public interest, in legal practice of European countries and legal doctrine is called administrative contract. As follows from above, the Custom here is acting not as a civil law person, but as public agency, therefore its actions and decision are administrative acts, which can be disputed under the order and time limits established by the administrative law'. See Judgment of the Lithuanian Senior Administrative Court of 25 Nov. 2005 in the administrative case No A-14-1479-05.*
21. Judgment of the LVAT of 24 Jan. 2017 in the administrative case No eA-424-575/2017.
22. Gytis Kuncevičius. *The Institute of Administrative Contract and Its Theoretical Grounding.* Summary of Doctoral Dissertation Social Sciences, Law (01 S), Mykolas Romeris University, p. 14.
23. Judgment of the LVAT of 6 May. 2008 in the administrative case No A-261-339-08; Judgment of the LVAT of 24 Jan. 2017 in the administrative case No eA-424-575/2017.
24. Judgment of the LVAT of *25 Nov. 2005* in the administrative case No *A-14-1479-05.*
25. Judgment of the LVAT of 3 Jun. 2013 in the administrative case No A-492-829-13.
26. Judgment of the LVAT of 15 Sept. 2016 in the administrative case eA-1578-662/2016.
27. Judgment of the LVAT of 6 May. 2008 in the administrative case No A-261-339-08.
28. Judgment of the LVAT of 14 Mar. 2013 in the administrative case No A-492-118-13.
29. Unfortunately, the regulation on public procurement seems to become so rigid and tight for the private suppliers in Lithuania and in fact pro-Governmental that one even may think about the recharacterisation of public procurement contracts to the public law contracts.

the scope of general civil contract law. However, in the case of public property contracts, the public law clearly dominates against the private law;[30] thus, the characterisation of those contracts as civil is highly debatable.

25. A general feature of administrative contracts is that those contracts should be concluded and performed under the standards laid down by the administrative law, including the unilateral right of public agency to modify terms of the contract and the possibility to agree on terms for the protection of public interest beyond the scope, which is normal for the civil contracts with a private party (clauses exorbitantes).[31] Under the current case law, general rules of civil contract law are applied to the performance of administrative contracts only taking into account the nature and attributes of administrative contracts, which limits freedom of parties.[32] Despite this delimitation, LVAT has affirmed subsidiary application of LCC even for the administrative contracts.[33]

26. Overall, the branch of administrative contracts in Lithuanian law is still evolving and, within the lack of comprehensive statutory regulation, is quite unclear. Although an administrative contract, as an agreement for use of *acta iure imperii*, may seem logical in theory, unclear and unbalanced regulation in practice may lead to the rising power of public bodies in contractual relationships and disregard to the private interests. My fear is that a privileged regime of administrative contract may evolve into the instrument of a self-protectionism of the powerful and interventionist State – alien to the free market economy, being cultivated in independent Lithuania.

30. It is even directly set in Lithuanian Law on the Management, Use and Disposal of State and Municipal Assets Art. 9 as the so-called public law principle, which means that transactions involving state and municipal assets must be concluded only in the cases and manner established by legal acts regulating the disposal of state and/or municipal assets. Therefore, freedom of contract is very limited in such cases.
31. *See* Colin C. Turpin. *International Encyclopedia of Comparative Law.* Vol. VII, ch. 4, 1982, Tübingen: Mohr (Siebeck), The Hague: Nijhoff, p. 27–29; Alan W. Mewett. *The Theory of Government Contracts.* McGill Law Journal, Vol. 5, 1959, p. 226.
32. Judgment of the LVAT of 14 Mar. 2013 in the administrative case No A-492-118-13.
33. Judgment of the LVAT of 6 May 2008 in the administrative case No A-261-339-08.

Introduction to the Law of Contracts

§1. Definition of Contract

27. According to LCC Article 6.154(1), a contract is an agreement of two or more persons to establish, modify or extinguish civil law relationships by which one or several persons obligate themselves to one or several other persons to perform certain actions (or to refrain from performing certain actions), while the latter persons obtain the corresponding claim. This is a general concept of contract, mainly used in civil law.

28. Two other branches of Lithuania law – labour law and administrative law – although in a more limited fashion, also deals with contracts. Therefore, definition presented above is not the sole one. Labour Code Article 32(1) defines employment contract as an agreement between employee and employer, under which employee obligates, being subordinate, to fulfil labour function for the benefit of employer, and employer obligates to pay salary in consideration. Also, as has been said before, Lithuanian case law introduced the concept of administrative contract, which in essence is understood as a bilateral administrative act concluded by the public body for the public interest under the public law and giving rise, change or end to the administrative law relationships. However, those special types of contracts concern undisputedly narrower province of contract law; therefore, analysis in this national report will further be carried out mostly about the civil contract law.

§2. Contract and Surrounding Legal Concepts

29. To become familiar with Lithuanian concept of civil contract, it is indispensable to understand its ties with surrounding legal concepts. The first important attribute of a civil contract is that it belongs to the more general category – transaction (*sandoris*). Transaction is defined broadly in LCC Article 1.63(1) as the action of person intended to create, modify or extinguish civil rights and duties. Transaction is species of juridical act (*Rechtsgeschäft, acte juridique*), a concept well known to other civil law jurisdictions. A contract is a bilateral or multilateral transaction,[34] but not unilateral as, for example, will or promissory note, because contract by its nature always must have more than one party. Therefore LCC Article 6.154(2) states that contracts shall be subject to the norms of LCC that regulate bilateral and multilateral transactions. It should be noted that most types of contracts concluded in practice are bilateral, and only few of them, such as joint venture agreements or company charters, are multilateral transactions, when concluded by three or more persons. General civil law rules on transactions are of extreme

34. A transaction is bilateral where the concerted will of two parties is a necessary condition for its formation and multilateral where the concerted will of three or more parties is a necessary condition for its formation (LCC Art. 1.63 (6 and 7)).

importance for the formation of valid contracts, especially those concerning substantial validity, such as error, fraud, illegality and formal requirements of transactions (LCC Article 1.63–1.96).

30. Another important aspect is that contracts in Lithuania are one of the sources of obligations (LCC Article 6.2), and general provisions on obligations shall likewise apply to contracts unless any exceptions are established by contract law itself (LCC Article 6.154(3)). Lithuanian legal doctrine follows classic Romanistic approach to the concept and doctrinal classifications of obligations.[35] Obligation (*prievolė*) by itself is not just a duty, but a whole legal relationship where one party (debtor) is bound to perform for the benefit of another party (creditor) a prescribed action or to refrain therefrom, and the creditor has the right to demand from the debtor the performance of his duty (LCC Article 6.1). Thus, irrespective of the type of obligation (contractual, tortious or other), generic definition of the obligee (active party) is a creditor, while the name of obligor is a debtor (passive party). Obligations which arise from the contracts are called contractual obligations. Other sources of obligations are unilateral transactions (emission of securities, legal tender, public promise of reward, etc.), torts (comprising of general tort and several specific torts), quasi-contracts (unjustified enrichment, performance not due, benevolent intervention) and statutes (the obligation to provide maintenance to minor children, obligation to provide compensation for the expropriation of property, etc.).[36] General law of obligations set in LCC Article 6.1–6.153 defines structural elements and modalities, performance, remedies and extinguishment of all obligations, including contractual obligations.

31. Yet, as the definition in LCC Article 6.154(1) implies, the contract is not only the source of obligations. Statutory definition does not limit contract to the relationships in personam, but indiscriminately concerns all civil law relationships, apparently including relationships *in rem*. Indeed, a civil contract is also one of the main tools for the creation, transfer and destruction of property rights, for example, security transaction (which is usually bilateral and therefore is a contract), creates security interests, such as hypothec (LCC Article 4.175(2)). At the same time, contract, even modifying *ius in rem*, should be distinguished from the act of *traditio*, which is a unilateral proprietary transaction (LCC Article 4.49) and a mode of the transfer of property rights.

35. General theory on obligations is presented in by far the most influential study on this topic in Lithuanian law provided by the academic Prof. V. Mikelėnas in his book *Prievolių teisė. Pirmoji dalis.* Justitia: Vilnius, 2002.

36. It is interesting that multilateral classification of sources prevails in Lithuanian legal thinking even though LCC by itself in Art. 6.2 (replicating Quebec CC Art. 1372) follows bilateral approach dividing obligations into transactional, i.e., stemming from legal acts, and non-transactional, i.e., stemming from other juridical facts. For the excellent overview of European private law on axes of classification according to the source of obligations, *see* Bénédicte Fauvarque-Cosson, Denis Mazeaud, *et al. European Contract Law: Materials for a Common Frame of Reference: Terminology, Guiding Principles, Model Rules.* Sellier, 2008, p. 66–100.

§3. THE ELEMENTS OF CONTRACT

I. Officially Recognised Elements

32. Philosophical background of the contemporary Lithuanian contract law is a classical libertarian theory of the autonomy of will. Consequently, contract law highly relies on the idea of consensualism and tries to abolish any unnecessary impediments to the freedom of choice and enterprise in private deals. For this purpose, law expressly prescribes that the following elements shall be sufficient to render a contract valid: an agreement of legally capable parties, and, when prescribed by laws, also a form of a contract (LCC Article 6.159). For the sake of clarity, a written form is the constituting element of the contract only where non-compliance with it has substantial consequences, i.e., invalidity. Therefore, the elements of the contract under Lithuanian law are at the least: first, an agreement; second, a capacity of all parties to enter the deal; and, third, formalities, where they are prescribed by law. In a more detailed fashion, these notions are disclosed in subsequent chapters of this book; however, Lithuanian notion of agreement needs separate discussion here.

II. Agreement

33. Structurally, the main element of contract under Lithuanian law is not a consent (*consentement*) as such, but broader notion of agreement, which encompasses not only the consent but also other important attributes. To become proper element of the contract, the agreement must: (1) be reached by the consensus, (2) be sufficient and (3) serious. These elements of an agreement at the same are the sub-elements of a contract.

34. Primary defining characteristic of an agreement presents its mechanics – the consensus, which is aligned will of the parties (*suderinta šalių valia*) and should be free from any defects. The criterion flows from the concept of a contract as a bilateral or multilateral transaction, used by the LCC, where contract is defined as transaction where the concerted will of two or more parties is a necessary condition for its formation (LCC Article 1.63(6–7), 6.154(2)). The argument of will is such common and important in Lithuanian doctrinal and judicial reasoning,[37] especially for the interpretation of contracts that one could say that the notion of will is a conceptual core of Lithuanian contract law. Respect of the will of parties requires that the contract should be only formed by mutual consent of both parties, which is usually expressed by the notions of offer and acceptance. The concept of will radiates through the notions of offer and acceptance, which are two separate unilateral voluntary transactions. Thus, a proposal for concluding a contract is qualified as an offer only if it indicates the intention of the offeror (LCC Article 6.167(1)), whereas

37. *See* Judgments of the Lithuanian Supreme Court of 15 May 2006 in the civil case No 3K-3-338/2006, of 4 Jan. 2007 in the civil case No 3K-3-150/2007 and of 25 Aug. 2008 in the civil case No 3K-3-304/2008; Aurimas Brazdeikis, *et al. Civilinė teisė. Bendroji dalis.* Justitia, 2009, p. 318–319.

the acceptance could only be evidenced where a conduct of the offeree indicates the assent to the offer. Silence or inactivity per se shall not imply acceptance of an offer (LCC Article 6.173(1)).

35. Second defining characteristic of an agreement is its sufficiency. This characteristic is about the content of agreement, which should meet the substantial requirement to contain all essential terms, necessary to conclude the contract. According to LCC Article 6.167(1), a proposal for concluding a contract is deemed to be an offer only if it is sufficiently definite. How much definite it should be is explained in LCC Article 6.162(2) according to which, where the parties agree on all essential terms of a contract, the contract shall be effective, even though the parties have reserved an agreement as to secondary terms. Hence, sufficient definite content of the offer even at initial contracting stage requires to clearly define the essential terms of the proposed contract. Failure to agree on essential terms means that the contract was not concluded at all. For instance, according to LCC Article 6.397(1), the price of the immovable being sold must be indicated in the real property sale contract, and if the price is not indicated in the contract, the contract shall be deemed not to have been concluded.

36. Although the particular standards for sufficiency may differ depending on the type of the contract, every contract should always contain the term on the prestation of obligation. A prestation (*prievolės dalykas*) is a subject matter of the obligation, i.e., behaviour of the debtor which is required to perform its obligation towards the creditor. Under LCC Article 6.3, the prestation of an obligation may be any action (active or passive) that is neither forbidden by law nor contrary to public order or good morals. The prestation of an obligation may relate to any property, even future property, provided that the property is determinate as to the kind and quantity or can be determined according to other criteria. The prestation of an obligation may have a monetary or non-monetary expression; it must nevertheless meet the correspondent interest of the creditor that is protected by law. The prestation of an obligation cannot be something that is impossible to perform (*impossibilium nulla obligatio est*). It is clear from the definition of the obligation and rules below that every obligation must have its prestation. In turn, it means that every contract which creates obligations must contain a clear agreement on the obligation, including its prestation. When the prestation of obligation is related to the assets, Lithuanian legal doctrine calls those assets an object of obligation.[38] It means that some types of obligations, i.e., obligations to give assets to the creditor (sales, lease, loan, franchise, gift, etc.), to create (construction and other works contracts) or increase them (trust contracts, etc.), can have prestation as both object *largo sensu* and object *stricto sensu*. However, the mandatory prerequisite of a contract's content is only prestation, while the object (in a narrow sense) only helps to define obligations which concern assets.

37. Third defining characteristic of an agreement is the seriousness expressed by intention to create legal relations, which affects willingness of the State to enforce

38. Valentinas Mikelėnas. *Prievolių teisė. Pirmoji dalis.* Justitia: Vilnius, 2002, p. 48.

them. The criterion of seriousness flows from the statutory definition of a contract, which expressly stresses the agreement to create, alter or end civil law relationships (LCC Article 6.154(1)). This sub-element is also included in the statutory definition of an offer because proposal for concluding a contract shall be deemed to be an offer if it indicates the intention of the offeror to be restricted in his rights by a contract and to be bound in the case of acceptance (LCC Article 6.167(1)). Hence, for the characterisation of an offer according to LCC Article 6.167, one should establish the intention to create legal, not just moral or other, relations. In effect, this requirement discriminates between legally binding agreements and unbinding ('gentlemen') agreements, such as an agreement to go for a date or to pray together. Agreements made for commercial purposes should be presumed as made with the intention to bound, except where parties make disclaimers stressing the non-binding nature of their agreement. Of course, such disclaimers do not prevent the rise of tortious or quasi-contractual obligations in parties' relations, for example, duty to return unjustified enrichment. Domestic agreements with family members and social agreements with friends or acquittances should be presumed as lacking the intention to be legally bound. Coalitions and other national political agreements normally should also lack this sub-element, except where they have pecuniary content presuming intent to create joint venture contract.

III. Question of Cause

38. As far as the relevance of cause (*causa contractus*) in Lithuanian contract law is concerned, the answer is not a straightforward one. The first draft of LCC, indeed, included cause as the necessary element of the contract,[39] but, following modern trend, it has disappeared in the final version of the LCC from the official list of elements.[40] The main reason is that direct function of cause – control of contractual terms to ensure legality and fairness – is performed by the other and more certain rules regarding substantial validity of the transactions, such as legality, public order and good morals, gross disparity, simulation, error, fraud and duress. However, some remnants and direct indications of the *causa contractus* in Lithuanian law still can be found. As it was mentioned below, under LCC Article 6.3, the prestation of an obligation must meet the correspondent interest of the creditor that is protected by law. Where parties agree on matters, which in reality concern no legally protected interest, for example, by simulating transfer of ownership, the contract is void. Even if statutory law at this point were silent, this consequence would naturally flow from the definition of a contract (LCC Article 6.154), which requires to agree on matters which are relevant and regulated by the law. If parties conclude an agreement on matters unregulated by law, for example when agree to go for a

39. Valentinas Mikelėnas. *Sutarčių teisė. Bendrieji sutarčių teisės klausimai: lyginamoji studija.* Vilnius: Justitia, 1996, p. 119.

40. Stasys Drazdauskas. *Bendrosios sutarčių teisės vienodinimo įtaka Lietuvos sutarčių teisei.* Doctoral dissertation (social sciences, law (01 S), Vilnius University, 2011, p. 198). Even French law during recent reforms has abandoned the notion of cause, which was always the iconic element of the French law. Solene Rowan. *The New French Law of Contract. In.* International & Comparative Law Quarterly. British Institute of International and Comparative Law, 2017.

date or cheer each other every day, no obligations arise. However, requirement to meet creditor interest is limited to rare situations where parties simulate or pretend to have contract, therefore, cannot be equated to the full extent effects of the cause doctrine. It is just a very limited fraction of it.

39. Much stronger indication of the cause is found in the general part of Lithuanian civil law regulating all civil transactions. To be precise, its source is not a statutory law, but legal doctrine, which usually makes distinction between causal and abstract transactions. Causal transactions in legal doctrine are defined as transactions which type or content enables to determine direct legal purpose desired by the parties. In other words, from causal transaction, one can see why it has been concluded. Most transactions, including sales, lease and works, according to the prevailing doctrine are called causal. All other transactions, which do not necessarily have apparent purpose or motive, such as promissory note and cheque, are abstract and valid only if so prescribed by law. Thus, the prevailing doctrinal position is that validity of most transactions can be challenged solely on the ground of the lack of cause and they only remain valid if statute lets them be abstract.[41] However, case law on this point is unsettled[42] and the problem is obvious – this position lacks statutory justification, as LCC itself and in general does not require cause neither for validity of transactions nor for the validity of contracts.[43] This position directly confronts LCC Article 6.159, which enlists elements of contract, and the principles of consensualism and *favor contractus*, which give priority to validity of contracts. On the contrary, proper interpretation of Lithuanian civil law should be that cause is prerequisite of transaction only in expressly prescribed cases, where it stems from the LCC.

40. Several notable examples may be presented and distinguished. First – as it flows from systemic analysis of LCC,[44] Lithuanian law has causal model of property transfer, where a cause is necessary requirement for the validity of property transfer (which is a separate unilateral proprietary transaction – *traditio*). The prerequisite for validity of a transfer here is not a *causa contractus* – a contract law concept – but a *causa traditionis* – a property law concept – which is a valid legal ground for the transfer of property. For instance, sales contract is *causa traditionis*, while underlying reason of parties for concluding sales contract would be *causa*

41. V. Staskonis, *et al. Civilinė teisė: vadovėlis.* Kaunas: Vijusta, 1998, p. 187; Aurimas Brazdeikis, *et al. Civilinė teisė. Bendroji dalis.* Justitia, 2009, p. 325–326; Leonas V. Papirtis, *et al. Civilinė teisė: bendroji dalis.* Vol. II, Mykolas Romeris University, 2005, p. 22.
42. Asta Dambrauskaitė, Agnė Tikniūtė, *et al. Lyginamoji sutarčių teisė: Lietuva europiniame kontekste.* Justitia, 2013, p. 46–48.
43. All doctrinal sources presenting this question in Lithuanian law cite or directly rely on Russian jurisprudence, despite that the notion of cause in Russian law has been accepted as the necessary element of contract long time ago (at least from 1835). *See* Olimpiad S. Ioffe. *Soviet civil law.* Kluwer Academic Publishers, 1988, p. 145–146; Christopher Osakwe. *Modern Russian Law of Contracts: A Functional Analysis.* Loyola of Los Angeles International and Comparative Law Review, Vol. 24, 2002, p. 142.
44. LCC Arts 1.63 (1, 3 and 4), 1.80, 1.95, 4.37, 4.39, 4.48 and 4.49(1).

contractus. As it follows from above, only *causa traditionis* would stand as a prerequisite for valid transaction of property transfer, while *causa contractus* remains in a shadow and acts only throughout other rules, such as illegality, gross disparity or simulation.

41. Second example is exceptional and shows strict application of *causa contractus* in Lithuanian law. There is a concept of insurable interest in the insurance law, which in essence is manifestation of a specific contractual cause. Insurable interest relates to the losses that the policyholder, the insured person or the beneficiary may incur upon occurrence of an insured event (Law on Insurance Article 2(14)). In other words, it is an interest to be insured from the losses. According to the Law on Insurance Article 92, a lawful interest of the policyholder or the insured person which may be expressed in money shall be an obligatory condition of an indemnity insurance contract. LCC Article 6.988(4) indiscriminately adds for all types of insurance contracts, including life insurance, that only the interests protected by law may be insured. If, for example, an insured person gets insurance policy which covers an event completely unrelated to him, for example Lithuanian farmer insures Amazon flood, no insurable interest exists if the farmer has no activities related to the Amazon river and cannot suffer loss.

42. There are other examples as well: a contract of novation, which is valid only if original contract, which largely defines *causa contractus* of novation, is also valid (LCC Article 6.141(3)); corresponding obligations in bilateral contracts as a *causa* for each other (a consideration in common law terms); various financial contracts of derivatives tied to an underlying factor, which should be lawful and possible, etc.

43. Summing up, while the fragments of cause are dispersed throughout the entire LCC, the notion of cause is not a general prerequisite for the validity of contract in Lithuanian civil law, therefore division of transactions into causal and abstract serves only explanatory function. Leaving aside some fragmented exceptions, legal effect cause creates only indirectly, i.e., being a basis to the most other contract law doctrines and rules. Seen from this angle, *causa contractus* is a very powerful principle, which indirectly coordinates the whole mechanics of contract law and as such deserves attention in most contractual cases even if no direct effect for it is prescribed by the LCC.

44. Besides purely national considerations, one should also take into account effect of EU financial law on the causality of transactions. Therefore, according to the fifth Money Laundering Directive[45] Article 18(2), notaries, banks, auditors and other obliged entities should examine, as far as reasonably possible, the background and purpose of all transactions that do not have an apparent economic or lawful purpose. It means that even if ordinary contract law does not directly require from the

45. Directive (EU) 2018/843 of the European Parliament and of the Council of 30 May 2018 amending Directive (EU) 2015/849 on the prevention of the use of the financial system for the purposes of money laundering or terrorist financing, and amending Directives 2009/138/EC and 2013/36/EU.

parties to show *causa contractus*, it still should be demonstrated for the notaries, who approve significant civil transactions.

45. Hence, every contract under Lithuanian law must have at least: (1) an agreement (made by mutual alignment of will, with intention to create legal relations and containing all essential terms of the contract, including the prestation of obligation) and (2) capacity of parties to enter the deal. In cases prescribed by law, the contract additionally must satisfy (3) formal terms, and, only in prescribed cases, must demonstrate its (4) cause.

§4. Historical Background of the Law of Contracts

I. Medieval Ages

46. Lithuanian state was established and consolidated in the first part of thirteenth century under the reign of King Mindaugas. In further two centuries, Lithuania arose to great military and political power, becoming the largest country in Europe. Prevailing socioeconomic system of that time in Europe was feudalism, which framed legal relationships around a land. Monarch was the owner of most land and stood at the top of the feudal pyramid, while lesser feudal lords (dukes, noblemen, knights) were its vassals and downstream formed a chain of seignior–vassal relationships by themselves. At the bottom of the pyramid were factual possessors of land – peasants. Peasants had various burdensome obligations towards their seigniors, who in turn had obligations towards their seigniors, etc. All these actors had varying forms of limited property rights over land used by peasants. Lithuanian contract law during feudalism was based on the customs, and contracts were mostly formed orally. At that time, there were only few literate people to write and even they used mainly Slavonic languages.

47. Particularity of medieval times was Magdeburg rights of self-governance in civil matters which were granted to Vilnius, Trakai, Kyiv, Minsk and some other cities by the privilege from Lithuanian Grand Duke. Under municipal laws, citizens were free to enter the contracts and set their terms, including agreement on payment and place of performance. Creditor rights were protected by pledge and suretyship. Contractual obligations did extinguish by proper performance, payment in deposit, assignment of claim, release from the obligation by creditor and in cases where performance was not possible any more due to reasons unrelated to debtor fault. Contracts of sales, loan, lease and works were widespread. Labour agreements were also used. Later, in concert with development of trade, contracts of company, carriage and custody were begun to be used.[46]

---

46. Mindaugas Maksimaitis, Stasys Vansevičius. *Lietuvos valstybės ir teisės istorija*. Justitia, 1997, p. *Ibid*, p. 103.

II. Renaissance

48. In the sixteenth century, during the Renaissance, Lithuanian Grand Duchy adopted remarkable legal achievement – three Lithuanian Statutes of 1529, 1566 and 1588. Those were collections of written legal rules, including the contract law, known and used as legislative example abroad. Statutes introduced formal requirements for conveyancing, i.e., property transfer agreement should be confirmed by noblemen witnesses which names were written down in the contract. Contractual parties with witnesses during conveyancing walked around the parcel of land. Other contracts should also be written down, but failure to meet this requirement did not bring invalidity. Contractual obligations should be performed only personally by the debtor. There was no solidary liability. Thus multiple debtors were liable only severally.[47] This period was graceful for Lithuanian contract law also because in 1641 within Vilnius University Law Faculty was established. One of the first in the faculty was Civil Law Department.

III. Industrial Age

49. Russian Empire along with Austria and Prussia in 1775, 1792 and 1795 three times divided and finally annexed internally weak Polish–Lithuanian Commonwealth. Despite that, Third Statute was applicable until 1840 when Russian laws came into force. The main source of Russian law from 1835 was the Digest of the Laws of the Russian Empire – a set of fifteen volumes with 60,000 articles—that entered into force. The civil law was codified in the tenth volume of the Digest of Laws, which was entitled Civil Laws (*Zakony Grazhdanskyje*) and consisted of four books: (1) *Family Rights and Obligations*; (2) *On the Procedure of Acquisition and Preservation of Property Rights in General*; (3) *On the Procedure of Acquisition and Preservation of Property Rights in Particular*; and (4) *Contractual Obligations*. The sources used by the drafters of the Civil Laws, along with Russian law, were Prussian (*Allgemeines Landrecht für die Preußischen Staaten* 1794), Austrian (*Allgemeines bürgerliches Gesetzbuch* 1810), and French (*Code civil* 1804). Although scholars usually emphasise the influence of the French Code, the less numerous borrowings from the Prussian Code were also rather important.[48] Civil laws emphasised classic principles of contract law – equality and consent of bargaining parties, freedom of contract and *pacta sunt servanda*. Contract formation included cause requirement; it was possible to conclude the contract at the notary.[49]

47. *Ibid*, p. 95. Vladas Staskonis, *et al. Civilinė teisė. Bendroji dalis.* Justitia, 2009, p. 76.
48. Asya Ostroukh. *Russian Society and Its Civil Codes: A Long Way to Civilian Civil Law.* Journal of Civil Law Studies. Vol. 6, 2013, p. 376–377.
49. Mindaugas Maksimaitis, Stasys Vansevičius. *Lietuvos valstybės ir teisės istorija.* Justitia, 1997, p. 196.

IV. Interwar Period

50. On 16 Feb. 1918, when World War I was going to the end and Russian Empire has collapsed, Lithuania declared its independence and Lithuanian State was re-established. During the interwar period in Lithuania, a bunch of different civil laws were still in force: Russian civil laws in the largest part of country, in the region on the left side of Nemunas River – French Code Civil, in the Klaipėda region – German BGB, in the Palanga and Zarasai – separate set of Russian civil laws designed for upper Baltic provinces (Code of laws of Baltic provinces).[50] This was abnormal and Government eventually composed special legislative commission which undertook task to prepare new Civil Code.[51] However, this was just years before World War II during which Lithuania suddenly suffered Soviet occupation, after that Nazi occupation then again Soviet reoccupation. In the aftermath, there was neither space for new Civil Code nor independent Lithuanian State any more.

V. Soviet Occupation

51. During Soviet occupation, Lithuanian economy was forcefully transformed into state command economy driven by the communist principles. Hallmarks of capitalism (which was the main ideological enemy of socialism), namely private property and free market, were eliminated, whereas wealthier people and society's middle class have suffered repressions. The official motto of nationalisation of private property and other reforms was 'a liberation of the working class from the capitalist yoke'. Lithuanian economy now was ruled by central planners, local Soviet loyalists and secret police (NKVD, MGB, KGB) officers. Private law was reframed accordingly – by almost eroding the property law and limiting contracting up to simple unsophisticated transactions.[52] The main source of contract law in Lithuania during Soviet period was Civil Code of 1964, which presented simplified version of European civil law highly diluted by the socialist doctrine. From the angle of juridical technique, Soviet civil law was the closest to the Germanic legal tradition.[53]

50. Mindaugas Maksimaitis. *Pabaltijo gubernijų vietinių įstatymų sąvadas*. Teisė: Mokslo darbai, t. 34, 2000, p. 17.
51. Valentinas Mikelenas. *Unification and Harmonisation of Law at the Turn of the Millennium: The Lithuanian Experience*. Uniform Law Review, Vol. 5, Issue 2, 2000, p. 245–246.
52. Soviet socialist law, according to Christopher Osakwe, totally bastardised European contract law tradition. *See* Christopher Osakwe. *Modern Russian Law of Contracts: A Functional Analysis*. Loyola of Los Angeles International and Comparative Law Review, Vol. 24, 2002, p. 121.
53. First Soviet civil codification has borrowed heavily from German and Swiss law, adding some peculiarly Soviet elements. In many ways, the Code was an improvement of the poorly organised civil law provisions of the Code of Laws of the Russian Empire. The Code was concise, well organised and used simple, clear language. Thus, it was ideal for a time when war, revolution and terror had created a shortage of educated lawyers and judges. The Code generally followed the principles of organisation of the 1900 German BGB. It began with a general part stating principles applicable to all parts of the Code. This section included subsections on dealing with natural and legal persons, things (property), transactions and periods of limitation. A section on obligations included subsections on general principles of obligations and on contracts. It also included subsections dealing with

However, Soviet contract law has retained the Romanic notion of *causa*,[54] which was a very helpful tool to subordinate all contracts under the communist ideology and was a heavy restraint to the freedom of contract. For example, Civil Code Article 5 stated that citizens and organisations, while exercising their rights and performing their duties, must obey laws and respect rules of common socialist life and morality principles of communism constructing society.

VI. Nowadays

52. Coinciding with the economic collapse of USSR, Lithuania regained independence and promptly returned to Western orientation. Extensive economic and legal reforms were unleashed in order to restore private property and market relations.[55] One of the remarkable achievements was adoption of new LCC in 2000, which came into force a year after, i.e., in 2001. LCC was prepared by the best civil law scholars in Lithuania, which were chaired by the Vilnius University Professor Valentinas Mikelėnas. The code is an interesting and unique mix of various Western private law ideas and principles, mostly, but not entirely, following Romanic and at less extent Germanic civil law tradition with a spicy flavour of some Common law doctrines. Thus, LCC after the period of Soviet law (which mostly used simplified and ideologised versions of Germanic civil law concepts) has returned the leading role of the Romanic tradition in Lithuanian civil law. The main sources used for the preparation of the LCC were Quebec CC, Netherlands Dutch Civil Code (BW), Russian Civil Code (ГК), EU law and international instruments, such as International Institute for the Unification of Private Law (UNIDROIT) conventions on international financial leasing and international factoring, UNIDROIT Principles of

---

particular types of contracts such as sales, barter, loan, rental and insurance. Further subsections dealt with different types of business entities – partnerships, joint-stock companies, etc. Also included in the section on obligations were obligations resulting from unjust enrichment and causing harm. There was a separate section on inheritance. The vast majority of the Code provisions were similar to those in Germany and Switzerland and thus fully suited for the limited private economy allowed during the New Economic policy. The new Soviet civil codes of the 1960s did not make significant changes in civil law. P. Maggs. *The Civil Codes of Central Eurasia: A Comparison. In Proceedings of the Central Eurasian Studies Society.* Fourth Annual Conference. Cambridge, 2003.

54. Olympiad S. Ioffe. *Soviet civil law.* Kluwer Academic Publishers, 1988, p. 145–146; Gyula Eörsi, Olympiad S. Ioffe. *International Encyclopedia of Comparative Law.* Vol. 7, *Contracts in general. Contract in the socialist economy.* Brill Archive, 1981, p. 22.

55. However, initial period of transformation was harsh as public institutions were unprepared to be empowered and free individuals. Level of organised crime gradually rose to extremity, and gangs were used to interfere into privatisations, create Ponzi schemes and racketeer entrepreneurs. Another, deeper problem, which Lithuania faces even today, is that Soviet period made its signature in the people's mentality. Society, which lived half century under the mandatory concept of single socialist community, suddenly shifted into individualistic culture, where one must care of himself without State paternalism. Entrepreneurship was for a long-time foreign concept for most of the population. During the transition, envy for more prosperous neighbours and suicide levels has raised, followed by economic emigration. Such vices, characteristic to late Soviet society, as corruption, protectionism, laziness and tendency to misappropriate other property still affects Lithuanian society. However, reforms, especially after joining the EU, are gradually taking their effect and Lithuanian economy is rising, while emigration is remaining a big challenge.

International Commercial Contracts (UNIDROIT PICC) and Principles of European Contract Law. Due to this, it is fair to say that today Lithuania has one of the most advanced systems of statutory contract law in Europe and gives an example of the compatibility of different contract law doctrines.

§5. Classification of Contracts

53. Legal classification empowers to break down heterogeneous concept of contract into more or less homogenous classes. This typology is not just an academic tool to understand various features of the multifaceted notion of contract but also an instrument to interpret and characterise contracts in practice.

54. LCC by itself prescribes several axes of contract classification. LCC Article 6.160(1) states that contracts may be unilateral and bilateral, onerous and gratuitous, consensual and real, contracts of successive performance and of instantaneous performance, consumer contracts and others, but these classifications are not the only ones.

I. Nominate and Innominate Contracts

55. From the structural point of view, the most important classification of contracts is their division into nominate and innominate contracts. Contract law, which takes by far the largest space in LCC, consists of general part applicable to all civil contracts and lengthy special part, where rules, having primacy against general contract law norms, on nominate contracts are included. There are also some other legislative acts fully or partly regulating specific types of contract, for instance Law on Concessions and Law on Markets in Financial Instruments, but main contract types are included in LCC. When contract is innominate, general rules of contract law apply in conjunction with specific rules of similar nominate contracts applied by analogy (LCC Article 1.8), where this (analogy) is possible. If, however, the contract is not purely innominate, but mixed, i.e., containing the elements of several nominate contracts, the rule is to simultaneously apply norms of these nominate contracts to the respective parts of the contract (the theory of combination), unless otherwise provided for by the agreement of the parties, or this contradicts the essence of the contract (LCC Article 6.156(3)). If in a mixed contract, elements of one nominate contract clearly dominate against the elements of other nominate contracts, rules of the nominate contract which elements dominate should apply (the theory of absorption).

II. Contracts with *In Rem* Effect and Pure Obligational Contracts

56. According to the patrimonial effects, civil contracts can be with *in rem* effect or pure obligational. This classification reflects consequences of transactions from the perspective of the core branches of civil law – property law and law of obligations. Contracts with *in rem* effect are those which modify (create and burden) or transfer property rights *erga omnes* in a way which exceeds simple creation of obligation. Contracts which modify property rights are agreements which create, change or destruct property rights – servitude, emphyteusis, superficies, usufruct, hypothec, pledge (charge) and other real encumbrances which are open to contracting (but only if express statutory provision permits encumbrance), as well as contract for works, for example construction contract, which leads to creation or destruction of property. Contracts with *in rem* effect constituting legal ground for the transfer of property rights (*causa traditionis*) *inter vivos* to another person (translatory contracts) are sales, exchange, rent, gift, loan, joint venture, contract for the transfer of exclusive (copy)rights, etc. Although untypically, depending on the content of agreement, even such contract as lease (in the form of hire purchase, including financial leasing) can become ground for the transfer.

57. Pure obligational contracts have effects only in personam and include contracts for use, for services, some contracts for works and other contracts. Contracts for use are legal ground to possess and use of property, including lease (with some exceptions), gratuitous use (loan for use), licencing agreements and franchise. Purely obligational contracts for works are those which normally by itself do not create or destruct property rights but improve customer's property. Contracts for services group includes general contract for provision of remunerative services and contracts for specific types of services – carriage, mandate, commission agency, property trust, deposit, financial services (bank account, bank deposit, loan, crediting, letter of credit, payment services, suretyship, documentary collection, investment services, derivatives and insurance contracts), etc. Other contracts are preliminary contract, agreements on non-competition, confidentiality, arbitration agreement, peaceful settlement, jurisdiction, etc.

III. Unilateral and Bilateral Contracts

58. Statutory distinction of contracts into unilateral and bilateral (synallagmatic) should not be confused with distinction of transactions into unilateral, bilateral and multilateral. The former distinction depends on the existence of corresponding obligations between parties, whereas latter depends purely on the number of transacting parties. Contract is always bilateral or even multilateral transaction. Hence, unilateral contracts are those where only one party has claim against other for the performance of contract. For instance, loan is unilateral contract, as only lender has a claim, whereas the borrower has an obligation to return principal amount with the interest. Other examples of unilateral contracts are: gift, gratuitous security interest (hypothec, pledge, charge) agreements, gratuitous deposit, gaming contract, etc. But most contracts are bilateral, i.e., where both parties have corresponding obligations. For example, sales, exchange, lease, remunerative services, works and insurance contracts, all are bilateral. Notion of multilateral contract does not exist. For example, articles of association signed between three founders of the company are multilateral transaction (as there are more than two parties of transaction) and at the same time bilateral contract (as every party has both – rights and duties).[56]

59. Significance of this distinction lies in the order of performance and remedies. Accordingly the counter-duties of the debtor and creditor must be performed by them concurrently unless otherwise provided for by laws, the contract or the essence of the obligation (LCC Article 6.39(3)). Where the parties are bound to perform a contract simultaneously, either party shall have the right to suspend performance until the other party begins to perform thereof. Where the parties are bound to perform a contract consecutively, the party who is to perform later shall be able to suspend its performance until the first party has performed his obligations (LCC Article 6.207(1–2)). Where the performance of an obligation that arises from a bilateral contract has become impossible for the cause not imputable to any of the parties, while neither laws nor a contract provides otherwise, none of the parties may require each other performance of the contract. In such case, each party shall have the right to claim restitution in kind without the corresponding counter-performance. Where, however, the performance of an obligation that arises from a bilateral contract has become impossible because of a circumstance imputable to this party himself, while neither laws nor a contract provides otherwise, the other party may revoke the contract and claim restitution in kind (to return everything that was performed), likewise compensate damages incurred by the non-performance of this obligation. But where the performance of an obligation that arises from a bilateral contract has become impossible due to circumstances imputable to the other party, the first party shall have the right to demand from the other party performance of the obligation and compensation of damage, including what has been accumulated due to the impossibility to perform the obligation (LCC Article 6.62).

56. Some Lithuanian company law scholars hold position that the articles of association by their legal nature are not a contract but instead a sui generis concept. *See* Lina Mikalonienė. *Bendrovės įstatų teisinė prigimtis.* Verslo ir teisės aktualijos. Mokslo darbai. 2011, Nr. 6 (2), p. 269–271. However, from the perspective of voluntarist contract law model, which prevails in Lithuania, there are no obstacles for the characterisation of a company article created by voluntary agreement of the founders as the contract *par excellence*. This position is further supported by the ECJ case law, which *expressis verbis* qualified company articles as a contract. ECJ has stated that already 'the Court held that the obligations imposed on a person in his capacity as member of an association were to be considered to be contractual obligations, on the ground that membership of an association created between the members close links of the same kind as those which are created between the parties to a contract. Similarly, the links between the shareholders of a company are comparable to those between the parties to a contract. The setting up of a company is the expression of the existence of a community of interests between the shareholders in the pursuit of a common objective. In order to achieve that objective each shareholder is assigned, as regards other shareholders and the organs of the company, rights and obligations set out in the company's statutes. It follows that, for the purposes of the application of the Brussels Convention, the company's statutes must be regarded as a contract covering both the relations between the shareholders and also the relations between them and the company they set up'. *See* Judgment of the ECJ of 10 Mar. 1992 in case C-214/89.

IV. Onerous and Gratuitous Contracts

60. Another statutory distinction is that drawn between onerous and gratuitous contracts. This distinction stresses the existence of the remuneration against contractual performance, or in other words, existence of counter-performance. In sharp contrast with common law, gratuitous transactions in Lithuanian law are contracts. For example, under a contract of gift, one party (donor) transfers by gratuitous title property in ownership or a pecuniary right (claim) to another party (donee) or relieves the donee of a pecuniary duty to himself or to a third person (LCC Article 6.465(1)). Where object of loan is not money, but fungibles, by default it is gratuitous, i.e., free of duty to pay interest (LCC Article 6.872(3)). Depending on the will of parties, gratuitous also may be agreements to create (not transfer, as it would equal gift) limited property rights (usufruct contract, pledge agreement), to administrate property, to give suretyship, etc. It goes from the following that gratuitous contracts are at the same time unilateral. But since *homo economicus* in the market does not give away his assets or energy without proper consideration, most contracts, such as insurance, lease, construction and loan of money, are onerous (*quid pro quo*). Significance of this dichotomy lies in the downgraded level of duty of care and legislative counterbalances to prevent abuses in gratuitous contracts. For instance, under LCC Article 4.242(5), the court, in appreciating the extent of civil liability of the administrator for the damage caused, and in view of the fact that the administrator has acted gratuitously and other important circumstances, may reduce the resulting damages. Another example is deposit. Where the contract of deposit is onerous, the depositary shall be in any case liable for the loss, shortage or damage of the things delivered to him, unless it was caused by force majeure. Where the contract of deposit is gratuitous, the depositary shall be liable only if he is at fault (LCC Article 6.845(2)). The first counterbalance is *actio Pauliana* – powerful remedy in practice used against fraudulent transactions of the debtor. Thus, if interests of creditor are prejudiced by the gratuitous transaction, it is treated as suspected transaction and may be annulled even if the third person is in good faith (LCC Article 6.66(2)). Another basic remedy – *actio rei vindicatio* – is also much easier for the claimant to get where contract for the property transfer is onerous because bona fides purchaser in such cases is not protected from vindication (LCC Article 4.96(3)).

V. Consensual and Real Contracts

61. Distinction of contracts into consensual and real is very important from the practical perspective because conclusion of consensual contracts materially differ from the conclusion of real contracts. The general rule, which stems from the principle of consensualism, is that all contracts are formed when capable parties wilfully agree to make a deal and sufficiently define the subject matter of the contract. However, even in Roman times, civil practice has shown that some situations are more prone to the abuse and, thus, require from the parties to take additional steps to bind each other. Therefore, under Lithuanian law, giving in payment, rent, ordinary loan, gratuitous use, deposit (with some exceptions), carriage of goods (except charter party), contractual trust, possessory pledge, gaming are contracts, which are concluded only after the thing, constituting the object of transaction, is transferred to the other party. Thus, if the lender signs ordinary loan contract (LCC Article 6.870) with the borrower but fails to transfer money, the lender commits precontractual tort (*culpa in contrahendo*), but not a breach of contract, because until the transfer of money parties have been signed only precontractual documents, not the contract in the legal sense. In this case, the borrower is entitled to claim reliance damages. In contrast, if the lender breaches the contract of crediting (LCC Article 6.881), which is a consensual subtype of loan, the borrower is entitled to claim expectation damages. It also should be noted that from the perspective of property law, restrictive regime of real contracts is limitation to the property transfer on *solo consensu* mode, which, in the case of movables, otherwise would be possible for all types of transactions (LCC Article 4.49).

VI. Contracts of Successive Performance and of Instantaneous Performance

62. Depending on the performance, contracts may be of successive performance and instantaneous performance. When a contract of successive and divisible performance is terminated or annulled, restitution is limited only to the future proceeds and does not cover performance which has already been used. For instance, after annulment of the lease contract, which was performed for a while, the lessor has no duty to return lease payments, which he has got from the lessee (LCC Article 6.222(2)).

VII. General Civil, Commercial and Consumer Contracts

63. According to the type of parties involved, contracts are classified into general civil contracts, commercial contracts and consumer contracts. Commercial contracts (B2B) are civil contracts between undertakings or between undertakings and public authorities which lead to the delivery of goods or the provision of services for remuneration (Directive 2011/7/EU of the European Parliament and of the Council of 16 Feb. 2011 on combating late payment in commercial transactions Article 2(1)), for example distribution, commercial agency, factoring, concession and agreements concluded based on public procurement. Consumer contracts (B2C) are civil contracts on the acquisition of goods or services concluded between natural persons (consumers) and persons which provide such goods or services (suppliers) for the purposes not related to the consumer's commercial or professional activities (LCC Article 6.228^1), i.e., for the satisfaction of the consumer's personal, family or household needs. As consumer contracts can be characterised not just simple everyday contracts, such as purchase of food or gasoline, but also more sophisticated by nature transactions, for instance, purchase of residential real property, copyrights of computer programs for personal computer and even investment in financial instruments, if these transactions are related to the purchaser's personal life, not a business.[57] All other contracts are general civil contracts, where both parties are consumers, who conclude contracts with each other usually on accidental manner, and this activity does not constitute business. Significance of this tripartite classification lies in the legal regime of each type of contract. For example, when a person gratuitously gives for use to her neighbour grasshopper or sells her car, it is general contract, and standard civil law rules apply. In commercial contracts, for example business joint venture, the freedom of contract is wider than in general civil contracts, and courts are ready to apply a broader scope of civil liability to commercial counterparties, who are treated as sophisticated enough to bear even big risks. In sharp contrast with these two types of contracts are consumer contracts, for example residential mortgage loan, where consumer is a weaker party protected by special rules (favourable jurisdiction, invalidity of unfair contract terms, etc.) against supplier who is better informed and have stronger bargaining position.

VIII. Imposed (Public) Contracts

64. On a similar justification related to the bargaining power of parties stands distinction of public contracts. These are not public law contracts, as one may think, but civil contracts, which are 'public' only in the sense of public necessity of resources, which some enterprises have. According to the Lithuanian contract law, a public contract is a contract concluded by a legal person (businessman) that renders services or sells goods to an indefinite number of persons, i.e., to everyone who makes a request (enterprises of transport, communications, electricity, heating, gas, water supply, access to the banking system and others). In rendering services or selling goods, any legal person (businessman) shall be bound to enter into contracts with every person who applies for those services, with the exception of cases approved in accordance with the procedure established by laws. When concluding public contracts, a legal person (businessman) may not privilege one or another person, except in cases provided for by the law. Prices and other terms of goods and services under public contracts must be equal to all consumers of the same category, except in cases expressly provided for by laws where preferential terms may be applied to the separate categories of consumers. In the cases established by laws, a legal person (businessman) shall be obliged to submit standard terms of a public contract to be approved by a relevant state institution. In the cases established by laws, public contracts may be concluded in accordance with standard terms approved by the corresponding state institution and obligatory to both parties (LCC Article 6.161).

65. These special rules on public contracts is an *ex ante* civil law solution of access to essential resource problem found in most markets. Under the competition

57. This characterisation still is a challenge for Lithuanian courts: initially courts had *ex ante* refused to characterise as consumers real estate buyers (this position was abandoned), and later the same happened with retail investors and gamblers. *See* Judgments of the Lithuanian Supreme Court of 6 Apr. 2007 in the civil case No 3K-3-156/2007, of 29 Sep. 2014 in the civil case No 3K-3-446/2014 and of 15 May 2015 in the civil case No 3K-7-168-687/2015; judgment of Šiauliai District Court of 3 Oct. 2016 in the civil case No 2S-918-267/2016.

law, refusal to supply is a form of the abuse of dominant position, which is strictly prohibited under Article 102 of the Treaty on the Functioning of the European Union (TFEU). According to the EC,[58] the concept of refusal to supply covers a broad range of practices, such as a refusal to supply products to existing or new customers,[59] refusal to license intellectual property rights,[60] including when the licence is necessary to provide interface information,[61] or refusal to grant access to an essential facility or a network.[62] In Lithuania, as in other post-socialist states, essential resource problem was especially important to solve because after the privatisation of state entities and properties, natural oligopolies (or even monopolies) quickly arose.

66. Thus, so-called public contracts in essence are imposed contracts, known also to some other European countries.[63] The problem from the perspective of a contract law theory is that they lack the basic element of a contract – voluntary agreement, thus may be called a contract with reservation and perhaps only superficially. Instead, imposed 'contract' could be characterised as the juridical fact which creates statutory obligations.

---

58. Communication from the Commission — Guidance on the Commission's enforcement priorities in applying Art. 82 of the EC Treaty to abusive exclusionary conduct by dominant undertakings (Text with EEA relevance). Official Journal C 45, 24.2.2009, p. 7–20.
59. Judgment of the ECJ of 6 Mar. 1974 in Joined Cases 6/73 and 7/73 *Istituto Chemioterapico Italiano* and *Commercial Solvents v. Commission*, 1974, ECR 223.
60. Judgments of the ECJ of 6 Apr. 1995 in Joined Cases C-241/91 P and C-242/91 *P Radio Telefis Eireann (RTE)* and *Independent Television Publications Ltd (ITP) v. Commission (Magill)*, 1995, ECR 743; Judgment of the Court (Fifth Chamber) of 29 Apr. 2004 in Case C-418/01 *IMS Health v. NDC Health*, 2004, ECR I-5039.
61. *See* Judgment of the Court of First Instance (Grand Chamber) of 17 Sep. 2007 in Case T-201/04 *Microsoft v. Commission*, 2007, ECR II-3601.
62. *See* EU European Commission (EC) Decision 94/19/EC of 21 Dec. 1993 in Case IV/34.689 *Sea Containers v. Stena Sealink* and Commission Decision 92/213/EEC of 26 Feb. 1992 in Case IV/33.544 *British Midland v. Aer Lingus*.
63. For instance, in Germany a legal duty to conclude a contract, which is seen as fundamental restriction of freedom of contract, is known under the notion of *Kontrahierungszwang*. The following are the two most important instances of *Kontrahierungszwang*. The first deals with public utilities such as electricity, gas, rail and aerial transportation, and in these cases, the consumer (or traveller) is, generally speaking, 'entitled' to have his offer to use these services accepted by the providers of these services. The second exception to the rule that the offeree is, in principle, entitled to refuse an offer to enter into a contract can be found in § 20 II (previously: § 26 II) of the Law Against Unfair Competition (*Gesetz gegen Wettbewerbsbeschränkungen*). This law, as the title suggests, prohibits certain discriminatory practices by enterprises that hold a dominant position in the market or operate restrictive price practices, thereby preventing smaller firms from having access to the market (similar considerations may arise in all EU Member States as a result of certain aspects of EC competition law, such as mandating access to facilities that are 'essential' to competition in downstream markets (e.g., non-replicable infrastructure such as high voltage transmission lines: *see* Judgment of the ECJ of 26 Nov. 1998 in Case C–7/97 *Oscar Bronner GmbH & Co KG v. Mediaprint Zeitungs- und Zeitschriftenverlag*, 1998, ECR I-7791) or in requiring 'non-abusive' licensing of intellectual property rights (*see* aforementioned Joined Cases C–241 and 242/91 *P Radio Telefis Eireann RTE*) and Independent Television Publications (*ITP) Ltd v. Commission*, 1995, ECR. I-743 (also known as 'Magill' or 'TV Guides')). *See* B.S. Markesinis, Hannes Unberath, Angus Johnston, Lord Bingham, Gunter Hirsch. *The German Law of Contract: A Comparative Treatise*. Hart Publishing, 2006, p. 70–71.

IX. Preliminary and Final Contracts

67. According to the finality of bonding, distinction is made between preliminary and final contracts. A preliminary contract is an agreement of parties by which they obligate themselves to conclude another – final – contract in future under the terms negotiated in the agreement. A preliminary contract must be made in writing. A preliminary contract which fails to meet the required terms of its form shall be null and void. In the preliminary contract, the parties shall be obliged to establish a time limit within which the final contract must be formed. In the event where such time limit is not established in the preliminary contract, the final contract must be formed within one year from the date of the conclusion of the preliminary contract. If after conclusion of the preliminary contract, a party without due grounds avoids or refuses to enter into a final contract, he shall be bound to compensate to the other party for damages inflicted. In the event where the parties fail to form a final contract within the time limit determined in the preliminary contract, the obligation to form that contract shall be extinguished (LCC Article 6.165). Lithuanian case law has created several limitations on remedies in case of the breach of preliminary contract. The Supreme Court has held that in contrast with final contracts preliminary contracts cannot be enforced to be specifically performed because this would force the obligor to enter a final contract in prejudice of his freedom of contract and also created controversial limitation on the unilateral termination of preliminary contract due to the fundamental breach, declaring that when preliminary contract is breached, this remedy is inapplicable.[64] The latter judicial finding has no ground in the substantial law and remains highly disputable.

X. Fiduciary Contracts

68. Lithuanian legal doctrine also uses the concept of fiduciary contracts. However, it understands the essence of these contracts purely literally and too broadly compared to the original meaning in Western jurisdictions. Fiduciary contracts in Lithuania usually are defined as contracts where one party especially trusts each other; therefore, outer relations must coincide with inner relations. For instance, the agent dealing with third parties in external relations must follow orders which she has got in internal relations from the principal.[65] As an example of fiduciary relations in Lithuania is usually given insurance contract on the reasoning that this is the relation of utmost trust.[66] Hence, resulting picture is unclear and questionable. It should be noted that distinct criteria for the characterisation of fiduciary relations is not just such elusive notion as mutual feeling of trust (it can be characteristic to

64. Judgments of the Lithuanian Supreme Court of 6 Nov. 2006 in the civil case No 3K-P-382/2006 and of 13 Jan. 2016 in the civil case No 3K-3-73-687/2016.
65. *See* Aurimas Brazdeikis, *et al. Civilinė teisė. Bendroji dalis.* Justitia, 2009, p. 327.
66. *See* Judgments of the Lithuanian Supreme Court of 14 Dec. 2005 in the civil case No 3K-3-675/2005; 27 Nov. 2006 in the civil case No 3K-3-600/2006; 17 Nov. 2008 in the civil case No 3K-3-518/2008, etc.

a lot of contracts), but concrete risk of misappropriation, which can arise when one party is entrusted by the powers or property of another.[67]

XI. Contracts by Mutual Agreement and Contracts of Adhesion

69. According to the manner of their conclusion, contracts are divided into contracts formed by mutual agreement and contracts of adhesion (LCC 6.160(2)). This classification is important for the interpretation and substantive controls of contracts. Contracting by mutual agreement is ideal model in terms of perfect market; however, not every party has enough economic power to bargain with another at arm's length. Very often, especially for consumer goods, contracts are formed by adhesion. Therefore, LCC Article 6.193(4) provides that in the event of doubt over terms of a contract, they shall be interpreted against the contracting party that has suggested thereof and in favour of the party that accepted those terms. In all cases, the terms of a contract shall be interpreted in favour of consumers and the adhering party. According to LCC Article 6.228^4, terms of a consumer contract which have not been individually negotiated shall be regarded as unfair and invalid if they cause a significant imbalance in the parties' rights and duties to the detriment of consumer rights and interests. And even in the commercial contracts, similar fairness controls, albeit at a limited extent, exist. Thus, a party who enters into a contract of adhesion where the standard terms are drawn up by the other party shall have the right to claim for dissolution or modification of that contract in the event where, even though the standard terms of the contract are not contrary to the law, they exclude the party's rights and possibilities that are commonly granted in a contract of that particular class, or exclude or limit civil liability of the party who prepared the standard terms, or establish other provisions which violate the principle of equality of parties, cause imbalance in the parties' interests, or are contrary to the criteria of reasonableness, good faith and justice (LCC Article 6.186(3)).

XII. Aleatory and Commutative Contracts

70. According to the definiteness of advantages that the parties obtain, contracts are divided into aleatory (where receiving of advantages and the amount of the obligation of the parties is uncertain and dependent on occurrence or non-occurrence of a certain event) and commutative contracts (where the advantages and the extent of the advantages obtained by the parties are certain and determinate at the time when the contract is formed) (LCC Article 6.160(3)). In practice, most types of contracts are commutative by nature. Separatist group of aleatory contracts consists of investment contracts (especially derivatives), insurance, rent for life, gambling and wagering – which are all contracts with a fair dose of uncertainty.

67. Tamar T Frankel. *Fiduciary Law.* Oxford University Press, 2010, pp. 4, 5; Laurynas Didžiulis. *Fiduciarinių pareigų instituto kilmė, esmė ir recepcija.* Teisė: Mokslo darbai, 2014, p. 97.

§6. CONTRACT AND TORT

71. Contract law and tort law are core areas of the law of obligations. Despite that legislation on contract law is much broader in scope than legislation on tort law, extensive case law surrounds both these branches. It is due to the fact that contracts (*sutartys*) and torts (*deliktai*) are the most common grounds for the obligations and related civil disputes to arise.

I. Contracts and Torts Are the Cornerstones of Civil Liability Law

72. Contracts and torts have another important common denominator – both these juridical acts[68] produce a common legal result – the obligation of civil liability. From the functional perspective, civil liability is a negative pecuniary reaction against civil wrong, which functions as a private sanction, applied in order to restore justice and deter wrongs.[69] According to the European Union Court of Justice (ECJ) and common law legal doctrine, civil liability is understood broadly as encompassing even restitutionary claims.[70] In Lithuanian private law, the notion of civil liability is narrower and traditionally associated only with compensation. LCC Article 6.245(1) defines civil liability as a pecuniary obligation where one party of which

68. According to the prevailing view in Lithuania, juridical fact is not the opposite notion to juridical act, but a more general category which encompass all facts of real life, which are associated with legal consequences. Juridical fact creates, changes and extinguishes legal relations. It is a trigger of all legal norms, despite the branch (*See* Stasys Vansevičius. *Valstybės ir teisės teorija: mokomoji priemonė*. Justitia, 2000, p. 217). All juridical acts may be either juridical acts (lawful and unlawful) or events (force majeure, *novus actus interveniens*, etc.), i.e., occurrences which do not fully depend on the person's will. Unlawful juridical acts are torts (delicts), breaches of contracts and other civil wrongs. Lawful juridical acts, in turn, may be either legal acts (transactions, administrative acts), which are wilful acts made with intention to create legal consequences, or operational acts (quasi-contracts, creation of artwork, etc.), i.e., acts of man, for whom law attaches consequences independently from any will of the person. Thus, the lawfulness is relevant only for the typology of juridical facts, but not as a prerequisite for the qualification of juridical acts. I believe that functionally this is more coherent and correct view than in jurisdictions, where juridical act is opposed to the juridical fact, because both torts and contracts are acts (actions or omissions to act) in legal sense, the main difference being their lawfulness.

69. On the concept of civil liability in Lithuanian and comparative law. *See* Valentinas Mikelėnas. *Civilinės atsakomybės problemos: lyginamieji aspektai*. Justitia, 1995, p. 38–42; Laurynas Didžiulis. *Finansų tarpininkų profesinė civilinė atsakomybė, kaip investuotojų apsaugos priemonė*. Doctoral thesis. Social sciences, law (01S). Vilnius: Vilnius university, 2014, p. 18; Helmut Koziol, *et al. Principles of European Tort Law. Volume 5. Unification of Tort Law: Damages*. Kluwer Law International, 2001, p. 185–187; Walter Van Gerven, Pierre Larouche; Jeremy Lever. *Cases, Materials and Text on National, Supranational and International Tort Law*. Oxford: Hart Publishing, 2000, p. 55; M. Stuart Madden. *Tort law through time and culture: themes of economic efficiency*. Exploring tort law. Cambridge University Press, 2005, p. 12–13; Graham Stephenson. *Sourcebook on tort law*. 2nd Ed., Cavendish Publishing Limited, 2000, p. 5–11; Vivienne Harpwood. *Modern tort law*. 7th. Ed., Routledge-Cavendish, 2009, p. 13–14; Willem H Van Boom; *et al. On the Intersection Between Tort Law and Regulatory Law – A Comparative Analysis*. Tort and regulatory law. Springer-Verlag/Wien, 2007, p. 426; Francesco Giglio. *The Foundations of Restitution for Wrongs*. Hart Publishing, 2007, p. 37–51.

70. *See* Judgment of the ECJ of 19 Dec. 2013 in Case C174/12; Richard Stone. *The Modern Law of Contract*. 7th Ed., 2009, p. 53.

shall have the right to claim for compensation of damage or demand payment of the penalty (fine, interest), and the other party shall be bound to make compensation for damage arising therefrom, or pay the penalty (fine, interest). According to LCC Article 6.245(2–4), civil liability is of two kinds: contractual liability and tortious (delictual) liability. Contractual liability is a pecuniary obligation resulting from a failure to perform a contract or from its defective performance where one party of the obligation has the right to claim for compensation of damage or demand payment of penalty (fine, interest), and the other party is bound to make compensation for damage, or to pay penalty (fine, interest) caused by the failure to perform the contract, or by a defective performance thereof. Tortious (delictual) liability is a pecuniary obligation which is not related to contractual relations, except in cases where it is established by laws that delictual liability shall also result from damage related to contractual relations. Thus, in Lithuanian law, as in other Romanic (from the perspective of patrimonial law) jurisdictions, there is strict delimitation between tort law and contract law, in favour of contract law (the principle of *non-cumul*).[71] Tort law is applicable to the contracts only in rare, statutory prescribed cases, such as in case of product liability (LCC Article 6.292). In turn, the significance of tort law is not such extensive as in other countries, where concurrence of claims is permitted, and, of course, risk for 'the death of contract' in Lithuania is very remote. Even more, in some cases, courts have pushed contractual liability even more forward, thus extending the boundaries of the contract law to the non-contractual realm.[72] However, in other cases, courts have failed to find the contract and applied

71. Similar position on concurrence of actions has been taken by ECJ in its judgment of 13 Mar. 2014 in Case C-548/12 (Brogsitter). The Court has ruled that a claim will concern 'matters relating to a contract' where the conduct complained of may be considered a breach of contract which may be established by taking into account the purpose of the contract. This would be the case where the interpretation of the contract is 'indispensable' in establishing whether the conduct complained of is lawful or not. It was for the national court to determine whether it has to take into account the contract to decide the action. *If that is the case, those civil claims concern 'matters relating to a contract' even if they are also claims in tort under the national law of another state.* As a result, if the place of performance of the contract is located in one contracting state, that state shall have jurisdiction in preference to another state in which a tort may have been committed under the latter state's national law. Therefore, the ECJ has established a weak form of *non-cumul* principle.
72. This controversial practice arose in post-crisis litigation after one notable financial scandal in Lithuania, where large number of retail investors sued major bank (DNB bank) for the precontractual misrepresentations, which induced them to subscribe equity-linked bonds issued by the same bank. High leverage for the subscriptions of bonds was provided by the bank and was secured with the mortgages on the investors' real estate. Bond coupons with the use of derivative element were linked to the equity markets. Such sophisticated investment scheme created considerable risks for the retail investors, which after the global financial meltdown of 2008–2010, were left without any profit, but with large debt against the bank in the form of loan interest. If court would apply the principle of *non-cumul* correctly in equity-linked bonds cases, where misrepresentations have occurred in precontractual stage, investor should base his (her) claim on the tort. The practical problem in the bonds litigation was, however, that the permissible defence against tort claims under the CC Art. 6.282 is not ordinary, but gross negligence. Therefore, in order to succeed investor must prove recklessness of the defendant, which is, of course, very difficult to achieve. To ease that burden the Supreme Court has chosen very strange and structurally inconsistent way. Instead of creating narrow exception in the application of the CC Art. 6.282, it without any sufficient explanations recharacterised tortious liability arising from precontractual wrongs as contractual liability and as a result extended contractual defence set in CC Art. 6.259 into extra-contractual realm. Such tremendous shift is not only

tort liability even where *de facto* contract existed; for example, liability of notary against client and liability of director against company is characterised by courts as tortious.[73]

II. Interplay

73. There are both interplay and differences between contract law and tort. First, the general part of law of obligations and general rules of civil liability equally apply to both – contractual and tortious obligations. Therefore, case law on torts refines general rules applicable also to contractual obligations, while contractual case law on common points also develops tort law. Second, tort law shields contractual obligations from various impairments and contributes to the completeness of regulation. In Lithuania, as in other Romanic jurisdictions, the general tort law rule[74] (LCC Article 6.263) is in force. Thus, the scope of tort law in the non-contractual realm is unlimited and covers all types of wrongs and losses. For instance, under Lithuanian tort law, pure economic loss, which also covers protection of purely contractual interests against third parties, in general, is fully recoverable (LCC Article 6.251(1)) and limited only on the grounds of causation (LCC Article 6.247) and equitable considerations (LCC Article 6.251(2)). Also, tort law protects contracts from the interference from the third party. Finally, tort law protects contractual parties during the precontractual and post-contractual stages, for example, by protecting confidential information even if the contract is not concluded yet or already has ended. Contract law, however, also can affect tortious liability; for example, parties may agree to reduce tortious liability on the extent permitted by law (LCC Article 6.252), to agree on the procedure, arbitration and settlement of the tort law disputes.

74. Tortious liability shares with contractual liability the same set of substantial elements, which are conditions for the civil liability to arise and as such constitute cause of civil liability action. In theory, there are four such conditions of civil liability: unlawful action (breach of contract, tort), fault, damage and causation, i.e., causal link between unlawful actions and damage (LCC Article 6.246–6.250). Since the fault is understood in objective sense, as a conformity with the standard of *bonus pater familias*, it coincides with breach of duty of care as a type of unlawful

---

ungrounded in substantive law but also has another side of a coin, as it creates deep practical problems, such as calculation of compensatory damages using positive (expectation) interest. This interest allows recovery of lost profit – untypical response against precontractual misrepresentations. Positive (expectation) interest sometimes even gives weaker protection against the capital loss than the negative (reliance) interest, which is tort law concept and much more suitable for the precontractual wrongs. Therefore, despite obvious desire to safeguard investors, judicial gameplay with fundamental private law concepts should be avoided, because it could lead to the undesirable consequences. *See* Judgment of the Lithuanian Supreme Court of 30 Jan. 2015 in the civil case No 3K-3-88-684/2015.

73. Judgments of the Lithuanian Supreme Court of 6 Oct. 2008 in the civil case No 3K-3-452/2008 and of 26 Nov. 2014 in the civil case No 3K-3-504/2014.

74. In Lithuania it is usually called 'the principle of general delict'. *See* Valentinas Mikelėnas. *Lietuvos Respublikos civilinio kodekso komentaras. Šeštoji knyga. Prievolių teisė.* Justitia, 2003, I t., p. 366.

action. Thus, in practice, the notion of fault is absorbed by another condition – unlawful action (being the type of it) and remains only a shadow of its former past. Fault, as independent notion, is more relevant, not as a ground for liability to arise,[75] but as criteria for the application of remedies; for example, the court in assessing the amount of non-pecuniary damage shall take into consideration, among other things, the gravity of the fault of the person by whom the damage is caused (LCC Article 6.251(2)). In general, despite different definitions, schema for both liabilities to arise is virtually the same. For example, unlawful action, as a condition for contractual liability is breach of a contract, whereas for tortious liability it is breach of the general duty of care or statute. However, contractual liability nowadays is often based not only on the express terms of contract but also by the implied terms stemming from the law itself. Thus, law, as a direct source of liability, is not the characterising criteria any more.

III. Practical Differences

75. Practical differences between two regimes exist in the application of liability, or in other words between contract law and tort law remedies. At this point, contract law tends to extend more than tort law. First, contract law offers stipulated damages including even penalty (LCC Article 6.258(1)), which are not permitted in the tort law. Second, contract law primarily protects positive (expectation) interest, i.e., value from the performance of contract, while tort law primarily protects negative (reliance) interest, i.e., interest to avoid any harmful relations with the defendant.[76] As a result, expectation damages include not only recovery of direct loss but also recovery of lost profits – untypical remedy in case of tort, where reliance damages prevail.[77] The application of tort law remedies, which are more limited in scope, are enhanced in other way: the defendant in tort litigation can only invoke defence of gross negligence or intent of plaintiff, while in contractual litigation, ordinary negligence on the part of plaintiff is sufficient to dismiss his claim (LCC Article 6.259, 6.282). This significant difference in the application of contributory fault defence, however, is compromised by the case law, which somehow failed to take it into account.[78]

§7. Contract and Quasi-contract

76. After the adoption of LCC, Lithuanian legal doctrine started to follow Romanic tradition by accepting a general notion of quasi-contract as an independent

75. Important exception is the company director's liability against creditors, where liability arises only if gross fault is established. *See* Judgment of the Lithuanian Supreme Court of 1 Feb. 2012 in the civil case No 3K-3-19/2012.
76. This division recently was acknowledged also in case law. *See* Judgment of the Lithuanian Supreme Court of 28 May 2015 in the civil case No 3K-3-327-687/2015.
77. Of course, reliance damages in some situations, such as in case of unsuccessful investment, can become more efficient remedy than expectation damages, but this 'cherry picking' in Lithuanian law is blocked by the aforementioned principle of *non-cumul*.
78. Judgment of the Lithuanian Supreme Court of 30 Jan. 2015 in the civil case No 3K-3-88-684/2015.

source of obligations.[79] Quasi-contracts, such as unjust enrichment or *negotiorum gestio*, are wilful and lawful acts, which give rise to obligations of the persons involved, when one person without the agreement confers on another a benefit to which he has no right. The absence of agreement separates quasi-contract from contract, while the lawful character of quasi-contract separates it from the tort.[80] Creation of quasi-contractual obligations is the manifestation of corrective justice and fairness in private relations.

77. Under Lithuanian law, quasi-contracts are strictly subsidiary in nature and as such are filling gaps of contract law. For example, if an insurer pays indemnity to the insured on a mistake, insured is obliged to return money on the ground of performance not due (*condictio indebiti*), which is a quasi-contract. The same result is where the contract is declared null and void – the restitution, which is quasi-contractual remedy, should take place (LCC Article 1.80(2)) because normal remedies of contract law are not applicable to extra-contractual situations.

§8. Contract and the Law of Property

I. Constitutional Aspect

78. Constitutional principles of inviolability of property (Lithuanian Constitution Article 23) and freedom of enterprise (Lithuanian Constitution Article 46) are the legal cornerstones of Lithuanian market economy. Lithuanian Constitutional Court has declared that freedom of contract is derived from these principles.[81] Indeed, a contract is a main tool for the owner to realise his right to dispose of property. This right together with right to possess and right to use contains the substance of ownership (LCC Article 4.37(1)). From the economic perspective, freedom of contract is crucially important to the property rights because the value of assets is enhanced by the possibility to exchange them for the other goods or work.

79. One of the biggest challenges after the declaration of independence in Lithuania was to establish versatile and functional property law system in private law instead of obscure one, inherited from Soviet regime, where public ownership dominated the economy. This was done in European way – by basing new property law system in the LCC on the Roman law foundations but taking into account main contemporary improvements.

79. Valentinas Mikelėnas. *Prievolių teisė. Pirmoji dalis.* Justitia: Vilnius, 2002, p. 63.
80. As famously pointed out by Stanford Professor Arthur M. Cathcart, 'these obligations occupy a field somewhere between contract and tort'. *See* Arthur M. Cathcart. *Nature and Extent of Quasi-Contractual Obligations. In.* Modern American Law, Vol. 7. American Law Blackstone Institute, 1921, p. 2.
81. Judgment of Lithuanian Republic Constitutional Court of 20 Nov. 1996.

II. *Numerus Clausus*

80. System of property (real) rights in Lithuania is restricted by *numerus clausus* principle and consists of ownership and limited property rights. Ownership is defined in LCC as the right to manage, possess, use and dispose of an object of ownership right at one's volition, without violating the laws and the rights and interests of other persons (LCC Article 4.37). Despite the inclusion of tripartite content into the above-mentioned definition, Lithuanian law recognises ownership not as 'a bundle of rights', but as the most comprehensive right a person, the owner, can have over property, which encompass all the lawful actions the owner is willing to take.

81. Limited property rights (*ius in re aliena*) are dismemberments of ownership which fall into two groups: rights to use and security interests. Rights to use are servitude, usufruct, superficies and emphyteusis. A servitude is a property right in respect of an immovable thing of another that is granted for the use of that thing (the servient thing) or a restriction of the right of the owner of that thing in order to ensure a proper utilisation of the thing in favour of which the servitude is established (the dominant thing) (LCC Article 4.111). Usufruct is the property right (the right of the usufructuary) of use and enjoyment, granted for a period of a person's life or for a certain period that may not be longer than a lifetime of a person, of a thing of another and of its fruits, products and revenues (LCC Article 4.141). The right of superficies is the property right to use the land of another for building construction works or to acquire and possess the land by the ownership right or by the right to use the subsoil (LCC Article 4.160). Emphyteusis is a property right to use the plot of land or other immovable of another provided the emphyteutic lessee does not aggravate its quality, does not undertake to build construction works, to plant perennial plants and perform other works thereon that durably increase its value both of the land used or any other immovable thing except upon the permission of the owner of the land (LCC Article 4. 165). Security interests are hypothec, charge (including pledge) and right of retention. Hypothec is a property right over immovable of another securing performance of a present or future pecuniary obligation, when the possession of collateral is not transferred to the creditor (LCC Article 4.170). A charge is a property right over movables of another securing the performance of an existing or future debt obligation (LCC Article 4.198). There are two subtypes of charge: non-possessory charge and pledge. Same as in the case of hypothec, agreement to create non-possessory charge must be approved by the notary[82] to become valid and registered in the public register in order to take effect against third parties, while the contract of pledge (possessory charge) can be concluded without any notarisation and is perfected by the possession of collateral (LCC Article 4.209). A right of retention is a property right of a lawful possessor, who has the claim against the owner, to retain the thing until his claim is satisfied (LCC Article 4.229). All security interests, except right of retention, may take consensual form, i.e., may be created, transferred or modified by the contract.

82. However, from 1 Jan. 2022, notarisation is no more required for transactions constituting non-possessory charges where such transactions are concluded between legal persons and expressed in a special electronic form.

82. There are some other concepts in Lithuanian law, such as property trust, possession and administration of property of another, which by some authors[83] or even by the laws[84] nominally are defined as independent property rights. However, despite the formal wording, this characterisation is highly disputable at best and cannot be accepted, since none of these concepts present stable antagonistic rights, which deserve to be called property rights *stricto sensu*. In fact, it is vice versa – property trust and administration of property of another are ownership protagonists, serving not as independent encumbrances *in rem*, but as the modes of the exercise of owner property rights. While a possession is purely antagonistic in character, during the incubation period (i.e., before transformation to the ownership), it is too prone and unstable to hold the status of independent property right because it can be easily destructed by the vindication action of the owner. Therefore, a more realistic and functional doctrinal view is to treat these concepts under the heading of *quasi*-property rights.

III. Interplay

83. In more general terms, obligation is a legal relationship which contains rights and duties of the parties, including a claim, which is the main right of the creditor to demand the performance of the debtor. By giving entitlement to the benefits which constitute subject matter of the obligation, claim contains definite economic value. Thus, besides the evident role of the structural element within relationship with debtor, at the same time claim under Lithuanian law is a species of property (LCC Article 4.38) and produces effects *erga omnes*. Proprietary side of the claim justifies the existence of the special actions – *actio Pauliana* (LCC Article 6.66) and oblique action (LCC Article 6.68), which *erga omnes* seek to reinstate quality of the claim against the diminution of its value by the debtor. Without the acknowledgement of dual nature of the notion of claim, it is impossible to explain legal nature of scriptural money, securities or other financial assets.

84. Property rights are the object of most contractual obligations. In this way, contracts are capable to modify (create and burden) or transfer property rights *erga omnes*, therefore to produce *in rem* effects. As it was mentioned above, contracts which modify property rights are agreements which create, modify or destruct absolute burdens of ownership – servitude, emphyteusis, superficies, usufruct, hypothec, pledge (charge) and other real encumbrances which are open to contracting (but only if express statutory provision permits encumbrance). Contracts with *in rem* effect constituting legal ground for the transfer of property rights (*causa traditionis*) *inter vivos* to another person (translatory contracts) are sales, exchange, rent, gift, loan, joint venture, contract for the transfer of exclusive (copy)rights, etc. Some translatory contracts may also carry out security function; for instance, factoring, leasing, repurchase agreement and retention of ownership are consensual security devices based on ownership.

83. Vytautas Pakalniškis, *et al. Daiktinė teisė*. Mykolas Romeris University, p. 31.
84. *See* LCC Art. 4.22(1); Law on the Real Property Register Art. 11.

85. Another field of interaction between property law and contract law is remedies. Where parties have contractual relations, such as lease or gratuitous use, remedies in personam – restitution and specific performance – usually replace vindication of the thing by the owner.[85] Loss done to the property, which was used during the existence of contract, may be remedied by the compensatory damages, which are contractual remedy. From the other angle, contractual claims, for instance, electronic money, may benefit from the protection *in rem* against third parties, for example, by the proprietary *actio declaratoria* or in some cases, where it is technically possible, even by vindication.

IV. Systemic Problems

86. Lithuanian experience has shown how complicated it can be to synchronise contract law with property law. Elaborated and sophisticated LCC's system of property rights has been impaired by the pitfalls of the economic transition period in Lithuania (which took place from the declaration of independence in 1990 until the enactment of the new LCC in 2000). During that time, mass privatisations took not only direct but also indirect way. When the demand of a land for the construction of private structures in the cities became very high, indirect privatisations were carried out on a very straightforward legal basis: private enterprises have acquired rights to use and develop State land on a basis of simple personal lease. Contracts of personal lease of land usually were concluded with State to the maximum possible period of ninety-nine years (Law on Land Article 9(3)) against very low price. Thus, personal lease, being temporary right in personam, in Lithuanian practice has been extensively used as the primary legal instrument for the development and long-term use of land, belonging to another. New LCC, while introduced more stable and elaborated limited property rights of use, such as superficies and emphyteusis, still preserved this primitive and prone structure of the rights over the land of another. LCC Article 6.550, even nowadays enables on the basis of personal lease to build and hold structures on the land of another. It goes without saying that this is problematic 'short-termism' because personal lease is simple personal right, which can be modified or terminated more easily compared with real lease (emphyteusis). Wide scope of personal lease in practice duplicates use of superficies and emphyteusis and compromises system of property rights over a land.[86]

---

85. *See* Judgment of the Lithuanian Supreme Court of 17 Feb. 2009 in the civil case No 3K-3-44/2009.
86. Moreover, some misconceptions over the rights to use land exist even within the internal logic of LCC, e.g., under LCC Art. 6.557(1), upon the expiry of the time limit of the land lease or upon its dissolution before the term, the owner of the land shall compensate the lessee for the erected buildings, construction works and installations, the construction of which was provided for in the land lease contract; where these constructions remain in the possession of the lessee by the right of ownership, the latter shall have the right to *the land servitude*, providing that it was stipulated in the land lease contract or the additional written agreement. Therefore, the right of servitude is used in unique and awkward way – as the substitute of superficies, which gives right to hold fixtures on the land of another.

§9. Contract and Trust

I. General Rules

87. It is interesting from the comparative perspective that, among other institutions, Romanic style LCC's fourth book (‘*Property Law*’), indeed, contains the general section on property trust (*turto patikėjimas*), supplemented by the rules of Russian origin in the LCC's sixth book (‘*Law of Obligations*’) on the contract of property trust. As trustee administers the property of another, fiduciary regime on the administration of property of another is subsidiary applicable to the relations of property trust (LCC Article 4.236(1)).

88. Property trust is defined as the right of the trustee to possess, use and dispose of property in the order and under terms defined by the settlor. To answer whether this institution can be characterised as ‘trust’ in the sense of Hague convention,[87] we need to take a closer examination.

89. Trust may be established for personal purposes, for private or public good either *inter vivos* by the law itself, administrative act, contract, court judgment or *mortis causa* by the will (LCC Article 4.106, 4.108). In Lithuanian economy, property trust is most often used in the public sector (public trust), where it is leading form of exercise of public ownership rights. In private sector, property trust (private trust) is used quite rare, with the exception where laws (especially financial regulation) mandatory prescribe use of trust.[88]

90. General property law rules on the trust are just few. The subjects of the trust (trustees) in the Republic of Lithuania include state or municipal enterprises, offices and organisations, as well as other legal and natural persons. The settlor or several settlors may appoint one or several trustees, as well as establish the procedure of their appointment and replacement (LCC Article 4.107). According to LCC Article 4.110, these subjects in protecting the property in possession enjoy *actiones in rem* established by LCC Article 4.95–4.99.

---

87. According to the Convention of 1 Jul. 1985 on the Law Applicable to Trusts and on their Recognition Art. 2, the term ‘trust’ refers to the legal relationships created – *inter vivos* or *mortis causa* – by a person, the settlor, when assets have been placed under the control of a trustee for the benefit of a beneficiary or for a specified purpose. A trust has the following characteristics: (a) the assets constitute a separate fund and are not a part of the trustee's own estate; (b) title to the trust assets stands in the name of the trustee or in the name of another person on behalf of the trustee; (c) the trustee has the power and the duty, in respect of which he is accountable, to manage, employ or dispose of the assets in accordance with the terms of the trust and the special duties imposed upon him by law. However, the reservation by the settlor of certain rights and powers and the fact that the trustee may himself have rights as a beneficiary are not necessarily inconsistent with the existence of a trust.

88. *See* Law on Markets in Financial Instruments Art. 13(8); Law on Collective Investment Undertakings Art. 39(2); Law on the Accumulation of Pensions 9 (2); Law on Protection of Interests of Private Companies Bondholders Art. 4–5.

II. Public and Private Trust

91. Laws further calibrate the content of property trust according to its type. LCC Article 4.109(1) prescribes that State or municipal enterprises, offices and organisations possess and use property duly entrusted to them by the State or municipality and dispose of it upon terms established by their statutes (regulations), as well as legal acts governing the activities of state or municipal enterprises, offices and organisations, without violating the law and other persons' rights and interests. Public trust[89] is further regulated by the special legislation, according to which the right of trust means the right of a state or municipal institution, the Bank of Lithuania, a state or municipal enterprise, establishment and organisation, in accordance with the procedure and terms laid down in their articles of association (regulations), as well as statutory acts regulating the activities of state or municipal enterprises, establishments and organisations, to manage and use the assets transferred by the State or municipalities and dispose of them without prejudice to laws and the rights and interests of other persons. Other legal persons shall manage, use and dispose of the assets transferred to them by the right of trust by the State or a municipality to the extent and in accordance with the procedure and terms specified in this law[90]

89. Lithuanian public trust in essence is renamed concept of operative management of State property, which was inherited from Soviet law. *See* Justas Sakavičius. *Turto patikėjimo teisės problematika Lietuvoje.* Doctoral thesis. Social sciences, law (01S), Mykolas Romeris University, 2012, p. 5.

90. According to this special law, State assets shall be transferred for the management, use and disposal by the right of trust in accordance with the procedure established by the Government unless the laws of the Republic of Lithuania provide otherwise. State assets shall be managed, used and disposed of by the right of trust by the manager of centrally managed state assets, state institutions, the Bank of Lithuania, state enterprises, establishments and organisations, as well as, in the cases specified in this law, by municipalities. The prescribed entities shall have the right to adopt decisions relating to the management, use and disposal of state assets, except for decisions relating to the transfer of assets into the ownership of other persons or restriction of the rights *in rem*, unless the laws of the Republic of Lithuania provide otherwise. In its decision to transfer state assets by the right of trust, the entity entitled to adopt decisions relating to the transfer of the state assets by the right of trust shall also have the right to establish other conditions relating to the management, use and disposal of the assets held in trust. State assets may be transferred to other legal persons by the right of trust under a trust contract only in the cases where state functions are assigned to them by laws. A decision on the transfer of the state assets by the right of trust to other legal persons shall be adopted by the Government. Such a decision must specify the state institution or establishment authorised to conclude a trust contract. Other legal persons to whom the state assets have been transferred under the trust contract may not transfer these assets to other persons by the right of ownership, pledge them or, in any other way, restrict the rights *in rem* to them, use them as a guarantee, surety or, in any other way, use them to secure the discharge of obligations assumed by them and by other persons, lease them, provide under loan for use or transfer them to other persons for use in any other way. These assets may only be used for the purpose of performing the functions assigned to them by laws. The trust contract may also provide for other restrictions. The trust contract shall expire in the cases laid down in the LCC. A state institution or establishment which concluded the trust contract must withdraw from the trust contract pursuant to LCC Art. 6.967(1)(5) if the legal person (trustee) is no longer in a position to perform (or renounces) the state functions for the purpose of performing whereof the assets were transferred under the trust contract. The state institution or establishment which concluded the trust contract must supervise the proper execution of the contract. Upon expiry of the trust contract, the assets shall be managed, used and disposed of by the right of trust by the state institution or establishment which signed the contract, unless established otherwise by the Government. The right of trust in respect of the transferred state assets shall arise as of transferring the

and in a trust contract (Law on the Management, use and disposal of State and municipal assets Article 2(10)). Private persons possess and use the property entrusted to them by the settlor and dispose of it to the extent and on terms and terms established in the legislation on trust, contract, will, court judgment or the law (LCC Article 4.109(2)).

III. Contractual Trust

92. As can be seen from above, one of the sources of a trust is a contract. Therefore, additional and quite elaborated statutory rules, mostly relevant for the private trust, are found in the special part of contract law. According to them, the trust contract is real in nature, i.e., concluded only if trust assets are transferred to the trustee LCC Article 6.953(1). The trust contract shall be made in writing, except in the case of immovables, where it should take a notary form. In a latter case, trust contract may be used against third persons only if registered with the public register. The non-compliance with the requirements for the form of the contract shall make the trust contract null and void (LCC Article 6.960). In addition, LCC Article 6.959 lists rules on the essential terms of the trust contract. Hence, the trust contract shall specify: (1) the property assigned by the trust; (2) the settlor, the trustee, and if the contract is made for the benefit of the third person (beneficiary) – the beneficiary; (3) the remuneration of the trustee and the procedure for its payment if the remuneration is set forth in the contract; and (4) the validity term of the contract. The trust contract shall be concluded for the term not exceeding twenty years. The law may also establish longer maximum terms for the validity of the contract. If upon expiration of the validity term of the contract neither party states its wish to terminate it, the contract shall be deemed extended on the same terms for the same term.

93. The founder of the trust (settlor) may be the owner of the property or any other person established by law who is vested with such right (LCC Article 6.957). The trustee may be a natural or legal person. The law may establish the persons who are not entitled to be trustees. The trustee may not be sole beneficiary under the trust contract (LCC Article 6.958).

94. The objects of the contractual trust may be movable and immovable things, securities or any other property. The State or municipal property which is possessed, used or disposed of by a State or municipal enterprise, institution or organisation shall not be assigned to any other person by the trust, except for the cases when such enterprise, institution or organisation is liquidated or reorganised, as well as other cases provided for by the law (LCC Article 6.956). To protect these assets, LCC Article 6.961 establishes the principle of segregation. Thus, the property assigned to the trustee by the trust shall be separated from the property of the settlor and the trustee. The trustee shall make and manage the accounting (the balance sheet) of the property assigned to it and shall open a separate bank account for

assets to the entity of the right of trust (trustee) and signing the act of transfer and acceptance of the assets (Law on the management, use and disposal of State and municipal assets Art. 10).

settlements. It shall be prohibited to recover from the property assigned by the trust subject to the actions brought by the creditors of the settlor, except for the cases when bankruptcy proceedings are instituted against the settlor or the settlor becomes insolvent. After institution of bankruptcy proceedings against the settlor or his becoming insolvent, the property trust shall expire and the property shall be returned to the settlor.

95. The trustee, complying with the law and contract, shall exercise the owner's rights to the property assigned to him by the trust (LCC Article 6.963(1)). The law or contract may impose guidelines and limitations on the rights of the trustee to possess, use or dispose of the property (LCC Article 6.954(2)). For example, the trustee should conclude the transactions, related to the property assigned to him by the property right, in his own name, but specifying that he acts as the trustee. The fact of the trust shall be disclosed in the form established for the transaction to be concluded. If the trustee fails to disclose this, he becomes personally liable against third persons (LCC Article 6.955). All the rights acquired by the trustee in exercising the owner's rights shall be an integral part of the property assigned to it. The obligations arising in the course of activities carried out by the trustee shall be fulfilled using the property assigned to him. The trustee shall be entitled to protect the trust in the same ways as are used while protecting the possession and the ownership right. The trustee shall submit the report on his activities to the settlor and the beneficiary in the procedure and terms established in the contract. If the term for submission of the report is not provided, the report shall be submitted once a year. The owner shall have the right to control the trustee's activities at any time (LCC Article 6.963(2–4)).

96. In general, the trustee must personally carry out his duties, i.e., possess, use and dispose of the property assigned to him. The trustee is entitled to authorise any other person to perform certain actions required in respect of possession of the property provided that this is stipulated in the contract or a prior written consent to that effect has been received from the settlor, or if it is necessary in order to protect the interests of the settlor or the beneficiary and it was not possible to receive the consent from the settlor within a reasonable term. The trustee shall be liable for the actions of the person whom he has authorised to perform such actions, as if it were the actions of the trustee himself (LCC Article 6.964). The trustee which has failed to duly, in the interests of the settlor and the beneficiary, take care of the property assigned to him shall indemnify to the beneficiary and the settlor the damages incurred due to the loss or damage of profit as well as the loss of income. The trustee shall be released from compensation of the damages if he proves that the loss has been incurred due to force majeure circumstances or the actions of the settlor or the beneficiary. If the trustee concludes the transaction in excess of the powers granted to him or in violation of limitations established in the contract, he shall be personally liable under such transaction. If any third persons did not or could not know about the abuse of powers or violation of limitations, this will cause the personal liability of the trustee. In such case, the settlor shall be entitled to claim from the trustee the compensation of the damages. The debts under obligations which accrued during possession, usage and disposal of the property by the trust shall be covered from the entrusted property. If such property is not sufficient, the recovery shall be made from the trustee's property, and when the latter property is not sufficient, from any other property of the settlor (LCC Article 6.965). The trustee is entitled to the remuneration set in the contract and compensation of obligatory expenses from the proceeds from the property assigned to him unless otherwise established in the contract (LCC Article 6.966).

97. The contractual trust shall expire in the following cases: (1) when the beneficiary dies or is liquidated, unless otherwise established in the contract; (2) when the beneficiary waives the benefit received under the contract, unless otherwise established in the contract; (3) when the trustee dies, is recognised as legally incapable of limited legal capacity or untraceable, or is liquidated; (4) when bankruptcy proceedings are instituted against the settlor; (5) when the settlor or the trustee waives the contract because the trustee is not in a position to fulfil the contract itself; and (6) when the settlor waives the contract on any other grounds and pays the trustee the remuneration established in the contract and compensates the necessary expenses incurred by virtue of termination of the contract. Any party that wishes to waive the contract shall give the other party six-month prior written notification to that effect unless the contract establishes any other term. Upon expiration of the trust contract, the trustee shall return the property to the settlor, unless otherwise established in the contract (LCC Article 6.967).

98. One should notice that rules presented by far are more or less standard rules of contract law, applicable for the particular type of nominate contracts. The problem is that these rules have not much in common with the concept of real trust. This impression is completely confirmed by LCC Article 6.953(2) under which the assignment of property to any other person by the trust shall not change the ownership of the property; the settlor shall remain the owner of the assigned property. This norm means that no trust *stricto sensu* in Lithuanian law really exists. Rule, which was copied from the Russian Г К Article 1012(1), undermines the very essence of the trust because real trust always involves ownership transfer to the trustee, who should manage property in favour of beneficiary. Apparently, one can try to defend this restriction on the ground that the concept of ownership in Lithuania is unitary and fragmentation of property rights is not allowed. However, this is denied by the fact that property transfer is equally characteristic for both – the full common law trust and its more limited civilian counterpart – *fiducia cum amico*; therefore, unitary model of ownership does not prevent the property transfer to the trustee.[91] In contrast with the logic of trust, Lithuanian model highlights the position of settlor, who remains the owner, thus leaving the trust structure prone to the insolvency of the settlor. It is also clear from the rules presented above that this trust

91. *See* Michele Graziadei; Ugo Mattei; Lionel Smith. *Commercial Trusts in European Commercial Trusts in European Private Law. Cambridge University Press, 2005*, p. 54 and 55, 105, 112, 113 and 157; Valerio Forti. *Comparing American Trust and French Fiducie.* The Columbia Journal of European Law, Vol. 17, 2011, p. 28–33; Stefan Grundmann. *Trust and Treuhand at the End of the 20th Century. Key Problems and Shift of Interests.* The American Journal of Comparative Law, Vol. 47, 1999, p. 401–428; Phillip Wood. *Principles of International Insolvency.* Sweet & Maxwell, 2007, p. 276–286; Jan Dalhuisen. *Dalhuisen on transnational comparative, commercial, financial, and trade*

structure gives no (even limited) property rights to the beneficiary, only personal right to claim damages for the breach of trust (LCC Article 6.965(1)). As to the nature of trustee's rights, these do not fit at all into the concept of property rights: they are neither ownership (this is prohibited by LCC) nor limited property rights because such trust is not antagonistic – it can be easily destructed by the settlor (LCC Article 6.967(6)) and does not actually encumber the ownership. It is evident that real purpose of a trust is directly the opposite – to serve as management device; therefore, the status of limited property right with respect to trustee's rights is a misconception.

99. Summing up, Lithuanian (or Russian) model of trust is only poor reflection of the real common law trust or even continental *fiducia*. In fact, it is just a wider version of indirect agency, constituting the relationship in personam, with superficial label of independent property right.

§10. Contract and Property Administration

100. Chapter XIV of the LCC fourth book '*Property Law*' regulates the activities of each person who administrates the property belonging by the ownership right to another unless law provides other rules of property administration (LCC Article 4.236). This distinct regime on the administration of property of another is directly taken from Quebec CC, where civilian contract of mandate was elaborated and enhanced by common law fiduciary principles to become supplementive regime of the general application for the various forms of property management.[92] However, by its legal nature, the administration of property of another is neither property right nor its independent encumbrance, just set of rules in personam which optimises the exercise of property rights through the other person.

101. According to the source, administration may be contractual and non-contractual, i.e., established by a court order, law and in cases provided for under LCC, by an administrative act. For example, insolvency administrator is a non-contractual administrator whose authority is based on the court order (Law on Corporate Insolvency Articles 34–35). Contractual administration may arise on the basis of mandate, commission agency, property trust, deposit or other contract, where obligor bears duty to manage property of another person. For example, LCC Article 6.757 prescribes that under a contract of mandate, the mandator may empower the mandatary to perform legal actions related to the administration of the mandator's property in total or a part thereof. Another example is as follows: the sequestrator shall have the right to perform any necessary act in respect of the

---

law. Vol. 2: Contract and Movable Property Law. 4th Ed., Hart Publishing, 2010, p. 449–452; Sjef Van Erp, Bram Akkermans; *et al. Cases, Materials and Text on Property Law.* Hart Publishing, 2012, p. 553–615.

92. *See* John E.C. Brierley; Roderick A. Macdonal (eds). *Quebec civil law: an introduction to Quebec private law.* E. Montgomery Publications, 1993, p. 171–173; Alexandru Mihnea Angheni. *The Legal Nature of the Administration of the Property of Others.* The International Conference Education and Creativity for a Knowledge Based Society – LAW, 2012, Titu Maiorescu University, p. 32–39.

sequestered thing which may be performed by a simple property administrator, with the exceptions established by agreement between the parties or court ruling (LCC Article 6.863(4)).

102. According to the extent, administration may be simple or full. A simple administration is when the administrator performs all the acts necessary for the preservation of the property or useful for the maintenance of the use for which the property is destined; a full property administration is established when the administrator is not only to preserve the property but also to increase it and to make it productive and to use it to a purpose in the best interests of the beneficiary. The kind of administration is established in the act constituting administration. If the kind of administration is not established in this act, it shall be deemed to be simple administration. In the case of simple administration, the administrator is bound to collect the fruits and revenues of the property, to register debts and to give valid acquittance for them from the property under his administration and to exercise other rights pertaining to the property operation and use. The administrator is entitled to make sound investments. Investments are presumed sound if the property is invested into immovables or sovereign securities. If securities are administrated, the administrator is entitled to vote and exercise other rights and obligations pertaining to securities. The administrator is not entitled to change the destination of the property unless he is authorised to make such a change by the court. With the authorisation of the court, the administrator may transfer the property to other persons for payment or to charge it with a pledge where it is necessary for the payment of the debts or the maintenance of the value of the property. The administrator may dispose of perishable property without an authorisation of the court (LCC Article 4.239–4.240, 4.248). In case of full administration, the administrator, in addition to the rights stipulated above, may transfer the property, invest, pledge, charge it with a property right or change its destination (LCC Article 4.241).

103. The administrator is a fiduciary and should, in carrying out his obligations, comply with laws and rules of the administration act. The administrator is not liable for loss of the property resulting from its normal depreciation and for the decrease of property value or the destruction of property due to force majeure. The administrator must carry out his obligations with prudence, honesty and solely in the best interests of the beneficiary. The administrator may not exercise his powers in his own interest or that of a third person. If the administrator himself is a beneficiary, he shall exercise his obligations in common interests of all beneficiaries by acting impartially and by respecting and equally protecting their rights. The administrator shall have the right to make claims related to the administration of property as well as to enter the case in relation to the administrated property initiated by other persons. The court, in appreciating the extent of civil liability of the administrator for the damage caused, and in view of the fact that the administrator has acted gratuitously and other important circumstances, may reduce the resulting damages (LCC Article 4.242). The administrator is prohibited from carrying out his functions in his own personal interest. The administrator must notify the beneficiary without delay about each conflict of interest. The administrator shall have no right to merge or mingle the property under administration with his own property, to use the administrated property or information related to the administration of the property in his interests except with the consent of the beneficiary or by the act establishing administration. The administrator shall have no right to transfer the administrated property to other persons gratuitously; he may not renounce any right belonging to the beneficiary with respect to the property administrated. The administrator shall have no right to acquire the administrated property except with the authorisation of the beneficiary or the court or acquire by succession (LCC Article 4.243).

104. In concluding transactions, the administrator is bound to indicate that he acts in the capacity of an administrator (LCC Article 4.237) with the exception that investments of property under administration should be made in the name of the beneficiary unless otherwise provided by the law or an act establishing administration (LCC Article 4.248). However, the latter rule is impossible during the execution of investment orders in the trading venues of financial markets, where transactions are carried out in the name of financial intermediary, which may act as administrator, not the client (owner of financial assets). The administrator is not personally liable towards third persons in respect of obligations arising from property administration, except if he binds himself in his own name. The administrator is personally liable towards third persons when he exceeds his powers unless the transaction was subsequently ratified by the beneficiary or a third person was aware of that fact that the administrator while acting exceeded his powers. The beneficiary is liable towards third persons for the damage caused by the fault of the administrator in carrying out his functions only up to the amount he has derived from the administrator. It shall be deemed that the administrator exceeds his powers if he has alone performed such actions that could have been only performed jointly with another person, except cases when he has performed such actions more advantageously than he has been requested to do (LCC Article 4.244).

105. From the revenues generated by the administrated property, the administrator is entitled to: (1) pay insurance premiums pertaining to administrated property; (2)cover costs of the property repairs and maintenance; (3) pay taxes payable on the administrated property; (4) use part of the property to cover depreciation expenses; and (5) discharge other obligations related to property administration. An administrator is bound to maintain the revenue and expenditure account. By the end of a calendar year, the administrator must render a detailed summary account of his administration. If there are several property administrators, they must render a joint account unless their duties have been divided.[93] An administrator must allow the

93. Where several administrators are charged with administration, all decisions pertaining to property administration are taken by a majority of them unless the law or the act establishing administration requires all of them to act jointly. If several administrators avoid taking a decision, the others may apply to the court for the authorisation to act individually or to modify a decision-making procedure. An administrator is presumed to have approved any decision made in his absence unless he makes his dissent known to the beneficiary and other administrators within a reasonable time after becoming aware of the decision. An administrator may delegate only specific acts to other persons or his representative. An administrator may delegate all his functions only to his co-administrators.

beneficiary to examine the books and other financial documents. Any interested person may apply to the court with a request that the account be audited (LCC Article 4.249).

106. The administrator is bound to make an inventory of the property, to insure the property against theft, fire and other elemental forces, to insure his own personal civil liability or to guarantee the performance of his obligations in some other way only when this is stipulated by law, the act establishing administration or a court judgment. Both the property and the civil liability of the administrator are insured at the expense of the beneficiary unless provided otherwise. If the administrator is bound to make the inventory, such an inventory shall contain the following: (1) the indication of the type, value, destination, location and individual characteristics of things; (2) securities and currency in cash; and (3) property related rights and obligations. The property described in the inventory is presumed to be in appropriate condition on the date of the preparation of the inventory unless it is proved otherwise. The administrator shall furnish the inventory to the person or the institution that entrusted him with the administration, copies of the inventory to the beneficiary and also to other persons he knows to have an interest. Any interested person has the right to contest the inventory and demand that a new inventory is prepared (LCC Article 4.245).

107. The property administrator is entitled to the remuneration fixed in the act establishing administration except cases when according to the law the administration is gratuitous. If in the act establishing administration the remuneration is not fixed, it is established by the court according to the market value of the services rendered by the administrator. If the administrator is not paid on time, he is entitled to keep the appropriate amount as remuneration for the administrative services rendered from the sum to be paid to the beneficiary, or to retain the property till the time he is paid. If there are several beneficiaries, they all are under a solidary obligation with respect to the payment of the remuneration to the administrator. A person acting without right or authorisation is not entitled to any remuneration (LCC Article 4.238).

108. The powers of a property administrator extinguish: upon his death, upon liquidation of the administrator as a legal person or upon the initiation of a bankruptcy case against him; when the administrator renounces his powers; by declaring an administrator incapable or partially capable; by his replacement; and by termination of administration. The administrator may renounce his powers. He shall

---

An administrator himself is accountable for the actions performed by such persons. All joint administrators are solidary liable for their administration unless their duties have been divided by the law, a court judgment or an act stabilising administration. In that event each administrator is liable for his own administration only. An administrator may be relieved of liability for the decision taken unless he immediately indicates his dissent to his co-administrators and notifies it to the beneficiary. The administrator may be relieved of liability if he proves that having declared to co-administrators his dissent he was unable for serious reasons to make his dissent known to the beneficiary. Administrators are accountable to the beneficiary for their acts, and when they delegate their duties to other persons, they are also accountable for the acts of persons selected by them (LCC Art. 4.246–4.247).

notify one month before a person or institution that appointed him, the beneficiary and other administrators, if there are several of them, about his resignation. The administrator who failed to give notice of his resignation in time shall cover losses due to his resignation unless he was unable to notify for serious reasons. A beneficiary or any other interested person concerned may apply for the replacement of an administrator if the administrator fails to fulfil his functions properly. Upon the death of the administrator, his successors are bound to give notice of the death without delay to the person or institution that appointed him and the beneficiary. His successors must preserve the property as far as possible till the appointment of a new administrator. In any case, the administrator shall render a report to a person (institution) that appointed him, the beneficiary, as well as other administrators, shall deliver over the property where it is and shall deliver over all that he has received in the performance of his duties, apart from remuneration for administration. If an administrator concludes a transaction after the termination of administration being unaware of it and when he could not be aware that the administration had terminated, such a transaction is valid and binding to the beneficiary. The same rule applies to transactions contracted that are required to preserve the administrated property. The beneficiary is also bound by transactions contracted by third persons with the administrator who were unaware that the administration had terminated (LCC Article 4.251–4.252).

§11. Good Faith and Fair Dealing

109. The principle of good faith and fair dealing (bona fides) is one of the most important and successful concepts established in Lithuanian contract law, in particular, and private law, in general. Most important in this respect and often applicable in the case law is LCC Article 1.5 which lays down rule of general application that in exercise of their rights and performance of their duties, the subjects of civil relationships shall act according to the principles of justice, reasonableness and good faith. In the cases when laws do not prevent subjects of civil legal relationships from determining their mutual rights and duties upon agreement between themselves, these subjects shall act in accordance with the principles of justice, reasonableness and good faith. If laws or an agreement between the parties provides for certain issues to be decided by a court according to its discretion, the court shall act in accordance with the principles of justice, reasonableness and good faith. In interpreting and applying laws, the court shall be guided by the principles of justice, reasonableness and good faith.

110. In addition, the general part of civil law provides illustrative examples of the express application of good faith principle: for instance, the property – object of the transaction that is annulled – may not be claimed from the third person in good faith, except in cases provided by the LCC itself (LCC Article 1.80(4)); a simulated transaction cannot be used as a defence by the contracting parties against third persons who in good faith have acquired rights from the simulated transaction (LCC

Article 1.87(3)); the fact of declaring voidable a transaction formed under the influence of fraud may not be invoked against third persons in good faith, except in cases established by the LCC (LCC Article 1.91(7)); etc.

111. Law of obligations, including contract law, is also full of imperatives and suggestions on the application of good faith and fair dealing. Thus, under LCC Article 6.4, the creditor and the debtor must conduct themselves in good faith, reasonably and justifiably both at the time the obligation is created and existing, and at the time it is under performance or extinguishment. Furthermore, in the event where the interest is established by laws, the parties may agree in writing upon a higher interest providing that such agreement is not contrary to laws or the principles of good faith and reasonableness (LCC Article 6.37(3)). The debtor who performs an obligation to a person who through the fault of the creditor is reasonably and in good faith deemed to be entitled to receive the performance shall be discharged from the performance of obligation to the creditor if he proves to have erred in good faith (LCC Article 6.45 (1)). The right of suspension of performance of an obligation must be used by the parties in good faith and reasonably (LCC Article 6.58(7)). A bilateral transaction may be annulled on the ground of *actio Pauliana* only in the case when the third person concluding the transaction with the debtor concerned was in bad faith, i.e., he knew or ought to have known that the transaction violates the rights of the debtor's creditor (LCC Article 6.66(2)). An obligation shall be extinguished by a set-off of a counterclaim which is of the same kind and its time limit has expired, or the time limit of its performance is not fixed, or it is defined by the moment of a demand to perform the obligation. A set-off or a refusal to make a set-off shall have no effect in respect of the rights acquired by a third person in good faith (LCC Article 6.130(1–2)). Expenses for the care and custody of the property subject to restitution incurred by the person who is bound to return the property shall be indemnified differently in respect of possessors in good faith and possessors in bad faith (LCC Article 6.150). During the precontractual relationships, parties shall conduct themselves in accordance with good faith. A party who begins negotiations or negotiates in bad faith shall be liable for the damages caused to the other party. It shall be considered bad faith for a party to enter into negotiations or continue them without intending to reach an agreement with the other party, likewise any other actions that do not conform to the criteria of good faith (LCC Article 6.163(1–3)). A consumer has the right to claim within the judicial procedure for invalidity of terms in a consumer contract that are contrary to the criterion of good faith (LCC Article 6.228^4(1)). A contract must be interpreted in accordance with good faith (LCC Article 6.193(1)) and so on.

112. More difficult task is the explanation of the notion of good faith and fair dealing. Lithuanian legal doctrine and case law, which follows it, usually explains this general notion using other similar general notions, such as justice and reasonableness. In this sense, good faith is the moral standard of legal relations explained by the objective and subjective criteria. Objectively, good faith is understood as human behaviour, corresponding to the requirements of reasonableness and justice, i.e., careful and considerate behaviour. Subjectively, good faith describes the mental state of a person in a current situation, depending on the person's age, education, experience and facts. To determine whether a person acted in good faith, it is necessary to apply both these criteria.[94]

113. If purely legal explanation may seem too philosophical and uncertain, alternatively good faith can be explained as the exact opposite to the economic notion – an opportunism. A party to a contract may be said to act opportunistically where it seeks, by stealth or by force, to change to its advantage and to the detriment of the other party or parties the division of the contract's joint gains that each party could normally look forward to at the time of contracting. It tries, in other words, to get 'more than its share'. Opportunism may involve getting a party to enter an agreement it would not willingly have signed if it had been fully informed (*ex ante* opportunism); it may also involve later exploiting unforeseen circumstances the contract does not provide for in order to change the division of gains implicitly agreed upon when the contract was entered into (*ex post* opportunism). In acting opportunistically, one party significantly exploits an asymmetry in the relationship among the parties to the detriment of the other party or parties.[95] Accordingly, there are two levels of unfairness. First is simple unfairness: when party has only ordinary duties of care, such as seller, lessor and lender, unfair exploitative behaviour amounts to the breach of contract and gives right to claim standard compensatory damages. Second is qualified unfairness: when agent, trustee or advisor having the duty of loyalty unfairly exploits its position, this amounts to the breach of fiduciary duties and entitles principal to claim even restitutionary damages.

§12. Style of Drafting

I. Drafting Contracts

114. Most contracts in Lithuania are quite simple, and contracts between unsophisticated parties have relatively short content. Usually, there is no need for very elaborated contracts because contracts are regulated by the comprehensive set of the LCC default rules and the main method for the interpretation of contracts is subjective, which denies the role of contract text as the sole source of evidence on the will of parties. The sharp contrast is the environment of legal services, where top Lithuanian business law firms are following English-American trends. Despite the virtues, by-product of this trend is a pattern to write long, sophisticated contracts, like those of common law. However, when the counterparty indifferently accepts and does not care about the proposed text of one-sided contract, this sometimes amounts into the problem of gross disparity. The same problem may be noticed in

94. Valentinas Mikelėnas, et al. *Lietuvos Respublikos civilinio kodekso komentaras. Pirmoji knyga. Bendrosios nuostatos*. Justitia, 2001, p. 77; Judgment of the Lithuanian Supreme Court of 19 Jun. 2013 in the civil case No 3K-3-336/2013.
95. Ejan Mackaay. *The civil law of contract. In* Contract law and economics. Encyclopedia of Law and Economics. 2 ed. Edward Elgar Publishing, 2011, p. 432.

consumer finance, when banks use lengthy sophisticated contracts, resembling the English style commercial contracts of project finance, under the rigorous principle 'take it or leave it', and consumers indiscriminately accept them.

II. Drafting Statutes

115. Legislative style in Lithuania to some extent is determined by Law on Legislative Framework, which lays down the principles of legislation technique, including clarity and systematicity. Clarity means that legal regulation provided for in legal acts must be logical, consistent, concise, comprehensive, accurate, clear and unambiguous. Systematicity means that legal provisions must be consistent with each other, legal acts of lower legal validity may not contradict legal acts of higher legal validity, the implementing legal acts of a law must be drawn up and adopted so that they enter into force together with the law or separate provisions thereof which are implemented by these legal acts (Law on Legislative Framework Article 3). As concern the trends of national legislation, those are sometimes contradictory. From one perspective, Lithuanian legislator, apparently influenced by the academia (which is the factual author of the main laws in the country) has codified the main legislation (Civil Code, Code of Civil Procedure, Criminal Code, Code of Criminal Procedure, Code of Administrative Offences, Labour Code, Road Transportation Code, etc.). In substance, codes are abstract, sophisticated, intelligent and very informative sources of law. However, the recent trend is the opposite – decodification is a very common practice, especially when EU law is transposed into national system. In the latter case, legislator does not always ask advice from academia on the coherent incorporation of new legislation in current laws. Quite often, a new set of rules becomes separate legislative act, which simply rewrites EU directives, despite that this routine, in the long run, deepens the fragmentation of private law. For example, instead of single Law on Hypothecary Finance, in Lithuanian there are two different laws: one, Law on Covered Bonds and Hypothecary Credit and, another, Law on Credit Related to Immovables, which transposes Mortgage Credit Directive (MCD).

§13. Sources of the Law of Contracts

116. Primary and most important national sources of contract law in Lithuania are statutes: first and foremost, written Constitution; second, parliamentary promulgated constitutional laws and ordinary laws; third, lower regulation adopted by Government and other public agencies within the boundaries fixed by higher legislation (laws). Secondary sources of contract law in Lithuania are case law, legal doctrine, soft law and *travaux preparatoires*.

117. Under the Constitution Article 138, international treaties ratified by the Seimas (Parliament of the Republic of Lithuania) are a constituent part of the legal system of the Republic of Lithuania. Thus, international sources of Lithuanian contract law are ratified international treaties, such as the United Nations Convention on

Contracts for the International Sale of Goods (CISG). However, even international treaties, which are not adjoined by the Republic of Lithuania, may become source of law if the parties choose them as the applicable law in their contract.

118. LCC is the main source and *primus inter pares* between ordinary (as opposed to constitutional) private law. LCC is based on the ideas of good faith, substantial justice, reasonableness, equality of persons' rights, inviolability of property, freedom of contract, non-interference in private relations, legal certainty, proportionality and legitimate expectations, prohibition to abuse a right, as well as the principles of comprehensive judicial protection of civil rights (LCC Article 1.2, 1.5). LCC covers main areas of private law and, following German pandectist approach, is divided into the General part (Book I – General Notions, Book II – Persons) and the Special part (Book III – Family Law, Book, IV – Property Law, Book V – Inheritance Law, Book VI – Law of Obligations). Respecting this special role of LCC, in the eventuality of contradictions between the LCC and other laws, the provisions of LCC apply, except in cases where LCC gives priority to the provisions of other laws. However, when implementing legal acts of the European Union (EU), other laws may lay down the norms, regulating civil law relationships, other than those laid down by the LCC. In this case, the LCC applies to the extent other laws do not specify otherwise. Contracts may be regulated by the decisions of the Government and legal acts of other state institutions only in the cases and to the extent expressly indicated by laws. Where legal acts of the Government or those of the other state institutions contradict the provisions of the LCC or the norms of other laws, the provisions of the LCC or those of the other laws prevail (LCC Article 1.3).

119. In the cases established by laws or agreed on in contracts, contracts are regulated by customs. However, the customs may not be applied if they are contrary to the mandatory legal norms or to the principles of good faith, reasonableness and justice (LCC Article 1.4).

Part I. General Part of the Law of Contract

Chapter 1. Formation

§1. Agreement and Quid Pro Quo

I. Offer and Acceptance

120. Lithuanian contract law lays down casuistic rules, influenced by the UNIDROIT PICC, on the standard way of contract formation by the acceptance of the binding offer. Thus, LCC Article 6.181(1) declares that contract shall be considered formed at the moment when the acceptance of the offeree to conclude the contract reaches the offeror unless it is otherwise provided for by the contract. According to their legal nature, both – offer and acceptance – are unilateral legal acts (unilateral transactions) and as such fall under the scrutiny of substantive validity of transactions, such as error, fraud and violence set in the General Part of LCC.

121. A proposal for concluding a contract is deemed to be an offer if it is sufficiently definite and indicates the intention of the offeror to be restricted in his rights by a contract and to be bound in the case of acceptance. An offer may be addressed to a definite person or to an indeterminate number of persons (offer to public) (LCC Article 6.167). Hence, two criteria are necessary for the characterisation of the offer: first, sufficient definite content of the offer, and second, intention to create legal relations. Former criteria even at initial stage requires to clearly define the essential terms of the contract including the prestation of contractual obligation, while the latter discriminates between legally binding agreements and unbinding acts, including 'gentleman' agreements, such as agreement to go to a date.[96]

96. Litigation on the characterisation of offer in Lithuanian courts arose in the context of pre-emption rights to acquire shares of common property and private companies. Under the LCC 4.79(1), co-owners enjoy the right to buy the share in sale of the common property at a price at which it is sold, and under the same conditions, except for cases when the sale takes the form of a public auction. Similarly, under the Law on Stock Companies Art. 47(2), the right of pre-emption to acquire all the shares offered for sale in a private limited liability company are vested in the shareholders who, on the day of receipt of the shareholder's notice of his intention to sell shares by a private limited liability company, held shares in the company. In both cases, the seller of a share shall inform the other co-owners or shareholders in written form about the intention to sell his shares to third parties, indicating the price and other conditions of sale. Disputes when recipients of these pre-emption rights tried to accept the notices about intention to sell as it were offers. Supreme Court rejected these

122. Lithuanian contract law follows the reception theory: an offer becomes effective only when received by the offeree (LCC Article 6.168(1)). An offer, acceptance, their revocation or any other declaration addressed to a given person is presumed to become known to him at the moment when they reach the place of residence or business (head office) or official e-mail box of that person unless the latter proves that not due to his fault or that of his employees it was impossible for him to receive the notice thereof (LCC Article 6.166).

123. An offer, even if it is irrevocable, may be annulled (withdrawn) by the offeror if the notice on the annulment reaches the offeree before or at the same time as the offer (LCC Article 6.168(2)). If this did not happen, from this moment until a contract is concluded, an offer may only be revoked. The revocation is effective if it reaches the offeree before he has dispatched the acceptance. However, an offer cannot be revoked if: (1) it is indicated therein, whether by stating a fixed time limit for acceptance or otherwise that it is irrevocable; and (2) there were reasonable grounds for the offeree to rely on the offer as being irrevocable, and he acted accordingly (LCC Article 6.169). The death, bankruptcy, liquidation or incapacity of the offeror or the offeree also render an offer to conclude a contract invalid if these events occur before acceptance is received by the offeror (LCC Article 6.172). In all other cases, an offer loses its effect only when the notice on its rejection reaches the offeror, or no reply to the offer is received within the time limit established (LCC Article 6.170).

124. An offer to the public is a proposal for concluding a contract where such proposal is addressed to everyone, also the display of goods with the indicated prices on the shelves in a shop or in the shop window, or a promise to pay for the performance of certain actions. Revocation of an offer to the public, if made in the same form as the offer, extinguishes the offer even though not all persons who are aware of the offer have received the notice on the revocation. Price lists, prospectuses with prices, priced catalogues, tariffs and other information materials are not considered an offer to the public unless there are exceptions established by laws (LCC Article 6.171). However, in consumer contracts, presentation of the things in advertisements, general circulation catalogues may be treated as a public offer, provided that the principal terms of the contract of purchase and sale are specified. Display of things in shop windows, on the counter or in other places of their sale, also demonstration of samples of the things or offering of information on the things on sale (description, catalogues, photographs, etc.) in the place of their sale, is considered as public offer, irrespective of whether or not the price of the thing or other terms of the contract of purchase and sale are indicated, unless the seller explicitly and unambiguously states that certain things are not for sale (LCC Article 6.352).

---

interpretations and stated that notice about intention to sell are not offer in the sense of LCC Art. 6.167, but simply proposal to use pre-emption right and start negotiations with the seller. This proposal would equal to offer only where it would be definite enough and the recipient named as the buyer. *See* Judgments of the Lithuanian Supreme Court of 8 Feb. 2007 in the civil case No 3K-7-133/2007 and of 5 May 2009 in the civil case No 3K-3-168/2009.

125. It flows from the legal nature of contract and the principle of freedom of contract that contract is a voluntary agreement, except in cases when the duty to enter into a contract is established by laws or a free will engagement (LCC Article 6.156(2)).[97] Therefore, the voluntary acceptance to enter into contractual bond is required from the recipient of the offer. A statement made by the offeree or any other conduct thereof indicating assent to the offer is considered acceptance. Silence or inactivity per se does not imply acceptance of an offer. An acceptance of an offer becomes effective when it reaches the offeror. If by virtue of the offer, or as a result of practices which the parties have established between themselves, or of existing usages, the possibility to accept an offer without notice to the offeror (by silence or by performing factual actions) is foreseen, the acceptance shall be legally effective from the moment when certain actions expressing the will of the offeree are performed (LCC Article 6.173). However, even if an agreement, for instance, to modify the existing contract under the standard terms may be concluded tacitly, the proposing party should clearly disclose this information and not mislead the other party.[98] Moreover, unsolicited supply of goods or provision of services to consumers is prohibited by LCC Article 6.228^{16} and the consumer has no duty to pay for such goods or services.

126. An offer must be accepted within the time limit fixed by the offeror, in the event where no time limit is fixed, within reasonable time having in regard concrete circumstances, including the capacities of the means of communication used by the parties. An oral offer must be accepted immediately unless, taking into account concrete circumstances, a different conclusion may be made (LCC Article 6.174). The time limit for acceptance indicated by the offeror in his telegram or a letter begins to run from the moment the telegram is handed in for dispatch, or from the date written on the letter, or if no date is indicated, from the date shown on the envelope. A time limit for acceptance indicated by the offeror by means of telecommunication terminal equipment begins to run from the moment when the offer reaches the offeree. Official holidays or non-working days should be included in calculating the time limit established for acceptance. However, if a notice of acceptance cannot be delivered to the offeror because the last day of the time limit falls on an official holiday or a non-working day, the period is extended until the first working day thereafter (LCC Article 6.175). A late acceptance is effective if the offeror without delay informs about it to the offeree or sends him a notice to that effect. If it is possible to be established from a letter or any other written notice containing a late acceptance that it was sent in time, and if under normal circumstances it would have reached the offeror in due time, the late acceptance is deemed to be effective unless the offeror without delay informs the offeree that his offer has been extinguished (LCC Article 6.176). The same as an offer, an acceptance becomes invalid if the notice on withdrawal reaches the offeror before or at the same time as the acceptance becomes effective (LCC Article 6.177).

97. ECJ has also stressed that contractual relations are not to be understood as covering a situation in which there is no obligation freely assumed by one party towards another. *See* ECJ judgment of 17 Jun. 1992 in the Case C-26/91.
98. Judgment of the Lithuania Supreme Court of 4 Sep. 2018 in the civil case No e3K-3-318-469/2018.

127. A reply to an offer which contains additions, limitations or other modifications of terms determined in the offer shall be considered a rejection of the offer and constitute a counter-offer. A reply to an offer which purports to be an acceptance but contains additional or different terms which do not alter the essence of the terms of the offer shall constitute an acceptance if the offeror, after receiving the reply, does not immediately object to such discrepancy. If the offeror does not object, the contract shall be deemed to be concluded under the terms of the offer with the modifications contained in the acceptance (LCC Article 6.178). The same is where the written confirmation which is sent by a party within a reasonable time after the conclusion of the contract and by which the fact of conclusion of the contract is confirmed contains additional or modified terms. Such terms shall become part of the contract unless they alter the terms of the contract essentially, or the recipient of such confirmation objects without delay to the amendments and supplements provided (LCC Article 6.180).

128. As to the 'battle of forms' LCC Article 6.179 states that where a contract is concluded by an interchange of standard terms of a contract made between both parties, it shall be considered that the contract is concluded on the basis of standard terms which are common in substance unless one party clearly indicates in advance his disagreement with the standard terms proposed by the other party, or informs without delay the other party of his disagreement after the standard terms are received by him.

129. The consensualism generally takes over the formalism in Lithuanian contract law, so the fact that the parties in the course of conclusion of a contract intentionally left certain terms to be agreed upon in future negotiations or mandated them to be determined by third persons does not prevent contractual relationships from coming into existence. The validity of a contract shall not be affected by the fact that subsequently the parties reached no agreement on the terms foreseen above, or the third persons failed to determine them, provided that there are other (alternative) means or ways of rendering those terms definite (LCC Article 6.182).

130. The place of contract formation shall be considered the place where the offeror's residence or his business is located unless otherwise provided for by laws or the contract. Where the receipt of the notice of acceptance by the offeror is not a necessary condition for the formation of a contract, such transaction shall be deemed to have been formed in the place of residence or business of the acceptor, or the place in which the factual actions of the acceptor were performed (LCC Article 1.69(2–3)).

131. Where in the course of negotiations one of the parties declares that he will not consider the contract concluded until it is agreed upon specific terms, or the agreement is correspondingly formalised, no contract shall be concluded before the agreement of parties is reached on those terms or in that form. Where a particular form is required by the law as a necessary condition of a contract, the contract shall be deemed to be formed from the moment when the agreement of the parties is expressed in that form. Where a transfer of a property is required in accordance with the law or the agreement of the parties as a necessary condition of a contract, the contract shall be considered formed from the moment when the relevant property is transferred (LCC Article 6.181(2–5)).

II. Intention to Create Legal Relations

132. It was already mentioned before that for the characterisation of the offer according to LCC Article 6.167, there should be established the intention to create legal, not just moral or other relations. This requirement discriminates between legally binding agreements and unbinding ('gentlemen') agreements, such as agreement to go on a date, or to pray together. This criterion naturally flows from the statutory definition of a contract, which expressly stresses the requirement to create, alter or end civil law relationships (LCC Article 6.154(1)) because rational law regulates only serious intentions for economic exchange. In effect, the intention to create legal relations is the element of agreement and thus sub-element of contract.

133. Accordingly, if the party of an unbinding agreement would sue its promisor in the court, the claim, as one which is unregulated by law at all, should not even be accepted by the court for the trial (CCP Article 137(2) 1).

134. Some agreements are such dangerous and abusive in character that they may, indeed, create legal relations, but not those desirable by the parties. For example, bribery, human trafficking and drug dealing are all agreements in technical sense, but instead of creating mutual civil obligations, they create criminal relations with the State leading to criminal punishment.

III. Consideration

A. Consideration Requirement Does Not Exist in Lithuanian Law

135. Under LCC Article 6.159, the following elements are sufficient to render a contract valid: an agreement of legally capable parties, and, when prescribed by laws, also a form of a contract.

136. Therefore, Lithuania belongs to civil law tradition and does not know the consideration requirement, applicable in common law countries. In addition, the classical civilian requirement of cause, except in cases expressly provided by law (e.g., insurable interest in insurance contracts) is also absent.

B. Gratuitous Promises

137. LCC Article 6.160(1) expressly states that contracts may be gratuitous. For example, under a contract of gift, one party (donor) transfers by gratuitous title property in ownership or a pecuniary right (claim) to another party (donee) or relieves the donee of a pecuniary duty to himself or to a third person (LCC Article 6.465(1)). Where object of loan is not money, but fungibles, by default it is gratuitous, i.e., free of duty to pay interest (LCC Article 6.872(3)). Gratuitous also are (or may be depending on the will of parties) prenuptial agreements, agreements to create (not transfer, as it would equal gift) limited property rights (usufruct contract, pledge contract), to administrate property, to give suretyship, etc. It goes from the following that gratuitous contracts are at the same time unilateral.

C. Natural Obligations

138. After the all-encompassing private law reform, which culminated by the adoption of LCC in 2000, Lithuanian legal doctrine, following Romanic sources,[99] quickly acknowledged the concept of natural obligation (*obligatio naturalis*). This is an intermediate category between legal and moral duties: it cannot be enforced, but voluntary performance by the debtor is legally valid and irrevocable.[100] For example, where a debtor performs his obligation after the expiration of the time limit of prescription, he shall have no right to claim restitution even if at the time of the performance of his obligation he did not know that the time limit of prescription had expired (LCC Article 1.133).

139. Supreme Court has also distinguished this type of obligation. In case where shareholder and director of liquidated company after its dissolution signed a note in which he promised for the creditor to cover debt of its former company, the courts dismissed creditor's claim against the successors of the former shareholder and director of the debtor. Courts have reasoned that he could not undertake the obligation, which had already been extinguished after the liquidation of company. Supreme Court has stressed that note created not legal, but only natural obligation, which cannot be actively enforced. Using doctrinal works, the Supreme Court has explained that natural obligation arises when parties are bound by the mutual moral duties, or one party feels moral duty to perform actions for the benefit of another. Law, without specifying particular sources of natural obligations, confers power to the court to characterise one or another relationship as the natural obligation. In contrast with legal obligation, performance of natural obligation cannot be enforced against debtor. However, under LCC Article 6.241(1) 3, property cannot be recovered as received without cause where it was transferred by a person who is aware of the absence of his duty to perform the obligation, or by a person who even though not bound to perform the obligation nevertheless makes the performance and where this conforms to the principles of good morals.[101]

140. The same is with property transferred for the purposes of performance of an obligation after the expiry of prescription – it cannot be reclaimed as transferred

99. Saul Litvinoff. *The Law of Obligations. Louisiana civil law treatise.* West Publishing Company, 1992.

100. Valentinas Mikelėnas. *Prievolių teisė. Pirmoji dalis.* Justitia: Vilnius, 2002, p. 24–36.

101. Judgment of the Lithuanian Supreme Court of 10 Feb. 2012 in the civil case No 3K-3-34/2012.

without legal cause (LCC Article 6.241(1) 2). In effect, natural obligation, albeit cannot be enforced, when performed voluntary, blocks a creation of quasi-contractual obligation.

IV. Modifications of the Contract

141. Modification of a contract is alteration of its terms, which is sometimes necessary where is a need to adapt the contractual obligations to the dynamics of social and economic life. There are two types of modification: voluntary and judicial. Voluntary modification is effected by an agreement of contractual parties (LCC Article 6.223(1)) and is characterised as independent contract. It goes without saying that freedom of contract and its general limitations apply also for the contracts to modify underlying contracts. Also, parties should comply with LCC Article 6.183 under which the contract formed in writing which contains a clause requiring any modification, supplementation or dissolution of the contract to be made only in writing cannot be otherwise modified, supplemented or dissolved. A party may be precluded by its conduct from invoking this clause to the extent that the other party has acted in reliance on that conduct. A contract concluded in the notarial form may be dissolved, modified or supplemented only in the notarial form. Besides, that are specific and very broad restrictions to change public procurement contracts under the casuistic rules set in Law on Public Procurement Article 89.

142. Another way to modify a contract is judicial. Hence, LCC Article 6.223 prescribes that on the demand of one of the parties, a court may modify the contract by its judgment, provided that the breach of the contract committed by the other party is fundamental, in other cases established by the contract or laws.

143. An action for modification of a contract may be brought only after a refusal of the other party to modify the contract, or if no notice upon proposal to modify the contract is received within thirty days unless a different procedure of modification is established by laws or the contract. A refusal of one party to perform the contract in part or in whole may be effected only in cases provided for by laws or the contract (LCC Article 6.223).

144. In case of a fundamental breach, the party is entitled to unilaterally terminate the contract (LCC Article 6.217). There is a legislative logic – if the party can use a stricter remedy (termination), it also should have right to use a milder one (modification). In determining whether a breach of a contract is fundamental, the following conditions must be taken into account: whether the aggrieved party is substantially deprived of what it was entitled to expect under the contract, except in cases when the other party did not foresee or could not have reasonably foreseen such result; whether, taking into consideration the nature of the contract, strict compliance with the conditions of the obligation is of essential importance; whether the breach is made intentionally or with gross negligence; whether the breach gives the aggrieved party the basis to suppose that it cannot rely on the normal future performance of a contract; and whether the breached party, which was preparing for performance or was effectuating the performance of the contract, would suffer significant damages if the contract were terminated.

145. Despite that LCC Article 6.223 does not directly address how the contract can be changed in case of fundamental breach, this change should bring fair and reasonable results (LCC Article 1.5) and keep (or reinstate) the equilibrium of the contract. However, in practice, when fundamental breach occurs more common remedy is unilateral termination of the contract than its modification.

146. Modification of the contract in case of fundamental breach is a legal sanction used in response to a contractual fault. However, there are cases where in prejudice to one or both parties the contractual terms do not adequately correspond to factual circumstances at such extent where the economic equilibrium of the contract is impaired. In these cases, even if no fault of the party exists, the principle of fairness requires to alter the terms of contract and reinstate economic equilibrium. The principle *pacta sunt servanda* is thus softened. In cases, where material inadequacy of obligations in the contract does not exist from the beginning, but arise later (*ex post*), the doctrine of *imprévision* (hardship) applies. Thus, where the performance of a contract becomes more difficult for one of the parties, this party is bound to perform the contract in accordance with the procedure set in LCC Article 6.204. Under this article, the performance of a contract is considered obstructed under such circumstances which fundamentally alter the balance of the contractual obligations, i.e., either the cost of performance has essentially increased or the value thereof has essentially diminished if: these circumstances occur or become known to the aggrieved party after the conclusion of the contract; these circumstances could not reasonably have been foreseen by the aggrieved party at the time of the conclusion of the contract; these circumstances are beyond the control of the aggrieved party; and the risk of occurrence of these circumstances was not assumed by the aggrieved party.

§2. Formal and Evidential Requirements

I. Formal Requirements

147. Main branches of civil patrimonial law are differently affected by formalism. The doctrine of formalism deservedly plays a dominant role in property law, where it, by creating additional burdens *ex ante*, enhances certainty and reduces *ex post* incentives to litigate, hoping to appropriate uncertain property rights. In the law of obligations, functionalism, which stresses dominance of substance against form, prevails. In contract law, functionalism embodies itself into the principle of consensualism and tries to suppress formalism until the minimum which is necessary in the market economy. Carefully calibrated interplay between these different attitudes facilitates both stable property rights and their efficient allocation by the contracts. Although after substantial reform Lithuanian contract law in general has reduced formalism, it still plays a notable role, especially in the fields of real property and company law.

148. According to LCC Article 6.159, when prescribed by laws, a form is a necessary element of a contract. Therefore, where a particular form is required by the law as a necessary condition of a contract, the contract shall be deemed to be formed from the moment when the agreement of the parties is expressed in that form (LCC Article 6.181).

149. In line with highly systemic character of LCC, the main requirements for the form of contracts are included in the general section on transactions in the first book of LCC. According to these rules, transactions shall be made in writing (in the ordinary or notarial form) or their formation may be implied from the actions. A transaction, in respect of which there is no specific form established by laws, shall be deemed to have been formed if the person demonstrates by his behaviour the will to form a transaction (a contract formed by actions) (LCC Article 1.71). Therefore, there are two main types of transaction form: written and non-written, i.e., based on verbal and other actions, which manifest alignment of parties will to enter mutual legal relationships. Furthermore, these types have their subtypes: written form is further distinguished into simple or notarial, whereas non-written form into verbal and based on conclusive actions. Written contracts in legal doctrine are called formal contracts, while other contracts are called factual contracts.

150. The general principle is that where the written form is not required by laws or by an agreement of the parties as a necessary condition for the forming of a transaction, the transaction may be formed verbally, for example, by direct conversation in meeting or by phone. Transactions resulting from the performance of a written contract may be formed verbally if this does not contradict laws or the contract (LCC Article 1.72). For instance, a contract of lease must be concluded in written form only where it is concluded for a period of more than one year (LCC Article 6.478). Another practical example is economic relationships between unmarried (cohabitant) couples, which are characterised as the factual contract of association (type of joint venture), solely to create legal protection for a weaker party, which in Lithuanian court practice is usually a housewife.[102] The purpose is to enable courts to declare constructed common household as common property under the LCC of both members of the former couple, not just of registered owner.

151. Written transactions should be made either by drawing up one document signed by all the parties or by the parties exchanging separate documents. Documents signed by the parties and transmitted by means of communication terminal equipment shall be conferred the same power as having been made in the written form, providing the protection of the text is guaranteed and the signature can be identified (LCC Article 1.73(2)). Transactions drawn up in writing must be signed by the contracting parties. Where a natural person due to physical defect, illness or any other reason cannot sign it himself, he may authorise another person to sign on his behalf. The signature of the latter must be witnessed by a notary; or the head or

102. *See* Judgments of the Lithuanian Supreme Court of 31 Oct. 2001 in the civil case No 3K-3-1029/2001 and of 14 Mar. 2014 in the civil case 3K-3-84/2014.

a deputy head of the enterprise, institution or organisation where the person concerned is employed or studies; or by the head physician or a deputy head physician of the inpatient medical institution where the person concerned undergoes treatment; or by the commander of the military unit or a deputy commander thereof if the transaction is made by a soldier; or by the master of a ship during the period of a long voyage; in addition, the reason for which the person entering into the transaction is unable to sign it himself must be indicated. Where the transaction is made by using telecommunication terminal equipment, in all cases there must be sufficient data for the ascertainment of the parties to the transaction. In the event of absence of such data, the parties, if a dispute arises, may not rely upon witnesses to prove the fact of transaction forming (LCC Article 1.76). Since it is important to apply those rules flexibly in the current digital environment, courts in practice are really open to identify written contract from various electronic evidence, such as files containing social media messages and e-mails. Moreover, consensualistic case law has accepted even unsigned text of contract, as a valid written transaction, where parties relied on and performed this contract as it had been perfectly signed.[103]

152. Special rules apply for electronic signature of contracts. Electronic signature means data in electronic form which is attached to or logically associated with other data in electronic form and which is used by the signatory to sign. Qualified electronic signature means an advanced electronic signature that is created by a qualified electronic signature creation device, and which is based on a qualified certificate for electronic signatures. According to the EU rules, an electronic signature shall not be denied legal effect and admissibility as evidence in legal proceedings solely on the grounds that it is in an electronic form or that it does not meet the requirements for qualified electronic signatures. A qualified electronic signature shall have the equivalent legal effect of a handwritten signature (EU Regulation No 910/2014 on electronic identification and trust services for electronic transactions in the internal market Article 25)Article.

153. Putting the facsimile on the document is not equal to the handwritten signature and does not replace it because such method prevents verification of the true signee and denies the whole reason to give legal significance to the signature.[104] Even more, the use of the facsimile to replicate the signature of another person formally resembles forgery of documents (Criminal Code Article 300) and should be avoided.

154. The parties may agree to adopt additional requirements for the written form of the transaction (signatures of certain persons, affixation of a stamp on the document, assignment of a special form for the document, etc.) and establish the legal

103. Judgment of the Lithuanian Supreme Court of 25 Nov. 2003 in the civil case No 3K-7-999/2003.
104. For instance, the Lithuanian Supreme Court has denied legal effect to the promissory note which was signed with facsimile instead of handwritten signature required by the strict rules of Law on Bills of Exchange and Promissory Notes. *See* Judgment of the Lithuania Supreme Court of 10 Mar. 2021 in the civil case No e3K-50-469/2021.

effects for non-compliance with such requirements. In the event of the parties failing to comply with the established requirements, the transaction shall not be considered formed, unless the parties agree otherwise (LCC Article 1.73(3)). In practice, additional requirements, including various steps of authorisation, are usual in the field of financial services, where is enhanced risk of fraud, money laundering, terrorist financing and loss of sensitive data.

155. LCC Article 1.73(1) prescribes non-exhaustive list of transactions, which should be made in writing. Therefore, written form is mandatory: for transactions made by natural persons where at the moment of their formation the value of the transaction exceeds EUR 1,500, except such transactions which are performed at the time of their formation; transactions on the formation of legal persons; contracts on sale of goods by instalments;[105] insurance contracts; arbitration agreements; contracts of lease of a movable thing for a term of over one year; preliminary contracts; contracts of life annuity (contracts of rent); compromise agreements; and other transactions whose mandatory simple written form is provided for by the LCC or other laws.

156. In the most strict and formal – notarial – form should be drawn up most important contracts (as a rule, with *in rem* effect): contracts on the transfer of the property rights in an immovable thing; transactions on the encumbrance of the property rights and of the immovable thing (except transactions which are concluded in the insolvency procedure); property trust contracts, gift of at least EUR 14,500; contracts for the partition of inherited real property; prenuptial and postnuptial agreements; loan contracts where lender lends at least EUR 3,000 as cash; contracts for the sale of private limited liability company shares, where the object of sale is at least 25 % of all shares or the price of shares is more than EUR 14,500; and other transactions which are to be notarised in accordance with the mandatory provisions of LCC (LCC Articles 1.74, 5.70, 6.469, 6.871, 6.960). It means that no other law (except laws of higher legal status – Constitution or constitutional laws) can create requirement on notarial form, which has no basis (legal ground or reference) in the LCC.

157. Even where notarial form is not mandatory, it can be opted in by the will of the parties. It means that transactions which are permitted by laws to be formed verbally may also be made in the written or notarial form, and transactions, the simple written form for which is mandatory, may also be formed in the notarial form (LCC Article 1.77).

158. It has already been said that when prescribed by law form is the necessary element of the contract. However, non-compliance with formal requirements not always results in invalidity of the contract, as it may seem. Absolute rigidity of the

105. The contract is instalment sale, where payment of price for goods is divided into at least two deferred instalments. *See* Judgment of the Lithuania Supreme Court of 1 Apr. 2022 in the civil case No e3K-3-72-421/2022.

contract law would be contrary to the idea of voluntarism, principle of consensualism and derivative principle – *favor contractus*. Thus, instead of strict and plain invalidity rule for every non-compliance, there is more elaboration as two types of consequences of non-compliance with mandatory legal form may arise: substantial and procedural. Substantial consequences are invalidity of the contract, whereas procedural consequences are evidential restrictions in the litigation. Indeed, under LCC Article 1.93, transaction not made in the form required by laws is void only in the case when such consequence is expressly indicated in the laws. Where any dispute arises upon the fact of forming or performance of a transaction which fails to meet the necessary requirements for its simple written form, the parties lose the right to use testimony of witnesses as evidence to prove the facts indicated above; in the cases expressly prescribed by the law, non-observance of the simple written form obligatory to a concrete kind of transactions causes the nullity of such transaction. But non-observance of the notarial form required by the law as a necessary condition of a transaction shall result in the nullity of the transaction in any case. Where one party in the whole or partly performs his obligations arising from a transaction that must be notarised, while the other party avoids the notarisation thereof, the court may, on the action of the party who has performed his obligations, declare such transaction valid. In such event, a subsequent notarisation of the transaction is not required. Where nullity of a transaction results from the lack of necessary requisites of its form as established by laws, the restitution should be applied. It is astonishing that in case of non-compliance with simple written form, no negative consequences may be applied by a court if they would contradict the principles of good faith, justice and reasonableness, in particular where: (1) there exists other written evidence, even though indirect, that proves the forming of the transaction; (2) written evidence to prove the fact of transaction forming has been lost not through the fault of the party; (3) taking into consideration the circumstances in which the transaction was formed, it was objectively impossible to form that transaction in writing; and (4) taking into consideration the interrelations between the parties, the nature of the transaction and other circumstances of importance to the proceedings, prohibition to invoke testimonies of witnesses would contradict to the principles of good faith, justice and reasonableness.

159. Considering these rules, it remains disputable whether the mandatory form of the contract is really an element of the contract, in a sense that without necessary structural element contract does not exist at all. It looks like that in case where only procedural consequences may be applied, form is not the element of the contract, but semi-element at best. Thus, form is the constituting element only for the solemn contracts, i.e., where non-compliance leads to invalidity.

160. Another important instrument of formalism is the requirement to register in the public registry various juridical facts, including transactions and other contracts. The main rationale for this is to use the property rights, transferred or modified with contracts, against third parties. Therefore, registration requirements serve mostly for the purposes of property law, not for the contract law itself, but since a contract is a main tool to redistribute property rights, these perfection requirements affect also the formation of contracts with *in rem* effect.

161. With respect to the legal registration of transactions, LCC Article 1.75 lays down a general rule that the laws may establish mandatory legal registration of certain transactions. But according to LCC Article 1.94, non-compliance of the requirement established by laws to perform legal registration of a transaction shall not result in nullity of the unregistered transaction, except in the cases prescribed by the LCC. In a more detailed fashion, a transaction shall produce its effects *inter partes* even if it is not registered in the mandatory order. In such instances, the rights and duties produce their effects between parties not from the moment of registration of the transaction but from the moment established by the law or agreement of the parties, except in cases where it is expressly determined by the LCC that the rights and duties of the parties shall arise only from the moment of registration of the transaction concerned; for example, contract of servitude according to LCC Article 4.124(2) comes to validity only after its perfection in the public registry. However, the parties to an unregistered transaction may not invoke the fact of transaction *erga omnes* and argue their rights against third persons by relying on other means of proof.

162. In addition, there are special rules with respect to competition between several acquirers of property, where it is transferred by unfair or negligent person under several duplicating contracts. Hence, if the same property rights or the same property is acquired by several acquirers, but only one of them registers that transaction, it shall be considered that the acquirer who has registered the transaction is vested with that thing or with the property rights in that property. If none of the acquirers registers the transaction, it shall be considered that the acquirer who is the first to form that transaction is vested with the rights indicated above. If several persons register their property rights or property rights in the same thing, the person who is the first to register that transaction shall be vested with these rights. Damage caused to persons by unlawful acts of the officials of state institutions or other organisations effectuating mandatory legal registration of transactions shall be compensated by the state (LCC Article 1.75).

163. Finally, one should take into account that under the Law on the State Language Article 9, all the transactions of legal and natural persons of the Republic of Lithuania shall be conducted in the state language. Translations into one or more languages may be attached to them. Transactions with persons of foreign states shall be conducted in the state language and another language acceptable to both parties. These rules create uncertainty about whether non-compliance with them leads to the invalidity of transaction. Indeed, in one case buyer of immovable unsuccessfully attacked transaction on the ground of non-compliance with language norms. The action was dismissed by lower courts on the reason that language rules are not imperative. Supreme Court has accepted this conclusion but quashed judgment on other grounds.[106] Taking into account a general picture of consensualistic Lithuanian contract law, it is difficult to imagine the opposite result. In other words, it is

106. Judgment of the Lithuanian Supreme Court of 20 Mar. 2014 in the civil case No 3K-3-150/2014.

hard to believe that during the dispute the court would complicate pursuit for justice and refuse to rely on the signed text by the parties solely on the reason that the contract was written and signed, for example, by two Lithuanian companies (i.e., Lithuanian nationals) only in English.

A. Contracts under Seal

164. In the common law, the 'deed' is a way of using the physical form in which an agreement is recorded in order to give it enforceability. The agreement is put in writing and, traditionally, 'sealed' by the party or parties to be bound to it. The 'seal' could take the form of a wax seal, a seal 'embossed' onto the document by a special stamp or simply the attachment of an adhesive paper seal (usually red). Such contracts were also known as 'contracts under seal' (in contrast to 'simple contracts' which use 'consideration' as the test of enforceability).[107]

165. According to LCC Article 1.73(3), besides general requirements, the parties may agree to adopt additional requirements for the written form of the transaction (signatures of certain persons, affixation of a stamp on the document, assignment of a special form for the document, etc.) and establish the legal effects for non-compliance with such requirements. In the event of the parties failing to comply with the established requirements, the transaction shall not be considered formed, unless the parties agree otherwise. Thus, despite that there are no substantial rules in Lithuanian law on contracts under seal comparable to those in common law, parties are free to use even such formalities as deeds if they see it necessary. However, it will have no substantial effect on the content of obligations.

B. 'Solemn' Contracts

166. As it was explained above, a formality is not always a requirement for the validity of the contract. It could also be that the legislator introduces a formality (including the written form) as a form of evidence. One speaks of contracts that need to be evidenced in writing, or of a form that is required *probationis causa* (with an eye to proof), as contrary to forms that are required in order to make the contract valid (*solemnitatis causa*).[108] Therefore, solemn are contracts, which are enforceable only when formalities are observed and no defences for this exist.[109] The rationale for solemn contracts should be obvious necessity to impose formal requirements, in order to prevent opportunism and avoid disputes and uncertainties in the most important and sensitive contracts.

167. Under Lithuanian law, solemn contracts are those for whom judicial or notarial approval is mandatory and simple written contracts, which are valid only

107. Richard Stone. *The Modern Law of Contract.* 7th Ed., 2009, p. 108.
108. Jan M. Smits. *Contract Law: A Comparative Introduction.* Edward Elgar Publishing, 2014, p. 108.
109. Bryan A. Garner, *et al. Black's Law Dictionary.* 9th ed., 2009, p. 1520.

made in writing. An example of a judicially approved contract is the contract of the spouses as to the consequences of divorce. According to LCC Article 3.53(3), while granting a divorce decree, the court shall approve the contract of the spouses as to the consequences of divorce providing for the maintenance payments for the children of minor age and each other, the residence of their minor children, their participation in the education of their children and their other property rights and duties. The content of the contract shall be incorporated in the judgment of divorce.

168. The notarial form is required for the contracts on the transfer of the property rights in an immovable thing; transactions on the encumbrance of the property rights and of the immovable thing (except transactions which are concluded in the insolvency procedure); property trust contracts, gift of at least EUR 14,500 EUR; contracts for the partition of inherited real property; prenuptial and postnuptial agreements; loan contracts where lender lends at least EUR 3,000 as cash; contracts for the sale of private limited liability company shares, where either the object of sale is at least 25% of all shares or the price of shares is more than EUR 14,500; and other transactions which are to be notarised in accordance with the mandatory provisions of LCC (LCC Articles 1.74, 5.70, 6.469, 6.871, 6.960). Simple written contracts which are solemn are contracts of suretyship, pledge, guarantee, earnest money, preliminary contract and other contracts, where strict requirements for the form are prescribed by the law (LCC Articles 4.209, 6.79, 6.91, 6.99, 6.165).

II. Evidential Requirements

169. Law of evidence is closely related to the contract law and constitutes its procedural continuum with respect to the proof of conclusion and performance of contracts. Besides that, law of evidence is extremely important to the interpretation of contracts because Lithuanian contract law employs subjective method of interpretation, which under the LCC 6.193 requires establishing the real intentions of the parties without being limited by the literal meaning of the words. No need to say, requirement to establish real intentions implies a broad spectrum and admissibility of evidence.

170. In Lithuania, some rules on evidence are included directly in LCC. For instance, under LCC Article 1.93(2), where any dispute arises upon the fact of forming or performance of a transaction which fails to meet the necessary requirements for its simple written form, the parties lose the right to use testimony of witnesses as evidence to prove the facts indicated above, except in the cases expressly prescribed by the law, where non-observance of the simple written form results in the nullity of such transaction. Therefore, the latter rule restricts admissibility of evidence. Another example is a set of presumptions included in the LCC, which are helping to solve questions related to the formation of contracts, for instance: upon the issue of uncertified securities, where the laws do not provide for otherwise, it shall be presumed pursuant to LCC Article 1.101(10) that the holder of the securities has entrusted the custodian with their custody upon the contract of deposit; if the creditor issues a quittance note for the principal sum, it shall be presumed that the interest and other costs have also been paid by the debtor (LCC Article 6.65(5)); and an offer, acceptance, their revocation or any other declaration addressed to a given person shall be presumed to become known to him at the moment when they reach the place of residence or business (head office) or official e-mail box of that person unless the latter proves that not due to his fault or that of his employees it was impossible for him to receive the notice thereof (LCC Article 6.166).

171. However, despite these and some other evidential rules found in the LCC, law of evidence belongs to the law of civil procedure and is included as a separate section in the CCP. Therefore, the process of proof should be carried out in accordance with the general rules of the CCP, which provides that the aim of proof is reasonable belief of a court on existence or non-existence of certain circumstances related to the question at issue (subject matter of the proceedings) based on examination and evaluation of case evidence (CCP Article 176).

172. Evidence in civil proceedings means any actual data serving as a basis for a court to state in the statutory procedure existence or non-existence of circumstances substantiating claims and replications of parties as well as other circumstances important for fair deciding on the case. The mentioned data shall be found out based on: statements of parties or third persons (in person or by representative), testimonies of witnesses, written evidence, real evidence, inspection protocols and expert reports. Written evidence encompasses documents, business or personal correspondence and other letters containing data on circumstances relevant to the case. Documents signed by participants in a proceeding and transmitted via telecommunication terminals in accordance with laws and other regulations shall be equal to a written form of a document. If written evidence is made in a language other than the official language, translation of the evidence certified in the established procedure shall be enclosed thereto. Legally obtained photo pictures, audio and video recordings may also serve as tools of proof. Actual data comprising state or official secrets may not serve as evidence in civil proceedings until and unless they are made public in the statutory procedure (CCP Articles 177, 197, 198).

173. Evidence should be examined in accordance with the principles of direct examination, literalism and concentration of case (CCP Article 183). The main principle in the procedure of proof is free evaluation of evidence, which gives broad discretion to the court to evaluate a diverse set of evidence. Thus, according to CCP Article 185, a court should judge on the case evidence in accordance with its self-belief based on comprehensive and unbiased examination of the evidence proven during the trial. No evidence shall have any pre-stipulated power over a court except for cases provided for in the CCP itself. The only example of *ex ante* priority of evidence over the other (and in effect restriction for the courts of evaluative discretion) is so-called official written evidence, which has prima facie power, i.e., has higher evidential value. To this category belong all authentic instruments issued by state and municipal authorities, approved by public officials within the limits of their competence and in accordance with requirements applied to the form of particular documents, such as the contracts approved by the notary. According to CPP Article 197(2), circumstances indicated in official written evidence shall be considered fully proved until and unless they are denied by other relevant proofs except for witness evidence. A ban to employ witness evidence shall not apply if this contradicts the principles of fairness, justice and reasonability. Evidential value of official written evidence may be statutorily conferred upon other documents as well.

A. *The Parol Evidence Rule*

174. The parol evidence rule prevails in the common law systems. Under this rule, where there is a written contract, extrinsic (parol) evidence cannot change the express terms laid down in that document. Extrinsic evidence includes oral statements, and written material such as draft contracts or letters, whether relating to pre-contract negotiations or the parties' post-contractual behaviour. The rule only prevents use of extrinsic evidence concerning the terms of a contract; where one side is seeking to prove whether or not a contract is valid (e.g., by claiming that there was no consideration, or that there was misrepresentation), extrinsic evidence may be used even though the actual contract has been put in writing.[110]

175. However, in Lithuania, as in other civilian jurisdictions this rule is absent. It is clear from LCC Article 6.193 according to which a contract must be interpreted in accordance with good faith. In interpreting a contract, it shall be necessary to seek the real intentions of the parties without being limited by the literal meaning of the words. In interpreting a contract, regard must also be taken of the preliminary negotiations between the parties, practices which the parties have established between themselves, the conduct of the parties subsequent to the conclusion of the contract and the existing usages.

B. *Function of the Notary*

176. As in other civil law jurisdictions, in Lithuania the system of Latin notary is in force, where notaries are expected to be the substantive private law practitioners of outstanding competence.[111] Under the Law on Notariate, a notary is a person authorised by the State, performing the functions set out in this law, which are aimed at preventing any illegal transactions and documents in civil law relationships. Notaries are appointed through public competition and dismissed by the Minister of Justice of the Republic of Lithuania. Prior to assuming office, a person appointed as a notary shall swear an oath administered by the Minister of Justice of the Republic of Lithuania.

177. A notary must hold a higher university degree in law and continuously improve his qualifications. The improvement of qualifications of notaries shall be

110. Catherine Elliott, Frances Quinn. *Contract Law*. 7th ed., Pearson Longman, 2009, p. 125–126.

111. On the concept of Latin notary *see* Pedro A. Malavet. *Counsel for the Situation: The Latin Notary, A Historical and Comparative Model. In.* Hastings International and Comparative Law Review, Vol. 19, 1996, p. 389–488.

organised by the Chamber of Notaries and coordinated by the Ministry of Justice of the Republic of Lithuania. Notaries shall undergo regular assessments. The assessment of notaries shall be carried out by the Chamber of Notaries.

178. Notarial acts may be performed only by a notary covered by compulsory insurance of notaries against professional civil liability. Notaries should exercise their powers disregarding any influence of public and administrative authorities and shall obey only laws. A notary cannot receive any remuneration other than a notary's fee, remuneration for work at the Chamber of Notaries or payment for teaching or creative activities. Notaries must ensure the confidentiality of notarial acts. Certificates about notarial acts and documents shall only be issued to legal and natural persons under whose authorisation or for whom notarial acts have been performed, or to the representatives of such persons. All records of a notary shall be kept in the state language. Transactions with foreign natural and legal persons shall be concluded in the state language and in another language acceptable to both the parties.

179. Notarial acts shall be performed at a notary office. The performance of notarial acts is only allowed at places other than the premises of a notary office where the person concerned is not able to come to a notary office for valid reasons (disease, disability or other cases) and requests a notary to arrive at his house, a medical or any other institution, where a notarial act is performed with the involvement of more than ten persons or where a notarial act is performed in a formal ceremony. Notarial acts should be performed immediately after the necessary documents have been submitted and the set fee has been collected. The performance of notarial acts may be postponed where additional information is required, but no longer than for ten calendar days. The notaries must explain the meaning and consequences of notarial acts to be performed to persons who want them to be performed. In the event of a complex transaction, a protocol of the conclusion (negotiation) of a transaction may be drafted, which shall be signed by the parties to the transaction and the notary.

180. Under the Law on Notariate Article 26, notaries perform the following notarial acts: (1) approve transactions; (2) issue certificates of succession; (3) issue certificates of title to a share in community property; (4) authenticate copies and extracts of documents; (5) authenticate signatures on documents; (6) authenticate the translation of documents from one language into another; (7) approve to the fact that a natural person is alive and at a particular place; (8) accept into custody wills which are equivalent to official wills and personal wills; (9) approve to the time of the submission of documents; (10) hand statements of natural and legal persons over to other natural and legal persons; (11) accept sums of money into the deposit account; (12) accept sea protests; (13) protest bills of exchange and cheques; (14) make executive inscriptions on protested or non-protestable bills of exchange and cheques; (15) make executive inscriptions on enforced recovery of the debt upon the mortgage (pledge) creditor's request; (16) draft or approve documents on the authenticity of data submitted to the Register of Legal Persons and approve that the legal person can be registered because the obligations set out by laws or the incorporation transaction have been fulfilled and the circumstances provided for by laws or incorporation documents have occurred; (17) approve to the compliance of incorporation documents of legal persons with the requirements of the laws; and (18) perform other notarial acts provided for by laws. It is recognised that facts contained in notarised documents are established and not subject to proof unless these documents (or parts thereof) have been invalidated in accordance with the procedure laid down by laws.

181. A notary shall approve contracts and other transactions in respect of which a mandatory notarial form is provided for by the LCC or other laws in the cases specified by the LCC, i.e., the contracts on the transfer of the property rights in an immovable thing; transactions on the encumbrance of the property rights and of the immovable thing (except transactions which are concluded in the insolvency procedure); property trust contracts, gift of at least EUR 14,500; contracts for the partition of inherited real property; prenuptial and postnuptial agreements; loan contracts where lender lends at least EUR 3,000 as cash; contracts for the sale of private limited liability company shares, where either the object of sale is at least 25% of all shares or the price of shares is more than EUR 14,500; and other transactions which are to be notarised in accordance with the mandatory provisions of LCC (LCC Articles 1.74, 5.70, 6.469, 6.871, 6.960). A notary may also approve transactions which under laws may be made in oral form or have to be made in ordinary written form. Transactions relating to the transfer of ownership of immovables or movables which are subject to legal registration under laws to another person, their lease or transfer for use in any other way, pledge or other rights *in rem* or their encumbrances shall be approved by a notary only after having established that this property belongs to the transferor by the ownership. A notary shall approve a transaction related to joint community property where in the cases specified by the LCC the transaction is made by both the spouses, or one of the spouses has the power of attorney granted by the other spouse to enter into such a transaction, or there is a written consent of the other spouse or authorisation of the court. A transaction relating to the transfer, mortgage of an immovable which is the personal property of one of the spouses but attributed to the family property, or any other encumbrance of rights *in rem* shall be approved by a notary only subject to a written consent of the other spouse. Where a family has minor children, a transaction in respect of an immovable which is treated as the family property shall be approved by a notary only subject to the authorisation of the court. In contracts on the transfer of ownership of an immovable, a notary shall specify the time (hours and minutes) of the conclusion of the contract. Such contracts shall also indicate that the ownership of the immovable shall pass to the acquirer from the moment of the transfer of the property, and parties to the contract may invoke the contract on the transfer of ownership of the immovable against third parties only where the fact of the passing of ownership under a transfer-acceptance deed or any other document has been registered in a public register in accordance with the procedure laid down by laws. Data about approved contracts shall be communicated by a notary to the manager of the public register within twenty-four hours from the moment of the approval of the contract in accordance with the procedure laid down by laws. When approving hypothec (pledge) contracts, a notary shall specify the time (hours and minutes) of the conclusion of the contract. Having approved the hypothec (pledge) transaction, the end of hypothec (pledge), having established enforced hypothec (pledge), a notary public forwards the data on the hypothec (pledge) to the Hypothec Register for registration in accordance with the provisions of the Hypothec register regulations.

182. A notary is liable in accordance with the procedure laid down by the LCC and Law on Notariate for damage caused to natural or legal persons by fault of his own, his agent and the staff of his notary office in the pursuit of notarial professional activities. The practical problem is that Lithuanian courts characterise liability of the notary against his clients as based on tort, despite the *non-cumul* rule (LCC Article 6.245(4)), which restricts application of tort rules to the contractual relations.[112] This apparently flows from the premise that there is no contract between the notary and the client. But this premise is wrong because it fails to insight *de facto* contract, which has all the attributes of professional services contract.

183. In addition, a notary is liable as a public official for violations of laws or other legal acts committed in the course of performing notarial acts, which are subject to criminal or administrative liability. Administrative supervision of the activities of notaries and their self-governing bodies is carried out by persons appointed by the Minister of Justice of the Republic of Lithuania. The Minister of Justice of the Republic of Lithuania or the Presidium of the Chamber of Notaries shall have the right to institute a disciplinary action against a notary for violations of the Law of the Republic of Lithuania on the Notarial Profession, legal acts approved by the Minister of Justice of the Republic of Lithuania and the Code of Honour (Ethics) of Notaries of the Republic of Lithuania.

184. However, despite these rules, the system of Lithuanian notaries still has some shortcomings. The main problem is that legislator delegated for notaries exceptional role in private law, but in practice notaries are very conservative, formalistic and reluctant to approve non-standard transactions. This practice in part is caused by the fear to lose professional chair because it is very difficult to get it as the number of notaries in the market is limited. In comparison, competition between members of similar legal profession – advocates (attorneys at law) – has grown tremendously during last decade, and this trend dramatically enhanced their competence. Of course, rigid style of Lithuanian notaries is to some extent is legitimate in the fields of property, family and inheritance law, where freedom of contract is restricted. However, this is totally not applicable to the company law, where the role of notaries in the mergers and acquisitions transactions has significantly increased, and at less extent applicable to the consensual security interests – hypothec, non-possessory charge and pledge, where freedom of contract was broadened during the recent reforms.

112. Judgment of the Lithuanian Supreme Court of 6 Oct. 2008 in the civil case No 3K-3-452/2008.

III. Burden of Proof

A. *General Procedural Framework*

185. Under the general rule on *onus probandi* set in CCP Article 178, the parties must prove the circumstances used as a basis to substantiate their claims and defences, except for circumstances that are considered to be existent without any need to prove them, i.e., legal presumptions, party's admissions, prejudicial facts and universally known facts. For example, if the debtor has concluded a suspected transaction with his spouse, children, parents or other close relatives, or if a suspected transaction has been made upon the payment of a debt that has not yet matured, it is presumed in the *actio Pauliana* litigation that the parties to a suspected transaction by whom interests of the creditor are violated were *mala fides* (LCC Article 6.67(1)). As for universally known facts, it is apparent that one has no need to prove such facts, as the fact, that Lithuania is in the European continent, or that a whole day has twenty-four hours. Prejudicial facts are proven in other legal procedure, such as in criminal trial; therefore, there is no need to repeat the proof of them. In addition, according to CCP Article 187, a party is entitled to admit the facts used as a basis by another party to substantiate the latter's claim or replication. A court may consider the admitted fact established, if it believes the admission is coherent with circumstances of the case and is not stated for deception, violence, threat, by mistake or in order to suppress the truth.

186. Accordingly, evidence shall be presented by parties and other participants in a proceeding. However, a court shall accept for hearing only such evidence that confirms or denies circumstances relevant to the case. From the other side, if the obtained evidence is not enough, the court may offer the parties and other participants in the proceeding to provide the court with corroborative evidence and fix a time limit for presentation thereof. The court is entitled to collect evidence on its own initiative (ex officio) exclusively in cases stipulated by the laws (CCP Article 179–180).

B. *Substantive Layers: Duty of Best Efforts and Duty of Result*

187. From the substantive point of view, proof is different depending on the obligation breached. Usually, personal duties are divided into the duties of best efforts and duties of result. The difference lies in the nature and intensity of particular duties. In general, the obligor should make the contractual expectations of obligee come true. That is why parties are going into contract at all. However, despite high expectations, in some contracts, such as medical, legal or other professional services, provider cannot objectively ensure achievement of expected result, all he can do is to ensure the most diligent performance possible. Performance of other contracts, such as of sale, deposit or mandate, does not so heavily depend on the external factors, third parties (e.g., courts, Government) or fortune in general. Hence, the threshold for liability is different. It is unjust to apply liability to the physician for the death of his patient, if he did all he could in that situation and despite that all efforts to cure patient were unsuccessful. In fact, liability solely for the failure to achieve result in these cases would provoke service providers to take unpredictable, risky or even illegal actions, such as to try experimental unapproved drugs to cure ill patient or bribe judge in order to win case for the client. From the other side, if seller despite his best efforts did not deliver the goods, there are no economic reasons to exclude him from liability because pattern of exclusion would lead to inefficient risk distribution in contracts and increased interruptions in commerce. Therefore, two types of obligations are distinguished in civil contract law – duty of best efforts (*obligation de moyens*) and duty of result (*obligation de résultat*).

188. According to the Romanic civilian sources, the essential difference between the two types of obligation lies therefore in the burden of proof. In both cases, the burden of showing that the debtor has not performed his obligation lies, as usual, on the creditor, but since in an *obligation de moyens* the failure to take care is an essential element in the non-performance, the burden of proof of fault lies on the creditor, whereas in an *obligation de résultat* the creditor has only to show that the result has not been achieved, and it is then for the debtor to show a *actus novus interveniens.*[113] It effectively means that breach of best efforts duty equals to fault, whereas breach of result duty leads to strict liability.[114]

189. Even more stricter or almost absolute obligations are so-called obligations to warranty (*obligation de garantie*), which are a subtype of obligations of result. Obligations of warranty are those of the highest intensity because the debtor may escape liability for non-performance only by proving fault of the creditor.[115]

190. The classification of obligations according to their intensity is accepted and used by Lithuanian legal doctrine.[116] Moreover, case law even overused it in one instance, where has declared the intensity of a duty as the criteria to distinguish services contracts from the works contracts. Hence, Supreme Court has assigned the duty of result as the describing characteristic of the works contract, while duty of best efforts was attributed to services contract.[117] Whereas this reasoning may have some limited explanatory role, intensity of obligations is very unreliable criterion of

---

113. Barry Nicholas. *French Law of Contract.* Butterworths, 1982, p. 50.
114. More on this from a functional and comparative perspective, *see* Bénédicte Fauvarque-Cosson, Denis Mazeaud, *et al. European Contract Law: Materials for a Common Frame of Reference: Terminology, Guiding Principles, Model Rules.* Sellier, 2008, p. 223–224; Ulrich Magnus, Hans W. Micklitz. *Comparative Analysis* of *National Liability Systems* for *Remedying Damage Caused* by *Defective Consumer Services.* Final report. Institut für Europäisches Wirtschafts und Verbraucherrecht, 2004, p. 106, 118; Benedicte Fauvarque-Cosson, Hugh Beale, Jacobien Rutgers, Denis Tallon, Stefan Vogenauer. *Cases, Materials and Text on Contract Law.* 2nd ed., Hart Publishing, 2010, p. 721–729; Pierre Widmer; *et al. Unification of Tort Law: Fault.* Kluwer Law International, 2005, p. 97.
115. *See* John E.C. Brierley; Roderick A. Macdonal (eds). *Quebec civil law: an introduction to Quebec private law.* E. Montgomery Publications, 1993, p. 386.
116. Valentinas Mikelėnas. *Prievolių teisė. Pirmoji dalis.* Justitia: Vilnius, 2002, p. 70–74.
117. Judgment of the Lithuanian Supreme Court of 5 Dec. 2012 in the civil case No 3K-3-543/2012 and of 16 Jan. 2013 in the civil case No 3K-3-110/2013.

characterisation. First, in both cases intensity really depends on particular agreement of parties because service contract may easily create obligation of result, while works contract may create obligation of best efforts. Second, works contract according to its legal nature is nothing more than special type of service contract (LCC Article 6.716(3)), and this distinction is superficial anyway.

§3. Liability and Negotiations

I. Precontractual Relations

191. Under the freedom of contract (LCC Article 6.156(2)), it is prohibited to force another person to conclude a contract, except in cases when the duty to enter into a contract is established by laws or a voluntary undertaking. Hence, parties shall be free to begin negotiations and negotiate and shall not be liable for failure to reach an agreement (LCC Article 6.163(2)). Negotiation and other relationships which are intended to lead to the contract are called precontractual relations.

192. Lithuanian legal doctrine, reflecting internationally known Dutch case law[118], usually distinguish the following stages of precontractual relations: (i) the initial or prior negotiations stage where the parties present each other and exchange their initial proposals; (ii) the second stage when the parties reach the principal consent and the legitimate belief that the contract will be concluded exists; and (iii) the final stage when all the key terms of the contract are agreed, but only some issues are left which do not allow the parties to conclude the main contract.[119] It is evident from contracting practice that not every negotiation takes this standard routine, which is more characteristic to the complex and lengthy corporate negotiations. Often there are peculiarities which deviate from this model, leaving it to serve simply as an academic example in university contract law courses.

II. Precontractual Obligations

193. Despite the general contractual freedom, Lithuanian law establishes important tortious and contractual obligations in precontractual relationships, which are intended to target unfair opportunism. Precontractual rules are totally new provisions of the LCC and were introduced for several reasons. First of all, the reality is that many contracts, especially commercial ones, are the result of protracted negotiations between the parties, and such a negative situation needs to be changed. Another reason was the lack of legislative provisions in this respect. This used to cause some difficulties for courts' practice; for example, there was no clarity as to

118. Judgment of Hoge Raad des Nederlanden of 18 Jun. 1982 in the civil case *Plas v. Valburg*, NJ 1983, 723.

119. Valentinas Mikelėnas. *Sutarčių teisė. Bendrieji sutarčių teisės klausimai: lyginamoji studija.* Vilnius: Justitia, 1996, p. 145–146, 168; Agnė Jakaitė. *Civilinė atsakomybė esant ikisutartiniams santykiams.* Doctoral dissertation. Vilnius University, 2012, p. 44–46.

how to qualify the precontractual agreements between the parties and how to resolve the issue of precontractual liability.[120]

194. Basic tort law rule, established in LCC Article 6.263, states that every person shall have the duty to abide by the rules of conduct so as not to cause damage to another by his actions (active actions or omissions). In the context of precontractual relations, this rule is further elaborated by LCC Article 6.163. Under this article, during the precontractual relationships, parties should conduct themselves in accordance with good faith. A party who begins negotiations or negotiates in bad faith shall be liable for the damage caused to the other party. It is bad faith for a party to enter into negotiations or continue them without real intentions to reach an agreement with the other party, likewise any other actions that do not conform to the criteria of good faith (LCC Article 6.163 (1,3)). For instance, it is unfair to bargain an already agreed matter, to enter into a knowingly invalid contract, to delay negotiations, to carry out undisclosed parallel negotiations, to hide real identity of party and – mostly important in practice – to withdraw from advanced negotiations without serious cause.

195. As to the freedom to withdraw from advanced negotiations, Lithuanian legal doctrine usually borrows scheme from the above-mentioned Dutch landmark case *Plas v. Valburg*, where the legal consequences depend on the stage of negotiations: (i) in an initial stage, the parties are free to break off negotiations, without any obligation to pay damages to the other party; (ii) in a continuing stage, a party may be free to break off negotiations, however, under the obligation to compensate the other party for expenses incurred; and (iii) in a final stage a party is not allowed to break off negotiations and violation of this obligation may give rise to compensation of the other party's expenses and also, if appropriate, the additional damages.[121] In assessing whether the negotiations are far advanced to bound the parties with *culpa in contrahendo* all the following facts and circumstances should be taken into consideration: the duration of negotiations, the stage of negotiations, the intensity of negotiations' process, the preliminary contracts and the reasonable and lawful belief that the contract will be concluded between the parties. The breach of such advanced negotiations is determined as justifiable only if the reasons are objective.[122]

196. In addition, under LCC Article 6.163(4), the parties shall be bound to disclose to each other the material information, i.e., which is of essential importance for the conclusion of a contract they have. Thus, parties should apply the test for materiality when deciding about provision of information. For example, in professional services material information concerns the risks of services: risk of fatal injury during the surgery; risk of capital loss in investment; and risk of dangerous

120. Valentinas Mikelėnas. *The Main Features of the New Lithuanian Contract Law System Based on the Civil Code of 2000.* Juridica International, Vol. 10, 2005, p. 46.
121. Judgment of Hoge Raad des Nederlanden of 18 Jun. 1982 in the civil case *Plas v. Valburg*, NJ 1983, 723.
122. Agnė Jakaitė. *Civilinė atsakomybė esant ikisutartiniams santykiams.* Doctoral dissertation. Vilnius University, 2012, p. 259.

counterclaim in litigation. In Lithuanian case law, precontractual misrepresentations were popular cause of action against banks during the waves of post-crisis financial services litigation.[123] For example, in *Snoras* case, which went even to the ECJ for preliminary ruling, investors concluded the investment agreements with banks 'Snoras' AB ('Snoras') for the acquisition of inflation-linked certificates of deposit and bonds. By decision of the Lithuanian Government of 16 November 2011, Snoras' business activities were suspended. On 24 November 2011, the Lithuanian central bank took a legal action with a view to insolvency proceedings being opened against Snoras. Then investors have brought legal proceedings seeking a declaration of invalidity in respect of the agreements they had concluded with Snoras. They claimed, in essence, that the bank had provided them with misleading and incomplete information concerning: (i) the application of the guarantee to the instruments purchased and (ii) Snoras' financial position.[124] In the aftermath, Supreme Court has dismissed actions related to invalidity of investment contracts due to the lack of materiality of misrepresentations, but protected part of investors (subscribers of certificates of deposit) on the other grounds.[125]

197. However, when during negotiations one party furnishes the other with confidential information, the party that has learned or received such information shall be under the duty not to disclose it or use it unlawfully for his own purposes, irrespective of whether a contract is subsequently concluded or not. The breach of confidentiality inflicts liability of the faulty party in damages suffered by the injured party. In such cases, the minimal amount of recoverable damages shall consist of monetary expression of benefit received (LCC Article 6.164).

198. Therefore, it is clear from above that Lithuania law has codified the content of *culpa in contrahendo* doctrine, formulated in the nineteenth century by the famous German lawyer Rudolf von Jhering.[126] Also, Lithuanian law establishes the complementary institution of *pactum de contrahendo*, i.e., preliminary contract, which is a source of organisational contractual obligations. By statutory definition,

123. *See* Judgments of the Lithuanian Supreme Court of 28 Jun. 2013 in the civil case No 3K-3-381/2013 and of 17 Mar. 2014 in the civil case No 3K-3-68/2014.

124. Judgment of the ECJ of 25 Jun. 2015 in Case C-671/13.

125. Judgment of the Lithuanian Supreme Court of 17 Nov. 2015 in the civil case No 3K-7-602-684/2015.

126. It should be recalled that in 1861, Rudolf von Jhering advanced the thesis that parties to precontractual negotiations are contractually bound to observe the 'necessary diligentia'. A party who commits a breach of this contractual obligation – a *culpa in contrahendo* (fault in contractual negotiation) – is therefore liable for reliance damages. Jhering himself was concerned primarily with such problems as the effect of *culpa* on contracts concluded by mistake and never applied his thesis to situations involving failed negotiations. It was a French scholar, Raymond Saleilles, who in 1907 advanced the view that after parties have entered into negotiations, both must act in good faith and neither can break off the negotiations 'arbitrarily' without compensating the other for reliance damages. German courts have, however, relied on Jhering's thesis as a basis of precontractual liability. According to the *Bundesgerichtshof*, fault in contractual negotiations that renders one liable for damages can also exist in that one party awakes in the other confidence in the imminent coming into existence of a contract subsequently not concluded and thus causes the latter party to incur expenses. *See* E. Allan Farnsworth. *Precontractual Liability and Preliminary Agreements: Fair Dealing and Failed Negotiations.* Columbia Law Review, Vol. 87, No. 2, 1987, p. 240.

a preliminary contract is an agreement of parties by which they bound themselves to conclude another – final – contract in future under the conditions negotiated in the agreement.[127] A preliminary contract must be made in writing. A preliminary contract which fails to meet the required conditions of its form shall be null and void. In the preliminary contract, the parties are bound to establish a time limit within which the final contract must be formed. In the event where such time limit is not established in the preliminary contract, the final contract must be formed within one year from the date of the conclusion of the preliminary contract. If after conclusion of the preliminary contract, a party without due grounds avoids or refuses to enter into a final contract, he shall be bound to pay to the other party damages. In the event where the parties fail to form a principal contract within the time limit determined in the preliminary contract, the obligation to form that contract is extinguished (LCC Article 6.165).

III. Remedies

199. According to LCC Article 6.163, a party who begins negotiations or negotiates in bad faith is liable to pay damages to the other party. Thus, the main response to precontractual wrongs under Lithuanian law is the application of civil liability. Remedy of specific performance is unavailable in the precontractual stage because forcing party in court to conclude the contract would undermine the freedom of contract. Under case law, even preliminary contracts, which in Lithuania are treated as contracts (albeit of organisational character), cannot be enforced for specific performance (*in natura*).[128]

200. Single exception is a preliminary contract for the purchase of a planned house by the consumer, where normal contractual remedies, including specific performance, are available.[129] Under this agreement, the seller – a legal person undertakes a duty to build the residential house or apartment provided in the contract by itself or upon enlisting the help of other persons and thereafter conclude with the buyer, which is a consumer, a contract for the sale of the residential house or apartment, whereas the buyer obligates himself to purchase the built house or apartment for the price indicated in the preliminary contract. It may also be stipulated in the preliminary contract that the buyer finances the construction of the residential house or apartment under the conditions provided in the contract whereas the seller shall perform the functions of customer. In this case, the buyer shall acquire the right of ownership to the residential house or apartment upon payment of the construction price provided in the preliminary contract. LCC Article 6.401 (1, 5).

127. Preliminary contract should be distinguished from the option contract, which is another type of precontractual agreement. An option is a contract whereby the parties agree that the offeror is bound by his offer for a specified period of time and that the offeree may accept within that time. According to Lithuanian civil law, financial options have status of investment security (LCC Art. 1.101).
128. Judgment of the Lithuanian Supreme Court of 6 Oct. 2008 in the civil case No 3K-3-455/2008.
129. Judgment of the Lithuanian Supreme Court of 23 Dec. 2008 in the civil case No 3K-3-608/2008.

201. There is an ongoing discussion in Lithuania concerning the legal nature of the precontractual liability. The prevailing view, which is mostly supported by the case law, is that precontractual liability in general is based on tort.[130] In cases where preliminary contract was breached, due to the principle of *non-cumul*, civil liability is contractual in nature.[131] Another group of authors opposes this view stressing the unique (sui generis) nature of precontractual liability, which by some is even called as the third type of civil liability. The main argument is that breach of precontractual agreement gives rise to reliance damages – tort remedy, not the expectation damages – contract remedy.[132] This argument, indeed, until recent shift in case law made sense because precontractual liability under Lithuanian case law and legal doctrine, closely following soft law sources, granted only reliance damages, *ex ante* excluding recovery of lost profits but including lost opportunities.[133]

202. However, limitation of precontractual liability to reliance (negative) interest is not decisive for the characterisation of the third liability type. First, under current civil liability system, there are only two types of civil liability (tortious and contractual), and these are delimitated by clear and strict Romanic rule of *non-cumul des responsabilités* (LCC Article 6.245(4)). The same clear-cut delineation, perfectly fitting for Lithuanian civil law, has been expressed also by the ECJ in the context of EU private international law. ECJ has stated that the obligation to make good the damage allegedly caused by the unjustified breaking off negotiations could derive only from breach of rules of law, in particular the rule which requires the parties to act in good faith in negotiations with a view to the formation of a contract. In those circumstances, it is clear that any liability which may follow from the failure to conclude the contract referred to in the main proceedings cannot be contractual. In circumstances characterised by the absence of obligations freely assumed by one party towards another on the occasion of negotiations with a view to the formation of a contract and by a possible breach of rules of law, in particular the rule which requires the parties to act in good faith in such negotiations, an action founded on the precontractual liability of the defendant is a matter relating to tort, delict or quasi-delict within the meaning of Article 5(3) of the Brussels Convention.[134] Second, the fact that liability in precontractual stage is untypically restricted to reliance (negative) interest is not the reason to recharacterise liability to the third type. Third, there is no need to 'reinvent the wheel' in Lithuanian law because both

130. Judgments of the Lithuanian Supreme Court of 12 Dec. 2002 in the civil case No 3K-7-1156/2002 and of 29 Sep. 2009 in the civil case No 3K-3-363/2009; etc.

131. Dalia Mikelėnienė, Valentinas Mikelėnas. *Lithuanian Contract Law.* International Encyclopedia of Laws. The Hague, Kluwer Law International, 2004, p. 97; Agnė Jakaitė. *Civilinė atsakomybė esant ikisutartiniams santykiams.* Doctoral dissertation. Vilnius University, 2012, pp. 91–92.

132. Stasys Drazdauskas. *Bendrosios sutarčių teisės vienodinimo įtaka Lietuvos sutarčių teisei.* Doctoral dissertation (social sciences, law (01 S), Vilnius University, 2011, p. 194); Dangutė Ambrasienė, Indrė Kryžiūtė. *Atsakomybės už preliminariosios sutarties nevykdymą problemos.* Jurisprudencija, Nr. 19(2), 2012, p. 579.

133. *See* Judgments of the Lithuanian Supreme Court of 19 Jan. 2005 in the civil case No 3K-3-38/2005 and of 6 Nov. 2006 in the civil case No 3K-P-382/2006. For doctrinal sources on the amount of precontractual damages, *see* Valentinas Mikelėnas. *Lietuvos Respublikos civilinio kodekso komentaras. Šeštoji knyga. Prievolių teisė.* Justitia, 2003, I t., p. 208.

134. Judgment of the ECJ of 17 Sep. 2002 in the Case C-334/00.

contract law and tort law enable recovery of pure economic loss, which is prevalent in precontractual relationships. Limitations of tort liability on the recovery of pure economic loss in some jurisdictions, such as Germany, forced courts to grant recovery on the theories floating somewhere between tort law and contract law;[135] however, as it was mentioned above, this limitation is not present in Lithuanian law.

203. From the other side, the characterisation of liability for breach of preliminary contract as contractual for several decades after enactment of LCC was also superficial. Outside cases of penalty clauses and specific preliminary contracts for the purchase of planned house by the consumer, precontractual remedies were focused to put plaintiff into a position where he did not conclude a breached preliminary contract with a defendant at all, i.e., were limited to reliance interest only. General exclusion of expectation damages is obviously alien to the main principles and philosophy of contract law focused on performance of agreed obligations. Thus, it may be concluded that despite nominal labelling as 'contractual liability', Lithuanian courts for breaches of preliminary agreements *de facto* had applied tortious liability focused on the protection of reliance interest.[136]

204. However, in 2022, the LSC has allowed the award of expectation and even restitutionary damages for the breach of the *pactum de contrahendo* in situation where party refused to perform preliminary agreement and sign principal contract.[137] This was a major shift from the former case law, significant not only in practical terms (giving wider variety of available precontractual remedies) but also in interplay between different contract law principles (*pacta sunt servanda* versus

135. B.S. Markesinis, Hannes Unberath, Angus Johnston, Lord Bingham, Gunter Hirsch. *The German Law of Contract: A Comparative Treatise*. Hart Publishing, 2006, pp. 92–108.

136. Some law and economics scholars have disputed the use of reliance interest in precontractual damages. For instance, R. Craswell argues that there is no economic rationale to prefer compensation of the reliance interest to other damage measures. Most damage measures, in fact, will give the parties incentives to rely too much, and the reliance measure could prove to be the worst of all in this respect. Instead, the proper damage measure should take into account all relevant economic variables that may be affected by the magnitude of compensation, in particular risk-bearing costs, incentives to search for contracting partners and incentives to investigate the profitability of the proposed deal. The preference for the reliance measure identified in the literature is probably motivated by the fact that the reliance measure is the minimum measure necessary to give optimal incentives to rely. However, parties in some situations may be willing to commit themselves to a larger damage measure, for example, in order to give their partner a positive signal of their willingness to conclude the deal. These observations seem to suggest that the choice of the optimal damage measure is possible only by carefully considering each particular set of case facts, so that it is neither desirable nor feasible to formulate a single, general solution. A similar intuition that the proper damage measure depends on the specific goals that need to be addressed in different contexts can also be found on the basis of O. Ben-Shahar's argument. The author presents his no-retraction principle as a liability rule that can be coupled with different damage measures 'depending on the underlying objectives that the remedy seeks to promote'. In the context of precontractual liability, where the social objective is to induce efficient reliance despite the risk of hold-up, however, O. Ben-Shahar specifically suggests that the reliance measure should apply. *See* Eleonora C. Melato. *Precontractual liability. In* Contract law and economics. Encyclopaedia of Law and Economics. 2 ed. Edward Elgar Publishing, 2011, pp. 27–28.

137. Judgments of the Lithuanian Supreme Court of 12 Sep. 2022 in the civil case No. e3K-3-188-1075/2022 and of 3 November 2022 in the civil case No e3K-3 241-381/2022.

freedom of contract) and even the nature of precontractual liability. As long as such case law granting an expectation remedy will continue in future, precontractual liability for the breach of the *pactum de contrahendo* could be rightly labelled in Lithuania as contractual one.

205. One should note that civil liability may arise not only where the party has unfairly abandoned negotiations and contract was not concluded at all but also where it has made precontractual wrongs which either has led to the losses despite the conclusion of valid contract or in addition to damage even made the concluded contract invalid. Civil liability in these cases also arises due to the precontractual wrongs and, according to the principle of *non-cumul*, is based on tort law, despite the subsequent conclusion of contract.[138] It means that reliance damages are normal remedies and injured party may not recover lost profits from the invalid contract, because this remedy would equalise void (voidable) contract with valid one. Instead, it can recover direct losses and lost opportunity to bargain. It should be noted that in contrast with conventional view[139], in some cases reliance damages may even exceed expectation damages, for instance, in the investment services where the proper investment in any case would be unsuccessful. In this example, reliance damages for precontractual wrongs would bring the invested capital to investor back thus enabling him to avoid unsuccessful investment, whereas expectation damages for the breach of contract would not be awarded due to the lack of causation as loss was anyway caused by unfortunate market events.

206. In Lithuanian contracting practice, especially in real estate market, very common instrument used to enforce preliminary contracts is penalty clause. Since case law and LCC (which have codified it) have prohibited use of earnest money to secure preliminary contracts (on the purely theoretical reason that earnest money evidences conclusion of a final contract which is absent in case of preliminary contract), this vacant place was promptly taken by the penalty clauses. These clauses often function in identical manner as earnest money: the buyer makes an advance payment; if the buyer will refuse to conclude a contract in breach of preliminary contract, a deposit will become a property of the seller as penalty; and if the seller will abandon the deal, he is liable to return the advance payment to the buyer and in addition to pay sum equal to the advance payment as penalty. So far, the transactional practice is satisfied with this solution; however, earnest money clause is much reliable instrument than penalty clause because former cannot be reduced in contrast with latter, which usually falls under judicial review. The only problem is that earnest money is inaccessible in precontractual stage.

138. However, courts in investment services litigation failed to take it into account and controversially characterised precontractual misrepresentations as a basis for contractual liability, despite the award of reliance damages. *See* Judgment of the Lithuanian Supreme Court of 30 Jan. 2015 in the civil case No 3K-3-88-684/2015.

139. *See* Paul G. Mahoney. *Contract Remedies: General.* Encyclopaedia of Law and Economics. Vol. III. The Regulation of Contracts. Cheltenham, Edward Elgar, 2000, p. 121.

207. Judicial scepticism against contractual remedies for the precontractual wrongs, such as expectation damages and specific enforcement of preliminary contract, is also seen in the field of the rescissory remedies. Albeit a party still may dispute validity of the preliminary contract, under the case law she cannot terminate the valid preliminary contract on the grounds of fundamental breach. Supreme Court has declared this remedy unavailable for the breach of preliminary contracts on the reasoning that injured party should invoke special remedy – compensatory damages set in LCC Article 6.163 and not the other remedies.[140]

208. Where the final contract was concluded, contractual remedy – termination of a contract – normally should be impossible for the precontractual wrongs, such as misrepresentations, because there was no contract at the moment of wrong. These wrongs normally are actionable with claims for annulment of contract on the grounds of invalidity. However, usual practice in financial and business transactions is to tie contractual terms – representations, warranties and covenants with the precontractual facts. This transactional technique in effect enables to terminate even the final contract due to precontractual behaviour which by agreement constitutes the breach of a final contract term.

140. Judgment of the Lithuanian Supreme Court of 13 Jan. 2016 in the civil case No 3K-3-73-687/2016.

Chapter 2. Terms of Substantive Validity

209. Contemporary Lithuanian contract law is based on the libertarian ideas of voluntarism and consensualism. Yet, within the consensualist conception of contract, one needs correctives for cases where consent is obviously not enlightened (error and fraud) or free (threat of violence). In contrast, in a strictly formalist system, such as Roman law was, there would be little need to correct regretted decisions. The formalities would ensure well-considered decisions and exclude ill-advised ones as well as subtle fraud and violence. Prospectively all parties expect to benefit by the projected transaction. Criminal law would take care of cases of outright fraud and violence. However, formalism entails important costs: it increases transaction costs and it limits the range of acceptable contracts. This would slow down markets and may deprive us of innovations, the gains from which, taken over all contracts, will surely suffice to offset a few regretted decisions. Modern legal systems rather bet on innovation and hence go by the principle of consensualism, both as to the variety of contracts that can validly be entered into – an open set – and as to the absence of formalism for doing so.[141] Thus, a set of substantive controls on contracting in Lithuanian civil law is necessary to correct transactional failures, while preserving economic benefits of consensualism. Substantive controls are focused on the capacity of parties, integrity of their consent and the lawful content of agreement.

§1. The Capacity of the Parties

210. The necessary element of a contract, among the proper agreement, is capacity of parties. Parties of the contract are always persons, not the assets, such as incorporated investment fund. Persons may be natural and legal. Although no statutory definition of natural person exists, a natural person is a citizen or other human. A legal (moral) person according to LCC Article 2.33(1) is a company, agency or organisation, which may in its name gain and enjoy rights, assume obligations and act as a party in a court. Rules on the capacity differ for natural and legal persons.

I. Natural Persons

211. A contract (or any other legal act) can only be validly concluded by someone who has the legal capacity to do so. The law does not consider everyone fit to have this capacity. Two categories of people qualify for not being legally capable: certain minors (in particular young children) and people with mental or behavioural disorders. It is important to realise which conflicting interests are at stake here. Legal incapacity (*incapacite de contracter, Geschäftsfähigkeit, handelingsonbekwaamheid*) is an instrument to protect parties who are presumed not to be able to

141. Ejan Mackaay. *The civil law of contract. In* Contract law and economics. Encyclopedia of Law and Economics. 2 ed. Edward Elgar Publishing, 2011, pp. 434–435.

take care of their own interests. But this interest to receive legal protection may conflict with two other interests. First, it would be odd if all transactions of a minor or a mentally ill person could be invalidated. For instance, to declare adults incapable means that they are no longer allowed to be responsible for their own acts, presenting a grave violation of their right to determine which life they want to lead. Second, the law has to balance the interests of the incapacitated person with those with whom they deal. In particular in the case of mentally ill persons, it is not always apparent to the outside world that a party is not capable of making a rational decision. Each jurisdiction balances these interests in its own way, but the starting point is the same everywhere: every natural person has the legal capacity to perform legal transactions.[142] This is equally true for Lithuania, where LCC Article 2.1, relying on the constitutional liberties, prescribes that every natural person shall have the full enjoyment of civil law rights. Restrictions on the civil capacity may not be imposed on anyone in any other manner except by express provision of law. Therefore, transactions and acts of public or municipality institutions or officials, which impose restrictions on the capacity, are deemed to be null and void except in cases where the said transactions and acts are prescribed by law (LCC Article 2.6).

212. Capacity of natural persons in Lithuania is categorised into to two types – passive capacity and active capacity. Passive capacity (*teisnumas*) in essence means that all people may equally have civil law rights and they always are subjects (rights holders), not the objects (assets) of transaction, as it had been in ancient times of slavery and still happens in the form of human trafficking. Latter situations are strictly prohibited by the criminal law. Thus, a passive capacity is a theoretical possibility to have civil rights and duties. Practical possibility to directly exercise civil rights and duties is called active capacity (*veiksnumas*).

A. *Passive Capacity*

213. Passive civil capacity of a natural person begins at the moment of his birth and ends at the moment of his death. The first independent breath is considered to be the birth of a natural person, whereas full and irreversible stoppage of blood circulation or stoppage of all brain functions is considered to be the death of a natural person. The beginning of rights prescribed by law to a conceived but yet unborn baby shall depend on the act of its birth. In the event of the impossibility to establish whether a baby was born alive or dead, it shall be presumed that it was born alive. Where certain ensuing legal consequences depend on the fact which of natural persons died at an earlier date and where it is impossible to establish the moment of the act of death of them each, it shall be presumed that the said natural persons died at the same time (LCC Article 2.2, 2.3).

214. As to the content of passive capacity, law prescribes that natural persons are entitled to property as the object of private ownership and shall enjoy the right

142. Jan M. Smits. *Contract Law: A Comparative Introduction.* Edward Elgar Publishing, 2014, pp. 91–92.

to engage in commercial activities, establish enterprises or other legal entities, inherit property and bequeath it, choose a sphere of activities and residence, have invention or industrial sample rights as well as other pecuniary and individual non-pecuniary rights, which are protected by the civil law. Natural persons who, in accordance with the procedure established by the law, are engaged in commercial activities shall be deemed to be entrepreneurs. Every person engaged in business or practising of his profession shall have to administer his property and everything related to his undertaking or practising of his profession as well as to safeguard documents and other information about his property, undertaking or practising of his profession in the manner, which would enable every person, having a legal interest, at any time, to receive comprehensive information about the property rights and obligations of the person in question (LCC Article 2.4).

215. Natural persons who want to pursue business activities without incorporation, i.e., forming company, must register in the tax authority as taxpayers (Law on Tax Administration Article 40(3)). This form of business falls under regime of so-called independent activity (*individuali veikla*), which, according to Law on Income Tax of Individuals Article 2(7) means an activity in pursuit whereof an individual aims at deriving income or any other economic benefit over a continuous period: (1) independent commercial or industrial activities of any nature, with the exception of activity involving sale and/or lease of property immovable by nature, and transactions in financial instruments; (2) independent creative, scientific and professional activities, including professional services, and other similar independent activities; (3) independent sports activities; and (4) independent performing activities.

B. Active Capacity

216. Another and more important in practice type of capacity of natural persons is active civil capacity, which is defined as a possibility of natural person not only to enjoy but also to fully exercise all his rights by his actions and assume obligations. Active civil capacity may be full, limited or absent, where a person is incapable. Incapable persons are minors until 14 years of age and mentally ill persons (but only in specific fields of activities), because they are treated as unable to understand the meaning of their actions or control them. Incapable persons only enjoy but do not directly exercise their rights. Of limited capacity are minors from 14 to 18 years of age (teenagers) and less mentally ill or addictive persons because their capability to understand the meaning of actions or control them is limited by immaturity, health or addictions.

217. Full active capacity of natural persons begins on attaining full age, i.e., when a natural person is of 18 years of age. However, there are two important exceptions related to age threshold. First, where the law provides for the possibility of a natural person to enter into marriage before he is 18, the person, who has not yet come of the given age, shall acquire full active civil capacity at the moment of entering into marriage. If at a later date this marriage is dissolved or nullity of marriage is declared for reasons not related to the age of the parties to marriage, a minor does not lose his full active civil capacity (LCC Article 2.5). Second, where a minor is 16 years of age the court may emancipate him after he or his guardian, parents, institutions of guardianship or he himself has filed a declaration to that effect with the court if there are sufficient grounds to believe that he may exercise all civil rights and discharge his obligations alone. In all cases a minor has to give his consent to be emancipated. The court may annul minor's emancipation on the request of parents or childcare institutions if exercising his rights and discharging his obligations a minor causes damage to his own or other persons' rights or lawful interests (LCC Article 2.9).

C. *Minors*

218. As it has been said above, active civil capacity of minors under 14 years of age is absent, i.e., they are deemed to be incapable for normal contracting and can enter only into simple transactions. According to LCC Article 2.7, contracts on behalf and in the name of minors under 14 years of age should be concluded by their parents or guardians. Upon entering into contracts and enforcing them, parents and guardians should have to act exceptionally in the interest of minors. Rights and obligations of parents and guardians in administering the property of minors are laid down in the provisions of Book III of the LCC. Minors under 14 years of age can enjoy the right to enter alone into contracts to meet their ordinary and usual needs, conclude contracts aiming at gratuitous personal gain, as well as conclude contracts related to the use of their own earnings or money provided by their legal representatives or other persons if the said contracts fail to have a prescribed notarial or any other specific form. Where a contract concluded by a minor under 14 years of age is not recognised to be null and void and where the said person becomes legally capable, the other party to the contract may apply in writing to the party to the contract, who has become legally capable, and request the approval of the contract within the time limits, which may not be shorter than one month, determined in the application. Where the person fails to notify about his refusal to approve the contract within the proposed time limits, he shall be deemed to have approved the contract. Liability over contractual obligations of minors, who are under 14 years of age, bears their legal representatives, unless they succeed in proving that they are not at fault for the breach of the said obligations.

219. Minors over 14 and under 18 years of age have only limited active capacity and according to LCC Article 2.8 can enter into contracts with the consent of parents or guardians. The form of consent must have to correspond to the form of the contract concluded. Contracts concluded without the consent of legal representatives are to be deemed valid if the consent of the legal representative is given after the contract has been concluded. Minors over 14 but under 18 years of age, in addition to the rights, which have minors under 14 years of age, have the right to dispose of their income and property acquired for that income, implement copyright to their works, inventions and industrial design as well as the right to enter into contracts alone to meet their ordinary and usual needs. However, where there are sufficient grounds, the court may be called upon to rule on an application filed by childcare institutions or other interested persons to impose restrictions on or divest minors, who are over 14 but under 18 years of age, of the right to dispose independently of their income and property. Minors over 14 but under 18 years of age are alone liable for their contractual obligations.

D. Adult Persons with Mental or Behavioural Disorders

220. In comparison to rules on minors, much more problematic in Lithuania seemed to be the regulation on capacity of mentally ill and addictive persons. Initially, limited capacity could only be established in cases where individuals were abusing alcohol, drugs or toxic substances, while persons with mental or intellectual disabilities had no capacity at all. According to some opinions, absolute absence of legal capacity failed to differentiate people and transformed them into 'legal objects' and 'social nobodies'. A strong impetus for reform came about after the European Court of Human Rights (ECHR) decision in the case of *D.D. v. Lithuania* (2012), where the applicant was represented by the Human Rights Monitoring Institute. The court criticised Lithuania for the fact that D.D. was not given the opportunity to participate in court proceedings regarding her legal capacity and was not informed on the consideration of the case related to her involuntary institutionalisation (violations of Articles 5 and 6 of the European Convention on Human Rights).[143] Legal amendments passed in 2015 bring change to Lithuania's regulations on incapacity, allowing persons with mental or intellectual disabilities to have the rights of limited capacity in some fields. The new regime allows for limited capacity in specific fields for persons that have mental or intellectual disabilities.[144] Legal reform in any case was inevitable because in 2010 Lithuania ratified the UN Convention on the Rights of Persons with Disabilities and its Optional Protocol and has since undertook obligation to ensure its effective implementation and to guarantee quality life for disabled persons.[145]

143. Judgment of ECHR of 14 Feb. 2012 in Case *D.D. v. Lithuania*.

144. The amendments, *inter alia,* provide for an annual review of a person's incapacity to be carried out by the newly formed Commission for Reviewing the Status of a Person Without Capacity. The new regulations allow parties to enter into an agreement for the provision of support in decision-making. Such agreements are considered to be a progressive way for persons with disabilities to enjoy their rights, as they leave the final decision to the persons themselves instead of letting others make decisions for them. The new amendments also establish the possibility of giving instructions prior to becoming incapacitated (the so-called living will). This will allow the person to appoint his guardian or tutor, leave instructions on matters of property and indicate what treatment he consents to in the potential event of his capacity becoming limited. Thus, the amendments abolish the possibility to declare a person incapable in all walks of life. However, the *Seimas* (Parliament) left open the possibility of declaring a person incapable of acting 'in a particular field' and leaving the decision-making in that field wholly up to his guardian. *See* https://www.liberties.eu/en/news/reform-incapacity-lithuania.

145. The Convention establishes the principle of equal recognition of persons with disabilities before the law. According to it, States Parties reaffirm that persons with disabilities have the right to recognition everywhere as persons before the law. States Parties shall recognise that persons with disabilities enjoy legal capacity on an equal basis with others in all aspects of life. States Parties shall

221. Under the current law (LCC Article 2.10, 2.11), there is no division into limited and full incapacity based predetermined source of disorder (either mental illness or serious addictions) any more. Instead all possible scenarios where an adult is not fully capable to understand his actions and to control them are handicapped under the general heading of mental or behavioural disorders and further distinguished according to the extent of illness. In addition, legal limitations on capacity are applied only for specific fields of social life and not for all legal matters. Hence, where due to mental disorder, such as mental weakness or insanity, the person cannot understand his actions and control them in certain prescribed fields, he should be declared in court as incapable in relevant fields. Where mental disorder, such as depression or serious addiction, only at limited extent affects ability of a person to understand his actions and control them, he should be declared in court as having limited capacity in certain prescribed fields. It means that under new regulation, even mentally ill persons may have limited capacity in certain fields of life if their illness is not grave enough. In all other fields of life, which are not mentioned in court's decision on incapacity or limited capacity, both incapable and limitedly capable persons retain full capacity.

E. Persons with Temporary or Recent Disorders (De Facto *Incapacity*)

222. The person becomes incapable or limitedly capable in certain fields only after declaratory judgment of court. Paradoxically, if a person has totally lost his sanity until he would be declared incapable by the court, he is treated as de jure fully capable to contract. Also, there may be situations when fully healthy and stable person gets in certain situations where he temporary loses clear mind, such as initial condition after car accident, street fight, death of relative, being drugged in hospital after surgery, heavily affected by alcohol, suffering from rapid depression and memory gaps. To remedy these situations, here is also another category of natural persons, so-called *de facto* incapable person, i.e., a capable natural person, who by reason of his state at the moment of the acts, was unable to comprehend the meaning of his acts or to control them (LCC Article 1.89).

---

take appropriate measures to provide access by persons with disabilities to the support they may require in exercising their legal capacity. States Parties shall ensure that all measures that relate to the exercise of legal capacity provide for appropriate and effective safeguards to prevent abuse in accordance with international human rights law. Such safeguards shall ensure that measures relating to the exercise of legal capacity respect the rights, will and preferences of the person, are free of conflict of interest and undue influence, are proportional and tailored to the person's circumstances, apply for the shortest time possible and are subject to regular review by a competent, independent and impartial authority or judicial body. The safeguards shall be proportional to the degree to which such measures affect the person's rights and interests. Subject to the provisions of this article, States Parties shall take all appropriate and effective measures to ensure the equal right of persons with disabilities to own or inherit property, to control their own financial affairs and to have equal access to bank loans, mortgages and other forms of financial credit and shall ensure that persons with disabilities are not arbitrarily deprived of their property (Art. 12).

F. Effects on Validity of Contracts

223. Rules on invalidity of a contract due to the lack of capacity are calibrated depending on who formed the contract – incapable person, person with limited capacity or temporary (*de facto*) incapable person.

224. First, there are invalidity rules on the contracts of incapable persons. A transaction is voidable if formed by a minor under 14 years of age, except in cases where the minor, within the limits imposed by his age and in accordance with LCC and other laws of the Republic of Lithuania, may enter into transactions alone to satisfy his ordinary and usual needs. A transaction is likewise voidable if it is made by a natural person who within the procedure established by laws is recognised as legally incapable in certain fields, in which transaction falls, because of mental or behavioural disorder. Besides the restitution of benefits, the legally capable party is obliged to compensate the expenses suffered by the other party, also any damage to the latter's property or loss thereof if the capable party knew or should have known about the incapacity of that other party. The invalidity of such transaction may be invoked by statutory representatives of the incapable person, also a public prosecutor. A transaction, if it is beneficial to the incapable person, may be ratified by the statutory representative of the latter in accordance with the procedure established by laws (LCC Article 1.84).

225. Second, there are invalidity rules on the contracts of persons with a limited capacity. A transaction upon the transfer of property or a property right that is formed by a natural person who due to mental or behavioural disorder has only limited capacity in certain fields, in which transaction falls, and without the consent of a curator, except small transactions to meet his ordinary and usual needs, can be declared voidable within the judicial procedure on the action of the curator or a prosecutor. If a transaction is declared voidable, the same consequences as with incapable persons should apply. However, after a transaction has been formed, a curator may ratify the transaction formed by the protected person alone during the period of his limited capacity for which he is required to be represented if such transaction is beneficial to the person with limited capacity (LCC Article 1.85). A transaction made by a minor from 14 to 18 years of age, where the law does not allow him to act without the consent of his parents or curators, may be declared void within the judicial procedure on the action of such minor's parents or curators, except for transactions into which the minor may, within the limits imposed by his age, enter alone in accordance with LCC and other laws. If a transaction is declared void, the same consequences as with incapable persons should apply. Statutory representatives of a minor can ratify a voidable transaction made without a proper consent, by giving their consent after the transaction has been formed, if such transaction is beneficial to the minor concerned (LCC Article 1.88).

226. Third, there are invalidity rules on the contracts of temporary (*de facto*) incapable persons. A transaction formed by a capable natural person may be annulled within the judicial procedure on the action of the natural person concerned if, due to his state at the moment of the transaction forming, he was unable to comprehend the meaning of his acts or to control them. Where the transaction is declared void, besides the restitution of benefits, the following additional consequences arise: the other party is bound to compensate to the party who at the moment of the transaction forming was unable to comprehend his own actions or to control them the expenses suffered, also any damage to his property or loss thereof, if this another party was aware or should have been aware of the state of the first contracting party (LCC Article 1.89).

II. Legal Persons

A. *Types of Legal Persons*

227. A legal (moral) person is a company, institution or organisation, which may in its name gain and enjoy rights, assume obligations and act as a party in a court (LCC Article 2.33). Direct participants in contractual relations, of course, are only natural persons because legal person is a superficial structure existing only in legal realm and having the legal capacity granted by the privilege of State on the practical and economic reasons. However, in the context of private law, the State is also treated as a legal person, which in private relations and actions (*acta iure gestionis*) has equal standing with other persons. Interestingly, the State even has its registered legal person code, which is 111105555. According to LCC Article 2.64(1), all legal persons should be registered in the public registry of legal persons (*Juridinių asmenų registras, JAR*).

228. As it flows from the statutory definition, set in LCC Article 2.33, there are three groups of legal persons: companies, institutions and organisations. Institutions are legal persons, which primary purpose is the fulfilment of public interests. For example, the Parliament (*Seimas*), the Government, ministries, the Army, courts and public agencies are all institutions. Organisations are legal persons, which primary purpose is to unite or empower their members in pursuit of some social, spiritual or citizenship goals. Examples of organisations are religious communities, associations and trade unions.

229. Companies are legal persons, which primary purpose is to seek profit from their commercial activities. As in other continental countries, Lithuanian companies mostly have concentrated ownership structure,[146] very often embodying family

146. Following the general trend of continental Europe shareholding structure in Lithuania is highly concentrated. From analysed thirty-three listed companies (all companies that have been listed on the NASDAQ OMX Vilnius stock exchange at the time of research) thirty had a single controlling shareholder (together with persons acting in concert, if any) holding at least 30% of voting rights and in twenty-five companies such shareholder held more than 50%. The median voting bloc of the largest shareholder (together with persons acting in concert, if any) was found to be 59.86%. These facts clearly point out that ownership is highly concentrated among the Lithuanian companies and is similar to the one in Belgium. *See* Paulius Miliauskas. *Company law aspects of shareholders' agreements in listed companies.* Doctoral dissertation. Vilnius, 2014, p. 97.

business. Biggest listed companies, which quite often are privatised former State companies owning important energy, infrastructure or manufacturing enterprises, are incorporated in the form of public limited liability company (*akcinė bendrovė*). This type of company is based on the model of traditional corporation. The capital of a public limited liability company capital is divided into shares and must be not less than EUR 25,000. Its shares may be offered and traded in publicly in compliance with the financial market regulation (Law on Companies Article 2(2)). Currently, there is no possibility to create no-par value shares, since all shares must have their nominal value (Law on Companies Article 38(2)). However, the most popular type of company in Lithuania is a private limited liability company, also sometimes called a joint-stock company (*uždaroji akcinė bendrovė*). The capital of a private limited liability company must be not less than EUR 2,500. The shares of the private limited liability company may not be offered and may not be traded in publicly; however, since the end of 2016 they can issue and publicly offer debt securities (Law on Companies Articles 2(4), 55(11)). These closed companies in essence are mix between the corporation and partnership; for instance, besides the limit on members of the company, there is also the pre-emption right of existing shareholders to acquire shares or converted bonds of the private limited liability company (Law on Companies Article 57). Other, less used in practice, legal forms of companies in Lithuania are state enterprises (*valstybės įmonės*), municipality enterprises (*savivaldybės įmonės*), small partnerships (*mažosios bendrijos*), commercial partnerships (*ūkinės bendrijos*), individual enterprises (*individualios įmonės*), etc. Small partnerships are limited liability companies with no capital requirements, thus are very suitable for start-ups. An important attribute of commercial partnerships and individual enterprises is that these are unlimited liability companies (LCC Article 2.50(4)).

230. Classification of legal persons into companies, institutions and organisations is mostly important from the organisational law perspective. However, as it is revealed below, for the purposes of the contract law the most important is another – statutory classification into public and private legal persons. According to LCC Article 2.34, legal persons are divided into public and private persons. Public legal persons are legal persons established by the state or municipalities, their institutions or other non-profit-seeking persons whose goal is to meet public interests (state and municipality enterprises, state or municipality institutions, public institutions, religious communities, etc.). Private legal persons are legal persons which aim at meeting private interests (private companies and partnerships).

B. The Capacity of Legal Persons

231. As the natural persons, legal persons also can choose a sphere of activities and residence, acquire, own and dispose property rights, conclude transactions, engage in commercial activities and establish other legal entities. According to LCC Article 2.75, legal capacity of legal persons may not be limited in any other manner except by express provision and procedure of law.[147] Legal capacity of an individual legal person may be limited only by the court judgment. In addition, it is prohibited to establish in legal acts, for discrimination purposes, different rights, obligations or privileges for separate legal persons (LCC Article 2.76). It is also prohibited for public or municipality institutions, in cases not prescribed by law, to use methods of administrative regulation of the activities of legal persons. Where, in accordance with the procedure prescribed by law, an emergency or martial law is declared or a certain territory is declared the region of disaster, legal persons must carry out the instructions of the Government or local self-government institution (LCC Article 2.80).

232. In contrast with natural persons, capacity of legal persons is not divided into active and passive. Instead, the emphasis for the classification of capacity is made here on another point – type of legal person – and according to this criterion the capacity is distinguished into general and special. Private legal persons have general (mostly unlimited) capacity. Therefore, LCC Article 2.75 prescribes that private legal persons may have or obtain any civil rights and assume duties except those which may emerge only when such characteristics of a natural person as gender, age and consanguinity are in place. Public legal persons have a special legal capacity; that is, they may have or obtain only such civil rights and assume such duties, which do not contradict with their incorporation documents or goals of activities. For example, if some activity is not expressly permitted in the incorporation documents and does not satisfy the goals of state enterprise, it cannot pursue this activity, despite the evident economic benefits achievable in doing so. In comparison, this activity would be limited for a private company only in express prohibition of it in the incorporation documents.

147. For example, in cases provided by law, legal persons may be engaged in a certain type of activities only after a licence has been granted in accordance with the procedure established by the law. A legal person must be in possession of all licences (permits) which are defined in the law as a necessary prerequisite for its activities. The Government approves licensing requirements for every licensed sphere of activities provided by law except as otherwise provided by other laws. Licensing requirements shall indicate the following: (1) licensed activities; (2) licensing institution and its authority; (3) documents for the issuance of a licence; (4) procedure and term for the investigation of documents; (5) types of licences, conditions of their issuance, re-issuance of a licence; (6) forms of licences; (7) procedure for the registration of issued licences; (8) cases of refusal to issue a licence; (9) conditions of licensed activities; (10) procedure for the supervision of the observance of the conditions of a licence; and (11) procedure and cases for the revocation and withdrawal of a licence. Regulations of licensing may provide for other requirements and a different procedure. Where the requirements specified in the regulations of licensing are fulfilled, an open-ended licence shall be issued. Except as otherwise provided by law, licence for the engagement in a certain activity or a written motivated refusal to issue a licence shall be submitted to an applicant within thirty days as of the day on which the documents for the issuance of a licence were produced. Refusal to issue a licence may not be based on the inexpediency of activities and has to be motivated. Upon the issuance of a licence, a legal person must supply information specified in the licensing requirements and related to the licensed activities or conditions predetermining the issuance thereof and allow the institution for the supervision of licensed activities to verify it. A state fee for the issuance of a licence shall not exceed the costs of the issuance of a licence and supervision thereof (LCC Art. 2.77–2.79).

233. After the incorporation, under LCC Article 2.81, legal persons obtain civil rights, assume civil duties and implement them through their bodies which are formed and act in accordance with laws and documents of incorporation of legal persons. Only natural persons may be members of managing bodies of a legal person, whereas both natural and legal persons may be members of other bodies. Authority and functions of the legal persons' bodies are established by the law and incorporation documents of a legal person, which regulate legal persons of a respective juridical form (LCC Article 2.82), for instance in the Law on the Stock Companies or in the Law on the Small Partnerships.

234. There are also rules for the contract made on behalf of legal person before the incorporation. According to LCC Article 1.83, where a transaction is made on behalf of a legal person that is not registered within the procedure established by laws, the natural person by whom such a transaction is made acquires the rights and assumes the duties arising from that transaction, providing there are no other grounds for declaring such transaction void. Where transactions are made on behalf of a legal person prior to its registration, the persons by whom these transactions are made shall be solidarily liable, unless the legal person, after it is registered, assumes the obligations resulting from those transactions. With this respect, LCC Article 2.61 provides that a managing body of a legal person or some other body defined in the incorporation document shall have the right to approve contracts, which in a legal person's name were concluded by other persons prior to the incorporation of a legal person. When such contract is concluded it should be indicated that it is concluded in a legal person's name and in its interests. Where such reference fails to be included the person who has concluded the contract and the legal person, whose managing body or some other body defined in the incorporation document approved the contract concluded in its interest, shall have solidary liability to discharge their contractual obligations.

C. Effects on the Validity of Contracts

235. Capacity rules have direct effect on the validity of contracts, but particular effect depends on the type of legal person and accordingly on the type of respective legal capacity. The ultra vires doctrine,[148] which sets aside contracts lacking the

148. The birth of the ultra vires rule in the context of limited liability companies may be traced back to English cases involving statutory companies, many of these companies having been formed to construct public utilities (e.g., railways and canals). Statutory companies were restricted in the pursuit of legitimate business activities by the particular statute that granted them a corporate status. Any act by a statutory company which contravened a limitation placed upon its capacity would be deemed ultra vires and void: *see*, e.g., the House of Lords' decision in *Eastern Counties Rlwy v. Hawkes* (1855) 5 HLC 331. The ultra vires rule of the common law was brought in by the courts to protect shareholders. It was thought that if a shareholder bought shares in a company which had as its main object publishing and allied activities, he would not want the directors of that company to start up a different kind of business because he wanted to put money in publishing. In more recent times, it has been realised that shareholders are not so fussy about the business the directors take the company into so long as it is ethical and makes profits from which to pay dividends and the price of the company's shares rises on the stock exchange as a result of its success. The people

capacity of legal person, impacts private legal persons less than public legal persons because former persons have general capacity, while latter persons have only limited capacity – special capacity.

236. Lithuanian rules on the general capacity of a legal person are constructed with respect to Article 9 of the former EU First Company Law Directive.[149] First, the directive has prescribed that acts done by the organs of the company shall be binding upon it even if those acts are not within the objects of the company, unless such acts exceed the powers that the law confers or allows to be conferred on those organs. However, Member States may provide that the company shall not be bound where such acts are outside the objects of the company, if it proves that the third party knew that the act was outside those objects or could not in view of the circumstances have been unaware of it; disclosure of the statutes shall not of itself be sufficient proof thereof. Second, the limits on the powers of the organs of the company, arising under the statutes or from a decision of the competent organs, may never be relied on as against third parties, even if they have been disclosed. Third, if the national law provides that authority to represent a company may, in derogation from the legal rules governing the subject, be conferred by the statutes on a single person or on several persons acting jointly, that law may provide that such a provision in the statutes may be relied on as against third parties on condition that it relates to the general power of representation; the question whether such a provision in the statutes can be relied on as against third parties shall be governed by Article 3 (on central registry).

237. Leaving marginal third rule aside, it is clear from above that under the EU company law, no limitation of organs' power to conclude contracts on behalf of a company is possible solely on the basis of company articles (statutes). Contracting restrictions exist only where limitation of powers is based on the law itself or (optional) if organs' act contravenes goals of the company (based in articles or law) and third party knew it. Thus, contracting restrictions set in the company articles may have impact on the validity of contract only where company articles define the goals of the company, which are compromised by the contract concluded with unfair counterparty. In other cases, company articles normally have no substantial effect

---

most affected by the ultra vires rule of the common law in more recent times were creditors who had supplied goods or services to a company for a purpose not contained in its objects clause. If the company was solvent, no doubt such creditors would be paid, but if it went into insolvent liquidation, they would not even be able to put in a claim. The liquidator would reject it as being based on a void transaction. Other creditors might get paid some part of their debts if the company had some funds, but the ultra vires creditors would get nothing. *See* Stephen Griffin, Michael Hirst, Peter Walton. *Company Law: Fundamental Principles.* Prentice Hall, 2005, p. 109; Charles Wild, Stuart Weinstein. *Smith and Keenans Company Law.* 14th Ed., Longman, 2009, pp. 72–73.

149. First Council Directive 68/151/EEC of 9 Mar. 1968 on coordination of safeguards which, for the protection of the interests of members and others, are required by Member States of companies within the meaning of the second paragraph of Art. 58 of the Treaty, with a view to making such safeguards equivalent throughout the Community. Currently those and other company law rules are codified in the Directive (EU) 2017/1132 of the European Parliament and of the Council of 14 Jun. 2017 relating to certain aspects of company law.

on the validity of contract. However, restrictions on the power of company bodies to conclude contracts set directly in law always should make the contract voidable.

238. However, these rules have been transposed into Lithuanian law with some distortions. LCC Article 1.82 prescribes that transactions made by the governing bodies of a private legal person in breach of the competence conferred on them by their incorporation documents or contradicting the goals of that legal person may be declared void only in the cases where it is proved that the other party acted in bad faith, i.e., he knew or should have known that the transaction was contrary to the goals of the legal person concerned. In such cases, the fact of announcement of the incorporation documents of the legal person concerned shall not be a sufficient proof of the other party's bad faith; therefore, the legal person shall be bound to prove that the other party deliberately acted in bad faith (LCC Article 2.74, 2.83–2.85). LCC Article 2.83 similarly states that contracts concluded by the managing bodies of a private legal person in overstepping their authority shall impose obligations on a legal person except in cases where it is proved that concluding the contract the third person was aware or due to certain circumstances may not have failed to be aware of the fact that the contract has been entered into by a managing body of a legal person who was not authorised to conclude it. Despite those limitations, according to LCC Article 2.83(2), ultra vires doctrine should be applied where quantitative representation has been established; that is, only some members of a managing body together or a member of a managing body and a representative together are authorised to act in the name of a legal person. Quantitative representation should have to be provided in the incorporation documents of a legal person, specified in the register of legal persons and publicised in accordance with the procedure established by the regulations of the register of legal persons.

239. Thus, Lithuanian law contradicts Article 9(1) of the Directive, because it suppresses the invalidating effect of ultra vires doctrine on the contracts made by exceeding the powers that the law confers or allows to be conferred on company organs (bodies). It means that under Lithuanian version of ultra vires, even contracts, which are concluded by the company bodies exceeding their competence set directly in the law, may escape invalidity. Nevertheless, as rightly pointed out in legal doctrine, this problem in practice is mitigated by the rules on illegality (LCC Article 1.80), which makes transactions void.[150] Another, but still unmitigated problem is the contradiction of LCC with Article 9(2) of the Directive, according to which the limits on the powers of the organs of the company, arising under the statutes or from a decision of the competent organs, may never be relied on as against third parties, even if they have been disclosed. In contrast, LCC permits reliance on

150. Andrius Smaliukas, Vaida Pacenkaitė. *Ultra vires doktrina naujajame Lietuvos Respublikos civiliniame kodekse. In.* Siuolaikinės civilinės teisės raidos tendencijos ir perspektyvos. Justitia, 2007, p. 83.

the restrictions of organs' powers solely in the company articles as the sufficient trigger for ultra vires with condition that counterparty knew about those restrictions.[151]

240. The exact meaning of goals (objects) of company is question of fact. In the rare occasion, where Supreme Court undertook to explain economic merits of LCC Article 1.82, it did reject claim for ultra vires and state that 'this ground of invalidity is not itself tied with commercial profitability of legal person transactions. Such factor would have impact on the transactions of legal person only where, in laws defining a capacity of legal person and its objects or in incorporation documents drafted according to such laws, a duty to conclude only commercially profitable transactions would be established. Otherwise the stability of legal relations would be in prejudice. It should be noted, that business cycles exist in economic activities, therefore it's impossible to guarantee neither consistent and stable profit, nor solely profitable transactions. If would be allowed to dispute transactions on the ground that they are simply unprofitable, huge uncertainty and instability thus would arise, because any commercially unprofitable transactions would become prone to attack. Where established in legal norms defining legal capacity of the legal persons or incorporation documents, with legal capacity can be incompatible only clear, evident disadvantage of a transaction, where leaving this transaction in force would mean clear injustice to the party of transaction. In this case, application of LCC Article 1.82 (taking into account also other circumstances) would be legitimate'.[152]

241. In case of contracts concluded by public legal persons, the doctrine of ultra vires has full and unrestricted effect. LCC Article 1.82 prescribes that transactions formed by public legal persons that are contrary to the goals of their activities may be declared void. In addition, LCC Article 2.84 states that contracts concluded by the managing bodies of a public legal person in overstepping their authority shall not impose obligations on a legal person. However, if at a later date, the person approves the contract, the contract shall become valid as of the day of its conclusion. A third person who, under those circumstances, has concluded a contract, which is not approved by a legal person, must redress the damage incurred on the third person, if he fails to prove that concluding the contract the third person was aware or due to certain circumstances may not have failed to be aware of the fact that the contract has been concluded in overstepping the authority of the managing body of a legal person. As in the case of private legal persons, publication and indication in the Register of legal persons of the authority of managing bodies of public

---

151. The conclusion that Lithuanian version of ultra vires permits reliance on company articles is unanimously supported by the Lithuanian legal doctrine and case law. *See* Gintautas Bartkus, *et al. Lietuvos Respublikos civilinio kodekso komentaras. Antroji knyga. Asmenys*. Justitia, 2002, p. 188; Alfonsas Vileita, *et al. Lietuvos Respublikos civilinio kodekso komentaras. Pirmoji knyga. Bendrosios nuostatos*. Justitia, 2001, pp. 188–189; *Aurimas Brazdeikis, et al. Civilinė teisė. Bendroji dalis*. Justitia, 2009, pp. 349–350. Judgment of the Lithuanian Supreme Court of 31 Oct. 2006 in the civil case No 3K-3-567/2006; Judgment of the Lithuanian Supreme Court of 3 Dec. 2007 in the civil case No 3K-3-534/2007.

152. Judgment of the Lithuanian Supreme Court of 16 Dec. 2011 in the civil case No 3K-3-511/2011.

legal persons which was stipulated in incorporation documents shall not affect the application of the ultra vires doctrine (LCC Article 2.85).

242. An action for the declaration of the contract as invalid on the ground of ultra vires may be brought by the legal person, the founder (founders) or a participant (participants) thereof. The laws may also specify other persons entitled to bring such an action, or special requirements which have to be met by the persons bringing such an action (e.g., holding of a certain number of shares (deciding votes)). Transactions annulled on ultra vires grounds are subject to the rules on restitution. Where a legal person fails to satisfy fully the claim of a third person, the person who has concluded the contract under circumstances laid down in paragraph 1 of the given Article shall take on subsidiary liability (LCC Article 1.82, 2.83).

§2. Defects of Consent

243. The contract creates legal claims and burdens parties with corresponding obligations, which may legitimately interfere within the party autonomy and significantly impact its property. Therefore, respect for the will of parties requires that the contract should be only formed by mutual consent of both parties, which is usually expressed by the notions of offer and acceptance. Where voluntary consent is missing, the contract lacks its main element – the agreement made by consent and thus becomes defective and open for annulment. From the other side, if contract law will allow to annul transactions on too subjectivist or arbitrary grounds, it will necessarily impede normal functioning and stability of markets. Therefore, proper balance between safeguards of party autonomy and markets efficiency there should be made.

244. Lithuanian law provides for several classical civilian grounds, modelled on UNIDROIT PICC, to remedy defects of consent. These are mistake, fraud, threat and gross disparity. Functionally, this list should be also extended by the unauthorised or malicious transactions, which are concluded by the agent, because in those cases consent a party (principal) is also defective.

245. However, if defect of consent is related to the facts, which came into existence after the transaction was formed, it is not proper ground for invalidity of the contract. For instance, the Supreme Court has held that evaluation of the mistake should be done according to the situation, which had existed during the formation of transaction, not that, which has come into existence after the conclusion of transaction.[153] Thus, situation, where person, who has given the consent for the cadastral survey and made no objections against it, despite having possibility to get familiar with the course of survey, later makes objection in court, is treated as change of will,

153. Judgments of the Lithuanian Supreme Court of 5 Sep. 2001 in the civil case No 3K-3-745/2001, of 26 Oct. 2005 in the civil case 3K-3-514/2005 and of 29 May 2006 in the civil case 3K-3-359/2006.

not the mistake.[154] The mistaken party in latter cases must assume the risk of negligent contracting or rely on other rules, such as resolutory condition and *imprevision*. This rule is equally applied to all cases of invalidity of transactions, not defects of consent.

I. Mistake

246. Lithuanian statutory law defines mistake as an erroneous assumption of the essential facts of the transaction that existed at the moment of the transaction forming. Thus, to make the contract voidable, mistake should be essential, i.e., test of materiality should be applied. This test promotes both legal certainty and economic efficiency.[155]

247. According to LCC Article 1.90, a mistake is essential where the error relates to the nature, object or any other essential terms of the contract itself, or the civil legal status of the other contracting party or any other circumstances, and where a person of normal diligence and attentiveness would not have made the transaction in a similar situation or would have made it on essentially different terms if he had known the real state of events. A mistake is likewise essential if both contracting parties are mistaken, or an error of one party induced the other party to err without the former's intention to deceive, or if one party was aware or should have been aware of the mistake committed by the other party, and the requirement addressed to the mistaken party to perform the transaction would contradict to the principles of good faith, justice and reasonableness. Essential mistake may also be related to the identity of the other party. Based on this, courts evaluate mistake on the criterion of reasonableness, i.e., actions of claimant should be evaluated in comparison with behaviour of diligent and prudent person in the same circumstances.[156]

248. However, a mistake may not be considered essential if it caused by gross negligence of the mistaken party or induced by circumstances the risk of which was

154. Judgment of the Lithuanian Supreme Court of 4 Jan. 2007 in the civil case 3K-3-150/2007.
155. Looking from the economic perspective, for a contract to produce a Pareto gain, each of the parties must, at least prospectively, expect to benefit by it. This expectation can only be realistic if the parties are abreast of the essential stakes of the projected contract. Should they be mistaken about them, the contract may not lead to a Pareto gain. In setting up rules dealing with mere mistakes, two pitfalls are to be avoided. In refusing to recognise an error, one would sanctify a relationship that does not create a Pareto gain and one needs to consider the incentive effect that will have on the errans: lots of precaution next time round; this is costly and slows down markets. If the law is to pursue welfare enhancements in private relationships, the contract better be redone. Conversely, were undoing a contract for alleged error to become too easy, legal certainty would be undermined: a purchaser will hesitate to undertake further transactions with the merchandise just bought if it may have to be returned to the seller; third persons may hesitate to buy it for the same reason. A seller cannot count on the profit made in a sale that the purchaser could easily undo. All of this slows down market operations. The law draws the line between these opposite forces by providing that only an error concerning the essentials is a cause for the contract to be called into question. *See* Ejan Mackaay. *The civil law of contract. In* Contract law and economics. Encyclopedia of Law and Economics. 2 ed. Edward Elgar Publishing, 2011, p. 435.
156. Judgment of the Lithuanian Supreme Court of 9 Oct. 2002 in the civil case 3K-3-1155/2002.

taken by the party upon himself or if, taking into account the concrete circumstances, the risk of mistake falls on that party in particular. A mistake resulting from the expression or transmission of a party's will should be deemed to be a mistake committed by that party himself.

249. In Lithuanian legal practice, mistake was very popular ground for action against banks misrepresentation during after-crisis financial mis-selling scandals. In DNB bank (now Luminor bank) cases, claimants were retail investors, who on the basis of MiFID protections (transposed in national law under the Law on Financial Instruments Markets) argued that bank has misled them by failing to properly disclose risks of the equity-linked bonds, which were issued by the bank. Initially, lower courts were willing to grant relief on this ground, but trend was reshaped into new direction when Supreme Court, albeit affirming multiple breaches of on the part of bank, finally rejected annulment claims. Supreme Court took into account personal characteristics of claimants (part of them were wealthy persons from business world) and concluded that negligent misrepresentations on the part of bank were not such misleading to constitute essential mistake, which makes transaction voidable.[157] In bank SNORAS case, the Supreme Court has also found misrepresentations on the part of the bank, but not on the substance of bank statements (related to the protection of retail investors under the depositors and investors protection scheme), which after the decision of ECJ turned out to be true,[158] but due to the misleading expressions of these statements in precontractual documentation. However, the Supreme Court again taking into account personal characteristics of the claimant and the nature of misleading statements did not find it to be essential enough to mislead the claimants.[159]

250. It should be noted that the LCC drafters and Lithuanian legal doctrine have tried to define clear boundaries of mistake in order to prevent broad application of this ground. However, case law seems to be moving into the opposite direction – by relaxing most of dogmatic constraints on the notion of mistake. Below several examples are presented.

251. UNIDROIT PICC Article 3.4, on the definition of mistake, was incorporated into LCC Article 1.90 only partly; that is, the LCC defines a mistake as erroneous assumption relating to facts only, not relating to law. Such partial acceptance of UNIDROIT PICC Article 3.4 could be explained by LCC Article 1.6, according to which ignorance of laws or improper understanding thereof does not exempt one from the application of the sanctions established therein and may not justify failure

157. Judgments of the Lithuanian Supreme Court of 17 Mar. 2014 in the civil case No 3K-3-68/2014; 20 May 2014 in the civil case No 3K-3-265/2014; 5 Sep. 2014 in the civil case No 3K-3-391/2014.
158. Judgment of the ECJ of 25 Jun. 2015 in Case C-671/13.
159. Judgment of the Lithuanian Supreme Court of 17 Nov. 2015 in the civil case No 3K-7-602-684/2015.

to comply with the requirements of laws, and likewise improper compliance therewith.[160] Despite this original intention of legislator, courts seem to have been willing to expand the notion of mistake including even mistakes related to the law. Suggestions on this have appeared in the Supreme Court general reasoning that: 'if party has concluded the transaction mistakenly understanding factual or legal circumstance, rules on the annulment of transaction on the ground of mistake, should apply';[161] 'before taking any legal act, person should evaluate possible consequences of such act. Transactions create rights and duties, therefore every person before transaction should check rights which he will acquire and obligations which he will assume. Erroneous vision on rights and duties cannot be declared as mistake if it has happened due to the party negligence'.[162] While these were just obiter dicta statements, several years later Supreme Court has quashed judgment of lower courts where they dismissed action of the buyers for the annulment of the land sales contract due to mistake on the possibility to build on purchased parcel of land, while in fact it was illegal. The Supreme Court has reasoned that since the right to build a house on the land was essential to the buyers and the mistake was essential.[163]

252. Another development in Lithuanian contract law is that the mistakes related to the value of goods are increasingly accepted in Lithuanian case law. Initial position of Supreme Court was restrictive; thus while it is possible, in principle, to err on the value of transaction, the mistake should be such which would prevent a prudent person from the conclusion of transaction at all or conclusion under the proposed terms. If price is much more favourable to one party, then when considering the mistake on the price, the circumstances, which had effect on the agreement on price, should be evaluated. If it would be clear that party of the contract assumes unjustified huge negative consequences, it could be treated as gross disparity.[164] Such position has left uncertainty whether a mistake could make the contract voidable under LCC Article 1.90 or the other remedies should apply. Nevertheless, later case law slightly moved in favour of annulment of contract on ground of mistake on value. For instance, the Supreme Court taking into account the premise that price is an essential term of the land sales contract equalised the essentiality of a mistake with the essentiality of a price as a contract term, thus enabling to rely on the mistake related to value of goods as a ground for annulment.[165] From the other side, a difference should be made between value of goods as such and perspectives of transaction for a party, because under case law if a party has correctly understood circumstances of a contract, but made a mistake on the perspectives of the contract,

160. Valentinas Mikelėnas. *The Influence of Instruments of Harmonisation of Private Law upon the Reform of Civil Law in Lithuania.* Juridica International, 2008 Vol. 14, p. 146.
161. Judgment of the Lithuanian Supreme Court of 27 Oct. 2008 in the civil case No 3K-3-504/2008.
162. Judgment of the Lithuanian Supreme Court of 24 Nov. 2011 in the civil case No 3K-3-85/2011.
163. Judgment of the Lithuanian Supreme Court of 22 Apr. 2015 in the civil case No 3K-3-229-248/2015.
164. Judgment of the Lithuanian Supreme Court of 24 Sep. 2003 in the civil case No 3K-3-863/2003.
165. Judgment of the Lithuanian Supreme Court of 4 Nov. 2008 in the civil case No 3K-3-252/2008.

contract due to mistake cannot be avoided.[166] However, real validity of this limitation makes doubt, since investment services litigation has shown that it is possible, in principle, to rely on the mistake due to the risks of transaction.[167]

253. The classical objection against mistakes related to the motives of a contract, which is fully maintained by the legal doctrine,[168] in case law is also supported, however with some carve-outs, which leave space even to these kinds of mistakes. The Supreme Court has held with this respect that motives being very individual and subjective by nature as well as unknown or irrelevant to the other party are not essential terms of transaction. The sole exception is where the transaction motives are incorporated into transaction as its essential terms.[169] For example, in one case claimants were elder parents, who gave as a gift immovables to the adult son, who was expected to become farmer, share gift with brothers (sisters) and take care of ill parents. After the gift contract was concluded, the son went abroad, failed to do what was expected from him and even is seeking to sell the property. The Supreme Court has dismissed this claim, which was related solely on motives, on the reasons that there was not a mistake, but change of mind on part of claimants.[170]

254. In sum, it seems that *ex ante* theoretical constraints on the legally relevant notion of mistake are continuously eroding in Lithuanian case law and are replaced by the *ex post* test of materiality, which should always be passed. In considering the materiality, courts often tend to rely on the essential terms of the contract, despite that under LCC, mistake on the essential terms is not the sole case of the essential mistake. Leaving aside the theoretical objections as to suitable application of the mentioned concepts, Lithuanian contract law in practice seems to share the position of the Principles on European Contract Law (PECL).

255. As to the remedies, a transaction resulting from the consent given by an essential mistake may be declared void by the judicial declaration on the person whose consent is vitiated action for its voidness. In the event of annulment of a transaction formed under the influence of an essential mistake, the restitution should apply. The party upon whose action the transaction is declared void may, in addition to the annulment, also claim from the other party compensation for the expenses incurred or the damage to his property or loss thereof if this party proves that the mistake was caused by the fault of the other party. Where it is not proved,

166. Judgments of the Lithuanian Supreme Court of 4 Jan. 2007 in the civil case No 3K-3-150/2007 and of 25 Nov. 2015 in the civil case No 3K-3-610-378/2015.
167. Judgments of the Lithuanian Supreme Court of 17 Mar. 2014 in the civil case No 3K-3-68/2014, of 20 May 2014 in the civil case No 3K-3-265/2014 and of 5 Sep. 2014 in the civil case No 3K-3-391/2014.
168. Alfonsas Vileita, *et al. Lietuvos Respublikos civilinio kodekso komentaras. Pirmoji knyga. Bendrosios nuostatos*. Justitia, 2001, p. 200.
169. Judgments of the Lithuanian Supreme Court of 5 Sep. 2001 in the civil case No 3K-3-745/2001, of 9 Oct. 2000 in the civil case 3K-3-974/2000 and of 19 Oct. 2005 in the civil case 3K-7-378/2005.
170. Judgment of the Lithuanian Supreme Court of 24 Nov. 2011 in the civil case No 3K-3-85/2011.

the party on whose action the transaction is declared void shall be bound to compensate to the other party the expenses incurred as well as the damage to his property or loss thereof.

256. However, under LCC Article 1.90(7), the mistaken party cannot claim the annulment of a contract where her rights and interests may be adequately protected by invoking other remedies. In some cases, this rule was highlighted by courts expressly, while in other cases it was implied from the effect of decisions. For example, the Supreme Court has ruled that if a person has suffered damage due to the fault of public auction organiser, he should demand damages from the organiser instead of resorting to the annulment remedy.[171] In aforementioned investment services, litigation concerning equity-linked bonds, although the Supreme Court was reluctant to expressly rely on LCC Article 1.90(7), it achieved exactly the same result by rejecting actions for annulment and suggested that more convenient remedy under the circumstances where both parties shared responsibility for investment losses was compensatory damages. The rationale of this redirection of case law was hidden in the different effects of the concurrent remedies: an action for declaration of a contract void employs inflexible all-or-nothing approach, which was inappropriate under current circumstances, whereas damages are flexible remedy, which may be awarded not only in full extent, but may be limited, as happens in case of contributory fault.

II. Fraud

257. According to LCC Article 1.91, a transaction may be declared void by a court on the action of the aggrieved party if it was entered into due to fraud. The fraud may result from the silence of a party, i.e., from concealment of such circumstances being aware of which the other contracting party would not have formed the transaction and which, within the principles of reasonableness, justice and good faith, had to be disclosed to the other party; fraud may also result from active actions by which it is desired to mislead the other contracting party concerning the effect of the transaction, essential terms thereof, civil legal capacity of the person who enters into the transaction and any other essential circumstances.

258. The Supreme Court has constantly defined the civil fraud as intentional misrepresentation towards counterparty related to the essential circumstances of the transaction, which may be expressed by active actions, as well as by concealment of significant circumstances of transaction with the intention to conclude transaction. Only those intentional actions may be declared as fraudulent acts, which have a determinative effect on the will of the party.[172] However, quite controversially the Supreme Court has also ruled that the contract may be annulled only where the circumstances prescribed in LCC Article 1.91, including civil fraud, have influenced

171. Judgment of the Lithuanian Supreme Court of 18 Feb. 2004 in the civil case No 3K-3-107/2004.
172. Judgments of the Lithuanian Supreme Court of 24 Oct. in the civil case No 2001 3K-3-1008/2001, of 21 Jan. 2002 the civil case 3K-3-353/2002, of 18 Sep. 2003 the civil case 3K-3-760/2003, of 11

the will of the counterparty, not her agent.[173] This collides with LCC Article 2.133(5) according to which, where the validity of a contract concluded by an agent is questioned due to a mistake, fraud, duress or threat, the existence or non-existence of the said circumstances shall be established with due regard to agent's will. It also collides with the position of the same court in the criminal cases, where a criminal fraud, which due to the criminal law principle *ultima ratio* should be defined more narrowly than a civil fraud, may be established irrespective who was misled – the counterparty or her agent.[174]

259. Generally, in the civil fraud cases, courts are evaluating whether the defendant did intentional and unfair actions (intentionally stated untrue information or concealed significant facts related to the essential elements of transaction with the intent to deceive the plaintiff), which motivated the plaintiff to conclude the transaction, but not the one he really wanted to conclude. It is also important to analyse behaviour of the misled party before, during and after the transaction. In deciding on the fraud, actions of both parties should be evaluated according to the principles of reasonableness, justice and fairness.[175] It is clear from above that the courts in order to find the fraud in the circumstances of the case must establish the essential character of misrepresentations; that is, test of materiality should be passed.

260. It is clear from above that the concept of fraud shares with the concept of mistake the misrepresentation element, in turn making it important to distinguish them. Regarding this, the Supreme Court has ruled that where facts show that misrepresentation although material, was without the intention to deceive, the court according to the law may annul the contract on the ground of mistake, instead of fraud.[176] Therefore, the necessary element of the fraud, which should be proved by the plaintiff, is a scienter.

261. LCC Article 1.91 also lays down two rules concerning the third parties. First, if a third person (but not the other party to the transaction) is guilty of fraud, duress or threatening, the transaction shall be declared void only in the cases where that other party was aware or should have been aware of those facts. Second, the fact of declaring void a transaction formed under the influence of fraud may not be invoked against third persons in good faith, except in cases established by LCC.

Dec. 2006 the civil case 3K-3-640/2006, of 5 Jul. 2007 the civil case 3K-3-306/2007, of 26 Mar. 2008 the civil case 3K-3-189/2008, of 27 Oct. 2008 the civil case 3K-3-458/2008 and of 22 Dec. 2008 the civil case 3K-3-609/2008.

173. Judgment of the Lithuanian Supreme Court of 25 Sep. 2002 in the civil case No 3K-3-1069/2002.

174. Judgment of the Lithuanian Supreme Court of 26 Feb. 2002 in the criminal case No Nr. 2K-188/2002.

175. Judgment of the Lithuanian Supreme Court of 20 Jun. 2005 in the civil case No 3K-3-349/2005, of 26 Oct. 2006 the civil case 3K-3-640/2006, of 4 Jan. 2007 the civil case 3K-3-150/2007, of 3 Apr. 2007 the civil case 3K-3-306/2007, of 5 Jul. 2007 the civil case 3K-3-306/2007, of 27 Oct. 2008 the civil case 3K-3-458/2008 and of 22 Dec. 2008 the civil case 3K-3-609/2008.

176. Judgment of the Lithuanian Supreme Court of 5 Jul. 2007 in the civil case No 3K-3-306/2007.

262. The fraud is highly socially undesired conduct which is countered by a set of legal remedies. Therefore, fraud not only may be remedied with annulment of contract and restitution but also may lead to tort liability in the form of compensatory damages, including compensation for non-pecuniary loss. Besides these civil consequences, fraud may also attract criminal liability even leading to imprisonment up to three years or in grave cases to eight years. In this respect, Lithuanian Criminal Code Article 182 defines criminal fraud as the situation where a person who, by deceit, acquires another's property for own benefit or the benefit of other persons or acquires a pecuniary right, avoids a pecuniary obligation or annuls it. The Supreme Court defines a deceit using these criteria: first, distortion of objective true, second, the purpose to deceive aggrieved person (to cause his mistake) and, third, the understanding of offender that he intentionally states untrue information.[177] Deceit by the false misstatements is called active deceit, whereas omission to inform (concealment of truth by silence) is called the passive deceit. To become criminal fraud the deceit, the same as in civil cases, should pass the test of materiality, i.e., must be of such nature, which causes harmful actions of the aggrieved party.[178] In addition to these general rules on criminal fraud, Lithuanian Criminal Code Article 207 separately prohibits credit fraud, i.e., situation where a person who, by deceit, obtains a credit, loan, subsidy, warranty or bank guarantee statement or another credit obligation. The difference from the general rules on fraud is that the credit fraud is already established when a person with a deceit obtains financing without any need to prove his intention to avoid undertaken obligations.

III. Misrepresentations

263. As follows from the preceding sections, misrepresentations can always attract at least some sort of civil law consequences under Lithuanian law if they were material in character and had misled the other party. Legal remedies apply irrespectively whether the misrepresentations were active (misstatements) or passive (failure to disclose information about the particular transaction) but are highly calibrated depending on the extent and existence of a fault on the part of the defendant.

264. In most egregious cases where misrepresentations were made with intent to defraud counterparty, in addition to reliance damages and annulment of contract on the ground of fraud, they may even lead to criminal liability under the Criminal Code Article 182 or 207. Where misrepresentations were negligent, reliance damages and annulment on the ground of mistake are available. Where misrepresentations were innocent, i.e., have been made without intent or negligence, annulment on the ground of mistake is the single remedy available to the misled party.

177. Judgment of the Lithuanian Supreme Court of 8 Jun. 2010 in the criminal case No 2K-335/2010.
178. Judgment of the Lithuanian Supreme Court of 18 May 2010 in the criminal case No 2K-203/2010.

IV. Improper Pressure

265. LCC Article 1.91(1) prescribes several grounds of contract invalidity related to wrongful pressure on the counterparty. These are violence, threat, economic duress and abuse of circumstances, where party in necessity assumes obligations under unfair conditions. Most mentioned acts are of a dangerous nature, therefore besides being ground of invalidity of contract are also torts and, in some cases, even crimes of health impairment, threatening to murder or cause a severe health impairment to a person or terrorisation of a person, restriction of freedom of a person's actions, extortion of property, (Criminal Code Articles 135–140, 145, 148, 181), etc.

266. In order to explain the concept of threat, LCC Article 1.91(4) uses the term 'real threatening', which is unjustifiable, or unlawful actions of the other party or a third person directed towards the person, property or reputation of the other contracting party, or that of his parents, children, spouse, grandparents, grandchildren or any other close relatives; the threatening actions must be of such nature as to impress a reasonable person and to cause him to fear that the person, property or reputation of the persons concerned may be exposed to damage and there is no other reasonable alternative except to enter into the transaction. Threatening shall also be deemed to be real where one party or a third person threatens to enforce measures of economic pressure against the other contracting party that is economically weaker or is in essence economically dependent in order to compel him to form a transaction under exceptionally economically disadvantageous conditions. In determining the occurrence of real threatening, the court shall take into account the age, economic and financial position, and the gender of the party towards whom the threat was directed, the nature of the threat and any other conditions significant for the case. The juridical technique of LCC Article 1.91 is not perfect, because part 1 of this article lists economic pressure as a separate ground, while part 4 includes it in the notion of real threatening.

267. According to the case law, economic duress makes contract voidable where all those criteria are satisfied: first, the person demanded to conclude the transaction; second, he threatened with economic consequences, which depends on his unfair actions; third, transaction is made under evidently unfavourable terms; and fourth, without the economic pressure transaction would not be concluded. However, submitting legal action to the court for the recovery of debt is not the economic duress.[179]

268. Although the notion of violence is not *expressis verbis* explained in the LCC, according to the legal doctrine, it means direct physical or psychical influence on the transacting person. It may be unlawful deprival of a personal liberty to move, beating, torture, life or health threatening. Violence should be significant and real;

179. Judgments of the Lithuanian Supreme Court of 19 Oct. 2005 in the civil case No 3K-7-378/2005 and of 6 Nov. 2006 in the civil case 3K-3-574/2006.

thus, it should impact that person according to her gender, age and condition, but not necessarily characterised as a crime.[180]

269. Abuse of circumstances leads to invalidity of a contract where one party is unfairly taking advantage of the vulnerable another party. The pressure is so unfairly exploiting the other party that abuse of circumstances *de facto* equals to the duress.[181] Case law holds that circumstances should be such hard to counterparty that it is forced to conclude a transaction on very unfavourable terms and defendant has known it.[182] It should be the case of necessity; for instance, where a person wants to help his dying close relative or has nothing to eat because of unemployment and his counterparty knowingly offers shark loan, it acts unfair and abuses circumstances which are so unfavourable for the first party.

270. In cases involving improper pressure, the transaction is voidable and unilateral restitution should take place. The aggrieved party may also claim reliance damages, including compensation of non-pecuniary loss. However, if a third person, but not the other party to the transaction, is guilty of violence or threat, the transaction can be declared voidable only in the cases where that other party was aware or should have been aware of those facts.

V. Gross Disparity

271. Lithuanian contract law to the list of substantive controls also adds the qualified version of *laesio enormis* doctrine, which in LCC is named the 'gross disparity of parties'.[183] According to LCC Article 6.228, a party may refuse the contract or a separate condition thereof if at the time of the conclusion of the contract,

---

180. Alfonsas Vileita, *et al. Lietuvos Respublikos civilinio kodekso komentaras. Pirmoji knyga. Bendrosios nuostatos*. Justitia, 2001, p. 204.
181. There are various reasons which militate for an extension of the concept of duress to cases of circumstantial pressure. The most obvious reason lies in the nature of duress as a defect of consent. If the legal institute of duress is designed to protect a contracting party's free consent, it is patently inconsistent with this objective if avoidance is granted when a party enters into a contract upon duress by a third person, whereas avoidance is denied when a party contracts due to circumstantial pressure. Obviously, in both instances the party's consent is equally vitiated and so the same legal remedy should be available. In other words, not treating both cases alike imply an arbitrary distinction that cannot be accounted for by the controlling objective, i.e., the protection of contracting parties' free consent. Another argument that speaks for an extension of duress follows from considerations of equity. In legal systems with a narrow concept of lesion or unconscionability, it would be inequitable if a party having entered into a contract under strong circumstantial pressure that impaired his free volition were left without any remedy. Naturally, in such instances courts will be tempted to avoid inequitable results by extending the scope of duress to cases of circumstantial pressure. *See* Ernst Kramer, Thomas Probst. *International Encyclopedia of Comparative Law.* Vol. 7. *Contracts in general. Defects in the Contracting Process.* Martinus Nijhoff Publishers, 2001, pp. 198–199.
182. Judgments of the Lithuanian Supreme Court of 21 Jan 2004 in the civil case No 3K-3-47/2004, of 22 Dec. 2008 in the civil case 3K-3-609/2008 and of 23 Mar. 2009 in the civil case 3K-3-86/2009.
183. On the original and qualified versions of the doctrine, *see* Benedicte Fauvarque-Cosson, Hugh Beale, Jacobien Rutgers, Denis Tallon, Stefan Vogenauer. *Cases, Materials and Text on Contract Law.* 2nd ed., Hart Publishing, 2010, pp. 564–582.

the contract or its term unjustifiably gives the other party excessive advantage. In such cases, among other circumstances, regard must also be paid to the fact that one party has taken unfair advantage of the other's dependent position, or the other party's economic difficulties, urgent needs, or the latter's economic weakness, lack of information or experience, his inadvertence or inexperience in negotiations; regard shall also be taken of the nature and purpose of the contract.

272. The gross disparity complements the *ex post* doctrine of *imprévision* by curing the hardship among the parties which exists *ex ante*. However, gross disparity differs from other *ex ante* grounds of invalidity by being the sole case in whole LCC where unilateral extrajudicial avoidance of a contract is allowed.[184] The particular difference from the abuse of circumstances (LCC Article 1.91) is that gross disparity does not require to prove the state of necessity on the part of the aggrieved party and functions even in less extreme cases. It differs from the standard terms defences (LCC Article 6.186, 6.228^4) because it gives relief and is not limited to the contracts of adhesion. Finally, gross disparity should be distinguished from the defence for the reduction of contractual penalties, because the latter defence provides special rules, which functionally substitute the remedy of gross disparity. For this reason, Lithuanian courts have refused to apply gross disparity rules for the reduction of contractual penalties.[185]

273. Besides a unilateral avoidance of contract, LCC Article 6.228 also prescribes additional remedies. Thus, upon the request of the party entitled to claim for invalidity of a contract or a separate term on the grounds of a gross disparity of parties, a court may revise the contract or its term and adapt them respectively in order to make the contract or its separate term meet the requirements of fairness and reasonable standards of fair dealing practices. The court may modify the contract or separate term also on the request of the party who has received a notice of the refusal from the contract if this party upon receiving the notice has immediately informed the other party about his request into the court, and the latter still has not refused from the contract.

VI. Defective Representation

274. A fundamental legal maxim of the agency law – *qui facit per alium facit per se* – implies that the principal acts through his agent and therefore agent actions equal actions of the principal. This is true so long as the agent expresses real will of the principal and does not act in his detriment or ultra vires. If the agent maliciously or without authorisation represents the principal, the party's will is defective since no normal agreement exists. It makes the contract voidable.

184. Valentinas Mikelėnas. *Lietuvos Respublikos civilinio kodekso komentaras. Šeštoji knyga. Prievolių teisė.* Justitia, 2003, I t., p. 305.
185. Judgment of the Lithuanian Supreme Court of 15 Mar. 2010 in the civil case No 3K-3-106/2010.

275. According to LCC Article 1.91(1), a transaction may be declared voidable by a court on the action of the aggrieved party if it was formed by a malicious agreement of the agent of one party with the other party. In order to annul the contract on this ground, case law requires to establish the intentional fault of both the agent and counterparty.[186] Accordingly, in addition to unilateral restitution, the aggrieved party may claim reliance damages, including compensation of non-pecuniary loss, *in solidum* also from both the agent and counterparty.

276. Another case is an unauthorised representation. LCC Article 1.92 prescribes that a transaction made by an agent outside the limitations of the authority conferred on him by laws or a contract may be declared voidable upon the action of the principal unless such transaction is ratified by the principal. LCC Article 2.133 states that where a contract was concluded without due authorisation, a person who has concluded the contract shall be liable for his contractual obligations to the other party to the contract, except in cases, where the said party to the contract was aware or had to be aware of the fact that the latter was not entitled to conclude the contract. However, where an agent acted in excess of his powers but in the manner which gave to a third person serious grounds to think that he was concluding a contract with a duly authorised agent, the contract shall be obligatory to the principal, except in cases where the other party to the contract was aware or had to be aware that an agent was exceeding his powers. In cases of unauthorised contracting, the aggrieved principal and bona fide third parties may claim damages from the agent: the principal is entitled to expectation damages due to breach of a mandate contract, while the third parties are limited to the reliance damages based on tort. In contrast with malicious representation, the compensation for non-pecuniary loss done by unauthorised trading is excluded.

§3. Other Terms of Validity

I. Existing and Licit Cause/Simulation

277. It has been presented in the first chapters of this book that only in prescribed cases the contract must demonstrate its cause. Examples of cause in Lithuanian contract law are: a concept of insurable interest in the insurance contract law (LCC Article 6.988(4)), which in essence is manifestation of specific contractual cause; a contract of novation, which is valid only if original contract, which largely defines *causa contractus* of novation, is also valid (LCC Article 6.141(3)); corresponding obligations in bilateral contracts as a *causa* for each other (a consideration in common law terms); and various financial contracts of derivatives tied to an underlying factor, which should be lawful and possible.

186. Judgment of the Lithuanian Supreme Court of in the civil case No Lietuvos Aukščiausiojo Teismo Civilinių bylų skyriaus teisėjų kolegijos 2009 m. rugsėjo 21 d. nutartis civilinėje byloje Nr. 3K-3-361/2009.

278. Therefore, while the fragments of cause are dispersed throughout the entire LCC, the notion of cause is not a general prerequisite for the validity of contracts in Lithuanian civil law. Leaving aside those fragmented exceptions, legal effect cause gives only indirectly – as a basis to the most other contract law doctrines and rules. Seen from this angle, *causa contractus* is a very powerful principle, which indirectly coordinates the whole mechanics of contract law and as such deserves attention in most contractual cases even if no direct effect for it is prescribed by the LCC.

279. Notable indirect manifestation of *causa contractus* is the notion of simulated contracts. There are two forms of simulation: absolute and partial. In case of absolute simulation, where a transaction is made for the sake of appearance without intention to create legal effects, it does not produce its effects between the parties and is void and restitution should be applied (LCC Article 1.86). In the case of partial simulation, where a transaction is formed to cover up another transaction, i.e., if the parties' intent to make a transaction is different from the simulated transaction, the rules applicable to the intended (real) transaction shall apply (LCC Article 1.87). For instance, a sales contract is simulated where the sole purpose of it is to disguise the actual contract of donation made in order to save social security benefits.[187] However, those are the consequences only *inter partes*. If the rights or lawful interests of third persons are violated by a simulated transaction, the third persons in defence of their rights shall be able to plead simulation against the parties of the simulated transaction.[188]

280. Similar to the legal consequences of simulation is the court's power to recharacterise legal transactions according to the real intentions of the parties (prevalence of substance over the form), which is quite common in Lithuania and other jurisdictions having subjective method of interpretation of contracts. However, these two situations should be distinguished. Nullity due to simulation is a more limited remedy compared to recharacterisation because in a latter case court does not need to establish fault (*mala fides*) of the parties. In contrast, there is an implied requirement to establish the intent of the parties to simulate transaction. Such moral downside of simulation causes more rigid consequences for the parties in comparison with an ordinary recharacterisation: recharacterisation of transaction has effects *erga omnes*, whereas the hidden transaction in case of simulation cannot be used against the third parties.

II. Determined or Determinable, Possible and Licit Object

281. Defining characteristic of an agreement, as the main element of the contract, is its sufficiency. This characteristic is related to the content of agreement,

187. Judgment of the Lithuania Supreme Court of 25 Jun. 2020 in the civil case No 3K-3-203-403/2020.
188. Judgment of the Lithuanian Supreme Court of 4 Apr. 2002 in the civil case No 3K-7-25/2002.

which should meet the substantial requirement to contain all essential terms, necessary to conclude the contract. Although the particular standards for sufficiency may differ depending on the type of the contract, every contract should always contain the term on the prestation of contractual obligation. A prestation (*prievolės dalykas*) is a subject matter of the obligation, i.e., behaviour of the debtor which is required to perform its obligation towards the creditor. Under LCC Article 6.3, the prestation of an obligation may be any action (active or passive) that is neither forbidden by law nor contrary to public order or good morals. The prestation of an obligation may relate to any property, even future property, provided that the property is determinate as to the kind and quantity, or can be determined according to other criteria. The prestation of an obligation may have a monetary or non-monetary expression; it must nevertheless meet the correspondent interest of the creditor that is protected by law. The prestation of an obligation cannot be something that is impossible to perform (*impossibilium nulla obligatio est*). It is clear from the definition of obligation and rules below that every obligation must have its prestation. In turn, it means that every contract which creates obligations must contain clear agreement on the obligation, including its prestation. When the prestation of obligation is related to the assets, Lithuanian legal doctrine calls these assets as an object of obligation.[189] It means that some types of obligations, i.e., obligations to give assets to the creditor (sales, lease, loan, franchise, gift, etc.), to create (construction and other works contracts) or increase them (trust contracts, etc.), can have both prestation as object *largo sensu* and object *stricto sensu*. However, the mandatory prerequisite of a contract's content is only prestation, while the object (in a narrow sense) only helps to define obligations which concern assets.

III. Initial Impossibility

282. *Ex ante* impossibility makes contract void without any further qualifications because in order for the agreement to be sufficient it must contain proper subject matter (prestation). LCC Article 6.3(4) prescribes that the subject matter of an obligation cannot be something that is impossible to perform. Since *impossibilium nulla obligatio est*, the contract lacks its main element – the agreement – which should encompass the subject matter of obligation. However, in one case Supreme Court has controversially declared assignment contract void on this ground solely on the reason that in time of contract formation seller had not yet owned the claim, which was sold.[190] This is incorrect reasoning, at least so far as there is nothing to prevent the seller from obtaining goods in the market or manufacturing them by himself and delivering them to the buyer. If one party is culpable for the conclusion of such contract, it should pay damages to the aggrieved party (LCC Article 6.263).

189. Valentinas Mikelėnas. *Prievolių teisė. Pirmoji dalis.* Justitia: Vilnius, 2002, p. 48.
190. Judgment of the Lithuanian Supreme Court of 30 Jun. 2008 in the civil case No 3K-3-199/2008.

IV. Illegality, Public Order and Good Morals

283. Freedom of contract finds its limits in mandatory law, public order and good morals. Even if contracting parties intend to be bound, and their consent is not affected by mistake, fraud, threat, duress or misrepresentation, their contract can still be void or unenforceable if its conclusion or performance violates a statute or fundamental principles of society.[191]

284. Probably the most common ground of invalidity of a contract in Lithuanian case law is illegality. According to LCC Article 1.80, any transaction that fails to meet the requirements of imperative statutory provisions is void and restitution should be applied. This ground is often invoked by claimants in spheres which are extensively regulated by the rules of public law (land use regulation, environmental, zoning and construction law, competition law, financial regulation, etc.), which by their nature are mostly imperative. Lesser number of imperative rules is also found in a private law, mostly in family law, consumer contract law and property law. Without any doubt, non-compliance with default rules does not lead to illegality because parties have the freedom of contract at their disposition to deviate from such rules (LCC Article 6.156). In addition, case law has softened the otherwise very broad scope of the illegality, as a ground to avoid transactions, by adding the requirement to establish violation of fundamental public interest, which requires to universally outlaw disputed transactions.[192]

285. Interesting issue, related to the illegality of contracts, concerns contracts concluded with a person lacking the administrative authorisation mandatory to start regulated activities, for example to provide financial services. Case law on this point seems to be arbitrarily different depending on the type of financial service concerned. Thus, in case, where defendant has provided investment services without authorisation, the contract was enforced by the courts without any hesitation.[193] In contrast, in insurance cases the Supreme Court has ruled that if insurance contract is concluded not with the insurance undertaking in meaning of the Law on Insurance, such contract is null and void.[194] It should be said that the first position is more in line with European trends.[195]

---

191. Jan M. Smits. *Contract Law: A Comparative Introduction.* Edward Elgar Publishing, 2014, p. 179.
192. Judgments of the Lithuanian Supreme Court of 4 May 2005 in the civil case No 3K-3-263/2005 and of 21 Sep. 2005 in the civil case No 3K-3-416/2005.
193. Judgment of the Lithuanian Supreme Court of 16 Apr. 2014 in the civil case No 3K-3-206/2014.
194. Judgment of the Lithuanian Supreme Court of 4 Jul. 2008 in the civil case 3K-3-320/2008.
195. As Prof. Michel Tison points out, EU Member States seem increasingly reluctant to attach stringent effects in civil law – under the form of nullity of contracts – to the absence of an authorisation by a financial institution. This is consistent with the legal nature of an authorisation requirement as supervisory-oriented instrument: the administrative authorisation should in the first place enable prudential supervisors to control *ex ante* whether an applicant financial institution satisfies the legal requirements for taking up a business as far as its internal organisation and financial soundness is concerned. Less convincing would be the approach to consider the authorisation as a precondition for recognising the capacity, as understood in contract law, of a person to enter into contracts. A similar reasoning applies for the civil law impact of prudential requirements: these rules are essentially concerned with the overall financial safety and soundness of a financial institution and will,

286. As concern public order and good morals, statutory law in contemporary times is of such extensive reach that in practice most situations prejudicing public order and good morals are already prohibited by one or another statute. However, as in other jurisdictions, Lithuanian civil law maintains residual category of public order and good morals (*bonos mores*), which constitutes independent ground for invalidity of a contract. LCC Article 1.81 prescribes that a transaction that is contrary to public order or norms of good morals is void. The Supreme Court has reasoned that the law does not define the notion of 'public order and good morals'; its content is multifaceted and concerns not only the actions but also their consequences. The impact on the society, State and private individuals should be evaluated.[196]

287. Public order (*ordre publique*)[197] is defined as encompassing main principles, which are the basis for the State legal system and functioning of State and society. Public order consists of imperative norms of constitutional, administrative and other branches of Lithuanian law.[198] The concept is universally used within the legal system and not reserved only for the formation of contracts. Public order is protected in main branches of Lithuanian law, such as constitutional law, civil law, private international law, arbitration law, administrative law and criminal law. For instance, according to Lithuanian Criminal Code Article 284 ('Violation of Public Order') a person who, by defiant conduct, threats, taunting or acts of vandalism, demonstrates disrespect to the surrounding people or the environment in a public place and thereby disrupts public peace or order shall be punished by community service or by a fine or by restriction of liberty or by arrest or by imprisonment for a term of up to two years.[199] Another example is as follows: according to the Law

---

as a rule, not determine the validity of individual contracts entered into by the supervised financial institution. Michel Tison. *The civil law effects of MiFID in a comparative law perspective*. Ghent University, Financial Law Institute Working Paper No. WP 2010-05, p. 8.

196. Judgment of the Lithuanian Supreme Court of 16 Jan. 2006 in the civil case No 3K-3-30/2006.

197. Historically, the concept of public order was taken to refer to provisions of the public law that were fundamental to the organisation of civil society; these were seen to include all the rules thought necessary to the institutional structure of the State and its organs. Increasing regulation in areas of labour standards, environmental degradation and agricultural protection has greatly expanded the scope of the concept of public order such that it is now common to distinguish between the traditional notion of political public order (*ordre public politique*) and the modern concept of economic public order (*ordre public economique*). John E.C. Brierley, Roderick A. Macdonal (eds). *Quebec civil law: an introduction to Quebec private law.* E. Montgomery Publications, 1993, p. 194–195.

198. *Aurimas Brazdeikis, et al. Civilinė teisė. Bendroji dalis.* Justitia, 2009, p. 348.

199. Interestingly, next to public order, there is also similar concept in Lithuanian law – 'public seriousness' (*viešoji rimtis*) violated by screaming, whistling, loudly singing and other noise creating activity in public places and during the night time – also at private places, if such activity interferes with peace of mind, rest or work of other people. Such behaviour is (and perhaps should be) prohibited as administrative violation by the Law on Administrative Violations Art. 488. However, having in mind potential overlaps with notion of public order, it is doubtful, whether such distinct concept is needed at all. The notion 'public seriousness' awkwardly presupposes some kind of closed society, police State and lack of individual freedoms, which is not true in independent Lithuania. Although this concept has been established only in the administrative law, it may be also used to attack transactions on the ground of illegality (LCC Art. 1.80) because rules of administrative offences law are imperative.

on Commercial Arbitration Article 50, the Court of Appeal of Lithuania may annul an arbitral award where the appellant party provides evidence that the arbitral award is in conflict with the public order of the Republic of Lithuania. According to the legal doctrine, transactions against public order are contracts with criminal content, transactions which hide evidence of a crime, creates illicit privileges, trades in chairs within the civil service, focuses on the evasion of taxes, facilitates hostile activities against Republic of Lithuania or its allies, making donations solely in order to get State accolades, etc.[200] For instance, the Supreme Court has found as violating public order the transaction which evades mandatory bailiff's order during the enforcement procedure,[201] public procurement contract which was concluded despite interim judicial prohibition to do it,[202] agreement fostering online poker gaming.[203] Purchases of academic theses by the students from the other persons to present them in the university as their own are prohibited in administrative law as administrative violations (Code of Administrative Violations Article 123) and in civil law as void transactions which violate public order.

288. The exact meaning of 'good morals' in liberal contemporary society is, indeed, interesting and a subtle question.[204] Since Lithuanian society is predominantly Christian, not surprisingly Lithuanian civil law doctrine admits that criteria of good morals in European culture are norms of Decalogue. The doctrinal examples of transactions against good morals are transactions related to the prostitution, trade in human body parts and tissues.[205] The Supreme Court has characterised as violating good morals, the transactions, where seized property was sold by the bailiff under very low price[206] or where purpose of the transaction was to maintain unequal parts of spouses' matrimonial property.[207]

289. It seems that Lithuanian legal doctrine views public order and good morals as subsidiary ground to illegality by stating that in case of violation of imperative norms, which is automatically violation of public order and good morals, LCC

200. Alfonsas Vileita, *et al. Lietuvos Respublikos civilinio kodekso komentaras. Pirmoji knyga. Bendrosios nuostatos*. Justitia, 2001, p. 185.
201. Judgment of the Lithuanian Supreme Court of 6 Apr. 2010 in the civil case No 3K-3-140/2010.
202. Judgment of the Lithuanian Supreme Court of 9 May 2011 in the civil case No 3K-3-231/2011.
203. Judgment of the Lithuania Supreme Court of 4 Nov. 2021 in the civil case No e3K-3-252-969/2021.
204. For instance, voluntary intimate relations between homosexual men in Soviet times were criminal offences, which according to the LSSR Criminal Code Art. 122 were punishable up to three years of imprisonment. Even today intimate relations between homosexual people by some parts of society are treated as immoral behaviour. However, even in purely hypothetical scenario where such public opinion would be prevailing in a society, it could have no legal effect due to constitutional prohibition to discriminate on the basis of sexual orientation (Lithuanian Constitution Art. 29).
205. Alfonsas Vileita, *et al. Lietuvos Respublikos civilinio kodekso komentaras. Pirmoji knyga. Bendrosios nuostatos*. Justitia, 2001, p. 185. In the Quebec legal doctrine, which had strong impact on the creators of LCC, concept good morals is to be understood as evoking the notion of right conduct as lived in society (social mores) and, however much influenced by religion, it is not a specifically religious notion (*la morale*). John E.C. Brierley, Roderick A. Macdonal (eds). *Quebec civil law: an introduction to Quebec private law.* E. Montgomery Publications, 1993, p. 194.
206. Judgment of the Lithuanian Supreme Court of 19 Jun. 2008 in the civil case No 3K-3-293/2008.
207. Judgment of the Lithuanian Supreme Court of 30 Dec. 2008 in the civil case No 3K-3-617/2008.

Article 1.80 (illegality) should be applicable.[208] There is also one judgment by the Supreme Court, which also equalised imperative norms with public order and by quashing judgment ordered lower court to apply imperative LCC 4.96 (bona fides acquisition defence) rule on top of Belgium property law, which governed the case.[209] However, the idea to mix imperative norms and public policy is not justified according to the scheme of LCC. First, public order, indeed, consists only from imperative (mandatory) rules, however, only from the most important ones. Not every set of imperative rules, especially of purely technical character, like vindication order, presupposes public order. There should also be fundamental values involved. Second, according to LCC Article 1.81, legal consequences for violation of public order may be stricter for parties, than in case of illegality, because in a former case court is instructed by the LCC itself to evaluate whether to apply restitution at all. The restitution in cases of violation of public order and good morals should not apply if both parties knew or should have known the transaction to be contrary to public order or good morals. However, unilateral or bilateral restitution may take place where its application is not contrary to the mandatory statutory provisions or good morals, i.e., where the purpose of the transaction contradicting public order or norms of good morals was not achieved, and the provisions of public law do not establish any property sanctions in regard to the parties to such transaction.

290. Having said that, it is evident that not the public order is subsidiary ground for avoidance, but quite the opposite – illegality is applied only where public order is not violated and ordinary consequences on the ground of illegality should follow.

V. Unenforceable Contracts

291. Unenforceable contracts in Lithuanian law are those which are void. For instance, in cases where games or wagers are prohibited by law, no action can be brought by the benefited party (winner) claiming the agreed sum to be paid; likewise, no recovery of the paid sum may be instituted by the losing party. The losing party has the right to recover what he has paid following the outcome of a game or wager where the loser is a minor, or in cases of compulsion, threat, fraud or any other unfair actions exercised against the losing party (LCC Article 6.243).

292. However, at some occasions even validly formed contracts may also be unenforceable. First, due to the privity of the contract, the contracts are not enforceable and even may be without any other effect against third parties. For instance, according to LCC Article 1.75 the parties to an unregistered transaction may not invoke the fact of transaction against third persons and argue their rights against third persons by relying on other means of proof.

208. Alfonsas Vileita, *et al. Lietuvos Respublikos civilinio kodekso komentaras. Pirmoji knyga. Bendrosios nuostatos*. Justitia, 2001, p. 185.
209. Judgment of the Lithuanian Supreme Court of 9 Nov. 2010 in the civil case No 3K-3-446/2010.

293. Second, due to protective rules the contracts may be unenforceable even *inter partes*. For instance, according to LCC Article 2.164, a commercial agent and a principal may provide in the contract that upon expiry of the contract the commercial agent shall not compete with the principal for no more than two years. However, a principal cannot enforce the provision of the contract on the prohibition of competition where: a principal terminates the contract without commercial agent's consent violating thereby the term of prior notification about the termination of a contract and fails to notify, without delay, the commercial agent about the important reasons for the termination thereof; a commercial agent terminates the contract for important reasons for which the principal is held liable and notifies the principal, without delay, thereof; and contract of a commercial agent and a principal has been terminated by a court judgment for reasons for which the principal is held liable.

§4. The Consequences of a Defect of Consent or a Lack of Substantive Validity

I. Avoidance of Contract: Limitations of the Remedy

294. The normal consequence of a defect of consent or a lack of substantive validity is invalidity of the contract. From the other side, Lithuanian civil law is focused on the stability of transactions; hence there are several limitations which tend to soften rigidity of avoidance.

295. First, LCC Article 6.189(1) provides that a contract formed in accordance with the provisions of the law and that is valid shall have the force of law between its parties. Obviously, it is not possible for a party either to unilaterally avoid a contract or to unilaterally refuse to perform an obligation that arises out of a contract (under LCC Article 6.59). For these reasons, the LCC working group decided not to accept the institute of avoidance of a contract, as provided by UNIDROIT PICC Article 3.14–3.17 because unilateral avoidance of a contract could lead to instability of civil relationships. As a result, the LCC provides that in the event of mistake, fraud or threat, the interested party must start court proceedings for the annulment of a contract.[210] The only exception is gross disparity of parties, where LCC Article 6.228 gives right to aggrieved party to unilaterally avoid the contract without the court judgment.[211]

296. Second, there are two types of nullity of a contract – absolute and relative. According to LCC Article 6.225, a contract is absolutely invalid (void contract) where a violation of the main principles of the Contract law made in forming a contract has breached not only of the interests of a party of the contract but also that of

210. Valentinas Mikelėnas. *The Influence of Instruments of Harmonisation of Private Law upon the Reform of Civil Law in Lithuania.* Juridica International, 2008 Vol. 14, p. 147.

211. Valentinas Mikelėnas. *Lietuvos Respublikos civilinio kodekso komentaras. Šeštoji knyga. Prievolių teisė.* Justitia, 2003, I t., p. 306.

the public interests. Void are illegal, contravening public order and simulated contracts. All other contracts may only be voidable. A contract is voidable (relatively invalid) where in contracting it one party acted in good faith, and the declaration of its nullity is necessary only for the protection of the private interest of the party in good faith.

297. A void contract may not be ratified by the parties later in contrast with a voidable contract which may be ratified by its parties (a party), provided that such ratification results from their express will. An action on the absolute nullity of a contract may be brought by any person whose rights and lawful interest are violated by such contract. The fact of an absolute nullity of a contract and legal effects of this fact may be stated by the court ex officio (on its own motion). An action on the avoidance of a contract may be brought by a contracting party in good faith which has sustained damage from entering into that contract, or by a third person in whose interest it is concluded, or by a person whose rights or lawful interests are violated by that contract.

298. Third, a contract may be not only fully invalid but also partially invalid. The nullity of a single term of a contract does not invoke the nullity of the entire contract, except in cases if it appears that the contracting parties would not have entered into the contract without the condition affected by nullity. In the case of a multilateral contract when there are two or more persons bound to perform an obligation, the nullity affecting one of the persons shall not import the nullity of the entire contract unless the participation of that person is necessary for the formation of the contract concerned.

299. Fourth, Lithuanian case law have restricted the claimants' disposition to avoid a contract due to defect of consent in financial markets litigation. In aforementioned DNB bank cases, initially most investors responded with the claims for the avoidance of the financial transactions – bonds subscription contracts, lending contracts and related mortgage agreements. The result in case of the avoidance of voidable contract under the CC Article 1.90(3) is full restitution of parties to the initial position where investor avoids losses completely. From the other side, in cases where transactions are not declared null by court investors are forced to bear all losses. This inflexible all-or-nothing approach leads to unsatisfactory and suboptimal results in cases where facts clearly show that both parties of transaction are at some extent responsible for the loss. These issues were addressed by the Supreme Court, which rejected above-mentioned all-or-nothing approach on the reasoning that despite civil wrongs made by the bank, avoidance of the transactions leads to the unfair results, because prohibits pro rata recovery depending on the fault of each party and provides legal instability. The Court suggested that much more adequate response in this situation would be award of damages and dismissed claims.[212] Investors who based their claims on the grounds of civil liability for the award of

212. Judgments of the Lithuanian Supreme Court of 17 Mar. 2014 in the civil case No Nr. 3K-3-68/2014; 20 May 2014 in the civil case No 3K-3-265/2014; 5 Sep. 2014 in the civil case No 3K-3-391/2014.

damages were more successful.[213] Later on, whole case law responding to that precedent established pattern to distribute losses from the investment in equity-linked bonds equally (50/50) for both parties, irrespective of the claim type.[214] These cases show judicial preference to satisfy civil liability claims instead of transaction avoidance claims for two acceptable reasons.[215] First, civil liability enables courts to reach much more individualised and fair result; second, in contrast with rescission of contract, civil liability does not impair the stability of the financial markets.

II. Retroactive Effect of Avoidance or Nullity

300. According to LCC Article 1.95, a transaction which has been annulled shall be deemed to be null and void *ab initio* (from the moment of its forming). Where from the content of a transaction follows that it is impossible to declare such transaction void *ab initio*, it may be declared void only for the future, i.e., from the time when the judgment acquires the authority of the final judgment (res judicata).

III. Restitution

301. LCC Article 1.80(2–4) prescribes a general order of restitution applicable for all cases of invalidity, unless for particular cases LCC provides special rules. Thus, when a transaction is invalid, each party shall be bound to restore to the other party everything he has received according to that transaction (restitution), and where it is impossible to restore in kind the received, the parties are bound to compensate the received to each other in money, unless the laws provide for other consequences of invalidity of the transaction. The rules of restitution are established by the law of obligations. The property – object of the transaction that is annulled – may not be claimed from the third person in good faith, except in cases provided for in LCC Article 4.96(1–3).[216]

---

213. Judgment of the Lithuanian Supreme Court of 22 May 2015 in the civil case No 3K-3-164-378/2015.

214. Judgments of the Lithuanian Supreme Court of 19 Nov. 2014 in the civil case No 3K-3-517 and of 3 Jul. 2015 in the civil case No 3K-3-208-248/2015.

215. For the evidence of this trend from the comparative perspective, *see* Marcel C.A. van den Nieuwenhuijzen; *et al. Financial Law in the Netherlands.* Kluwer Law International, 2010, p. 439; Joel Seligman, Louis Loss, Troy Paredes. *Securities regulation.* 4 ed. Wolters Kluwer Law & Business/Aspen Publishers, 2006, p. 4116–4119; Judgment of the Italian Supreme Court of 19 Dec. 2007 in the case No 26724 (Parmalat).

216. LCC Art. 4.96 prescribes that if a movable thing was acquired upon payment from a person who had no right to transfer this property, and the acquirer did not and could not know this (acquirer in good faith), the owner shall have the right to vindicate the thing from the acquirer only if the thing belongs to the owner or to a person to whom the owner had given it in possession, if the thing was lost or stolen from one of these, or if it stopped being in their possession against their volition. The owner may vindicate the thing within three years from the moment of the loss of the thing. Immovable thing may not be vindicated from an acquirer in good faith with the exception of cases when the owner had lost such thing due to a crime committed by other persons. If a thing was acquired

302. If transaction is contrary to public order or norms of good morals, the restitution shall not apply if both parties knew or should have known the transaction to be contrary to public order or good morals. Unilateral or bilateral restitution may take place where its application is not contrary to the mandatory statutory provisions or good morals, i.e., where the purpose of the transaction contradicting public order or norms of good morals was not achieved and the provisions of public law (criminal law, administrative law) do not establish any pecuniary sanctions in regard to the parties to such transaction (LCC Article 1.81).

303. Under Lithuanian law, restitution of prestations should be applied by the court on its own motion (ex officio) immediately after it satisfies action of invalidity (LCC Article 1.78(5)). Moreover, Supreme Court has ruled that in case where (primary) restitution is inapplicable, the court ex officio should apply the restitution on the alternative ground – performance not due (LCC Article 6.237) or at least reverse the unjustified enrichment (LCC Article 6.242).[217]

304. Restitution of prestations being remedy in personam is shaped and subordinated to the privity of a contract. Therefore, if the benefit by A, performing the invalid contract to creditor B, is conferred on the third person C, the duty to restore property still owns the contractual counterparty B. 'Leapfrogging' where the enriched third party C is directly responsible against A in such cases only is possible on a basis of subsidiary restitution of a performance not due (LCC Article 6.237) if it has no independent valid cause for enrichment from B.

305. Similarly, restitution against the third party is limited also in a stipulation for a benefit of a third party C (LCC Article 6.191), despite the fact that C after the acceptance of the claim, actually becomes an additional creditor in a contract. Since third-party beneficiary falls into the ambit of the contract, from the first glance, it should directly return the benefit to the performed party A. However, if a third party received the stipulated benefit in a good faith, it is protected from the restitution by LCC Article 6.153(3), according to which actions in favour of a third person in good

---

without recompense from a person who had no right to transfer its ownership, the owner shall have the right to vindicate the thing in all cases. This rule shall apply to movable as well as immovable things.

217. *See* Judgment of the Lithuanian Supreme Court of 22 Dec. 2016 in the civil case No 3K-3-529-916/2016. In this case, service contract for the benefit of a third party was declared void. At the time of judgment, the services were already supplied for a third party, but unpaid. The Supreme Court has struggled to apply the primary restitution, because in view of the Court it should be normally be applicable only where both parties exchange the performances. Instead, the Court has tried to apply the recovery on the basis of performance not due (which is also restitution), however, taking in regard that services were supplied not to the counterparty (customer), but to the third party, recovery from whom was not appropriate on the policy reasons, made conclusion that this remedy is also inapplicable. Finally, the Court has ruled that enrichment is indirect and should be recoverable by the general action on unjustified enrichment (LCC Art. 6.242). In my view, this judicial acrobatic in search for the alternative for the primary restitution was completely unnecessary, because in this case primary restitution was easily applicable as a recovery of performance value, because such option is expressly prescribed by LCC Art. 6.146.

faith may be invoked against a person who claims for restitution. It means that primary restitution should normally take place between original parties of the contract, unless C, who has received performance, was in bad faith.

IV. Damages

306. Civil liability for precontractual wrongs is based on doctrine *culpa in contrahendo* (LCC Article 6.163). Precontractual wrongs, according to *non-cumul* principle (LCC Article 6.245), in Lithuanian are characterised as torts. The normal remedy in such cases is reliance damages, which includes compensation of direct losses and value of lost opportunity.

307. Where from the content of a transaction, for example lease, follows that it is impossible to declare such transaction void *ab initio* and it may be declared void only for the future, the damages are for expectation, if cause of action consists breach of the contract, which was avoided only to the future. However, the expectation damages should cover only profits lost during the period when contract had been valid.

308. Besides the general liability rules, LCC also directly prescribes special rules for damages concerning some grounds of invalidity. Thus, in the cases where a transaction formed by a natural incapable or only partially capable person (LCC Article 1.84) is avoided, in addition to the restitution, the legally capable party is obliged to compensate the expenses suffered by the other party, also any damage to the latter's property or loss thereof if the capable party knew or should have known about the incapacity of that other party.

309. Similarly, according to LCC Article 1.89, in case of avoided contract, made by a person who was unable to comprehend his own actions or to control them, the other party is bound to compensate the party who at the moment of the transaction forming was unable to comprehend his own actions or to control them the expenses suffered, also any damage to his property or loss thereof, if this another party was aware or should have been aware of the state of the first contracting party.

310. In the event of annulment of a transaction formed under the influence of a mistake, the mistaken party, in addition to the annulment, also claim from the other party compensation for the expenses incurred or the damage to his property or loss thereof if this party proves that the mistake was caused by the fault of the other party. Where it is not proved, the mistaken party is bound to compensate to the other party the expenses incurred as well as the damage to its property or loss thereof (LCC Article 1.90).

311. In cases of inappropriate pressure (fraud, violence, economic pressure, etc.), the defendant is bound to restore to the aggrieved party everything he has received according to that transaction, and where it is impossible to restore in kind, it must be compensated in money. In addition, the guilty party shall be bound to compensate to the aggrieved person all the expenses incurred. Where a transaction is avoided by reason of fraud, violence, economic pressure, real threatening or malicious agreement made between the agent of one party and the other party, the aggrieved party may, in addition, claim compensation of non-pecuniary damage (LCC Article 1.91).

V. Judicial Revision

312. Substantive defects of the contract formation may be remedied not only with avoidance but also with change of a contract. Such is the case with gross disparity. According to LCC Article 6.228, upon the request of the party entitled to claim for invalidity of a contract or a separate condition thereof on the ground of gross disparity, a court may revise the contract or its condition and adapt them respectively in order to make the contract or its separate condition meet the requirements of fairness and reasonable standards of fair dealing practices. The court may modify the contract or separate conditions thereof also on the request of the party who has received a notice of the refusal from the contract if this party upon receiving the notice has immediately informed the other party about his request to the court, and the latter still has not refused from the contract. However, in practice, aggrieved party rarely chooses this option and instead proceeds with annulment remedy.

Chapter 3. The Contents of a Contract

313. The content of a contract consists of its clauses (terms), which in essence are mini agreements on a particular contractual issue. Whereas in a perfect world, the content of contract should always match Arrow–Debreu ideal by being complete and free from imperfections;[218] in practice, it is impossible and highly impracticable to achieve. Almost all contracts in real life are incomplete and are left to be supplemented with default rules of law. In addition, not every contract is fair enough to be enforced without hesitation of the judge with high integrity. Thus, there are two main issues related to the content of contract: first, its sufficiency and, second, fairness of its terms.

314. Sufficiency of agreement is important not just in the sense of completeness, as is stressed by Arrow–Debreu ideal, but, first, as a minimum amount of agreed terms necessary for the formation of a valid contract. Contractual obligations may arise only from the sufficient agreement. If the contract terms are insufficient, there is no contract at all.

315. Another problem is the fairness of contract's content. There are a lot of contracts, especially in Lithuanian banking industry, which are sufficient and detailed, but lacking fair allocation of rights and duties of both parties. The goal of Lithuanian contract law is not only to facilitate efficient exchange of goods and services but also to ensure fairness in economic transactions by providing mandatory rules to limit freedom of contract and safeguarding weaker party. Therefore, the control of the substance of agreement enables to achieve goals of contract law and ensure substantive fairness in private relations.

---

218. The search for contract terms that yield efficient outcomes is the subject of a prodigious theoretical literature in economics. The customary starting point for that enquiry is the complete contingent claims contract associated with the work of Arrow and Debreu. Although originally conceived as an analytical tool for modelling competitive equilibrium rather than as a theory of contracting per se, the efficiency properties associated with contingent trade in the Arrow–Debreu framework made complete contingent claims contracts – contracts specifying the physical characteristics, date, location and price of a commodity for every future state of nature – appealing to contract theorists as an archetype against which to compare more realistic agreements: Arrow–Debreu complete contingent claims contracts represent what transactors would write in an ideal world free from 'imperfections'. The complete contingent contract is an (imaginary) contract that would spell out in complete detail the exact legal rights and duties of each party under every possible state of affairs. If any contract ever succeeded in reaching this endpoint, the law's default rules would then be irrelevant, as no issue would ever arise that could not be settled by the terms of the contract itself. *See* Richard Craswell. Contract Law: General Theories *In.* Encyclopedia of Law and Economics, Vol. III. The Regulation of Contracts, Cheltenham, Edward Elgar, 2000, p. 1; Scott E. Masten. Contractual Choice *In.* Encyclopedia of Law and Economics, Vol. III. The Regulation of Contracts, Cheltenham, Edward Elgar, 2000, p. 27.

§1. THE DIFFERENT CLAUSES

316. The content of a contract is composed of various clauses, which differ not only by their own content but also by the type. Lithuanian contract law doctrine uses classical civilian classification of contract terms into essential, ordinary and incidental.[219]

317. Essential terms (*essentialia negotii*) are those which are necessary minimum for the contract to exist. The contract always must include a prestation of obligation and, depending on the type of the contract, other mandatory prescribed clauses. For instance, according to the Lithuanian constitutional law, the contract for a sale of public property to a private person should contain terms and security interests, which would guarantee to ensure effective, rational and generating value privatisation process, as well as ensure compliance with principles of equality, inviolability of property, proportionality and legitimate expectations.[220] Another example is immovable sales contract, where LCC Article 6.397 requires agreeing on the price; therefore, if the price is not indicated in the contract, the contract is deemed not to have been concluded. The otherwise ordinary or accidental clause can get the character of essential term also by the will of the parties, where they remark the essentiality of clause in the text of agreement in order to attract extensive remedial consequences for the breach of such terms. Where the parties agree on all essential terms of a contract, the contract is effective, even though the parties have reserved an agreement as to secondary terms. If the parties do not reach their agreement on the secondary terms, the dispute may be resolved within the judicial proceedings taking regard to the nature of the contract, non-mandatory norms, usages, the principles of justice, reasonableness and good faith.

318. Ordinary terms (*normalia negotii*) are the terms which are imposed by the supplementary rules of law despite the will of parties (if such rules are imperative) or on points where parties were silent (if such rules are default). In the strict sense, these are not terms of the contract as such, but statutory rules of supplementation. For example, if parties have not expressly agreed on the quality of goods, LCC Article 6.197 prescribes that the quality of performance must fall with a quality that is reasonable and not lower than average in the concrete circumstances. The source of such term is not the contract, but the law itself, therefore ordinary terms are terms implied in law.

319. Accidental terms (*accidentalia negotii*) are those terms which otherwise would not be applicable, but parties decide to include them into the contract for their convenience. For example, there is no general duty to provide insurance in the sale of goods; however, parties may agree that such insurance cover should be obtained by one of them (LCC Article 6.316). Where the parties stress essentiality of the accidental term in the contract or precontractual documentation, such term becomes an essential term.

---

219. V. Staskonis, *et al. Civilinė teisė: vadovėlis.* Kaunas: Vijusta, 1998, p. 383-385.
220. Judgment of the Lithuanian Republic Constitutional Court of 24 Oct. 2012.

I. Ascertaining of Express Terms

320. LCC Article 6.196 provides that the terms of the contract may be express or implied. Express are those terms which are directly expressed in the contract itself. It encompasses clauses in the main contractual documentation as well as in any other durable medium, characterised as the component part of the contract. Latter option is possible because Lithuanian law allows subjective method of interpretation of contract, does not know parol evidence rule and forbids integration clauses (LCC Article 6.193). Therefore, the text of the contract may be aggregated from various sources into single binding mosaic. For example, in one case, the court has characterised as directly agreed term the price which was achieved and recorded during the conversation of parties within social media platform.[221]

321. Sometimes the law by itself prescribes necessary list of terms, which should be expressly included in the contract. For example, according to LCC Article 6.401, the following should be indicated in the preliminary contract of sale of a planned house or apartment: (1) the buyer's right to repudiate the preliminary contract within ten days from the date of conclusion of the contract; (2) the price of the planned house or apartment and the terms and conditions of its revision or changing; (3) description of the subject matter of the contract and the works which the seller must perform; (4) time limits of construction of the residential house or apartment; (5) encumbrances of the right to the residential house or apartment (both present and future); (6) the contractor, architect, engineer and other persons who will carry out and supervise the construction work; and (7) legal status of the land plot on which the house or apartment will be built and the rights to the land plot of the buyer of the house or apartment.

II. Implied Terms

322. Contractual terms may be implied in law and fact. Terms implied in law are imposed by default rules and other supplementary rules of law. For example, default rule in LCC Article 6.198 on the price of movable creates a contractual term implied in law that the parties should be considered, in the absence of any indication to the contrary, to have made reference to the price commonly charged at the moment of the conclusion of the contract for such performance in comparable circumstances in the sphere of business concerned, or if such price does not exist, to a reasonable price. This is, of course, a very broad understanding of the implied terms, which confuses them with supplementary rules of law.

323. Implied terms *par excellence* are terms implied in fact, i.e., those which follow not from the law itself, but from the essence and purpose of the contract, the nature of relationships established between the parties, the criteria of good faith, reasonableness and justice, as defined in LCC Article 6.196. For instance, the Supreme Court has ruled that reimbursement for ancillary and fortuitous expenses

221. Judgment of the Vilnius County Court of 18 Oct. 2017 in the civil case No 2-11633-545/2017.

of the freight forwarder should be covered by the implied term of contract where such recourse is not regulated by the express terms of contract or direct rules of contract law.[222]

III. Standard Terms and Exemption Clauses

324. Under Lithuanian law, standard terms are such provisions which are prepared in advance for general and repeated use by one contracting party without their content being negotiated with another party, and which are used in the formation of contracts without negotiation with the other party. LCC Article 6.185 provides that standard terms prepared by one of the parties are binding to the other if the latter was provided with an adequate opportunity of getting acquainted with the said terms. In the event where both parties to a contract are companies (businessmen), it is considered that the other party was provided with the opportunity to get acquainted with the said terms if: (1) the party who prepared the standard terms delivered thereof in written form to the other party before or at the time of signing the contract; (2) the party who prepared the standard terms informed the other party before the signing of the contract that the contract would be formed in accordance with standard terms which were accessible to the other party in the place indicated by the party who prepared the standard terms; and (3) a copy of standard terms was offered to be sent to the other party if requested.

325. Use of standard terms is contracting technique, which significantly saves transaction costs and in effect may lower the price of goods and services; however quite often they are also used as an instrument of abuse for the detriment of a weaker party, as is clearly evident in 'take it or leave it' situations. Therefore, in the event of conflict between standard terms and non-standard terms, preference shall be given to the latter, i.e., to those which have been individually negotiated by the parties (LCC Article 6.187). In the event of doubt over terms of a contract, they shall be interpreted against the contracting party that has suggested thereof, and in favour of the party that accepted those terms (LCC Article 6.193). Moreover, no surprising term contained in a standard term contract, i.e., such term that the other party could not reasonably expect to be included in the contract, should be effective. Standard term shall not be considered surprising if they were expressly accepted by the party when they were duly disclosed thereto. In determining whether a term is of surprising character, regard must be taken of its content, wording and form of expression. A party who enters into a contract of adhesion where the standard terms are drawn up by the other party shall have the right to claim for dissolution or modification of that contract in the event where, even though the standard terms of the contract are not contrary to the law, they exclude the party's rights and possibilities that are commonly granted in a contract of that particular class, or exclude or limit civil liability of the party who prepared the standard terms, or establish other provisions which

222. Judgment of the Lithuanian Supreme Court of 23 Nov. 2010 in the civil case No 3K-3-462/2010.

violate the principle of equality of parties, cause imbalance in the parties' interests, or are contrary to the criteria of reasonableness, good faith and justice (LCC Article 6.186).

326. In addition to those general rules, Lithuanian law provides special rules calibrated for the specific types of contracts, which are aimed to mitigate abuses of standard terms for the detriment of a weaker party.[223]

327. In the case of the so-called public contracts, which are imposed on a legal person (businessman) that renders services or sells goods to an indefinite number of persons, i.e., to everyone who makes a request (enterprises of transport, communications, electricity, heating, gas, water supply, access to the banking system and others), a legal person (businessman) may be obliged to submit standard terms of a public contract to be approved by a relevant state institution. In the cases established by laws, public contracts may be concluded in accordance with standard terms approved by the corresponding state institution and obligatory to both parties (LCC Article 6.161).

223. There is however, a vivid challenge for the legislator and courts to properly identify weaker party. It is stressed in Lithuanian jurisprudence that cases when one of the parties is considered to be in a weaker position are also possible in commercial contractual relations, so the protection of such party when the court controls the content of the commercial contract is inevitable. However, the measures of such intervention into contractual relations have to be applied in a limited manner, taking into consideration the peculiarities of such relations. In consumer contract law the need for the protection of weaker party is grounded by limited ability of the consumer to negotiate with a businessman, the lack of information and special knowledge, the need to consume which is determined by his physical characteristics, the impact of advertisements and the fact that he concludes the contracts without the purpose to gain profit. In commercial contractual relationships the need of priority protection of weaker party interests has to be grounded on the lack of information and special knowledge of such party, yet other criteria should not be applied. The size of legal entity (including its yearly turnover and (or) yearly balance and the number of employees) should not be decisive criteria in the process of determining weaker party position in the commercial contractual relationship. These criteria, first, are intended to be used as finance and economic measures of small and medium size business promotion. For this reason, they should not influence the regulation of commercial contractual relations and the weaker party determination in them. When analysing which criteria could mean the stronger party position in commercial contractual relationship it has been concluded that the peculiarities of such relations are best reflected by the factor of permanent commercial activity which also is closely related to the better position determined by the available information and special knowledge. This means that a party should be considered as having the stronger position in those transactions which are normally concluded in its permanent business activity, because such party has or at least it can reasonably be expected for it to have more information and special knowledge in the respective trade sector. Whereas, the position of a businessman who concludes a single and incidental contract in a business field which is extraneous for him should be considered as weaker. *See* Viktorija Budreckienė. *Teisminės komercinių sutarčių turinio kontrolės ribos.* Doctoral thesis. Mykolas Romeris University, 2016, p. 278–279. However, the evaluation of informational asymmetry as sole criterion for the identification of a weaker party in commercial contracts is insufficient as it ignores the market power of some companies, which can unfairly exploit even the most experienced and informed counterparties, having less market power.

328. As concern commercial contracts, EU Late Payments Directive[224] Article 7 provides that a contractual term or a practice relating to the date or period for payment, the rate of interest for late payment or the compensation for recovery costs is either unenforceable or gives rise to a claim for damages if it is grossly unfair to the creditor. In determining whether a contractual term or a practice is grossly unfair to the creditor, within the meaning of the first subparagraph, all circumstances of the case shall be considered, including: (a) any gross deviation from good commercial practice, contrary to good faith and fair dealing; (b) the nature of the product or the service; and (c) whether the debtor has any objective reason to deviate from the statutory rate of interest for late payment, from the payment period as or from the fixed sum. A contractual term or a practice which excludes interest for late payment or compensation for recovery costs shall be presumed to be grossly unfair. This rule has been implemented in Lithuanian in the Law on the Prevention of Late Payment in Commercial Transactions Article 9. Lithuanian law as available remedies has selected judicial declaration of term or practice as unfair and award of compensatory damages. This means that statutory law does not give ground to invalidate unfair terms. In my opinion, the damages remedy is insufficient because instead of invalidation of unfair term and thus *ex ante* avoiding detrimental financial effect, the legislator has chosen to enable for such damage to exist, but cure with the *ex post* remedy.

329. Consumer protection in case of unfair standard terms in Lithuania is based on the rules of EU Unfair Terms in Consumer Contracts Directive,[225] which is transposed into LCC Article 6.228^4. According to those rules, a consumer has the right to claim for invalidity of terms in a consumer contract that are contrary to the criterion of good faith. Terms of a consumer contract which have not been individually negotiated shall be regarded as unfair if they cause a significant imbalance in the parties' rights and duties to the detriment of consumer rights and interests, i.e., the terms which: (1) exclude or limit the civil liability of a seller or service supplier for damage caused by the death of a consumer or impairment of his health, likewise for the damage caused to his property; (2) exclude or limit the rights of a consumer vis-à-vis a seller, service supplier or another party in the event of total or partial non-performance or improper performance by the seller or service supplier of any of the contractual obligations; (3) make contractual terms binding on the consumer whereas contractual obligations of the seller or service supplier are subject to other terms, the realisation of which depends solely on the latter's own will; (4) permit the seller or service supplier to retain sums paid by the consumer where the latter decides not to conclude a contract or refuses to perform it without providing for any rights of the consumer to receive in compensation the sums of the same amount from the seller or service supplier when they unilaterally dissolve the contract; (5) establish a disproportionately high civil liability of the consumer who fails to fulfil his obligation or fulfils it improperly; (6) authorise the seller or service supplier to dissolve the contract unilaterally or rescind it at any time, and no adequate facility

224. Directive 2011/7/EU of the European Parliament and of the Council of 16 Feb. 2011 on combating late payment in commercial transactions.
225. Council Directive 93/13/EEC of 5 Apr. 1993 on unfair terms in consumer contracts.

is granted to the consumer, or provide the seller or service supplier with the right not to compensate the consumer for the amounts received therefrom before the performance of the contract in the event where the seller or service supplier unilaterally dissolve or rescind the contract; (7) enable the seller or service supplier to dissolve an indeterminate contract without any reasonable grounds without due notification of the consumer about such dissolution; (8) entitle the seller or service supplier with the right to unilaterally extend a fixed-term contract automatically, or establish unreasonably short time limit for the consumer to express his opinion upon the extension of the contract, or set forth a requirement for the consumer to express his assent or dissent upon the extending of the contract unreasonably early; (9) irrevocably bind the consumer to the terms with which he had no real opportunity of becoming acquainted before the conclusion of the contract; (10) enable the seller or service supplier to alter the terms of the contract unilaterally without there being any contractual or sufficient grounds; (11) enable the seller or service supplier unilaterally and without any sufficient grounds to modify any characteristics of the good or services to be provided; (12) entitle the seller or service supplier with the right to unilaterally determine the prices of goods and services at the time of their provision, or allow the seller of goods or supplier of services to unilaterally increase the price without providing the consumer with the right to cancel the contract in the case where the final price is higher than that stipulated in the contract. This provision shall not apply for contracts in respect of securities or other financial documents, or for contracts on alienation of things or provision of services where the price is dependent upon the fluctuation of exchange rates or indexes on the exchange, and is beyond the control of the seller or service supplier, likewise for purchase–sale contracts for foreign currencies, travellers cheques or international money orders expressed in a foreign currency; (13) entitle the seller or service supplier with the right to unilaterally determine whether the goods supplied or services rendered are in conformity with the requirements of the contract; (14) provide the seller or service supplier with the exclusive right to interpret the contract; (15) limit the duty of the seller or service supplier to perform obligations undertaken by their agents, or render such obligation subject to compliance with a particular formality; (16) obligate the consumer to fulfil all his obligations to the seller or service supplier even in the event of total or partial non-performance by the seller or service supplier of their own obligations; (17) provide the seller or service supplier with the right of transferring their rights and obligations under the contract without the consumer's consent, where such transferring may reduce the guarantees for the consumer; and (18) exclude or hinder the consumer's right to bring action or exercise any other remedy (by requiring the consumer to take disputes exclusively to arbitration, restricting the use of evidence, by imposing on him the burden of proof, etc.).

330. Terms are considered as not having been individually negotiated where the consumer is deprived of the possibility to influence the process of their preparation, in particular where such terms are determined in advance in the standard contract prepared by the seller or service supplier. In the event where certain terms in the contract prepared in advance were individually negotiated, the provisions established in LCC Article 6.228[4] shall apply to other terms of such contract. The burden of proof that such terms were individually negotiated shall rest upon the seller or service supplier. The assessment whether a term of a contract is unfair shall be effectuated taking in regard the nature of the goods and services stipulated in the contract, as well as other circumstances which existed at the time of contract forming and exerted influence thereupon, likewise any other terms of that contract or those of other contract it depends upon. The terms which define the subject matter of a contract, likewise those related to the conformity between the good sold or a service rendered and the price thereof ought not to be subjected to assessment from the point of view of unfairness where they are expressed clearly and understandably. Contract terms which coincide with the statutory rules are also excluded from such assessment. Any written term of a consumer contract must be expressed clearly and understandably. In the event of doubt over the terms of a contract, the rule of the interpretation of contracts, laid down in LCC Article 6.193, should apply. This rule shall not apply in the case of consumer collective redress, when prohibition of the use of the drawn-up standard terms of contracts is sought. In the event where a court acknowledges a certain term (terms) of a contract not fair, it shall have no effect from the moment when the contract was formed while the remaining terms of the contract shall continue to be binding on the parties, providing that a further performance of the contract is still possible after the elimination of the unfair term. Consumer claims for avoidance of unfair terms are not subject to limitation (prescription) of actions at all, except for claims to recover unduly paid money under such contracts, which are subject to the general limitation (prescription) term. The consumer whose interests are violated by the application of unfair terms shall be entitled to apply also to institutions for the protection of consumer rights. The institutions for the protection of consumer rights are entitled to control the standard terms of contracts and challenge unfair terms in the consumer contracts.

331. Lastly, standard terms in practice are often used in order to limit civil liability of the stronger party. In this respect LCC Article 6.252 prescribes that an agreement of the parties upon exclusion of civil liability for the damage suffered by the debtor's intentional fault or gross negligence, as well as any agreement concerning the limitation of the amount of civil liability for damages sustained by the reasons indicated above is null and void. It is prohibited to exclude or limit civil liability for impairment of health, deprivation of life or non-pecuniary damage caused to another. The mandatory legal norms establishing civil liability, as well as the form or amount thereof, cannot be modified by an agreement of the parties. Although the LCC is silent on this point, it should be equally impossible to limit liability for the breach of essential obligations in such manner that those obligations would be left without any normal means of enforcement. For example, if the contract will exclude liability for the negligent breach of duty of care, such duty may become unprotected and illusive.[226]

226. Some Lithuanian authors propose that in determining whether the limitation of the liability for damage caused by ordinary negligence is admissible and whether the exclusion clause corresponds to the requirements of the good faith principle, several factors should be taken into account: the nature of the contractual obligation breached; existence of the fiduciary relationships between the parties; in the sphere of which party's activity arise the risk of the emergence of the loss and which of the

IV. Penalty Clauses

332. Penalty (*poena*) is a popular clause in Lithuanian contracting practice. It is the tool of civil liability enhancement, when the parties in advance agree and set the sum of possible damages. As such they are the form of contractual liability. From the other side, preventive effect of the penalty clauses, which motivates debtor to perform properly in order to avoid penalties, even caused them to be characterised by LCC Article 6.70 and Lithuanian legal doctrine as the form of personal security.[227] This dual nature of penalties is stressed in the LCC, where penalties are regulated in both the chapter on the personal security (LCC Article 6.71–6.75) and the chapter on contractual liability (LCC Article 6.258). It could be argued whether such characterisation, inherited from Soviet law (Civil Code of 1964 Article 194), is functionally correct because there is no third person or specifically encumbered assets to create the security. If the sole fact, that debtor is motivated to perform, because of penalty fear, would be sufficient for the characterisation of security, it should equally mean that other remedies, such as compensatory damages or criminal punishment for fraud, are also forms of security.

333. Interestingly, Lithuanian legal doctrine and case law have continuously stated that penalties under Lithuanian law cannot be punitive in nature; they can be only inclusive. Punitive penalties are described as such where the creditor may recover both at the same time – the sum of penalty and the compensatory damages. Inclusive penalties are such where the penalty sum and compensatory damages encompass each other, and the creditor may recover only one of these sums.[228] However, the acceptance only of inclusive penalties just stresses unavailability of recovery of both forms of contractual liability – compensatory damages and penalties, apparently because it leads to unjust enrichment of the claimant. But this does not mean that penalties, as they are known in civil law countries, do not provide

---

parties has a better possibility to manage the risk; the party's access to insurance against the risk of the emergence of the loss; the contractual price; the manner of the conclusion of the contract and of the incorporation of particular contractual provision (individually negotiated or standard terms); the possibilities of the parties to negotiate a contract and to choose another supplier, etc. Moreover, in such a case it is not enough merely to demonstrate a breach of essential contractual obligation or existing fiduciary relations between the parties, while examining whether exemption clause is fair. It is necessary to assess the entirety of all the circumstances determined in the particular case. *See* Rūta Lazauskaitė. *Contractual liability limitations that depend on the will of the parties.* Summary of Doctoral Dissertation. Vilnius: Mykolas Romeris University, 2011, pp. 14–15.

227. Valentinas Mikelėnas. *Lietuvos Respublikos civilinio kodekso komentaras. Šeštoji knyga. Prievolių teisė.* Justitia, 2003, I t., p. 114.

228. Dangutė Ambrasienė, *et al. Civilinė teisė. Prievolių teisė.* Mykolo Romerio Universitetas, 2004, p. 67; Judgment of the Lithuanian Supreme Court of 8 May 2015 in the civil case No 3K-3-267-916/2015.

punitive function under Lithuanian law. The sole fact that courts by upholding penalty clauses have awarded amounts significantly exceeding the actual loss suffered[229] means that this extra sum is monetary punishment for the non-performing debtor. Thus, the statement that penalties under Lithuanian law cannot be punitive is inherently misleading.

334. Rules of LCC on the penalty clauses are modelled according to the resolution of the European Council on the Penal clauses in civil law.[230] LCC Article 6.71 defines a penalty as a sum of money determined by laws or a contract which the debtor shall be bound to pay to the creditor in the case of failure to perform an obligation, or defective performance thereof (fine, forfeit). The penalty may be established in the form of a concrete sum of money or expressed in percentage terms on the amount of the secured obligation. The penalty stipulated for a delay in performance of an obligation may be established for every day, week, month, etc., that exceeds the time limit of the performance. The penalty clause must be made in writing; however, non-compliance with this formality requirement does not make the clause invalid, just prevents use of witnesses for the proof of agreement on the penalty clause (LCC 1.93, 6.72).

335. The penalty is an accessory obligation, the validity of which totally depends on the validity of the principal obligation. Thus, where the transaction from which the obligation has arisen is declared void within the procedure established by laws, any agreement upon the security of performance of such an obligation by way of penalty shall be equally void (LCC Article 6.74).[231]

336. Where an obligation with a penal clause is established, the creditor may not demand both the real performance of the principal obligation and the penalty, except in cases when the debtor is in delay of the performance of the obligation. Any stipulation of parties contrary to this rule is void, with the exceptions provided by the LCC in respect of certain types of contracts. For example, in case of failure by the trader to perform its obligation under the consumer contract, the payment of penalty does not release the trader from performance of the obligation in kind (LCC

229. *See*, for instance, Judgment of the Lithuanian Supreme Court of 12 Oct. 2007 in the civil case No 3K-7-304/2007.

230. Penal clauses in civil law: resolution (78) 3 adopted by the Committee of Ministers of the Council of Europe on 20 Jan. 1978 and explanatory memorandum Strasbourg: Council of Europe, 1978.

231. However, Vilnius District Court in the public procurement litigation has ignored an accessory character of the penalties. The claims were brought by the central procuring agency, which has agreed for penalties in a preliminary agreement with suppliers. According to those agreements the supplier who has fundamentally breached the public procurement contract should pay penalties to the central procuring agency. The courts have controversially satisfied those claims failing to take into account that after the conclusion of procurement contract the preliminary agreements have reached their purpose by proper performance and came to the end (LCC Art. 6.123). With respect to obligations stemming from the preliminary agreements, penalties were accessory obligations, thus the end of the preliminary agreements automatically should have extinguished penalties clauses. *See* Judgments of the Vilnius District Court of 3 Jul. 2015 in the civil case No. e2A-2358-345/2015, of 18 Sep. 2015 in the civil case No e2A-1827 619/2015 and of 23 Mar. 2017 in the civil case No. e2A-1 101-656/2017.

Article 6.228[15]). In any case, the sum stipulated in the penal clause shall be included into damages in the case where compensatory damages are claimed.

337. The amount of penalty stipulated may be reduced by the court when it is manifestly excessive, or if the creditor has already benefited from partial performance of the obligation, though the sum may not be reduced below the damages payable for the failure to perform the obligation or for defective performance thereof. No reduction of the penalty paid shall be allowed (LCC Article 6.73). It should be noted that this rule in recent case law has been interpreted in a way which have significantly suppressed the efficiency of penalties. Normally, one of the main practical advantages of penalty clauses is relief of the creditor from his duty to prove damage, since penalty in essence is agreed sanction. However, under current case law, when the creditor claims penalties in the court, the debtor responds with actual damage defence, i.e., states that penalties are manifestly excessive compared to actual damages. Then the courts reallocate burden on the plaintiff to prove the actual damage in order to assess whether debtor's defence is really valid.[232] Now the plaintiff is burdened to prove actual loss as in the case of ordinary damages claim. This makes penalty less efficient remedy.

338. The burden to prove the fact of performance of the principal obligation in a proper way is placed on the debtor by whom the obligation to pay the penalty is disputed on the basis of assertion that the obligation has already been performed by him (LCC Article 6.75).

V. Arbitration Clauses

339. Commercial arbitration in Lithuania is understood as a method of resolving a commercial dispute, where natural or legal persons, as mutually agreed, refer or undertake to refer to an arbitrator/arbitrators, appointed by the agreement of the parties or according to the procedure established by arbitration law, rather than to a court to have their dispute resolved by an arbitral award binding on the parties, whether administered by a permanent arbitral institution (institutional arbitration) or in the form of ad hoc arbitration. Special Law on Commercial Arbitration, based on the United Nations Commission on International Trade Law (UNCITRAL) Model Law on International Commercial Arbitration (1985), with amendments as adopted in 2006, regulates arbitral proceedings taking place on the territory of the Republic of Lithuania, sets requirements for the form and content of an arbitration agreement; defines constitution and competence of an arbitral tribunal, application of interim measures and delivery of a preliminary order, arbitral awards and closure of proceedings without an award being made on its merits, setting aside of an arbitral award, recognition and enforcement of foreign arbitral awards on the territory of the

232. *See* Judgment of the Lithuanian Supreme Court of 3 May 2016 in the civil case No 3K-3-235-690/2016.

Republic of Lithuania; and regulates other issues related to arbitration. Also, Lithuania in 1995 ratified the 1958 New York Convention (Convention on the Recognition and Enforcement of Foreign Arbitral Awards).

340. Arbitration agreement means an agreement between two parties or more to submit to arbitration all or certain disputes which have arisen, or which may arise between them in respect of a defined legal relationship, whether contractual or not, and which may be subject to arbitral proceedings. The state, a municipality or other public legal persons may also enter into an arbitration agreement. Therefore, from the contract law perspective, arbitration agreement is a procedural contract with purely obligational effects.

341. An arbitration agreement may be in the form of an arbitration clause in a contract or in the form of a separate agreement as ad hoc submission between the parties. Latter type of arbitration agreement in Lithuania is called a compromise.[233]

342. As to the *ratione materiae* of arbitration agreement, the general rule is that all commercial disputes may be settled by arbitration. Commercial dispute is any disagreement of the parties over a fact and/or matters of law arising out of contractual or non-contractual legal relations, including but not limited to supply of goods or services, distribution, commercial agency, factoring, lease, contracting, consulting, engineering services, licensing, investment, financing, banking, insurance, concession, creation and involvement in a joint venture, any other type of industrial or business cooperation, payment of damages caused by breach of rule of competition law, contracts concluded on the basis of public procurement and carriage of goods or passengers by air, sea and road. However, arbitration may not settle disputes that are subject to the administrative procedure or hear cases that fall within the remit of the Constitutional Court of the Republic of Lithuania. Disputes arising from family legal relations and disputes concerning registration of patents, trademarks and design may not be submitted to arbitration. Disputes arising from employment and consumer contracts may not be submitted to arbitration except for the cases where an arbitration agreement is concluded after the dispute has arisen. Disputes may not be submitted to arbitration where one of the parties to a dispute is a state or municipal enterprise, also a state or municipal institution or organisation, with the exception of the Bank of Lithuania, unless a prior consent to an arbitration agreement has been given by the founder of this enterprise, institution or organisation. The Government of the Republic of Lithuania or a state institution authorised thereby may, in accordance with the regular procedure, enter into an arbitration agreement concerning disputes arising out of commercial contracts concluded by the Government or a state institution authorised thereby.

343. Rules on arbitration agreements in Lithuania are highly consensualist and even exceeds the overall level of consensualism in general Lithuanian contract law. An arbitration agreement must be concluded in writing and be deemed valid if: (1)

233. Gediminas Dominas, Valentinas Mikelėnas. *Tarptautinis komercinis arbitražas*. Vilnius: Justitia, 1995, p. 110.

executed as a joint document signed by the parties; or (2) concluded in an exchange by the parties of letters, which may be transmitted by electronic communications terminals provided that the integrity and authenticity of information so transmitted is ensured, or of other documents recording the fact of entering into such an agreement; or (3) concluded by using electronic communications terminals provided that the integrity and authenticity of information so transmitted is ensured and the content of the transmission is made available for later access; or (4) the parties submit to each other a claim and a statement of defence in which the existence of the arbitration agreement is alleged by one party and not denied by another; or (5) there is other written proof of conclusion or recognition by the parties of the arbitration agreement. A reference in a contract between the parties to a document containing an arbitration clause shall constitute an arbitration agreement provided that the contract or document is in conformity with the requirements to the form of an agreement (Law on Commercial Arbitration Article 10).

344. Since arbitration is a form of alternative dispute resolution (ADR), which is acknowledged and promoted by the State itself, upon the receipt of a claim in relation to a matter that is the subject of an arbitration agreement between the parties, a court shall refuse to admit it. Where the fact of the conclusion of the arbitration agreement is established after the admission by the court of the claim, the court shall not consider the claim related to the matter that is the subject of the arbitration agreement. An arbitration agreement may be judicially recognised null and void at the request of one of the parties, on the general grounds for recognising transactions null and void, or if any breach of rules on arbitrability and form of agreement has been established. After commencing arbitral proceedings, the issue of invalidity of an arbitration agreement shall be handled only according to the principle of 'competence of competence', i.e., an arbitral tribunal may rule on its own jurisdiction, including the cases where doubts arise with respect to the existence or validity of an arbitration agreement. For this purpose, an arbitration clause, which forms part of a contract, must be treated as an agreement independent of the other terms of the contract. A decision by the arbitral tribunal that the contract is null and void shall not entail *ipso jure* the invalidity of the arbitration clause. According to the Law on Commercial Arbitration Article 11, a court must suspend the hearing of a case if the case may not be heard before the resolution of an arbitration case.

§2. Interpretation

345. Interpretation of contracts is of crucial practical importance because it defines from which sources and how can be determined a binding content of the contract. If the real shared intentions should be established, then the scope of evidentiary sources is unlimited in contract law and limited only by the evidence generally admissible by the procedural law. From the other side, if the law pragmatically focuses on the reliance of parties, then the evidence is already restricted by special rules in substantive contract law, which reduce evidentiary sources exclusively to the signed contractual documentation. Thus, the rules on the interpretation of contracts are tightly related to the scope of permissible evidence.

346. In Lithuania, the rules on the interpretation of contracts were introduced only by the new LCC in 2000, as the previous Civil Code did not include any provisions in this respect. Some methods of interpretation of contracts were developed by legal doctrine and courts' practice, these factors being of great value and serving as a useful contribution in the drafting of the relevant chapter of the LCC.[234]

347. LCC establish rules on the interpretation of contracts, which are characteristic to the other civil law jurisdictions. Pursuant to LCC Article 6.193, a contract must be interpreted in accordance with good faith. In interpreting a contract, it shall be necessary to seek for the real intentions of the parties without being limited by the literal meaning of the words. In interpreting a contract, regard must also be taken of the preliminary negotiations between the parties, practices which the parties have established between themselves, the conduct of the parties subsequent to the conclusion of the contract and the existing usages. In the event where the real intentions of the parties cannot be established, the contract must be interpreted in accordance with the meaning that could be attributed in the same circumstances by reasonable persons in the corresponding position as the parties.

348. It basically means that LCC establishes the subjective (contextualist) method of interpretation as a prevailing one. Since Lithuanian contract law is based on the overreaching theory of will, this choice of LCC drafters is unsurprising and correct, at least in theory. From the other side, the issue here is the ability of courts to correctly interpret contracts and decide that parties have really had in mind.[235] An obvious difficulty with subjective approach is that the 'actual' intention of a party can never be established: even a psychological or neuroscientific investigation into a party's mind is not likely to uncover the historical intention as it existed at the time of concluding the contract.[236] This obstacle has even provoked some authors in Lithuanian legal doctrine to conclude that for the interpretation of contracts, the objective method should be applicable, unless both parties agree that the text of contract does not reflect the real meaning of it, or one of the parties knew, or should have known, at the time of contracting, that the other party gives other

234. Valentinas Mikelėnas. *The Main Features of the New Lithuanian Contract Law System Based on the Civil Code of 2000.* Juridica International, Vol. 10, 2005, p. 49.

235. In law and economics, one of the main criticisms of courts taking too contextualist an approach to interpreting and implying contractual terms is the problem of court error and incompetence. At one extreme, if courts make no errors in importing contextualist evidence, then such evidence should always be allowed, at least if the cost of producing such evidence is not too high. At the other extreme, if courts make too many mistakes in interpreting or implying terms, then textualism becomes superior if the transaction costs of contracting are lower than the expected savings resulting from fewer court errors (Eric Posner, 1998, pp. 542–544). If courts make the methodological error of choosing contextualism in situations of high court error, then the parties will respond by attempting to contract around the court's rules through detailed language or broad merger clauses, by avoiding courts (for example, arbitration) or contracts (for example, vertical integration), or by engaging in inefficient contractual behaviour to adjust to the court's erroneous legal standard. *See* George M. Cohen. *Implied Terms and Interpretation in Contract Law. In.* Encyclopedia of Law and Economics, Vol. III. The Regulation of Contracts, Cheltenham, Edward Elgar, 2000, p. 94.

236. *Ibid.*

and not ordinary meaning to the content of contract.[237] The task to interpret Lithuanian rules on the on the interpretation of contracts has been undertaken even by the UK Court of Appeal, who has remarked that the use of the expression 'subjective intention' is apt to mislead. Unless the parties share a common intention which they have communicated to each other or some common intention which can be attributed to them (e.g., an intention derived from words to which they have both assented) there can be no meeting of minds and no recognisable agreement between them. The expression 'subjective intention' is often used to mean the private intention of one party, which may or may not be the same as that of the other and may or may not have been communicated to him. To search for the subjective intentions of the parties in that sense is therefore a pointless exercise, but neither party suggested that that is what Lithuanian law requires. On the contrary, the proper approach under Lithuanian law is to ascertain the parties' real intentions, that is their actual common intentions, by reference not only to the language of the document in which their agreement is expressed but also to such other evidence as may be of assistance. That may take the form of precontractual negotiations and post-contractual conduct as well as the surrounding circumstances, existing usages and any communications between them. The exercise is essentially objective in nature; it does not involve disregarding the language of the document but construing it in a way which most fully and accurately gives effect to the parties' real agreement.[238] This is mostly correct interpretation how Lithuanian law works in practice, because, first, the courts are seeking to establish common intention of parties, otherwise there is no consensus and contract at all and, second, starting point and basis for the interpretation of contract is the text of it. However, prevalence of theory of will in Lithuanian contract law forces courts to give undisputed priority for the intentions of parties whenever it is possible according to the collected evidence, not just to use those intentions for the ancillary supplementation of the document text. Thus, it is really possible for Lithuanian courts to replace clause set in the text of the contract with unwritten term, which was formed within a set of different means of communication (phone text messages and social media messages, verbal statements made to the third parties, video recordings, etc.), showing shared will to agree differently than expressed in the finally signed text.

349. LCC Article 6.193 also prescribes that all terms of a contract shall be interpreted taking into account their interrelation, the nature and purpose of the contract, and the circumstances under which it was formed. In interpreting a contract, regard must also be taken of the ordinary terms, irrespective of their expression in the contract. In the event of doubt over notions which may have several meanings, these notions must be understood in the sense most suitable to the nature, essence and subject matter of the contract. In the event of doubt over terms of a contract, they shall be interpreted against the contracting party that has suggested thereof, and in

237. Stasys Drazdauskas. *Bendrosios sutarčių teisės vienodinimo įtaka Lietuvos sutarčių teisei.* Doctoral dissertation (social sciences, law (01 S), Vilnius University, 2011, pp. 246–247).
238. Judgment of the England and Wales Court of Appeal of 13 Nov. 2006 in the civil case *Svenska Petroleum Exploration AB v. Lithuania & Anor*, [2006] EWCA Civ 1529.

favour of the party that accepted those terms (rule *contra proferentem*). In all cases, the terms of a contract shall be interpreted in favour of consumers and the adhering party.

350. Where the parties have left without being discussed certain terms, which are necessary for the performance of a contract, such gaps in the contract upon the demand of one of the parties may be eliminated by a court in determining appropriate terms by taking into regard non-mandatory legal norms, the intentions of the parties, the purpose and essence of the contract, the criteria of good faith, reasonableness and justice. Where a contract is drawn up in two or more languages and all the language versions are of equal legal power, in case of discrepancy between the language versions, preference shall be given to the version which was the first to be drawn up (LCC Article 6.194–6.195).

§3. Conditional Contracts

351. From the transactional perspective, a condition is a type of the term of contract, which forms part of its content. Structurally, conditions are sort of modalities of contractual obligation, others being terms, multiple parties, multiple prestations, etc.

352. Pursuant to LCC Article 6.30, an obligation is conditional where its arising, modification or extinction is made dependent on whether or not a certain circumstance occurs in the future. It flows from the definition that a condition is a possible future event, occurrence of which is uncertain. If it is a present event, then no condition exists. Accordingly, an obligation is not conditional if its extinction depends on an event that, unknown to the parties, had already occurred at the time when the debtor accepted the conditional obligation. If it is a certain event, for example, sunrise in Vilnius, the modality is not a condition, but a term. Also, in contrast with a suspensive term, until suspensive condition has occurred, the obligation is not created. The period until the condition occurs (*pendente conditione*) is a kind of legal phenomena because although the valid contract exists, it has not created yet any obligations. According to LCC Article 6.30, the conditional nature of an obligation does not prevent the rights that arise from it being alienable and inheritable; however, this rule in the legal doctrine is understood only as the transfer of future claims, occurrence of which has the retroactive effect *inter partes*.[239] Finally, a condition can be only such circumstance, the existence or non-existence of which is possible.

239. Valentinas Mikelėnas. *Lietuvos Respublikos civilinio kodekso komentaras. Šeštoji knyga. Prievolių teisė.* Justitia, 2003, I t., p. 53. The Lithuanian Supreme Court has recently given the retroactive effect for transfer clauses even with respect to third parties; however, such reasoning sharply contradicts fundamentals of property law in both – specificity and publicity – aspects, since it acknowledges the existence of property rights on the claim without their object and permits to use them against third parties without proper publication. *See* Judgment of the Lithuania Supreme Court of 13 Feb. 2020 in the civil case No e3K-3-24-969/2020.

353. Lithuanian legal doctrine makes distinctions of conditions into positive and negative, suspensive and resolutory, casual and potestative, express and implied, etc.[240] From all this taxonomy, most important distinction is between suspensive and resolutory conditions, based on the effects of conditions of the contractual obligations. Where a transaction is concluded with a suspensive condition, when the arising of rights and duties therefrom is conditioned by the parties upon an uncertain event. If transaction is concluded with a resolutory condition, the extinguishment of rights and duties arising therefrom is conditioned by the parties upon an uncertain event (LCC Article 1.66). This distinction is of crucial importance also in other respects. If a condition had already been fulfilled at the time when the transaction was formed, such transaction shall be unconditional in the case of a suspensive condition, and null and void in the case of a resolutory condition. If non-fulfilment of the conditions was already certain at the time when the transaction was formed, such transaction shall be unconditional in the case of a suspensive condition, and null and void in the case of a resolutory condition. A transaction subject to a suspensive condition which is impossible objectively shall be null and void; a transaction subject to a resolutory condition which is objectively impossible shall be unconditional. A transaction subject to a suspensive condition shall be null and void if the condition is dependent solely upon the will of the debtor (LCC Article 1.68).

354. LCC provides set of requirements for the condition to provide desired legal effects. A condition shall have to be lawful and not contrary to the public order and good morals. A condition which is unlawful, contrary to the public order or good morals, or which is impossible shall be null and void and shall render the obligation which depends upon it null and void. The obligation whose arising depends upon a potestative condition, i.e., at the absolute discretion of the debtor shall be null and void. However, if the condition consists of exercising or not exercising appropriate actions, the obligation shall be valid even where the exercising or not exercising the action is at the sole discretion of the debtor (LCC Article 6.31).

355. There are also rules in the LCC on the occurrence of conditions. In the event where no time limit has been fixed for the fulfilment of a condition, the condition may be fulfilled at any time. If it becomes certain that the condition may not be fulfilled at all, it shall be deemed to be not fulfilled. Where the arising, modification or extinction of an obligation is dependent upon a condition that certain circumstances will not occur within a given time, the condition shall be considered having occurred once the determined time has elapsed without the certain circumstance having occurred, also when before the elapse of the time it becomes certain that the circumstance is not bound to occur altogether. Where no time limit has been fixed, the condition shall not be considered fulfilled until it becomes certain that the circumstance will not occur. Where the appearance of a condition is unfairly hindered by a party to whom the condition is disadvantageous, this condition shall be

240. For an excellent presentation of the taxonomy of contractual conditions. *See* Valentinas Mikelėnas. *Prievolių teisė. Pirmoji dalis.* Justitia: Vilnius, 2002, pp. 84–105.

considered as having existed. Where the appearance of a condition is unfairly facilitated by a party to whom the condition is advantageous, this condition shall be considered as not having existed (LCC Article 1.67, 6.32).

Chapter 4. Privity of Contract

§1. The Rule of Privity of Contract

356. Privity of contract is a very important stabilising principle of Lithuanian contract law, which enables to control the scope of contractual obligations and mitigate the effect of opposing core principles of contract law – freedom of contract and *pacta sunt servanda*. In effect, the contractual arrangements are mostly unlimited in *ratione materiae* and have the force of law, but their effect is restricted in *ratione personae*, thus creating obligation only *inter partes*. Therefore, the contractual rights have the relative character. This is in stark contrast with property rights, which are restricted in *ratione materiae* by the *numerus clausus* principle, but unrestricted in *ratione personae* due to the absolute character of property rights (LCC Article 4.20).

357. The rule of privity of contract in Lithuanian contract law is found in LCC Article 6.189, which prescribes that a contract which is formed in accordance with the provisions of laws and is valid shall have the force of law between its parties. The contract shall bind the parties not only as to what it expressly provides but also as to all the consequences deriving from its nature or determined by laws. The parties may agree that the contract shall apply to their relationships arisen before that contract was concluded.

I. Third Parties and the Contract

358. Although the privity of contract is paramount principle in Lithuanian contract law, there are a set of exceptions characteristic for most of the contemporary civilian jurisdictions and explained by the need for a flexibility in economic relations.

359. One could notice that main instance where contract creates effects against third parties is the formation of contracts with *in rem* effects, because such contracts create, transfer, modify or destruct property rights. However, binding effects on the third parties are provided not by the contract itself, but by the property right, which belongs to the subject matter of the contract. For example, under LCC Article 6.411, under the contract of instalment (credit) the seller retains the right of ownership to the thing which is being sold until the payment of the full sale price set in the contract, but reservation of title has an effect against third persons if the purchase–sale contract has been registered in the public register according to the procedure prescribed by law. In this case, the seller's contractual remedies would be useless against the third persons, but he may well defend its property rights by all means available to the owner, as he has retained the ownership.

360. Another similar instance is the concept of real obligation (*propter rem*), which stems from some kinds of contracts, such as lease, gratuitous use, rent, contracts for the establishment of servitude, usufruct, *emphyteusis*, *superficies*. Real obligation, being attached and following the particular property rather than person, burdens property rights and can be created only in cases prescribed by the law. For example, under LCC Article 6.643, in the event where lender sells the thing or transfers it for onerous use to a third person, the rights and duties under the previous contract of loan for use shall pass to the new owner or user if that contract, in the case of it being subject to registration, was registered in the Public Register in accordance with the procedure established by laws, or the new owner and user knew or should have known about it at the time of concluding the contract. Under LCC Article 6.417, the seller of property under the repurchase agreement may redeem the property from any third party, if agreement was perfected in the public register. Nonetheless, real obligations lack absolute character and are not full-fledged property rights, because they can be effectively used only against the other contract parties, not the whole world, and has no priority against other obligational rights.

361. Some contracts even create obligations, non-performance of which depending on the circumstances may give rise to the double civil wrong – breach of contract against the counterparty and tort against third persons at the same time. Examples are contracts for a provision of medical services, contracts for the management of a company and mandate for administration of property of another.

362. If parties simulate contract by concluding apparent contract, which conceals real one, third parties may be misled. Therefore, in order to protect reliance of the third parties LCC improves the position of third parties in Article 1.87, permitting third parties to plead simulation against the parties of the simulated transaction. A simulated transaction cannot be used as a defence by the contracting parties against third persons who in good faith have acquired rights from the simulated transaction.

363. Other third-party situations in Lithuanian contract law encompass conferral of right for the third person, change of parties in contract, change of parties in performance, legal remedies against third persons. Most important of those instances are discussed hereinafter.

II. Contract for the Benefit of a Third Party

364. Contract for the benefit of a third party is a bright achievement of Germanic legal tradition, which first appeared in Lithuania during the interwar period, where in Klaipėda region German Civil Code (BGB) was in force. As the institution was known also to the Soviet civil law, which widely used Germanic concepts, it was in force in Lithuania during the Soviet occupation. Drafters of the current LCC have retained basic rule, supplementing it with additional rules taken from UNIDROIT PICC. Today stipulation in favour of third party is mostly used in the Lithuanian economy in the contracts of carriage, insurance, public financing of medical services and trust.

365. Contract for the benefit of a third party (stipulation for another) enables to simplify transactions and save costs.[241] According to the contemporary civilian doctrine, the most significant legal effect of the stipulation for another is the immediate creation of a right in favour of the third-party beneficiary to enforce performance of the promise in his favour by the promisor without the need to implead the stipulator/promisee. The third-party beneficiary benefits from any security granted by the promisor for performance of the benefit. There is a clear contractual relationship between the stipulator/promisee and promisor. The stipulation for another is subject to the normal rules for the formation of contract.[242] Those views in most respects are reflected in LCC Article 6.191 and shared by the Lithuanian legal doctrine.[243]

366. Pursuant to LCC Article 6.191, if a contracting party has made a stipulation in a contract for the benefit of a third person, the stipulation shall give both the contracting party and the third-person beneficiary the right to demand performance of the agreed obligation unless otherwise provided for by laws or contract or appears from the essence of the obligation. In the case of the refusal by the third person to avail himself of the stipulation, the stipulator himself may exercise this right if it is in compliance with laws or the contract and does not contradict the essence of the obligation. The stipulation for the benefit of a third person may be revoked by the stipulator as long as the third-person beneficiary has not declared of his assent to accept it. If the performance is to be made to a third person only after the death of the stipulator, the latter can revoke the benefit by a testament (will). A contracting party who is bound to perform an obligation shall be able to set up against the third-person beneficiary such defences as he could have set up against the stipulator.

---

241. The clauses of the contract which establish a third party as a beneficiary often have similar economic effects with the clauses of an assignment contract that transfers the rights arising from a contract to a third person, with no synchronous delegation of the duties (if they exist). It is apparent that the existence of two different ways of transferring contractual rights are due to the desire of the parties to economise on transaction costs. A contract which confers rights to a third party is economising on transaction costs by reducing the number of deeds necessary for the transfer of these rights from the promisee to the third party. At the same time, it creates a greater sense of security for the third party whose claim against the promisor may not be attacked as non-assignable. Thus, with a third-party beneficiary clause, there is no need for an additional assignment contract. The third party may obtain the rights of the assignee without the extra transaction costs. Evidently, this is only possible when all information is available before the contract for the benefit of the third party is concluded, and the promisor expressly agrees to the substitution. The *ex ante* agreement of the promisor is an indication that the transaction is efficient and that the relations among the three parties are well functioning. It is obvious that the unenforceability of third-party clauses in a given legal order seems rather anomalous. *See* Aristides N. Hatzis *Rights and Obligations of Third Parties. In.* Encyclopedia of Law and Economics, Vol. III. The Regulation of Contracts, Cheltenham, Edward Elgar, 2000, pp. 202–203.
242. Martin Boodman. *Third-Party Beneficiaries in Quebec Civil Law.* Canadian Business Law Journal, Vol. 35, 2001, pp. 220–222.
243. Valentinas Mikelėnas. *Lietuvos Respublikos civilinio kodekso komentaras. Šeštoji knyga. Prievolių teisė.* Justitia, 2003, I t., p. 246; Edita Borevičienė. *Sutartis trečiojo asmens naudai.* Doctoral dissertation. Mykolas Romeris University, 2013, pp. 34–35.

367. Stipulation for another should be distinguished from the similar situation – promise for another, which does not give independent contractual claim for the third party. According to LCC Article 6.190(2), if one of the contracting parties by a contract made in his own name promise that a third person will undertake to perform an obligation or any other action, in the event where the third person fails to perform the obligation or any other action as promised, the contracting party – the promisor – shall himself be bound to perform the obligation or any other action agreed, and to compensate for damage suffered by the other contracting party.

368. Although it is denied by some Lithuanian authors,[244] in essence, stipulation for another is an offer from the existing parties for the third party to enjoin the contract under the special status defined by the stipulation. After the acceptance, which depending on circumstances may be tacit (LCC Article 6.173), the contractual obligation is changed, thus becoming multiparty relationship with a third party as additional and sui generis creditor. It is the reason why the stipulation for the benefit of a third person may be revoked by the stipulator only until the third-person beneficiary has not declared of his assent to accept it. The opposite view that the claim of a third person arises immediately after stipulation and even before the acceptance would contradict the legal maxim *invito non datur beneficium*, according to which nobody can be constrained to accept a benefit. There could be various reasons for rejecting an apparent benefit. The recipient may have personal reasons for not wishing to be under any moral obligation to the person trying to confer the benefit. Or the benefit may come with inherent burdens or disadvantages.[245]

369. As in UNIDROIT PICC, LCC Article 6.191 only requires that the beneficiary must be identifiable with adequate certainty by the contract, but there is no requirement for a beneficiary to be in existence at the time the contract is made. However, one should take into account that Lithuanian version of the contract for the benefit of a third party differs from the UNIDROIT PICC in respect of the benefit, other than right. Pursuant to LCC Article 6.191, stipulation for another gives the third-person beneficiary only the right to demand performance, as LCC Article 6.191 is silent on the benefit conferred as an exclusion or limitation of the third party's liability to one of the contracting parties. Despite this, parties are free agree to discharge third party and such agreement, when transmitted to the third party should be characterised as the offer to release debtor (third party) from the whole or part of obligation under LCC Article 6.129.

§2. Transfer of Contractual Rights

370. The contractual rights (claims) are the component part of the patrimony, which by definition is a totality of economic assets and liabilities belonging to the

244. Edita Borevičienė. Sutartis trečiojo asmens naudai. Doctoral dissertation. Mykolas Romeris University, 2013, pp. 30–36.
245. Christian Von Bar, Eric Clive, *et al. Principles, Definitions and Model Rules of European Private Law. Draft Common Frame of Reference (DCFR).* Full ed., Sellier, 2009, p. 343.

person. Claims have economic value because they correspond to the debtor's pecuniary obligations to give (*dare*), to do something valuable to the creditor (*facere*) or to sustain from the actions, which are disadvantageous to him (*non facere*). In this respect, claims are property and belong to the active side of the patrimony, whereas obligations rest on the passive side of it. All property under LCC Article 4.38 taxonomy are either corporeal (*res corporales*) or incorporeal (*res incorporales*). Contractual claims, being creation of human mind and social consensus rather than nature, are the species of incorporeal property.

371. According to the rules of Lithuanian property law, owner has the right to possess, use and dispose of a property at his free discretion, without violating the laws and the rights and interests of other persons. The owner enjoys the right to pass the entire object of ownership rights or a part thereof to another person, or only specific rights (LCC Article 4.37). The most common occurrence of derivative property acquisition is a singular transfer *inter vivos* done by the transfer transaction (*traditio*), which is based on the underlying contract. In addition, the property may be transferred together with all the patrimony in case of universal acquisition of property rights by succession, corporate merger (division) or sale of enterprise. LCC Article 4.48–4.49 prescribes that the ownership may be transferred to another person only by the owner or by a person given such powers by the owner. The new owner acquires such rights and obligations regarding the transferred property as had the former owner of the property (*nemo dat quod non habet* rule) if the laws and the contract do not stipulate otherwise. The acquirer of a property acquires the ownership to the thing property at the moment it is transferred to him, provided the laws or the contract does not stipulate otherwise. This is the general transfer regime provided by the property law and by default applicable to the transfer of property rights.

372. Special regime is applicable for the transfer of claims and obligations – the key categories of the law of obligations. The reason for this special regime lies in the apparent need to tailor legal rules for the particularities of obligational relationships: the debtor needs to know who the creditor is while the creditor needs to control who is the debtor. In Lithuanian legal theory, the transfer of contractual rights is analysed almost exclusive from the perspective of the law of obligations, where it is the part of the broader rubric called *the change of parties in obligation.*[246]

373. Considering the system and logic of LCC, singular change of parties in contractual relationship may take four forms: assignment of claim, personal subrogation, delegation of debt and transfer of a contract. Those are singular changes of parties' *par excellence*, because they do not interrupt the existence of contractual relationship.

246. P. Rasimavičius, *et al. Civilinė teisė: vadovėlis*. Kaunas: Vijusta, 1998, pp. 373–374. Such one-sided approach and failure to take into account the proprietary side of the claim caused controversial findings in the case law, for example that the scriptural money is not money at all. *See* Judgments of the Lithuanian Supreme Court of 18 Sep. 2014 in the civil case No 3K-3-400/2014 and of 3 Feb. 2016 in the civil case No. 3K-3-2-969/2016.

I. Assignment of Claim

374. Contract for assignment of claim (*cessio*) is a widely used transaction in EU countries, including Lithuania, especially in the field of financial services. Assignment is indispensable for factoring transactions and is the main technique in structured finance to carry out securitisation schemes.[247]

375. Under LCC Article 6.101, a creditor may without the consent of the debtor assign to another person all or a part of the claim provided that the transfer does not contradict to laws or the contract, or the claim is not related to the person of the creditor. This formulation means that Lithuanian law allows anti-assignment clauses (*pactum de non cedendo*) with full *erga omnes* effect.[248] The assignment of the claim may not infringe the rights of the debtor and render his obligation more onerous. By effect of the assignment, the claim is transferred to the assignee with the security rights and other accessory rights. A future claim shall be likewise subject to assignment. In the event where the person of the creditor is of the essential importance to the debtor, the creditor shall be prohibited to assign the claim without the consent of the debtor. However, the assignment of a claim, which cannot be executed is prohibited. Judges, public prosecutors and advocates cannot become assignees of claims in respect of which litigation has arisen in the court within whose jurisdiction they exercise their functions. It is prohibited to assign a claim inseparably related to the person of the creditor (claim for maintenance, claim for compensation of damage caused by impairment of health or loss of life) (LCC Article 6.102).

376. Formation of an assignment contract is subject to the same formalities as prescribed for the creation of assigned claim. The creditor who has assigned his

247. According to the draft Regulation of the European Parliament and of the Council laying down common rules on securitisation and creating a European framework for simple, transparent and standardised securitisation and amending Directives 2009/65/EC, 2009/138/EC, 2011/61/EU and Regulations (EC) No 1060/2009 and (EU) No 648/2012 Art. 2(1), securitisation means a transaction or scheme, whereby the credit risk associated with an exposure or pool of exposures is tranched, having both of the following characteristics: (a) payments in the transaction or scheme are dependent upon the performance of the exposures or pool of exposures; and (b) the subordination of tranches determines the distribution of losses during the ongoing life of the transaction or scheme.

248. Those clauses, besides being controversial as to their effect on the third parties, are seen by some authors as a major barrier to use of receivables in financing transactions. While such clauses can make sense in such exceptional cases, where the personality of the creditor is of importance to the obligor, their endorsement in commercial contracts merely restricts the right of the originator to dispose of the property belonging to him and provides strong economic actors with tools to exploit their position on account of the weaker ones, who are forced to enter into contracts with anti-assignment clauses. *See* Lina Aleknaitė. *The prospects of asset securitization in Lithuania in the light of experiences from the United States of America and Europe.* Vilniaus universiteto leidykla, 2010, p. 99. Currently, non-assignment clauses are unenforceable only in case of factoring, where LCC Art. 6.907 provides that the assignment of the monetary claim to the financier shall be also valid in cases when the agreement made between the client and the debtor prohibits or limits such act. This rule does not release the client from the obligations and liability against the debtor for the breach of the condition of the agreement which prohibits or limits the assignment of the claim.

claim to another person is bound to hand over to the new creditor the documentary evidence pertaining to the claim and the accessory rights, including the right to receive interest. If such documents remain of importance to the previous creditor, the new creditor shall only be entitled to copies thereof confirmed within the established order. Assignment of a claim, the performance of which is secured by a pledge (hypothec), must be inscribed in the public register. In this case, the previous and the new creditors shall be obliged to take measures in order to ensure that relevant inscriptions are made in the public register. In the event of the assignment of the universality of claims, the previous creditor is obliged to deliver to the new creditor any pledged property which is under his control. All expenses related to the official registration and delivering of the documents stipulated in should be covered by the new creditor unless otherwise provided for by the contract. A claim confirmed by a bearer security issued by the debtor shall be assigned by handing over the bearer security to the new creditor. In this case, the debtor shall be bound to perform the obligation to any person who hands over the security to him. In this event, the debtor shall neither be entitled to setting up any objections or defences other than a claim for acknowledging the nullity of the bearer security. A creditor who has been dispossessed of a bearer security against his will may prevent the debtor from performing the obligation to the person who presents the security exclusively by means of instituting judicial proceedings (LCC Article 6.103, 6.104).

377. The assignor (previous creditor) is responsible against the assignee (new creditor) for the invalidity of the assigned claim, though he shall not be liable for the debtor's non-performance of the obligation arising from this claim, except in the cases when the assignor gives a surety to the assignee for the debtor. When the claim is assigned gratuitously, it shall be deemed that the assignor affirms that the claim exists and is owned by him even if such affirmation is not provided for by the contract (statutory warranty), with the exception of cases where the assignee acquired the claim at his own risk, or at the time of the assignment, he knew or should have known of the uncertain nature of the claim. Where the claim is assigned onerously, the assignor is responsible only for the insolvency of the debtor that existed at the time of the assignment, and only to the extent of the amount he received for that assignment (LCC Article 6.105).

378. Although the creditor may assign a claim without the consent of the debtor, the fact of the assignment of the claim may be invoked against third persons and the debtor from the moment when the debtor has consented for assignment, or received a copy of the document or any other evidence of the fact of the assignment of the claim.[249] Where the place of the debtor's whereabouts is unknown, the assignment of the claim may be announced by public notice. The assignment of the claim which is registered in the Public Register within the order established by laws

249. LCC rules on perfection of assignment are criticised in the legal doctrine as unsuitable for asset securitisation. Critique is based on the proposition that the main barrier to use cession for the transfer of large amounts of receivables to the 'special purpose vehicle' (SPV) is the requirement to notify the obligor to render assignment effective against third persons. Perfection of assignment is necessary to make sure to investors that the SPV has rights to assets backing their securities and which cannot be eradicated by originator's subsequent transfer of these assets to another assignee.

should be announced in accordance with the legal procedure and the fact of the assignment shall be registered in the Public Register. The assignment of a claim cannot be set up by the creditor against the debtor if the creditor gives a notice of this assignment to the debtor, even if the assignment would have not occurred or would have been declared void. The handing over of the contract on the assignment of the claim to the assignee and presentation of that contract to the debtor shall also be deemed to constitute a notice. A notice on the assignment of the claim may be renounced only with the consent of the assignee. The debtor shall be bound to perform the obligation to the assignee only if the latter together with the expression of his demand presents the contract on the assignment of the claim. Refusal from the obligation or a demand of the performance thereof by the assignee shall have no effect without presentation of a contract on the assignment. This rule shall not apply if the assignee has notified the debtor of the assignment of the claim in writing (LCC Article 6.109).

379. In the event of failure to inform the debtor that the claim has been assigned, the performance of the obligation in favour of the assignor is deemed to be proper. If the claim has been assigned several times, the performance of the obligation in favour of any subsequent creditor shall be deemed to be right. In the case of a dispute over the property rights on claim, the debtor shall have the right to refuse payment to any concrete creditor and perform the obligation by depositing a sum into the depository account of a notary office, bank or any other credit institution. In the instances where the debtor pays the debt being aware of the dispute, he is acting at his own risk. Nevertheless, in any case, the debtor has the right to set up against the assignee all the defences which he was entitled to set up against the assignor at the time of receiving the notice about the assignment of the claim. After the assignment of the claim and handing over of a bearer instrument, the debtor who has issued the bearer instrument has no right to set up defences against the assignee based upon the assertion that the obligation is simulated or false, or the assignment is prohibited if at the time of the assignment of the claim the assignee did not and could not know of these circumstances. In the event where after the assignment of the claim the debtor brings an action against the assignor for the annulment of the legal fact from which the obligation arises, the debtor is bound to inform about that the assignee, except in the cases when the annulment of that legal fact cannot be invoked against the assignee. The debtor who has the right to a counterclaim against the assignor can avail himself of a set-off against the assignee, except in the cases where at the time of acquisition of the right to the counterclaim the debtor knew of the assignment of the claim, or the time limit for the recovery of the assigned claim

---

It can be seen from the experiences of the other jurisdictions that requirement of obligor notification hampers the use of receivables for financing purposes. Therefore, asset securitisation can proceed only if the legislature eliminates such requirement or businesses and with the help of courts can develop a way to evade it. Perfection by notification of the obligor also limits the variety of receivables that can be assigned. Before the identity of the potential obligor is known, receivables are unassignable, because it is not clear who to notify. As a consequence, such constructions used in other jurisdictions, as bulk assignment or global assignment, become impossible. *See* ALEKNAITĪ, Lina. *The prospects of asset securitization in Lithuania in the light of experiences from the United States of America and Europe.* Vilniaus universiteto leidykla, 2010, p. 99.

expired after he became aware of its assignment, or after the expiration of the time limit allotted for the recovery of the assigned claim (LCC Article 6.106–6.108).

II. Transfer of Contract

380. Transfer of a contract is situation where a party to a contract agrees with a third person to completely substitute the party to the relationship. The whole contract may be transferred together with whole patrimony of the person (LCC Article 6.122) where such patrimony moves from one person to another, as in case of succession, corporate merger (division) or sale of enterprise. Apart from the above-mentioned universal transfers, contract may be transferred in a singular way. Generally, singular transfer of a contract in the Lithuanian law is carried out by the simultaneous assignment of claim (*cessio*) and transfer of the corresponding debt (*cessio debitis*) to the third party. It means that this change should comply with both rules – on assignment of claim and transfer of debt. As rules of assignment of claim were explained in the previous section, there is a need only to present those on the transfer of debt.

381. Contractual transfer and assumption of a debt must be made in writing (LCC Article 6.118). As the creditor has interest in the debtor's solvency and qualities of performance, LCC Article 6.116 prescribes that debt may be transferred by the debtor exclusively with the consent of the creditor. It means that all bilateral contracts may be transferred only with consent of the counterparty. The consent should be given only after the creditor is notified of the intended transfer by the debtor and the person who assumes the debt. Until the creditor has consented, the contract may be modified or terminated by the parties. After the consent of the creditor is received, the contract between the initial and the new debtor may not be modified. The creditor's consent for transfer of the debt may be given in advance. The creditor has no right to revoke his consent given in advance unless he has reserved this right in the said consent. If the creditor has not given his consent, the debt is not transferred. In the event where the debtor and the person who assumes the debt establish a time limit during which the consent of the creditor must be given, the consent may be given within the period provided. If no consent of the creditor is given within the established time limit, it is deemed that the creditor has not consented to the transfer of the debt. Pending the response by the creditor, the person who assumes the debt shall be bound to the debtor for the performance of the obligation in favour of the creditor.

382. The new debtor has the right to invoke against the creditor all the defences based upon the relationship between the creditor and the initial debtor, except to set-off the claim of the initial debtor. The new debtor cannot invoke against the creditor the defences based upon the relationship between the initial debtor and the new debtor which formed the basis for the transfer of the debt (LCC Article 6.119).

383. Upon the change of the debtor in the effect of the assumption of a debt, all accessory rights of the creditor remain unchanged if they are not purely personal in respect of the initial debtor. Thus, upon the transfer of a debt secured by proprietary security, the security interest to the property of the debtor remains valid. Suretyship and pledge granted by a third person is extinguished by the transfer of the debt if the surety or the pledgor do not expressly state their consent to be liable for the new debtor (LCC Article 6.117, 6.120).

384. If a contract of transfer of debt is avoided, the obligations of the initial creditor, likewise all his accessory rights and responsibilities arising therefrom are restored, though the rights of third persons in good faith should be retained. The creditor has the claim against the person who has assumed the debt compensation of damage resulting from the invalidity of contract of transfer of debt, except in the instances where the invalidity of that contract and the resulting losses were not caused by the transferee's fault (LCC Article 6.121).

385. Apart from the general rules, special regime for the transfer of some types of financial contracts is set in the financial law. For instance, by a written agreement and upon obtaining an authorisation from the supervisory authority, an insurance undertaking has the right to transfer its rights and duties under insurance contracts (all contracts or any part thereof) to another insurance undertaking. For such transfer, the policyholder's consent is not required, but an insurance undertaking must publicly announce about its intention to transfer rights and duties under insurance contracts and the policyholder has the right to terminate the insurance contract within one month from the transfer of the rights and duties (Law on Insurance Article 49–50). Special provisions exist also in other financial laws, for instance in Law on Consumer Credit Article 22^1, Law on Credit Relating to Immovable Property Article 33.

III. Personal Subrogation

386. Subrogation, from the first years of application of new LCC, has been one of the clumsiest topics in Lithuanian private law. The reason for this is ambiguous language of LCC, incoherent explanations in legal doctrine and lack of clarity in case law. Two different positions compete in Lithuania: one view presents personal subrogation as the specific manifestation of recourse, another one explains personal subrogation as the complete opposite of recourse. First position is backed by the language of LCC and is expressed in leading doctrinal works on law of obligations,[250] while the latter positions stem from the case law and subsequent legal doctrine.[251] As inconsistency lies in explanations of all of those positions, there is a need to rely

250. Valentinas Mikelėnas. *Lietuvos Respublikos civilinio kodekso komentaras. Šeštoji knyga. Prievoliųteisė*. Justitia, 2003, I t., p. 153; Dangutė Ambrasienė, *et al. Civilinė teisė. Prievolių teisė*. Mykolo Romerio Universitetas, 2004, p. 86.

251. *See* Judgments of the Lithuanian Supreme Court of 24 Oct. 2005 in the civil case No 3K-3-503/2005 and of 10 Feb. 2009 in the civil case No 3K-3-46/2009; Valentinas Mikelėnas, Armanas Abramavičius. *Autotransporto priemonių valdytojų teisinė atsakomybė*. Registrų centras, 2010, pp. 474–495.

on functional and comparative analysis, taking into account the concept of subrogation in the Quebec CC, which, together with Russian ГК, was the main source of LCC personal subrogation rules.

387. Subrogation (*subrogare*) in essence is substitution. It may be real, such as in case of floating charge, or personal, as in case of insurance. Personal subrogation is the substitution of a third person who performs the obligation instead of a debtor to the rights of a creditor. Legal policy behind the personal subrogation is a need to avoid the unjust enrichment. By the legal nature subrogation is, indeed, type of recourse, however, derivative one.[252] Whereas primary recourse rests on the contractual or quasi-contractual rights stemming from the third party's own patrimony, subrogatory recourse is derivative because it is derived from the patrimony of the creditor. Subrogation as type of recourse is understood also in the DCFR.[253] Thus, the first position, which is based on the language of LCC and is expressed in leading doctrinal works, is the correct one.

388. In contrast with primary recourse, which creates new and default legal relationship, personal subrogation produces change of parties of the existing obligation fully maintaining its attributes. During the personal subrogation third party 'steps into another's shoes', i.e., enters into position of the creditor together with all his rights and peculiarities. Thus, solidarity, indivisibility or other modality of obligation, security rights, limitations of claims, interest rate and other attributes of legal relationship are passed from the creditor to the third party.

389. As in other Romanic jurisdictions, civil law prescribes two separate sources of subrogation – contract and law (LCC Article 6.111). LCC sixth book's chapter VII on subrogation is titled 'transfer of a claim to a third person within the order of recourse (subrogation)'. This chapter contains two separate articles on grounds of subrogation: LCC Article 6.112 ('cases of subrogation') and LCC Article 6.114 ('subrogation by operation of law'). Such wording, taking into account two possible sources of subrogation, indicates that while LCC Article 6.114 by no doubt prescribes cases of legal subrogation, LCC Article 6.112 prescribes cases of contractual subrogation. This is totally misunderstood by Lithuanian courts, who tend to explain subrogation exclusively as *cessio legis*, i.e., legal assignment of rights,[254] despite the express rules in the LCC on the contractual subrogation.

390. According to LCC Article 6.112, a claim is transferred to a third person by way of subrogation if: (1) the claim is satisfied from the property of the third person; (2) the obligation is performed for the debtor by the third person whose property was pledged in securing the performance of obligation; (3) the third person performs the obligation for the debtor in order to prevent seizure of property, even

252. Johann Andreas Dieckmann. *Normative Basis of Subrogation and Comparative Law: Select Explanations in the Common Law, Civil Law and in Mixed Legal Systems of the Guarantor's Right to Derivative Recourse*. Tulane European and Civil Law Forum, Vol. 27, 2012, p. 53.
253. Christian Von Bar, Eric Clive, *et al. Principles, Definitions and Model Rules of European Private Law. Draft Common Frame of Reference (DCFR)*. Full ed., Sellier, 2009, p. 986.
254. Judgment of the Lithuanian Supreme Court of Sep. 2006 in the civil case No 3K-3-457/2006.

though the property does not belong to him, where the seizure would make him lose whatever rights he has in that property; and (4) the debtor and the third person who has paid the debt concludes a contract upon the payment of the debt, provided that the creditor knew of this contract at the time of payment, or had been notified thereof. Definitely, to list cases of contractual subrogation, having in force the freedom of contract, is unnecessary, but, anyway, this list can serve as the illustration of contractual subrogation cases.[255] From the list first three cases apparently concern third-party contract with the creditor, whereas only the last one concerns contract with the debtor. The contract should be done in writing (LCC Article 6.111). As the performance extinguishes the obligation (LCC Article 6.123), contract of subrogation, in order to be valid, should be concluded before or at the same time when performance takes place. In contrast with assignment, subrogation, even contractual, is triggered only when third party makes performance, therefore initial transfer *solo consensu* of the claim (LCC Article 4.49) under the contractual subrogation is impossible and should be done by the assignment. Consent of residual party in contractual subrogation (debtor's in creditor's signed subrogation or creditor's in debtor's signed subrogation) is not required. This is another difference from assignment where the claim can be transferred only with consent of the creditor (LCC Article 6.101). Lastly, contractual subrogation does not imply any guarantee as to the validity of a claim as in the case in assignment (LCC Article 6.105).

391. In the vast majority of instances, a person who performs the obligation of another does not need to obtain a contractual subrogation by the creditor or the debtor because the law by its direct operation subrogates that person to the right and action of the creditor. The instances of legal subrogation, however, are exclusively enumerated in the law since that kind of subrogation derogates from the well-established principle that no one may acquire the right of another without the concurrence of both the will of the person who acquires the right and that of the one who transfers it.[256] With this respect, LCC Article 6.114 prescribes grounds of legal subrogation, which are almost identical to the ones in other Civil codes of Romanic tradition, for example French Code Civil Article 1251, Quebec CC 1656 and Louisiana CC 1829. Hence, according to LCC Article 6.114, a claim should be transferred to a third person according to subrogation by operation of law in the following cases: (1) in favour of the creditor who pays the debt to another creditor whose claim has preference to his by virtue of its securement in the form of a pledge (hypothec) or by the priority of claim; (2) in favour of the acquirer of the property when he performs an obligation towards the creditor whose claim is secured by a pledge (hypothec) on that property; (3) in favour of a person who performs the obligation to which he is bound with other debtors, or has reasonable interest in the performance thereof; (4) in favour of a heir who at his expense performs the obligation of succession for which he was not bound; and (5) in other cases provided for by

255. Another example of contractual subrogation is a contract of sale where the buyer subrogates himself to the seller's rights in warranty (LCC Art. 6.317) against other persons.
256. Saul Litvinoff. *Subrogation.* Louisiana Law Review, Vol. 50, 1990, pp. 1163–1164.

law.[257] In addition, LCC Article 6.101(4), transplanted from the Russian ГК Article 387, provides that a claim is transferred to another person on the grounds of law in the following cases: where the rights of the creditor under a court judgment are delegated to another person if such possibility is provided for by laws; where the surety or the pledgor of the debtor, who are not parties to the secured obligation, perform the obligation for the debtor; and where within the procedure of recourse the rights of the creditor connected with the debtor responsible for the insurance event are transferred to an insurance company.

392. As can be surprisingly noticed from all the aforementioned rules, subrogation for the guarantor after performance of its obligation, in contrast with co-debtors and sureties, is not granted by the Lithuanian statutory law. LCC Article 6.90(3), which mentions recourse of the guarantor, and case law also speak only about ordinary recourse, without any indication about the personal subrogation.[258] This significant difference is caused by the modified construction of LCC Article 6.114(3) in comparison with its preparatory sources: whereas Western codes speak about a person who pays a debt to which he is bound *with others* or *for others*,[259] LCC speaks about a person who performs the obligation to which he is bound *with other* debtors. This means that guarantor who pays a debt to which he is bound for other should not subrogate into the creditor's position. Another peculiar difference is that subrogation according to the Western sources, for example Quebec CC Article 1656(3), takes place, where a person pays a debt to which he is bound with others or for others *and* which he has an interest in paying. In contrast, LCC Article 6.114(3) prescribes that subrogation takes place in favour of a person who performs the obligation to which he is bound with other debtors, *or* has reasonable interest in the performance thereof. Therefore, LCC Article 6.114(3) from the one side per se does not allow a subrogation for the security providers, but from the other side very broadens scope of subrogatory recourse in other instances: it does not require sufficient interest in cases of common obligation and gives subrogation solely on the sufficient interest to perform for another (LCC Article 6.51) or even the controversial general right (not a duty as in case of guarantee) to perform for another in order to get the subrogation (LCC Article 6.50). Hence, with respect to subrogation, LCC

257. For example, LCC Art. 6.1015 on the acquisition of the rights of the insured to compensation of the damage onto the insurer (subrogation) provides that unless the insurance agreement provides for otherwise the right to claim the paid amounts from the person liable for the damage incurred shall pass over to the insurer who has paid the insurance indemnify. If the damage has been made by malice, the claim right shall pass over to the insurer notwithstanding the fact that the subrogation is prohibited by the insurance agreement. Subrogation shall not apply in case of insurance against accidents and illness, civil liability insurance, as well as in other cases prescribed by laws. Having passed over to the insurer, the claim right shall be implemented in compliance with the rules establishing the relations between the insured (the beneficiary) and the person liable for the loss. The insured (the beneficiary) shall transfer to the insurer all the information which is required for the insurer to duly implement the assigned claim right. If the insured (the beneficiary) refused his claim or if it became impossible to implement such right through the fault of the insured (the beneficiary), the insurer shall be released, fully or in part, from the payment of the insurance indemnity and shall be entitled to request to refund the indemnity which had already been paid.

258. Judgment of the Lithuanian Supreme Court of 16 Nov. 2015 in the civil case No 3K-7-301-706/2015.

259. *See* French CC Art. 1251; Quebec CC 1656.

has established casuistic, fragmentary and unnecessary deviations from the authentic Romanic sources, which should be revised.

393. As subrogation is a ground for acquisition of property rights on the claims, general maxim of property law – *nemo dat quod non habet* – applies. This maxim is specifically repeated in LCC Article 6.113, which states that a third person who is subrogated to the rights of the creditor shall not obtain more rights than the subrogating creditor. Sometimes, subrogation even may be limited in content, i.e., the subrogation in case of solidary debt owed by several debtors does not retain solidarity of the remaining debtors, because LCC Article 6.9 prescribes that a co-debtor who has performed the solidary obligation has the right to recover within the procedure of recourse from his co-debtors their respective shares that correspond to the equal portions from the performed, with his participatory share deducted unless otherwise provided for by laws or agreement.

394. Another problem, symptomatic for subrogation in most jurisdictions, is found in cases where creditor was paid only in part. If this happens, the question is whether the original creditor and third party (new creditor) share the claim on parity or on priority basis. Unfortunately, the issue is not covered in the LCC chapter on subrogation, which overall is quite obscure. However, the Supreme Court in case, where third party partly repaid loan to the hypothecary creditor instead of the debtor, has ruled that the third party has subrogated into the respective part of creditor's position, but its subrogatory claim is subordinated to the residual part of creditor's original claim.[260] In this way, the Supreme Court has given effect to the old adage that subrogation should not operate against the subrogated person (*nemo contra se subrogare censetur*), although on the highly debatable reasoning.[261]

IV. Functional Equivalents and Similar Situations

395. Previously analysed situations are changes of parties' *par excellence*, because they do not interrupt the existence of contractual relationship. In addition, there are various functional equivalents and similar situations where during the factual change either a contract comes to an end or no formal change occurs at all.

---

260. *See* Judgment of the Lithuanian Supreme Court of 23 Jun. 2015 in the civil case 3K-7-276-469/2015.

261. The Court ruled that the hypothec is divisible obligation, which in case of personal subrogation together with the secured claim has split into two separate hypothecs: old one has remained in the patrimony of the original creditor, whereas the third party has acquired the seceded part. As the older hypothec always has the priority against newer hypothec (LCC 4.193), third party's claim is subordinated during the hypothecary enforcement against the older claim belonging to the creditor. In my opinion, this is disputable reasoning. First, the Supreme Court by making such interpretation has made references into Quebec CC and DCFR, which, in contrast with LCC, has express rules on the priority of original creditor against the subrogatory creditor. Second, the hypothec, by its nature, is not an obligation, but indivisible property right; thus, the subrogation does not produce any split of the hypothec but only creates co-ownership of it. Third, such reasoning has no, even arbitrary, ground where the obligation is unsecured and the general *in paritas creditorum* rule applies, instead of priority in time.

A. Primary Recourse

396. Similar to the statutory subrogation and often confused with it in Lithuania is the primary recourse (*regressus*). Primary recourse is personal right of the debtor because it stems from his personal patrimony on various grounds of reimbursement in personam. In contrast with subrogation, primary recourse is original acquisition of property rights on claim; thus, no security interests, solidarity and other attributes of past obligation are imputed to the right of recourse. As right of recourse is a new and default obligation, LCC Article 1.127(4) provides that extinctive prescription of claims arising from recourse obligation shall start its run from the moment when the principal obligation is performed.

397. It should be noted that in Lithuanian legal thought, which was formed during the transitional (pre-LCC) period, recourse was seen as unitary category, which arises when one person pays for another.[262] However, after enactment of LCC, Lithuanian civil law was brought into the Western legal tradition and such simplified explanations no longer adequately reflects the law.

398. Within the analytic framework of current Lithuanian patrimonial law, which follows neo-Romanic taxonomy of sources of obligations, recourse does not have status as independent source of obligations. Depending on the situation, recourse may arise from the contract, quasi-contract, statute and even tort. For instance, in case of mandate contract, the mandator is obliged to compensate to the mandatary for any expenses which were necessary for due fulfilment of the mandate and in addition any loss (if there is no fault of the mandatary in his actions and other persons are not bound to compensate it) incurred in the fulfilment of the mandate (LCC Article 6.761). If there were no contract at all and other person has incurred loss by prudently managing affairs of another, the quasi-contract of managing the affairs of another (*negotiorum gestio*) may arise. According to LCC Article 6.233, when the management of the affairs of another person has been rightly undertaken and conformed to the principal's interests, the principal must reimburse the manager for all the useful and necessary expenses incurred and compensate for the damages suffered by reason of the management of his affairs, irrespective of whether the desired result has been attained. Where the person has managed the affairs of another believing to be managing his own affairs, the quasi-contract of unjust enrichment arises and the person who has enriched himself without any legal cause at the expense of another must indemnify the latter for his losses in the amount of the unjust enrichment (LCC Article 6.236, 6.242). Where the person has wrongfully induced another to manage his affairs, for example to salvage his ship, or pay his debts, the basis of primary recourse is tort (LCC Article 6.263).

399. Other examples of primary recourse are: default recourse of the guarantor in the absence of agreement on subrogation (LCC Article 6.90);[263] the cases of

262. P. Rasimavičius, *et al. Civilinė teisė: vadovėlis.* Kaunas: Vijusta, 1998, pp. 372–373.
263. Judgment of the Lithuanian Supreme Court of 16 Nov. 2015 in the civil case No 3K-7-301-706/2015.

vicarious liability of employer or hirer who has paid damages arising from wrongs of its employees or subordinates (LCC Article 6.280); and right of social security institutions, which have paid insurance payments, against the person by whom the damage was caused, except in the cases where insurance premiums on behalf of the aggrieved person were paid by the same person who caused the damage (LCC Article 6.290)[264].

B. Subjective Novation

400. Subjective novation is a contract, which extinguishes original obligation and in place of it creates a new obligation with another creditor or debtor. According to LCC Article 6.141, novation is not presumed, and the intention to effect it must be expressed clearly and unequivocally in all cases. Novation is possible only if the original obligation is valid. It is prohibited to apply novation for the obligations to compensate for damage incurred by reason of bodily injury or death, also for the obligations the performance of which is connected exceptionally with the person of the parties.

401. LCC 6.141 regulates two types of subjective novation. First is the *expromissio*, i.e., change of the passive side of obligation, where an obligation is extinguished when the parties by their agreement substitute the existing obligation with a new obligation where a new debtor is substituted for the initial debtor who is discharged by the creditor. In such a case, novation may be effected without the consent of the initial debtor. However, the situation of imperfect delegation (*delegatio solvendi*), where creditor assumes claim against the new debtor without releasing first one, is not expressly covered in the LCC. In such a case, depending on the exact intent of parties, other rules of LCC should apply, for instance, where the creditor has retained the original debtor as a debtor in case the new debtor does not perform properly, those on suretyship (LCC Article 6.76.). However, if the creditor agreed with new debtor on *expromissio*, but later fraudulently maintained first debtor in obligation, contract of novation is fundamentally breached and may be terminated by the new debtor. But in no case the new debtor may invoke against the creditor the defences which he could have raised against the initial debtor, nor the defences which the initial debtor had against the creditor. Though, the debtor may claim for the nullity of the transaction from which his obligation results (LCC Article 6.144).

402. Second type of subjective novation is change of the active side of obligation, i.e., where a new creditor is substituted for the previous creditor towards whom the debtor is discharged. If the old creditor refuses to discharge the debtor, novation may be avoided on the grounds of error or terminated due to fundamental breach where the discharge was promised by the new creditor.

264. Judgments of the Lithuanian Supreme Court of 1 Oct. 2014 in the civil case No 3K-3-405/2014, of 12 Dec. 2014 in the civil case No 3K-3-552/2014 and of 23 Dec. 2014 in the civil case No 3K-3-564/2014.

403. Main shortcoming and cause of unpopularity of subjective novation in Lithuanian commercial practice is its negative influence upon accessory rights. LCC prescribes that right of pledge (hypothec) also other accessory rights arising from the original obligation are extinguished by novation, except in the cases where the parties agree to preserve them. If novation is made between the creditor and one of the solidary debtors with the effect of discharging from the performance of the obligation all other co-debtors, the right of pledge (hypothec) and other accessory rights arising from the original obligation may be retained only in respect of the property of the debtor who makes the new obligation (novation) with the creditor. Where novation is effected by substituting a new debtor for the initial debtor who is discharged from the performance of the obligation, pledge (hypothec) by which the performance of the obligation is secured, may not be transferred to the property of the new debtor. Pledge (hypothec) attached to the property of the discharged initial debtor may be retained only with the consent of the initial debtor. In the event where a new debtor acquires from the initial debtor a thing, the rights to which are encumbered by pledge (hypothec), the pledge (hypothec) shall be retained if the new debtor consents thereto. In the event of novation of a creditor and a principal debtor, a surety of the debtor shall be released from the performance of the obligation. An obligation shall not be extinguished if the creditor requires participation of the surety in the novation and the surety refuses (LCC Article 6.143, 6.144).

C. *Third Parties in Performance*

404. The obligation normally should be performed by the debtor to the creditor. However, in the developed market, quite often this is not the case, and the parties may either assign or delegate the performance to the third parties. In those cases, no formal change of parties occurs, only change in performance.

405. As concern the assignment of performance, LCC Article 6.44 provides that the obligation must be performed to the creditor, or to his representative, or to the person designated by the creditor, or to the person obliged by laws or the court to accept such performance. Performance of an obligation made to a person not entitled to accept it shall be deemed to be an appropriate performance if the creditor ratifies it or factually obtains the full performance from the person concerned.

406. In case of delegation of performance, the obligation can be performed in part or in full by a third person, except in the cases when pursuant to the agreement of the parties, or the essence of the obligation, it must be performed by the debtor personally (LCC Article 6.50).

§3. Subcontracting

407. According to the definition, subcontract is a secondary contract made by a party to the primary contract for carrying out the primary contract, or a part of it.

Subcontractor is one who is awarded a portion of an existing contract by a contractor, especially a general contractor. For example, a contractor who builds houses typically retains subcontractors to perform speciality work such as installing plumbing, laying carpet, making cabinetry, and landscaping – each subcontractor is paid a somewhat lesser sum than the contractor receives for the work.[265] Hence, in essence, subcontracting is the same as delegation of performance, presented above. Subcontracting presupposes the chain of contracts – original contract and subcontract – both of which are subordinated to the privity of contract. Accordingly, there are no direct contractual relations between the creditor and subcontractor.

408. The main statutory rule for subcontracting is that the obligation can, indeed, be performed in part or in full by a subcontractor, except in the cases when pursuant to the agreement of the parties, or the essence of the obligation, it must be performed by the debtor personally (LCC Article 6.50). But if the debtor in performance of the obligation uses assistance of other persons, he is liable for the actions of those persons as for his own (LCC Article 6.38). For instance, in case of works contracts, LCC Article 6.650 provides that unless the duty of the works contractor to fulfil the work provided for in the contract personally arises from the laws or works contract, the works contractor shall have the right to involve other persons (subcontractors) to perform his obligations. In the event where subcontractors are involved for the performance of the task, the works contractor shall act in the capacity of a general works contractor. The works contractor who has involved subcontractors to perform a contract of works in violation of laws or the rules established in the contract shall be liable before the customer for any damages caused by the subcontractors in the performance of the contract. The general works contractor shall be liable before the customer for the failure to perform or improper performance of the obligations by the subcontractors, and before subcontractors, for the failure to perform or improper performance of the obligations by the customer. Unless otherwise provided for by laws or the contract, the customer and the subcontractor shall have no right to raise monetary claims to one another connected with the violation of the contracts concluded by each of them with the general works contractor. With the consent of the general works contractor, the customer shall have the right to conclude contracts for fulfilment of concrete work with other persons. In this event, those persons shall be directly liable before the customer for the failure to perform or improper performance of the contract.

§4. Remedies Against Third Parties

409. The contractual claim for the performance of the contract at the same is species of intangible property, value of which may be reduced by the wrongs involving the third parties. Thus, in addition to the remedies against debtor, statutory law provides special remedies for the situations where the quality of a claim is protected or enhanced by the special actions against third parties.

265. Bryan A. Garner, *et al. Black's Law Dictionary*. 9th ed., 2009, p. 373, 1560.

I. Damages for Interference with Contract

410. The contract gives rise to the obligation, which is defined in as a legal relationship one party of which (debtor) is bound to perform for the benefit of another party (creditor) a determined action or to refrain therefrom, and the creditor has the right to demand from the debtor the performance of his duty (LCC Article 6.1). Whereas creditor's rights, stemming from contract, are protected against the debtor by the contract law, against third parties they are protected by the general tort law rule, which states that every person have the duty to abide by the rules of conduct so as not to cause damage to another by his actions (active actions or refrainment from acting). Any bodily or property damage caused to another person and, in the cases established by the law, non-pecuniary damage must be fully compensated by the liable person (LCC Article 6.263).

411. In addition, Law on Competition Article 15 prohibits the actions of unfair competition, stating that undertakings are prohibited from performing any actions contrary to fair business practices and good usages if such actions may be detrimental to the competitive potential of another undertaking, including proposal for the employees of the competing undertaking to terminate their employment contracts or refrain from performing all or part of their work-related duties, seeking self-benefit or inflicting damage on that undertaking.

412. Therefore, interference with contract infringes both the general requirements for honest business practice and principles of fair competition. In Lithuania one can claim damages and request for a suspension of such unfair actions. Legal action is directed against a third party that induced non-performance of a contract. If a party to a contract suffers damage due to third party's behaviour and decides to defend its rights in court, the court will have to ascertain certain findings in accordance with Lithuanian tort law.

413. First, the defendant's actions must be unfair, i.e., the fact of inducing non-performance of a contract must be proved. According to the general tort rule imposed in LCC Article 6.263, such an inducement is illegal. There can be various forms of inducement in practice, both explicit (e.g., open persuasion not to fulfil the contract) and implicit. For instance, in one ruling the Supreme Court stated that poaching employees can take place both in open form, suggesting termination of an employment agreement, and in hidden form, i.e., when an attractive offer is made, such as a low-interest loan, to the headhunted employee.[266] In another classic case, the Supreme Court awarded damages since the defendant, the director of the plaintiff's company dismissed a majority of employees and soon after hired these employees in his own company.[267] It should be noted that it is difficult to prove a violation, i.e., the actual luring. However, the Supreme Court has facilitated suits

266. Judgment of the Lithuanian Supreme Court of 25 Apr. 2005 in the civil case No 3K-3-223/2005.
267. Judgment of the Lithuanian Supreme Court of 24 Apr. 2002 in the civil case No 3K-3-581/2002.

against poaching by indicating that just the fact of proposing to terminate an agreement is sufficient to prove wrongfulness, and the luring is judged by objective circumstances and not just subjective explanations of the former partners. Thus, a partner does not have to be finally lured away, since a sole attempt to do so may suffice for a successful legal action. Second, it must be proved that damage was incurred as a result of the third party's actions. If the real cause of damage is other factors, like poor relationships or miscommunication of the parties, then damages are not recoverable. Third, a claim can be satisfied only if the defendant was or should have been aware that he or she was violating the rights of the plaintiff, i.e., was acting with intention. Fourth, the exact amount of loss incurred in form of costs and lost profit by the plaintiff must be proved. For instance, if as a result of inducement to breach the contract the plaintiff lost his main supplier or distributor, which in turn resulted in the reduction of the number of consumers.

II. *Actio Pauliana*

414. One of the most powerful remedies and limits of freedom of contract in Lithuanian civil law is *actio Pauliana*.[268] This is revocatory action, transplanted from Quebec law, for avoidance of preferential or other fraudulent transactions made by the debtor to conceal or transfer the assets beyond the reach of its creditors.[269] The purpose of this action is case of insolvency procedures is to avoid the fraudulent transactions and return the transferred assets to the debtor's patrimony. If the debtor is not bankrupt, the assets are transferred directly to the creditor and what's left should be returned to their owner – the debtor.

415. As in most other Romanic jurisdictions, revocatory action in Lithuania is included not in the insolvency law, but directly in the Civil Code. Thus, under LCC Article 6.66, a creditor has the right to challenge transactions made by a debtor,

268. In around 150 to 125 BC, a praetor named Paulus, about whom little is known, contributed to the removal of the excessive adherence to formalities from the earliest civil actions by creating a procedure that was personal and discretionary in nature, which enabled a creditor to revoke any acts carried out fraudulently and to his detriment by a debtor. Centuries later, the Digest consolidated the most sophisticated version of the *actio Pauliana*, by merging it, in its classical form, with the *interdictum fraudatorium*. From that time, the *actio pauliana* was based on the concepts of *alienatio* (alienation), *eventus fraudis* (detriment), *fraus* (fraud) and *participatio fraudis* (knowledge of the fraud). *See* Opinion of Mr Advocate General Ruiz-Jarabo Colomer delivered on 16 Oct. 2008 in ECJ Case C-339/07.

269. However, LCC differs from the original version of *actio Pauliana* prescribed in Quebec CC in one important aspect. Since this remedy is intended to protect only the plaintiff against the fraudulent actions of his debtor, under Quebec law the contract remains valid between the debtor and the third party. The only effect *actio Pauliana* produces with respect to a contract is limited to a judicial declaration that the contract may not be set up against the plaintiff. According to Quebec CC 1636, where it is declared that a juridical act may not be set up against the creditor, it may not be set up against any other creditors who were entitled to institute the action and who intervened in it to protect their rights; all may have the property forming the subject of the juridical act seized and sold and may be paid in proportion to their claims, subject to the rights of prior or hypothecary creditors. *See* Vincent Karim. *Les obligations.* 4e éd. Montréal: Wilson & Lafleur, 2015, vol. 2, p. 994–995, 1060.

where the debtor was not bound to make them and where they violate the rights of the creditor, while the debtor knew or ought to have known that prejudice to the creditor would result from that transaction (*actio Pauliana*). The creditor's rights shall be considered violated if by such transaction the debtor renders himself insolvent or by which, being insolvent, he grants preference to another creditor, or the rights of the creditor are infringed in any other way. A gratuitous transaction may be annulled by revocatory action irrespectively of whether the third person is in good or bad faith. However, a bilateral transaction may be annulled only in the case when the third person concluding the transaction with the debtor concerned was in bad faith, i.e., he knew or ought to have known that the transaction violates the rights of the debtor's creditor. The scope of revocatory action is very broad since cause of this action uses the notion of transaction, which is broadly understood in LCC Article 1.63 as any voluntary act made in order to create, modify or extinguish civil law rights and duties. Hence, not just contracts, but unilateral transactions, such as payments or other performance may be challenged by the *actio Pauliana*. From the other side, legal acts which are not transaction, for example refusal to accept gift, cannot be attacked with revocatory action.

416. The case law has crystallised a cause of revocatory action abstractly defined in LCC Article 6.66. According to the Supreme Court, preconditions for this action are: (1) the creditor has undisputed and valid claim against debtor; (2) the disputed transaction prejudices creditor rights; (3) the debtor has no duty to make disputed transactions; (4) the debtor was dishonest because knew or should have known that the transaction is prejudicial for the creditor; and (5) third party in case of bilateral onerous transaction was also dishonest.[270] In general, Lithuanian courts are very sympathetic to this remedy and grant it even in extreme cases.[271]

417. To ease the burden of proof even more, LCC Article 6.67 prescribes set of bad faith presumptions. Therefore, it is presumed that the parties to a transaction by whom interests of the creditor are violated were in bad faith if: (1) the debtor has concluded a transaction with his spouse, children, parents or other close relatives; (2) the debtor has made a transaction with a legal person in which his spouse, children, one of the parents or any other close relative is the director, a member or a

---

270. *See* Judgments of the Lithuanian Supreme Court of 6 Nov. 2012 in the civil case No 3K-P-311/2012 and of 1 Feb. 2017 in the civil case No 3K-3-3-695/2017.

271. Striking example of abusive use of revocatory action is judgment, where appellate court annulled postnuptial agreement, which changed community property regime *ex nunc* into individual property regime between spouses, solely on the reason that agreement reduces the scope of assets available for the personal creditor of one spouse and this was unnecessary transaction. The court failed to take into account LCC Art. 4.93(2) according to which nobody has the right to demand that an owner against his own will to join property with that of another owner. The obligation was personal for one of the spouses and agreement only took force into the future, without any division or partition of existing property. Thus, the court has allowed for the creditor to interfere into family relations and with *actio Pauliana* retain spouses against their will in the community property regime. Surprisingly, the Supreme Court case selection panel has refused to take accept this case for the review on the ground that this situation does not contain any legal problems worth of cassation. *See* Judgment of Vilnius District Court of 30 Mar. 2017 in the civil case No e2A-222-580/2017.

participant of its managing body who either directly or indirectly hold by the right of ownership at least 50% of the issued shares (portion of shares owned by a shareholder, contributions, etc.); (3) the debtor, who is a legal person, has concluded a transaction with a natural person who is the director or a member of the managing body of that legal person, or with his spouse, children, one of the parents or any other close relative; (4) the value of the prestation which had to be performed by the debtor considerably exceeds the prestation presented by the other party to the transaction (disproportion of counter-obligations); (5) a transaction has been made upon the payment of a debt that has not yet matured; (6) the debtor, who is a legal person, has made a transaction with a natural person who either himself, or his spouse, children, parents, or any other close relative, or jointly with them are the participants of that legal person and hold directly or indirectly by the right of ownership at least 50% of the shares (portion of shares owned by a shareholder, contributions, etc.) of that legal person; (7) the debtor, who is a legal person, has concluded a transaction with another legal person which is controlled by the debtor, or if the director or a member of the managing body of one of the parties to the transaction is a person who directly or indirectly, separately or jointly with his spouse, children, parents or close relatives hold by the right of ownership at least 50% of the issued shares (portion of shares owned by a shareholder, contributions, etc.) of the other legal person or of the issued shares (portion of shares owned by a shareholder, contributions, etc.) in both legal persons; and (8) the debtor, who is a legal person, has made a transaction with an association of legal persons or with any other corporation where the debtor is a member.

418. The creditor has the right to bring an action upon the annulment of the transaction on the ground of *actio Pauliana* within one-year prescription. This time limit shall be calculated from the day on which the creditor learned or ought to have learned of the transaction which violates his rights. The annulment of the transaction shall have legal effects only in respect of the creditor who brought the action upon the annulment of the transaction and only to the extent that is necessary to remove the prejudice experienced by the creditor. The annulment of the transaction should not have effect upon the rights of third persons in good faith to the property which was the object of the annulled transaction.

III. Oblique Action

419. Another similar remedy, taken from Quebec law, is an oblique action. This action targets not the active fraudulent behaviour of the debtor, as in case of *actio Pauliana*, but dishonest passiveness, i.e., prejudicial omission to enforce debtor's patrimonial rights against third parties. The remedy is not limited to one-year prescription period as *actio Pauliana*, thus may be brought in intervals applicable to the particular remedy demanded by the oblique action, which usually are much longer. However, if debtor is not bankrupt, oblique action is not such extensive remedy as *actio Pauliana*, because in the former case the assets are returned to the debtor's patrimony and used for the benefit of all creditors, whereas in the latter case, they are straightforwardly used to satisfy the claim of the plaintiff.

420. According to LCC Article 6.68, a creditor whose right to claim against the debtor is certain and exigible shall be entitled to exercise the rights of the debtor by bringing an action in the debtor's name in the event where the debtor fails to implement these rights himself, or refuses to exercise them to the prejudice of the creditor's interests (an oblique action). An oblique action may be brought only in the instances when the creditor is necessitated to protect his rights (in the event of the debtor's insolvency, bankruptcy proceedings instituted against him, or in any other special events) and under the condition that the time limit for the performance of obligations matured prior to the institution of the action. The creditor shall have no right to demand exercising of such debtor's rights which are related exceptionally with the person of the debtor. A person against whom an oblique action of the creditor is brought may set up against the creditor all the objections and defences he could have set up against the debtor. Upon the satisfaction of an oblique action, the recovered property shall be set-off into the property of the debtor and shall benefit all his creditors.

421. The Supreme Court has reasoned that in case of oblique action, creditor enforces debtor's rights against third party, which is debtor of the plaintiff's debtor. Therefore, the main attribute of oblique action is that right to initiate civil dispute in court is given to the qualified person who has no direct claim against defendant. Oblique action may be brought under the following circumstances. First, the creditor has a valid, certain and liquid claim. Second, the debtor has a patrimonial right, which he refuses to enforce, i.e., delays or avoids demanding performance, chooses inappropriate remedies, etc. Third, debtor's patrimonial right is also certain, valid and executable; that is, defendant has the obligation and is the debtor of the debtor of plaintiff. Fourth, passiveness of the debtor prejudices the interests of the creditor. Accordingly, an oblique action cannot be brought where debtor has enough assets to satisfy claim of the creditor.[272]

422. From this judicial explanation, one can notice the uncertainty of its oblique action's scope under Lithuania law. The thing is that oblique action structurally is placed in the law of obligations and is explained in case law as an action against 'debtor's debtor' implying that enforced claim should be founded in law of obligations, since the notion 'debtor' is the category of law of obligations. However, this is misleading since LCC by itself does not limit scope of the action to enforce only the rights in personam. Actually, there are two distinct patrimonial rights. First is the plaintiff's right against his dishonestly passive debtor, which value is protected by the oblique action. This right is necessarily claim in personam, as it flows from the obligational relationship between the creditor and debtor. Second right is enforced by oblique action against the defendant who owes some kind of duty against the plaintiff's debtor. That right is patrimonial is not necessarily found in the

272. *See,* for instance, Judgments of the Lithuanian Supreme Court of 16 Apr. 2007 in the civil case No 3K-3-146/2007, of 29 May 2008 in the civil case No 3K-3-312/2008 and of 7 Dec. 2012 in the civil case No 3K-3-520/2012.

law of obligations. It also may be right stemming from the other branches of patrimonial law. For example, right to accept succession[273] or vindicate property from adverse possession may well be enforced by the oblique action.

423. Special form of oblique action is a shareholder derivative action for damages, brought by the Law on Stock Companies Article 16, which provides that a shareholder has a non-pecuniary right to refer to the court with a claim requesting to redress damage incurred on a company resulting from nonfeasance or malfeasance by the manager of the company and members of the board of their duties prescribed by law and the articles of association of the company as well as in other cases laid down by law. However, the Supreme Court has ruled that although a derivative action by its legal nature may be treated as specific form of oblique action devoted for corporate litigation, nevertheless it is still special remedy for whom general rules of LCC Article 6.68 are not applicable.[274] This is, indeed, a correct ruling because direct application of general rules concerning certainty and liquidity of claims, which are a precondition for the satisfaction of oblique action, would make derivative action for damages inaccessible in most cases due to difficulties showing certainty and liquidity of protected claims.

IV. Direct Action Against Third Party

424. Most contractual actions are direct because they are directly brought by the creditor against the debtor. Contractual actions against third parties normally are not available due to the privity of contract. Legal protection is available for the plaintiff only indirectly – on the basis of oblique action, if all requirements for its satisfaction are met. However, in rare cases, law provides exceptional option for party of the contract to directly sue third party, which is not the party of the contract. This is so-called direct action (*d'action directe*), which is used to enforce plaintiff's own right against the third party, given directly by the law as the exception to the privity of contract. In contrast with stipulation for another, direct action is based on the statutory law, not the agreement.

425. The reasons to make such exceptions by granting relief against third party are based on practicality and economic considerations, which may vary. For instance, in case of financial leasing, the seller is directly bound towards the lessee with respect to all claims resulting from the sales contract related to the leased assets (with respect to the quality and completeness of the property, handover period, etc.). Save to the duty to pay for the acquired property, the lessee enjoys all rights and duties of the buyer to the same extent as if he were party to the sales contract. However, the lessee does not have the right to terminate the sales contract without the consent of the lessor (LCC Article 6.573). This rule is explained by the nature of financial leasing as the form of title finance, where the lessee is the 'economic owner', who actually possesses and uses leased assets, whereas lessor is only the

273. Judgment of the Lithuanian Supreme Court of 29 May 2008 in the civil case No 3K-3-312/2008.
274. Judgment of the Lithuanian Supreme Court of 14 Feb. 2013 in the civil case No 3K-3-23/2013.

'formal owner', since its right of ownership serves just as a security interest. This sophisticated structure of patrimonial relationships cannot optimally function with standard remedies, that is why the lessee has the right to directly claim against the seller, who has no contract with the lessee.[275] Another example is the sublease. In general, due to the privity of contract, the lessee is responsible towards the lessor for the wrongs done by the sub-lessee. However, if a sub-lessee fundamentally breaches the sublease contract and inflicts damage by his actions to the lessor or to other lawful users of that thing, the lessor has the right to demand termination of the sublease (LCC Article 6.490). This right apparently seeks to directly protect property rights of the lessor, thus avoiding the two separate civil procedures based on the same contractual chain.

275. Even if such claim would not directly be prescribed in the LCC, it would nevertheless flow from the sales contract, which is concluded by the seller and lessor in favour of lessee. Thus, the regimes of direct action and of stipulation in favour of third party in some situations may coincide.

Chapter 5. Performance and the End of the Contract

§1. Performance of Contract

426. Basic goals of contract law are: (1) to facilitate efficient exchange of goods and services as well as (2) to ensure fairness in economic transactions. The first goal of contract law is achieved mostly throughout the rules on the performance of the contracts and is supported by the other rules, i.e., on the security interests, remedies, simplified debt recovery procedure, etc.

427. Performance of contracts in Lithuanian law is regulated by the mix of general rules on transactions, obligations and contracts applicable for all contracts in conjunction with special provisions of contract law applicable specifically for nominate contracts.

428. Performance of obligation is the second stage in the life of obligation, preceded by the rise of obligation and succeeded by the extinguishment of it (*solutio*). Performance may be voluntary or enforced by the bailiff under the executory law. In case of voluntary performance, the same performance by its legal nature is a separate legal transaction – unilateral transaction. This is important because it allows to control the performance of a contract against the defects of the will under the general validity rules applicable to all transactions. For example, LCC Article 6.73(2) provides that the amount of stipulated penalty may be reduced by the court when it is manifestly excessive, or if the creditor has already benefited from partial performance of the obligation, though the sum may not be reduced below the damages payable for the failure to perform the obligation or for defective performance thereof. No reduction of the penalty paid shall be allowed. This one last sentence, taken in isolation, could lead to the reasoning that even penalty which is paid by the threat is not recoverable by the aggrieved party. That is why it is inevitable to apply general validity rules with respect to performance of contracts in order to mitigate such kind of situations.

429. Basic rule on the performance of obligations – LCC Article 6.38 – states that obligations must be performed in good faith, properly and without delay, pursuant to the requirements indicated in laws or the contract, and in case of absence of relevant requirements, obligations must be performed in accordance with the criteria of reasonableness. Each of the parties shall be obliged to perform his obligations in the thriftiest way possible and render every kind of assistance to the other party in performing his obligations (obligation of the parties to cooperate). If the debtor in performance of the obligation uses assistance of other persons, he shall be liable for the actions of those persons as for his own. Similarly, LCC Article 6.200 prescribes that a contract must be performed by the parties in a proper way and good faith. In performing a contract, each party shall be bound to contribute to and to cooperate with the other party. The parties shall be bound to use the most economical means in the performance of the contract.

430. Where according to a contract or its nature, a party in exercising certain actions is bound to make the best effort in the performance of a contract this party shall be bound to make such effort as a reasonable person would make in the same circumstances. Thus, in the event where the performance of an obligation is inherent in the exercise of professional activity of one of the parties, such as physician, lawyer and auditor, the requirements with respect to the nature of that professional activity shall also have to be observed by the party concerned, i.e., party should act as *bonus profesionalis.*

431. As the rules on the performance of obligations are detailed and sometimes may seem confusing, Lithuanian legal doctrine uses set of the principles of: (1) proper performance, (2) performance in kind, (3) economy of performance and (4) cooperation of parties as the analytical framework for the understanding and applying detailed statutory rules.[276]

I. Proper Performance of Obligations

432. The principle of proper performance of obligations is important in two respects – legal and economic. From the economic perspective, proper performance of contract means successful exchange of goods or services and creation of added value. Failed performance disturbs the normal exchange of goods in the market and creates losses. From the legal perspective, proper performance extinguishes legal obligations, whereas improper performance goes against the principle of *pacta sunt servanda* and creates civil liability of non-performing party.

433. According to LCC Article 6.123, an obligation is extinguished by its proper performance. It shall likewise be extinguished where a creditor has accepted the performance of a different kind in substitution for the one originally called for. After the acceptance of performance by the creditor, the burden of proof of non-performance or the improper performance thereof shall fall on the creditor. Extinction of an obligation by a proper performance entails termination of all accessory rights and liabilities arising from this obligation.

434. Thus, it is clear from above that to extinguish obligations performance must be proper. It means that the performance should totally comply with the mode, quality, quantity, time, place, recipient and other requirements of performance of contractual obligations. Even slightest unjustified nonconformity with these principles technically constitutes a breach of the contract (LCC Article 6.205).

435. The debtor must perform the obligation in an agreed manner, for example, the seller must properly deliver the goods, the lessee must timely pay rent and the supplier must equip the distributor. A debtor may not without the consent of the creditor free himself from the obligation by a performance different from that which is set in the contract or law, notwithstanding the value of the performance. Where

276. P. Rasimavičius, *et al. Civilinė teisė: vadovėlis.* Kaunas: Vijusta, 1998, p. 415.

the creditor has consented to accept a different performance, the obligation is extinguished. The mutual duties of the debtor and creditor must be performed by them concurrently unless otherwise provided for by laws, the contract or the essence of the obligation (LCC Article 6.39). The creditor has the right to refuse accepting a partial performance of an obligation unless otherwise provided for by laws or the contract. In the event where the debtor disputes a part of an obligation, he is obliged to accept the performance of that part of the obligation which is not disputed. However, the creditor reserves the right to demand performance of the remaining part of the obligation (LCC Article 6.40).

436. As to the quality of performance of an obligation, when the object of an obligation is a generic thing, the debtor must deliver a thing of the same kind, but not below the average quality required for the kind concerned unless otherwise provided for by laws or a contract. When the prestation of an obligation is an individually specified thing, the debtor is liable for any deterioration of the quality of that thing if such worsening occurs through his own fault (LCC Article 6.41). An obligation to deliver an individually specified thing shall include the duty to safeguard it until delivery unless otherwise provided for in the contract (LCC Article 6.43).

437. According to LCC Article 6.52, an obligation shall be performed at the place expressly indicated in the contract or laws, or which may be inferred from the essence of the obligation. However, in the event where no place of performance is indicated, the following rules shall apply: (1) the obligation to deliver an individually specified thing shall be performed at the place where the thing was situated when the obligation arose; (2) the obligation to deliver an immovable thing shall be performed at the place where the thing is situated; (3) the obligation to deliver a thing specified as to the kind shall be performed at the place of residence or business of the debtor; (4) a monetary obligation shall be performed at the place of residence or business of the creditor at the time of maturity of the obligation. In the event of change of place of residence or business of the creditor since the time of the arising of the obligation, which has caused additional expenses of performance to the debtor, the creditor shall be bound to compensate the debtor for such additional expenses. Upon the request of the creditor, a monetary obligation may also be performed in the territory of another state where the place of residence or business of the creditor is located at the time of payment, or the state where the creditor's residence was at the time when the obligation arose. However, where the required performance would be rendered substantially more onerous in the consequence, the debtor may refuse to satisfy such requirement of the creditor and execute performance in the place of the creditor's residence or his business at the time when the obligation arose; and (5) all other obligations shall be performed in the place of the debtor's residence or business at the time of maturity of the time limit for the performance of the obligation.

438. If the time limit for the performance of an obligation is not established in the contract, or it is determined by the moment of demand to perform the obligation, the creditor shall have the right to demand it at any time, and the debtor shall have the right to perform the obligation at any time. Though, when a certain time limit is necessitated by the nature of the obligation, the manner or place of its performance, it may be fixed by the court upon the demand of one of the parties. The obligation whose time limit of performance is not determined must be performed by the debtor within seven days from the day when the creditor requested the performance unless a different time limit of performance results from laws or the essence of the contract. In such cases, the time limit for performance must be reasonable and enable the debtor to perform the obligation properly. The debtor shall have the right to perform the obligation before the expiry of the time limit determined for its performance unless this is prohibited by laws, the contract, or is contrary to the essence of the obligation (LCC Article 6.53).

439. In addition, LCC in Article 6.44–6.51 sets detailed rules as to the persons involved in the performance. Therefore, the obligation must be performed to the creditor, or to his representative, or to the person designated by the creditor, or to the person obliged by laws or the court to accept such performance. Performance of an obligation made to a person not entitled to accept it shall be deemed to be an appropriate performance if the creditor ratifies it or factually obtains the full performance from the person concerned. Performance of an obligation shall not be deemed to be carried out in a proper way if the debtor, during its performance in respect of one of his creditors, infringes the interests of his other creditor who is granted the right to demand the arrest of the property of the debtor.

440. The debtor who performs an obligation to a person who through the fault of the creditor is reasonably and in good faith deemed to be entitled to receive the performance is discharged from the performance of obligation to the creditor if he proves to have erred in good faith. The erroneous creditor who has accepted performance shall be obliged to restore it to the true creditor or to the debtor in accordance with the rules on the unjustified enrichment. The debtor has the right to suspend performance upon substantial and reasonable grounds for doubt whether the person with respect to whom the obligation is being performed has the right to accept this performance, and if the latter upon the demand of the debtor fails to present the necessary proof of his right to claim. The debtor also has the right to suspend performance of the obligation if the creditor fails to perform his counter-obligation and where the counter-obligations of the debtor and creditor are connected in such a manner which justifies the suspension of the performance of the obligation. But the debtor has no right to suspend performance of the obligation where the creditor cannot perform his obligation through the fault of the debtor himself, likewise when the creditor cannot perform his obligation due to circumstances beyond his control.

441. Performance made to a creditor without capacity to accept it is valid only to such extent if the debtor proves that the performance truly conforms to the best interests of the incapable person and is to the advantage thereof. Where the obligation is performed without considering that the creditor due to certain reasons (arrest, etc.) was unable to accept the performance personally, the debtor shall be bound to perform such obligation anew and shall have the right of recourse against the creditor to demand the return of what has already been transferred. If the obligation is performed by an incapable debtor, such performance cannot be disputed upon the grounds of the debtor's incapacity.

442. The debtor cannot dispute performance of an obligation made by the transfer of property he had no right to dispose of, except in the cases when he himself offers to make performance by a transfer of property he has the right to dispose of, and if such change of prestation does not violate the interests of the creditor. The creditor to whom the property of another has been transferred by the debtor in performance of an obligation has the right to dispute such performance and claim damages.

443. An obligation can be performed in part or in full by a third person; except in the cases when pursuant to the agreement of the parties, or the essence of the obligation, it must be performed by the debtor personally. The third person who has performed the obligation shall acquire the rights of a creditor with respect to the debtor. The creditor may refuse acceptance of the performance offered by a third person if the debtor has notified him of his objection to such performance. The exception is the case where the exaction against the property of the debtor has been taken by the creditor, the claim of the creditor may be satisfied by third persons who by the reason of such exaction may be deprived of certain rights to that property. The same right shall belong to the person who possesses the property if by the reason of exaction the right of possession may be lost by him. A claim of the creditor may also be satisfied by depositing the money into the depository account of a notary, a bank or any other credit institution, or by setting off counterclaims.

444. According to LCC Article 6.57, the expenses related to the performance of an obligation should be charged to the debtor unless otherwise provided for by laws or a contract. Any person bound to furnish security of performance of an obligation which is not specified by the contract as to the manner or form has the right at his own discretion to choose particular means of security adequate to the essence of the obligation or a form of security established by laws (LCC Article 6.42).

445. LCC Article 6.54 establishes statutory cascade rule for the allocation of payments, which is default and can be changed by the agreement. Thus, unless otherwise agreed by the parties, payments received by the creditor in result of performance of an obligation shall be imputed first to the creditor's expenses related to the tender. Second in line payments shall be imputed to interests in accordance with the sequence of their maturity. Third in line payments shall be imputed to a penalty. Fourth in line payments shall be imputed to the performance of the principal obligation. A creditor has the right to reject an offer to pay if the debtor indicates a different order of payments, as well as to reject the full repayment of the principal obligation if the current interest at maturity is not paid at the same time.

446. A debtor who owes several debts of the same kind to the same creditor may declare at the time of payment which debt he intends to satisfy. Though the debtor shall have no right without the consent of the creditor to impute a payment to an obligation not yet due in preference to a debt at maturity. In the absence of such declaration of the debtor, or a different agreement between the parties, it shall be considered that the payment is imputed first to the debt at maturity. In the event of several debts at maturity, where none of them is secured, it shall be considered that the payment is imputed to the debt that was the first to reach maturity. Where several debts are due, it shall be considered that the payment is imputed to the one having the security. Among several secured debts, the payment shall be imputed first to the debt which is most burdensome to the debtor, and in the event of all the debts being equally burdensome, to the one that was the first to reach maturity. In the instances where none of these criteria may be applied, imputation shall be made in proportion to all the debts. These rules also apply when the debtor's obligation to the creditor consists of the supply of goods or services, to the extent that this does not contradict to the essence of the obligation (LCC Article 6.55).

447. In addition to this, payments under Lithuanian law are subordinated to a pre-established row of priority. This row was included directly in the LCC after the financial crisis of 2008–2011 and strictly enforced by courts as a policy measure to combat fraudulent insolvencies. The row applies during a pre-insolvency period and does not impact rows of insolvency law. Thus, according to the LCC 6.930^1, a debtor who has insufficient funds to satisfy all submitted claims should pay its debts in this priority: (1) under the executory documents for the recovery of debt arising from the personal injury and maintenance; (2) under the executory documents for the recovery of payoff arising from the labour and copyright agreements; (3) under the payment documents requiring to pay sums owed to the public budget and State monetary funds; (4) under the executory documents for the recovery of other debts; and (5) under the payment documents for the recovery of debt in a calendar order. Payments for the same level creditors should be distributed in a calendar order. Non-compliance with this order leads to invalidity of the disputed payment under LCC Article 1.80 (illegal transactions)[277] and in extreme cases even may attract criminal liability.[278] In order to nullify a transaction, a plaintiff must only show that there were (1) insufficient funds and (2) creditors of higher level. Thus, in practice, this remedy duplicates the *actio Pauliana*, however, without any real possibilities for the honest creditor to defend against this action. Despite its good purposes in theory, the payment sequence remedy makes exception to the *in paritas creditorum* principle and is very controversial from the economic point of view because may compromise efforts to rescue businesses facing liquidity problems: the company will be forced to pay workers first, leaving less possibilities to purchase raw materials from the suppliers in order to continue and safeguard its business.

277. Judgment of the Lithuanian Supreme Court of in the civil case No Lietuvos Aukščiausiojo Teismo Civilinių bylų skyriaus 2017 m. spalio 12 d. nutartis civilinėje byloje Nr. e3K-3-351-611/2017

278. Criminal Code Art. 208 prohibits crime of 'dishonesty of a debtor' basically stressing that a person who, owing to a difficult economic situation or insolvency, when facing obvious bankruptcy and being unable to meet all creditors' claims, meets claims of only one or several of them or secures claims of one or several creditors and thereby incurs pecuniary damage to the remaining creditors shall be punished by a fine or by imprisonment for a term of up to two years.

448. The debtor has no burden to prove that payment money belongs to him.[279] The payment may be done by the third party, such as bank, directly to the creditor instead of the debtor, thus avoiding ownership of funds by the debtor.

449. The debtor has the right to perform a monetary obligation by depositing the debt into the deposit account of a notary, a bank or any other credit institution if: (1) the creditor or any other person authorised to accept the performance cannot be found at the place where the obligation is to be performed; (2) the creditor is incapable and a guardian is not appointed to him; (3) the creditor avoids accepting the performance of the obligation; and (4) the creditor is not clear, as the right to accept the performance is being disputed by several persons. A deposit of the sum necessary for the performance of an obligation into a deposit account is considered a proper performance of the obligation. A notary, a bank or any other credit institution, into account of which the money is deposited, shall be obliged within a reasonable time to inform the creditor accordingly. Where the object of an obligation is a thing, and the creditor refuses to accept performance, the debtor shall be obliged to make a tender and determine the time limit for the acceptance of performance. In the case of the creditor's failure to accept performance of the obligation within the established time limit, he shall be considered to be in default. In this event, the creditor shall bear the costs of the preservation of the thing. The creditor shall also bear the risk of loss or deterioration of a thing. If a thing is perishable, the debtor may sell it and deposit the proceeds. Performance of an obligation in deposit releases the debtor from the payment of interest or any other dues in the future. An interest or any other sums calculated from the day of deposit shall be due to the creditor. However, if the deposit is made to obtain performance of the obligation of the creditor that is correlative to the obligation the debtor intends to perform by the deposit, the received interest and other sums shall belong to the debtor until the deposit is accepted by the creditor. The deposited sums of money may be withdrawn by a debtor as long as the performance has not been accepted by the creditor. If the debtor withdraws the deposited sums from the deposit account, he shall not be considered to have performed the obligation. Where the deposit of a sum of money is made during judicial proceedings, the debtor may withdraw such deposited sum only upon the authorisation of the court. In addition, the withdrawal may not be effectuated by the debtor if this would impair the rights of third persons or the interests of solidary debtors or sureties. In the event of bankruptcy, funds accumulated in the deposit account shall not be calculated into the property of the bank or of any other credit institution from which the claims of the creditors are satisfied under the procedure of bankruptcy (LCC Article 6.56).

II. Finality of Performance of Financial Obligations

450. Special issue related to the proper performance is the finality of performance of the financial obligations. For the sake of clarity, the notion of finality is

279. *Judgment of the Lithuania Supreme Court of 7 Oct. 2021 in the civil case No. e3K-3-230-701/ 2021.*

more important to financial law, than to general private law; nevertheless, it is still the matter of contract law and is explained here.

451. In the world of financial intermediation, it may seem unclear when the obligation to transfer financial assets is finally performed and extinguished – at the time the client's proper order to the financial institution is made, or at the time when such order is executed by the client's bank, or at the time when funds are credited into recipients account. In general, Lithuanian statutory law is silent on this point. The exception is a contract of loan, which under LCC Article 6.873(5) is repaid only when the borrower's funds are transferred to the lender or credited to his bank account. Another exception comes from public law, according to which taxes are paid only when a credit institution or any other payment services provider carrying out the relevant instructions given by the taxpayer, credits an account of tax administrator (Law on Tax Administration Article 83(2)). As concerns general standard, case law of ECJ is an excellent example of the rational application of law and should also be followed in cases involving national law. In the case concerning the interpretation of EU Late Payment Directive[280] the ECJ has ruled that a debtor's payment is regarded as late, for the purposes of entitlement to interest for late payment, where the creditor does not have the sum owed at his disposal on the due date. In the case of payment by bank transfer, only the crediting of the amount due to the creditor's account will enable him to have that sum at his disposal. However, the debtor must not be held liable for delays for which he is not responsible. In other words, Directive itself excludes interest for late payment in cases where the late payment is not the result of the debtor's conduct, as he has diligently taken into account the periods normally necessary for execution of a bank transfer.[281]

452. Another crucial aspect of the finality principle is the immunity of financial transactions against the intrusion of insolvency law. According to the EU Settlement Finality Directive Article 3 and 5, transfer orders and netting shall be legally enforceable and, even in the event of insolvency proceedings against a participant, shall be binding on third parties, provided that transfer orders were entered into a system before the moment of opening of such insolvency proceedings. No law, regulation, rule or practice on the setting aside of contracts and transactions concluded before the moment of opening of insolvency proceedings shall lead to the unwinding of a netting. A transfer order may not be revoked by a participant in a system, nor by a third party, from the moment defined by the rules of that system.

453. The same principle is also established in the EU Financial Collateral Directive with respect to financial collateral and close-out netting agreements. The Directive's Articles 7 and 8 state that a close-out netting provision should take effect notwithstanding the commencement or continuation of winding-up proceedings or reorganisation measures in respect of the collateral provider and/or the collateral taker and notwithstanding any purported assignment, judicial or other attachment or

280. Directive 2000/35/EC of the European Parliament and of the Council of 29 Jun. 2000 on combating late payment in commercial transactions.
281. Judgment of the ECJ of 3 Apr. 2008 in the Case C-306/06 (*Deutsche Telekom*).

other disposition of or in respect of such rights. A financial collateral arrangement, as well as the provision of financial collateral under such arrangement, may not be declared invalid or void or be reversed on the sole basis that the financial collateral arrangement has come into existence, or the financial collateral has been provided: (a) on the day of the commencement of winding-up proceedings or reorganisation measures, but prior to the order or decree making that commencement; or (b) in a prescribed period prior to, and defined by reference to, the commencement of such proceedings or measures or by reference to the making of any order or decree or the taking of any other action or occurrence of any other event in the course of such proceedings or measures.

III. Performance in Kind

454. Performance in kind means that the obligation should be performed as agreed, and no substitutes are allowed. Thus, there is no easy recourse for the debtor to the payment of compensatory damages in lieu of performance as in common law countries. Lithuanian as the other civilian jurisdictions instead prefers specific performance, however not in such a strict form as in Soviet times any more. Within the socialist planned economy, which was present in Lithuania during the Soviet occupation, supply chains tightly depended on each other, so break in one transaction automatically caused shortage of goods in the subsequent transactions and the economy as a whole. The market was either absent or very limited at best; thus, no alternatives were easily available to the aggrieved party. In contrast, in the current economic system, which is based on free market, there is no need for absolute adherence to the performance in kind any more, as substitutes usually are normally available. Despite this performance in kind remains the general rule of the performance of contractual obligations.

455. Under Lithuanian contract law, the adherence to the principle of performance in kind depends on the type of obligation. In the event where a party fails to perform his monetary obligation, the other party shall have the right to demand performance in kind; thus no alternatives are available. However, if a party fails to perform his non-monetary obligation, the other party may demand performance in kind, except in one of these cases where: (1) performance of a contractual obligation in kind is impossible legitimately or in fact; (2) performance of a contractual obligation in kind would be greatly burdensome or expensive for the debtor; (3) the party entitled to performance may reasonably obtain performance from another source; (4) the party entitled to performance does not demand that performance within a reasonable time after he became or should have become aware of the non-performance of the contract; and (5) the non-performed obligation is of exclusively personal character.

IV. Economy of Performance

456. The goal of economic activities is an efficient exchange of goods and services. In order to achieve this, the contracts should be performed in a rational way, i.e., either by extracting maximum value from the fixed means or by extracting fixed (agreed) value by minimum means.

457. This logic is reflected in several articles in the LCC. Hence, according to LCC Article 6.38(3) each party is obliged to perform its obligations in the most economical way possible and render every kind of assistance to the other party in performing his obligations (obligation of the parties to cooperate). The same is repeated in LCC Article 6.200(3), which states that the parties shall be bound to use the most economical means in the performance of the contract. However, this does not intend that quality of performance should suffer; thus, when the subject matter of an obligation is a generic thing, the debtor must deliver a thing of the same kind, but not below the average in quality required for the kind concerned unless otherwise provided for by laws or a contract (LCC Article 6.41). Another rule of economy of performance is found in the institution of works contracts, where LCC Article 6.654(1) prescribes that in the event where the actual expenses of the contractor prove to be lower than those taken into account in determining the price of work, the contractor shall retain the right to the payment for work as established in the contract of works unless the customer proves that the economies produced negative effect on the quality of work as determined in the contract. A distribution of the economies received may be provided for in the contract. It is seen from above that while this rule is efficiency related, it is differently calibrated since enhances personal incentives on part of contractor and gives him extra value from the proper and economical performance.

V. Cooperation of Parties

458. Hesitation to cooperate creates transactions costs and is unfair for the counterparty. These economic and legal reasons make the duty to cooperate imperative. Hence, LCC Article 6.38(3) states that each party is obliged to render every kind of assistance to the other party in performing its obligations (obligation of the parties to cooperate). LCC Article 6.200(2) restates that in performance of a contract, each party shall be bound to contribute to and to cooperate with the other party.

459. Failure to cooperate amounts to the breach of contract. For instance, LCC Article 6.64(1) 1 prescribes that the creditor is in default when the debtor cannot perform the obligation in the result of insufficient cooperation between the creditor and the debtor, or through any other fault of the creditor.

460. In addition to these general rules, there are a lot of dispersed rules in the statutory law, which stress the importance of cooperation. For example, under the *Nachfrist* procedure, the party failing to perform a contract may at its own expense cure any defects of performance only if the aggrieved party has no lawful interest in refusing cure. During that period, the aggrieved party shall be bound to cooperate with the other party during the whole period of the elimination of defects (LCC 6.208). Another example is the cooperation of parties to a construction contract. In the course of performing a construction contract, parties to the contract are obliged to cooperate (duty of cooperation). In the event of appearance of obstacles which hinder proper performance of the contract, each of the parties to the contract shall be obliged to take all reasonable measures within his control to eliminate such obstacles. The party which fails to perform this duty shall be deprived of the right to claim compensation of damage caused by the non-elimination of the relevant obstacles. Expenses incurred by a party in eliminating the obstacles should be taken by the other party in the instances and amounts determined in the construction contract (LCC Article 6.691). Under LCC Article 6.761, the mandator shall be obliged to cooperate with the mandatary to facilitate the fulfilment of the mandate by the latter.

§2. Breach of Contract

461. The breach of contract is a type of civil wrong, which entitles aggrieved party to use legal remedies against the party in breach. Breach of a contract is an unjustified failure to perform any of the obligations arising from the contract, including improper performance and delay of a time limit of performance (LCC Article 6.205). Thus, a breach of a contract is any behaviour of the party, which unjustifiably deviates from expressively agreed or implied terms of the contract.

462. There is a taxonomy of breaches according to Lithuanian contract doctrine.[282] By the intensity three types of breaches are distinguished: ordinary, material and fundamental breach. Ordinary breach is minor or at least non-substantial failure to perform any of the obligations arising from the contract, such as slight delay of time in performance or insignificant incompatibility of delivered assortment with agreed assortment. In case of ordinary breach, the aggrieved party is entitled to specific performance and damages but not to the termination or modification of contract or suspension of performance.

463. Material breach (LCC Article 6.217(2)1) is unjustified non-performance of a contract, where an aggrieved party is substantially deprived of what it is entitled under the contract, for example, where the buyer does not get substantial part of the goods sold to her. In case of material breach, the aggrieved party is entitled to specific performance, damages, suspension of performance but not to the termination or modification of contract. Material breach besides from being the sole ground for application of contractual remedies is also main criterion for the characterisation of breach as fundamental one.

282. *See* Laurynas Didžiulis. *Numatomo sutarties pažeidimo doktrina: samprata, kvalifikavimo pagrindai ir teisinis poveikis.* Teisės problemos, 2007, Nr. 1. p. 46–78.

464. Fundamental breach (LCC Article 6.217) is most severe breach of contract, which entitles the aggrieved party to full set of contractual remedies, including the modification and even unilateral termination of contract. In determining whether a breach of a contract is fundamental, the following conditions must be taken into account: materiality of breach, i.e., whether the aggrieved party is substantially deprived of what it was entitled to expect under the contract, except in cases when the other party did not foresee or could not have reasonably foreseen such result; whether, taking into consideration the nature of the contract, strict compliance with the conditions of the obligation is of essential importance; whether the breach is made intentionally or with gross negligence; whether the breach gives the aggrieved party the basis to suppose that it cannot rely in the normal future performance of a contract; and whether the breached party, which was preparing for performance or was effectuating the performance of the contract, would suffer significant damages if the contract were terminated. In contrast with UNIDROIT PICC, under Lithuanian law, only a fundamental breach entitles to the termination of contract but not a broader category of fundamental non-performance, which includes also justified fundamental non-performance. Latter situation is free of such consequences leading to the end of the contract, unless it equals to fortuitous events mitigated by the other rules (force majeure, *imprevision*).

465. According to the timing, breaches may be either actual or anticipatory. Actual breach is one which has already happened, whereas anticipatory breach is one which should probably happen in some future time. The difference is that in case of anticipatory breach only anticipatory fundamental breach entitles to the remedies and lesser kinds of breaches do not. Thus, LCC Article 6.219 prescribes that if prior to the date when performance falls due it is reasonable to think that there will be a fundamental breach by one of the parties, the other party may terminate the contract. Usually, there is an uncertainty regarding the fundamentality and anticipation of future breach; therefore, LCC Article 6.220 gives to a party which reasonably believes that there may be a fundamental breach by the other party, the right to demand the latter to present an assurance of due performance. The party may suspend performance of his obligations under the contract until the first party has provided the assurance that he will faithfully exercise a proper performance of the contract. Where the assurance is not received within a reasonable time, the party demanding thereof may terminate the contract.

466. And, finally, according to the breaching party, breaches may take form of either the debtor's default or the creditor's default, and this classification is relevant for both unilateral and bilateral contracts. LCC Article 6.63 prescribes that a debtor is in default (*mora debitoris*) where: (1) the conditions of a contract are not performed, or are being performed improperly; (2) the debtor fails to perform the obligation within the established time limit; (3) the creditor with valid reason files a suit against him, or addresses him in an extrajudicial demand to perform the obligation; (4) the creditor demands performance of the obligation within a reasonable time established by him, but the debtor failed to perform the obligation within this time limit; (5) the debtor informs the creditor before the expiry of a time limit of his intention not to perform the obligation; and (6) performance of the obligation has become impossible due to the debtor's fault. The debtor is liable from the moment he is considered to be in default for any damages suffered by the creditor, except in the cases when the debtor is released from the performance of the obligation. In the event where the time limit for the performance of an obligation is not fixed, the debtor shall be considered to be in default from the moment when the creditor made a demand in writing to perform the obligation and fixed the time limit for the performance, but the debtor has failed to perform the obligation within that time limit. The debtor is liable for all the consequences of the impossibility to perform the obligation after it was violated by the debtor, except in cases where the performance of the obligation has been rendered impossible through the fault of the creditor. After the violation of an obligation committed by the debtor, the creditor has the right to refuse acceptance of the tender offered by the debtor if the debtor does not offer the compensation of damage sustained by the creditor in the result of the violation of obligation.

467. Pursuant to LCC Article 6.64, the creditor is in default (*mora creditoris*) when: (1) the debtor cannot perform the obligation in the result of insufficient cooperation between the creditor and the debtor, or through any other fault of the creditor; and (2) the creditor through his own fault fails to perform his duty to the debtor; thus the debtor justifiably suspends performance of the obligation. In the event of default of the creditor, the debtor can file a suit and demand to be released from the performance of the obligation in whole or in part, conditionally or unconditionally. If the creditor violates the obligation, the debtor shall be considered not to have violated it. The debtor may not be considered in violation of the obligation as long as the creditor is considered to have violated it. The debtor has the right to demand compensation for the damages incurred in the result of the violation of obligation committed by the creditor.

§3. Impossibility, Frustration and Hardship

468. As the principle *pacta sunt servanda* is firmly rooted in the various articles of the LCC, illegitimate refuse to perform the contract is a breach which gives rise to the contractual liability. Such attitude significantly adds to the efficiency of Lithuanian contract law and national economy. There are very few exceptions to this purely legalistic principle, and most of them are backed by the other fundamental and morality principle of contract law – good faith. It would, indeed, be unfair to require the performance from the debtor, where he is facing unexpected circumstances, which complicates normal performance of the contract making it either totally impossible, or highly impracticable. Therefore, Lithuanian contract law provides two affirmative defences to the claim based on the strict application of the *pacta sunt servanda* principle – the doctrines of force majeure and *imprévision*.

I. Impossibility

469. Taking into regard taxonomy, impossibility to perform the contract may be *ex ante* and *ex post*. *Ex ante* impossibility makes contract void without any further qualifications because in order for agreement to be sufficient it must contain proper subject matter (prestation). In this respect, LCC Article 6.3(4) prescribes that the subject matter of an obligation cannot be something that is impossible to perform. Since *impossibilium nulla obligatio est*, the contract lacks its main element – the agreement – which should encompass the subject matter of obligation. However, Supreme Court in one case has controversially declared contract void on this ground solely on the reason that in time of contract formation seller had not yet owned the asset (claim), which was sold.[283] This is incorrect reasoning, at least so far as there is nothing to prevent the seller from obtaining goods in the market or manufacturing them by himself and delivering them to the buyer. If one party is culpable for the conclusion of such contract, it should pay damages to the aggrieved party (LCC Article 6.263).

470. *Ex post* impossibility to perform the contract is divided into two cases: impossibility due to the force majeure (innocent impossibility) and impossibility imputable to the debtor (culpable impossibility). As concerns the culpable *ex post* impossibility, LCC Article 6.62 provides that where the performance of an obligation that arises from a bilateral contract has become impossible because of a circumstance imputable to the party himself, while neither laws nor a contract provides otherwise, the other party may revoke the contract and claim restitution in kind (to return everything that was performed), likewise compensate damage incurred by the non-performance of this obligation. Where the performance of an obligation that arises from a bilateral contract has become impossible due to circumstances imputable to the other party, the first party shall have the right to demand from the other party performance of the obligation and compensation of damage, including what has been accumulated due to the impossibility to perform the obligation (LCC Article 6.62).

471. The rule on innocent *ex post* impossibility in Lithuanian contract law, following the Romanic tradition, is called irresistible force or force majeure. Synonymous expressions *vis major* and *cas fortuit* are rarely, if at all, used. Rules on force majeure at large are based on UNIDROIT PICC.

472. LCC lays down three separate yet interrelated descriptions of force majeure. First, according to LCC Article 6.212(1), a party is exempted from liability for breach of a contract if it proves that the breach was due to the circumstances which were beyond its control and could not have been reasonably expected by it at the time of the conclusion of the contract, and the arising of such circumstances or consequences thereof could not be prevented. Second, under LCC Article 6.127(1), an obligation is extinguished when its performance becomes impossible as a consequence of irresistible force which is not imputable to the debtor. And third,

283. Judgment of the Lithuanian Supreme Court of 30 Jun. 2008 in the civil case No 3K-3-199/2008.

according to LCC Article 6.253, which prescribes list of civil liability exemptions, an irresistible force is unavoidable events that cannot be controlled or escaped by the debtor, and which were not and could not have been foreseen. It is evident that all three definitions, being more or less elaborate, are similar and do not conflict with each other. Those definitions, taking into account case law of Lithuanian civil courts[284] and legal doctrine,[285] are stressing strict and objective attitude of force majeure.[286]

473. In comparison, despite the characterisation of force majeure in ECJ case law dealing with application of various EU legal acts is largely similar to Lithuanian definition, it is not limited to purely objective attitude, thus affirming the possibility of broader understanding of force majeure. ECJ has ruled that although the notion of force majeure is not predicated on absolute impossibility, it nevertheless requires the non-performance of the act in question to be attributable to circumstances, beyond the control of the party claiming force majeure, which are abnormal and unforeseeable and the consequences of which could not have been avoided despite the exercise of all due diligence.[287] However, as the concept of force majeure is not identical in the different branches of law and the various fields of application, the significance of this concept must be determined on the basis of the legal framework within which it is intended to take effect.[288]

474. To establish the force majeure as an affirmative defence in Lithuanian contract law, the defendant should prove three classic properties of the fortuitous events, which prevented performance: externality, unforeseeability and irresistibility.

475. Externality (*externalité*) means that the events are not imputable to the debtor's fault or risk. If, for instance, enterprise workers start to strike due to the harsh labour conditions, it is within sphere of debtor's control, and it must therefore assume the liability for non-performance. Similarly, the debtor who has delayed performance should be liable towards the creditor for the impossibility to perform the obligation which accidentally results from the delay (LCC Article 6.260(2)).

476. According to the strictly objective attitude, which has clearly prevailed during the first decade of LCC application, Lithuanian civil courts most likely would not treat the illness of debtor as force majeure, even when it has suddenly and unexpectedly occurred without the fault of debtor, because it is his personal issue. However, in such Western jurisdictions as France and US, death or illness, though

284. *See* Judgment of the Lithuanian Supreme Court of 8 Oct. 2003 in the civil case No 3K-3-931/2003.
285. Valentinas Mikelėnas. *Lietuvos Respublikos civilinio kodekso komentaras. Šeštoji knyga. Prievolių teisė.* Justitia, 2003, I t., pp. 283–286.
286. The defence of force majeure is also known in Lithuanian tax law. *See* Judgments of the LVAT of 9 Feb. 2005 in the administrative case No A15 – 141/2005 and of 21 Mar. 2011 in the administrative case No. A556 – 319/2011.
287. Judgment of the ECJ of 8 Mar. 1988 in the Case 296/86.
288. Judgment of the ECJ of 11 Jul. 1968 in the Case C-4/68.

apparently subjective since they are personal to the obligor, is regarded as objective. The reason for that conclusion is that no other person in the obligor's situation could have overcome such an obstacle, which meets the requirement of generality that makes impossibility objective.[289] Latter position seems to be prevailing also in the EU law. Thus, under the Parental Leave Directive's[290] Clause 7:1, workers should be entitled to time off from work, in accordance with national legislation, collective agreements and/or practice, on grounds of force majeure for urgent family reasons in cases of sickness or accident making the immediate presence of the worker indispensable. Another example is EC Rural Development Implementing Regulation,[291] which in Article 39 had stated that Member States may recognise, in particular, the following categories of force majeure: (a) death of the farmer; (b) long-term professional incapacity of the farmer; (f) an epizootic disease affecting all or part of the farmer's livestock. Applying this Regulation, LVAT has quashed judgment of first instance court, which declared illness of the farmer as force majeure, however, on the other grounds and seems to have tacitly accepted this type of force majeure even in Lithuanian law.[292]

477. Unforeseeability (*imprévisibilité*) criterion requires that events should be fortuitous (*cas fortuit*), i.e., not expected at the moment of contract formation. Since all events in theory are possible, the key here is not abstract possibility, but realistic probability of occurrence weighed by the reasonable person, i.e., such who is not too optimistic but not too pessimistic either. In practice, this requirement is most difficult to meet because courts tend to use very objectivist approach and most often holds that debtor could foresee one or another event pleaded by debtor as fortuitous. For example, fire in the building, highly frozen land in the winter and heavy rainstorms were treated as foreseeable and normal under Lithuanian climate.[293] Almost all cases where lower courts have found force majeure were quashed by the Supreme Court mostly on the lack of unforeseeability. Exceptional is one civil case on Convention on the Contract for the International Carriage of Goods by Road (CMR) matters, where the Supreme Court has declared as the fortuitous and unavoidable the robbery of goods in truck by the criminals, who masked themselves as policemen and falsely stopped the truck driver.[294] However, such events as US stock markets 'Flash Crash' of 2010, nationalisation of Lithuanian bank Snoras by the end of 2011, Ukraine political crisis and subsequent hostilities in 2014 and various terror attacks in US and Western Europe, so far as they are connected

289. Saul Litvinoff. *Law Of Obligations. Louisiana Civil Law Treatise.* 2d ed., 2017, § 16.20.
290. Council Directive 2010/18/EU of 8 Mar. 2010 implementing the revised Framework Agreement on parental leave.
291. Commission Regulation (EC) No 817/2004 of 29 Apr. 2004 laying down detailed rules for the application of Council Regulation (EC) No 1257/1999 on support for rural development from the European Agricultural Guidance and Guarantee Fund (EAGGF).
292. Judgment of the LVAT of 27 May 2011 in the administrative case No. A-525-2175-11.
293. Judgments of the Lithuanian Supreme Court of 4 Feb. 2004 in the civil case No 3K-3-83/2004, of 4 Oct. 2010 in the civil case No 3K-3-370/2010 and of 5 Feb. 2014 in the civil case No. 3K-3-1/2014.
294. Judgment of the Lithuanian Supreme Court of 9 Jan. 2002 in the civil case No. 3K-3-29/2002.

to the application of Lithuanian contract law, may be legitimately regarded as fortuitous even to a very objectivistic and diligent observer.

478. Irresistibility (*irrésistibilité*) means that the event should make the performance for the debtor impossible despite of the exercise of all due care. If debtor can perform his obligations but incurring altered expenses, this is not force majeure and situation can only be mitigated by the rules on impracticability, i.e., *rebus sic stantibus* doctrine. Irresistible force may be acts of God (cyclones, earthquakes, uncontrollable and spreading fire, dangerous viruses, etc.), acts of man (war, riots, sectoral strikes, etc.) and acts of State (sudden policy change, licencing, statutory prohibition, quarantine, etc.). If some obstacles, despite their power, may be controlled by the acceptable means, they are not treated as force majeure. For example, if Government agency prohibits some contracts, but it is possible to easily freeze this order in court, it is not force majeure. Equally, if the seller has faced unexpected circumstances, which have destroyed generic goods held by him, he must procure the same goods in the market and deliver them to the buyer.

479. The global coronavirus pandemic already in 2020 has shown that the same cause may spill over and create a group of related fortuitous events with different effects on contracts. For instance, SARS-CoV-2 is a virus responsible for COVID-19 disease which caused State action in the form of quarantine restrictions. Coronavirus (SARS-CoV-2) and COVID-19 disease are biological impediments (acts of God), whereas quarantine is legal one (act of State). For instance, during the period of extreme contagion, there may be a necessity to suspend the enjoyment of leased office premises in order to prevent the spread of the virus between company employees. In such a case, a virus itself is impediment. If virus will affect the debtor and he will become ill due to COVID-19 disease by not being able to perform the personal obligation, then the COVID-19 will be the impediment of the contract. Finally, where State adopts quarantine measures and restricts use of business premises, it may equal to another type of contractual impediment. Therefore, the Lithuanian Supreme Court has relieved the lessee, who could not use the leased property due to quarantine, from its obligations on the basis of force majeure.[295]

480. According to LCC Article 6.212, an irresistible force (force majeure) does not include such circumstances as absence of goods in the market needed for the performance of the obligation, or lack of the necessary financial resources on the part of the party, or violation of their own obligations committed by the counterparties of the debtor. Here LCC shares the position of ECJ who had not regarded a failure by an exporter's business partner to fulfil his contractual obligations as an

---

295. Judgment of the Lithuania Supreme Court of 24 Mar. 2022 in the civil case No. e3K-3-66-313/2022. The judgment is fair and welcome, however based on surprising reasoning for the civilian contract law – the frustration of contractual purpose. In my opinion, the court should not introduce such alien reasoning and instead rely on the understanding that quarantine restrictions to use leased property mean that due to State action the lessee cannot fulfil its duty to ensure that the lessor is able to normally use the leased premises (LCC Art. 6.483(1)). Therefore, force majeure in such a case affects obligation of the lessor, not the lessee, and there is no need to refer to the doctrine of frustration.

abnormal and unforeseeable circumstance. The exporter is fully at liberty to select his trading partners and it is up to him to take the appropriate precautions, either by including the necessary clauses in the contracts in question or by effecting appropriate insurance[296] The ECJ had not even recognised fraudulent conduct on the part of the exporter's contracting partner as constituting force majeure.[297]

481. The force majeure is a strong defence since it extinguishes obligations of parties and exonerates debtor from liability if he has failed to perform contract due to fortuitous event. The burden of proof of an irresistible force falls on the debtor. The party who failed to perform a contract is obliged to inform the other party about the arising of fortuitous event and its influence on the possibility to perform the contract. In the event where the notice is not received by the other party within a reasonable time after the non-performing party became or should have become aware of the fortuitous event, he shall be bound to compensate the damage resulting from the non-receipt of the notice. This does not deprive a party of exercising the right to terminate the contract, or to suspend its performance, or to require due interest (LCC Article 6.127, 6.212).

482. According to LCC Article 6.212, in the event where the fortuitous event is temporary, the non-performing party shall be exempted from liability only for such a period which is reasonable taking in regard the effect of that event on the performance of the contract. It should be noted that the ECJ shares the same position, stressing that where it is possible to attribute an act to force majeure, the effects of that attribution can only last a certain time, namely the time which is in fact needed in order for an administration exercising a normal degree of diligence to put an end to the crisis which has arisen for reasons outside its control.[298] In the event where the performance was rendered impossible only in part, the debtor shall be discharged from the obligation upon performing that part whose performance is still possible.

483. Because force majeure extinguishes obligations, none of the parties may require each other performance of the contract. In such case, each party have the right to claim restitution in kind without the corresponding counter-performance. The debtor in a bilateral contract who has been released by impossibility of performance is bound to return all the benefits which he has received from the other party, and he shall have no right to claim performance of the remaining part of the unperformed obligation of the creditor in accordance with the contract.

484. If the performance of the obligation has become impossible by reason of unlawful acts of institutions of the state authority or a local self-government, the parties may claim for compensation of damage from the state or the municipality

296. Judgments of the ECJ of 27 Oct. 1987 in the Case 109/86 (Theodorakis) and of 9 Aug. 1994 in the Case C-347/93 (Boterlux).
297. Judgment of the ECJ of 8 Mar. 1988 in the Case 296/86 (McNicholl and Others).
298. Judgment of the ECJ of 11 Jul. 1985 in the Case 101/84 (*Commission v. Italy*).

budget. When such act is annulled, the obligation shall revive unless otherwise conditioned by the contract of the parties or the essence of the obligation, or the creditor has already lost interest therein (LCC Article 6.62).

A. *Hardship*

485. Where inadequacy of obligations in the contract exists from the beginning (*ex ante*), the doctrine of gross disparity (*laesio enormis*) applies. However, where material inadequacy of obligations in the contract does not exist from the beginning and contract is perfectly valid, but arise later (*ex post*), then the doctrine of *imprévision* or hardship (sometimes also called *rebus sic stantibus* stressing its Canon law origins) applies. The focus of the doctrine is to mitigate harsh consequences of commercial impracticability by loosening strict application of *pacta sunt servanda* principle, in cases where literal performance of the contract would be unfair to one party. Thus, where the performance of a contract becomes more difficult for one of the parties, this party is bound to perform the contract in accordance with the procedure set in LCC Article 6.204. Under this article, the performance of a contract is considered obstructed under such circumstances which fundamentally alter the balance of the contractual obligations, i.e., either the cost of performance has essentially increased or the value thereof has essentially diminished if: these circumstances occur or become known to the aggrieved party after the conclusion of the contract; these circumstances could not reasonably have been foreseen by the aggrieved party at the time of the conclusion of the contract; these circumstances are beyond the control of the aggrieved party; and the risk of occurrence of these circumstances was not assumed by the aggrieved party.

486. Some cases of *imprévision* are defined directly in statutory law. For instance, in the event of essential growth of the price of materials or equipment, or also of the services rendered to the independent work contractor by third persons, and the independent work contractor was not able to predict such increase at the time when the contract was concluded, the independent work contractor shall have the right to demand an increase of the established price of work or to dissolve the contract in accordance with the provisions of hardship (LCC Article 6.653(6)). Another example is as follows: the independent work contractor has the right to demand a revision of the price of the contract if for reasons beyond his control the actual price of the work has increased by more than 15% (LCC Article 6.653(2)). In practice, obligors heavily relied on the doctrine of *imprévision* during the global economic crisis of 2008–2010, which severely hit the Lithuanian economy. Courts normally refused to satisfy these claims and adhered to strict compliance to the contract, on the reason that these circumstances could reasonably have been foreseen by the aggrieved party at the time of the conclusion of the contract; however there were exceptions.[299]

---

299. *See* Judgment of the Lithuanian Supreme Court of 31 May 2011 in the civil case No 3K-3-265/2011. The parties of this case in 2002 have concluded a fixed-term commercial premises lease agreement that was supposed to end in 2019. In 2009, the tenant requested a court to amend the

487. The practical effect of *imprévision* doctrine is that in the event where the performance of a contract becomes obstructed, the aggrieved party shall have the right to make a request to the other party for the modification of the contract. Such request shall have to be made immediately after the occurrence of obstructions and the grounds on which the request is based indicated therein. The request for modification of the contract shall not in itself entitle the aggrieved party with the right to suspend performance of the contract. Where within a reasonable time the parties fail to reach an agreement on the modification of the contractual obligations, any of them may bring an action into a court.[300] The court may: (1) terminate the contract and establish the date and terms of its dissolution; and (2) modify the conditions of the contract with a view to restoring the balance of the contractual obligations of the parties. According to the case law, where party relies on the *imprévision*, the court has power to terminate the contract under LCC Article 6.204 on its own initiative even without the particular claim for termination of contract.[301] This gives broad powers to the court, which are untypical for the commercial litigation especially in the light of the principle of free disposition (CCP Article 13).

---

contract and restore the contractual balance by decreasing the rent payment from LTL 50 per 1 m^2 to LTL 33 per 1 m^2. The tenant explained that by the time the parties had concluded the contract, the tenant could not have foreseen the world financial crisis starting in 2008. Due to this crisis, the lease prices in the market decreased by 30%–40%, thus the contract needed to be adjusted. The courts of lower instance granted the tenant's claim and amended the contract, and the Lithuanian Supreme Court confirmed the decisions of the lower courts. It attributed this situation to a fundamental diminution of value which in the courts' view amounted to hardship. The court's decision to declare hardship in this situation was criticised by the legal doctrine on the following reasons: (1) it is doubtful whether the numeric expression of the alteration of the contractual equilibrium (30%–40%) should be qualified as fundamental. Only in exceptional cases may a threshold which is lower than 50% be justified, and it is submitted that no such exceptional situation existed in the Lithuanian case; and (2) the alternative fundamental alteration criteria could not be applied here either because the debtor was not trying to prove the threat of the company's financial ruin, and there was no threat to the debtor's personnel or property. *See* Daniel Girsberger, Paulius Zapolskis. *Fundamental Alteration of the Contractual Equilibrium under Hardship Exemption*. Jurisprudence. 2012, 19(1), p. 133.

300. As to the efficiency of this remedy, law and economics scholars point out that courts can complete the contract with respect to those remote risks the parties could not foresee at the time of contracting, according to the principles of efficient risk allocation. The benefit of specific allocation may be reproduced if a court later allocates *ex post* the once-remote risk, but only if the ruling is predictable. The judicial allocation of losses cannot yield the intended efficiency benefits of efficient precaution and insurance unless it can be predicted *ex ante*. The superior risk bearer analysis must play with sets of criteria that often cut in opposite directions and call for information that is often unverifiable. As a result, parties may well contract *ex ante* to avoid the additional risk of judicial intervention or may overinvest in precautions. Excuse rules conditioned on unobservable or unverifiable information will be unusable by courts and rejected by future contracting parties. The concern with conditioning judicial allocation of risk on verifiable factors, in particular, seems to be a persuasive explanation for the greater inclination of the courts to excuse performance in cases where it has become impossible (e.g., by the destruction of the subject matter or because of government regulation) rather than impracticable. As a normative matter, the courts should intervene to allocate remote risks when the incompleteness of the contract is due only to contracting costs, and not to obstacles of verification. *See* George Triantis. *Unforeseen Contingencies. Risk Allocation in Contracts. Encyclopedia of Law and Economics*. Edward Elgar, 2000, pp. 111–112.

301. Judgment of the Lithuania Supreme Court of 14 Oct. 2020 in the civil case No. e3K-3-39-378/2020.

B. Frustration of Purpose

488. As Lithuania is civil law jurisdiction, the doctrine of frustration is not in use here and its role is played by the above-mentioned doctrines of force majeure and *imprévision.*

489. From the other token, there are some dispersed rules in the special part of contract law, which focus on the frustration of creditor's purpose in the contract, albeit without merging into the general doctrine of frustration, known in common law jurisdictions. Here frustration does not play exonerating role for the debtor, but quite the opposite – reduce ways for him to avoid liability in case of non-performance by cutting creditors burdens to keep the contract alive (*favor contractus*). Thus, under LCC Article 6.260(3), the creditor has the right to refuse performance offered to him after the delay and may claim for damage caused by the delay in performance where the debtor's default by delay in performance results in the creditor's frustration of any interest in that performance. This rule is repeated in the LCC chapter on works contracts, under which, in the event of the breach of the time limits of the fulfilment of the whole work under the works contract, the customer shall have the right to refuse acceptance of the work fulfilled in result of performance of the whole obligation and claim damages from the contractor related to the delay in performance in the cases where the performance of the obligation due to the delay became of no significance for the customer (LCC Article 6.652(4)). In the loan for use (*commodatum*) contract, where accessories and documents were not transferred for loan recipient, and without them the thing cannot be used for its designation, or its use without the accessories and documents loses value for the loan recipient, the latter shall have the right to require such accessories and documents to be granted to him by the lender, or to dissolve the contract and demand from the lender compensation for the damages suffered (LCC Article 6.633(3)).

490. The frustration of a creditor's purpose is also seen in the so-called *Nachfrist* procedure, i.e., the party failing to perform a contract may at its own expense cure any defects of performance only if the aggrieved party has no lawful interest in refusing cure (LCC 6.208(1) 2). And, of course, it plays important role in establishing materiality of breach of contract; thus, in determining whether a breach of a contract is fundamental, one must take into account whether the aggrieved party is substantially deprived of what he was entitled to expect under the contract, except in cases when the other party did not foresee or could not have reasonably foreseen such result (LCC Article 6.217(2)1).

§4. The End of the Contract

491. The end of the contract[302] means that principal contractual claims and obligations are extinguished. However, contract is fully extinguished only where

302. For the sake of clarity, the end of the contract is incorrect term in a strict legal sense because the contract is mutual juridical act and as such it either was validly formed or not. As juridical fact, it

breaches of it have not created additional legal relations because if they have occurred, remedial obligations, such as duty to pay damages, still bind parties. This latter situation is called 'limited end of the contract'.

492. The end of the contract should not be confused with avoidance of it. As it was analysed in previous chapters, there are grounds to avoid the contract on the lack of substantive elements, such as agreement made by consent. In those cases, the contract is deemed as never existed at all and there is no need, and even room, to talk about the end of contract, since something may come to an end only if it did exist.[303] As for the end of a contract, there are number of grounds in Lithuanian law, which voluntary and even the involuntary extinguish the valid contractual obligations.

I. Voluntary Grounds

A. *Proper Performance*

493. Performance of obligation is the second stage in the life of contractual obligation, preceded by the rise of obligation and succeeded by the extinguishment of it (*solutio*). According to LCC Article 6.123, an obligation is extinguished by its proper performance. It is likewise extinguished where a creditor has accepted the performance of a different kind in substitution for the one originally called for. After the acceptance of performance by the creditor, the burden of proof of non-performance or the improper performance thereof falls on the creditor.

494. Extinction of an obligation by a proper performance entails termination of all accessory rights and liabilities arising from this obligation, for instance, suretyship, charge, pledge, hypothec, right of retention and even ordinary guarantee, since in Lithuanian law in fact it is accessory to the secured claim (LCC Article 6.92(5)). Non-accessory instruments, such as promissory notes, guarantees on first demand or bearer hypothecs, are independent, at least in theory, from the secured claim and should survive the *solutio*. Whereas their use in latter cases should be undisturbed, abuses and other improper uses are mitigated by the tort law and law of unjust enrichment remedies.

---

cannot extinguish and what actually extinguish is the legal relationships (obligations), which arise from the contract. Thus, such phrases as the end of the contract and termination of the contract are used for simplicity of legal language and in fact means the end of contractual relationship (obligation) or the termination of it. However, for reader's convenience, we will use traditional term, such as the end of the contract alternatively with the correct one – the end of contractual obligation.

303. The same logic is with the occurrence of a resolutory condition, which makes the obligation non-existent *ab initio*. Nevertheless, a resolutory condition is briefly presented in this chapter for the sake of comparison with a resolutory term.

B. Discharge by Agreement, Including Gratuitous Release

495. Freedom of contract permits parties not only to create but also to alter and even extinguish a contract (partly or in whole) by the agreement, which is a separate contract (contract of discharge). Such contract may be concluded in any form, except in cases where its obligatory written or notary form is established for the arising of the obligation (LCC Article 6.125), for example, by unilateral termination of contract (LCC Article 6.217). In practice, discharge by agreement may be an efficient bilateral alternative to the unilateral ways of discharge. Unilateral discharge is often complicated by the lack of mutuality in particular or flexibility in general, as clearly evident in cases of set-off or termination due to the breach of contract. Consensual discharge is quite often used in the dispute settlement agreements and may involve novation.

496. The contract may be discharged by onerous or gratuitous act. Onerous release is a bilateral contract regulated by the general rules on consensual discharge (LCC Article 6.125). Gratuitous discharge is called release and is regulated in LCC Article 6.129, which provides that an obligation is extinguished where the creditor releases his debtor from performance of his obligation or declares non-existence of the obligation if such release does not violate the rights of third persons towards the property of the creditor. Release must be expressed in a clear and unequivocal manner.

497. According to the principle *invito non datur beneficium*, nobody can be constrained to accept a benefit. There could be various reasons for rejecting an apparent benefit. The recipient may have personal reasons for not wishing to be under any moral obligation to the person trying to confer the benefit. Or the benefit may come with inherent burdens or disadvantages.[304] Therefore gratuitous release of a debtor from contractual obligation requires the consent of both parties and constitutes contract of gift (LCC Article 6.465). From the one side, such limitation to the surrender of claim is in stark contrast to the general regime of abandonment of property, which normally is unilateral. From the other side, discharge of a debtor is beneficial to him; therefore, the creditor's offer addressed to the debtor regarding the latter's release from performance of an obligation shall be considered accepted if it is not rejected by the debtor immediately upon receipt, i.e., the acceptance for a discharge contract is implied (LCC Article 6.173(3)).[305]

304. Christian Von Bar, Eric Clive, *et al. Principles, Definitions and Model Rules of European Private Law. Draft Common Frame of Reference (DCFR).* Full ed., Sellier, 2009, p. 343.

305. One should note that although LCC Art. 6.129(5) adopts the rule of implied acceptance only for onerous discharge and is silent on the gratuitous discharge, this rule should be applied vice versa, i.e., only for gratuitous discharge. First, a contract of gift requires consent of both parties, including the donee (debtor in discharged obligation). Second, for onerous discharge such rule can hardly be applicable if at all because onerous discharge is a bilateral contract – unsuitable to be formed by implied acceptance, especially where it includes novation, which is not presumed and should be expressly agreed by parties (LCC Art. 6.141). Therefore, it seems that LCC Art. 6.129(5) contains a drafting mistake, which may have happened due to incorrect translation from foreign sources.

498. Release is presumed to be complete unless clearly stipulated by the creditor to be partial. A creditor shall be presumed to grant a debtor release of the debt where the creditor voluntarily surrenders the document evidencing the debt to the debtor unless the circumstances indicate that the document evidencing the debt has been surrendered to the debtor after he has performed the obligation. The creditor's offer addressed to the debtor regarding the latter's onerous release from performance of an obligation shall be considered accepted if it is not rejected by the debtor immediately upon receipt. In the event where an obligation is solidary, release granted to one of the solidary debtors shall release the other co-debtors only from the performance of the discharged person's part. Express release granted by one of the solidary creditors to a debtor shall release the debtor only from the performance of that part in which the claim of that creditor can be brought. Express renunciation of a pledge (hypothec) or any other kind of security of performance of obligation made by a creditor shall not constitute any grounds for acknowledging that the debtor has been released from performance of the principal obligation.

C. Set-Off

499. An obligation can be extinguished by a set-off of a corresponding claim which is of the same kind and its time limit has expired, or the time limit of its performance is not fixed, or it is defined by the moment of a demand to perform the obligation. A set-off or a refusal to make a set-off shall have no effect in respect of the rights acquired by a third person in good faith (LCC Article 6.130). The Supreme Court has constantly rephrased this sentence as meaning that to set-off both parties should have corresponding, valid, exigible and certain claims of the same kind.[306]

500. A set-off, which is unilateral remedy and form of self-help, should be distinguished from the similar categories of netting and clearing, which also end obligations, although in a more sophisticated manner. Clearing means the process of establishing positions, including the calculation of net obligations, and ensuring that financial instruments, cash, or both, are available to secure the exposures arising from those positions (Article 2(3) of the European Market Infrastructure Regulation (EMIR)).[307] Clearing follows after a trade confirmation and matching and involves transmitting, reconciling and, in some cases, confirming transfer orders prior to settlement, potentially including the netting of orders and the establishment of final positions for settlement. Netting in the EU law is described as the conversion into one net claim or one net obligation of claims and obligations resulting from transfer orders which a participant or participants either issue to, or receive from, one or

306. Judgments of the Lithuanian Supreme Court of 11 Dec. 2006 in the civil case No. 3K-3-624/2006, of 26 Jun. 2009 in the civil case No. 3K-3-293/2009, of 19 Apr. 2010 in the civil case No. 3K-3-179/2010, of 19 Sep. 2013 in the civil case No. 3K-3-445/2013, of 23 Dec. in the civil case No. 3K-3-710/2013, etc.

307. Regulation (EU) No. 648/2012 of the European Parliament and of the Council of 4 Jul. 2012 on OTC derivatives, central counterparties and trade repositories.

more other participants with the result that only a net claim can be demanded or a net obligation be owed (Article 2(k) of the Settlement Finality Directive). It is narrow understanding on netting. In essence, netting is the agreed offsetting of mutual obligations by participants in a system. This process involves the calculation of net settlement positions and their legal reduction to a (bilateral or multilateral) net amount. Simple clearing without netting is settling trades one by one on a gross basis. Clearing can be done with position netting, i.e., simple calculation and set-off mutual obligations, which deals with liquidity risk. Clearing also can be done with netting by novation, where obligations derived from individual transfer orders are netted and replaced by a new obligation by the agreement of parties. Netting by novation usually is effected through a central counterparty (CCP), i.e., a legal person that interposes itself between the counterparties to the contracts traded on one or more financial markets, becoming the buyer to every seller and the seller to every buyer (Article 2(1) EMIR). CCP deals with liquidity and credit risk, but absorbs credit risk to itself, hence must obtain an authorisation and is supervised by national supervisory authority. Close-out netting is a special form of netting which follows certain contractually agreed events (such as the opening of insolvency proceedings), whereby all existing obligations are accelerated such that they become due immediately. Special rules on the close-out netting are included in the Law on Financial Collateral Arrangements.

501. As to the procedure of a set-off, the declaration of intention made by one party shall be sufficient for the effectuation of a set-off. No special legal action is needed. A set-off shall be effectuated by notifying about thereof the other party to the obligation. The notification shall be deemed of no effect where the set-off is made dependable upon a certain condition, or a time limit established thereto. Where the creditor possesses documentary evidence of the debt issued by the debtor, the set-off shall be effected by inscribing the declaration of a set-off in the document and by remitting it to the debtor. If a set-off does not cover the entire claim, or where the creditor still needs the documentary evidence of the debt to exercise his other rights, the creditor may retain the document with the inscription upon the set-off, though the creditor must also furnish the debtor with a written notice of the set-off (LCC Article 6.131).

502. A period of grace granted to the debtor for payment of one of the debts does not prevent the application of a set-off. The fact that the obligation must be performed in a different place shall not prevent the application of a set-off. In this event, the party to the obligation who avails himself of the right of a set-off shall be obliged to compensate for the damages suffered by the other party as a consequence of the obligation not being performed at the place agreed (LCC Article 6.132–6.133).

503. According to LCC Article 6.134, the following claims cannot be set-off: (1) claims disputed within the judicial proceedings; (2) claims arising from a contract for the constitution of a life annuity; (3) claims the performance of which is connected with the person of a concrete creditor; (4) claims for damage suffered by reason of bodily injury or death; (5) claims against the state; though, the state may effect a set-off; (6) where the subject matter of an obligation is property which is exempt from seizure; and (7) other claims, in the cases established by laws. A debtor shall not be entitled with the right of a set-off if he is bound to pay damages resulting from his actions performed with the intention to harm.

504. Special rules are applicable for the set-off in multiparty situations. First, a surety may refuse to satisfy the claim of the creditor if the principal debtor is entitled with the right of a set-off. A surety shall have the right to effect a set-off for what the creditor owes to the principal debtor, i.e., by considering the relationships between the creditor and the debtor, but the principal debtor may not effect a set-off in the interrelations of the creditor and the surety, i.e., for what the creditor owes to the surety (LCC Article 6.135). Second, there a claim is assigned, the debtor shall have the right to use for a set-off his claim against the previous creditor for the satisfaction of a claim of the new creditor (assignee) if the time limit of the debtor's claim expired before the day when the notice about the assignment of the claim was received by him, or if the time limit is not established, or if it is defined by the moment of a demand to perform the obligation (LCC Article 6.136). Third, a solidary debtor may not use a set-off for what the creditor owes to his co-debtor, except for the share of that co-debtor in the solidary debt. A debtor (whether solidary or not) may not use a set-off against one of the solidary creditors for what another co-creditor owes him, except for the share of that co-creditor in the solidary debt (LCC Article 6.137). Fourth, a person who has assumed an obligation in favour of a third person shall have no right to use his own claim against the other party to the obligation for a set-off to relieve himself (LCC Article 6.139).

505. In a multidebt situation, set-off is subordinated to the principle of cascade. LCC Article 6.138 provides that where several debts are owed by one debtor to the same creditor, a set-off shall be effected by applying rules of priority of imputation of payment established in LCC Article 6.54–6.55.

506. Having in mind the extreme importance of set-off for financial risk management, relevant question is whether Lithuanian law permits insolvency set-off. The sources of Lithuanian contract law on this point give a contradictory answer. For instance, LCC Article 6.140 seems to depart from Romanic tradition of patrimonial law by providing that after a debtor is proved to be insolvent, the claims of the creditors may be used for a set-off even though they are not due unless otherwise provided for by laws. Although the LCC seems to permit the insolvency set-off in Lithuania, however, this is wrong impression, since set-off now is directly prohibited by insolvency acts – Law on Corporate Insolvency Article 28 and Law of Bankruptcy of the Natural Persons Article 6. Even before direct statutory prohibitions came into force, case law did not allow set-off in corporate bankruptcy procedures on the reasoning that after the beginning of bankruptcy proceeding it is prohibited to perform all financial obligations and set-off would be prejudicial to other creditors.[308] Although, a set-off is prohibited against the insolvent company,

308. *See* Judgments of the Lithuanian Supreme Court of 13 Mar. 2001 in the civil case No. 3K-7-95/2001, of 28 Jan. 2008 in the civil case No. 3K-3-31/2008, of 18 Dec. 2009 in the civil case No.

there are exceptions in favour of some creditors. First, according to the Law on Tax Administration Article 87, right of set-off have tax authorities, i.e., State. Despite apparent unequal playing field for private market actors and the State, Constitutional Court has defended such privilege as legitimate on the basis of public interest.[309] However, such right exists only with respect to tax claims which have arose until the insolvency proceedings (Law on Corporate Insolvency Article 28).[310] Second, due to the insolvency of major national bank 'Snoras', such right from 2012 until the August of 2014 was set in the Law on Banks Article 85 in favour of retail investors and depositors to set-off their claims against claims of insolvent banks stemming from the loan contracts, but up to the qualified amount and in qualified circumstances. Third, right of set-off is given to financial institutions on the basis of close-out netting agreements (Law on Financial Collateral Arrangements Articles 12–13). Fourth, set-off is possible in the payments and settlement systems (Law on Payments and Settlements Finality Article 7). Fifth, set-off against insolvent bank is valid if transaction falls under the foreign applicable law permitting insolvency set-off, for example English law (Law on Banks Article 93(4)). This brief overview shows that leaving aside some marginal exceptions, only State and financial institutions can benefit from the insolvency set-off in Lithuania, whereas other creditors are left without such remedy. With this respect, Lithuania can be called the Romanic pro-debtor jurisdiction, but with controversially privileged position of State and financial institutions.

D. Unilateral Termination

507. According to LCC Article 6.125, an obligation may be extinguished by a unilateral statement of the party to the obligation only in cases provided for in law or a contract. The main instance where a contract may be terminated without the consent of other party on the basis of law is the fundamental breach. In this event, termination is unilateral and is executed as self-help remedy. However, the other party may contest termination on the lack of the fundamental breach. The Supreme Court has adopted the view of legal doctrine[311] by ruling that since a contract is a mutual transaction, it can be unilaterally terminated only in cases prescribed by law because act of termination is unilateral transaction and cannot end bilateral transaction.[312] Where the party declares about the termination, but the breach is not fundamental, the contract still exists and the party, which has tried to terminate the contract, by itself is in repudiation of contract (LCC Article 6.219).

3K-3-591/2009, etc. The Supreme Court's reasoning did rest on the premise that set-off in effect is performance of financial obligations. In light of LCC, this premise is obviously flawed because set-off is independent ground for extinguishment of obligations without performance and not the type of performance.

309. Judgment of the Lithuanian Republic Constitutional Court of 5 Jul. 2013.

310. Also *see* Judgment of the Lithuanian Supreme Court of 2 Jun. 2015 in the civil case No. 3K-3-354-969/2015.

311. Laurynas Didžiulis. *Numatomo sutarties pažeidimo doktrina: samprata, kvalifikavimo pagrindai ir teisinis poveikis.* Teisės problemos, 2007, Nr. 1. p. 52.

312. Judgment of the Lithuanian Supreme Court of 26 Jun. 2012 in the civil case No. 3K-7-297/2012.

508. If contract is not fundamentally breached, it may be unilaterally terminated only within the judicial proceedings resulting from an action of the interested party (LCC Article 6.217(4)). For example, in case of *imprevision*, the contract may be terminated only by the court decision (LCC Article 6.204). Another instance where a party should sustain from self-help and ask for judicial relief is the termination of contract after the expiry of additional period for performance if the breach was not fundamental (LCC Article 6.209(3)).

E. Novation

509. Novation (*novatio*) is ancient consensual technique used to change structural elements of the obligation by creating new and modified obligation instead of a former one. Where the intention is to change parties, novation is called subjective; in other cases, novation is objective. LCC Article 6.141 prescribes that an obligation is extinguished when the parties by their agreement substitute the existing obligation with a new obligation of different subject matter or different kind of performance. But novation shall also be effected where a new debtor is substituted for the initial debtor who is discharged by the creditor. In such a case, novation may be effected without the consent of the initial debtor. Such conduct where by the effect of a new contract, a new creditor is substituted for the previous creditor towards whom the debtor is discharged shall likewise be considered novation. However, it is prohibited to apply novation for the obligations to compensate for damage incurred by reason of bodily injury or death, also for the obligations the performance of which is connected exceptionally with the person of the parties.

510. Novation is not presumed; thus, *animus novandi* must be expressed clearly and unequivocally in all cases. Novation is possible only if the original obligation is valid; thus, novation is one of the rare exceptions, where *causa contractus* in Lithuanian law is a necessary element of a contract. According to LCC Article 6.142, any extension or contraction of the time limit of performance of an obligation, the issuance or change of a document confirming the existence of the obligation and any other accessory modifications of an obligation is not considered novation. For example, in case law novation was found where parties have changed the object of obligation (horse) and other terms of primary obligation,[313] also where parties replaced the statutory obligation to pay damages with obligation from the loan agreement.[314]

511. The question may arise whether the contract of giving in payment (*datio in solutum*) produces the objective novation. According to LCC Article 6.436, under the contract of giving in payment, the debtor transfers his property which is not pledged to a creditor to the latter's ownership in payment of his monetary or any other pecuniary debt. The person who transfers property according to the contract

313. Judgment of the Lithuanian Supreme Court of 25 Oct. 2012 in the civil case No. 3K-3-441/2012.
314. Judgment of the Vilnius District Court of 18 Oct. 2017 in the civil case No. e2-3690-661/17.

of giving in payment (debtor) assumes all duties of a seller. Despite doctrinal controversies,[315] the giving in payment (*datio in solutum*) under Lithuanian law also should be characterised as novation because LCC lists it under the category of nominate contracts, what presupposes the creation of new contract instead of the original contract from which payment obligation had arose. Moreover, the contract of giving in payment is concluded only at the moment when the property is delivered to the creditor, which means that this contract is real one and is concluded only when the other – original contract – is extinguished by proper performance.

512. Main shortcoming of novation is its negative influence upon creditor's accessory rights. LCC prescribes that right of pledge (hypothec) and other accessory rights arising from the original obligation are extinguished by novation, except in the cases where the parties agree to preserve them. If novation is made between the creditor and one of the solidary debtors with the effect of discharging from the performance of the obligation all other co-debtors, the right of pledge (hypothec) and other accessory rights arising from the original obligation may be retained only in respect of the property of the debtor who makes the new obligation (novation) with the creditor. Where novation is effected by substituting a new debtor for the initial debtor who is discharged from the performance of the obligation, pledge (hypothec) by which the performance of the obligation is secured may not be transferred to the property of the new debtor. Pledge (hypothec) attached to the property of the discharged initial debtor may be retained only with the consent of the initial debtor. In the event where a new debtor acquires from the initial debtor a thing, the rights to which are encumbered by pledge (hypothec), the pledge (hypothec) shall be retained if the new debtor consents thereto. In the event of novation of a creditor and a principal debtor, a surety of the debtor shall be released from the performance of the obligation. An obligation shall not be extinguished if the creditor requires participation of the surety in the novation and the surety refuses (LCC Article 6.143, 6.144).

---

315. One position in civilian legal doctrine is that a giving in payment does not affect a novation because the giving in payment does not create a new obligation. This position is premised on the theory that 'as a matter of law, a giving in payment is effective only upon delivery of the thing to the obligee, at which moment the obligor puts an end to is obligation without subjecting himself to a new one'. The other position is that as one of the modes of extinguishing an obligation, every giving in payment involves, even without the parties realising it, an implied novation. The obligee to a giving in payment consents to substitute the obligor's original performance with a new performance having a different object. This substitution of performances operates as an objective novation. Delivery of the thing extinguishes the obligor's prior obligation and creates a new obligation to transfer ownership of the thing. Such new obligation lasts only an instant, but the rapidity of the transactions which succeed each other do not change their nature. The giving in payment also satisfies the requirement that the parties intend to effect a novation. The giving in payment presupposes the intention to novate, since, according to its definition, the creditor renounces his old action in exchange for the one that is given him. *See* Jason P. Bergeron. *Watkins v. Freeway Motors – A Need to Clarify the Principle of Novation.* Louisiana Law Review Vol. 58, 1998, pp. 1249–1250.

II. Involuntary Grounds

A. Resolutory Modality

513. An obligation with a resolutory term is an obligation whose duration is fixed by laws or agreements of the parties and which is extinguished by the expiry of the fixed term (LCC Article 6.33). Therefore, LCC Article 6.124 states that an obligation is extinguished by the expiry of a resolutory time limit which is a condition for the termination of the obligation. For instance, the statutory twelve-month term to pay for subscribed shares of the company (Law on Stock Companies Article 45(12)) is resolutory. If such a term is expired, the contract comes to an end.[316]

514. Although it is not mentioned in the LCC chapter devoted for general provisions on extinction of obligations,[317] the contractual obligation is also extinguished in case of a resolutory condition. LCC Article 1.66(3) provides that a transaction is deemed to be concluded with a resolutory condition if the extinguishment of rights and duties arising therefrom is conditioned by the parties upon an uncertain event. Since occurrence of resolutory condition has retroactive effect and puts things back as if the obligation had not existed, technically speaking this is not 'the end', but 'extinguishment' of obligation ab initio. However, parties are free to agree that resolutory condition has effects only *ex nunc*. In such case resolutory condition, without doubt, puts the contract to an end.

B. Force Majeure

515. According to LCC Article 6.127, an obligation shall be extinguished when its performance becomes impossible as a consequence of superior force which is not imputable to the debtor. An obligation shall extinguish upon these grounds only in that event if the superior force arose before the obligation was violated by the debtor. The burden of proof of a superior force shall fall on the debtor. In the event where the performance was rendered impossible only in part, the debtor shall be discharged from the obligation upon performing that part whose performance is still possible. Force majeure is analysed in a more detailed manner in previous sections of this book.

C. The End of the Person

516. An obligation is extinguished upon the death of a party only if that obligation is purely personal (*intuitu personae*). Therefore, in case of death of a debtor,

316. Judgment of the Lithuania Supreme Court of 23 June 2021 in the civil case No. e3K-3-208-1075/2021.

317. In contrast, French CC Art. 1234 expressly attributes resolutory condition to the grounds of extinguishment of obligations.

an obligation is extinguished if it cannot be performed without the participation of the debtor himself, or if in any other way is inseparably connected with the person of the debtor. Accordingly, an obligation is extinguished upon the death of a creditor where the performance of the obligation was assigned to the creditor personally, or where it is in any other way inseparably connected with the person of the creditor (LCC Article 6.128).

517. An obligation is extinguished upon the liquidation of a legal person (a creditor or a debtor) except where it is stipulated by laws that the obligation must be performed by other persons; for example, in the case of unlimited liability company, such as a personal enterprise or commercial partnership, the obligations pass into the patrimony of members of liquidated companies (LCC Article 2.50(4)).

D. Confusion

518. An obligation shall be extinguished where the qualities of creditor and debtor are united in the same person. Where confusion ceases to exist, the obligation shall be restored unless it has been extinguished upon other grounds. The confusion of the qualities of the parties to the obligation shall not affect the rights of third persons. An obligation cannot extinguish by confusion if the claim and the debt are related to separate and unconnected property. In the event of suretyship, confusion of the qualities of creditor and debtor shall result in the extinction of the suretyship. Confusion of the qualities of surety and creditor or of surety and principal debtor shall not be the grounds for the extinction of the principal obligation. Confusion of the qualities of creditor and one of the solidary debtors or of debtor and one of the solidary creditors shall be the grounds for the extinction of the obligation only to the extent of the share of that solidary debtor or solidary creditor. A pledge (hypothec) shall be extinguished by confusion of qualities of the hypothecary creditor and the owner of the pledged property. Nevertheless, if a creditor is evicted for a cause which is not imputable to him, the pledge (hypothec) shall revive (LCC Article 6.126).

Chapter 6. Remedies

§1. General Provisions

519. It has been analysed below that a contract, even if formed, may be nevertheless avoided *ab initio* by the declaratory actions, based on the LCC general rules on transactions, such as those on error, illegality or public order. Such actions usually attract restitution of prestations.

520. In addition, Lithuanian law of obligations provides remedial framework for the enforcement of valid contracts and protection of creditor rights against non-performing debtor. To this category belongs specific performance, expectation damages, penalties, withholding of performance, termination of contract, restitution of prestations, etc. Obligational remedies are actions in personam as they are used only against debtor. Since personal remedies usually are effective as long as defendant is solvent, possible proprietary remedies, such as *rei vindicatio*, also should not be underestimated. Latter remedies occasionally could be the only ones, which offer effective protection even in the case of financially distressed defendant, for instance, where lessee of other precarious possessor is under insolvency seizure.

§2. Specific Performance and Injunctions: *Astreinte*

521. Considering availability of specific performance remedy *in abstracto*, we should recall that performance in kind is a technical principle of Lithuanian law of obligations (derived from a more fundamental and abstract principle – *pacta sunt servanda*), which requires that the obligations should be performed as agreed and normally no substitutes are allowed. The right to obtain performance includes the right to demand a repair or replacement of a defective performance, or elimination of defects in performance by other means (LCC Article 6.214). Where the debtor is failing to provide contractual performance voluntarily, it may be ordered by the court and enforced by the bailiff. There is no easy recourse for the debtor to the payment of compensatory damages in lieu of performance as in common law countries. Lithuania as the other civilian jurisdictions instead prefers specific performance, however not in such a strict form as in Soviet times any more.[318] In the current economic system, which is based on free market, there is no need for absolute adherence to the performance in kind any more, as substitutes usually are normally available. Despite this, performance in kind remains the general rule of the performance of contractual obligations.

318. Within the socialist planned economy, which was present in Lithuania during the Soviet occupation, supply chains tightly depended one on each other, so break in one transaction automatically caused shortage of goods in the subsequent transactions and the economy as whole. The market was either absent or very limited at best, thus no alternatives were easily available to the aggrieved party.

522. Availability of specific performance remedy *in concreto* depends on the type of obligation. According to LCC Article 6.213, where a party fails to perform his monetary obligation, the other party shall have the right to demand performance in kind, thus no alternatives are available. However, Lithuanian Court of Appeal in case concerning specific performance of crediting (consensual contract of loan) contract has ruled that although statutory law does not expressly provide for exceptions, it does not preclude exceptions on the basis of reasonableness, justice and fairness (LCC Article 1.5).[319] As the decision clearly creates broad exception and goes against the statutory law, it is questionable whether the Supreme Court will upheld such reasoning when similar case will go under the cassation.

523. If a party fails to perform its non-monetary obligation, normally, the other party may also demand performance in kind in a specifically prescribed manner. For instance, where a debtor fails to perform an obligation that entails doing a certain work, the creditor has the right to perform that work himself at the debtor's expense within a reasonable time and for a reasonable price unless otherwise established by laws or a contract, or he may claim damages. In these instances, the creditor has the right to file a suit and demand the creditor to pay in advance the amount necessary for performing the work. Where a debtor fails to perform an obligation that entails performing a certain work or actions which can be performed exclusively by the debtor personally, the court may upon the demand of the creditor exact a fine from the debtor in favour of the creditor (*astreinte*). According to Lithuanian legal doctrine, *astreinte* is a civil liability in the form of judicial penalty (LCC Article 6.70), analogous to statutory penalty and contractual penalty.[320] The amount of judicial penalty is determined by the court. The fine may be exacted in a lump sum, or payable for every delayed day until the full performance of the obligation by the debtor. Fine should not be applicable in the instances where the violated rights of the creditor can be defended by other forms of protection of rights, likewise where the performance of the obligation was rendered impossible not through the fault of the debtor (LCC Article 6.61).

524. Where a debtor fails to perform the obligation to deliver an individually determined thing to the creditor's ownership or possession thereof by the right of trust or use, the creditor has the right to demand that thing to be delivered. This right becomes extinct upon the thing concerned being handed over to another creditor

319. The court has dismissed the claim of debtor because after the contract formation until the court of first instance order to pay the money more than two years have passed, and during this time conditions for crediting could have been changed. *Inter alia* court has stressed the importance of responsible lending and dismissed the claim. *See* Judgment of the Lithuanian Court of Appeal of 6 Dec. 2011 in the civil case No 2A-512/2011. This reasoning seems to be wrong because the principle of responsible lending is applicable only before the conclusion of lending contract not after it. After the contract is concluded, it should be performed as agreed and no exceptions on the basis of responsible lending should be available, because it will lead to the violation of contract law rules. Performance of the contract in such cases should be mitigated by the contract law itself, which provides for both general (withholding of performance) and special grounds (refusal to grant credit) to refuse to lend money.

320. Valentinas Mikelėnas. *Lietuvos Respublikos civilinio kodekso komentaras. Šeštoji knyga. Prievolių teisė.* Justitia, 2003, I t., p. 115.

with the same kind of right. Until the thing is not handed over, the priority to receive it shall belong to the creditor in whose favour the obligation arose first of all, and in the event where it is impossible to be ascertained, to the creditor who was the first to bring the action. The creditor who cannot avail himself of the right to force the performance of the obligation in kind shall be entitled only to compensation of damage. Where a penalty is stipulated by the contract, the creditor shall have the right within his choice to claim either payment of the penalty or delivery of the individually determined thing (LCC Article 6.60).

525. Remedy of specific performance is normally unavailable in the precontractual stage, because forcing party in court to conclude the contract would undermine the freedom of contract. Under case law, even preliminary contracts, which in Lithuania are treated as contracts (albeit of organisational character), cannot be enforced for specific performance (*in natura*).[321] Single exception is a preliminary contract for the purchase of planned house by the consumer according to LCC Article 6.401, where normal contractual remedies, including specific performance, are available.[322]

526. In addition, because Lithuanian law on the specific performance remedy is modelled on UNIDROIT PICC, there are a set of general exceptions reflecting, albeit at limited extent, common law attitude to the remedy. Under LCC Article 6.213, a court may refuse to grant the remedy in one of these cases where: (1) performance of a contractual obligation in kind is impossible legally or in fact; (2) performance of a contractual obligation in kind would be greatly burdensome or expensive for the debtor; (3) the party entitled to performance may reasonably obtain performance from another source; (4) the party entitled to performance does not demand that performance within a reasonable time after he became or should have become aware of the non-performance of the contract; and (5) the non-performed obligation is of exclusively personal character. Obviously, the trickiest exception is one stating that the party entitled to performance may reasonably obtain performance from another source. This exception in UNIDROIT PICC is explained by the reason that many goods and services are of a standard kind, i.e., the same goods or services are offered by many suppliers. If a contract for such staple goods or standard services is not performed, most customers will not wish to waste time and effort extracting the contractual performance from the other party. Instead, they will go into the market, obtain substitute goods or services and claim damages for non-performance. However, the word 'reasonably' indicates that the mere fact that the same performance can be obtained from another source is not in itself sufficient, since the aggrieved party could not in certain circumstances reasonably be expected to have recourse to an alternative supplier.[323]

---

321. Judgment of the Lithuanian Supreme Court of 6 Oct. 2008 in the civil case No. 3K-3-455/2008.
322. Judgment of the Lithuanian Supreme Court of 23 Dec. 2008 in the civil case No. 3K-3-608/2008.
323. Michael Joachim Bonell, Roy Goode, Reinhard Zimmermann, *et al. UNIDROIT Principles of International Commercial Contracts. Text and Official Comment.* UNIDROIT, Rome, 2016, pp. 245–246.

527. Where the creditor does not have the right to demand for the performance in kind, the creditor may require other remedies to be invoked. But if no exceptions are applicable, the court will satisfy creditor's claim. By awarding the property in kind, the court should indicate in the judgment the value of the property, which must be exacted from the defendant, should it turn out during the enforcement of the judgment that the property awarded does not exist (CCP Article 272). If the property exists and court's order to enforce specific performance is ignored by the debtor intentionally, similarly as in common law, the debtor may face criminal liability.[324] In addition, LCC Article 6.215 provides for a fine for non-performance of the requirement to perform an obligation in kind (*astreinte*). Hence, where the debtor fails to comply with the judgment of a court ordering the performance in kind an obligation under the contract, the court shall impose a fine upon the debtor. The amount of a fine shall be established by a court with regard to concrete circumstances of the case. The fine may be imposed in the form of a lump sum payment or in the form of payment of interest on the delayed payments for every day exceeded. The fine shall be exacted in favour of the creditor. Exaction of the fine shall not release the debtor from the obligation to compensate for damages.

528. In order to provisionally secure claim for specific performance during and even two weeks before the litigation period, CCP Article 145 offers interim measures, such as seizure of an immovable thing of the defendant; entry in the Public Register on prohibition to transfer the title; seizure of movable things, money or property rights owned by the defendant and possessed by the defendant or third persons; detention of a thing owned by the defendant; appointment of an administrator of defendant's property; and prohibition of the defendant to take part in certain transactions or take other particular actions. In any case, a court shall pass a motivated ruling as to application of provisional measures. The ruling must specify the provisional measure, its scope, procedure and ways of enforcement. In case of seizure of assets, the court's ruling must contain provisions as to safekeeping, management and usage of such assets.

§3. Termination

529. In general, a contract may be terminated only within the judicial proceedings resulting from an action of the interested party based on the contractual or statutory ground of termination. For example, according to LCC Article 6.479, the lessor has the right to bring an action into a court for the termination of a contract of lease before time if: (1) the lessee uses the thing in breach of the contract or not according to the designation of the thing; (2) the lessee intentionally or through negligence worsens the state of the thing; (3) the lessee fails to pay the payment of

324. The offence is a special one and not a crime of contempt of court as is in UK. According to Lithuanian Criminal Code Art. 245, a person who fails to comply with a court's decision in civil case is considered to have committed a criminal violation and shall be punished by community service or by a fine or by restriction of liberty or by arrest.

lease; (4) the lessee fails to perform capital repair in those cases where the laws or the contract obligate him to do so; and (5) there exist other grounds provided for by the contract of lease.

530. According to LCC Article 6.125, an obligation may be extinguished by a unilateral statement of the party to the obligation only in cases provided for in law or a contract. Single statutory exception to the judicial way of termination is a case of fundamental breach (LCC Article 6.217). Fundamental breach is a most severe possible breach of contract, entitling the aggrieved party to full set of contractual remedies, including unilateral termination of contract. In determining whether a breach of a contract is fundamental, the following conditions must be taken into account: materiality of breach, i.e., whether the aggrieved party is substantially deprived of what it was entitled to expect under the contract, except in cases when the other party did not foresee or could not have reasonably foreseen such result; whether, taking into consideration the nature of the contract, strict compliance with the conditions of the obligation is of essential importance; whether the breach is made intentionally or with gross negligence; whether the breach gives the aggrieved party the basis to suppose that it cannot rely in the normal future performance of a contract; and whether the breached party, which was preparing for performance or was effectuating the performance of the contract, would suffer significant damages if the contract were terminated.

531. As unilateral out-of-court termination is a self-help remedy, it should be carried out by strictly observing LCC rules. According to LCC 6.218, the party shall be bound to give the other party notice of termination in advance within the time limit established by the contract; if the contract does not indicate such time limit, the notice of termination must be given within thirty days. Where the party who has fundamentally breached the contract submits an offer to perform the contract before the termination thereof, but this offer is belated or otherwise does not conform to the requirements of the contract, the aggrieved party loses his right to terminate the contract unilaterally unless he gives notice to the other party within a reasonable time after he became or ought to have become aware of the offer to perform the contract, or such offer fails to conform to a proper performance of the contract (LCC Article 6.218).

532. Those rules are of a great practical importance because the other party may contest unilateral out-of-court termination both on the lack of the fundamental breach and on non-observance of termination procedure. The Supreme Court has adopted the view of legal doctrine[325] by ruling that since a contract is mutual transaction it can be unilaterally terminated only in cases prescribed by law, because act of termination is unilateral transaction and cannot end bilateral transaction.[326] Where the party declares about the termination, but the breach is not fundamental, the contract still exists and the party, which has tried to terminate the contract, by

325. Didžiulis, Laurynas. *Numatomo sutarties pažeidimo doktrina: samprata, kvalifikavimo pagrindai ir teisinis poveikis.* Vilniaus universitetas. Teisės problemos, 2007, Nr. 1. p. 52.
326. Judgment of the Lithuanian Supreme Court of 26 Jun. 2012 in the civil case No. 3K-7-297/2012.

itself is in repudiation of contract (LCC Article 6.219). The party may contest bilateral out-of-court termination on grounds of invalidity of transactions.

533. The effect of termination is described in LCC Article 6.221, according to which a termination of the contract releases both parties from the performance of the contract. Termination of a contract does not preclude the right of claim for damages for non-performance of the contract, as well as the right of claim for penalty. Termination of the contract does not affect its conditions which establish the procedure of settlement of disputes, nor the validity of any other conditions which, taking in regard to their nature, are to be in force even after dissolution. Also, party of the terminated contract may claim restitution (LCC Article 6.222).

§4. *Exceptio Non Adimpleti Contractus* and Withholding Performance

534. *Exceptio non adimpleti contractus* is a defence of the debtor by proving that the creditor did not perform its contractual duties. The root of this defence lies in the imperative of fairness, which would be denied if one party could successfully sue another party without taking into regard the fact that the former by itself has breached its contractual duties. Thus, simple biblical truth 'do to others as you would have them do to you'[327] is embodied in this defence.

535. *Exceptio non adimpleti contractus* produces several effects under Lithuanian contract law. First, according to LCC Article 6.206, one party may not rely on the non-performance of the other party to the extent where such non-performance was caused by the first party's actions or inactivity, or by any other event as to which the first party bears the risk.

536. Second, such party is in breach by itself, because LCC Article 6.64 provides that the creditor is in default (*mora creditoris*) when: (1) the debtor cannot perform the obligation in the result of insufficient cooperation between the creditor and the debtor, or through any other fault of the creditor; and (2) the creditor through his own fault fails to perform his duty to the debtor; thus the debtor justifiably suspends performance of the obligation. In the event of default of the creditor, the debtor can file a suit and demand to be released from the performance of the obligation in whole or in part, conditionally or unconditionally. If the creditor violates the obligation, the debtor shall be considered not to have violated it. The debtor may not be considered in violation of the obligation as long as the creditor is considered to have violated it. The debtor has the right to demand compensation for the damage incurred in the result of the violation of obligation committed by the creditor.

327. Holy Bible, Luke 6:31.

537. Third, non-performance of obligation gives right to other party to withhold (suspend) its own performance as a form of self-help. Where the contractual obligation is counter-performed, and the party who is the first to make actions of performance fails to perform his obligation, or where it is evident that the party will delay the performance of the obligation, or if the creditor refuses to issue a quittance, to remit the documentary evidence of the debt or to inscribe in the quittance annotation about the impossibility to remit that document, the other party shall have the right to suspend the performance of his counter-obligation, or refuse to perform it altogether, inform of this to the other party and claim damages. No right of suspension shall exist where: (1) the other party produces adequate security of performance of his obligation and this will not bring about groundless delay of performance of the obligation; (2) the performance of the obligation of the other party is impossible for the reason beyond the control thereof; and (3) the performance of the obligation of the other party is prevented by the fault of the opposite party. In the event of a contractual obligation being not performed in full by one of its parties, the other party also has the right to suspend the counter-performance of his obligation, or to refuse performance to the degree correspondent to that non-performed by the party obliged to perform first. Where a party performs his counter-obligation before the party who is to perform first, the latter shall be bound to perform his obligation. The right to suspend performance of a bilateral obligation shall become extinct when the other party to the obligation presents adequate security for the performance of his obligation. The right to suspend performance of any obligation may also be invoked against the creditors of the other party to the obligation. The right of suspension of performance of an obligation must be used by the parties in good faith and reasonably (LCC Article 6.58, 6.65, 6.207).

538. Similar remedy to withholding of performance is a non-consensual security interest *in rem* – the right of retention (*ius retentionis*). According to LCC Article 4.229, a lawful possessor who has the claim in respect of the owner of the thing belonging to another is entitled to retain the thing until his claim is satisfied. In contrast to withholding of performance, which is a personal remedy, right of retention is a limited property right and once created can be used against the whole world (*erga omnes*). Also, the right of retention is not limited to bilateral obligations and may be well used in unilateral obligations. It is not divisible, and the possessor may retain the entire thing until his claim is fully satisfied (LCC Article 4.230), whereas withholding of performance should be applied only to the degree correspondent to that non-performed by the party obliged to perform first. From the other side, the right of retention may not be exercised before the term for performance of the obligation, while it is in principle possible to withhold the performance before the before the term (LCC Article 6.58). Another weakness of *ius retentionis* is CCP Article 748, according to which the right of retention comes to an end where execution of decisions is directed at retained thing. This rule creates space for easy destruction of right of retention by simulating enforcement and redirecting it against the retained thing – the option which is normally not possible in case of withholding of performance.

§5. Faulty Behaviour of the Debtor

539. Faulty behaviour of the debtor (default) constitutes breach of a contract and as such is ground for contractual remedies, including expectation damages. In general, breach of a contract is failure to perform any of the obligations arising from the contract, including defective performance and delay of a time limit of performance (LCC Article 6.205). In particular, a debtor is in default where: (1) the conditions of a contract are not performed, or are being performed improperly; (2) the debtor fails to perform the obligation within the established time limit; (3) the creditor with valid reason files a suit against him, or addresses him in an extrajudicial demand to perform the obligation; (4) the creditor demands performance of the obligation within a reasonable time established by him, but the debtor failed to perform the obligation within this time limit; (5) the debtor informs the creditor before the expiry of a time limit of his intention not to perform the obligation; and (6) performance of the obligation has become impossible due to the debtor's fault. The debtor shall be liable from the moment he is considered to be in default for any damages suffered by the creditor, except in the cases when the debtor is released from the performance of the obligation (LCC Article 6.63).

540. Where the time limit for the performance of an obligation is not fixed, the debtor is in default from the moment when the creditor made a demand in writing to perform the obligation and fixed the time limit for the performance, but the debtor has failed to perform the obligation within that time limit. The debtor is liable for all the consequences of the impossibility to perform the obligation after it was breached by the debtor, except in cases where the performance of the obligation has been rendered impossible through the fault of the creditor. After the breach of an obligation committed by the debtor, the creditor has the right to refuse acceptance of the tender offered by the debtor if the debtor does not concurrently offer compensation of damage sustained by the creditor in the result of the breach of obligation.

§6. Limitation of Actions

541. With few exceptions,[328] legal actions in Lithuanian law are limited by extinctive prescription. According to LCC Article 1.124, prescription of a legal action is a time period established by laws during which a person can defend his violated right by bringing an action.[329] It is an affirmative defence, based on a substantive rather than procedural law. The character of an affirmative defence means that the sole commencement of the extinctive prescription term does not automatically extinguish the legal claim, and defendant during the trial should ask the court to dismiss the claim on the basis of the extinctive prescription (LCC Article 1.126).

328. For example, claims of depositors for repayment of their accounts deposited in a bank or any other credit institution are not subject to prescription, according to LCC Art. 1.134.

329. Limitation of claims is not the sole incident of extinctive prescription in Lithuanian law. For example, LCC Art. 4.136 regulates extinction of a servitude through prescription.

In turn, the existence of legal claim, despite the commencement of prescription, precludes restitution where a debtor performs his obligation after the expiration of the time limit of prescription even if at the time of the performance he did not know that the time limit of prescription has expired (LCC Article 1.133).

542. Limitation of actions is governed by the substantive law applicable in determining the rights and obligations of the participants in the relevant civil legal relationship (LCC Article 1.59). Rules on limitation of actions are imperative; therefore, any agreement of the parties with an intention to modify legal regulation of prescription, i.e., to modify the time limit and the calculation thereof, is prohibited. Also, prescription may not be renounced in advance.

543. Pursuant to LCC Article 1.125, general prescription comprises a period of ten years. Claims for specific performance, avoidance or termination of a contract, restitution of prestations, use of quasi-contractual remedies, etc., all fall under such term. As the exception to the general prescription period, LCC calibrates particular kinds of claims, for whom abridged prescription is applicable. For instance, abridged one-month prescription applies to claims arising from the results of tender. Abridged six-month prescription applies in respect of claims arising from the penalties. The same abridged six-month prescription applies with respect to claims arising from the relationships between communication companies and their clients regarding dispatches sent within the territory of Lithuania with the exception of one-month prescription when the dispatches were sent abroad. Abridged one-year prescription applies with respect to insurance claims, *actio Pauliana*, claims for defects of work under the works contracts and the actions for revocation of gift by the donor or by his heirs. Abridged two-year prescription applies for claims arising from defects in the goods, services or digital content. Abridged three-year prescription applies with respect to claims for the compensation of damage and claims for avoidance of residential lease contract. Abridged five-year prescription shall be applied with respect to claims for the recovery of interest and any other periodical payments. Other laws or applicable international treaties may also prescribe prescription terms; for instance, according to CMR Convention Article 32, the period of limitation for an action arising out of carriage under Convention is one year. Nevertheless, in the case of wilful misconduct, or such default as in accordance with the law of the court or tribunal seized of the case is considered as equivalent to wilful misconduct, the period of limitation is three years.

544. Prescription starts its run from the day on which the right to bring an action may be enforced. Normally, the right to bring an action arises from the day on which a person becomes aware or should have become aware of the breach of his right. But this is just general rule, and the application highly depends on the nature of claim; for instance, as the sole occurrence of wrong is not sufficient cause of action in damages claims, prescription does not run until the occurrence of loss.[330] Where there is a time limit established for the performance of an obligation, prescription of

330. Judgment of the Lithuanian Supreme Court of 28 Dec. 2017 in the civil case No. e3K-3-457-684/2017.

a claim arising from such obligation starts its run upon the expiry of the time limit allotted for the performance of that obligation. Where a time limit for the performance of an obligation is not established, prescription runs from the moment when a claim to perform the obligation is brought. Subrogation and other substitution of persons in an obligation does not affect the course of prescription – the time limit and the procedure of its calculation, unless laws provide for otherwise. In contrast, prescription of claims arising from primary recourse shall start its run from the moment when the principal obligation is performed. In the event of a continuous breach, i.e., it happens every day (a person fails to perform the actions he is bound to perform, or performs the actions he has no right to perform or does not discontinue another violation), prescription for actions brought upon activity or inactivity that occurred on a concrete day shall start its run from that every day (LCC Article 1.127).

545. It has been explained above that legal action should be accepted by the court irrespective of the expiry of prescription. The expiration of prescription may produce legal effects, i.e., dismissal of the claim, only if invoked as an affirmative defence by a party to the defendant. Due to the principle of accessoriness, expiration of prescription with respect to the principal claim shall have the same effect likewise on the accessory claims (penalty, pledge, suretyship, etc.), even though the prescription of the latter may not have expired. Nonetheless, if the court acknowledges the time limit of prescription as expired due to important reasons, the violated right must be protected and the expired time limit restored (LCC Article 1.131, 1.135).

§7. Damages and Exemption Clauses

I. General Framework of Lithuanian Civil Liability System

546. In Lithuanian law, damages are a form of application of civil liability. Thus, damages remedy is strictly related to the concept of civil liability. Whereas in some countries 'civil liability' is just a vague notion meaning non-criminal liability in case of breach of law, in Lithuanian law civil liability has fixed definition, which clearly distinguishes damages from other remedies.

547. According to LCC Article 6.245, civil liability is a pecuniary obligation one party of which shall have the right to claim for compensation of damage or demand payment of the penalty (fine, interest), and the other party shall be bound to make compensation for damage arising therefrom, or pay the penalty (fine, interest). Based on such definition, civil liability in Lithuanian case law is usually understood as providing only compensation[331] and sometimes prevention or education,[332] thus excluding punishment and restitution. However, such narrow view sometimes fails to fully reflect whole remedial system of the LCC itself, and fundamentals of some

331. Judgment of the Lithuanian Supreme Court of 9 May 2012 in the civil case No. 3K-3-214/2012.
332. Judgment of the Lithuanian Supreme Court of 17 Nov. 2008 in the civil case No. 3K-7-496/2008.

remedies and at some point is misleading.[333] For instance, contractual penalty not only covers loss in advance (as stipulated damages) but also may provide extra monetary punishment for breaching party. The same is with compensation of non-pecuniary loss, which is basically vague notion and, in practice, may include some punishment elements. Default interest in Lithuanian case law called 'compensatory interest' for the non-performance of monetary obligations (moratory damages) is not 'compensatory' at all where there are no present market possibilities to profit from such money, and the whole interest is just presumed loss, more similar to penalty than compensatory damages. Another example is *de facto* restitution provided in the form of damages, thus restitutionary damages, because LCC Article 6.249(2) expressly permits the plaintiff to include defendant's wrongful gains into award of damages. Moreover, there are cases where Lithuanian courts *de facto* have awarded nominal damages, which have nothing in common with real compensation, only with satisfaction.[334] Despite this limited diversity of heads of damages, compensation remains main goal of civil liability in general and of damages in particular.

548. Lithuanian private law has unified notion of civil liability, encompassing both tort law and contract law damages, as well as contractual penalties. These two areas are delimitated by the principle of *non-cumul*, which restricts application of tort law remedies in contractual relations. This is clearly established in LCC Article 6.245, according to which contractual liability is a pecuniary obligation resulting from a failure to perform a contract or from its defective performance where one party of the obligation has the right to claim for compensation of damage or demand

333. In my opinion, in order to maintain the efficiency of civil liability, it is crucial to move away from narrow and outdated approach about civil liability as solely compensatory instrument and start to interpret its functions more broadly. Being type of legal liability, civil liability is a negative pecuniary reaction to the civil wrong, functioning as private legal sanction applied in order to restore justice and deter other wrongs. From a functional perspective, the civil liability is related to two legally significant aims: the implementation (restoration) of justice by awarding damages (thereby realising the individual function of civil liability) and the enforcement of lawful conduct by coordinating behaviour of general public (realising the social function of civil liability). The individual function of civil liability is carried out between the defendant and the claimant by restoring or implementing justice. In the context of civil liability, the justice is primarily implemented by compensating the claimant. The significance of the compensatory function is that civil liability restores the claimant's pecuniary position, which in turn allows him to safely withdraw from the market or continue its activities. Furthermore, the individual function of civil liability can be realised by restoring to previous position also the defendant, if he benefits from the wrongs. It is important to demotivate the defendant, especially if he has the fiduciary obligations against the claimant. The social function of civil liability seeks to ensure the desired public behaviour and avoid the undesired one, which is legally considered to be unlawful. The preventive effect is extremely relevant for the wealthy persons, which tend to be more emotionally attached to wealth than others; therefore, monetary sanctions have a serious impact on them. The efficiency of civil liability prevents the occurrence of damage and helps to reach specific aims of the financial regulation. Moreover, the concept of civil liability decreases both individual and social costs of behaviour by limiting economically inefficient (harmful) conduct.

334. *See*, for example, Judgments of the Vilnius City Court of 8 Dec. of 2011 in the civil case No 2A-350-262/2011 (one litas (former Lithuanian currency unit) for the illegal entry into the premises of the plaintiff), of Klaipėda District Court of 19 Dec. 2013 in the civil case No 2A-1546-460/2013 (one litas for the offensive comments in the social media about two prosecutors), etc.

payment of penalty (fine, interest), and the other party is bound to make compensation for damage, or to pay penalty (fine, interest) caused by the failure to perform the contract, or by a defective performance thereof. Non-contractual (tortious) liability is a pecuniary obligation which is not related to contractual relations, except in cases where it is established by laws that tortious liability shall also result from damage related to contractual relations. Tort law in contractual disputes is applicable where loss stems from precontractual wrongs, void contracts, wrongs against third parties, post-contractual wrongs and only in specifically prescribed cases in contractual situations, like in case of product liability (LCC Article 6.292).[335] The principle of *non-cumul* in Lithuanian case law is applied quite strictly. It has even included the protection of a negative interest into the scope of contractual damages in order to exclude tort liability between counterparties in tort-like situations.[336]

549. Civil liability has two stages in its life cycle: first, civil liability obligation arises under prescribed conditions (so-called conditions of civil liability) and, second, civil liability is applied in form of damages or penalty, if no justifications are present. Civil liability arises where its conditions, constituting cause of action, are present and no notice to the other party or approval by the court is needed for this. The civil liability conditions are as follows: civil wrong, fault, loss and causal link. Normally, all of those conditions, except fault, should be proved by the plaintiff (*actori incumbit probatio*).

550. Civil wrong in Lithuanian law comes under the heading of 'unlawful actions'. LCC Article 6.246 broadly prescribes that civil liability arises from non-performance of a duty established by laws or a contract (unlawful refrainment from acting), or from performance of actions that are prohibited by laws or a contract (unlawful acting), or from violation of the general duty to behave with care. Those are primary liability duties, breach of whom creates secondary duty – civil liability to repair loss. Damage caused by completely lawful actions must be compensated only in cases expressly specified by laws, for example for establishment of servitude (LCC Article 4.129) or expropriation of property (LCC Article 4.100). Also, it may be established by laws that a person shall be bound to compensate damage he has not caused himself but is responsible for the actions of another person who inflicted the damage (vicarious liability).

551. In addition to unlawful actions, LCC includes the element of fault as an independent condition of civil liability. According to LCC Article 6.248, civil liability shall arise only upon the existence of the fault of the obligated person, except in the cases established by laws or a contract when civil liability arises without fault. The fault of a debtor shall be presumed, except in the cases established by laws.

335. It means that in Lithuanian law, there is no space for erosion of contract law by tort law remedies, as is evidenced in US law by the notable Grant Gilmore's notion – 'the death of contract'. *See* Grant Gilmore. *The Death of Contract.* Columbus: Ohio State University Press, 1974.

336. In a particular case, Lithuanian Supreme Court has characterised liability of a railway works contractor as contractual in the case where locomotive of the customer collided with the excavator of the subcontractor who was performing the works contract. *See* Judgment of the Lithuania Supreme Court of 24 Mar. 2021 in the civil case No. e3K-3-44-313/2021.

Fault may be intentional or constitute negligence. A person is in fault where taking into account the essence of the obligation and other circumstances he failed to behave with the care and caution necessary in the corresponding conditions. Where damage has also been caused through the fault of the creditor himself, the repairable damages shall be diminished in proportion to the degree of gravity of the creditor's fault committed, or the debtor can be released from civil liability.

552. It can be seen from above that the notion of fault *stricto sensu* is expressed in objective (as non-compliance with *bonus pater familias* standard) rather than subjective way (as defendant's mental relationship with his wrong); hence notion of fault duplicates with the breach of duty of care as type of unlawful actions. This creates deep practical problems because if negligent conduct is attributed to the condition of unlawful actions, it should be proved by the plaintiff, whereas if it belongs to the condition of fault, it is presumed and burden of proof lies on the defendant to deny his fault.[337] Case law has varied on such attribution in different types of cases creating different results,[338] however, without any persuasive analytical reasoning that why such attribution is granted in favour of preferred civil liability condition. Taking into account functional, historical and comparative perspective,[339] more pragmatic and accurate way is to accept the erosion of fault, its gradual merger with the condition of unlawfulness and treat fault as a type of civil wrong, the other one being innocent wrong in case of strict liability. Normally, fault as an independent condition of civil liability is not appropriate, because it not only creates aforementioned uncertainty for the attribution of negligent conduct but also distorts coherence in a whole system of civil obligations.[340] Fault recovers its significance only in prescribed situations, where gross negligence or intent is a necessary condition of liability. For instance, according to case law, company director's liability against third parties may arise only if gross fault (intent or gross negligence) is present.[341] The same is with tort of abuse of process, where gross fault is implied in cause of action (LCC Article 1.137, CCP Article 95).

---

337. Such problem is present also in other jurisdictions, which distinguish fault and unlawfulness as separate conditions. *See* Pierre Widmer; *et al. Unification of Tort Law: Fault.* Kluwer Law International, 2005, p. 356.
338. Judgments of the Lithuanian Supreme Court where negligent conduct was attributed to the fault: of 26 Sep. 2011 in the civil case No 3K-3-356/2011; of 20 Apr. 2012 in the civil case No. 3K-3-92/2012; of 26 Jun. 2009 in the civil case No 3K-3-304/2009; of 21 Jun. 2006 in the civil case No 3K-3-422/2006; etc. Judgments of the Lithuanian Supreme Court where negligent conduct was attributed to the unlawfulness: of 31 Mar. 2003 in the civil case No. 3K-3-438/2003; of 25 Apr. 2005 in the civil case No 3K-3-222/2005; of 21 Feb. 2011 in the civil case No 3K-3-59/2011; of 13 Feb. 2012 in the civil case No 3K-3-6/2012; etc.
339. *See* Bénédicte Fauvarque-Cosson, Denis Mazeaud, *et al. European Contract Law: Materials for a Common Frame of Reference: Terminology, Guiding Principles, Model Rules.* Sellier, 2008, p. 279; Pierre Widmer, *et al. Unification of Tort Law: Fault.* Kluwer Law International, 2005, p. 341.
340. Suppose, the parties have agreed for the obligation to achieve specific result (*obligation de resultat*), instead of obligation to make best efforts (*obligation de moyens*). If such obligation is breached, the independent requirement of fault would mean that liability would be applicable if at least negligence (failure to make best efforts) is established. The fault, in such scenario, will soften contractual liability in conflict with a contract itself.
341. *See* Judgment of the Lithuanian Supreme Court of 1 Feb. 2012 in the civil case No 3K-3-19/2012.

553. Next condition of civil liability is damage (loss), which may be pecuniary and non-pecuniary. According to LCC Article 6.249, pecuniary damage includes the amount of the loss or damage of property sustained by a person and the expenses incurred (direct damage) as well as the lost profits, i.e., the profit he would have received if unlawful actions had not been committed. Where the amount of damage cannot be proved by the party with precision, it shall be assessed by a court. If the person who is liable towards another has derived benefit from his unlawful actions, upon the demand of the creditor the benefit received may be attributed to damages. The court may postpone the evaluation of damage which has not yet occurred or may evaluate future damage upon assessment of its real probability. In such cases, the court may adjudge either to pay a lump sum or to make instalment payments, or it may obligate the debtor to furnish security upon compensation for damage. In addition to the direct damage and the lost profits, damages shall comprise: (1) reasonable costs to prevent or mitigate damage; (2) reasonable costs incurred in assessing civil liability and damage; and (3) reasonable costs incurred in the process of recovering damages within extrajudicial procedure. Damage is assessed according to the prices valid on the day when the court judgment was passed unless the law or the nature of the obligation requires the application of prices that were valid on the day the damage arose or on the day when the action was brought. In case where one and the same action has created both damage and benefit for the aggrieved person, the benefit received may, to the extent that this does not contradict to the criteria of reasonableness, good faith and justice, be computed into damages.

554. Non-pecuniary damage includes a person's suffering, emotional experiences, inconveniences, mental shock, emotional depression, humiliation, deterioration of reputation, diminution of possibilities to associate with others, etc., evaluated by a court in terms of money. Non-pecuniary damage shall be compensated in all cases where it is incurred due to crime, health impairment or deprivation of life. Non-pecuniary damage can be compensated in other cases only if it is directly provided by statutory law. From the perspective of contract law, most important statutory ground to claim non-pecuniary loss is set in the Law on the Protection of Consumers Article 3(1) 5, which entitles consumers to seek redress for non-pecuniary loss even in cases unrelated to personal injury or crime, for example, where newlyweds did not get their photos from the photographers after their wedding.[342]

555. The court in assessing the amount of non-pecuniary damage shall take into consideration the consequences of such damage sustained, the gravity of the fault of the person by whom the damage is caused, his financial status, the amount of pecuniary damage sustained by the aggrieved person, also any other circumstances of importance for the case, likewise to the criteria of good faith, justice and reasonableness (LCC Article 6.250).

556. Last, but not least, condition of civil liability is a causation. According to LCC Article 6.247, only such damage can be compensable which is related to

342. *See* Judgment of the Klaipėda City Court of 2 Jul. 2012 in the civil case No. 2-100-613/2012.

actions (acting or refrainment from acting) giving rise to civil liability of the debtor in such a manner that the damage, taking into account its nature and that of the civil liability, can be imputed to the debtor as a result of his actions (acting or refrainment from acting). Lithuanian courts often explain causation as twofold: factual and legal;[343] however, they have used this distinction so far mostly as an abstract introduction into case reasoning, than a real workable tool. Most civil liability cases in Lithuania were solved within the test of *conditio sine qua non*, with a small number of exceptions where factual causation was extended by 'indirect causation'.[344] Latter instance of causation is rare manifestation of legal causation in Lithuanian case law. However, 'indirect causation' should not be confused with the synonymous term known in French law, which limits cause in fact by cutting down causal link as inadequate. Lithuanian version of indirect causation works the opposite way – it extends liability beyond the scope of definite factual causation by attributing claimants' loss to the defendants' wrong even if such wrong did not unequivocally produce loss but substantially affected the arousal of it. Therefore, it seems that Lithuanian courts under the label 'indirect causation' have introduced into Lithuanian law the substantial factor doctrine, known in American tort law.[345]

557. Second stage in the life of a civil liability is its performance. Performance may be voluntary or enforced by courts.[346] In the latter case, liability is said to be 'applied'. During this stage two things should be done.

558. First, even if conditions for civil liability are established, court should check whether affirmative defences are successfully proved by the defendant or otherwise established. Affirmative defences which completely or in part may release a person from his civil liability are: intervening cause (force majeure, actions of state and actions of a third party), actions of the aggrieved party, state of necessity necessary defence and self-help. Force majeure are unavoidable events that cannot be controlled or escaped by the debtor, and which were not and could not have been foreseen (LCC Article 6.212). Actions of state are binding and unforeseen actions (acts) of public authorities which render the performance of an obligation impossible and which could not be disputed by the parties. Activities of a third person are injurious actions (acting or refrainment from acting) committed by a person for whom neither the creditor nor the debtor is liable. Actions of the aggrieved person are the actions committed through the fault of the aggrieved person himself and resulting in the appearance or increase of his damages. Such actions may be

343. *See* Judgments of the Lithuanian Supreme Court of 30 Mar. 2005 in the civil case No 3K-3-206/2005, of 9 Nov. 2005 in the civil case No. 3K-3-556/2005, of 11 Dec. 2007 in the civil case No 3K-3-554/2007, of 9 Jun. 2008 m. in the civil case No 3K-3-322/2008; etc.

344. *See* Judgments of the Lithuanian Supreme Court of 17 Apr. 2002 in the civil case No 3K-3-614, of 3 Sep. 2003 in the civil case No. 3K-3-764/2003, of 9 Mar. 2005 in the civil case No. 3K-3-156/2005, of 26 Nov. 2007 in the civil case No. 3K-7-345/2007, of 10 Nov. 2008 in the civil case No. 3K-3-476/2008.

345. On the substantial factor doctrine in US law, *see* Deborah DeMott. *Causation in the Fiduciary Realm*. Boston University Law Review, vol. 91, pp. 864–865.

346. In terms of constitutionality, quite anomalous is power granted by the Code of Administrative Violations Art. 644 to police and other administrative institutions to award out-of-court compensation, for loss made by administrative offences, together with administrative sanction.

expressed in the form of consent of the aggrieved person to suffer the damage or to assume the risk. This consent of the aggrieved person may be the grounds for exemption from civil liability only under condition that such consent and causing of damage is not contrary to mandatory legal norms, public order, good morals, the criteria of good faith, reasonableness and justice. The state of necessity is the actions of a person by which he is compelled to cause damage in order to avert danger to himself, to other persons or to their rights, as well as to the interests of the society or the state by avoiding imminent occurrence of greater damage to the person who has already sustained damage or to any other person, providing that causing the damage in the concrete circumstances was the only way of avoiding greater damage. The court, taking into consideration the circumstances of the case and acting in accordance with the principles of good faith and justice, may obligate the damage to be compensated by the person in whose interests the injurious act was committed. Necessary defence is considered to be the actions committed by a person with the purpose of defending himself or another person, property, inviolability of dwelling, other rights, interests of the society or the state against commenced or imminent unlawful dangerous assault, providing that such actions do not exceed the limits of necessary defence. Self-help is considered to be the actions of a person by which he lawfully enforces his right in the instances where competent authorities fail to provide timely assistance and where without such actions the implementation of that right would be rendered impossible or essentially obstructed. Nevertheless, a person who employs self-help unlawfully or without due cause shall have to compensate the damage caused. For instance, self-help is unilateral termination, suspension of performance, set-off and retention of goods.

559. Other grounds for exemption from civil liability or for the non-application thereof may be established by laws or the agreements of the parties. For instance, ratification defence against claim for unauthorised trading stems from the principal's right to ratify unauthorised transaction according to LCC Article 2.136.

560. As to the agreements of parties upon exclusion or limitation of civil liability, LCC Article 6.252 prescribes that an agreement of the parties upon exclusion of civil liability for damages (damage) sustained by the reason of the debtor's intentional fault or gross negligence, as well as any agreement concerning the limitation of the amount of civil liability for damages sustained by the reasons indicated above shall be null and void. It shall be prohibited to exclude or limit civil liability for impairment of health, deprivation of life or non-pecuniary damage caused to another. The mandatory legal norms establishing civil liability, as well as the form or amount thereof, cannot be modified by an agreement of the parties.

561. Second, civil liability is applied in the form of damages, penalty or reparation in kind. Latter remedy is very rarely used in Lithuanian civil litigation, because claimants usually ask for monetary award – damages or penalties. Damages may be distinguished into compensatory, i.e., based on plaintiff's loss (LCC Article 6.249(1)) and restitutionary, i.e., based on defendant's wrongful gains (LCC Article 6.249(2)). Main principle in law of damages is *restitutio ad integrum*. According to LCC Article 6.251, the damage incurred must be compensated in full, except in cases when limited liability is established by laws or a contract. However, the court, having considered the nature of liability, the financial status of the parties and their interrelation, may reduce the amount of damages if awarding full compensation would lead to unacceptable and grave consequences. However, the reduction may not exceed the amount for which the debtor has or ought to have covered his civil liability by compulsory insurance. Where contract is breached, compensatory damages protect expectation interest, i.e., interest of the creditor in performance of obligation by the debtor. Therefore, contractual compensatory damages are called expectation damages and seek to put the claimant in position where contract would be perfectly performed. Such basis for damages is progressive, and next to out-of-pocket damages enables award of lost profits, however may be a weak remedy in case of failed markets. If tort is committed, normal remedy is reliance damages, which seeks to put plaintiff into a position where he has no prejudicial contact with defendant at all. Reliance damages are regressive, hence normally do not award lost profits, however, by focusing on the stability of plaintiffs' position offer stronger protection in case of failed markets. Finally, restitutionary damages protect restitutionary interest and may be perfect remedy to disgorge ill-gotten gains by the dishonest fiduciaries.

II. Contractual Damages

562. Distinction of liability into primary and secondary duties is properly reflected in the rules of LCC. According to LCC Article 6.256, every person shall have a duty to perform his contractual obligations in a proper way and without delay. Where the performance of a contract falls within professional activities of one of the parties, the party concerned must perform the contract in accordance also with the requirements attached to that professional activity. Those are the primary duties of liability.

563. Where a person fails to perform his contractual obligation or performs it defectively, he shall be liable to compensation for damage caused to the other contracting party and/or pay a penalty (fine, interest). A debtor who engages the services of third persons in performance of his obligation is liable towards the creditor where non-performance of the obligation or defective performance thereof results from the fault of the third persons concerned unless the law or the contract provides for the liability of the direct executor. Those rules reflect secondary duties of liability, which in essence are contractual liability itself.

564. In contrast with common law jurisdictions and leading soft law instruments (UNIDROIT PICC Article 7.4.1 and DCFR Article III.–3:701), normally contractual liability under Lithuanian law is applicable only for a fault. As an exception, strict liability regime is applicable for an enterprise (businessman). If such person fails to perform its contractual obligation or performs it defectively, it shall be liable in all cases unless it proves that non-performance or defective performance of the obligation has resulted from a superior force unless it is otherwise provided for by laws or the contract. However, strict liability regime is softened by the rule that the non-performing party (enterprise or businessman) shall be liable only for the damage which it foresaw or could reasonably have foreseen at the time of the conclusion of the contract as being likely to result from the non-performance of obligation. This last rule creates a subtle difference for the establishment of legal causation in the case of businessman's strict liability in comparison with a general fault-based regime for other debtors because latter by examining legal causation also takes into account foreseeability, but at the moment of breach, whereas in strict liability regime foreseeability is tied to the more remote moment of contract formation. It is clear that before the breach it is much easier for debtor to foresee future events, than at the time of contract formation. It follows that under Lithuanian contract law it is easier to establish legal causation under general fault-based regime than in case of businessman's strict liability.

565. Damages are to be assessed either in the currency in which the monetary obligation was expressed or in the currency in which the loss was suffered, whichever is more appropriate to the parties according to the circumstances of the case. Unless otherwise agreed, interest on the damage for non-performance of an obligation shall be calculated from the time of the non-performance. Where the aggrieved party dissolves the contract on the grounds that the other party has violated it and makes a replacement contract within a reasonable time, it may claim from the accountable party the difference between the contract price and the price of the replacement contract as well as damages for any further loss (LCC Article 6.258). It is not required for the replacement contract to have identical terms as the original one; it is sufficient that the new contract can economically replace the original one. For instance, the original work contract may be replaced by an alternative work contract with shorter time limits to perform work.[347]

566. A debtor is deemed to be in delay of performance where he fails to perform it before the expiry of the time limit established for the performance of the obligation. The debtor who is in delay is liable towards the creditor for the compensation of damage caused by the delay in performance, as well as for the impossibility to perform the obligation which accidentally results from the delay. The creditor has the right to refuse performance offered to him after the delay therein and may claim for damages caused by the delay in performance where the debtor's default by delay in performance results in the creditor's loss of any interest in that performance. The debtor is not considered to be in delay as long as the obligation cannot be performed as a consequence of delay in the performance made by the creditor himself (LCC Article 6.260).

567. In order to balance contractual liability, LCC expressly provides a defence of contributory fault and establishes duty to mitigate damage. Hence, according to LCC Article 6.259, in case of the non-performance of an obligation or defective performance thereof resulting from the fault of both parties, the liability of the debtor may be correspondingly reduced, or the debtor may be fully relieved from liability.

347. Judgment of the Lithuania Supreme Court of 15 Dec. 2021 in the civil case No. e3K-3-325-378/2021.

In contrast, contributory fault defence in tort law is possible only in case of creditor's gross fault (LCC Article 6.282). The defence should also be applied to the cases where a creditor through his own intentional fault or negligence contributes to the failure in the performance of the contractual obligation or the increase of damage caused by its defective performance, likewise when the creditor through his intentional fault or negligence failed to take any measures to reduce the damage. The defence applies also in the cases where the liability of the debtor for the non-performance of the obligation or for its defective performance arises in accordance with laws or the contract irrespective of the existence of his fault. A creditor is in delay of performance if he refuses to accept the proper performance proposed by a debtor or fails to perform the actions until the performance of which the debtor could not perform his obligations. Where the creditor is in delay, the debtor acquires the right to be compensated for damage caused by the delay unless the creditor proves that the time limit which has been set for the performance lapsed without the obligation having been performed neither through the fault of the creditor himself nor through the fault of the persons obligated by laws or authorised by the creditor to accept the performance. With regard to monetary obligations, the debtor should not be obliged to pay interest (penalty) for the period of the creditor's delay (LCC Article 6.262).

III. Default Interest

568. Special rules are applicable for delay of the performance of monetary obligations. A specific feature of all monetary obligations is their potential to generate interest on a prescribed rate. Interest on obligations may be fixed by laws or agreements of the parties. Where the interest is established by laws, the parties may agree in writing upon a higher interest providing that such agreement is not contrary to laws or the principles of good faith and reasonableness. Interests are of two types: payment interest and default interest (in French tradition labelled as 'moratory damages'). Payment interest accrues if a party lawfully, i.e., without any breach of a contract, holds money gotten from another, as in the case of a loan. Default interest accrues in case of unlawful holding of money owed to another, as in case of unjustified delay to pay for services. In principle, default interest on a monetary obligation is payable even without any evidence of loss.[348] Thus, the debtor who is in delay of the performance of an obligation to pay a sum of money is bound to pay default interest resulting from the contracts or laws which is considered to be minimal damages.

348. Default interest for the non-performance of monetary obligations in Lithuanian case law is called 'compensatory interest'. *See* Judgment of the Lithuanian Supreme Court of 8 Jun. 2012 in the civil case No. 3K-3-283/2012. Such label may be misleading, because the default interest may not be 'compensatory' at all where there are no current market possibilities to profit from such money and the whole interest is just presumed loss, more similar to *ex ante* fixed penalty than *ex post* compensatory damages.

569. According to LCC Article 6.210, a debtor is bound to pay an interest at the rate of 5% per annum upon the sum of money subject to the non-performed obligation unless any other rate of interest has been established by the law or contract. Where both parties are businessmen or private legal persons, the interest at the rate of 6% per annum shall be payable for a delay in payment unless any other rate of interest has been established by the law or contract. The last rule nowadays is rarely used because according to special Law on the Prevention of Late Payment in Commercial Transactions, where a debtor fails to meet his monetary obligation in a commercial contract, the payable interest rate consists of simple interest for late payment at a rate which is equal to the sum of the reference rate[349] and at least eight percentage points. The creditor is entitled to interest for late payment where the creditor has fulfilled its contractual and legal obligations and has not received the amount due on time, unless the debtor is not responsible for the delay. In addition, the creditor is entitled to obtain from the debtor, as a minimum, a fixed sum of EUR 40 (Law on the Prevention of Late Payment in Commercial Transactions Article 7) and recovery of any other damage he is able to prove.

570. Default interest accruing during the period from the breach until the commencement of the case in the court is pretrial interest. After the commencement of the case in the court, pretrial interest is replaced by the procedural interest on the same rate based on LCC Article 6.37(2), according to which the debtor may be asked to pay a certain interest established by laws on the sum adjudged to the creditor for the period from the moment of the commencement of the case in the court until the final execution of the judgment. This is understandable because both pretrial and procedural interests are manifestations of the same default interest and should not duplicate each other. It is prohibited to calculate interest on the interest calculated previously (double interest), except in the cases established by laws or agreement of the parties if such agreement is not contrary to the requirements of good faith, reasonableness and justice. This rule only precludes calculation of the double interest of the same type, for example default interest from the default interest, and is inapplicable where default interest accrues from failure to pay payment interest. However, in the case of loan, LCC Article 6.874 controversially permits capitalisation of procedural interest on top of pretrial interest.[350]

571. Another practical issue is concurrence between default interest and stipulated penalty for delay expressed on a daily basis. This issue is solved by LCC Article 6.258, according to which where a claim for compensation of damage is being made, the penalty shall be included in the damages. It means that the creditor

349. Reference rate means either the interest rate applied by the European Central Bank to its most recent main refinancing operations or the marginal interest rate resulting from variable-rate tender procedures for the most recent main refinancing operations of the European Central Bank.

350. In case of failure by the borrower to repay timely the amount of the loan, the borrower must pay the pretrial interest established in LCC Art. 6.210 hereof from the day when the amount of the loan had to be repaid until the day of its actual repayment, notwithstanding the payment of the procedural interest set forth in LCC Art. 6.37 hereof, unless otherwise established in the loan agreement.

may not claim both at once – penalty and default interest – for the same breach but may elect and claim only one of those sums, apparently the bigger one.[351]

§8. Restitution

I. Legal Nature and Types of Restitution

572. Restitution *largo sensu* is a legal remedy used to avoid or reverse unjustified enrichment and assessed by reference to the benefit obtained by the defendant. Whereas in common law, restitution represents a unified body of law,[352] in civil law jurisdictions, it is calibrated and dispersed bundle of rules.[353] Despite this, there is sign of recent trend to unify and systematise this remedy within the civilian private law,[354] and this trend directly relates to Lithuanian law which establishes a unified

351. Judgment of the Lithuanian Supreme Court of 12 Oct. 2007 in the civil case No 3K-7-304/2007.
352. The common law of restitution is concerned with all claims where the remedy which the claimant seeks is assessed with reference to the defendant's gain. Such remedies are available in three situations: first, where it can be shown that the defendant has been unjustly enriched – here the only remedies which are available are personal restitutionary remedies; second, where the defendant has committed a wrong for which restitutionary relief may be available – here the remedy may be restitutionary, but it can also be compensatory; finally, where the claimant wishes to vindicate his or her property rights – here the remedy is typically restitutionary and, depending on whether or not the defendant retains property in which the claimant has a proprietary interest, the restitutionary remedy will either be proprietary or personal. Thus, the common law of restitution is not confined to the law of unjust enrichment but is simply a body of law concerning a common category of remedies which may be awarded in particular circumstances. There are a number of common principles and questions of policy which relate to all restitutionary claims regardless of the cause of action. *See* Graham Virgo. *The Principles of the Law of Restitution.* 3 ed., Oxford University Press, 2015, p. 17–18.
353. For example, as before the amendments of French *Code civil* in 2016 has noted S. Whittaker, the French law of restitution contains a striking paradox. For a while it recognises *enrichissement sans cause* as a distinct and 'general' ground of recovery, and the wider picture of the French law of restitution (if we can properly call it that) is remarkably disparate and unsystematic, in particular when compared to its law of contract and delict. There has, moreover, been in general little attempt to relate, let alone to integrate, the various legal grounds of the reversal of unjust or unjustified enrichments. Nowhere is the resulting diversity more apparent than in the measure or rather various measures of recovery which are permitted in French law. Thus, in the case of recovery of undue payments, the measure of recovery depends, in particular, on a distinction between the defendant's good or bad faith or other fault; a minor's restitutionary obligation under a rescinded contract is restricted to any surviving value and the defendant to a claim based on *enrichissement sans cause* is in principle liable for the *lesser* sum as between the cost of the procuring of the defendant's enrichment and any increase in value which it may have caused the defendant. This diversity and lack of overall justifying principle may well in part be due to the way in which the Code was written, but it may also be due to the special role given to the principle of *enrichissement sans cause* in French law as a specific and independent, but therefore necessarily severely restricted, cause of recovery. The expression *obligations de restitution* is not, therefore, used to refer to the body of law concerning the reversal of unjust enrichments in the way in which 'restitution' is in English law. *See* J. Bell, S. Boyron and S. Whittaker. *Principles of French Law.* 2nd ed., Oxford University Press, 2008, p. 420–422.
354. Best examples are Quebec Civil Code of 1991 and amendments of French *Code civil* in 2016, which created a separate section for a restitution within the law of obligations.

concept of restitution as a remedy. This is because Lithuanian civil law has borrowed the 'restitution of prestations' from the Quebec civil law, which is remedy in personam created in order to generally cover all situations where the restitution of performances is possible (invalidity, termination of contract, force majeure, etc.) and also serve as default instrument where particular law provides for the reimbursement of costs incurred by a party but does not provide the terms or extent for it.[355] As restitution of prestations has a much narrower scope of application (it does not cover restitution for wrongs, restitution *in rem* and even general cases of unjustified enrichment)[356] in contrast with the concept of restitution *largo sensu* prevailing in common law,[357] and therefore fixed meaning, it is called here restitution *stricto sensu.*

573. Without denying its apparent quasi-contractual roots, according to the scheme of LCC based on Quebec law, restitution of prestations is a special self-standing institution of law of obligations, which belongs neither to unjust enrichment nor to contract.[358] Chapter X on restitution *stricto sensu* in the sixth book of LCC provides general rules for all cases, where performances should be reversed: where a person is bound to return to another person the property he has received either unlawfully or by error, or as a result of the transaction[359] according to which the property has been received by him being avoided *ab initio*, or as a result of the obligation becoming impossible to perform because of *a* force majeure (LCC Article 6.145). The restitution is also applicable in case of termination of a contract (LCC Article 6.222). It is clear that all listed situations involve cases of *condictio indebiti*, i.e., performance not due, but there is an important *summa divisio* between all those grounds of restitution. The first part of them (avoidance, termination, force majeure) are special cases involving contractual situations where rules of restitution of prestations are applied in a primary manner and general quasi-contractual rules of *condictio indebiti* (LCC Article 6.237) only in a subsidiary (gap-filling) manner. The second part consists of all other performance not due cases, such as payment

355. Vincent Karim. *Les obligations.* 4e éd. Montréal: Wilson & Lafleur, 2015, vol. 2, p. 1384.
356. There are also other instances of restitution in Lithuanian law, which do not belong to personal restitution of prestations but rather are cases of proprietary restitution. One of them is expressly called 'limited restitution', in a case law is a restitution of property, nationalised during the Soviet occupation. This type of restitution is regulated by the Law on the Restoration of the Rights of Ownership of Citizens to the Existing Real Property. Other instance, is a criminal restitution called 'illegal enrichment' (Criminal code Art. 189^1) used to disgorge crime based revenues. Due to the strong proprietary effect, both those types of restitution *largo sensu* came under the scrutiny of the Constitutional Court. *See*, for instance, Judgments of the Lithuanian Republic Constitutional Court of 19 Jun. 2012 and of 15 Mar. 2017.
357. In Lithuanian law, those three instances of the common law restitution are covered by the special remedies: restitutionary damages as a civil liability remedy (LCC Art. 6.249(2)), vindication as property law remedy (LCC Art. 4.95) and recovery of unjustified enrichment, which is an independent quasi-contractual remedy (LCC Art. 6.242).
358. Lionel Smith. *Property, subsidiarity and unjust enrichment. In.* Unjustified Enrichment: Key Issues in Comparative Perspective. Cambridge University Press 2004, p. 600.
359. Under the case law, restitution of prestations is applied also where the administrative act under which the property was transferred is declared void. *See* Judgments of the Lithuanian Supreme Court of 1 Dec. 2004 in the civil case No 3K-3-662/2004, of 15 in the civil case No, of May 2006 in the civil case No 3K-3-328/2006, of 6 Jun. 2007 in the civil case No 3K-3-149/2007.

by error, falling into general scope of LCC Article 6.237. It flows from above that performance not due is not a separate remedy, but a quasi-contract, which is remedied by the restitution of prestations and from which all other cases of restitution in contract law (avoidance, termination, force majeure) are derived. For the sake of simplicity, we refer for special cases as grounds for primary restitution of prestations and for other cases as grounds for subsidiary (quasi-contractual) restitution of prestations. Primary restitution further may be divided into contractual, applicable to reverse benefits conferred on the basis of a terminated valid contract, and non-contractual, applicable to reverse benefits conferred on the basis of an invalid contract.

574. In case law, however, terminology is oversimplified to such an extent which distorts the overall scheme of LCC: the term 'restitution' is used only with respect to primary restitution, whereas subsidiary restitution based on performance not due is not understood as a restitution, but as a separate remedy set in LCC Article 6.237.[360] This leads to a confusing reasoning that recovery of a performance not due is possible only in cases, where restitution, as a primary remedy, is inapplicable. Such reasoning, if taken literally, is *contra legem* because LCC Article 6.145 expressly prescribes for a restitution, *inter alia,* where a person is bound to return to another person the property he has received either unlawfully[361] or by error.

575. In cases, where property is returned to both parties of the contract, restitution is called bilateral, whereas in case where property is returned to only one party it is unilateral restitution. Later case of restitution may be where only one party has performed its obligations or where bilateral restitution would be against the public order or good morals (LCC Article 1.81).

II. General Order of Restitution

576. Restitution should be applied where provided and as provided by statutory law. However, in exceptional cases, LCC Article 6.145 gives to the court an equitable discretion to modify the mode of restitution or refuse restitution altogether where it would render undue and unfair aggravation for one party and, accordingly, undue advantage to the other party. Also, according to the Supreme Court, the

---

360. *See* Judgments of the Lithuanian Supreme Court of 22 Feb. 2006 in the civil case No 3K-3-140/2006 and of 29 May 2009 in the civil case No 3K-3-253/2009.

361. It should be noted, however, that according to the Quebec CC Art. 1699, restitution of prestations takes place where a person is bound by law to return to another person the property he has received, either *without right* or in error. Thus, the wording is slightly different, because LCC uses term 'unlawfully', instead of 'without right'. Nevertheless, in LCC commentary, written by chief drafter of LCC, it is affirmed that performance not due (LCC Art. 6.237) falls into the scope of restitution of prestations. *See* Valentinas Mikelėnas. *Lietuvos Respublikos civilinio kodekso komentaras. Šeštoji knyga. Prievolių teisė.* Justitia, 2003, I t., p. 185. Therefore, this difference is nothing more than just a matter of translation.

defendant in case of the special restitution may invoke the defences against the action based on performance not due (LCC Article 6.241),[362] i.e., general restitution action.

577. As to the modes of restitution, it should be made in kind, except in the instances where this is impossible or it would cause serious inconveniences for the parties. In these cases, restitution shall be effectuated by payment in monetary equivalent. Monetary equivalent shall be estimated according to prices that were valid at the time when the debtor received what he is liable to restore. In the case of destruction or alienation of property subject to restitution, the person shall be bound to compensate for the value of the property which was at the time when the property was received, destroyed or alienated, or at the time of its restitution, taking in regard whichever value is the lowest. In the event of the person liable to make restitution being in bad faith, or where the restitution is due to his fault, he shall be bound to return the highest value of the property (LCC Article 6.146–6.147).

578. If the property is destroyed by a force majeure, the restitution shall not be applied, though the debtor shall be bound to assign to the creditor the claim for indemnity for the lost property, or to deliver him the indemnity he has received for the destroyed property. In the event where the debtor is in bad faith, or the restitution is due to his fault, he shall be bound to return the value of the property calculated in accordance with the rules provided in LCC Article 6.147(2), except in the cases where the debtor proves that the property would have been destroyed even if it had been in the possession of the creditor. Where the property has suffered partial loss or any other depreciation in value, the debtor shall be bound to pay the creditor monetary equivalence of such partial loss or to indemnify the depreciation in value of the property unless it results from normal wear and tear of the property (LCC Article 6.148–6.149).

579. Expenses for the care and custody of the property subject to restitution incurred by the person who is bound to return the property shall be indemnified in accordance with the provisions of property law applicable in respect of possessors in good faith and possessors in bad faith (LCC Article 4.97). The fruits and revenues of the property subject to restitution shall belong to the person bound to make restitution. This person shall bear all the expenses incurred in the production of those fruits and revenues. In the event where the person bound to make restitution is in bad faith, or if the restitution is due to his fault, he shall be obliged to return the fruits and revenues also to indemnify the creditor for any benefit he has derived from the property. Nevertheless, the creditor must compensate to such person for the necessary expenses incurred by him in producing the fruits and revenues (LCC Article 6.150–6.151).

---

362. Judgment of the Lithuanian Supreme Court of 23 Apr. 2009 in the civil case No 3K-7-90/2009.

580. According to LCC Article 6.152, costs of restitution shall be borne by both parties in equal shares unless they have agreed otherwise. In the event where one party is in bad faith, or the restitution is due to his fault, all costs of restitution shall be borne by that party alone.

III. Restitution and Third Parties

581. Third persons in good faith who in accordance with a transaction of alienation by onerous title acquire property subject to restitution shall be able to invoke this transaction against a person who claims for restitution. Third persons in good faith who in accordance with a transaction of alienation by gratuitous title acquire property subject to restitution shall not be able to invoke this transaction against a person who claims for restitution if the time limit of prescription is not exceeded by the latter. Any other actions performed in favour of a third person in good faith may be invoked against a person who claims for restitution (LCC Article 6.153). The Supreme Court has clarified that third-party protection against the personal restitution does not equal protection of bona fide acquirers against the vindication, where the court analyses whether acquirer knew (or should have known) about sales circumstances. Restitution, instead, is focused on the maintenance of equilibrium of parties' interests on the basis of equitable discretion of the court.[363] This reasoning stems from the idea that vindication is a remedy *in rem* and as such should be used only against third parties, whereas restitution is a remedy in personam and should be used only between the parties of an obligation; hence, as bona fide acquisition is a defence only against the vindication, it should not preclude the restitution *inter partes*.

582. Thus, if the contract is avoided or terminated it does not mean that the only response will be personal restitution. Accordingly, nothing precludes the bona fide acquirer protection in a chain of invalid contracts if the plaintiff and the defendant were not counterpartying to a contract, because in such a case a recovery would be judicially characterised as a vindication and subsequently destroyed by the bona fides defence. Moreover, the priority of restitution in contractual relations in any case should not block the vindication against the insolvent counterparty, because in case of insolvency the recovery of thing *de facto* becomes not a claim against the counterparty any more, but a claim against the third parties – other creditors. Otherwise the constitutional principle of inviolability of property (Lithuanian Constitution Article 23) would be prejudiced.

583. Despite strict delimitation between personal restitution and vindication in Lithuanian case law, there are still possibilities to initiate personal restitution against third persons and use bona fides defence on the basis of LCC Article 6.153. First, where A's property, unlawfully transferred by the insolvent counterparty B to third

363. Judgments of the Lithuanian Supreme Court of 22 Oct. 2007 in the civil case No 3K-3-413/2007, 3 Dec. 2007 in the civil case No 3K-3-525/2007 and of 23 Apr. 2009 in the civil case No 3K-7-90/2009.

party C in good faith, is generic and not segregated, but still existing. In such case primary remedies fail: vindication due to the lack of specificity and primary restitution due to insolvency of the counterparty. The residual option in such case is to claim subsidiary (quasi-contractual) restitution from C on the basis of performance not due (LCC Article 6.237). In such a case, the proprietary cause for enrichment of C is absent, but if he was in good faith and acquired property onerously, the restitution will be blocked by LCC Article 6.153. Second, where plaintiff A successfully attacks transaction of B and C and, without vindicating it for himself, triggers the personal restitution to return property from C into the patrimony of B. Third, where restitution is claimed against the beneficiary in the stipulation for a benefit of a third party (LCC Article 6.191). Third party in such a contract *de facto* is the additional creditor, therefore direct remedy against it is the personal restitution. However, if a third party was in good faith and acquired property onerously, it is protected by LCC Article 6.153.

IV. Peculiarities of Contractual Restitution

584. Under Lithuanian law, the contractual restitution is applicable only by the claim of the plaintiff submitted in legal action, whereas non-contractual restitution should be applied by the court on its own motion (ex officio) when it satisfies action of invalidity (LCC Article 1.78(5)).

585. Pursuant to LCC Article 6.222, upon termination of the contract, each of the parties shall have the right to claim the return of whatever he has supplied the other party under the contract if this party concurrently makes the return of whatever he has received from the latter. If restitution in kind is not possible or appropriate to the parties due to modification of the subject matter of the contract, a compensation of value of what has been received must be made in money, provided that such compensation does not contradict the criteria of reasonableness, good faith and justice. If the performance of a contract is successive and divisible (lease, services, etc.), the party may claim restitution only of what has been received after the termination of the contract. Restitution shall not affect the rights and duties of third persons in good faith, except in the cases established in LCC.

586. Restitution is also mentioned in the special part of Lithuanian contract law. For instance, according to LCC Article 6.472(3), revocation of a gift obligates the donee to restore to the donor the property he has received under the contract of gift in accordance with the provisions of restitution if this property still exists at the moment of revocation of the gift.

Part II. Specific Contracts

Chapter 1. Agency

587. In a pandectist manner, inspired by German law, LCC regulates agency (representation) relationships by distinguishing general rules applicable for all types of direct representation and rules applicable for specific types of agency. General rules are found in a second book of LCC '*Persons*' (LCC Article 2.132–2.151) and are more focused on external aspects of agency, while rules on specific agency types, with exception of commercial agency (LCC Article 2.152–2.168), are found in other books of LCC (LCC Article 6.756–6.765, 6.780–6.795, etc.) and more focused on internal aspects of agency. Internal aspect concerns relationships between agent and principal, whereas external aspect concerns relationships between third parties on the one hand and agent or principal on the other hand.

588. There are several axes for agency classification. According to the legal ground, agency may be contractual (e.g., contract of mandate,), statutory (e.g., guardian of incapable person), judicial (e.g., judgment to adopt the representative) or administrative (e.g., administrative order to represent Government).

589. According to the legal environment in which agent acts, agency may be substantive, where agent is involved in the contractual or other substantive law relationships, and procedural, where representative, usually advocate, represents its client in the legal proceedings. External aspects of the latter type of agency are regulated by procedural law.

590. According to the person in which name agent is contracting, agency may be direct and indirect. In direct agency the agent acts in the name of principal by disclosing fact of representation. In mandate, commercial agency, joint venture and most other occasions agency relations are direct. Indirect agency exists where agent acts in its own name, but on behalf of the principal.[364] Main type of indirect agency is commission agency (LCC Article 6.780–6.795), but, in my opinion, not the sole one. It has been analysed in preceding chapters of this book that Lithuanian version of trust is not the real trust, but just a wider version of indirect agency, constituting

364. Interestingly, one may find rule in LCC Art. 2.132, which states that persons who act in their own name although in the interest of other person shall not be deemed to be agents (sales intermediaries, etc.). Such rule should not be understood literally, but only as restricting scope of LCC Art. 2.132–2.151 only for direct agency.

the relationship in personam, with superficial label of independent property right. It should be noted that Lithuanian law do not use the similar distinction into disclosed and undisclosed agency, which may be found in common law jurisdictions and UNIDROIT PICC. Thus, even if it is disclosed for the third party that particular person acts on behalf of another person, but in his own name, contract is formed between that person, as indirect agent, and third party (LCC Article 6.780(2)). In my opinion, opting for such more formalistic model in LCC was a good choice, because it gives more certainty for the market than alternative model based on disclosure.[365]

§1. General Rules on Agency

591. A fundamental legal maxim of the agency law – *qui facit per alium facit per se* – implies that the principal acts through his agent and therefore agent actions equal actions of the principal. Therefore, a legal act made by an agent in the principal's name without exceeding authority directly creates, modifies and destructs the rights and duties of a principal (LCC Article 2.133). Even in indirect agency, where commission agent directly assumes personal rights and duties in a contract with third person, he still has power to directly acquire and dispose of the principal's property rights (LCC Article 6.786(1), 6.785(3–4)).

I. Authority of Agents

592. Authority of agent be either express or implied from circumstances. Express authority is normally granted by a power of attorney – unilateral legal act – the main purpose of which is the disclosure of agency fact for the third persons. Usually, according to LCC Article 2.137, power of attorney is a written document granted by a person (principal) to other person (authorised agent) to represent a principal in establishing and maintaining relations with the third persons. The following powers of attorney should be even notarised: power of attorney to conclude contracts for whom a notarial form is obligatory; power of attorney to represent natural person in actions with legal persons; power of attorney to possess, use or dispose of real property of a natural person.[366] However, there is no duty to notarise the power of attorney to represent natural person in actions with legal persons if the document is created in electronic form and registered in a public register (LCC Article 2.138). To avoid unnecessary restrictions for the contracting, duty to notarise the power of attorney to represent natural person in actions with legal persons should only be mandatory for the cases where agent concludes legal acts – transactions – which bind principal, but not just makes factual acts, like transmission of information or requests in the name of principal. It would be awkward to apply this

365. More on this in the light of investment services, *see* Laurynas Didžiulis. *Investicinių pavedimų priėmimo, perdavimo ir vykdymo civilinis teisinis kvalifikavimas.* Teisė: Mokslo darbai. Vol. 100, 2016, p. 45–46.

366. Powers of attorney verified by a notary must be registered in a public register.

rule also in cases, where the client is represented by professional service provider, whose professional status is given by the statute, for example, advocate (Law on Advocacy), insurance broker (Law on Insurance) and financial intermediary (Law on Markets in Financial Instruments). Power of attorney granted by a legal person is signed by executives and, in the event that the legal person must have a stamp, be stamped by the head thereof (LCC Article 2.140). Powers of attorney may be issued for unspecified legal acts or just for specific acts. Former instruments are called general powers of attorney, whereas the latter are called specific powers of attorney. An authorised agent who holds the general power of attorney has the right to perform only those actions, which are necessary for the protection of principal's property and property interests as well as supervision of principal's property (LCC Article 2.137(2)). Subtype of a general power of attorney is *prokura*, i.e., a power of attorney, which a legal person (entrepreneur) grants to his employee or other person to perform, in principal's name and in his interests, all legal acts related to legal person's (entrepreneur's) undertaking (LCC Article 2.176).

593. The significance of power is attorney lies in its ability to easily disclose the fact and extent of agency, without disclosing internal aspects of it, which may be confidential. Therefore, LCC Article 2.143 gives right for the third person to request an agent to present his power of attorney and its copy. Power of attorney may not only be formed and evidenced as a separate document – unilateral legal act of principal – but also be inferred from an agency contract. For instance, CCP Article 57, applicable for a representative by mandate, prescribes that rights and liabilities of an attorney or an attorney's assistant and the scope of the same shall be confirmed by a written agreement with the client. Another example is joint venture, where in case of relations with the third persons, the right of a partner to conclude the transactions on behalf of all the partners may be proved by the power of attorney issued by the remaining partners or the contract of joint venture.

594. The period of the power of attorney may be fixed or open-ended. Where the period of the power of attorney fails to be indicated, the power of attorney shall be valid for one year as of the day on which it was granted. Power of attorney which fails to indicate the date when it was granted shall be deemed invalid (LCC Article 2.142). However, even during the period of validity, power of attorney may be revoked by both principal and agent, unless irrevocable power of attorney has been granted (LCC Article 2.146). As agency relations are based on trust and mandate given by the principal, common sense dictates that irrevocability should be applicable only against agent, not the principal. Hence, even the irrevocable power of attorney should be open form termination by the principal in order to avoid trading without mandate and obvious mismatch of internal and external agency relations leading to conflict of interests.[367] In addition, according to LCC Article 2.147, power of attorney expires: upon termination of a legal person who was vested with

---

367. There are also the opposite opinions expressed in Lithuanian legal doctrine, which states that such revocation should be ineffective. *See* Vytautas Mizaras, *et al. Lietuvos Respublikos civilinio kodekso komentaras. Antroji knyga. Asmenys.* Justitia, 2002, p. 286; Agnė Tikniūtė, *et al. Lyginamoji sutarčių teisė: Lietuva europiniame kontekste.* Justitia, 2013, p. 196.

power of attorney or where the said person was instituted a bankruptcy; and upon the death, recognition of legal incapacity, partial capacity or absence of a natural person who was vested with the power of attorney.

595. Agent's authority may also be implied. LCC Article 2.133(2–3) prescribes that rights of an agent may also arise from the circumstances under which an agent acts (salesperson in retail trade, cashier, etc.). In the event that behaviour of a person gives reasonable grounds for the third persons to think that he has appointed the other person to be his agent, contracts concluded by the said person in principal's name shall be binding for the principal. Consequently, where an agent fails to inform that he acts in principal's name and in his interests, the principal will acquire the rights and assume the duties arising from the contract where the other party to the contract was in a position to understand from the circumstances that the contract was concluded with an agent, mostly because circumstances revealed that person has intended to act in the name of another. Of course, this last rule should be applied narrowly as concerning only situations where agent did not reveal in which name he acts at all, because if he expressly stated that he is acting in his own name, the agent should be counterparty despite the disclosure of agency relations (LCC Article 6.780(2)). Thus, any implications about agency relations from circumstances should only fill the gaps of express statements about the relations of parties, not overrule them. In other words, express statements on agency should have priority against implied considerations.

596. Authority of agent may also be real or ostensible (fake). Actual authority is where agent's competence to contract with third parties in the name of principal is matched by the powers given to him in internal relations with the principal, for instance, where agent's transactions are fully permitted in the contract of mandate. In this case, there is harmony between internal and external agency relations. Ostensible authority is where it only appears for the third parties that agent has actual power to act in the name of principal, but in fact no such power was given to this person by the principal. This is in contrast with implied authority, where do exist internal relations giving real authority to the agent. Again, as in case of implied authority, LCC Article 2.133(2) should be applicable, which states that where a behaviour of a person gives reasonable grounds for the third persons to think that he has appointed the other person to be his agent, contracts concluded by the said person in principal's name shall be binding for the principal. This rule is adopted in order to protect reliance of honest third parties, therefore should not be applicable in cases, where the third party was aware or had to be aware of the fact that the so-called agent was not entitled to conclude the contract.

597. Similar consequences arise in cases of exceeded actual authority, for instance where stockbroker makes unauthorised trading with client's assets, which means that authority to transact in part was real and in another part was fake. LCC Article 2.133(8–9) states that where a contract was concluded without due authorisation, a person who has concluded the contract shall be liable for his contractual obligations to the other party to the contract, except in cases, where the said party to the contract was aware or had to be aware of the fact that the latter was not entitled to conclude the contract. However, where an agent acted in excess of his powers but in the manner which gave to a third person serious grounds to think that he was concluding a contract with a duly authorised agent, the contract shall be obligatory to the principal, except in cases where the other party to the contract was aware or had to be aware that an agent was exceeding his powers. In cases of unauthorised trading, among other remedies, the aggrieved principal and bona fide third parties also may claim damages from the agent: the principal is entitled to expectation damages due to breach of a mandate contract, while the third parties are limited to the reliance damages based on tort. In contrast with malicious representation, the compensation for non-pecuniary loss done by unauthorised trading is excluded.

598. In order to promote stability of transactions made through the agents, Lithuanian law uses concept of ratification. According to LCC Article 2.133(6), where a contract has been concluded by a person, who has not been authorised to do so, the principal must bear the consequences thereof only when the principal ratifies the contract. The other party to the contract may, in this case, request to ratify the contract within its established time limit, which may not be shorter than fourteen days. Where no reply has been received within the established time limit the contract shall be deemed not ratified. The ratification of a contract has a retroactive effect, i.e., it shall be deemed valid as of the day of its conclusion. It should be noted that ratification not only makes the contract valid from the day of its formation but also acts as affirmative defence by the agent against principal's actions for damages.

II. Fiduciary Relationships with Principal

599. As agent is in strict fiduciary relations with principal,[368] he should be loyal to him. In particular, he may not conclude contracts in the principal's name either with himself or with a person, whom he represents at the given time, as well as his spouse, parents, children or other close relatives. Such contracts, upon the principal's request, may be deemed null and void. An agent may not conclude a contract which a principal himself is not authorised to conclude. Where, in violation of the rights conferred, an agent enters into a contract, which contravenes the interests of a principal, such contract, upon the principal's request, may be deemed void in the cases where a third person was aware or had to be aware of the conflict of interests. A person may not act as an agent of both parties to the contract. This provision, however, shall not be applied in the cases where contractual obligations are performed as well as in the cases where both parties to the contract express their will explicitly that the agent has to act in the interests of both parties (LCC Article 2.134–2.135).

600. If the agent maliciously or without authorisation represents the principal, the party's will is defective, since no normal agreement exists. It makes the contract voidable. According to LCC Article 1.91(1), a transaction may be declared voidable

368. Judgment of the Lithuanian Supreme Court of 19 Nov. 2001 in the civil case No 3K-3-1010/2001.

by a court on the action of the aggrieved party if it was formed by a malicious agreement of the agent of one party with the other party. In order to annul the contract on this ground, case law requires to establish the intentional fault of both the agent and counterparty.[369] Accordingly, in addition to unilateral restitution, the aggrieved party may claim reliance damages, including compensation of non-pecuniary loss, *in solidum* also from both the agent and counterparty.

601. Fiduciary character of agency relations also requires from the agent to personally perform the acts, which he has been authorised to perform. According to LCC Article 2.145, he may delegate authority to the other person to perform the said acts only in the cases where such right has been conferred upon him by the authority he was vested with or where under certain circumstances he is forced to do so to protect the principal's interests. A reauthorised person shall enjoy the same rights and assume the same obligations as an agent in respect of a principal and the third persons. The form of power of attorney which is given by reauthorisation shall have to conform to the form of the power of attorney, which has been granted. The term of power of attorney granted by reauthorisation may not exceed the term of power of attorney, which formed the basis for granting it. A person, who delegates his authority to the other person, shall have to notify a principal thereof and supply the necessary data about the person who was delegated the authority. Where the authorised agent fails to discharge the given obligation, he shall be liable for the actions of the person, to whom he delegated his authority, as for his own actions. Where an authorised agent has been appointed as per principal's instructions, an agent shall not be liable for the authorised agent's actions, except in the cases where the agent was aware of the fact that the person who was appointed as authorised agent was dishonest and unreliable but failed to notify the principal thereof.

602. Agent also has a fiduciary duty to account, i.e., after the acts of representation an agent must present a report to a principal about his activities and give an account of everything he received in his mission to the principal (LCC Article 2.150).

603. As concerns obligations of the principal, he has a duty to cooperate with agent (LCC Article 6.200) and must reimburse all agent's expenses related to his mission, as well as to offer remuneration with the exception where the law or the contract provide for a free of charge representation (LCC Article 2.151).

§2. Main Types of Agency Contracts

604. In this section, main types of agency contracts – mandate, commercial agency and commission agency – are analysed. All those contracts are consensual,

369. Judgment of the Lithuanian Supreme Court of 21 Sep. 2009 in the civil case No 3K-3-361/2009.

onerous, bilateral (with the exception to mandate, which may be gratuitous and unilateral), commutative and purely obligational. Other contracts creating internal agency relations, such as trust or joint venture, were explored in the preceding parts of this book.

I. Mandate

605. Mandate (*mandatum*) contract is the simplest and probably most important type of agency contract in everyday life of Lithuanian society. Mandates everyday are given to spouses, employees, corporate executives, lawyers, property administrators (including insolvency administrators), insurance brokers, credit intermediaries, portfolio managers and other direct representatives. LCC norms on mandate contract are transplanted from Quebec CC.

606. Under a contract of mandate, one party (mandatary) takes an obligation to perform in the name of and at the expense of another party (mandator) prescribed legal acts in respect of third persons. The powers granted to the mandatary and the written document confirming thereof is called a power of attorney. Under a contract of mandate, the mandator may empower the mandatary to perform legal acts related to the defence of the mandator, execute administration of the mandator's property in total or a part thereof, perform procedural actions on behalf of the mandator in the court and other institutions, as well to as do any other legal acts. The person's consent to assume the mandate may be expressed explicitly or, taking in regard the concrete circumstances, by silence (LCC Article 6.756, 6.757).

607. A contract of mandate may be either by gratuitous title or by onerous title. A contract of mandate entered into by natural persons is presumed to be by gratuitous title, except in cases where the action performed by the mandatary on behalf of another person constitutes professional or business activity of the mandatary. In the instances where one or both parties to a contract of mandate are entrepreneurs, the contract is presumed to be given by onerous title. In the instances where the contract is onerous, the amount of the mandatary's remuneration is determined by the contract of mandate or laws. In the event where neither the contract nor laws determine the amount of the remuneration, the payment is determined taking into consideration usages, market prices, the character and duration of the services rendered, recommendations of the professional association of the persons engaged in rendering relevant services and other circumstances. The mandatary acting as a commercial agent has the right of retention with respect to things subject to transfer to the mandator until the latter fully remunerates the mandatary for the services rendered (LCC Article 6.758).

608. The mandatary is under duty to perform the mandate given to him in accordance with the instructions of the mandator. The instructions of the mandator must be lawful, practical and definite. The mandatary shall have the right to deviate from the instructions of the mandator if under the circumstances of the case this is necessary for the interests of the mandator and the mandatary could not enquire in advance of the mandator or did not receive any reply to his enquiry within a reasonable period (LCC Article 6.759). A mandatary is obliged to fulfil the mandate in good faith and with prudence and diligence in the best interests of the mandator, as well as to avoid any conflict between his personal interests and those of the mandator. A mandatary is obliged to fulfil the mandate personally, except in cases where the contract provides for exceptions, as well as where the law permits a substitution of mandatory. During the mandate, the mandatary is obliged to furnish the mandator, upon the latter's request or where the concrete circumstances warrant it without any request, with all the information concerning the course of the performance of mandate. Having fulfilled the mandate, the mandatary is obliged without delay to inform the mandator accordingly, submit a report with documents of justification appended, and return the power of attorney unless otherwise provided for by the contract. The mandatary is obliged to transfer to the mandator without delay everything received in the performance of the mandate. Where in the instances provided for by the contract, the law or usages, the mandatary takes assistance of third persons for the performance of the mandate, he is liable towards the mandator for the actions of those persons and is bound to compensate for any damage caused to the mandator by the actions thereof. In the instances where a mandate is performed by several mandataries, they are solidarity liable towards the mandator unless otherwise provided for by the contract. The mandatary shall have no right to use for his own interests the information or property obtained in fulfilling the mandate, except in cases provided for by the law or contract, likewise when the mandator gives his consent to such use. In the instances where the mandatary fails to perform this duty, he is obliged to compensate to the mandator for the damages incurred by him in the result, likewise to return everything that is considered to be his unjust enrichment; in the cases where he has unlawfully used a thing or money, he is obliged to pay accordingly the payment for lease or the interest on the sums used (LCC Article 6.760).

609. The mandator is obliged to cooperate with the mandatary to facilitate the fulfilment of the mandate by the latter. The mandator is obliged without delay to accept from the mandatary everything performed by him in accordance with the contract of mandate. Unless otherwise provided for by the contract, the mandator is obliged to advance to the mandatary the means necessary for the fulfilment of the mandate, compensate to the mandatary for any expenses which were necessary for due fulfilment of the mandate and, in case of necessity, to issue advance payment needed to cover expenses related to the fulfilment of the mandate. Upon the due fulfilment of the mandate by the mandatary, the mandator is obliged to pay remuneration to the former if the contract is onerous. The mandator is obliged to compensate the mandatary for any damage incurred in the fulfilment of the mandate in the events where there is no fault of the mandatary in his actions, and other persons liable for the damage are not bound to compensate for it (LCC Article 6.761).

610. In addition to the general grounds of the extinction of obligations, a contract of mandate comes to an end as a consequence of: (1) revocation of the power of attorney by the mandator; (2) renunciation of the power of attorney by the mandatary (LCC Article 2.146); (3) expiry of the time limit of the power of attorney;

(4) death of a party to the contract; (5) liquidation of one of the parties to the contract of mandate; (6) initiation of bankruptcy proceedings against one of the parties; and (7) one of the parties is acknowledged incapable, of limited capacity or missing. In the instances where the mandator appoints a new mandatary for the performance of the same actions, the contract of mandate is considered terminated from the moment when the first mandatary is notified about the appointment of a new mandatary. In the instances where the mandator due to his health or other serious reasons is unable to revoke the power of attorney on his own, any interested person or a public prosecutor shall have the right to apply to the court for the revocation of the power of attorney in the instances where it is necessary for the interest of the mandator, or the public interest (LCC Article 6.763).

II. Commercial Agency

611. Commercial agency contract has evolved from a contract of mandate, but today is so distinct that regulated separately from the latter. A commercial agent is an independent person whose basic business activity is to permanently act for payment as intermediary for a principal in conclusion of contracts or conclusion of contracts in the principal's name and at the principal's expense. LCC rules on commercial agency implement EU directive 86/653/EEC of 18 December 1986 on the coordination of the laws of the Member States relating to self-employed commercial agents.

612. Commercial agent's rights and obligations may be established in writing or orally. Only upon conclusion of a contract in writing shall the following conditions be valid and shall establish: (1) restrictions on the civil liability of an agent or a principal or a complete exemption from civil liability; (2) prohibition of competition after the contract has been terminated; (3) conditions for the termination of a contract; (4) exclusive rights of a commercial agent; and (5) ratio of the commercial agent's right to remuneration to the performance of a contract (LCC Article 2.154).

613. A principal and an agent may, in a contract, establish such competition restricting conditions, for instance, which grants a commercial agent an exclusive right to conclude contracts in principal's name on a certain territory or with a certain group of consumers which are not prohibited by the provisions of the competition law (LCC Article 2.152). A commercial agent and a principal may provide in the contract that upon expiry of the contract the commercial agent shall not compete with the principal for no more than two years. The given provision may be agreed upon in writing. Restriction of competition may be related only to a certain territory or certain kinds of goods and services or a group of customers and a territory, which were entrusted to the commercial agent. A principal shall enjoy the right to waive, in writing, in a unilateral manner, the prohibition of competition until the end of a contract. Where a contract provides for the prohibition of competition a commercial agent shall enjoy the right to compensation for all the period of the prohibition thereof. The amount of compensation is fixed by the agreement of both parties. The court has authority, upon commercial agent's request, to declare full or partial invalidity of the provision on the prohibition of competition where, taking into consideration the commercial agent's lawful interests, the said provision causes him serious damage (LCC Article 2.164).

614. As in cases of other agency contracts, LCC provides for a list of duties for both parties. Thus, a commercial agent must: (1) carry out in good faith and carefully comply with all principal's reasonable instructions, be loyal to the principal and act exclusively in the principal's interest; (2) notify the principal, on a regular basis, about contracts, which are being or have been concluded, as well as supply other important information related to his own and principal's business; (3) keep principal's commercial secrets during the term of validity of a contract and upon its expiry; (4) where such condition has been set in the contract, avoid competition with the principal; (5) compensate the losses damages incurred on the principal; and (6) upon the expiry of a contract, return to the principal all documents, property and other things which were handed over by the principal (LCC Article 2.156). Prior to commencing his activities, a commercial agent must insure his civil liability against possible damage which, as a result of his activities, may be incurred on the principal or the third persons (LCC Article 2.153). A principal must: (1) supply the commercial agent with requisite documents and information (price lists, samples of commodities, advertising materials, standard conditions of contracts, etc.); (2) notify the commercial agent, without delay, about his consent or refusal to enter into a specific contract or enforce perform it, as well as about alterations of or supplements to the conditions of the contract; (3) notify, without delay, the commercial agent about the approval or a refusal to approve a contract, which the commercial agent concluded without due authority; (4) pay a salary as provided in the contract; and (5) supply the commercial agent with information requested for the performance of the agency contract and especially notify about the existence of a lesser number of trade contracts than the commercial agent might expect (LCC Article 2.157).

615. A commercial agency contract for indefinite period may be terminated on each party's initiative subject to the condition that the other party has been notified about the termination thereof within the following term: (1) a month before – where the contract was valid for one year; (2) two months before – where the contract was valid for no more than two years; (3) three months before – where the contract was valid for no more than three years; and (4) four months before – where the contract was valid for more than three years. Each party also has the right to terminate even a fixed period contract before the expiry of its term where there are compelling reasons to do so. Waiver of the given right is null and void. Where the contract is terminated for reasons, for which the other party is liable, the latter shall have to compensate for the losses damages inflicted by the termination of the contract (LCC Article 2.165, 2.166).

III. Commission Agency

616. Archetype of indirect agency in civil law is the contract of commission agency. In this contract, the fact of internal agency relations is not disclosed to third persons, which makes this contract distinct from mandate. Commission agency is widely and successfully used in business environment, such as in retail stores and stock exchange markets. It would be impossible to conclude investment transactions directly between a vast number of retail investors, who would never reach eligibility criteria laid down by financial regulation,[370] instead of supervised financial entities, which are perfectly capable of trading in their own name, but for the client's behalf. In contrast with mandate, rules on commission agency in Lithuanian law are transplanted from Russian ГК.

617. Under a contract of commission agency, one party (commission agent) is obliged to conclude upon mandate of another party (principal) for remuneration one or several transactions in his own name but at the expense of the principal. According to LCC Article 6.780, a commission agent acquires the rights and duties in respect of the transaction concluded by the commission agent with a third person, even though the principal was also disclosed to the third person or entered into direct relations with the third person with respect to the performance of the transaction.

618. A contract of commission agency may be concluded for a fixed or indeterminate term. A contract of commission agency may be concluded with or without specifying the territory of the performance thereof, likewise with or without a duty of the principal not to grant to third persons the right to conclude a contract in his interests and at his expense, the conclusion of which has been entrusted to the commission agent. A contract of commission agency may or may not specify the things that are the subject matter of the contract. The peculiarities of separate types of a contract of commission agency may be determined by laws. In the instances where parties to a contract of commission agency are enterprises (entrepreneurs), the contract of commission may only provide for such conditions to limit competition which are not prohibited by the competition law.

619. The principal must pay remuneration to the commission agent. In the event where the commission agent acted as surety for the performance of the transaction by a third person, he is also to pay additional remuneration to the commission agent in the amount established in the contract. If the amount of the remuneration for commission or the additional remuneration is not established in the contract, it is determined in accordance with the general contract law provisions. In the event of failure to perform a contract of commission agency due to reasons responsibility for which

370. According to MiFID II Art. 53(3), regulated markets may admit as members or participants investment firms, credit institutions and other persons who: (a) are of sufficient good repute; (b) have a sufficient level of trading ability, competence and experience; (c) have, where applicable, adequate organisational arrangements; and (d) have sufficient resources for the role they are to perform, taking into account the different financial arrangements that the regulated market may have established in order to guarantee the adequate settlement of transactions.

falls upon the principal, the commission agent shall retain his right to remuneration for the commission as well as compensation for the expenses incurred (LCC Article 6.781).

620. A commission agent must perform the commission order on the conditions most advantageous to the principal in accordance with the instructions of the principal, and in the absence of such instructions, in accordance with the customary business practices. In the instances where the commission agent concluded a transaction on conditions more advantageous than those specified by the principal, the additional advantage derived from the transaction is enjoyed by the commission agent unless otherwise provided for by the contract. The commission agent shall not be liable towards the principal for the failure of a third person to perform a transaction concluded with him at the expense of the principal, except in cases when the commission agent acted as surety for the performance of the transaction by the third person or failed to display the necessary caution in the selection of the third person as a party to the transaction. In the event of the failure of a third person to perform a transaction concluded with the commission agent, the latter is obliged to immediately inform the principal thereof, collect the necessary evidence and at the demand of the principal assign the right of claim to him in respect of that transaction (LCC Article 6.782, 6.783).

621. In contrast with a contract of mandate, default rule laid down in LCC Article 6.784 is that the commission agent has the right for the purpose of performing the contract of commission to conclude a contract of sub-commission with another person. Nevertheless, even in such instances the commission agent remains liable towards the principal for the actions of the sub-commission agent. Under a contract of sub-commission, the commission agent shall acquire the rights and duties of a principal with respect to the sub-commission agent. Upon the termination of a contract of sub-commission, the principal shall have no right without the consent of the commission agent to enter into direct relations with the sub-commission agent unless otherwise provided for by the contract sub-commission.

622. It is usually stressed that the main difference between direct and indirect representation is that in former case party to the contract becomes principal, while in the latter case it is agent. However, this is true only with respect to in personam and not for *in rem* relations. LCC Article 6.786 prescribes that things received by the commission agent from the principal or acquired at the expense of the latter is the ownership of the principal from the moment of the transfer. The commission agent shall have the right of retention in respect of the things which are situated with him and which are subject to transfer to the principal or to the person indicated by the latter if the principal fails to perform his obligations in respect of the commission agent. In the event where the principal is declared insolvent (bankruptcy proceedings have been started against him), the commission agent shall lose the right of retention and acquire the right of pledge in respect of the thing concerned, while his claims for the amount of the thing retained is satisfied together with the claims secured by the pledge.

623. Upon the performance of the commission, the commission agent is obliged to submit a report to the principal and transfer to him everything he received under the commission, likewise to transfer upon the demand of the principal all the rights acquired by the principal in respect of a third person arising from the transaction concluded by the commission agent. In the instances where the principal has objections with regard to the report, he must inform the commission agent accordingly within three months from the date of receipt of the report. Otherwise, the report is considered to be accepted unless there is another agreement (LCC Article 6.789).

624. The principal is obliged to: (1) accept from the commission agent everything received under the commission; (2) inspect the thing acquired for him by the commission agent and notify the latter without delay about any defects discovered in the thing; and (3) relieve the commission agent from the commitments assumed by him to a third person in the performance of the commission (LCC Article 6.790). Moreover, the principal is obliged, in addition to the commission payment and in relevant instances, also additional payment for the suretyship assumed (*del credere*), to compensate the commission agent for the necessary expenses incurred by him in the performance of the commission unless otherwise provided for by the agreement between the parties. The commission agent shall have no right to demand compensation for the deposit of a thing of the principal situated with him unless otherwise provided for by the law or the contract (LCC Article 6.791).

625. A contract of commission agency shall terminate as a consequence of: (1) refusal of the principal to perform the contract of commission; (2) refusal of the commission agent to perform the contract of commission in the cases provided for by the law or contract; and (3) death of the commission agent, acknowledgement thereof to be incapable, of limited capacity or to be missing, liquidation thereof or declared insolvent (initiation of bankruptcy proceedings). In the event where bankruptcy proceedings are initiated against the commission agent, all the rights and duties with regard to a transaction concluded by him under the instructions of the principal shall pass to the principal (LCC Article 6.792).

§3. Peculiarities of Agency in International Sale of Goods

626. LCC provides special section on external agency relations, rules of which are based on the UNIDROIT Geneva Convention on Agency in the International Sale of Goods of 1983. The Convention was adopted in order to complement UN Rome Convention on Contracts for the International Sale of Goods. Provisions of the section are applied only in the cases where an international contract of purchase and sale of goods has been concluded and is performed; a principal and the third person reside in different states. Rules are not applicable for contracts concerning the shares or other securities traded in the stock exchange, commodities sold by auction and the activities of statutory representatives as well as activities of representatives appointed by the decision of the court or an administrative institution.

627. According to LCC Article 2.170, rights and obligations of an agent may be express or implied in specific circumstances. An agent shall be vested with authority to perform any acts, which under specific circumstances are necessary to carry out principal's instruction properly. Rights and obligations of an agent may be presented in any form, and any mode of proof may be used to prove their content. Where an agent acts in principal's name and in his interests without overstepping his authority and where the third person was aware or had to be aware that he was concluding the contract with an agent, the principal shall achieve the rights and assume obligations arising under the contract. Rights and obligations arising under a contract concluded by the agent shall be imposed on an agent and not a principal where: the third person failed to know and was not obliged to know that the contract was concluded with an agent (undisclosed agency); and specific circumstances (e.g., provision of the contract) confirm that the agent, not the principal, intended to achieve rights and assume obligations arising under the contract. Where an agent fails to discharge his obligations to the principal, the principal may exercise the rights, achieved by the agent, and related to the third person, by taking into consideration the right of the third person to use protective measures against the agent. Where the agent fails to discharge his obligations to the third person, the said person shall be vested with authority to exercise his rights, achieved against the agent, and related to the principal, by taking into account the right of the agent to use protective measures against the third person as well as the principal's right to use protective measures against the agent. Rights may be exercised if the principal, the agent and the third person have been respectively notified thereof. Upon the receipt of the said notification, the third person or the principal may not waive the obligations linking them with the agent. Where an agent fails to discharge his obligations to the third person through a principal's fault, the agent must reveal principal's name to the third person. Where the third person fails to discharge his obligations to the agent, the agent must reveal the third person's name to the principal. A principal may not exercise the rights achieved by the agent and related to the third person, where the third person proves that he would not have concluded the contract if he had known who the principal was (LCC Article 2.171). Where a person acts without due authority or outside his authority, his actions shall have no legal consequences for the principal. In such cases rights and obligations of the said person and the third person shall be achieved. This rule should not be applied in cases where principal's behaviour gave reasonable grounds for the third person to think that the agent had due authority and has not exceeded his powers (LCC Article 2.172).

Chapter 2. Bailment

628. Bailment relationships in Lithuania are organised around the ancient Roman contract of deposit (*depositum*). Under the contract of deposit, one party (the depositary) obligates himself to keep in his possession property delivered to him by the other party (depositor) and to restore it to the depositor after having taken reasonable care thereof, whereas the depositor undertakes to pay a reward if this is required under the contract.

629. Main source of deposit contract law in Lithuania is LCC, whose chapter on deposit is the copy of corresponding Russian ГК rules and in part resembles former Soviet legislation. Again, the style of contractual legislation is highly detailed and systematic: there are general rules in LCC Article 6.830–6.850 and rules for special types of deposit. Those are warehousing (LCC Article 6.851–6.869), sequestration (LCC Article 6.863), pawnshop deposit (LCC Article 6.864), hotel deposit (LCC Article 6.865), deposit of tangibles in a bank (LCC Article 6.866–867), deposit of lost luggage (LCC Article 6.868) and cloakroom deposit (LCC Article 6.869). In addition, LCC refers to deposit of securities (LCC Article 1.101), performance of obligations in the deposit facility (LCC Article 6.56), as well as bank account (LCC Article 6.913), all of which are special or derivative forms of deposit contract. Also, Lithuania is a member of the 1962 Convention on the Liability of Hotel-Keepers concerning the Property of their Guests.

630. The contract for deposit is mostly a two-faced contract. It flows from the statutory definition that by default it is gratuitous, however under agreement between parties, a contract of deposit may be onerous. Also, in general, it is a real contract, because is formed only from the moment of delivery of the thing to the depositary. Deposit, despite of being real contract, may be bilateral where it is onerous. Where the depositary is a legal person (businessman) for whom safekeeping constitutes one of the activities it/he engages in (professional depositary), the contract for deposit or the documents of incorporation of the legal person may provide for the depositary's obligation to accept into possession from the depositor a thing at the date specified in the contract. In a last case, the contract consensual and bilateral, but the remedy of specific performance is limited because having undertaken to accept a thing for safekeeping, the depositary has no right to require the delivery of the thing to him for safekeeping. However, the depositor, who fails to deliver the thing for safekeeping within the time period set in the contract, is bound to indemnify the depositary for any loss failure to deliver the property may have caused him, unless otherwise established in the contract. The depositor is released from the liability if he notifies the depositary of his refusal to deliver the thing within a reasonable time. Unless otherwise established in the contract, the depositary has the right to refuse to accept the thing for safekeeping if it has not been delivered to him/it within the time period set in the contract (LCC Article 6.833). The contract for deposit normally is purely obligational; however, it may create *in rem* effects where things were mixed with other things of the same type and quality delivered for deposit by other persons (*depositum irregulare*). In such cases, the ownership of deposited property is transferred to the depositary, who acquires personal duty to restore the quantity of the things of the same type and quality which is provided for in the contract.[371]

631. An important aspect of deposit is its relationship with other contracts for services. In theory, the essence of deposit is to transfer property for a custodian, who will use organisational measures to safeguard the property and give it back to the client. Real character of deposit requires that depositary should get from the client factual possession of property or at least part of it. For instance, where the client holds car in the guarded parking place, without handing over the keys of the car to the storehouse, it creates limited factual possession to the depositary – which only excludes other people from the car (negative exclusivity) but gives no access to lawfully drive the car (no positive exclusivity). Thus, transfer of possession or part of it is a *conditio sine qua non* for the creation of deposit, which is a real contract. If no transfer of possession has taken place, for example, in case of premises surveillance and security services, there is no deposit, but simple contract for services. Another important feature of deposit is safeguard measures, which do not always exist in other services. For example, where car is parked within the unguarded parking lot it is the contract for lease of parking space, not the contract of deposit. Nevertheless, in practice those rules, stemming from the system of LCC, are not always followed. For example, in the case of real property surveillance and security services, Supreme Court has controversially ruled that the contract is deposit,[372] whereas in the case of car held within guarded parking lot found the general service contract (LCC Article 6.716).[373]

632. LCC Article 6.830, as in cases of most of the nominate contracts, defines an object of the deposit contract quite narrowly – as encompassing only things and this case only movable things. However, as concerns the tangibility, there are no reasons for such limited application of the deposit contract, especially keeping in mind that we live in the era of digitalisation and Lithuanian property law, by having no *numerus clausus* of property law objects, understands the concept of property very widely (LCC Article 4.38). Even more, the LCC by itself denies this narrow concept of the property under deposit, because the custody of investment securities, which are immaterial, expressly calls the deposit (LCC 1.101). Thus, even *res incorporales*, such as specific data files and databases, should be eligible property for the deposit contract. As concerns the mobility of property, the statutory definition of deposit contract again is slightly misleading, because indeed according to the general rule the deposit contract may be concluded only for the movable assets, but with

371. It has been established in European private law from the Roman times that *depositum* implies a depositor's right to retrieve his assets *in specie*, while under *depositum irregulare*, all the depositor's property rights are transferred to the custodian. *See* Reinhard Zimmermann. *The Law of Obligations: Roman Foundations of the Civilian Tradition Roman Foundations*. Oxford University Press, 1996, p. 216; Matthias Haentjens. *Harmonisation of securities law: custody and transfer of securities in European private law*. Doctoral thesis. Amsterdam University, 2007, p. 321.
372. Judgment of the Lithuanian Supreme Court of 18 Mar. 2002 in the civil case No 3K-3-452/2002.
373. Judgment of the Lithuanian Supreme Court of 15 Apr. 2016 in the civil case No 3K-3-233-421/2016.

two exceptions. First, the specific type of deposit contract is sequestration, which may cover also immovables (LCC Article 6.863). Second, immovables by law, but movables by nature, are registrable aircraft and ships (LCC Article 1.98), which are mobile and perfectly suitable property for the transfer for custody purposes, hence should be eligible object for the contract of deposit.

633. Form of the contract of deposit should match the following requirements. A contract of deposit concluded by natural persons must be in writing if the value of the property is over EUR 1,500. If the contract of deposit provides for the depositary's obligation to accept the thing into possession for safekeeping in future, the contract must be in writing in all cases. A contract of deposit shall be recognised as having been concluded in writing if the delivery of a thing to the depositary is certified by: (1) a receipt or any other document issued by the depositary; and (2) a token (number) or any other sign. Failure to abide by the ordinary written form shall not deprive the parties of the right to rely on the evidence presented by witnesses in case of a dispute regarding the identity of the thing that has been delivered for safekeeping and restored (LCC Article 6.831).

§1. Obligations of Parties

634. The depositary has duty of care with respect to deposited property. According to LCC Article 6.832, the depositary shall use all available means to ensure the preservation of the thing put in his possession. The depositary is bound to take care of the thing in accordance with the conditions of safekeeping set in the contract. Where the conditions of safekeeping are not set in the contract or not all conditions are set, the depositary is bound to preserve the thing under such conditions which would ensure maximum protection of the thing. In all cases, the depositary is bound to ensure that he/it fulfils the requirements for implementation of safety measures (fire prevention, sanitary, etc.), laid down in laws and other legal acts. In the case of gratuitous deposit, the depositary is bound to take as much care of the thing as he would take of his own things. Unless the contract establishes otherwise, the depositary shall have no right to make use of the thing deposited with him/it or to permit the use thereof by other persons. The depositary may not require the depositor to prove that he is the owner of the thing delivered for safekeeping or require such proof of the person to whom the thing is to be restored. The depositary is bound to restore the thing to the depositor on demand, even before the expiry of the period of deposit. The depositary shall have the right to request that the person to whom the thing is returned produce a receipt or any other document evidencing conclusion of the contract of deposit and the person's right to withdraw the thing.

635. The depositary is bound to preserve the thing for the period of deposit set in the contract. Where the period of deposit is not set in the contract and cannot be set under the conditions of the contract, the depositary must preserve the thing until the restoration thereof is demanded by the depositor or any other person entitled to withdraw the thing. Where it is stipulated that the period of deposit expires from the moment the restoration thereof is demanded, the depositary shall be entitled, upon the expiration of the time period of deposit customary under the conditions, to demand that the depositor withdraw the thing within a reasonable time from the receipt of such a notice (LCC Article 6.834).

636. Another obligation of the depositary is to return to the depositor or any other person authorised by him the identical thing that was delivered to the depositary. The thing must be returned in the same condition in which it was handed over for safekeeping, having regard to its normal wear and tear, amortisation or change due to its natural qualities. Unless otherwise established by the contract of deposit, together with the thing the depositary is bound to restore to the depositor the fruits and revenues received therefrom in the course of its safekeeping. The thing shall be restored at the place where it was handed over for safekeeping, unless the contract establishes otherwise. Where the deposit is gratuitous, the cost of restoration of the thing shall be borne by the depositor. Where deposit is onerous, the cost of restitution shall be borne by the depositary (LCC Article 6.844).

637. The depositary is liable for the loss, shortage or damage of the things delivered to him/it. Where the contract of deposit is onerous, the depositary shall be in any case liable for the loss, shortage or damage of the things delivered to him, unless it was caused by force majeure. Where the contract of deposit is gratuitous, the depositary shall be liable only if he/it is at fault. A professional depositary is strictly liable in any case, except where the thing was lost or damaged due to or by force majeure. The depositary shall be liable for the loss, deficiency or damage of the thing after the arising of the depositor's obligation to withdraw the thing only where there has been the depositary's malice or gross negligence. Where the depositary's heir or other legal representative sells in good faith the thing delivered for safekeeping without his knowledge, the heir or other legal representative is bound only to return the price he has received or to assign to the depositor his claim against the purchaser in good faith if the price has not been paid. The depositary is bound to compensate the depositor for all damage connected with the loss, deficiency of or damage to the thing. Where the contract of deposit is gratuitous, the depositary shall be liable for: (1) the loss or shortage of the thing in the amount of the value of the thing or of the missing part thereof; and (2) the damage to the thing in the amount of the reduction of the value of the thing. Where due to the damage of the thing the value thereof has been reduced to the extent that it may no longer be used for its previous purpose, the depositor shall have the right to refuse withdrawing the thing and to demand the depositary compensate for the value of the thing and for all losses, unless otherwise established by the contract (LCC Article 6.845–6.846).

638. As for the obligations of the depositor, where the contract of deposit is onerous, the depositor is bound to pay the depositary a remuneration upon the termination of safekeeping. The parties may agree that payment shall be effected in parts at fixed intervals, upon the expiration of the time period set in the contract. Where payment of remuneration at regular intervals has been agreed upon, the depositary's failure to effect payment for more than one period shall entitle the depositary to terminate the contract and to demand from the depositor immediate withdrawal of the thing. If the contract of deposit expires before the date set in the contract due to circumstances which are outside the depositary's remit, he/it shall be entitled to the portion of remuneration corresponding to the duration of safekeeping and, in cases of hazardous things, to the full amount of the remuneration. In case the contract of deposit expires due to the circumstances that are within the depositary's remit, he/it shall have no right to demand payment of remuneration and is bound to refund the depositor the amounts paid. In case of failure by the depositor to withdraw the thing upon the expiration of the period of deposit, he/it is bound to pay an appropriate remuneration for continued safekeeping of the thing. The above rule shall also be applicable where the depositor is bound to withdraw the thing prior to the expiry of the period of the contract of deposit. The depositary shall have the right to retain the thing delivered to him/it for safekeeping until he/it is paid full amount of the remuneration by the depositor (LCC Article 6.840).

639. Also, the depositor must reimburse the depository of expenses related to safekeeping. Pursuant to default rule in LCC Article 6.841, the depositary's expenses related to the safekeeping of the thing shall be entered in the reward for deposit. If the contract of deposit is gratuitous, the depositor is bound to reimburse the depositary for the necessary expenses related to safekeeping, unless otherwise established by the law or the contract.

640. Upon the expiry of the period of the contract of deposit as well as of the period fixed by the depositary for withdrawing the thing, the depositor must forthwith withdraw the thing delivered for safekeeping. In a case of failure by the depositor to withdraw the thing, the depositary shall have the right, upon giving the depositor a written notice to the effect, at his/its own discretion to sell the thing in his/its custody for the local market price. If the price of the thing kept in custody is over of EUR 600, the depositary shall have the right to sell it only by auction. The proceeds from sale of the thing shall be transferred to the depositor upon deducting therefrom the amounts due to the depositary (LCC Article 6.843).

641. Finally, the depositor is bound to compensate for the damage inflicted on the depositary due to the qualities of the thing kept in custody if the depositary did not and could not know of the qualities when accepting the thing for safekeeping, whereas the depositor knew or should have known thereof (LCC Article 6.847).

§2. Special Types of Deposit

642. LCC rules are calibrated for various types of deposits. Apart from regular and irregular deposits, explained above, there are statutory deposit, urgent deposit, warehousing, sequestration, pawnshop deposit, hotel deposit, deposit of tangibles into a bank, deposit of lost luggage, cloakroom deposit, deposit facility for the performance of obligations, custody of securities and bank account.

I. Urgent Deposit

643. Urgent deposit takes place where a person is compelled by an unforeseen and unavoidable urgent necessity (accident, natural disaster, etc.) to entrust the custody of his property to another person. In case of an urgent deposit, the depositary may not refuse to accept the thing for safekeeping without a serious reason. In case of an urgent deposit, the depositary shall be liable in the same manner as a depositary under the contract of gratuitous deposit. The delivery of a patient's things in a health or guardianship (curatorship) institution is presumed to be an urgent deposit (LCC Article 6.849).

II. Statutory Deposit

644. LCC Article 6.850 prescribes that rules of LCC section on a contract of deposit must also be applied with respect to deposit obligations which arise under law, unless the law establishes otherwise. For instance, pursuant to CCP Article 683, a bailiff ordinarily should leave the attached property in the possession of the person who possessed it when he attached the property. However, if necessary, a bailiff at any stage of the proceeding may hand the attached property over to the safekeeping of another person as well as to the judgment creditor. These persons must perform the duties of its keeper.

645. Sometimes courts characterise as statutory deposit situation where, according to Law on Safety of Road Traffic Article 33, a vehicle may be towed by the police to the parking lot company, if that vehicle creates risk to health or life of traffic participants and other people or interferes with safe traffic of vehicles or pedestrians and violates requirements of the legal acts.[374] However, most often this is not a statutory but contractual deposit created by agreement between police and parking lot company.

III. Warehousing

646. Indispensable for logistics business is warehousing contract. On the basis of a warehouse contract, the warehouse (the warehouse-keeper) undertakes to safeguard for consideration the goods deposited with it/him by the owner/depositor of the goods and to return them to the specified person after safekeeping. For the purposes of this section, the warehouse shall be considered to be a legal person (businessman) whose principal type of activity is safekeeping of goods and provision of other services connected with the safekeeping of goods. The warehouse contract shall be executed by issuing a warehouse certificate (LCC Article 6.851).

---

374. Judgment of the Klaipėda City Court of 11 Aug. 2017 in the civil case No e2-9006-323/2017.

647. Having received the goods for safekeeping, the warehouse issues one of the following documents confirming the warehouse contract: (1) double warehouse certificate; (2) ordinary warehouse certificate; and (3) warehouse receipt. A double warehouse certificate consists of two parts – warehouse certificate and pledge certificate (LCC Article 6.857) – which shall be separable. A double warehouse certificate, each one of its two parts and an ordinary warehouse certificate are negotiable instruments. Goods received for safekeeping with a double warehouse certificate, if the parts thereof have been separated, or with an ordinary warehouse certificate may be an object of pledge during the period of safekeeping by way of pledging the corresponding certificate (LCC Article 6.856).

648. LCC Article 6.862 states that if the law or the contract establishes the right of the warehouse to dispose of the things deposited for safekeeping, the rules regulating the loan contract (LCC Chapter XLIII) shall also be applicable to the relationships between the parties, but the place and time of release of the things shall be governed by provisions of the deposit contract.

IV. Sequestration

649. Sequestration is a contract of deposit by which two or more persons who are in dispute over the right to a thing place the thing in the hands of another person chosen by them (sequestrator). The person shall bind himself to return the thing, once the issue is decided, to the person who will then be entitled to it. The object of sequestration may be an immovable thing as well as a movable thing. The parties shall elect the sequestrator by mutual agreement. They may elect one of them to act as sequestrator. Where the parties disagree on the election of the sequestrator, he shall be appointed by the court hearing the dispute. A person may be appointed sequestrator only with his consent. The sequestrator shall have the right to perform any urgent act in respect of the sequestered thing which may be performed by a simple property administrator, save for the exceptions established by agreement between the parties or court ruling. The sequestrator shall be entitled to remuneration unless otherwise stipulated by the contract or court order. The sequestrator shall restitute the thing to the person specified in the court judgment or order. In the event of the contract of transaction, the thing shall be restored to the persons specified in the contract of transaction. Upon the termination of sequestration, the sequestrator shall render an account of his management of the property and deliver it to the parties or the court. Where a person is appointed the sequestrator of the attached property by the court, the court bailiff, tax administrator or any other officer, in such case the sequestration shall be subject, in addition to the provisions of LCC, also to those laid down in the CCP (LCC Article 6.863).

V. Pawnshop Deposit

650. A contract for depositing things owned by a natural person with a pawnshop is a public (imposed) contract. A contract for depositing things with a pawnshop shall be certified by a pawn ticket issued to the pawnor. The price of the things deposited with the pawnshop shall be set by agreement between the parties. The pawnshop is bound to insure, at its expense and for the benefit of the pawnor, the thing deposited with it for the amount equal to the price of the thing set by agreement between the parties. Where a thing deposited with the pawnshop is not redeemed within the time period set in the contract, the pawnshop is bound to keep the thing for one more month at the pawnor's expense. Upon the expiration of the said time period, the pawnshop shall have the right to sell the thing. The proceeds of such sale shall be used to cover the expenses of the pawnshop which may have arisen in relation to the storing of the thing and other amounts due to it, while the balance shall be repaid by the pawnshop to the pawnor (LCC Article 6.864).

VI. Hotel Deposit

651. According to LCC Article 6.865, a hotel is liable, without a special agreement with the person who lodges with it, in the same manner as a depositary, for the loss, deficiency or damage of the personal effects of the said person. The hotel is entitled to retain, as security for payment of the cost of lodging and services actually provided by the hotel, the effects brought into the hotel by the guest. The hotel is liable for the loss, shortage or damage of the things which: (1) during the person's lodging with the hotel were kept in the hotel room or at any other place in the hotel; (2) were entrusted by the hotel guest as deposit to the hotel staff for safekeeping within the hotel or outside it; and (3) were placed as deposit at the hotel for a reasonable time starting from the moment the person takes up lodging with the hotel and until his departure. Where the property has not been deposited with the hotel, with the exception of the cases where the hotel has refused to receive the property which the hotel is bound to receive for safe custody, the civil liability for the damage, destruction or loss of the things of a person who stays at the hotel shall be limited to the price, multiplied by one hundred, paid for the overnight lodging at the hotel by the person who stays at the hotel. The civil liability for the damage, destruction or loss of one thing of a person who stays at the hotel shall be limited to the price, multiplied by fifty, paid for the overnight lodging at the hotel by the person who stays at the hotel. The hotel is liable and its civil liability shall not be limited where the damage, destruction or loss of the property is caused through the fault of the hotel or any person for whose actions the hotel is responsible. The hotel is bound to accept for deposit sums of money, jewellery and other valuable articles brought by the hotel guests, unless the things are dangerous to the people around or, giving their size or excessive value, are cumbersome to the hotel and its guests. A hotel, accepting for deposit sums or money or other valuable articles, may require them to be placed in special marked receptacles. Unless the hotel administration is immediately notified by the person lodging in the hotel of the loss, shortage of or damage to his things, the hotel shall be released from liability for failure to preserve the things. The hotel shall not be liable for failure to preserve the things, if this was due to the fault of the owner of the things, the persons accompanying him or invited to the hotel or due to superior force or because of the qualities of the thing. Neither shall the hotel be liable for failure to preserve the vehicles of the hotel guests left outside the hotel's guarded parking lot, and the things or animals left in the said vehicles. An agreement between the parties or a unilateral statement by the hotel that the hotel is not liable for the safety of the things of its guests or establishing a limited liability shall be null and void. Those rules also are applicable to the deposit of things with motels, rest homes, residential care homes, sanatoria and other similar institutions.

VII. Deposit of Lost Luggage

652. Under LCC Article 6.868, luggage offices of transport companies are bound to accept for safekeeping personal effects of passengers and other persons, irrespective of whether or not the passenger possesses travelling tickets. The contract of deposit in left luggage offices of transport companies is a public contract. Conclusion of the contract of deposit in a left luggage office (except for automatic safety deposit boxes) shall be confirmed by issuing the depositor with a receipt or token. In case of loss of the receipt or token, the thing shall be released to the depositor after he proves his ownership of the thing. Time period of safekeeping of the thing in the left luggage office shall be set by agreement between the parties. Transport companies may set maximum time periods for the safekeeping with possible extension as per agreement between the parties. Things that are not retrieved within the set period shall be stored for one more month and thereafter sold. In case of loss, shortage or damage of the delivered things, the transport company shall within twenty-four hours after the filing of the claim compensate for the value specified when the depositor delivered the things for safekeeping.

VIII. Cloakroom Deposit

653. According to LCC Article 6.869, it is presumed that the safekeeping of things in cloakrooms is gratuitous, except in cases when the things are delivered upon explicit agreement of deposit for a reward. Irrespective of whether the contract of deposit is onerous, or not, the depositary must take all measures within his power in order to ensure the safekeeping of the things delivered to the cloakroom. Those rules shall also apply in the cases when natural persons leave their outer clothing, headgear and other similar things in enterprises, institutions, organisations or means of transport in the places designated for the purpose without a special delivery thereof for safekeeping.

IX. Deposit Facility for the Performance of Obligations

654. According to LCC Article 6.56, the debtor has the right to perform a monetary obligation by depositing the debt into the deposit account of a notary, a bank or any other credit institution if: (1) the creditor or any other person authorised to accept the performance cannot be found at the place where the obligation is to be performed; (2) the creditor is incapable and a guardian is not appointed to him; (3) the creditor avoids accepting the performance of the obligation; and (4) the creditor is not clear, as the right to accept the performance is being disputed by several persons. Performance of an obligation into the deposit releases the debtor from the payment of interest or any other dues in the future.

X. Deposit of Tangibles into a Bank

655. Today banks play a crucial role by safekeeping intangible items, especially money and securities. Nonetheless, banks still engage in a custody of tangible property and LCC provides two articles for deposit of things with a bank.

656. LCC Article 6.866 provides that a bank has the right to accept for deposit securities, precious metals and precious stones, other valuables and documents. The contract of deposit of things with a bank for safekeeping shall be certified by the storage certificate issued to the depositor by the bank.

657. In addition, the contract of deposit may provide for the safekeeping of the client's valuable items in the individual bank vault (department of the vault, isolated bank vault) allotted for use by the customer. Under the contract of deposit of valuable items for safekeeping in an individual bank vault, the client shall have the right to place the valuable items in the vault and take them from the vault by himself. The bank shall issue the client with the key to the vault and the customer's identification card or any other document certifying the customer's right to enter the bank depository where the client's individual vault is located and to open the vault. The contract of deposit may also provide for the client's right to work in the bank with the valuable items deposited in the bank vault. The bank shall accept from the client the valuable items to be deposited in the vault and shall also supervise their placement in and withdrawal from the vault and shall hand over to the client the valuable items taken from the vault. Where the contract establishes that the customer shall use the vault personally, the bank must ensure the client an opportunity to place the valuable in the vault and withdraw them from the vault unattended by anyone, bank employees included. The bank must also ensure the client's free entry into the bank depository where his individual vault is located. Unless otherwise provided by the contract of deposit, the bank shall be released from liability for the failure to preserve the valuable items placed in the individual vault if it proves that under the conditions of storage no person was allowed access to the contents of the vault without the client's knowledge or that the valuable items were lost due to superior force. Where under the contract the individual vault is allotted for use to another person and the liability of the bank for the preservation of the valuable items placed in the vault is not established, the rules regulating the contract of lease shall apply to the contract of the type (LCC Article 6.867).

XI. Custody of Financial Assets

658. Custody of money and financial instruments is of crucial importance because those financial assets nowadays form the largest part of assets within the whole economy.

659. It has been said already that the contract for deposit normally is purely obligational, but it may create *in rem* effects where things were mixed with other things of the same type and quality delivered for deposit by other persons (*depositum irregulare*). In such cases, the ownership of deposited property is transferred to the depositary, who under LCC Article 6.835 acquires personal duty to restore the quantity of the things of the same type and quality which is provided for in the contract. It means that *actio depositi* in case of irregular deposit is only personal remedy, which is inefficient against other creditors in case of depository insolvency.

A. Money in Bank Deposit and Bank Account

660. Historically, irregular deposit of money was the precursor to the creation of a contract of bank deposit. However, its evolution was gradually overtaken by the contract of loan and it is a mistake to equalise those monetary transactions today. The main difference between them is that the purpose of bank deposit contract is to lend money to the bank and get the interest on lent sum, whereas in the deposit, even irregular, the person who has the primary interest to put money into the bank is the client, not the bank. In short, in the deposit, the client wants to put money in the bank, while in loan it is the bank which wants the client's money.[375] Bank deposit in this respect, obviously, is functional equivalent of loan, not the deposit contract, a similar name of them being only historical connotation. From the other side, irregular deposit contract gave rise to another crucially important banking contract – bank account, which has retained purpose and character those of deposit, not the loan.

661. By the bank account agreement, the bank undertakes to accept and enter the money into the account opened by the client (the owner of the account), follow the client's instructions concerning the transfer and payment of certain amounts from the account, also to carry out any other operations performed by the bank, and

375. Widely discussed cases of negative bank interest rates followed by the ECB stimulus policy, where banks' negative base interest rate meant that bank should pay for giving money to the client and such unexpected premium erased bank's profit (margin interest rate), may be explained in legal terms only as the evolvement of deposit element in purely lending relationships. It should be noted that Lithuanian case law on the basis of the freedom of contract has acknowledged the possibility for the client to get paid for using loan money; however, as such relationships are unusual, such agreement is subject to clear and unequivocal term in the contract. Such agreement may not be identified solely on the basis of mathematical formula in the contract for a calculation of interest rate. *See* Judgments of the Lithuanian Supreme Court of 14 Apr. 2021 in the civil case No. e3K-3-87-611/2021 and of 30 Jun. 2021 in the civil case No. e3K-3-200-823/2021. However, such reasoning is not convincing, since it without any statutory ground limits contract term only to express term with direct statement on the negative interest rates and fails taking into account not only equality of parties but also enrichment of a bank which transfers only costs, not a benefit, originated in the interbank market on the same base interest rate clause. Inclusion of such a clause in the loan is justified as a part of the external lending costs which are automatically transferred to the client. Therefore, it is not clear the same clause should work only unilaterally. Having this in mind, it is naïve to think that banks will agree to include clauses in such a direct form as it has described. In sum, the Lithuanian Supreme Court, although in theory affirmed negative interest rates, in practical terms has denied the practical possibility to apply them.

the client undertakes to pay the bank for the services and operations effected. The bank may dispose of the funds in the client's account provided that it secures the client's right to freely dispose of such funds. The bank shall have no right to determine and control the use of the money by the client or impose any other limitations of the client's right to dispose of the funds in the account, except as provided in the law or the bank account agreement (LCC Article 6.913). It is prohibited to restrict the client's possibility to dispose of the funds in the account, except for the cases when the funds in the account are attached or if the operations performed by the bank are suspended in the cases and procedure prescribed by laws.

662. Similarly as some other special types of a deposit contract, bank account contract is a public (imposed) contract, because LCC 6.914 states that the bank has no right to refuse to open the account if the possibility for its opening is set forth in the law, operational documents of the bank or the licence issued to the bank, except for the cases when such refusal is permitted by laws.

B. Custody of Investors' Assets

663. In order to safeguard and promote investments, statutory law provides exceptions for the usual *depositum irregulare* consequences[376] as concern the custody of financial assets. First, there are so-called depository accounts, where account holders hold money belonging to their clients or third parties.[377] For instance, Law on Advocacy Article 50 prescribes that funds temporarily held by advocates but owned by other persons shall be accounted separately and kept in deposit accounts of advocates. It is prohibited to execute recovery from the funds kept in these accounts in respect of the obligations of the advocate.

664. Similar rules are established also within some financial laws. Most important for the investment services is Markets in Financial Instruments Law which transposes into Lithuanian law Directive 2014/65/EU of the European Parliament

376. Looking from the comparative law perspective, if a bank or investment firm does not record the individual numbers of the securities it holds for each client separately, or, more generally, if these securities are not in any way identifiable as a specific client's property, most civil law jurisdictions will deem these securities to form part of that bank's or investment firm's (own) property. It has dramatic consequences: without specific legislation having been enacted or special measures having been taken, the commingling of securities to which multiple clients are entitled would mean that those securities are deemed to be part of the bankruptcy estate in the event the bank or the investment firm that holds those securities falls bankrupt. Civil law jurisdictions therefore need both legal and operational rules to accomplish asset segregation and client protection. In common law jurisdictions, as a general rule, client securities do not form part of the property of a bank or an investment firm, at least in as far as the bank's or the investment firm's administration holds the securities for the benefit of clients. Such securities form part of a statutory trust and thus take free of the bank's or the investment firm's own creditors' claims. Common law jurisdictions therefore need operational rules to achieve asset segregation and client protection. *See* Matthias Haentjens, Pierre de Gioia-Carabellese. *European Banking and Financial Law*. Routledge, 2015, p. 161.

377. *See* Judgment of the Lithuanian Supreme Court of 9 Mar. 2017 in the civil case No e3K-3-124-611/2017.

and of the Council on markets in financial instruments (MiFID II) and which in Article 16 (17) states that a financial brokerage firm (in MiFID terminology – investment firm) shall, when holding funds belonging to clients, make adequate arrangements to safeguard the clients' rights and, except in the case of licensed credit institutions, prevent the use of client funds for its own account. Clients' funds transferred to the financial brokerage firm for the purpose of acquisition of financial instruments and clients' funds generated from the sale of financial instruments owned by the client shall be the client's property upon which no enforcement may be levied in respect of the indebtedness of the financial brokerage firm. Even more, in this case *depositum irregulare* principle is not applicable at all, because under the same article a financial brokerage firm must hold clients' funds in credit institution not on the deposit, but on a trust basis segregated from its own funds. And for the trust contract, imperative rule in LCC Article 6.953(2) prohibits the transfer of ownership to trustee. This implies that in case of bank insolvency, money of investors should be returned to them on a superpriority basis as assets falling outside of the bankruptcy estate.

665. Nevertheless, an application of trust for the custody of investors' money is just a partial solution because under LCC Article 1.101 (10), upon the issue of dematerialised securities, where the laws do not provide for otherwise, it shall be presumed pursuant to LCC that the holder of the securities has entrusted the accountant with their keep upon the contract of deposit. The rights, obligations and liability of the keeper shall be determined in accordance with the provisions of LCC applicable to the contract of deposit. Therefore, part of investors financial assets is held under the contract of deposit and other part under the contract of property trust. The practical difference of such regime would normally be that under the property trust contract, property of assets remains within client, while under the irregular deposit it passes to depositary. Fortunately, this problem is solved by the Markets in Financial Instruments Law Article 106(5), which states that the administrator of the financial brokerage firm shall return to the firm's clients their cash funds either held at the firm or deposited in client accounts with a credit institution managed by the financial brokerage firm and shall transfer the management of the personal accounts of financial instruments to another account manager designated by the client. This rule indirectly means that in the case of custody of financial instruments, the ownership of assets is left within the patrimony of the client, thus making second exception from usual *depositum irregulare* consequences.

666. As concern custody of investment funds assets, financial law is even more intrusive and rectifying general regime of deposit contract law. Law on Collective Investment Undertakings, which transposes UCITS directive[378] into Lithuanian law, requires investment funds to hold their assets at depositary, who may be only credit institution (Article 31). Law on Collective Investment Undertakings Article 32

378. Directive 2014/91/EU of the European Parliament and of the Council of 23 Jul. 2014 amending Directive 2009/65/EC on the coordination of laws, regulations and administrative provisions relating to undertakings for collective investment in transferable securities (UCITS) as regards depositary functions, remuneration policies and sanctions.

transposes UCITS directive Article 22(8), which prescribes that in the event of insolvency of the depositary and/or of any third party located in the Union to which custody of UCITS assets has been delegated, the assets of a UCITS held in custody are unavailable for distribution among, or realisation for the benefit of, creditors of such a depositary and/or such a third party.

Chapter 3. Gaming and Wagering

667. Gaming business gets through the hard way to legalisation in post-socialist society since games of chance for money have connotations of greed, easy enrichment and speculation – evil notions for the former regime, which still highly affected the mentality of Lithuanian society during the first years of independence. The legalisation of gaming in 2001, after more than a decade of independent State, was really a rational choice, because, as a rule of thumb, if State does not legalise and supervise those activities, they still exist, however, usually owned and controlled by organised crime. Without doubt, the industry runs businesses risky of abuse of money laundering, fraud and pathologic attraction leading to over-indebtedness and personal insolvency of gamers. Therefore, next to private law legislation on gaming and wagering, there is a clear public interest for administrative regulation of gaming entities to exist.

668. Games of chance in Lithuania are briefly regulated by LCC, which establishes the obligations stemming from such games, and special laws. Law on Gaming of 2001 establishes the conditions and procedure for the operation of gaming in the Republic of Lithuania, whereas the Law on Lotteries of 2003 regulates the conditions and procedure for operating lotteries in the country.[379] The purpose of the Law on Lotteries is to ensure the fulfilment of obligations undertaken by lottery operators in respect of players and to ensure the protection of the rights of players and lottery operators. The gaming industry in Lithuania is supervised and licences are issued by the State Gaming Control Commission (Law on Gaming Article 4). The same is with big lottery organisations, which are licensed and supervised by the State Gaming Control Commission, except for small lottery (up to EUR 30,000) operators, who are licensed and supervised by an executive body of the municipality in the territory of which the lottery will be conducted (Law on Lotteries Article 4, 23).

669. The whole framework of obligations in Lithuanian private law regarding games of chance is overlapped and at some point odd. The main mystery is that LCC rules on gaming and wagering are established not in the contract law section, but in quasi-contractual section titled 'obligation arising from other sources'. In

379. ECJ in the judgment of 24 Mar. 1994 in the case C-275/92 (*Schindler*) has admitted that lotteries are subject to particularly strict regulation and close control by the public authorities in the various Member States of the Community. However, they are not totally prohibited in those States. On the contrary, they are commonplace. In particular, although in principle lotteries are prohibited in the United Kingdom, small-scale lotteries for charitable and similar purposes are permitted, and, since the enactment of the appropriate law in 1993, so is the national lottery. In these circumstances, lotteries cannot be regarded as activities whose harmful nature causes them to be prohibited in all the Member States and whose position under Community law may be likened to that of activities involving illegal products even though the law of certain Member States treats gaming contracts as void. Even if the morality of lotteries is at least questionable, it is not for the Court to substitute its assessment for that of the legislatures of the Member States where that activity is practised legally.

legal doctrine, gaming and wagering without additional explanation are also characterised as quasi-contracts.[380] However, this characterisation goes in conflict with the whole system of civil obligations in the same LCC and fails to take into account special laws. But, as it is confirmed by the same doctrinal authors and the courts,[381] quasi-contracts may be only lawful acts. This is important because according to Law on Gaming Article 10, it is prohibited to operate gaming which is not provided for in this Law or to operate it in violation of the procedure established in this Law. Similarly, according to Law on Lotteries Article 17, it is prohibited to operate lotteries not indicated in this Law or to operate them in violation to the procedure established by this Law. It means that illegal operation of gaming, wagering and lotteries is a tort, not the quasi-contract. From the other side, if operation of gaming, wagering and lotteries is carried out in legal way, they give rise to the contractual obligations, which, as all other contractual obligation, only in subsidiary manner may be supplemented by quasi-contractual obligations stemming for performance not due (*condictio indebiti*) and unjustified enrichment (*actio de in rem verso*).

§1. Gambling and Wagering

670. Gambling and wagering falls under the regulatory concept of gaming. Gaming means the playing of a game or mutual betting in accordance with established regulations where the participants seek to win *money* by voluntarily risking a stake and where winnings or losses depend on chance, an occurrence of any event or the outcome of a sporting event (Law on Gaming Article 2). According to LCC Article 6.243, no obligations shall arise on the ground of gambling and wagering, except in cases established by laws. Claims from gambling and wagering are not protected in court, except in cases established by laws. Such cases, as it has been said may be contract or tort, but with some exceptions presented below.

671. When gaming is carried out legally it constitutes an aleatory contract, where a player – natural person – exchanges money for the chance to win more money. As gaming normally is a form of adult leisure, unrelated to their business, trade and profession, provided by business enterprise it should be characterised as

380. Valentinas Mikelėnas. *Prievolių teisė. Pirmoji dalis.* Justitia: Vilnius, 2002, p. 63. Possible explanation for such position could be the case law of the French *Cour de Cassation,* which has ruled that certain unfair commercial practices can be counteracted by a recourse to French CC Art. 1371 (the general definition of quasi-contracts). The subject matter of these judgments were ostensible notifications to consumers that they had won lottery prizes. The *Cour de Cassation* has held that such communications may establish a quasi-contract between the sender and the addressee. However, this new type of quasi-contract appears to be a construction sui generis between the law of contract and tort law and seems more closely related to the law of *culpa in contrahendo* (itself often interpreted as a quasi-contractual construction, giving a completely different meaning to the term) than it does to the law of quasi-contracts in the traditional meaning of the concept derived from Roman origin. *See* Christian von Bar, Walter de Gruyter. *Benevolent Intervention in Another's Affairs.* Sellier, 2006, p. 91.

381. Valentinas Mikelėnas. *Prievolių teisė. Pirmoji dalis.* Justitia: Vilnius, 2002, p. 63; Judgment of the Kaunas District Court of 18 Jan. 2013 in the criminal case No 1A-72-317/2013.

consumer contract.[382] Usually, such contracts are concluded by actions, not in the written form. The gaming is a unilateral real contract, because gaming organiser cannot contractually force the player to play or bet (it would be contrary to public order), and the whole gaming is carried out only where a player puts tokens (money) on the table, in the machine slot or transfers money to online casino.

672. To protect players, Law on Gaming Article 10 prescribes additional rules having impact on the contract law. Hence, a gaming company is prohibited from ensuring the fulfilment of the obligations undertaken by other entities as well as from granting any kind of loans to other persons. It is prohibited to use bank (debit, credit) cards for payment and instal ATM machines in premises where gaming is operated. Economic and commercial activities other than catering, sale of drinks, concert activity and currency exchange shall be prohibited on the premises where machine gaming, bingo and table games are operated. A gaming company shall be prohibited from manufacturing, assembling from parts or repairing gaming devices, developing new or modifying the existing gaming algorithm programs. A gaming company may not be the founder or shareholder of other companies. Very important safeguard measure of players is their right to ask State Gaming Control Commission for disallowance to play games of chance for at least six months. Where no period is mentioned in the players' submission, law presumes for disallowance of particular player for two years. Incompetent persons are also not allowed to play.

673. If gaming is prohibited by laws,[383] no action can be brought by the benefited party (winner) claiming the agreed sum to be paid; likewise, no recovery of the paid sum may be instituted by the losing party (loser). Hence, LCC Article 6.243 penalises loser and restricts possible causes of recovery for him only for situations

382. This feature of gaming contract is not always properly understood by the courts. In one case, court has refused to characterise gaming contracts as consumer contracts and grant favourable jurisdiction, solely relying on LCC $6.228^3(2)$, which states that rules of particular LCC chapter on consumer contract law are not applicable to games of chance. However, this chapter simply transposes Consumer Rights Directive 2011/83/EU together with its exclusions and does not preclude other consumer law protections for such contracts. This is clearly evident from Recital 31 of the directive stating that 'gambling should be excluded from the scope of this Directive. Gambling activities are those which involve wagering at stake with pecuniary value in games of chance, including lotteries, gambling in casinos and betting transactions. Member States should be able to adopt other, including more stringent, consumer protection measures in relation to such activities'. *See* Judgment of Siauliai District Court of 3 Oct. 2016 in the civil case No 2S-918-267/2016.

383. For instance, according to Law on Gaming Art. 10, gaming is completely outlawed in: residential houses, except those where non-residential premises located on the ground floor have been adapted for other activity according to the design and use of the building and which have a separate entrance from the street, which does not coincide with the stairwell entrance; preschool establishments; general education schools; vocational training establishments; higher schools; higher educational establishments; additional and non-formal educational establishments; healthcare establishments; children's sanatoriums; cultural establishments; libraries; theatres; museums and exhibition halls; credit and other financial institutions; shops, except for betting and totalisator stations in shopping centres which are designated not only for shop activities and which, according to the building layout plan, have separate premises; state and municipal institutions and establishments; cinemas, railway and bus stations, airports, seaports, except for machine gaming where it is operated in separate premises which are not related to the direct functions of such establishments; and post offices, except for betting and totalisator stations established therein.

where the loser is a minor, or in cases of compulsion, threat, fraud, or any other unfair actions exercised against the losing party. For instance, if gaming organiser, in contravention to ask for disallowance, still allows the addicted player to play, such gaming is illegal and void, and player may return lost money on the basis of tort law damages.[384]

§2. Lottery

674. Lottery is a game conducted in accordance with the established rules where the player purchases tickets to win *money or goods*. Pursuant to LCC Article 6.244, lottery can constitute a basis for obligations if organised and carried out within the procedure established by laws. Equally with gaming, where lotteries are organised pursuant to the procedure established by laws, a contract between the organiser and the participant of a lottery or other game shall be considered concluded. The lottery contract is unilateral, aleatory consumer contract and also real. The contract is formed in the form of either a ticket of the lottery or a receipt or any other document indicated in the regulations for the organisation of the lottery. Lottery ticket is a document or recording (numbers and/or symbols chosen by the player, time of recording, the player's telephone number and/or code), which is identifiable (providing evidence of participation in a lottery) in the database of a lottery's computer system. Prizes are paid out or delivered only upon the presentation of a lottery ticket. Depending on facts, lottery ticket may be characterised as negotiable instrument in the sense of LCC Article 1.101. Regulations for the organisation of the lottery should be approved by the organiser of the lottery. The regulations must contain information about the time of the lottery, rules for determining the winner, the amount of the prize and the procedure of its payment. The regulations must be publicly accessible. Where the organiser of a lottery refuses to organise it at the established time, the participants of such lottery have the right to demand from the organiser compensation of actual damage caused by the cancellation of the lottery, as well as by the postponement of the period of time allotted for the organisation of the events concerned. The organiser is bound to pay to the persons who are acknowledged as winners in accordance with the regulations of the lottery the winnings in the amount and form (in money or in kind) established by the regulations. The winning must be paid within the time limit established by the regulations and, where such time limit is not established, it must be paid within one month from the ascertainment of the results of the lottery. If the organiser of a lottery fails to perform his duty indicated above, the winner has the right to demand from the organiser payment of the winning and compensation of damage. However, in contrast with gambling and wagering, recovery of lost funds in illegal lottery contracts, according to LCC Article 6.244, is permissible in all cases, without additional restrictions.

675. LCC Article 6.244 by enabling recovery in illegal lottery contracts, oddly makes reference to the quasi-contracts of performance not due (LCC Article 6.237)

384. Judgment of the Klaipėda District Court of 19 Jan. 2017 in the civil case No 2A-15-730/2017.

and unjustified enrichment (LCC Article 6.242), thus overriding the general scheme of the civil obligations in LCC. In my opinion, this reference is erroneous and should be replaced with reference to the general tort law rule (LCC Article 6.263). Also, it is disputable, whether the separate treatment of gaming and lotteries in two different LCC articles providing for different civil consequences is justified. In my opinion, LCC Article 6.243 is not necessary at all, because, in essence lottery is just third form of gaming, next to gambling and wagering, and, at least for the purposes of civil law, principles set in LCC Article 6.244 should be equally applicable to all forms of gaming.

Chapter 4. Sales

676. Sales (*emptio-venditio*) formalises and enforces exchange of property, and as such, it is the main contract type in every economy, being it socialist or capitalist. During the communism period in Lithuania, the seller of consumer goods was usually the State and its enterprises, whereas in todays' market economy, it is private enterprises. Due to diversification of economic activities in independent Lithuania and as a result – much wider variety of contracts – sale of property now shares its popularity with few other types of contracts, prima facie loans and supply of other services, around which substantial contractual litigation in contemporary Lithuania takes place.[385] This, of course, at no instance means decline of sales contract, which having in mind everyday's amount of consumer and financial sales, evidently remains the most common contract in Lithuanian markets.

677. Market demand for legal certainty in intra-trade relations is an apparent leitmotif justifying currently detailed regulation of sales contract in LCC. Indeed, Lithuanian sales law is clearly more detailed in comparison to most of foreign codifications of hard and soft law, including, Dutch BW, German BGB, French *Code Civil*, Swiss CO, Russian ГК, DCFR, Common European Sales Law, etc. The other less noble and more technical reason for such extent was the apparent desire of LCC drafters to put all wisdom of Quebec CC, Russian ГК[386] and CISG into single chapter, without sacrificing the content of those sources. The result is extensive and even casuistic sales law seeks to provide answers to most of the questions in sales relationships. Meanwhile, case law surprisingly shows that sales law produces comparatively lesser amount of difficult legal questions compared to some other institutions of LCC. This juridical technique, where general rules on sales offer comprehensive regulation applicable for all sales, but calibration of specific sale types enables to satisfy needs of turbulent markets and to transfer even very sophisticated assets, at least by far seems to be successful.

678. Main source of sales law in Lithuania is LCC, which provides the general rules (LCC Article 6.305–6.349) and rules for specific sale types. Those specific types are consumer sale (LCC Article 6.350–6.370),[387] wholesale sale (LCC Article 6.371–379), sale on public procurement (LCC Article 6.380–6.382, Law on Public

385. For example, according to official judicial statistics of 2021, in Lithuania from 36,000 new contractual disputes 10,065 were initiated from loans, 8,418 from sales, 10,818 from supply of services, 2,464 from lease and 359 from construction works. *See* http://www.teismai.lt/lt/visuomenei-ir-ziniasklaidai/statistika/106.

386. The sources of the new Russian Code are the Civil Code of the RSFSR of 1964, the Fundamental Principles of Civil Legislation of the USSR of 1991, four classical civil codes (German, Swiss, French and Italian), two of the newer codes (of Québec and of the Netherlands), the Draft of the Civil Code of the Russian Empire of 1913, and international private law (e.g., Vienna Convention on International Sale of Property). Asya Ostroukh. Russian Society and its Civil Codes: A Long Way to Civilian Civil Law. Journal of Civil Law Studies, Vol. 6, No 1, 2013, p. 394.

387. Closely related to the consumer sales contract is the novel concept of supply of digital content, which is based on the EU law – Directive 2011/83/EU of the European Parliament and of the Council of 25 Oct. 2011 on consumer rights (CRD) and Directive (EU) 2019/770 of the European Parliament and of the Council of 20 May 2019 on certain aspects concerning contracts for the supply

Procurement), energy sale (LCC Article 6.383–6.391), immovable sale (LCC Article 6.392–6.401), enterprise sale (LCC Article 6.402–6.410), instalment sale (LCC Article 6.411–6.416), sale with right of redemption (LCC Article 6.417–6.418), auction sale (LCC Article 6.419–6.424) and sale of rights (LCC Article 6.425–6.427). In addition to general transactional and contractual rules, sales are also regulated by tort law, which provides for liability for defective production in consumer sales (LCC Article 6.292–6.300). There are also special laws, which regulate sales, most notable of them being Constitutional Law on the Subjects, Procedure, Terms and Conditions and Restrictions of the Acquisition into Ownership of Land Plots, provided for in paragraph 2 of Article 47 of the Constitution of the Republic of Lithuania, which regulates the conditions, according to whom foreign subjects may be permitted to acquire into ownership land, internal waters and forests in Lithuania. Other specific laws are Law on Financial Instruments Market, Law on the Privatisation of Shares Owned by the State and Municipalities, etc. On the top of national law, sales are highly affected by EU law and trade policy and an international law, in particular, the CISG, which was ratified by Lithuania already in 1995.

§1. Sales Contracts in General

679. In evaluating style of sales law in a given jurisdiction, the crucial point is the place of *caveat emptor* principle. Lithuania in this respect is purely continental jurisdiction, which suppress this principle quite extensively as a sacrifice for an overriding principle of good faith. It is the active duty of the seller to reveal all the facts, which are required to know about the condition and status of property, not the duty of the buyer to make due diligence. The seller has statutory obligation of warranty and even in commercial contracts is liable for the defects thereof unless he proves that the defects appeared after the delivery of the things to the buyer due to improper use or violation of the rules of preservation thereof or through the fault of third persons or as a result of superior force. Of course, according to LCC, the buyer has right to inspect the property, at any place, at any time or in any manner which correspond to the criteria of reasonableness, but it may be at the same time risky action because the seller is not bound to warrant against any latent defect known to the buyer or any apparent defect that can be perceived by a prudent and diligent

of digital content directive (DCD). However, in contrast to Directive (EU) 2019/771 of the European Parliament and of the Council of 20 May 2019 on certain aspects concerning contracts for the sale of goods (SGD), the rules of the DCD were implemented in Chapter XVIII[1] titled 'Consumer contracts for supply of digital content directive', i.e., in the general part of the contract law. In my opinion, this is not only incongruent but also a conceptually wrong choice, because contracts of supply of digital content by their nature are new types of *contractus nominatus*. Instead, rules on digital content from CRD and DCD should have been aligned and codified in the special part of contract law next to rules on consumer sales of movables based on SGD. This would have brought more clarity and logic within the whole structure of LCC and better reflect the equivalence between two types of consumer contracts – supply of digital content and sales of tangible movables. *See* Laurynas Didžiulis, '*EU Digital Content Directive And Evolution Of Lithuanian Contract Law*', 12 Journal of Intellectual Property, Information Technology and E-Commerce Law (2021), pp. 260–270.

buyer without any need of expert inspection. Thus, if the buyer has done due diligence, the probability that court will say 'the buyer should have known about those defects' arises. Clear exception is business due diligence, where Supreme Court has ruled that shares are specific assets and buyer, which has failed to do due diligence, was careless.[388] Nevertheless, the picture is quite clear – LCC puts emphasis on the seller than the buyer to ensure the sale is successful. In my opinion, this is really a rational attitude because seller knows better her property than the stranger buyer, and burden of disclosure on the part of seller simply reduces transaction costs by avoiding the need for extensive due diligence. Hence *caveat vendor*!

680. The essence of the sale is exchange of property for money. In this respect, sale is different from very similar contract – barter, which is exchange of property for other property. However, both contracts are so similar that LCC 6.432 provides for subsidiary application of sales rules for barter contracts. Although barter is a sign of primitive economy and used mostly in simple domestic transactions, during the initial stage of credit crunch of 2008–2010, its popularity in Lithuanian business practice had been on the rise.

681. Sale is consensual, bilateral, onerous, commutative contract with *in rem* effect – the transfer of property rights. Therefore, so-called leasing contracts, the main purpose of which is to transfer the ownership at the end of property use, are not lease, but instalment sale, according to the case law and legal doctrine.[389]

682. In general, movable sales are informal contracts, i.e., may be concluded in verbal form or form of gestures. For instance, according to LCC Article 6.384, where under the energy sales contract the subscriber is a natural person who uses energy for domestic consumption, the contract shall be deemed concluded from the moment the consumer equipment is connected to the energy transmission network. Immovable sales should be notarised (LCC Article 6.393), except for crops or standing timber, which may be transferred in equal manner as movables (LCC Article 4.2). If real property falls under the regime of family assets and family has minor child, sale is perfected only with approval of court (LCC Article 3.85). Usually, the only essential term of a contract in the case of movable sales is the prestation, while in sales of immovables and instalment sales, it is also the price (LCC Article 6.397, 6.404, 6.413) and some additional requirements in specific sale situations: an agreement of use rights over the land where building is sold separately from land (LCC Article 6.394) and enlistment of inhabitants of sold residential property (LCC Article 6.400). Without those terms and execution of formalities the contract is not formed.

---

388. *See* Judgments of the Lithuanian Supreme Court of 28 Nov. 2005 in the civil case No 3K-3-614/2005, of 16 Oct. 2006 in the civil case No. 3K-3-558/2006 and of 3 Apr. 2007 in the civil case No. 3K-3-145/2007.

389. *See* Laurynas Didžiulis, Janina Stripeikienė. *Aktualūs finansinės nuomos (lizingo) instituto taikymo klausimai. In.* Privatinės teisės doktrina ir praktika: Liber Amicorum Vytautui Pakalniškiui. Vilnius: Mykolas Romeris University, 2014, p. 319–335; Judgment of the Lithuanian Supreme Court of 9 Jan. 2013 in the civil case No 3K-3-154/2013.

I. The Seller's Obligations

683. Principal obligations of seller are: (1) duty to transfer the title to property; (2) duty to transfer the possession of property; (3) duty to transfer the documents accompanying property; and (4) warranty the title and conformity of property. Other obligations may also be established; for instance, parties may agree that seller must insure sold property.

A. Duty to Transfer the Title to Property

684. The purpose of sales contract, from purely legal perspective, is to transfer the ownership of goods from seller to buyer against payment. There is always the opposite movement of goods against money, both of them being the different classes property. This translatory function of sales contract is achieved according to rules of property law. In the universe of property law, sales contract is an independent ground for derivative acquisition of property rights by transfer (LCC Article 4.47). Hence, the sales contract is *causa traditionis* without which in a causal transfer system, present in Lithuania, no property passes to the buyer. Without the contract, property rights may be created on the transferred property only by way of original acquisition, such as bona fides acquisition, acquisitive prescription and confiscation.

685. In order to transfer the title, besides the existence of the contract itself, Lithuanian property law also requires two additional conditions to exist: seller's right to dispose and transfer in proper mode (*modus*).

686. As to the right to dispose, LCC Article 4.48 states that the right of ownership may be transferred to another person only by the owner of a thing or by a person given such powers by the owner. But even the owner may not have the right to dispose, if it has been temporarily seized by the order of court, the hypothec contract (LCC Article 4.170) or on the other ground.

687. As for transfer mode, LCC Article 4.49 prescribes that the acquirer of a thing (property) acquires the ownership right to the thing (property) as of the moment these are transferred to him, provided the laws or the contract does not stipulate otherwise. Thus, there are two possibilities: real transfer act (*traditio*), as a default rule, and consensual transfer clause (*solo consensus*), as a contractual carve-out. Real transfer is unilateral proprietary transaction, carried out by the seller in order to transfer the property. Real transfer may involve transfer of actual possession (*traditio possesorium*) or may be simply symbolic (*traditio symbolica*), i.e., executed by signing of transfer deed. It should be noted that transfer act in any case is unilateral act of seller, which only should be accepted by, not formed with, the buyer; therefore, it is inaccurate to characterise it as bilateral transaction. As the transfer act is proprietary transaction, it should be distinguished from the contract itself, which is an obligational transaction, according to which execution of such transfer is a civil obligation of the seller.

688. Consensual transfer clause is an option for parties, permitted in all cases where real transfer is not mandatory. In consensual transfer mode, the transfer of ownership is effected by the sole agreement on immediate transfer included in the sales contract. Thus, the sales contract by itself transfers ownership and no additional proprietary transaction is required. This mode seems to be attractive; however, it may also create additional problems such as legal uncertainties when ownership is transferred in advance without actual identification of purchased property, shift of seller's insolvency risk on the buyer and additional amount of related litigation. For this reason, law restricts the use of consensual transfer and sticks to the real transfer in cases of transfer of immovables (LCC 6.393), negotiable financial assets (LCC Article 1.101, 6.922, 6.933) and registrable property (LCC Article 4.49(4)), like cars. Transfer *solo consensu* may also be restricted where property are dangerous (guns, drugs, poison, etc.), and administrative permit is required for a transfer (LCC Article 4.51). Whereas it is fully possible to contract on sale of future non-registrable property (LCC Article 4.49(4)), the ownership passes only when such property are created and specified, because, first, derivative acquisition by sale is possible only after original acquisition by creation has happened and, second, property should be specified enough in order to attach ownership rights to them.

689. In *solo consensu* mode, the transfer of ownership precedes the transfer of possession, which happens later. But there can also be the opposite situations, where possession precedes the ownership. First, quite simple situation is where at the time of sale the possession already belongs to the buyer. In such event, ownership passes immediately (*brevi manu traditio*), since possession has been already transferred. Even more, according to LCC Article 6.309, the promise of sale of a thing, for instance in a preliminary contract,[390] with delivery thereof to the future buyer for actual possession is equivalent to sale of the thing.

690. Second, sophistication of ordinary transfer regime is possible by LCC Article 4.49(3), which permits contract to stipulate that the ownership right shall pass to the acquirer only after the latter shall have carried out a condition established in the contract. For example, in financial markets usual and at some point even mandatory technique to mitigate risk is to employ delivery versus payment (DvP)[391] rule, instead of default free-of-payment regime (FoP).[392] Such condition is applied on the top of applicable mode of transfer – transfer by delivery or mere agreement – by suspending the transfer until the occurrence of condition. As such, this technique is characterised as title-based security interest securing obligations in

390. Judgment of the Lithuanian Supreme Court of 6 Nov. 2006 in the civil case No 3K-P-382/2006.

391. Delivery versus payment or DvP means a securities settlement mechanism which links a transfer of securities with a transfer of cash in a way that the delivery of securities occurs if and only if the corresponding transfer of cash occurs and vice versa. Regulation (EU) No. 909/2014 of the European Parliament and of the Council of 23 Jul. 2014 on improving securities settlement in the EU and on central securities depositories No 909/2014 Art. 39(7) prescribes that all securities transactions against cash between direct participants in a securities settlement system operated by a central securities depository (CSD) and settled in that securities settlement system shall be settled on a DvP basis.

392. Judgment of the Lithuanian Supreme Court of 18 Oct. 2013 in the civil case No. 3K-3-493/2013.

the sense of LCC Article 6.70. According to LCC 6.431, under the sales contract with a reservation clause regarding the right of ownership, the seller shall retain the right of ownership to the thing being sold until the performance by the buyer of the obligations provided for in the contract. Under a contract with a reservation clause relating to the right of ownership, the buyer shall have no right of disposal of the thing being sold until he fulfils all the conditions specified in the contract. Specific instance of title reservation is instalment sale, under which the seller retains the right of ownership to the thing which is being sold until the payment of the full sale price set in the contract, unless the contract provides otherwise. A reservation of ownership in respect of the thing which is not subject to registration, acquired for the service or operation of an enterprise, has an effect against third person only if the purchase–sale contract has been registered in the public register according to the procedure prescribed by law (LCC Article 6.411). However, if the buyer has paid more than a half or the price of the thing, the seller shall have no right to take back the thing, unless the contract provides otherwise. Where the right of ownership passes to the buyer from the moment of delivery of the thing, it shall be considered from the moment of delivery of the thing to the buyer until the payment of the full price that the thing has been charged to the seller seeking to secure performance of obligations by the buyer (legal charge (hypothec), unless the contract provides otherwise (LCC Article 6.414)). In any case, as reservation of title is a security interest with *in rem* effects, it should be perfected by registration in order to use it against third parties, otherwise the transaction will be prone to bona fide acquirers.

691. After the transfer, the new owner acquires such rights and obligations regarding the property as had the former owner of the thing property, if the laws and the contract do not stipulate otherwise (*nemo dat quod non habet* rule, LCC Article 4.49).

B. Duty to Transfer the Possession of Property

692. The obligation to deliver the things is performed when the seller puts the buyer in possession of the things or consents to his taking possession of it and all disturbances are removed. Unless otherwise provided by the contract, the seller is bound to deliver the things together with all their accessories in condition it is at the time of formation of the contract of sale (LCC Article 6.317).

693. Transfer of possession is important for sales contract in three aspects: first, it is the default way to transfer the ownership and exercise the respective obligation; second, even in transfer of ownership in *solo consensu* mode, possession is a necessary prerequisite to fully enjoy and exercise ownership rights – the apparent purpose of buyer; third, in a sale with reservation of title possession is precondition for use of property until the final transfer of title. Thus, duty to transfer possession is distinct from that for the transfer of title.

694. According to LCC Article 4.50, delivery of a thing should give the acquirer the opportunity to use the thing transferred according to its purpose, with due regard to the condition of the thing and to its legal status. The transfer is the passing into ownership of a thing to the acquirer, as well as the passing over of a thing, given without the duty to deliver to the destination, to a transport company for delivery to the acquirer and delivery by post to the acquirer, if the laws and the contract do not provide for differently. Transfer of a bill of lading or another document testifying to the disposal thereof equals to the transfer of the thing. Delivery expenses are assumed by the seller, unless the contract provides otherwise (LCC Article 6.317).

695. Pursuant to LCC Article 6.398, transfer of an immovable thing is executed by the transfer-acceptance deed or any other document provided for in the contract, signed by the seller and buyer. Unless otherwise provided for by the laws or contract, the seller's obligation to transfer the immovable thing shall be deemed performed from the moment of transfer of the thing to the buyer and signing of the relevant document regarding the transfer thereof. Where one of the parties to the contract avoids signing the document of transfer specified in the contract, it shall be deemed that the buyer refuses to accept and the seller refuses to transfer the thing.

696. In international trade contracts, parties usually specify sale terms, including delivery place, using International Commercial Terms of International Chamber of Commerce (INCOTERMS). Nonetheless, if the seller is not bound to deliver the things at any other particular place, pursuant to LCC Article 6.318, his obligation to deliver consists: (1) if the contract sale involves carriage of the things – in handing the things over to the first carrier for transmission to the buyer, unless otherwise provided in the contract; (2) if the contract relates to specific things to be drawn from a specific stock or to be manufactured, and at the time of the conclusion of the contract the parties knew thereof – in placing the things at the disposal of the buyer or the person indicated by him at the place of the reserve or manufacture; and (3) in other cases – in placing the things at the buyer's disposal at the place where the seller had his place of business or residence at the time of the conclusion of the contract or where the things are transmitted to the person indicated by the buyer. The fruits and revenue from the things belong to the buyer from the time of delivery of the things.

C. Duty to Transfer the Documents Accompanying Property

697. Together with the property seller is bound to surrender to the buyer the related documents in his possession. If the seller himself needs the above documents for enforcing other rights not related to the things sold, the seller is bound to deliver to the buyer copies of the documents validated in the established manner (LCC Article 6.318).

D. Warranty of the Title and Conformity of Property

698. Seller warrants to the buyer the title and conformity of property. Title is legal quality, while conformity is factual quality of property.[393] Warranty may be statutory, as a minimum protection for every buyer, and contractual, as a voluntary extension of statutory warranty.

699. According to LCC Article 6.317, the seller's warranty of ownership and quality of the things exists of right whether or not these warranties are stipulated in the contract of sale (statutory warranty).

700. Seller's statutory duty to give warranty of ownership of the property is further established in LCC Article 6.321, according to which the seller is bound to warrant the buyer that the things delivered is free from any right or claim of any third party, unless the buyer agreed in advance to accept the things subject to that right or claim, whereas the seller gave a due notice thereof to the buyer. The seller is bound to discharge the things of all pledge (hypothecs) irrespective of the registration of the pledge or hypothec, unless the buyer, after he has been given notice by the seller of the encumbrances, agrees to buy the things. The seller is bound to warrant the buyer that the delivered things have not been seized and is not an object of a legal action, also that the seller has not been deprived of the right to dispose of the things or that there are no encumbrances. The seller of an immovable thing is a warrantor towards the buyer for any violation or restrictions of public law affecting the thing which are exceptions to the ordinary law of ownership. Where at the time of the sale the seller has duly given notice to the buyer of the encroachment by the third persons on the things being delivered or of these encumbrances or where such rights of the third persons or such encumbrances have been registered in the public registers, the buyer may not invoke the circumstance that the seller has breached his obligation. Where the seller breaches his obligations specified above, the buyer is entitled to demand reduction of the price or to rescind the contract, unless the seller proves that the buyer was aware or could not be unaware of the rights of the third persons to the things or these encumbrances.

701. Statutory conformity requirements in respect of the property are set in LCC Article 6.327, according to which the thing which is being sold must be of the quantity, quality and other description required by the contract or, where the contract contains no specific requirements, correspond to the regular requirements. The seller shall not be liable for any lack of conformity of the thing if at the time of the conclusion of the contract the buyer knew or could not have been unaware of such lack of conformity. The seller shall be liable under the contract and LCC for any lack of conformity which exists at the time when the right of ownership passes to the buyer, even though the lack of conformity becomes apparent only after that time. The seller

393. The concept of 'legal quality' is known to Germanic legal tradition (*See* BGB Art. 435) and in Lithuanian legal doctrine was introduced by notable Lithuanian private law scholar – Prof. V. Mizaras. *See* V. Mizaras. *Pirkimo-pardavimo sutartinių santykių reguliavimas Civiliniame kodekse.* Justitia, 2003, nr. 5, p. 10.

shall be also liable for any lack of conformity which occurs after the time when the right of ownership passes to the buyer and which is due to a breach of any of the seller's obligations, including a breach of any warranty that for a period of time the things will remain fit for their ordinary purpose or for some particular purpose or will retain specified qualities or characteristics. The buyer shall forfeit the right to rely on a lack of conformity of the things if he does not give notice to the seller specifying the nature of the lack of conformity within a reasonable time after he has discovered or ought to have discovered it.

702. In consumer sales, unless proved otherwise, any lack of conformity which becomes apparent within one year of delivery of the goods shall be presumed to have existed at the time of delivery unless this presumption is incompatible with the nature of the goods or the nature of the lack of conformity (LCC Article 6.364).

II. The Buyer's Obligations

703. Principal obligations of buyer are: (1) duty to pay the price; and (2) duty to accept the property and documents. Other obligations may also be established; for instance, parties may agree that buyer must insure sold property.

A. *Duty to Pay the Price*

704. A price is not an essential term of movables sales contract under Lithuanian contract law. LCC Article 6.313 provides that the price of the thing being sold shall be stipulated by agreement between the parties. Where the price is not stipulated in the contract of purchase–sale either expressly or impliedly, or the manner for stipulating the price is not agreed by the contract, it shall be considered, unless otherwise agreed by the parties, that the parties have impliedly made reference to the price generally charged at the time of the conclusion of the contract for such thing sold under comparable circumstances in the trade concerned and, where the price is non-existent, the price meeting the criteria of reasonableness. Where the price must be stipulated according to the weight of the things, it shall be determined by the net weight, unless otherwise agreed by the parties. If the price is to be stipulated by one of the parties and the price fixed in the said manner clearly fails to meet the criteria of reasonableness, the price in the contract must be replaced by a price meeting the criteria of reasonableness regardless of the agreement between the parties. Where the price is to be stipulated by a third person, but he does not or cannot fix the price, the price which meets the criteria of reasonableness shall be deemed to be the price of the contract. Where the price is to be stipulated on the basis of criteria which are non-existent or have disappeared or which cannot be established, the price shall be fixed on the basis of the criteria of the closest value. Where the contract provides that the price must be changed having regard to certain indices affecting the price (cost, expenses, etc.) without, however, referring to the procedure for price change, the price shall be determined according to the ratio of the indices at the moment of conclusion of the contract and delivery of the thing. If the seller delays delivery of the thing, the price shall be fixed according to the ratio of the said indices at the moment of conclusion of the contract and delivery of the thing provided in the contract. However, in immovables sales contract and instalment sales, price is an essential term (LCC Article 6.397, 6.404, 6.413).

705. LCC also provides detailed rules for the manner in which price should be paid. Thus, unless bound to pay the price at a specified place, the buyer must pay the seller the price at the place of delivery of the thing. Unless bound to pay the price at a specified time, the buyer must pay the price at the time of delivery under the contract of the thing or documents of disposal thereof to the buyer. The buyer is not obligated to pay the price before he has had an opportunity to examine the things, except where the agreement between the parties provides otherwise. Unless otherwise provided by the contract, the buyer must pay the entire price in a lump sum. If the buyer fails to pay for the things delivered to him by the set date, the seller shall be entitled to demand payment of the price and interest prescribed by law or under contract. If the buyer refuses to accept delivery of the thing and to pay the sale price, the seller may, at his discretion, demand from the buyer the payment of the price or refuse to perform the contract. Where the seller is bound under contract to deliver to the buyer not only the things for which the buyer has not yet paid the price, but also other things, the seller may suspend the delivery of the latter things until the buyer pays the whole of the price of the previously delivered things, unless otherwise provided by law or the contract (LCC Article 6.314). In case of the dispute, the buyer has a burden to prove the payment of price.[394]

706. Additional rules on the payment of price are established in LCC chapter on payments and special Law on Payments, which transposes EU Payment Services Directive II.[395] Pursuant to LCC Article 6.929, payments with participation of natural persons who are not engaged in economic-commercial activities may be effected only in cash without limitation of the amount, or in non-cash. Payments between legal persons and payments with participation of natural persons who are engaged in economic-commercial activities shall be effected in non-cash and in the cases and procedure prescribed by laws – in cash as well. Payment in non-cash shall be effected through banks with which appropriate accounts are opened, unless otherwise established in the law or unless limited by the used payment forms. Payments by checks and bills of exchange shall be accordingly regulated by the Law on Checks and Law on Bills of Exchange and Promissory Notes. Payments in non-cash shall be effected using payment orders, letters of credit, checks, bills of exchange, collection and other means of payment established by laws. The parties shall be entitled to choose and determine any means of mutual payment (LCC Article 6.930). Whereas LCC understands payment as settlement of monetary obligations, Law on Payments, being legislation of more technical nature, characterises

394. Judgment of the Lithuania Supreme Court of 24 Feb. 2021 in the civil case No. e3K-7-125-378/2021.

395. Directive (EU) 2015/2366 of the European Parliament and of the Council of 25 Nov. 2015 on payment services in the internal market, amending Directives 2002/65/EC, 2009/110/EC and 2013/36/EU and Regulation (EU) No. 1093/2010, and repealing Directive 2007/64/EC (Text with EEA relevance).

as payment any act, initiated by the payer or on his behalf or by the payee, of placing, transferring or withdrawing funds, irrespective of any underlying obligations between the payer and the payee.

B. Duty to Accept the Property and Documents

707. Principles of good faith and fair dealing require parties to cooperate, especially when a seller performs its duty to deliver the property and accompanying documents to the buyer. Thus, LCC Article 6.346 obliges the buyer to accept the delivered things, unless he is entitled to demand replacement of the things or termination of the contract. Unless otherwise provided by laws or the contract, the buyer is bound to take such measures and perform such actions which are required under the usually stated demands seeking to ensure due delivery and acceptance of things. Where the buyer, in breach of his obligation, does not accept or refuses to accept things, the seller has the right to demand that the buyer accept the things or refuse to perform the contract. Also, the seller may perform obligations into deposit. Pursuant to LCC Article 6.56, the debtor shall be obliged to make a proposal and determine the time limit for the acceptance of performance. In the case of the creditor's failure to accept performance of the obligation within the established time limit, he is in default. In this event, the creditor shall bear the costs of the preservation of the thing. The creditor shall also bear the risk of loss or deterioration of a thing. If a thing is perishable, the debtor may sell it and deposit the proceeds into the account of a notary or credit institution. A deposit of the sum necessary for the performance of an obligation into a deposit account is considered a proper performance of the obligation.

708. However, if the buyer has the right under the law or the contract to return to the seller the property delivered to him, the buyer must take such steps as are reasonable in the circumstances to preserve the property subject to be returned until their return. In this case the buyer is entitled to retain them until he has been reimbursed his reasonable expenses by the seller. If the dispatched things subject to be returned have been placed at the buyer's disposal at their destination, he is bound to return them at his own expense, unless the seller or his agent is present at the destination or provided this does not cause the buyer unreasonable inconvenience or unreasonable expense.

III. Risk of Accidental Damage to the Property

709. Pursuant to the Lithuanian property law, the risk of accidental damage of a thing being transferred shall pass to the acquirer at the moment that he acquires the ownership rights, unless otherwise stipulated by law or by contract. If the transferor misses the deadline to transfer the thing or the acquirer misses the deadline to receive the thing, the risk of accidental damage for the thing shall be upon the party that has missed the deadline, unless otherwise stipulated by law or by contract (LCC Article 4.52).

710. Those rules are further elaborated by contract law, in particular by LCC Article 6.320, which also provides the general rule that the risk of accidental perishing of or damage to the things shall pass to the buyer from the moment when the seller is deemed under the contract or law to have been duly discharged of his duty to deliver the things, regardless of the time of passing of the ownership. But the risk of accidental perishing of or damage to the things sold during the carriage thereof shall pass to the buyer from the time the contract is made, unless the contract or custom of the trade provides otherwise. The term of the contract that the risk of accidental perishing of or damage to the things passes to the buyer after the handling of the thing to the first carrier may be recognised as null and void at the buyer's request if at the time of entry into the sales contract the seller knew or should have known that the things had perished or had been damaged; however, he did not notify the buyer thereof. If the things perished or were damaged after their sale through no fault of the seller, the buyer must pay the price to the seller. The above rule shall also apply in cases where the seller was unable to deliver the things to the buyer due to the latter's insufficient cooperation with the seller and for this reason was in breach of the contract. Where the subject matter of contract are things characterised by description of the kind of the things and the buyer refuses to accept the things or is otherwise in breach of the contract, the risk of accidental perishing of or damage to the things shall transfer to the buyer from the moment when the seller identifies the things and notifies the buyer thereof. If the buyer brings a justified action for the nullity of the contract or replacement of the things, the risk of accidental perishing of or damage to the things shall be borne by the seller. If the risk of accidental perishing of or damage to the things stays with the seller even after the delivery thereof to the buyer, the seller shall be liable for the perishing of or damage to the things, even though this might have been caused by reason of the actions of the buyer. However, from the moment the buyer could have reasonably foreseen that he had to return the things to the buyer he shall be responsible for the safekeeping thereof.

IV. Remedies

711. Besides the usual remedies in personam, such as specific performance, avoidance of contract, withholding of performance or award of damages, sales law provides several sets of specific remedies calibrated to various non-performances, including the failure to deliver the property of proper assortment, packaging, quantity or quality. In practice, the most important issues related to breach of sales contract are delivery of defective property and failure to pay the price.

712. According to LCC Article 6.334, there the things sold do not correspond to the quality requirements and the seller did not discuss the defects with the buyer, upon buying things of unsatisfactory quality the buyer shall be entitled to demand, at his own choice; (1) to replace the thing which is characterised in the contract by its kind by the thing of satisfactory quality unless the defects are minor or appeared due to the fault of the buyer; (2) to reduce the price; (3) that the seller eliminates the defects within a reasonable time without any additional payment or reimburses the buyer's expenses for the elimination of defects if these may be eliminated; and

(4) to restore the price and repudiate the contract, where the sale of things of unsatisfactory quality is an essential breach of contract. If the bought things perished by reason of a latent defect that existed at the time of conclusion of the contract of purchase–sale, the seller is bound to restore the price. If the loss results from force majeure, or is due to the fault of the buyer, the buyer shall deduct from his claim the value of the things in the condition they were in at the time of the loss. If the things perished by reason of a latent defect of which the seller was aware or could not have been unaware, he is bound not only to restore the price but also to pay all damages suffered by the buyer. The conditions of the contract excluding or limiting the seller's liability for the defects of the things shall be null and void unless he has disclosed to the buyer the defects of which the seller was aware or could not have been unaware or in the case where a buyer buys things at his own risk from a seller who is not a professional seller.

713. The sold property may also lack legal quality, i.e., the 'clean' legal title to the property. Such defect may even lead to a situation where sold property is revendicated from the buyer. Hence, pursuant to LCC Article 6.323, where the court revendicates against the buyer the thing sold on the grounds which appeared due to non-performance of the contract, the seller must restore the price and pay the damages suffered by the buyer, unless the seller proves that the buyer was aware or could not have been unaware of the grounds. Agreement between the parties to exclude or limit the liability of the seller shall be null and void if the seller, being aware that the third person has rights to the thing under sale, fails to notify the buyer thereof.

714. The buyer is bound to notify the seller of the breach of any term of the contract specifying the quality, quantity, range, completeness, containers and packaging of the things within the time period fixed by law or contract or where the time period is not fixed – within a reasonable time after the breach of a certain term was discovered or, in view of the type and purpose of the things, ought to have been discovered. In case of failure by the buyer to notify the seller of the breach, the seller shall have the right to refuse to fully or in part meet the buyer's demands to replace the things, to deliver the missing things, to eliminate the defects of the things, to complete the things, to pack the things or deliver them in containers or to replace the containers or packaging, provided that he proves that following the breach of the obligation by the buyer his demands can no longer be met or that meeting of the demands would cause the seller unreasonable expenses compared to those the seller would have incurred if the buyer duly notified the seller of the breach of the contract. If the seller was aware or could not have been unaware of the nonconformity of the things delivered by him to the conditions of the contract of purchase–sale, he shall lose the right to invoke those rules.

715. According to LCC Article 6.338, where the time period of warranty of quality or fitness for use of the item of the thing has not been established, the buyer may file claims regarding the defects of the thing within a reasonable time but not later than within two years from the day of sale of the thing, unless a longer time period is provided by law or the contract. The time period for filing claims in respect of the defects of the thing transported or conveyed by post shall run from the day of arrival of the thing to the appointed destination. Where the time period of warranty of quality of the thing has not been fixed, claims regarding the defect of the thing may be filed, provided the defects are established within the period of warranty. If the period of warranty of quality valid for the component parts is shorter than the period of warranty of quality of the principal thing, the claim regarding the defects of the component part may be filed within the period of warranty of quality of the principal thing. Where a period of warranty of quality applied in respect of the component part is longer than that of the principal thing, a claim regarding the defects of the component part discovered within the period of warranty may be filed regardless of the expiration of the period of warranty of quality of the principal thing. The buyer may file claims regarding a thing, in respect of which a time period of fitness for use has been fixed, provided the defects are discovered within the time period of fitness for use of the thing. Where the period of warranty of quality fixed for a thing in the contract is less than two years and the defects of the thing are discovered after the expiration of the time period but not after the lapse of two years from the day of delivery of the thing, the seller shall be liable for the defects of the thing if the buyer proves that the defect appeared before the delivery of the thing or due to the reasons which appeared before the delivery and for which the seller is liable.

716. Time limits established in LCC Article 6.338 (which is based on Russian ГК Article 477) are resolutory and applicable for the submission of legal demands to the seller. In addition, time limit to sue seller in the court on the basis of extinctive prescription is two years, according to LCC Article 1.125. A lot of controversies have continuously surrounded relationship between those two types of time limits. The question is when time limit to sue buyer actually begins – after identification of defects, after submission of out-of-court legal demand to the seller or after the rejection of legal demands by the seller? The LCC by itself is silent with respect to sales contracts, but, interestingly, in the case of very similar rules for works contracts expressly states that the prescription shall commence from the date of the statement concerning the defects is made (LCC Article 6.667). If applied also for sales contracts, such calculation would be a prudent one, because after the submission of legal demand, both parties know about the defects and the seller should be ready to prepare for litigation in case where seller withholds answer or even rejects this demand. However, the position in the case law is different and clearly more favourable to the buyer – extinctive prescription begins to run only where the buyer gets the rejection of its legal demand or no answer in the reasonable time limit at all from the seller.[396]

717. Additional protection for the consumers in sales contracts is offered by the tort law. LCC chapter on defective production, which transposes EU Defective

396. *See* Judgment of the Lithuanian Supreme Court of 12 Mar. 2015 in the civil case No. 3K-3-137-706/2015.

production directive,[397] states that producer is bound to compensate for damage caused by defective products or defective services. A product is defective if it does not conform to the safety requirements which a consumer could reasonably expect thereof. Whether a product is defective or not shall be determined on the basis of the following criteria: (1) given characteristics (advertisement) of a product; (2) whether a product (services) may be used for the intended purpose; (3) time when a product was put into circulation; (4) defects of the construction or composition of a product, or any other defects thereof; and (5) other circumstances. However, a product cannot be considered of defective quality for the sole reason that a better product has subsequently been put into circulation. According to LCC Article 6.295, damage must be compensated if the aggrieved person proves the occurrence of damage, existence of defects in the product (service) and the causal link between the defects and the damages. Thus, the defective production liability is strict.

718. As concerns protection of the seller against failure to pay the price, in addition to general rules on specific performance of monetary obligations, LCC Article 6.345 provides that where the movable things have already been delivered to the buyer, but the latter fails to pay the sale price, the seller shall have the right to repudiate the contract, notifying the buyer thereof in writing and recover the things. If only a part of the price has not been paid, the seller may recover only the unpaid part of the thing, provided the thing is divisible. The seller shall retain the right of recovery only until the things are in the country of their delivery or have not passed into the hands of a third person or of a hypothecary creditor or the usufructuary right has not been laid down. In case of insolvency of the buyer, the seller cannot recover the things for which the price has not been paid if within a reasonable time the buyer's administrator offers to pay the price or presents a guarantee of performance of the obligation.

§2. Specific Types of Sale Contracts

719. Specific types of sale are sale of movables for consumers (LCC Article 6.350–6.370), wholesale sale (LCC Article 6.371–6.379), sale on public procurement (LCC Article 6.380–6.382, Law on Public Procurement), energy sale (LCC Article 6.383–6.391), immovable sale (LCC Article 6.392–6.401), enterprise sale (LCC Article 6.402–6.410), instalment sale (LCC Article 6.411–6.416), sale with right of redemption (LCC Article 6.417–6.418), auction sale (LCC Article 6.419–6.424) and sale of rights (LCC Article 6.425–6.427). Here we will explore only some of them.

I. Wholesale Sale

720. Under the contract of wholesale sale, the seller who is the person engaged in trade, or his agent undertakes to deliver on the fixed date things manufactured or

397. Council Directive 85/374/EEC of 25 Jul. 1985 on the approximation of the laws, regulations and administrative provisions of the Member States concerning liability for defective products.

purchased by him into the ownership (trust) of the buyer for the latter's business needs or other needs not related to personal, family or household need whereas the buyer obligates himself to pay the price.

721. Where a long-term contract has been concluded for the sale of things, under which things are delivered in lots and the period of time for the delivery of things is not provided in the contract, the lots of things shall be delivered on a monthly basis in equal parts, unless a different conclusion is to be drawn having regard to the custom of the trade or the essence of the obligation. In case of failure by the seller to deliver all things within the specified period of time, the things that have not been delivered by the due date must be delivered within the remaining time period/periods, except where the contracts provide otherwise (LCC Article 6.372).

722. If the means of transportation and terms of transportation of the things by the seller to the buyer are not specified in the contract, the seller is bound to arrange for carriage of the things by means of transportation appropriate in the circumstances and according to the usual terms for such transportation, unless it is reasonable to infer otherwise in view of the custom of the trade or the essence of the obligation. The contract may stipulate the buyer's obligation to take over the things from the stock at the seller's place of business or any other place (warehouse, railway station, etc.) The buyer must take necessary measures to ensure that all delivered things are accepted in due manner within the time period fixed in the contract or where the time period is not fixed – within a reasonable time and to examine the quantity and quality of the things according to the procedure set in the contract and promptly notify the seller of the discovered defects and deficiency in the quantity. Where the buyer is bound to receive the things from the carriers' organisation, he must check conformity of the things with the information given in the shipping documents and accept the things in accordance with the regulations of the means of transportation (LCC Article 6.373, 6.374). Unless otherwise provided in the contract, the buyer must return to the seller at his own expense the returnable containers and packaging in which the things were delivered. Other containers shall be returned only in cases provided for in the contract (LCC Article 6.377).

723. Where the things transferred by the seller are of inferior improper quality or completeness, the buyer may use usual remedies, except in cases where the seller upon the receipt of the buyer's notice promptly replaces the things of inferior improper quality with quality things or delivers the product in its completeness. A breach of the contract committed by the seller shall be deemed fundamental if: (1) the delivered things are of inferior improper quality and their defects cannot be eliminated within the time period the buyer finds acceptable; and (2) the seller has more than twice missed the deadline set for the delivery of the things where under the long-term contract the things had to be delivered within the fixed time limits. The buyer shall be considered to have committed a fundamental breach of contract and the seller shall acquire the right to a unilateral rescission of the contract if the buyer: (1) has more than twice failed to make timely payment for the things delivered when due; and (2) has more than twice failed to take possession of the things delivered on the set date.

II. Sale of Immovables

724. Immovables sales are one of the most important contracts for Lithuanian economy. According to the basic rules of Lithuanian property law, land and other things which are connected with land and which cannot be moved from one place to another without change of their purpose and essential reduction of their value are immovables (buildings, equipment, perennial plants and other things which, according to their purpose and nature, are deemed to be immovable). Ships and aircraft, the mandatory legal registration for which is established by laws, are also considered to be immovables. Any other property may also be attributed to immovables by the laws (LCC Article 1.98).

725. A contract for the sale of an immovable is subject to notarial approval, and non-compliance with the requirements of the form renders the contract null and void. It may be invoked against third persons only in the event of it being registered in the public register according to the procedure established by laws. The contract for sale of an immovable shall contain express price clause and information specifying the immovable which the seller is bound under contract to transfer to the buyer, also indication of the location of the thing in the relevant land plot or location of the immovable being sold in another immovable. The price of the land plot being sold shall include the price of the buildings, construction works, installations, plantations and other objects located on the plot, unless the laws and contract provide otherwise. A contract in which price clause and specification of property is absent cannot be approved by a notary and, if approved, is null and void (LCC Article 6.393, 6.396, 6.397).

726. Ownership over the immovable passes to the buyer from the moment of delivery of the thing, which is evidenced by the transfer-acceptance deed or any other document provided for in the contract, signed by the seller and buyer. If any of the parties avoids registering the fact of passing of ownership of the immovable, the court may, at the request of the other party, adopt a decision on the registration of the contract. In such case, the contract shall be registered based on the court decision. The party which avoided without any reason to register the passing of ownership right, must compensate the other party for the damage incurred (LCC Article 6.393, 6.398).

727. Immovable sales are complex transactions, which complicate even more where land is sold without fixtures, or fixtures are sold without land. Lithuanian civil law provides several rules in order to preserve *superficies solo cedit* principle and prevent property disputes in such situations. Thus, under the contract for sale of a building, installation or other immovable the seller shall transfer to the buyer, together with the right of ownership to the thing, the patrimonial rights to the part of the land plot, which is occupied by the thing and which is necessary for the thing to be fit for the purpose it would ordinarily be used. Where the seller is the owner of the land plot on which the immovable being sold is situated, the buyer shall be transferred the rights of ownership to the land plot or the right of land lease or right of superficies, whatever is provided by the contract. A contract in which the rights of the buyer to the land plot are not contemplated may not be certified by a notary and if certified, shall be null and void. Where the owner of the immovable is not the owner of the land plot on which the thing is situated, he may sell the immovable without the consent of the owner of the land plot only provided this is in compliance with the conditions of use of the land plot set down by laws and (or) the contract. In the event of sale of such an immovable the buyer shall acquire the right to use the appropriate part of the land plot under the same terms and conditions as the seller of the immovable. In the event of sale of a land plot containing buildings, construction works, installations, plantations or other objects, the issue of passing of the right of ownership therein must be contemplated in the contract. If the issue is not contemplated in the contract, the right of ownership in the buildings, construction works, installations, plantations or other objects situated on the land plot shall be deemed to have passed to the buyer of the land plot. If the land plot containing buildings or other immovables belonging to the seller by the right of ownership is sold without transferring to the buyer the rights of ownership in the above-mentioned immovable, the seller shall retain the right to use the part of the land plot which is occupied by the immovable and is necessary for the use thereof by the right of superficies or any other right and under the terms and conditions provided for in the contract. Where the seller's right to use a part of the land plot and the conditions of use are not contemplated in the contract of sale, the servitude shall be established for the seller with respect to the part of the land plot which is occupied by the immovable and which is necessary for it to be used for the purpose it would ordinarily be used (LCC Article 6.394, 6.395).

728. Where the seller transfers to the buyer under the contract of sale of an immovable a thing of improper quality, usual remedies of the seller shall be applicable, except with respect to the buyer's right to request replacement of the thing of improper quality with a thing of proper quality. The circumstance that the buyer accepted an immovable which does not conform with the terms and conditions of the contract shall not constitute grounds for releasing the seller from liability for improper performance of the contract even in the cases where such nonconformity was contemplated in the document of transfer of the thing (LCC Article 6.398, 6.399).

729. Unique legal regime, which allows to agree on transfer of even future realty (normally this is forbidden by LCC 4.49), is provided by LCC Article 6.401, which regulates sale of a planned house or apartment to consumer. The buyer – a natural person – may conclude a preliminary contract for the sale of a planned residential house or apartment whereby the seller – a legal person – obligates itself to build the residential house or apartment provided in the contract by itself or upon enlisting the help of other persons and thereafter conclude with the buyer a contract for the sale of the residential house or apartment, whereas the buyer obligates himself to purchase the built house or apartment for the price indicated in the preliminary contract. The following shall be indicated in the preliminary contract: (1) the buyer's right to repudiate the preliminary contract within ten days from the date of conclusion of the contract; (2) the price of the planned house or apartment and the terms and conditions of its revision or changing; (3) description of the subject matter of the contract and the works which the seller must perform; (4) time limits of construction of the residential house or apartment; (5) encumbrances of the right to the residential house or apartment (both present and future); (6) the contractor, architect, engineer and other persons who will carry out and supervise the construction work; and (7) legal status of the land plot on which the house or apartment will be built and the rights to the land plot of the buyer of the house or apartment. The project of the residential house, its estimate and other documents shall constitute an inseparable part of the preliminary contract. It may also be stipulated in the preliminary contract that the buyer finances the construction of the residential house or apartment under the conditions provided in the contract whereas the seller shall perform the functions of customer. In this case the buyer shall acquire the right of ownership to the residential house or apartment upon payment of the construction price provided in the preliminary contract.

III. Sale of Enterprise

730. Private equity firms and other corporate investors usually acquire companies by purchasing main package its shares. Alternative way, which is more complex and costlier but still used in some occasions, is acquisition of the enterprise, i.e., the patrimony of a company, which is treated as immovable by LCC Article 1.110(1). Under the enterprise sales contract, the seller obligates himself to transfer to the buyer by the right of ownership as an object of property the whole enterprise or a substantial part thereof, with the exception of the rights and duties which the seller has no right to transfer to other persons, while the buyer obligates himself to accept the said object and to pay the price.

731. The right to the name of the firm, trade name or service name or to other marks identifying the seller or his goods or services supplied by him also to the rights possessed by the seller under the licence agreement shall pass to the buyer, unless otherwise provided by the contract. The seller's rights which he acquired under licences shall be transferred to the buyer only provided the possibility of such transfer has been stipulated by the laws or the licence. The transfer to the buyer alongside the enterprise of obligations which he cannot perform since he does not have a licence for the performance of such obligations shall not release the seller from liability to creditors for non-performance of obligations. In such cases, the seller and buyer shall be jointly liable to creditors for non-performance of the obligations (LCC Article 6.402).

732. The enterprise sales contract must be a written document, signed by both parties, approved by the notary and be accompanied by the requisite accompanying documents. The contract must specify the compositions of assets of the enterprise being sold and the price of the enterprise as well as the person who shall be paid and who shall settle with the creditors of the enterprise. The following accompanying documents must be drawn up, agreed between the parties and signed before the signing of the contract: (1) deed of inventory of the enterprise assets; (2) the balance sheet of the enterprise; (3) the opinion of the independent auditor regarding the composition and price of the assets of the enterprise; and (4) the list of debts (obligations) of the enterprise, specifying the amount of the debt, time limits of performance and kinds of security of the obligations, creditors and their addresses. Non-compliance with the requirements of the form of the contract renders the contract null and void. The contract of sale of an enterprise may be set up against the third parties only provided it has been registered in the public register in the manner established by law and relevant amendments have been made in the register of legal persons (LCC Article 6.403, 6.404).

733. The buyer must not later than twenty days before the conclusion of the contract notify in writing all creditors of the enterprise named in the list of enterprise debts (obligations) of the intended sale of the enterprise. In the event of failure by the buyer to fulfil the above duty, the seller's creditors shall have the right to submit their claims directly to the buyer. The buyer shall pay part of the price provided for in the contract to the person specified in the contract, who shall be charged to settle with the creditors of the enterprise, while the remaining amount shall be paid to the seller. Only a bank, other credit institution or insurance company may be chosen by the parties as the person to be charged with settling with the creditors. The buyer is relieved from this duty if he presents to all creditors of the enterprise an acceptable security for the satisfaction of claims (LCC Article 6.405).

734. Pursuant to LCC Article 6.407, the seller shall transfer the enterprise to the buyer under the deed of transfer-acceptance. The deed shall contain information relating to the enterprise and its assets, the condition of its assets, obligations of the parties to the creditors of the enterprise and the performance thereof. Unless the contract provides otherwise, the seller shall be bound to prepare the enterprise for sale and draw up the deed of transfer-acceptance at his own expense. The enterprise is transferred to the buyer from the moment the deed of transfer-acceptance is signed by both parties. The risk of accidental perishing of or damage to the assets of the enterprise shall pass to the buyer from the moment of signing of the deed of transfer-acceptance of the enterprise. Where the contract provides that the seller shall retain the right of ownership to the enterprise until the buyer pays the full amount of the price or until he/it fulfils other conditions, the buyer shall be entitled to use the assets of the enterprise and the incidental rights to the extent and in the manner that is required for the purpose for which the enterprise was acquired.

735. Where the enterprise is transferred and accepted under the transfer-acceptance deed in which the defects of the enterprise or its assets are specified, the buyer shall be entitled to demand reduction of the price if under the contract he is not entitled to present any other demands in such a case. The buyer shall be entitled to demand reduction of the price if he has been assigned the seller's debts (obligations) not specified in the contract or enterprise transfer-acceptance deed, except in cases where the seller proves that the buyer was aware or could not be unaware of the debts (obligations) at the moment of conclusion of the contract and transfer of the enterprise. If the seller receives the buyer's notification of discovery of defects of the transferred assets or of the fact that certain assets provided for in the contract are altogether missing, the seller shall have the right to promptly replace the assets of inferior quality with other analogous assets of proper quality or to offer to the buyer the missing assets. Where the defects of the enterprise for which the seller is liable render the enterprise unfit for the use indicated in the contract and the defects cannot be eliminated or the seller did not eliminate them within the fixed time period, the buyer shall have the right to apply to the court for the dissolution or revision of the contract and compensation for the damage (LCC Article 6.408).

IV. Auction Sale

736. Sale of things by auction means a sale by which things are offered for sale to several persons through the intermediary – the auctioneer – and the contract is deemed concluded with the buyer – the bidder – of the highest price for the thing offered for sale. An auction sale may be either voluntary or forced. The forced auction is regulated by the procedural law.

737. The seller may fix the reserve price of the thing offered for sale and any other conditions of the auction. However, the conditions of the auction that have not been communicated to the bidders may not be set up against the bidders, save in the cases where the auctioneer announced the conditions to the bidders before receiving bids. The seller shall have the right to refuse to disclose his identity but, if his identity is not disclosed to the successful bidder, the auctioneer shall become bound by all the obligations of the seller to the successful bidder. The bidder shall have no right to withdraw his bid. The contract of sale by auction is concluded when the auctioneer announces this by the fall of his hammer or any other customary action. If at the moment when the completion of the auction sale of the thing is announced by the fall of the auctioneer's hammer, a new bid is received, the auctioneer shall have the right to extend the auction or declare the thing sold for the last price bid before the fall of the hammer. Entry of the bid and the name of the successful bidder makes proof of the sale. In the absence of such an entry proof by testimony by the witnesses shall be admissible. In case an immovable is sold at the auction, a contract in the form prescribed by law must be within ten days from the sale concluded between the seller and the buyer (LCC Article 6.420, 6.421).

738. The buyer must pay the price according to the procedure and within the time limits prescribed by the conditions of the auction. If the buyer does not pay the price in compliance with the established procedure and within the set time limits, the auctioneer shall be entitled to exercise all rights of the buyer. Moreover, the auctioneer may, in addition to the ordinary remedies of a seller, announce, after a notice given to the buyer within a reasonable time, that he is holding a new auction for the resale of the thing. In such event a false bidder may not bid again at a new auction. He is bound to cover the auctioneer's expenses incidental to arranging and holding a new auction and also pay the difference in prices if the thing was resold at a lesser price than the price false bidder did not pay (LCC Article 6.422).

739. As concern a forced auction, CCP Article 715 provides controversial rule that from the moment when memorandum of sale at auction is signed, it is held that duty to transfer property is performed properly and from this moment he acquires ownership to transferred property. In cases where possession is still in the hands of the debtor or third party, this rule, despite being *lex specialis*, makes fictitious statements, lowers value of property sold in a forced auction and contravenes the whole logic of substantive legislation, in particular LCC Article 4.50, which states that the transfer of a property gives the acquirer the opportunity to use the property transferred according to its purpose, with due regard to the condition of the property and to its legal status. The practical problem is that after the forced auction buyer is forced to initiate eviction proceedings in new legal proceedings against unlawful possessors, while this second round of unnecessary substantive litigation would be absent if bailiff not only would sell seized property but also actually (not just in legal fiction) deliver its possession to buyer.

V. Sale of Rights

740. General rules for transfer of claims are established in the general part of Lithuanian law of obligations. In addition, LCC lays down special rules for sale of succession rights and litigious rights.

741. A person who, upon accepting the property received by succession, sells rights of succession without specifying in detail the property affected, is bound to warrant to the buyer only his quality as an heir. The seller is bound to hand over to the buyer all the fruits and revenues he has received from the succession together with the capital of any claim due and the price of any things he has sold which formed part of the succession. The buyer is bound to reimburse the seller for the expenses incidental to accepting the succession and pay the amounts due to the seller from the succession. The buyer is bound to reimburse the seller for the debts of the succession that he has paid. The buyer shall also pay the debts of the succession for which the seller is liable (LCC Article 6.426).

742. A right is litigious when it is contested by a person bringing an action or there is reason to presume that such an action maybe brought. No advocate, judge, notary or bailiff or their family members or close relatives may acquire contested litigious rights. Contracts concluded by the above persons for sale of litigious rights shall be null and void. Where litigious rights are sold, the person from whom they are claimed is fully discharged by paying to the buyer the sale price, the cost related to the sale and interest on the price. This right of redemption may not be exercised, where the sale is made to a creditor in payment of what is due to him or to a coheir or co-owner of the rights sold. Nor may the right of redemption be exercised where a court has rendered a judgment affirming the right sold (LCC Article 6.427).

Chapter 5. Construction Contracts, Hire of Work and Skills

743. Construction contracts, hire of work and skills all may be generalised as contracts for supply of services. Next to set of contracts involving specific types of services (mandate, deposit, carriage, lease, distribution, factoring, etc.) Lithuanian contract law presents two types of services contracts, which are of rather general nature and encompass contracts for hire of work and skills, including building contracts. Those contracts are contract for supply of remunerated services and works (processing) contract. Both types of contracts are civil contracts, where supplier (contractor) acts as an independent party – enterprise or entrepreneur – on its own commercial risk and no subordination against customer exists. It distinguishes civil contracts for hire of work and skills from employment contracts, based on subordination of employee and commercial risk taking by employer, regulated by Lithuanian Labour Code. Therefore, LCC expressly states that the independent work contractor and customer shall not be connected by subordination or any other dependence relationship (LCC 6.645), also, that the provisions of LCC chapter on service contracts shall apply only for those services, in respect of which no relationship of employment or other subordination exists between the provider of services and the client.

744. In contrast with France, Quebec or DCFR, general services contracts are separately regulated in two different chapters of LCC. Regimes of both contracts accordingly differ by level of particularity, character of obligations, liability, time periods for extinctive prescription, etc.[398] LCC general service contracts legislation is a new institution composed from mix of rules which may be found in Quebec CC, Russian ГК and Dutch BW, whereas works contracts legislation is based mostly on Russian ГК and in part resembles former Soviet legislation. Although there is an obvious need to be capable to distinguish one contract from another, such task in practice is not easy to achieve. Let us explore this issue little bit further.

745. Pursuant to LCC Article 6.716, the contract for services is a contract by which one party to the contract (the provider of services) undertakes to provide to

398. According to R. Zimmermann, the separation of contracts for services and works has been taken over from the pandectists. They referred to *locatio conductio rei* (letting and hiring of things), *locatio conductio operarum* (letting and hiring of services) and *locatio conductio operis* (letting and hiring of work). The Roman lawyers, however, did not draw these distinctions. They did not think in terms of three different transactions, but accommodated all of them within the framework of one single contract called *locatio conductio*. There are a variety of marginal cases where it can be very difficult to decide on which side of the borderline between *locatio conductio operis* and *operarum* they fall. These difficulties continue to persist in all those modern legal systems which have adopted the trichotomy of contracts grafted on to the Roman *locatio conductio* by the writers of the *ius commune*. Take, for example, the legal relationship between physician and patient. It is normally taken to be a contract of service by the modern German courts: the contract only obliges the physician to carry out, *lege artis*, an indicated medical treatment; it is not intended to make him liable for the success of such treatment. But it is very doubtful whether the same applies if a physician accepts a patient for sterilisation. *See* Reinhard Zimmermann. *The Law of Obligations: Roman Foundations of the Civilian Tradition.* Oxford University Press, 1996, p. 338, 395.

the other party to the contract (the client) by commission of the latter certain services of a non-material nature (intellectual) or other types which are not related to the creation of a material object (to perform certain actions or pursue certain activities), and the client undertakes to pay for the services provided. Whereas under a contract of independent work, one party (independent work contractor) undertakes an obligation to perform certain work at his own risk in accordance with the task of another party (customer), and transfer the results thereof to the customer, while the latter shall be obliged to accept the work performed and pay for it. A contract of independent work may be concluded for the manufacture or transfer of the results of a certain work, or for the fulfilment of any other work with the ensuing transfer of the results created in the process of this work to the customer (LCC Article 6.644, 6.645).

746. Initially, the Supreme Court of Lithuania had held that dividing line between contracts for work and for services is corporeal character of works, in contrast to incorporeal character of services.[399] Similar position was expressed also in legal doctrine.[400] Interestingly, the same criterion is used in Italian law.[401] Later on, the Supreme Court has turned for another dividing criterion, which is used in German law[402] – the intensity of obligation.[403] Thus, contract for work is such where parties have agreed for obligation of result, whereas in a services contract parties have agreed for an obligation of efforts. In my opinion, both those criteria, although helpful, are not sufficient or specific enough to serve as a decisive basis for a characterisation. Take, for instance, tangibility as a criterion. The problem arises where intangible goods (movies, computer programs, design, survey reports, digital assets, etc.) are to be created under the contract. There is no sense why rules on the works for a creation of intangible goods should be different from the rules on the creation of tangible goods. From the other token, having in mind, that regime of a contract

399. Judgment of the Lithuanian Supreme Court of 19 Oct. 2005 in the civil case No. 3K-3-494/2005.
400. Andrius Kabišaitis. *Paslaugų sutartis – Lietuvos civilinės teisės naujovė.* Justitia, 2003, Nr. 5(47), pp. 3–4.
401. Jan M. Barendrecht; *et al. Service Contracts. Principles of European Law.* Sellier, 2007, p. 151, 327.
402. In German law, the main difference between the contract for services and the contract for work (*Werkvertrag*, § 632) is that a contract for services does not stipulate an obligation to achieve a specific result. The employee merely promises to perform the act required of him in the contract. This becomes obvious if typical examples of contracts for services are analysed. § 611 covers what has been called the 'free' contract for services (in the sense of being less closely regulated) and also 'labour contracts' (*Arbeitsverträge*). The first category includes, for instance, a contract with a solicitor or a contract for treatment concluded with a medical doctor (*Arztvertrag*). In both these cases, the person 'hired' to provide the services is, generally speaking, only required to perform the service *lege artis* but does not (and usually cannot) promise a particular outcome (e.g., that the disputed litigation is won or that the patient regains his health). This does not mean that contracts with such professionals may never come under § 632. Occasionally, they do involve the promise of a result (what French lawyers refer to as an *obligation de resultat*): for instance, the promise of a solicitor to draft contract terms. *See* B.S. Markesinis, Hannes Unberath, Angus Johnston, Lord Bingham, Gunter Hirsch. *The German Law of Contract: A Comparative Treatise*. Hart Publishing, 2006, p. 153.
403. Judgment of the Lithuanian Supreme Court of 5 Dec. 2012 in the civil case No 3K-3-543/2012 and of 16 Jan. 2013 in the civil case No 3K-3-110/2013.

for works is tailored for the creation or modification and acceptance of some independent object, criterion of tangibility would lead to a characterisation of some services provided with physical means, for instance masseuse, veterinary or barber, and in effect awkward regulation as a works contract. Another criterion, intensity of obligation by itself is also imperfect, because, first, parties may agree for a result in a pure services contract and, second, contractor may undertake only best efforts to do some works. In such cases, the whole logic of such distinguishment and regulation is easily overturned and is left without any clear and reasonable basis.

747. Instead, in my opinion, it is more accurate and convenient in light of LCC rules to use as the distinguishing criterion the agreement on the creation, modification or destruction of property for customer. Where such element is present, i.e., parties have agreed to create, modify (repair, improve, change) or destruct tangible or intangible property, the contract should be characterised as a contract for works. Medical treatment, cosmetologist's services, hairkeeping, masseuse, etc., then automatically do not fall into works, because human body is not a property. Veterinary services, even if they are about healing biologic property, by LCC are expressly regulated as services, not works. In addition, legal, audit, consultancy, personal healthcare, information, education, tourist or other remunerative services, to the exclusion of the scientific research, experimental, development or technological work, mandate, commission agency, carriage, freight forwarding, deposit, bank deposit, bank account, payments and trust management are also regulated as provision of services (LCC Article 6.716). As preservation of asset quality (cleaning a snowfall, housekeeping, technical maintenance (as opposed to repair and improvement) of computers and other machines) does not change the property physical characteristics, it does not fall under the contract of works and constitutes pure service. However, the sole modification of property, which occurs in a contract for work, does not always create effect on related property rights. The performance of works contract creates *in rem* effects only where property is created, transferred, destructed or common property is improved (with permission of co-owners).

§1. Contract of Work

748. Contract of work (*rangos sutartis*) is a consensual, bilateral, onerous, commutative civil contract, which in some instances, presented above, may create *in rem* effects, while in other instances remaining purely obligational contract. Property law aspect is expressly mentioned in LCC Article 6.645(2), according to whom, where a contract of work is concluded for the manufacture of a thing, the contractor together with the manufactured thing shall transfer to the customer the rights thereto. Contract of work differs from a sales contract by the type of obligations: in contract of works a fundamental obligation is to do (*facere*), whereas in sales the obligation is to give (*dare*). For mixed situations, the characterisation test is established in LCC Article LCC 6.645(4), pursuant to which, where the character and value of the work fulfilled being relatively insignificant in comparison with the value of the manufactured, purchased or converted thing, the contract shall be deemed to be not that of work, but a sales contract. Thus, in case of concurrence the contract works prevail against the sales, unless works are of insignificant value compared to value of goods. This may be seen as protective regime for the contractor because responsibility of a customer and his overall involvement in a contract of work is more extensive compared to that of the buyer in sales contact. Essential term in a work contract is a prestation (subject matter), while the price is not; hence parties may leave to decide on it later or in case dispute the price will be determined by the court. Also, there are no special formal requirements for a formation of work contract.

I. Rules Common for All Contracts of Work

749. Principal obligation of a contractor is duty to do a work and usually create result, whereas principal obligations of customer are duty to accept the works and pay the price. Ancillary duties of parties are duties to cooperate and inform, for instance, duty of customer to supply contractor with materials where it is the responsibility of customer, duty to inform contractor about risks and change of circumstances, etc.

750. Normally the contractor has the right to involve other persons (subcontractors) to perform his obligations. In the event where subcontractors are involved for the performance of the task, the contractor shall act in the capacity of a general contractor. The contractor who has involved subcontractors to perform a contract of work in violation of laws or the rules established in the contract shall be liable before the customer for any damages caused by the subcontractors in the performance of the contract. The general contractor shall be liable before the customer for the failure to perform or improper performance of the obligations by the subcontractors, and before subcontractors, for the failure to perform or improper performance of the obligations by the customer. Unless otherwise provided for by laws or the contract, the customer and the subcontractor shall have no right to raise monetary claims to one another connected with the violation of the contracts concluded by each of them with the general contractor. With the consent of the general contractor, the customer shall have the right to conclude contracts for fulfilment of concrete work with other persons. In this event, those persons shall be directly liable before the customer for the failure to perform or improper performance of the contract.

751. Unless otherwise provided for by the contract, the contractor must fulfil the work agreed in the contract from his own materials and by his means and forces. In fulfilling the work from his own materials, the contractor is liable for any inferior quality of the materials. In the event of the materials supplied by the customer, he is also obliged to transfer to contractor the documents certifying the conformity of the materials. Where the materials supplied by the customer being not fit for use, or defective, of which the contractor must know, the contractor is obliged to immediately notify the customer thereof. The risk of accidental perishing or damaging of materials or equipment transferred for the fulfilment of work is borne by the party granting them, while the risk of accidental perishing or damaging of the result of the work fully completed or that of its intermediary stage shall be borne by the contractor until the acceptance thereof by the customer. As to the time limits for the fulfilment of work, the beginning and ending of the fulfilment of the work shall be indicated in the contract of work. The parties may also determine the time limits for completing concrete stages of work (intermediate time limits). The contractor shall be liable for a violation of both the beginning and the ending of work, likewise for the violation of the intermediate time limits. The customer shall have the right to refuse acceptance of the work fulfilled in result of performance of the whole obligation and claim damage from the contractor arising from the delay in performance in the cases where the performance of the obligation due to the delay became of no significance for the customer.

752. The contracts of work usually specify the price of the work subject to fulfilment or the methods and criteria of its calculation. However, in cases where the price is not specified in the contract, it still can be determined in accordance with the default rules of LCC pointing to the average market price for such type of works. The price of work specified in the contract may be determined by drawing up a definite or approximate estimate. In the instances when the work is fulfilled in accordance with the estimate drawn up by the contractor, the estimate shall enter into force and become part of the contract of work from the moment it is confirmed by the customer. In the event where a necessity arises to fulfil additional work or for any other important reasons the contractor has to increase the price of some individual stages of the work, he shall be obliged to inform the customer thereof in time. If the customer refuses to increase the price, the contractor has the right to revoke the contract. In this event, the contractor shall have the right to demand from the customer payment for the work fulfilled. The contractor who failed to inform the customer in time about the necessity to increase the price shall be obliged to perform the contract for the price foreseen therein. In the instances where a definite price for the work to be fulfilled is indicated in the contract, the contractor shall have no right to increase the price, nor the customer to reduce it. The same provision applies for those instances where at the moment of concluding the contract of work, it was not possible to determine the exact amount of work subject to fulfilment nor all the expenses necessary for the fulfilment of work. In the event of essential growth of the price of materials or equipment, or also of the services rendered to the contractor by third persons, and the contractor was not able to predict such increase at the time when the contract was concluded, the contractor shall have the right to demand an increase of the established price of work or to dissolve the contract in accordance with the provisions established in LCC Article 6.204 (*rebus sic stantibus*). In the event where the actual expenses of the contractor prove to be lower than those taken into account in determining the price of work, the contractor shall retain the right to the payment for work as established in the contract of work unless the customer proves that the economies produced negative effect on the quality of work as determined in the contract.

753. In practice, of crucial importance is the stage of acceptance of contractors' works. This is because the risk of collateral damage and associated costs are transferred to the customer, who is then obliged to pay the contractor the stipulated price.

The price becomes payable after the final acceptance of the results of work on condition that the work is fulfilled properly and on time or with the consent of the customer before time, unless preliminary payment for work fulfilled or individual stages thereof has been provided for in the contract of work. LCC Article 6.662 lays down detailed and formal rules on the acceptance of work. According to them, the customer is obliged within the periods and in the procedure provided for in the contract of work to inspect with the participation of the contractor and accept the work fulfilled (its result). In the event of discovering any deviations from the conditions of the contract which worsen the quality of the result of the work, or any other defects in the work, the customer must immediately inform the contractor accordingly. The acceptance of the work fulfilled must be formalised by drawing up an act by which the customer certifies an unconditional acceptance, or that with a reservation clause, and the contractor transference of the work fulfilled. The customer, having discovered defects of the work in the course of acceptance, shall be able to rely upon the fact of the defects only in the instances where in the act or any other document certifying the acceptance of the work fulfilled these defects were recorded, or the right of a subsequent claim on the part of the customer concerning their elimination is stipulated. The customer having accepted the work without verification shall be deprived of the right to rely upon the defects which could have been discovered by ordinary means of acceptance of the work (obvious defects). The customer having discovered after the acceptance of the work defects thereof or any deviations from the contract which could not have been discovered by ordinary means of acceptance of the work (latent defects), likewise those intentionally concealed by the contractor shall be obliged to notify the contractor thereof within reasonable time after their discovery. In the event where a dispute arises between the contractor and the customer because of the defects of the work, each party shall have the right to demand expert examination.

754. The quality of the work fulfilled by the contractor must conform to the conditions of the contract of work and, in the absence of any determination of quality in the contract, to the requirements ordinarily presented for work of the respective nature. The result of work fulfilled must at the moment of transfer to the customer possess the properties specified in the contract of work or determined requirements usually presented, and within the limits of a reasonable period be fit for use in accordance with its designation. Where obligatory requirements for work to be fulfilled are established by the law or the contract of work, the contractor, acting as a businessman, shall be obliged to comply with those requirements. The parties may establish in the contract of work a duty of the contractor to fulfil the work in accordance with higher requirements than the existent obligatory requirements.

755. Where the work is fulfilled with deviations from the conditions of the contract, which renders the result of the work unfit to be used in accordance with its designation as determined in the contracts or worsens its possibilities (conditions) to be used in accordance with its designation and, where the designation is not specified in the contract – in accordance with its ordinary use, the customer shall have the right, unless otherwise provided for by the law or the contract, at his choice to require from the contractor: (1) elimination of defects without compensation within a reasonable period; (2) reduction of the price established for work; and (3) compensation of his expenses for elimination of the defects when the right of the customer to eliminate them has been provided for in the contract of work. The contractor shall have the right instead of eliminating the defects to fulfil the work anew without compensation and compensate to the customer damages caused by the delay of performance. In this event, the customer shall be obliged to return the result of work previously transferred to him to the contractor if by the character of the work such return is possible. In the event of the failure of the contractor to eliminate the deviations from the contract or other defects within a reasonable time, or the defects prove to be essential and cannot be eliminated, the customer shall have the right to dissolve the contract and claim the compensation of damage. The conditions of a contract of work which relieve the contractor from liability for certain defects shall not exempt him from liability if the customer proves that such defects were caused by the fault or gross negligence of the contractor. In the event where the work was performed from the materials of the contractor, the contractor shall be liable for the improper quality of those materials as a seller under a purchase–sale contract.

756. The same as in sales contracts, where warranty period is not established, the defects of the result of the work must be determined within a reasonable time but not exceeding the limit of two years from the date when the result of the work was transferred unless other time limits are provided for by the law or the contract of work. Unless otherwise provided for by the contract of work, the warranty period shall start its run from the moment when the result of work was accepted or should have been accepted by the customer. However, the prescription for claims arising in connection with defects of the work fulfilled is longer than in sales and according to LCC Article 6.667 constitutes one year. In the instances where according to the contract of work the result of work was accepted in parts, the prescription shall commence from the date of acceptance of the results of work as a whole. In the event where a warranty period is established by the law or contract of work, and the statement concerning the defects was presented within that warranty period, the prescription shall commence from the date of the statement concerning the defects.

II. Construction Contract

757. The most important specie of work contract in expanding the Lithuanian economy is construction contract. Under a construction contract, the contractor is obliged, within the period established in the contract, to build a determined construction work according to the task of the customer or to fulfil another construction work, while the customer shall take an obligation to create the necessary conditions for the contractor in order to fulfil the work, to accept the result of the work performed and pay the price stipulated in the contract. A construction contract may be concluded for the construction or reconstruction of enterprises, construction works, dwelling houses and other structures and also for the fulfilment of assembly, capital repair of buildings or installations, launching or any other work.

758. As the building process has significant impact on the environment, urban planning and safety, it is extensively regulated by public law, which is mandatory in nature and rules of which may not be contracted out. Therefore, the contractor when performing construction is obliged to comply with the requirements of public law concerning the protection of environment and ensuring safety of work. In particular, contractor is obliged to perform the construction work in accordance with the requirements established in the construction and zoning law, technical regulations and the contract (contractual documentation, e.g., FIDIC[404] or ICE[405] standard terms) determining the price of work and quality requirements applicable to the construction works (work). The contractor is liable for the violation of these requirements. But a duty to get building permission is sole responsibility of a customer according to Law on Construction Article 2 (87).

759. The customer has the right to make changes in the contractual documentation on condition that the price of the additional work caused by this does not exceed 15% of the total price of construction specified in the contract, and those changes do not alter the character of the work provided for in the contract. The parties may also provide for other conditions for making changes in the contractual documentation. But the contractor accordingly has the right to demand a revision of the price of the contract if for reasons beyond his control the actual price of the work has increased by more than 15% (*rebus sic stantibus*).

760. The customer is obliged in a timely way to provide a land plot for construction (construction site). The size and state of the land plot provided must conform to the conditions specified in the construction contract and enable the timely commencement, normal conducting and timely completion of the construction by the contractor. The customer is also obliged in the instances and according to procedure provided for by the contract to transfer for the use of the contractor buildings and installations, grant transportation services, instal temporary electric power or water supply networks, obtain the permits granting the contractor with the right to perform certain work, as well as render other services provided for in the contract.

761. Although there is no legal subordination between parties in civil contracts, the customer has the right to provide limited control and supervision over the course and the quality of construction work being fulfilled, compliance with the schedules of construction work, the quality of the materials supplied by the contractor and the use of the materials provided by the customer. In implementing this right, the customer has no right to interfere in the commercial activity of the contractor.

762. The customer on having received the notification of the contractor concerning the readiness for handing over the results of the work or, if this is provided in the contract, a stage of the work fulfilled is obliged to immediately embark upon

404. FIDIC is the International Federation of Consulting Engineers, residing in Geneva.
405. ICE is the Institution of Civil Engineers, residing in London.

the acceptance thereof. The contractor is liable for any deviations from the requirements of the technical construction regulations and also for the failure to achieve the indicators of the objects of construction specified in these documents or the contract (productive capacity of the enterprise, resistance, etc.). In the event of the reconstruction of construction works and installations, the contractor is liable for any reduction or loss of reliability, durability and resistance of the construction works or installation. The contractor is not liable for minor deviations from the technical construction regulations made with the consent of the customer if he proves that these deviations have not influenced the quality of the construction object and will not bring about negative consequences.

763. The contractor, unless otherwise provided for in the construction contract, must ensure throughout the whole warranty period the compliance of the object of construction to the indicators established in the technical construction regulations and its fitness for use for the designation specified in the contract. According to LCC Article 6.698, the contractor, architect and the technical supervisor of the construction is liable for the collapse of the object or defects if the object collapsed or the defects were discovered within the time limit of: (1) five years; (2) ten years, in existence of hidden constructions of the construction works (structures of construction works, pipelines, etc.); and (3) twenty years, in existence of intentionally concealed defects. The time limits specified above shall start their run from the day when the result of the work is handed over.

764. The contractor, architect and the technical supervisor of the construction is respectively liable for the collapse of a construction work and the resultant damage if the object collapsed due to the defects in the design, structures of construction work or the performance of construction work, likewise due to unsuitable ground.

§2. Service Contract

765. Service contract (*paslaugų sutartis*) is a consensual, bilateral, onerous, commutative and purely obligational civil contract. There are no special formal requirements for the formation of a service contract.

766. As in a work contract, an essential term in a service contract is a prestation (subject matter), while the express agreement on price is not necessary; hence parties may leave to decide on it later or in case dispute the price will be determined by the court. However, since the typical contract for services is only bilateral and onerous, it must encompass the duty of the client to pay for the services provided. It means, there should be an express or implied agreement on the remuneration of services; otherwise, the provision of services will not lead to the binding typical contract for services. For instance, remunerative character of the contract may be proved by the evidence showing that parties understood that there is a payment for the services and accepted that.[406] Of course, parties are also free to create the contract on gratuitous services, however, being atypical such contract should be express and could attract rules on typical service contracts (LCC sixth book XXXV chapter) only by analogy.

767. The obligations of service provider are obligations to do (*dare*). Since it is not employment, but a civil contract, the provider of services is free to choose the methods and measures to perform the contract. However, in contrast with a contract for work, the default rule is that the provider of services must personally provide the services. Even where according to the nature of services the provider of services may employ third persons to perform the contract, the provider of services is personally liable to the client for the proper performance of the contract. Where the services are provided by more than one person, all providers of services shall be liable for the proper performance of the contract, to the exclusion of the cases where the default of the contract or improper performance of the contract occurred through no fault of anyone of them.

768. Pursuant to LCC Article 6.718, the provider of services has professional and (or) fiduciary duties to be honest and reasonable in the provision of services, so as to serve best the interests of the client. Having regard to the type of services, the provider of services must act, in the provision of services, in accordance with established practices and standards applicable to the relevant profession, for example auditors code of conduct. The provider of services must provide the services in accordance with the terms of the contract and following the instructions of the client. If the instructions of the client are in violation of laws, established rules of the professional activities, standards, professional ethics or the terms of the contract, the provider of services shall have the right to refuse to carry out such instructions and to terminate the contract. The provider of services shall have the right to deviate from the terms of the contract or the instructions of the client, where specific circumstances necessitate such a deviation for the interests of the client or in order to discharge the latter's commission, and where the contractor was not able to inform the client thereof in advance. In this case, the contractor must notify the client of the deviations as soon as the circumstances permit. If the contract provides for the obligation on the part of the provider of services to achieve a certain result, the provider of services may be relieved from liability because of the non-performance of the said obligation only where the provider of services could not meet such obligation for reasons of force majeure.

769. Before the contract for services is entered into, the provider of services is bound to provide the client with detailed information concerning the nature of the services that are provided, the terms of their provision, the price of the services, the schedule for the services, possible consequences and any information which has influence on the client's determination may have to enter into the contract. In the event of public services rendered, or where the provision of the services constitutes

406. Judgment of the Lithuania Supreme Court of 17 Dec. 2019 in the civil case No. e3K-3-381-684/2019.

business of the provider of services, the client shall be provided with the conditions of public access to the information either at the head office of the provider of services or at any other place freely accessible to each possible client.

770. The price of the services may be fixed by agreement of the parties and may be modified after the conclusion of the contract only in accordance with the terms of the contract and in cases stipulated in the contract. The client is bound to pay the increased price of the services exceeding the price fixed at the time the contract is entered into only in the event the provider of services furnishes proof that such increase was essential to ensure the proper performance of the contract and to the extent that such increase could not be foreseen at the time the contract was entered into. The client shall pay for the services rendered within a given time and following the procedure agreed in the contract. Unless the contract provides otherwise, the client is bound to pay the whole price when the contracted services are provided. By agreement between the parties, part of the price may be paid at the time the contract is entered into or at any agreed time thereafter, and the final settlement shall be effected upon the performance of the contract by the provider of services. If the performance of the contract is impossible through the fault of the client, the client must pay the whole price fixed in the contract, unless the contract provides otherwise. If the performance of the contract is impossible as a result of the circumstances for which no party to the contract may be held responsible, the client is bound to remunerate the provider of services for the actual expenses incurred by the latter, unless the contract provides otherwise. The client shall also reimburse the provider of services for the expenses incurred by the latter and related to the performance of the contract to the extent that such expenses are not covered by the price of the services. The client is also bound to reimburse the provider of services for the latter's losses related to the provision of the service, incurred at the time of the provision of the services in the event of unforeseen specific circumstances, for which the provider of services shall not be responsible. Where the provision of certain services constitutes professional activities (business) of their provider, the client is bound to reimburse such provider for the losses incurred by the latter only in the event the losses result from specific circumstances not covered by a normal risk characteristic to a certain type of profession or business. If the services are provided by commission of two or more than two clients, all the clients shall bear solidary liability to the provider of services.

771. Unless the contract for services provides otherwise, the provider of services: (1) shall, at the request of the client, communicate to him all information on the services rendered and progress in their provision; (2) shall, at the request of the client, forthwith submit a report to the client on the services rendered or progress in their provision; and (3) shall forthwith furnish to the client all what the provider of services has received during the provision of services for the benefit of the client.

772. According to LCC Article 6.721, the client has the right to unilaterally terminate the contract even though the provision of the services by the provider is already in progress. In this case, the client is bound to pay to the provider of services part of the agreed price in proportion to the services rendered and to pay other reasonable expenses made by the provider of services for the purpose of the performance of the contract before the date of receipt of the notice of termination of the contract from the client. But the provider of services may unilaterally terminate the contract for important reasons only. In this case, the provider of services must fully reimburse the client for the losses incurred.

773. The death of the client does not terminate the contract unless it has been entered into specifically in view of the personal qualifications of the client, or the performance of the contract thereby becomes impossible or useless. The contract on the said grounds shall be terminated from the date the provider of services was informed or had reasonable grounds to be aware of the death of the client. The provider of services must, in all cases, ensure that all adequate measures available to him are taken to protect the interests of the client. The contract shall be terminated by the death or incapacity of the provider of services unless analogous services may be adequately continued by his successors who are entitled thereto. The successors of the provider of services, who are informed of the commission, must ensure that all adequate measures available to them are taken to protect the interests of the client.

Chapter 6. Lease, Commercial and Agricultural Leases

774. Lease of property (*locatio conductio rei*) is one of the most important contracts in Lithuania, which allows for a temporary enjoyment of a property of another. Residential lease is very important for younger people, who have no money or financial history to get credit for their own house. Industrial and financial lease helps to cheaply expand industrial capacities of business enterprises, whereas lease of public land is even functioning as simple business stimulation instrument.

775. Lease contract is consensual, bilateral, onerous and commutative contract with a successive performance. Legal nature of lease in Lithuania, as in other civil law jurisdictions, is usually presented as purely obligational. But this issue should never be oversimplified because there are at least several instances, where lease provides varying *in rem* effects. First, registered lease is a real obligation (*propter rem*), which follows leased property and binds new owner (LCC Article 6.494). Despite this soft proprietary effect lease remains obligation, which has no *erga omnes* effect on third parties. Second, Lithuanian law next to ordinary lease presents emphyteutic lease (LCC Article 4.165), which is not an obligation, but a property right. Third, hybrid models of ordinary lease, such as hire purchase in general (LCC Article 6.503) and financial lease in particular (LCC Article 6.567), are ownership-based security devices and often become grounds for a transfer of the ownership at the end of lease period. Fourth, Lithuanian case law controversially gives right for a lessee to directly sue third parties with property law remedies – negatory actions[407] – without any involvement of the owner, for whom such actions should only belong. It should be noted that statutory law does not support such sharing of owner remedies without his direct mandate. Fifth, ordinary loan of land (LCC Article 6.545), regulated by law of obligations, enables lease of land up to ninety-nine years and even gives right for a lessee to build and maintain its fixtures on the land of another. It means that ordinary lease of land mimics qualities of limited property rights for use – emphyteutic lease (*emphyteusis*) and right to build (*superficies*). Nonetheless, those qualities of land lease should be seen not as virtues, but as vices of LCC disturbing its internal logic and undermining demand for the above-mentioned property right. The negative result of it is that property developers in Lithuania prefer to opt for more familiar but less stable ordinary lease.

776. LCC extensively regulates lease contracts, by providing general rules (LCC Article 6.477–6.503) for all ordinary lease contracts and rules for specific types of ordinary lease (LCC Article 6.504–6.628). Specific types of lease in LCC are consumer lease (LCC Article 6.504–6.511), transport lease (LCC Article 6.512–6.529), industrial lease (LCC Article 6.530–6.535), enterprise lease (LCC Article 6.536–6.544), land lease (LCC Article 6.545–6.566), financial leasing (LCC Article 6.567–6.574) and very detailed and consumer protective – residential lease (LCC Article 6.575–6.628). LCC rules on ordinary lease, with some exceptions, is a loose copy of the same rules within Russian ГК, which are a remodelled and upgraded

407. Judgments of the Lithuanian Supreme Court of 12 Dec. 2005 in the civil case No 3K-3-659/2005 and of 22 Dec. 2009 in the civil case No 3K-3-575/2009.

version of Soviet legislation on lease. Neither of those LCC rules directly apply to emphyteutic lease, which is property right *par excellence* and has its own distinct regime. Lease rules only by analogy may be applied to other lease equivalents, for example, licence contracts, where intellectual property rights are given for a temporary use (Law on Trademarks Article 2 (10)),[408] or affreightment contracts, which is a carriage service of giving limited use of vessel or part of it (LCC Article 6.810). Lease of public property is regulated by the special Law on Management, Use and Disposal of State and Municipal Assets, whereas Law on Land regulates lease of public land.

§1. General Regime for Ordinary (Obligational) Lease

I. Concept and Duration of a Contract

777. Under ordinary lease contract, one party (lessor) shall be obliged to grant to the lessee a thing for payment in temporary possession and use, and the other party (lessee) shall obligate himself to pay a lease payment. Although, according to LCC an object of a lease may be only durable things, other durable property in intangible form (digital assets, rights for radio frequency, etc.) may also be the object of lease, unless expressly reserved by statute for other types of contracts, for example, licencing contracts.[409] The kinds of property, the leasing of which is not permitted, may be established by law. A property or its features enabling to define the property which is to be transferred by the lessor to the lessee must be specified in the contract of lease and cannot be fungible. In the absence of such features in the contract, and if the object of lease cannot be determined according to other features, the contract of lease shall not be considered concluded. A lessor may be the owner of the property under lease or persons empowered by laws or by the owner to lease out a property owned by another person.

778. According to LCC Article 6.478, a contract of lease for a period of more than one year must be concluded in written form. A contract of lease for immovable things for a period of more than one year may be invoked against third persons only in the event if it is registered in the Public Register in accordance with the procedure established by laws.

779. By prescribing period of a lease, LCC Article 6.479 establishes rule against perpetuities: a contract of lease may be fixed-term or concluded for an indefinite period, but in all cases the period of lease may not exceed one hundred years. A period of a contract of lease shall be determined by the agreement of the parties. If

408. In Lithuanian private law, licencing contracts are understood quite specifically. First, they concern only intellectual property, and, second, they may give even exclusive use of property, thus fully resembling and de facto being intellectual property lease.

409. But even the intellectual property rights, which in Lithuania is leased under the licencing contracts, may be leased under the ordinary lease in case of lease of enterprise, which encompass also intellectual property rights.

the period of the contract of lease has not been determined in the contract, the contract of lease shall be considered to have been concluded for an indefinite period. Other periods may be established by laws for the leasing of property which is owed by the state. If, however, parties extend the term of lease, it may be a sign that relationships of parties outgrew those of lease and the court may recharacterise lease to other contracts, such as sales.

780. If the contract of lease is indeterminate, both of the parties shall have the right at any time to repudiate the contract having warned the other party one month in advance, and in the event of the lease of immovable things, three months in advance. A more extensive period may be established in the contract of lease for the issue of warning about the termination thereof. A contract of lease shall be considered to become concluded for an indefinite period where the lessee continues to use the property for more than ten days after the expiry of the period of the contract without any opposition from the lessor (LCC Article 6.480–6.481).

II. Obligations of Parties

781. The parties have a bundle of obligations, which may be summarised as follows: the lessor has duty of delivery with warranty against defects, duty to ensure peaceful enjoyment of property and duty of maintenance, whereas lessor has duty to pay the rent and duty of care, including maintenance of leased property.

782. The lessor is obliged to deliver property to the lessee in the state corresponding to the terms of the contract and designation of the property. The lessor shall be bound to guarantee that the thing is fit to be used for the purpose for which it is leased throughout the whole period of the lease. The incomes, fruits, livestock increase received from the leased thing shall belong to the lessee unless otherwise provided for by the contract. The lessor shall not be held liable for the defects of the property leased which were stipulated by him when concluding the contract. The lessor shall be obliged to deliver to the lessee the documents relating to the thing leased and appurtenances thereof (technical passport, certificate of quality, etc.) which are necessary for the use of that thing unless otherwise provided for by the contract. Neither the lessor nor the lessee may change the form and designation of the leased property during the period of the lease. In the event of the failure of the lessor to deliver into the use of the lessee the leased thing, its documents and accessories, the lessee shall have the right to recover this thing from the lessor and to claim damages caused by the delay of performance or to demand dissolution of the contract and compensation of damage caused by the non-performance of the contract (LCC Article 6.483–6.484). In addition, the lessor has the duty to ensure peaceful enjoyment of property without any disturbances from him, other lessors, State or third parties.

783. The lessor is liable for defects of the thing leased out which wholly or partially obstruct the use thereof for its designation even in those instances where the lessor was not aware of those defects at the time of concluding the contract. In the event of discovery of such defects, the lessee shall have the right at his choice: (1) demand from the lessor either elimination of those defects without compensation or a commensurate reduction of the lease payment, or compensation of the expenses of the lessee incurred in the elimination of the defects; (2) withhold the amount of expenses incurred for the elimination of defects from the lease payment if the lessor was informed of this in advance; and (3) demand the termination of the contract before time (LCC Article 6.485).

784. Principal obligation of lessee is duty to pay rent (lease payment) on time. Parties are free to agree on a broad spectrum of considerations which are compatible with the concept of lease. Pursuant to LCC Article 6.487, upon the agreement of the parties, the lease payment may be established in the following forms: (1) in a fixed sum of money which must be paid in a lump sum or in instalments; (2) in a portion of the products, fruits or incomes received from the use of the leased thing; (3) by certain services supplied to the lessor by the lessee; (4) by the duty of the lessee to improve the state of the leased thing at his own expense; and (5) by the duty of the lessee to transfer to the lessor a thing stipulated in the contract into his ownership or on lease. The parties may agree on a combination of these forms or may establish another form of calculating the lease payment.[410] If the concrete amount of the lease payment or the method of its calculation is not determined in the contract, each of the parties to the contract shall have the right to apply to a court with the request to appoint independent experts for determination of the amount of the lease payment. Unless otherwise provided for by laws or the contract, he has the right to demand a commensurate reduction of the lease payment if due to circumstances for which he is not responsible, conditions of the use of the thing established in the contract or the state of the thing have essentially got worse.

785. Also, the lessee has a contractual duty of care. He must use the leased thing in accordance with the contract and designation of the thing. The lessee is obliged to use the leased thing in such a way as not to hinder the use of that thing by other lawful users. The lessee shall be liable towards the lessor and other lessees. In addition, the lessee shall be liable for actions of other persons he entitles with the right or possibility to use the leased thing. Where one of the lessees violates the duty of care, the other lessees may obtain a reduction of the lease payment if the lessor has been notified of the hindrances. The lessor has the right without interfering with the rights of the lessee to check if the lessee uses the leased thing in a proper way. In addition, the lessor shall have the right to show the leased thing to a prospective lessee or acquirer (LCC Article 6.489).

786. Duty of maintenance of property is shared among parties. The lessor is obliged to make capital repair at his own expense of the leased thing, while the lesse is obliged to maintain the leased thing in a proper state and to bear expenses for the maintenance of this thing and to make its current repair at his own expense, unless

410. For instance, in one case tenant paid rent for a land lease with money, crops, firewood and other goods. *See* Judgment of the Lithuania Supreme Court of 15 Oct. 2020 in the civil case No. e3K-3-260-684/2020.

otherwise provided for by laws or the contract. Violation by the lessor of the duty shall vest the lessee with the right, upon obtaining the authorisation of the court, to make the capital repair and to recover from the lessor the price of the repair, or to withhold it from the lease payment, or to dissolute the contract and claim damages caused by failure to perform the contract. In this event, the lessee shall be bound to submit to the lessor the estimate and account of the work of capital repair. The lessee shall be obliged to provide for all the conditions necessary for the proper performance of the duty of the lessor. In the performance of his maintenance duty, the lessor shall have the right to require from the lessee to temporarily desist from the use of the leased thing if the capital repair is necessary and urgent. If the capital repair is not urgent and the lessee does not agree to be temporarily dispossessed of the leased thing, the lessor must obtain the authorisation of the court for the temporary restriction of the lessee's right to use the leased thing. The lessee whose right to use the leased thing is restricted shall have the right to obtain reduction of the lease payment, to demand compensation, or to apply for the dissolution of the contract of lease (LCC Article 6.492). From the other hand, the lessee, on becoming aware of damage or any other serious defects of the leased thing for the elimination of which urgent capital repair is necessary, shall be bound immediately to inform the lessor thereof. In the event where the lessor, after he was informed by the lessee, fails to eliminate the defects, the lessee shall have the right to undertake the necessary repair work even without the authorisation of the court if it is necessary to ensure the preservation of the leased thing; in doing so the lessee shall inform the lessor accordingly and subsequently submit to him the document confirming the value of the performed work as well as the replaced parts of the thing. Where necessary, the lessee may perform the inevitable repair of the thing by withholding the amount of the expenses from his payment of lease (LCC Article 6.493).

III. Third Parties

787. An ordinary lease of a thing is obligation, which does not affect the rights of third persons to that thing. Thus, the lessor before concluding a contract of lease is obliged to inform the lessee about all rights of third persons to the thing upon lease (pledge, servitude, usufruct, etc.). If the lessor fails to perform this duty, the lessee shall have the right to demand a reduction of lease payment or dissolution of the contract and compensation of damage (LCC Article 6.486). In addition, the lessor, in selling or in any other way transferring a leased thing, as well as pledging it or otherwise encumbering the right of ownership thereto, shall be bound to inform the purchaser of the thing or the party of any other contract about the contract of lease in operation, likewise to inform the lessee of the intended sale, any other alienation of the thing, or of the encumbrance of the right thereto (LCC Article 6.495).

788. LCC Article 6.494 offers possibility to upgrade by perfection personal lease obligation up to real obligation (*propter rem*), which follows the leased property. According to this article, transfer of the right of ownership of the leased thing from the lessor to another person shall preserve validity of the registrable contract of lease towards the new owner/shall preserve the registrable contract of lease being in force towards the new owner, provided the rights resulting from that/such contract of lease are registered in the Public Register within the procedure established by laws. But the transfer of the right of ownership to the leased property from the lessor to another person shall be the grounds for the termination of the contract of lease in case of a demand of the lessee. In the event of death of a lessee – natural person – who was leasing an immovable thing, his rights and duties under the contract of lease shall be passed to his heirs unless otherwise provided for by laws or the contract. In such event, the lessor shall have no right to refuse the heir of the deceased lessee the assignment of the rights and duties of the previous lessee for the remaining period of the lease, except in the cases when the conclusion of the contract was conditioned by the personal qualities of the lessee. However, in the event of expropriation of the thing for public interests, the contract of lease shall terminate at the moment from which the new owner of the expropriated thing (possessor) acquires possession of that thing. This rule flows from property law, because expropriation is original acquisition of property rights, which extinguishes all former burdens, including real obligations.

789. Another important feature of lease, concerning third parties, is the preferential right of the lessee to renew a contract of lease. Pursuant to LCC Article 6.482, the lessee who has duly performed his duties accepted according to the contract of lease shall have a preferential right before other persons to renew the contract upon the expiry of the period thereof. The lessor must inform the lessee in writing within the period determined in the contract of the latter's right to conclude a contract of lease for a new term, and if such period is not determined in the contract, within a reasonable period before the termination of the contract of lease. When concluding a contract of lease for a new period, the conditions of the contract may be modified by the agreement of the parties. If the lessor refused to conclude a contract with the lessee for a new period, but within a year from the termination of the contract of lease concluded a contract of lease upon the same thing with another person without informing the previous lessee, the latter shall have the right at his choice to claim either the transfer to him of the rights and duties of the lessee under the contract of lease concluded or compensation of damage incurred in the result of the refusal to conclude a contract of lease for a new period. It should be noted that this rule is an element of the overall protective regime of the lessee, which is usually weaker than lessor even in commercial lease, for example, where business start-up leases business office from big property developer. It promotes stability of economic relationships, lessee's goodwill associated with business place and safeguards its investments into lease property, which according to standard market practice otherwise would not be compensated. This statutory rule is protective and binding even third parties. Thus, if it would be possible to contract-out, the lessor would for sure do in its standard contract terms. Unfortunately, those features were not held as important by the Supreme Court, which has ruled that in commercial contracts, parties are free to contract-out from the pre-emption right of the lessee.[411]

411. Judgment of the Lithuanian Supreme Court of 7 Feb. 2018 in the civil case No e3K-3-23-611/2018.

790. A right to lease is an item of non-tangible property. Therefore, the lessee shall have the right upon the written consent of the lessor obtained in advance to assign his rights and duties under the contract of lease, to pledge the right of lease or to transfer it as a property contribution or to effectuate any other encumbrance thereof unless otherwise provided for by the contract of lease (LCC Article 6.491). Nonetheless, the lessee has the right to sublease the leased thing only with the written consent of the lessor unless otherwise provided for by the contract. The contract of sublease may not be concluded for a period exceeding the period of the contract of lease. A refusal of the lessor to consent to the sublease of the thing must be reasonably motivated. If the lessor refuses to consent without any reasonable grounds, the lessee shall have the right to dissolve the contract before its expiry. If the consent of the lessor for the sublease of a thing is not necessary, the lessee before concluding the contract of sublease shall be bound to inform the lessor about the contract of sublease and the sub-lessee. If the contract of lease is void, the contract of sublease shall also be void. The lessee shall be liable towards the lessor both in the event of sublease and the lease for use. If a sub-lessee violates the contract of sublease in essence and inflicts damage by his actions to the lessor or to other lawful users of that thing, the lessor shall have the right to demand dissolution of the contract of sublease. In the event where the lessor fails to perform his obligations in accordance with the contract of lease, the sub-lessee may also submit a claim on behalf of the lessee (LCC Article 6.490).

IV. Termination and Restitution

791. A contract of lease with a fixed term is terminated upon expiry of its time limit unless it is renewed by the parties by forming/making/entering into a new agreement or by tacit renewal. In addition to cases of fundamental breach prescribed in LCC Article 6.217, the lessor has the right to bring an action into a court for the dissolution of a contract of lease before time if: (1) the lessee uses the thing in violation of the contract or not according to the designation of the thing; (2) the lessee intentionally or through negligence worsens the state of the thing; (3) the lessee fails to pay the payment of lease; (4) the lessee fails to perform capital repair in those cases where the laws or the contract obligate him to do so; and (5) there exist other grounds provided for by the contract of lease. The lessor shall have the right to demand dissolution of the contract of lease before time only after having sent a written warning to the lessee about the necessity to perform the obligation or eliminate violations within reasonable time; however, the lessee after reception of such warning failed within reasonable time to perform the obligation or to eliminate the violations. Equivalently, in addition to cases of fundamental breach prescribed in LCC Article 6.217, the lessee also has the right to bring an action to a court for dissolution of a contract of lease before time if: (1) the lessor fails to carry out the repair he is obliged to; (2) the thing by virtue of circumstances for which the lessee is not liable becomes not fit for use; (3) the lessor fails to transfer the thing to the lessee or hinders the use of the thing in accordance with its designation and the conditions of the contract; (4) the thing transferred has defects which were not stipulated by the lessor and were unknown to the lessee and which render the thing impossible to be used in accordance with its designation and the conditions of the contract; and (5) there exist other grounds provided for by the contract of lease (LCC Article 6.497, 6.498).

792. Upon the termination of the contract of lease, the lessee shall be bound to return the thing to the lessor in the state he received it, taking into account normal wear and tear, or in the state agreed in the contract. In the event where the lessee returns the thing after the term, the lessor shall have the right to demand the lease payment for the entire time of the delay and compensation for damage incurred by such delay. In the event of the failure on the part of the lessee to return the leased thing, he shall be bound to compensate to the lessor the amount of the value of that thing, likewise to effectuate the payment of lease and compensate for other damages incurred by the lessor. In the event of the lessee causing deterioration of the leased thing, he shall be bound to compensate to the lessor damages caused by the deterioration, except in the cases where the lessee proves that the deterioration occurred not due to his fault. In the instances where the lessee with the permission of the lessor has made improvements of the leased thing, he shall have the right to compensation of the necessary expenses incurred by him for that purpose. In the event where the improvements made by the lessee without the permission of the lessor are separable without harm to the leased thing, and where the lessor does not agree to compensate for them, they may be taken out by the lessee. The value of improvements which are not separable without harm to the leased thing made by the lessee without the permission of the lessor shall not be subject to obligatory compensation. The lessee is liable for the loss of a thing unless he proves that the loss was not due to his fault or that of the persons he, upon the permission of the lessor, granted the right of use of the leased thing or allowed access thereto. The lessee is not liable for the loss of an immovable thing by the reason of fire unless it is proved that the fire occurred due to his fault or that of the persons he, upon the permission of the lessor, granted the right of use of the leased thing or allowed access thereto (LCC Article 6.499–6.502).

§2. Commercial Leases

793. There are several types of commercial leases, the most important or interesting being the industrial lease (LCC Article 6.530–6.535), enterprise lease (LCC Article 6.536–6.544) and financial lease (LCC Article 6.567–6.574).

I. Industrial Lease

794. Under a contract of industrial lease, the lessor undertakes an obligation to transfer for payment a building, construction works or machinery to the lessee in temporary possession and use or temporary use, while the lessee undertakes an obligation to pay the payment of lease. According to LCC Article 6.531, such contract must be formed in written form and may be invoked against third persons only if registered in the Public Register.

795. The transfer of a building, construction works or machinery and the acceptance thereof shall be effectuated under the act of transfer-acceptance. The act shall be signed by both parties. Unless otherwise provided for by laws or the contract, the obligation of the lessor to transfer the building, construction works or machinery to the lessee is performed after the factual granting of the building, construction works or machinery to the lessee or upon the signing of the act of transfer-acceptance. In the event of one party of the contract avoiding to sign the act of transfer-acceptance of a building, construction works or machinery under the conditions agreed in the contract of lease, it shall be considered as a refusal respectively of the lessor to perform his obligation with regard to the transfer of the relevant building, construction works or machinery or of the lessee to accept them. Upon the termination of a contract, they must be returned to the lessor by the same manner.

796. Pursuant to LCC Article 6.532, the rights of the use of that part of the land plot which is occupied by the relevant buildings, construction works and machineries and is necessary for the use in accordance with their designation shall pass to the lessee simultaneously with the transfer of the subject matter of the lease. In the event where the lessor is the owner of the land plot on which the leased buildings, construction works or machineries are situated, the land plot shall be provided for the use of the lessee under the right of lease or on any other right stipulated in the contract of lease of buildings, construction works and machineries. In the event where the rights of the lessee to the land plot occupied by the relevant buildings, construction works or machineries are not determined in the contract of lease, it shall be deemed that the lessee is granted for the period of the lease of the respective immovables the right to use gratuitously that part of land plot which is necessary for the use of buildings, construction works and machineries in accordance with their designation. The lease of buildings, construction works or machineries situated on a land plot which does not belong to the lessor by the right of ownership shall be permitted without the consent of the owner of this plot exclusively where this is not contrary to laws or the contract between the owner of the plot and the lessor of the buildings, construction works and machineries. In the event where the land plot occupied by the leased buildings, construction works or machineries is sold or transferred under any other grounds into the possession of another person under the right of ownership, the lessee shall retain the right to use that part of land plot which is necessary for the use of buildings, construction works and machineries in accordance with their designation under the same terms as existed before the alienation of the land plot into the ownership of another person, providing the contract of lease was registered in the Public Register in accordance with the procedure established by laws (LCC Article 6.533).

797. Accordingly, the payment of industrial lease established in the contract shall include payment for the use of the land plot on which the leased buildings, construction works or machineries are situated unless otherwise provided for by laws or the contract of lease. In the instances where the payment of lease has been established per unit of space of the building, construction works or machinery or any other dimension thereof, the lease payment shall be determined by proceeding from the actual size of the leased building, construction works or machinery (LCC Article 6.534).

II. Enterprise Lease

798. An enterprise is a universality of assets and debts, belonging to the person who is engaged in business (seeking profit), which may be the object of property rights and as such may be sold, pledged or leased. According to LCC Article 1.110, an enterprise is considered to be an immovable thing. Being the patrimony, an enterprise should be distinguished from its holder – the business company.

799. LCC Article 6.536 provides that under a contract of lease of enterprise, the lessor shall take an obligation to grant to the lessee in temporary possession and use for payment an enterprise as a business patrimony, while the lessee undertakes an obligation to pay the payment of lease. The granting of an enterprise as a business patrimony to the lessee shall also comprise a transfer of the plot of land, buildings, construction works, installations, equipment, other means of production specified in the contract, raw materials, stocks, working capital, rights to the use of land, water and other natural resources, buildings, construction works or installations, likewise any other property rights connected with the enterprise, the rights to the product or service mark and the name of the firm as well as other exclusive rights. The transfer of an enterprise as a business patrimony shall also comprise the assignment of the rights to claim and obligation of debts determined in the contract of lease. The transfer of the rights of possession and use of property which is in the ownership of other persons, likewise the transfer of rights of possession and use of land and other natural resources shall be effectuated in accordance with the procedure established by laws.

800. This type of transaction is not very common in business practice, because the demand for temporary use of business it is quite low, while the procedure is very burdensome. Huge obstacle is LCC Article 6.537 requirement that the lessor of an enterprise shall be obliged before the transfer thereof to the lessee to notify in writing the creditors of the enterprise about its lease. A creditor of the enterprise who has not been informed about the lease of the enterprise has the right to bring the specific performance, termination and damages claims against the lessor within the period of one year from the date when he became aware or should have become aware of the lease of the enterprise.

801. LCC provides for a mandatory form of a contract of lease of enterprise, which must be concluded in written form by means of drawing up one document. The failure to comply with the requirements to the form of the contract of lease of enterprise shall render the contract null and void. A contract of lease of enterprise may be invoked against third persons only where it has been registered in the public registers of real property and of legal persons (LCC Article 6.538).

802. The transfer and return of a leased enterprise are effectuated under the act of transfer-acceptance. Normally, the lessee has the right without the consent of the lessor to sell, exchange, transfer temporary use raw materials, stocks, manufactured products which are part of the property of the leased enterprise, sublease them and transfer his rights and obligations in respect of those valuables under the contract of lease, on condition that this does not entail violation of the provisions of the contract of lease of enterprise and reduction of the value of the enterprise. But the lessee has no right without the consent of the lessor to make changes in the leased enterprise as a business patrimony, perform its reconstruction, modernisation, expansion of its capacity, technical re-equipping or introduce any other transformations. The lessee of an enterprise shall be obliged within the entire period of operation of the contract of lease to ensure proper technical state of the enterprise and to perform its current and even capital repair. The lessee shall be obliged to bear all the expenses related to the exploitation of the leased enterprise, to pay for the insurance of the property of the enterprise and any effectuate other payments unless otherwise provided for by the contract of lease of the enterprise.

III. Financial Lease

803. From the perspective of financial law, financial lease is a possessory title finance arrangement which secures creditors rights, and, according to Law on Financial Institutions Article 3, is a type of financial services. From the perspective of civil law, financial lease is a subtype of hire purchase (LCC Article 6.503) agreements. Legislation on the financial lease in LCC, with some deviations, is modelled according to UNIDROIT Convention on International Financial Leasing, signed in Ottawa in 1988. LCC Article 6.567 defines leasing (financial lease) as an agreement whereby one party (the lessor) undertakes to acquire from a third party, on the specifications of another party (the lessee), a thing and place it, in return for payment, at the possession of the lessee for business purposes provided that upon payment of the total amount provided for in the leasing agreement the equipment will pass to the ownership of the lessee, unless otherwise provided for by the agreement. The provisions of LCC chapter on leasing also apply *mutatis mutandis* in cases where the lessor is the owner of the leased property. Obvious shortcoming of leasing definition in the LCC is the inclusion of the property transfer in the concept of leasing, which makes it difficult to distinguish leasing from sales contracts. This has been firmly mitigated by case law and legal doctrine, which recharacterised so-called leasing contracts, the main purpose of which is to transfer the ownership at the end of property use, as not lease, but instalment sale.[412] The leasing is exclusively commercial contract, but in practice analogous contracts are concluded also with consumers. The Supreme Court of Lithuania has correctly ruled on this that 'leasing

412. *See* Laurynas Didžiulis, Janina Stripeikienė. *Aktualūs finansinės nuomos (lizingo) instituto taikymo klausimai. In.* Privatinės teisės doktrina ir praktika: Liber Amicorum Vytautui Pakalniškiui. Vilnius: Mykolas Romeris University, 2014, p. 319–335; Judgment of the Lithuanian Supreme Court of 9 Jan. 2013 in the civil case No 3K-3-154/2013.

contracts' concluded with consumers are not financial lease but general instances of hire purchase.[413]

804. The object of the leasing agreement may be any non-consumable movable or immovable thing with the exception of land and natural resources. The lessor may transfer all or part of his rights related to the leasing agreement and its object to third parties. Such transfer of rights shall be without prejudice to the lessor's obligations under the leasing agreement where the time limit for meeting such obligations is due before transfer of such obligations to third parties and shall be without prejudice as to the substance of the leasing agreement. The lessee may transfer the right to the use of the object of the leasing agreement or any other right under the leasing agreement only subject to a prior written consent of the lessor. Unless otherwise provided for by the leasing agreement, the lessor may not, without a written consent of the lessee, pledge the leasing object (LCC Article 6.568).

805. Because the lessee is an economic owner of leased property,[414] the risk of accidental damage to the thing (the object of the leasing agreement) shall pass to the lessee as from the moment when such thing is transferred over to him, unless otherwise provided for by the leasing agreement. The lessee shall assume all costs in relation to the maintenance and repair of the thing. Usually the lessor, who is just formal owner for security purposes, is not liable to the lessee for the defects of the object of the agreement with the exception of cases where the lessee relied on the lessor's experience and knowledge and also where the lessor intervened in the selection of the seller and the object of the agreement. The lessee must use and maintain the thing with diligence and due care and keep it in the condition in which it was handed over to him subject to fair wear and tear and to any modification agreed by the parties in the agreement. Where the lessee fails to comply with the duty provided for in paragraph 4, the lessor shall have the right to require the payment of the total price of the agreement or termination of the agreement and redress of damages (LCC Article 6.571). For the same reason, the lessee is liable for any damages incurred by third parties as a result of the use of the object of the leasing agreement. The seller is directly bound towards the lessee with respect to all claims resulting from the purchase–sale agreement of the object of leasing (with respect to the quality and completeness of the property, handover period, etc.). Save to the duty to pay for the acquired property, the lessee shall enjoy all rights and duties of the buyer provided for in this book to the same extent as if he were party to the purchase–sale agreement. However, the lessee shall not have the right to terminate the purchase–sale agreement without the consent of the lessor (LCC Article 6.573).

413. According to LCC Art. 6.503, it may be provided for by laws or the contract of lease that the leased thing shall pass to the ownership of the lessee upon the expiry of the time limit of the contract of lease or before the expiry thereof if the lessee pays the entire amount of the price stipulated by the contract of sale by instalment. If the condition on the purchase of the leased thing is not provided in the contract, it may be established by an additional agreement of the parties in which they may agree upon the set-off of the previously paid lease payment against the price of the thing. A prohibition of purchase of the leased thing may be established by laws or the contract.

414. Vytautas Mizaras. Lizingo sutarties sampratos aiškinimas pagal Civilinį kodeksą. Justitia. 2003, Vol. 1–2 (43–44), p. 5.

806. As the leasing is title finance arrangement giving superpriority rights for the lessor,[415] it should be perfected in order to get full legal effect. Thus, LCC prescribes that the lessor's rights of ownership in the object of the leasing agreement which is not subject to registration shall be valid against third parties only if the leasing agreement has been registered under the procedure provided for by laws. It means that in the case of the lessee's bankruptcy, the lessor's rights shall be valid against the lessee's creditors and the administrator only if the leasing agreement has been registered under the procedure provided for by laws.

807. Where the lessee is in fundamental breach of the leasing agreement, the lessor must require in writing that the lessee eliminates, within a reasonable time limit, the infringement if this is possible taking into account specific circumstances. Where the lessee's default continues, the lessor shall have the right to require accelerated payment of rentals or to terminate the leasing agreement. Where the leasing agreement is terminated, the lessor shall have the right to require that the object of the agreement is returned to him and to recover such damages as will place the lessor in the position in which he would have been had the lessee duly performed the agreement (LCC Article 6.574).

§3. Agricultural Leases

808. There are two types of leases relevant for agricultural use – ordinary lease of land and emphyteutic lease. Where public land is leased, special rules apply.

I. Ordinary Lease of Land

809. Under a land lease contract, one party (lessor) shall take an obligation to transfer for payment a plot of land to the other party (lessee) in temporary possession and use for the purposes specified in the contract and under conditions established therein, while the lessee undertakes an obligation to pay the payment of land rent indicated in the contract. The subject matter of a land lease contract is a plot (parcel) of land (or a part thereof) in the state or private ownership formed in accordance with the project of land use planning or any other detailed document of territorial planning and registered in the Public Register within the procedure established by laws. In the event of a plot of land belonging to several persons under the right of co-ownership, the land plot concerned may be leased upon the written consent of all the co-owners.

810. According to LCC Article 6.547, a land lease contract shall have to be formed in written form. A land lease contract may be invoked by the parties against third persons only if it is registered in the Public Register within the procedure established by laws. A land lease contract shall have to be appended with the plan of the land plot to be leased, and in the event of the land to be leased for the period

415. Judgment of the Lithuanian Supreme Court of 3 Mar. 2009 in the civil case No 3K-3-91/2009.

of up to three years, with the scheme of the land plot. These documents shall form an inseparable part of the land lease contract.

811. The duration of a contract of lease of public land shall be established upon the agreement between the lessor and the lessee; nevertheless, the term may not exceed ninety-nine years. Where the land plot pursuant to the territorial planning documents is allocated to be used for public needs, such land plot shall be leased only for a period until it is expropriated for the purposes intended. In the event of the contract being concluded for a longer period, it shall be deemed to be concluded only for the duration until the expropriation of the land plot.

812. LCC Article 6.550 prescribes content of land lease contracts. The following must be stated in a land lease contract: (1) the lessor of the land; (2) the lessee of the land; (3) the data on the object of the land lease registered in the Land Cadastre and the Public Register; (4) duration of the lease of land; (5) the principal particular purpose of land use; (6) conditions of use of the construction works and installations situated on the leased land and belonging to the owner of the land or any other persons under the right of ownership, as well as the conditions of erecting new buildings, construction works, building of roads and water reservoirs, or other conditions, likewise the intended use of the buildings or installations upon the expiry of the time limit of the land lease contract; (7) conditions of use of the surface and subterranean waters, mineral resources (with the exception of amber, oil, natural gas and quartz-sand) found in the land plot to the extent that they are not contrary to laws; (8) special conditions of the use of land; (9) restrictions of the use of land; (10) land servitudes and other property rights; (11) payment for the land lease. It shall include payment for the land reclamation installations, roads, bridges, engineering equipment, etc., likewise indexing of the payment in the event of the lease of public land; (12) other commitments of the lessor and the lessee related to the use of the land plot and its return upon the expiry of the land lease contract; and (13) liability for the infringements of the land lease contract. From the other token, a land lease contract may not provide for: (1) authorisation issued to the lessee to represent the owner of the land and dispose of the private land of this owner and any other immovable property situated therein; and (2) the right of a lessee of land in private ownership to change the principal particular purpose of land utilisation. The conditions of the land lease contract which determine the manner of the use of the leased land may not contradict to the interests of environment, those of the owners or users of the neighbouring land plots, as well as to the public interests.

813. As for public land, pursuant to LCC Article 6.551, it should be leased only by auction to a person who offers the highest payment for the lease of land. Public land may be leased without the auction in the instances when it is built over by buildings, construction works or installation that belong to private persons by the right of ownership or are leased by them, likewise in other cases provided for by laws. Law on Land Article 9 further defines by providing that such possibility exists only where structures or facilities owned by the right of ownership, or leased, by natural and legal persons are located on it (except for temporary structures, engineering networks and structures without a clear functional dependence or of unspecified use or nature of economic activities and which serve the main structure or facility or its appurtenance). Land parcels whereon structures or facilities leased by natural or legal persons are located shall be leased only for a term of lease of these structures or facilities. The leased land parcels shall be of the size stipulated in the territorial planning documents or landholding projects, and required for operating the structures or facilities pursuant to their primary purpose indicated in the Real Property Cadastre.

814. As concerns the maintenance of land, the lessor is obliged to repair at his own expense land reclamation installations, roads, bridges and other engineering facilities owned by him. In the event where the lessor fails to perform this duty, which renders the land plot impossible to be used for its designation, the lessee has the right to terminate the contract. In the instances where the lessor fails to perform the repair work acknowledged by relevant public authorities as indispensable and immediate, the lessee shall have the right to perform the repair work himself and exact from the lessor within judicial proceedings repair expenses necessary to ensure the functioning of the leased property. The lessee is prohibited to perform any actions in the leased land plot which might bring about destruction or pollution of the fertile layer of soil. Usually, the lessee is obliged at his own expense to perform within the procedure established by laws minor maintenance work of the land reclamation installations, roads, bridges and other engineering facilities belonging to the lessor, to preserve protective and other signs, likewise to ensure the compliance with the environment requirements in the territory. In the event where the lessee fails to perform these duties, the lessor shall have the right to exact within the judicial proceedings from the lessee the funds necessary for the performance of the indicated work, damages and terminate the land lease contract. In the event of improper use of agricultural lands by the lessee with resultant deterioration of their quality, the lessee of the land shall be obliged to compensate to the lessor the damage caused (LCC Article 6.555, 6.556).

815. Upon the expiry of the time limit of the land lease or upon its termination before the term, the owner of the land shall compensate the lessee for the erected buildings, construction works and installations, the construction of which was provided for in the land lease contract; where these constructions remain in the possession of the lessee by the right of ownership, the latter shall have the right to the land servitude, providing that it was stipulated in the land lease contract or the additional written agreement. In the event where the buildings, construction works and installations were erected without permission, or where the erected buildings, construction works and installations were not stipulated in the land lease contract, the lessee shall be obliged to demolish them and restore the land plot. If the lessee fails to comply, this shall be executed by the lessor at the expense of the former, while the buildings, construction works and installations concerned shall pass to the lessor by the right of ownership, providing the constructions conform to the requirements established in the territorial planning documents and are legitimised in accordance with the procedure established by laws (LCC Article 6.557).

816. A land lease contract, according to LCC Article 6.562, is terminated: (1) upon expiry of the time limit of lease; (2) after the death of the lessor of land where his heirs do assume the rights and duties related to the lease contract, or in the case of absence of any heirs; (3) upon liquidation of the legal person that was the lessor of the land; (4) when the land under lease is sold, gifted or by any other way alienated to the lessee; and (5) upon agreement of the parties. Moreover, in the event of the land being expropriated for public needs, the land lease contract shall be terminated, and the damage incurred by the lessor and the lessee compensated in accordance with the procedure established by laws. A land lease contract may also be terminated at the demand of the lessor before the expiry of its time limit: (1) if the lessee of the land fails to use the land in conformity with the contract or the principal particular purpose of land use; (2) if the lessee of the land fails to execute payment for the land lease within the period of three months from the payment date established in the land lease contract; and (3) in other instances provided for by laws. Where the lease of agricultural land being terminated before the expiry of its time limit at the demand of the lessor, the harvest shall be gathered by the lessee, or the lessor shall compensate the lessee for the damage incurred due to the termination of the contract (LCC Article 6.564). A lease contract of agricultural land may be dissolved before the expiry of its time limit at the demand of the lessee upon prior notification of the lessor not later than three months before the termination, and not later than two months before the termination of a contract of the lease of any other land (LCC Article 6.565).

II. Emphyteutic Lease

817. Emphyteutic lease, or simply emphyteusis is not a contractual obligation, but property right to use the plot of land or other immovable of another provided the emphyteutic lessee does not aggravate its quality, does not undertake to build construction works, to plant perennial plants and perform other works thereon that durably increase its value both of the land used or any other immovable thing except upon the permission of the owner of the land. Emphyteusis may be established for a fixed or an indefinite period. The duration of emphyteusis may not be less than ten years. When the owner or the emphyteutic lessee changes, emphyteusis remains due, provided assignees use the leased thing properly and fulfil other obligations stipulated in the contract constituting emphyteusis (LCC Article 4.165).

818. Since emphyteusis is a property right, its content according to *numerus clausus* principle is mandatory prescribed by law, and freedom of contract is permitted only where law expressly says so. Pursuant to LCC Article 4.168, the lessee shall use the leased immovable thing as its owner; however, he shall not increase its value essentially, he also is not entitled to change its destination without the permission of the owner, unless the contract constituting emphyteusis provides otherwise. If emphyteusis is established in respect of land, the contract constituting emphyteusis may stipulate the right of the lessee to build construction works or plant plants necessary for the use of the land in accordance with its destination. The emphyteutic lessee is bound to preserve and repair the immovable at his own expense. Unless provided otherwise, the emphyteutic lessee enjoys the fruits produced by an immovable thing. The contract constituting emphyteusis may stipulate that the emphyteutic lessee is not entitled to assign his rights to another person or divide emphyteusis without the consent of the owner. Unless the contract constituting emphyteusis provides otherwise, the emphyteutic lessee has the right to sublease. The sub-lessee shall not have more rights than the emphyteutic lessee. The sublease terminates upon the end of emphyteusis.

819. Emphyteusis is extinguished: (1) by the expiry of the term; (2) by the loss of the object of emphyteusis; (3) by the extinction of emphyteusis by a court judgment; (4) by the union of the qualities of owner and emphyteutic lessee in the same person; (5) by non-user for ten years; and (6) by a mutual agreement of parties. On the initiative of the owner and the emphyteutic lessee, grounds for premature extinction of the emphyteusis may be stipulated in the contract constituting emphyteusis. Emphyteusis may be modified or cancelled by a court judgment on the request of either the owner or the emphyteutic lessee, provided that unforeseen circumstances appear whereby it is impossible to use the thing in conformity with two earlier conditions. Upon the extinction of emphyteusis, the emphyteutic lessee is bound to return to the owner the object of emphyteusis. The emphyteutic lessee is to be reimbursed for the value of the improvements of the object of emphyteusis, provided that the improvements have been made upon the consent of the owner. The emphyteutic lessee is entitled to suspend the transfer of the object of emphyteusis till the time when the owner repays the compensation. The owner can retain the thing belonging to the emphyteutic lessee till the time the lessee settles accounts with him. If the contract constituting emphyteusis stipulated the right of the emphyteutic lessee to build construction works or plant plants necessary for the use of the land in accordance to its destination, at the extinction of emphyteusis, the emphyteutic lessee can remove construction works or plants, if he returns the land to its former condition and unless the contract constituting emphyteusis provides otherwise.

§4. Lease as a Model for Gratuitous Use

820. Under classical civilian reasoning, based on Roman law, gratuitous temporary use of property belonging to another is called a loan for use.[416] In my opinion, this classification is misleading and wrongly organised because a so-called loan for use has more in common with lease, than with loan. Both former contracts concern transfer of possession of non-consumable goods for temporary use, the basic difference is that 'loan for use' is gratuitous, while a lease is onerous contract.[417] This tight connection is reflected by LCC Article 6.629, which states that provisions of paragraphs 2 and 3 of LCC Article 6.477 (object of the contract), LCC Article 6.478 (formalities), 6.479 (duration), 6.481 (tacit renewal), paragraphs 1 and 2 of LCC

416. Christian Von Bar, Eric Clive, *et al. Principles, Definitions and Model Rules of European Private Law. Draft Common Frame of Reference (DCFR).* Full ed., Sellier, 2009, p. 2456.
417. *See* Judgment of the Lithuanian Supreme Court of 13 Oct. 2008 in the civil case No 3K-3-481/2008.

Article 6.489 (lessee's duty of careful use), and LCC Article 6.501 (improvement of a thing) – all of them designed to lease contracts – should apply correspondingly to a contract of 'loan for use'. In contrast, ordinary loan is a legal ground for a transfer of ownership of the fungible property, which at the end of the contract should be returned to the property of the creditor. It means that ordinary loan produces direct *in rem* effect (change of ownership), whereas 'loan for use' is purely obligational contract. Therefore, I see as an advantage that 'loan for use' in Lithuanian language within the text of LCC is called *panauda* (use) and not *paskola* (loan).

821. Under a contract of gratuitous use, one party (giver) transfers a durable property for temporary gratuitous possession and use to another party (user) while the user takes an obligation to return this property in the same state in which he was received taking into account normal wear and tear, or in a state stipulated in the contract (LCC Article 6.629). Gratuitous use is a real, unilateral and gratuitous contract. Real (and accordingly unilateral) character gratuitous use bears from its historic origins related to a contract of loan. But, especially taking into account reasoning presented above, this is perhaps single feature which today connects those contracts. Due to real character of a contract, agreement as such is not sufficient ground to form the contract, thus failure to honour a promise to transfer a property for gratuitous use without adequate grounds only gives the user the claim for compensation of expenses incurred in relation with the acceptance of the transferable property for gratuitous use (LCC Article 6.631).

822. In order to avoid corporate abuses, LCC Article 6.630 provides limitation on forming a contract of gratuitous use by stating that profit-seeking legal persons shall have no right to transfer a property under a contract of gratuitous use to persons who are founders, participants or members of the bodies of those legal persons.

823. The giver must transfer a property to the user in a state corresponding to the conditions of the contract of gratuitous use and the designation thereof. The giver is liable for defects of the property granted for gratuitous use which he intentionally or through gross negligence did not stipulate when concluding the contract for use, as well as for the damage caused to the user by these defects.

824. In contrast with ordinary lease, but similarly as with emphyteutic lease, the user is obliged not only to maintain and preserve the property transferred to him under the contract but also to perform current and even capital repair, and to bear all expenses for the maintenance thereof unless otherwise provided for by the contract (LCC Article 6.636). Also, the user bears the risk of accidental perishing or damaging of the property if the property perished or was damaged while being used for other purposes than those indicated in the contract or transferred to a third person without prior written consent of the giver. The user also bears the risk of accidental perishing or damaging of the property if he continued using the property after the expiry of the time limit of the contract of gratuitous use, or taking into account the actual circumstances, he could have saved the property by using his own property but failed to do that (LCC Article 6.638). Moreover, the user has no right of retention in respect of a property transferred to him, except in cases where the obligation of the giver entails compensation of necessary and immediate expenses related to the preservation of the property (LCC Article 6.640).

825. Grounds for the end of gratuitous use are defined broadly in LCC, because such use is burden on property of another without any monetary consideration and stability of a contract is not safeguarded at such extent as of onerous contracts. Thus, the giver has the right to demand termination of the contract before time in the instances where the user: (1) uses the property not in accordance with its designation; (2) does not fulfil the duty to maintain and preserve the property; (3) essentially worsens the state of the property; and (4) transfers the property to third persons without the consent of the giver. The giver also has the right to demand termination of the contract of gratuitous use before time in the instances where due to unpredicted and extraordinary circumstances the property is urgently and inevitably needed by the giver himself. The user has the right to demand termination of the contract before time: (1) in the event where defects of the property are discovered, which make the normal use of the property impossible or obstructed and about the existence of which he did not know or could not have known at the time of concluding the contract; (2) if the property by virtue of circumstances for which the user is not liable becomes not fit for use in accordance with its designation; (3) if at the time of concluding the contract the giver failed to warn him about the rights of third persons in that property; and (4) in the event of the failure of the giver to transfer the auxiliaries or documents related to the property (LCC Article 6.641). In addition, each of the parties to a contract of the gratuitous has the right at any time to terminate an indeterminate contract of the gratuitous use having notified the other party thereof three months beforehand unless other time limit has been provided for by the contract. Even more, as the gratuitous use serves only the interests of user, he has the right at any time to revoke a fixed-term contract of the gratuitous use having notified the other party about the intended revocation of the contract at least one month beforehand (LCC Article 6.642). Therefore, if parties want to create more stable and prolonged transaction for unremunerated use, they should contract for usufruct (LCC Article 4.141) instead of gratuitous use.

826. Gratuitous use is very similar contract to lease, and this is clearly seen by equal possibility to upgrade by perfection both contracts to creating real obligations, which follow property, not the person (*propter rem*). Hence, LCC Article 6.643 prescribes that the giver has the right to sell the property or transfer it for onerous use to a third person. In this event, the rights and duties under the previous contract of gratuitous use pass to the new owner or user if that contract, in the case of it being subject to registration, was registered in the Public Register in accordance with the procedure established by laws, or the new owner and user knew or should have known about it at the time of concluding the contract. Interestingly, that last possibility to follow property even in case of unregistered gratuitous use, if the new owner and user knew or should have known about it at the time of concluding the contract, is not available in case of lease (LCC Article 6.494).

Chapter 7. Compromise Settlements

827. Contract of peaceful settlement (*taikos sutartis*) is regulated in both substantive and procedural law. General features of settlement contract are established within the LCC rules on contract law, whereas procedural laws currently provide for particularities of settlement within civil and administrative procedures. Before the repeal of criminal trial on the basis of private accusation from 2017, peaceful settlement also has existed in criminal procedure. A settlement is a consensual, commutative and often bilateral and onerous contract, which is capable to produce *in rem* effects if parties wish so.

828. Pursuant to LCC Article 6.983, by the peaceful settlement agreement the parties shall resolve, by making mutual allowances, an existing judicial dispute, preclude a judicial dispute in the future, resolve an issue of enforcement of the court judgment or any other controversial matters.[418] The obligation of the parties arising from the peaceful settlement agreement in respect of its subject matter is indivisible. According to LCC Article 6.985, the peaceful settlement agreement, upon approval by the court, has the effect of the final judgment (*res judicata*) and is an enforceable document. In concert with this rule, procedural law forbids a court from accepting a statement of claim if there is a court ruling to approve the settlement of the parties, and if a civil case had been mistakenly initiated, the court after getting familiar with the fact of settlement must immediately terminate civil proceedings on the case (CCP Article 137, 293). Moreover, the Supreme Court has ruled that even without the approval by the court, peaceful settlement has binding force as a contract (*pacta sunt servanda*) and the court must resolve the case according to such agreement.[419] Power of *res iudicata* is, of course, greater than that of *pacta sunt servanda*, because former principle forbids even questioning the validity of approved settlement outside the appeal procedure, whereas the latter principle does not preclude attack on settlement contract by new legal action.

829. Depending on the facts, peaceful settlement may create novation, change of contract and even waiver of rights. In any case, the effect of valid peaceful settlement agreement may be far-reaching – the party to a dispute may *ex post* waive[420] its constitutional (Constitution Article 30) and human right (European Convention on Human Rights Article 6) to a trial. Therefore, LCC sets plenty of rules regarding

---

418. CCP Art. 140 provides that at any stage of the procedure, the parties may settle the case. The text of the written settlement of the parties shall be annexed to the case and an oral application shall be recorded in the minutes of the court session and signed by the parties. Prior to approving the settlement of the parties, the court shall explain to the parties the consequences of these procedural actions and in approving the settlement shall make a ruling, by which the case shall be discontinued. The ruling must indicate the conditions of the settlement of the parties, which is being approved. If the court does not approve the settlement of the parties, it shall make a reasoned ruling concerning it.
419. Judgment of the Lithuanian Supreme Court of 26 Jun. 2015 in the civil case No 3K-3-409-701-2015.
420. *Ex ante* waiver of civil procedural and substantive rights is void in all cases according to CCP Art. 5 and LCC Art. 1.137(5).

the validity of peaceful settlement agreement. Thus, the peaceful settlement agreement shall be in made in writing. The non-compliance with such requirement makes the agreement null and void. The peaceful settlement agreement regarding the legal status or legal capacity of persons, regarding the matters regulated by the imperative norms of law, as well as regarding the matters related to public order, is void. The peaceful settlement agreement may be avoided due to gross disparity of its parties (LCC Article 6.228), as well as on other grounds of invalidity of transactions. If the peaceful settlement agreement is based on the transaction which was not in force at the time of making of the peaceful settlement agreement, such peaceful settlement agreement is void. If the peaceful settlement agreement is made based on written documents which later appear as fake, such peaceful settlement agreement is also void. The peaceful settlement agreement is void if at the moment of making of the peaceful settlement agreement one or both parties did not know that the issue, which is the subject matter of the peaceful settlement agreement, had already been resolved by the res judicata court judgment. The peaceful settlement agreement is void if after its execution there appear the documents confirming that one of the parties to the peaceful settlement agreement is not or was not entitled to what is recognised as belonging to it by the peaceful settlement agreement. The error of the parties in respect of the legal norms, except for the imperative legal norms, is not the ground to recognise the peaceful settlement agreement as void.

Chapter 8. Suretyship

830. Contract of suretyship (*adpromissio*) is an ancient Roman instrument used for a security of debtor's obligations. Suretyship is based upon the simple idea of imposing a sanction on a person other than the debtor where the latter fails to perform an obligation or comply with a duty.[421] Since it is a general form of personal security and is often given by the natural persons, which bear huge risk, the policy of suretyship law is based on social considerations. This is necessary in order to avoid problems related to the increase of insolvency of households and start-up companies. That is why the regulation of suretyship in Lithuanian statutory law is protective and full of traps for the creditor's claim, i.e., there are relatively many grounds in the LCC for a surety to avoid or reduce its responsibility under the suretyship contract. In contrast, another form of personal security – guarantee – is suited for business purposes. As the policy of guarantee law is based on the commercial element, it is liberal and regulation is quite relaxed.[422] Having in mind general character of suretyship and following the good practice of leading civilian jurisdictions, in case of uncertainty, it should be presumed that parties have agreed on the suretyship than on the guarantee unless the personal security is provided by the financial institution.[423]

---

421. This is most apparent if one considers primitive forms of suretyship, or non-contractual forms such as judicial suretyship. The sanctions imposed on the surety have evolved through time, and have generally taken the same forms as those imposed on a defaulting debtor. Thus, hostage-taking is one of the earliest examples of suretyship, and it existed contemporaneously with imprisonment for debt: the surety was held prisoner by the creditor until the debtor paid his debt. In times where a debtor could be sold as a slave, so could a surety. A close analogy was drawn between suretyship and the pledge of a thing, since the creditor gained control over the surety's body as if it were a thing (i.e., *plegerie*). In some instances, the rules on suretyship provided that the surety was to be imprisoned, sold, mutilated, or even put to death instead of the debtor. In such cases, the creditor who had accepted a surety had no recourse against the debtor. If the surety died, that put an end to any possible legal action by the creditor. The sanctions to which the surety was exposed could not be exercised against his heirs. *See* Michelle Cumyn. *Responsibility for Another's Debt: Suretyship, Solidarity, and Imperfect Delegation.* McGill Law Journal, Vol. 55, No 2, 2010, p. 223.
422. In the Lithuanian legal doctrine, guarantee is characterised as an independent obligation and in this respect is opposed to the suretyship, which is dependant obligation. *See* Valentinas Mikelėnas. *Lietuvos Respublikos civilinio kodekso komentaras. Šeštoji knyga. Prievolių teisė.* Justitia, 2003, I t., p. 132. However, this position is not supported by LCC itself, Art. 6.92(5) of whom states that 'where it becomes known to the guarantor that the principal obligation secured by the guarantee has been performed fully, or has been terminated on other grounds, or has been acknowledged null and void, he must immediately notify of this the creditor and the debtor. In the event where after such notification the guarantor receives a repeated demand of the creditor to perform the obligation, he shall be obliged to satisfy thereof only upon the presentation by the creditor proof that the obligation has not been terminated and continues to be valid'. As can be seen from above, there is albeit hidden, but undeniable accessoriness of guarantee towards secured obligation.
423. For example, in France if it is doubtful whether a dependent personal security or another kind of personal security has been assumed, the qualification with the weaker effect, i.e., a dependent personal security will be chosen. If the security provider is a consumer, this interpretation guideline is even more strictly respected. Also under German law, if after applying the principles of interpretation (CC §§ 133, 157) a doubt remains, a dependent personal security is assumed since this is the regular legal type of personal security and since the security provider is in this way best protected, especially by the formal requirement of a writing according to CC § 766 (cf. Staudinger/Horn §

831. Suretyship is consensual, onerous or gratuitous, accessory and commutative contract.[424] According to the statutory definition, suretyship is a contract by which the surety binds himself to be liable towards the creditor of another person gratuitously or for a remuneration in the event where the person in whose favour suretyship is granted fails to perform the obligation in whole or in part. Suretyship is an accessory obligation (dependent upon the obligation of the principal debtor for which it has been entered into). Suretyship is terminated upon the extinguishment of the principal obligation or it having been declared void suretyship must be contracted in written form. Non-observance of this requirement shall result in the voidability of the contract (LCC Article 6.75–6.76, 6.79).

832. Suretyship may be granted for an obligation irrespective of the request of the person for whose obligation it is being granted, also irrespective of the identity of the person who binds himself. A person may become surety either for the principal debtor or for his surety. The creditor shall have the right to require a concrete person to be a surety. In the case where the creditor does not express such a requirement, the debtor shall offer a person with sufficient property to perform the obligation to act as surety. Where a debtor is bound to furnish suretyship on the grounds of laws (legal surety) or a court judgment (judicial surety), he may present other adequate security of the obligation instead suretyship. Disputes on whether the property of the surety is sufficient and whether the security offered is adequate shall be decided by the court (LCC Article 6.77).

833. Obligations secured by suretyship are an already existing obligation and those which will arise in future, but in any event, suretyship may be applied only for the performance of a sufficiently specified obligation. Suretyship may also be contracted for a part of the principal obligation. Suretyship may not be contracted for an amount in excess of that owed by the debtor. Suretyship may not be contracted under any other onerous conditions. Where the sum secured by suretyship extends beyond the limits of the debt for which it was contracted, it must be diminished till the amount of the debt. Suretyship shall extend to all the accessories of the principal obligation (LCC Article 6.78).

834. The debtor who has performed the obligation secured by suretyship shall be bound to immediately inform the surety about the performance. Otherwise the surety who in his turn has performed the obligation himself shall retain the right of

765 no. 24). *See* Christian Von Bar, Eric Clive, *et al. Principles, Definitions and Model Rules of European Private Law. Draft Common Frame of Reference (DCFR).* Full ed., Sellier, 2009, pp. 2582–2583.

424. Unlike insurance, a surety obligation is not an aleatory contract. Some foreign courts have, indeed, confused suretyship with insurance by mistaking the obligation of the surety as an obligation to hold harmless the principal. The surety has no such obligation. To the contrary, the principal must exonerate and reimburse the surety. The contract surety does not underwrite a contractor based on some actuarial determination of the risk for the appropriate premium. Instead, contract bonds, like loans, are written based on the financial integrity of the principal, premised on the idea that no losses should follow. *See* T. Scott Leo. *The Construction Contract Surety and Some Suretyship Defenses.* William & Mary Law Review, Vol. 34 1993, pp. 1231–1232.

recourse against the debtor. In this case, the debtor may recover from the creditor only what has been received by him that is not due. In addition, at the demand of the surety, the creditor is bound to provide him with information in respect of the content and the conditions of the principal obligation, also with information regarding its performance.

835. If the debtor fails to perform the obligation, both the debtor and the surety are liable as solidary debtors towards the creditor for the fulfilment of this obligation unless otherwise provided for by the contract of suretyship. The surety is liable to the same extent as the debtor (for the payment of interest and penalty, compensation for damages) unless otherwise established by the contract of suretyship. Where several persons become sureties of the same debtor for the same debt, they shall be solidarily liable unless otherwise provided for by the contract of suretyship.

836. According to LCC Article 6.82, in the event where the creditor brings an action against the surety, the latter shall be bound to implead the debtor. Otherwise, the debtor shall have the right in the case of a counterclaim brought by the surety to set up against the creditor all the defences he is entitled to. The surety shall have the right to set up against the creditor all the defences which could be set up by the principal debtor. The surety shall not lose his right to set up such defences even when the debtor refuses his defences or admits his obligation. The surety may avail himself of all other rights which may be exercised by the debtor (dispute a debt, apply a set-off, suspend performance of the obligation, etc.), with the exception of those which are exceptionally related to the person of the debtor. A postponement of the performance of obligation granted to the debtor by the creditor shall also apply to the surety.

837. The surety has the right to demand from the creditor enforcement to be directed first on concrete property of the principal debtor, except in the cases where the surety has expressly renounced this right. Where the creditor failed to comply with the instruction of the surety, and did not levy the exaction first to the indicated concrete property of the principle debtor, the creditor shall be liable for any subsequent insolvency of the principle debtor up to the value of the property indicated. These rules do not apply in the instances of solidary liability of the principal debtor and the surety towards the creditor (LCC Article 6.80–6.81). Where the creditor refuses his priority right in the satisfaction of his claim or declines any other security of the obligation established in his favour, the surety shall be released from liability if the creditor would have been able to satisfy his claim by exercising the refused rights (LCC Article 6.86).

838. All the rights of the creditor arising from a certain obligation shall pass to the surety by whom that obligation has been performed. The surety who has bound himself at the request of the debtor or with his consent and who has performed the obligation shall have additional right to claim from the principal debtor compensation for all damage incurred in relation with the suretyship; he may also charge interest on the sum paid to the creditor even if the principal debt is not producing interest. A surety who has bound himself without the consent of the debtor may only claim from him what the debtor would have been bound to pay, including damages, if there had been no suretyship. Every of several co-sureties shall have the right by way of recourse to claim from the debtor what he has paid. However, if those sums cannot be recovered from the debtor, a co-surety who has performed shall have the right of recourse against other co-sureties for their respective portions. After the surety has performed the obligation, the creditor shall be bound to deliver him the documents confirming the right of claim against the debtor, as well as the rights by which such claim is secured. In the event where the surety fails to inform the principal debtor that he has performed the obligation, he shall have no right of recourse against the principal debtor who, being unaware of this performance, effectuates it repeatedly. The same effects will be produced in the case if the surety performs the obligation without informing the principal debtor at the time when the principal debtor has already acquired the right to set up against the claim of the creditor defences that could have enabled him to have the debt declared extinguished. Nevertheless, in both these cases the surety should retain his right of claim for recovery of the sums that were not due to the creditor (LCC Article 6.83–6.84).

839. A suretyship shall be terminated at the time of extinguishment of the obligation which was secured by it. A suretyship shall also be terminated by the death of the surety. If the qualities of a surety and debtor are united in the same person, the suretyship shall remain in force if the creditor has an interest in its continuation. Unless the contract of suretyship provides for otherwise, suretyship shall be terminated if the obligation is changed in essence, and such change without the consent of the surety results in the increase of his liability, or in any other consequences unfavourable thereto. Suretyship shall be terminated if the debt according to the secured obligation is assumed by another person and the surety does not give his consent to the creditor to extend suretyship over in respect of the new debtor. Suretyship shall be terminated where the creditor without any grounds refuses to accept a proper performance of the obligation offered by the debtor or the surety (LCC Article 6.87).

840. In case of a suretyship contracted for a determinate period or with a view of performing an obligation with a fixed term shall be terminated if the creditor does not bring an action against the surety within three months from the day on which the contract of suretyship or the time limit of performance of the obligation expires. Where suretyship by which the future obligation is secured is contracted for a fixed period, it shall terminate on the day of maturity of the time limit of suretyship if the obligation did not arise before the expiration of this time limit. Where the suretyship is contracted for an indeterminate period, or where the time limit of performance of the obligation is not indicated, nor determined by the moment of demand for performance, the default rule is that the suretyship comes to the end upon the expiry of two years from the day on which the contract of suretyship was formed if the creditor does not bring an action against the surety within this time limit. Where a future obligation is secured by the suretyship contracted for an indeterminate period, the surety may by his unilateral notice dissolve it upon expiry of three years from its contraction if during the three years the obligation did not become exigible.

The surety must immediately inform in writing the debtor and the creditor of the dissolution of suretyship (LCC Article 6.88–6.89).

841. Those rules clearly show the protective framework of the LCC suretyship rules, which is especially important in the absence of general principle of the proportional security in the Lithuanian statutory law. Such gap and underdeveloped case law have given space for abusive practice of overcollateralisation in Lithuanian credit practice which in turn has impaired the limited liability regime of the private companies. It has become even usual practice for credit institutions to require the suretyship of the dominant shareholder or the director as the prerequisite for the corporate loan. The Bank of Lithuania, who is the supervisory authority and possesses huge influence on the behaviour of financial institutions, in one of its regulatory technical acts has mitigated such policy by requiring from credit institutions to refrain from taking personal security exceeding surety's unencumbered assets.[425] Of course, this is the right step and the problem is worth attention, because it leads to social problems related to the increased insolvency of households and worsened start-up business conditions. However, it is difficult to treat this problem without strict application of the general principle of proportional security in the case law of courts.

842. Despite pro-debtor legal policy expressed in the LCC, Lithuanian case law during the first decade of the LCC application slightly moved towards the pro-creditor direction. Most importantly, the Supreme Court has ruled that the creditor who has a bundle of security rights, including suretyship, is free to elect the most appropriate one to use in a given moment.[426] Thus, even the creditor, who has tolerated non-performance of the debtor and did not enforce business charge when the debtor was still solvent, may rely on the suretyship after the debtor became insolvent. In effect, the surety was forced to bear the risk of non-successful workout of the debtor, who has given collateral.[427] Actions of surety are limited and may be tightly controlled by the creditor on the basis of *actio Pauliana*.[428] Extreme example of pro-creditor attitude is the disapplication of LCC Article 6.88(1), which states that where the creditor does not bring an action against the surety within three months from the day on which the contract of suretyship or the time limit of performance of the obligation expires, by the Supreme Court. The Court has *contra legem* ruled that the time limit for the performance of obligation does not expire until the moment of its proper performance if contract states that suretyship lasts until then,[429] making the surety always be liable because in case of non-performance time limit will never be expired. From the other side, the Supreme Court, in case where the debtor went into bankruptcy and due to insolvency limitations accrual of penalties was suspended, has strictly safeguarded accessoriness of suretyship in scope. The Court has rejected claim of the creditor against surety for

425. Bank of Lithuania Boards Decision adopting Regulations for the organisation of internal control and risk assessment (management) Art. 36^1–36^6.
426. Judgment of the Lithuanian Supreme Court of 29 Dec. 2011 in the civil case No 3K-P-537/2011.
427. Judgment of the Lithuanian Supreme Court of 28 Feb. 2014 in the civil case No 3K-3-56/2014.
428. Judgment of the Lithuanian Supreme Court of 10 Apr. 2012 in the civil case No 3K-3-86/2012.
429. Judgment of the Lithuanian Supreme Court of 18 May 2009 in the civil case No 3K-7-229/2009.

the accrual of penalties on the reason that the accessory obligation of the surety cannot become larger than principal obligation of the debtor.[430] Overall, case law has demonstrated conservativism and adherence to the classical principle of *pacta sunt servanda* mitigated by another classical principle of *accessorium sequitur principale* but leaving aside potential social problems related to the suretyship.[431] From the other side, these are the good news for financial institutions, which are doing business in Lithuania.

430. Judgment of the Lithuanian Supreme Court of 29 Dec. 2011 in the civil case No 3K-P-537/2011.

431. Other Lithuanian authors also advocate a more effective protection of weaker non-professional sureties that allows the preclusion of negative social consequences of over-indebtedness. They have argued that currently Lithuanian courts are permitted to exercise considerable discretion, e.g., by amending the contents of the contract in question. In essence, they tend to adopt a sui generis approach whereby they decide on those contractual rights and obligations which are fair and those which are not. In this respect, a purposive interpretation of general clauses of the CC that are aimed at protecting a weaker contracting party from unfair disadvantage may enhance the level of protection of non-professional sureties without introducing special new statutory regulations. On the other hand, the consistency of case law is no less important. All business participants should have clear rules regarding which transactions can be put at stake. If, at the time of the conclusion of the suretyship contract, a creditor already anticipates that the provided suretyship could be struck down in the future, he/she should probably consider some other means of securing the transaction or increase the price of the transaction in order to offset possible losses of risky deals. *See* Andrius Smaliukas; Gintautas Šulija. Report on Lithuania. *In. Regulating Unfair Banking Practices in Europe– The Case of Personal Suretyships*, Oxford University Press, 2010, p. 414.

Chapter 9. Pledge

843. In contemporary Lithuanian law, pledge is a limited property right *par excellence* and not simply the contract.[432] Since detailed analysis of property rights is beyond scope of this book on contracts, pledge will be presented here only from the birds view and analysis will focus more on contractual aspects of the pledge.

§1. Pledge in General

I. *In Rem* Aspects

844. Pledge (*pignus*) is a possessory security interest, regulated by LCC Article 4.198–4.228, which in Lithuania is available only over the movables. Other types of security interests in Lithuania are non-possessory charge over movables, hypothec (mortgage) over immovables together with an accessory movable and right of retention over the property possessed by the creditor. Pledge, non-possessory charge and hypothec may be both contractual and legal, whereas right of retention may arise only by operation of law and may not be contracted out. The ownership right, as the most comprehensive right a person may have over the property, may also be used as proprietary security device in so-called title finance transactions (financial lease, factoring, repurchase agreements, etc.) and in retention of title transactions. Thus, Lithuanian law follows not a functionalistic, but a modern formalistic approach on the security interests.[433] In addition, there are other security devices – suretyship, guarantee, credit risk insurance, etc. – which are personal and not proprietary security transactions. It is important to distinguish personal and proprietary security, because proprietary security has priority against personal claims (*ius preferendi*), but its varieties and contents are limited by the *numerus clausus*, transparency and other property law principles.

432. In contrast, during Soviet times in Lithuania and even now in in Russian civil law pledge has been viewed more often as a contract. This is not least because of the location of rules regulating pledge. The issue is that while the existing 1994 RF Civil Code was being drafted, lawmakers unfortunately used the approach applied in the 1964 RSFSR Civil Code and included rules concerning pledge in the section entitled Law of Obligations. The draftsmen of the 1964 RSFSR Civil Code adopted this position most likely because the section Law of *Rights in Rem* that was included in the 1922 RSFSR Civil Code and included rules regulating pledge was repealed (it was not needed) in the course of adopting the new code, and the rules regulating pledge had to find a 'new home' somewhere; the section Law of Obligations probably seemed to the authors of the code to be the most appropriate place (because pledge is indeed a form of security for obligations). *See* R.S. Bevzenko. *Battle for the Law of Real Security: the Third Step in Reforming Russian Pledge Law.* Civil Law Herald, 2015, Vol. 15. Issue 2, p. 6.

433. LCC crystallised the concept of Lithuanian secured transactions law: Lithuania did not opt the functionalistic approach of US Uniform Commercial Code (UCC) Art. 9, yet it pursued the wholesale formalistic reform, now also reflecting the experience of the civil law revision in Quebec. Consequently, LCC covered not only the charges *stricto sensu* but also their functional equivalents – the so-called quasi-security interests, which, apart from generally being registered in a single registry, might bear some incidents of a charge. *See* Andrius Smaliukas. *Property and Trust Law in Lithuania.* Wolters Kluwer, 2017, p. 205.

845. One principle of property law deserves special attention with respect to pledge. It is the principle of accessoriness, which is set to control abuse and other misuse of pledge. Lithuanian property law, in general, provides for strict accessoriness of security rights, because pursuant to LCC Article 4.198(3) validity of the pledge depends on the validity of secured obligation. However the needs of credit market influenced Lithuanian legislator in 2012 reform[434] to relax those constraints and now there is a possibility to create non-possessory bearer charge, which may be created unilaterally by the owner. It is not dependent on the secured obligation but may not be used against third parties without the registration of the creditor in public registry (LCC Article 4.210). Even more advanced relaxation of accessoriness would be possible if LCC would allow a possibility of certification of bearer charge into negotiable instrument. In such a case, charge would be open for assignment to third persons separately from the secured obligation. However, such possibility is reserved by LCC only for hypothec (LCC 4.189(3)).

846. A pledge is indivisible property right, even if secured obligation be divisible. A pledge may secure any present or future pecuniary obligation together with payment interest. However, default interest (moratory damages) and penalties for delay should be expressly agreed in the contract and are allowed only under the maximum amount pledge (LCC Article 4.200). This kind of pledge functions as follows. Parties in the security agreement, which should expressly state that it creates maximum amount pledge, agree only for the maximum amount of secured obligations. Exact amount of secured obligation is fixed only later, on a date provided by agreement or by a bailiff during the enforcement of pledge. However, the amount of secured obligations after the fixation stops accruing.

847. The object of pledge, according to LCC Article 4.201, may be any existing or future corporeal or incorporeal movable, together with its accessories and non-separated fruits. The exceptions are things in respect of which under the existing laws enforcement may not be levied, for instance *res extra commercium*, as well as movable things that together with immovables have been encumbered by hypothec. Common property may be pledged only upon a written consent of all co-owners.

848. It should be noted that LCC also provides for a possibility to secure even universality of assets. Enterprise, as patrimony of a company, is immovable by law (LCC Article 1.110) and as such is eligible collateral only for a hypothec (LCC Article 4.177). Other universalities of assets, for example, money in a bank account, business stockpiles or goods in circulation, being movable property, may be encumbered only by pledge or non-possessory charge. The collateral of such floating charge is sufficiently defined by writing down set of encumbered assets, without specifying each of them. During the ordinary course of business, collateral owner

434. Reform of 2012 was a coherent and comprehensive effort to reform and harmonise both security over movable and immovable property. The drafters of new Lithuanian secured transaction laws, *inter alia,* relied on the UNCITRAL Legislative Guide on Secured Transactions. Reform was not functionalistic – it further expanded the modern formalistic approach taken by the drafters of the Civil Code in early 2000s. *See* Andrius Smaliukas. *Property and Trust Law in Lithuania.* Wolters Kluwer, 2017, p. 207.

(debtor or third party) may dispose encumbered assets if this does not lower the overall value of collateral. When he transacts lawfully, pledge extinguishes for transferred assets and originates for newly acquired assets. Thus, principle of specificity is relaxed and real subrogation takes place, but only if collateral owner does not abuse its right to dispose those assets. If he concludes unfair transactions, for example, during the suspect period sells liquid assets for a low price, the pledge follows the asset, thus eliminating the need (and space) for *actio Pauliana*.

II. In Personam Aspects

849. Pledge is created voluntary where the owner of collateral makes act – pledge transaction. This transaction is always a contract since possession of the pledge by the creditor will reveal who is a creditor and demonstrate not just unilateral statement on the encumbrance property, but agreement of parties on pledge. LCC Article 4.210(4) which states that bearer security gets *erga omnes* effect only after the entry of the creditor's identity in public registry, even more confirms this conclusion. Indeed, it would be highly impracticable for parties of pledge, which is possessory security, to additionally perfect it in public register.

850. Pledge contract is solemn, real, unilateral or bilateral, onerous or gratuitous, commutative contract with *in rem* effects. Agreement on pledge may be formed either as separate contract or included in the secured contract. In any case, it should be formed at least in simple (non-notary) writing, otherwise the contract is void. In contrast to non-possessory charge contract, it is a real contract, because in order to form it (and also create the pledge itself), delivery of collateral to the possession of creditor is required (LCC Article 4.209(1)). Gratuitous pledge contract is unilateral, because transfer of possession to the creditor (pledgee) is a prerequisite for the creation of contract and after this act only pledgee has an obligation. Thus, the creditor in secured obligation and holder of pledge is at the same time the debtor in pledge contract – pledgee, who has real obligation to safekeep (LCC Article 4.214) and personal obligation to return property back to the pledgor after the proper satisfaction of claim. Usually pledge is gratuitous, but also may be onerous, where pledgor has obligation towards pledgee to pay for safekeeping or improvement of collateral. Undisputedly, pledge contract provides *in rem* effects, because it decomposes ownership and creates limited property right – the pledge. Pledge is created solely by the conclusion of written pledge contract if possession has been delivered, unless suspensive conditions are agreed between parties. In such a case, conditional pledge contract is formed and perfectly valid, but is of limited content, because obligations from it and pledge itself are not created until the prescribed conditions occur.

851. Agreement is main element of any contract, including that of pledge. As to the sufficiency of pledge agreement, LCC Article 4.210 mandatorily prescribes that it should include: time and place of formation; pledgor, debtor, creditor and their addresses; description of collateral; secured obligation and its amount; period for debt performance. Conditional pledge and maximum amount pledge agreements should include express indication about their types. It is obvious that conditional pledge agreement must include condition. Where collateral is encumbered by additional pledge, it should be mentioned in pledge agreement. After the reform in 2012, Lithuanian security law became more flexible and less formalistic, which is perfectly evidenced by the fact that LCC no longer requires to use formal pledge deeds, as mandatory prescribed form of pledge agreements.

852. Contemporary Lithuanian civil legislation which legitimately rejected obligational basis of pledge went to another extreme. It now solely focuses on proprietary aspects of it set in LCC book on property law and, unfortunately, is scarce on personal aspects other than formation of pledge contract. With respect to pledge contract there are no special rules in contract law, only general ones. However, there are important questions, such as duty to safekeep property, to return it after the satisfaction of claim, remuneration for safekeeping and duty to reimburse expenses and cover losses, which normally belongs to the law of obligations.

853. LCC Article 4.201(4) provides that risk of accidental perishing and loss of collateral shall bear pledgor, i.e., owner, unless pledge contract or statute establishes otherwise. This rule is counterbalanced by the duty of possessor to take proper care of collateral (LCC Article 4.214). He is liable for the safekeeping if he fails to prove that the thing has been lost or damaged without fault of his. This person has no right to use the collateral unless otherwise provided by law or the pledge contract. It is clear from the wording above that duty to safekeep collateral is a real obligation of the possessor, which follows the collateral in whatever hands it is.

854. As concern pledgee's duty to return collateral after the satisfaction of claim, remuneration for safekeeping, reimbursement of expenses and compensation of losses, these are not expressly mentioned in LCC. Legal doctrine and case law are also scarce on those important points.[435] However, in order to avoid legal gaps and taking into account obvious similarities of possession in pledge and in deposit, the respective rules on deposit should be applicable by analogy to the pledge contract. Thus, for instance: for the personal claim of pledgor against the pledgee (creditor) to return collateral after the extinction of pledge back (*actio pigneraticia*), LCC Article 6.844 should be applicable; for the personal pledgee's claim against pledgor to pay remuneration (if agreed), compensation of damage and expenses for safekeeping (*actio pigneraticia contraria*) LCC Article 6.840, 6.841, 6.842, 6.847 should be applied; etc. In addition, general in personam remedies may be used; for example, pledgor may offset secured obligation against obligation of pledgee (creditor) to compensate the collateral damage.

---

435. Legal writings just made reference to the general rules of civil liability in case of collateral damage, whereas Lithuanian Supreme Court has ruled *in abstracto* that after the transfer of collateral to the creditor he became its possessor, but does not acquire rights for the administration of collateral, which could entitle him to use collateral and get revenues from it. *See* D. Petrauskaitė. *Lietuvos Respublikos civilinio kodekso komentaras. Ketvirtoji knyga. Daiktinė teisė. XII skyrius. Įkeitimas (5).* Justitia, 2004, No. 5 (53), pp. 6–7; Judgment of the Lithuanian Supreme Court of 16 Jul. 2004 in the civil case No 3K-3-334/2004.

855. Pledge gives legal ground for titular possession, therefore *actio pigneraticia* is possible only after the extinction of pledge (LCC Article 4.224) and only against pledgee. Where the thing was transferred to the third party, vindication *in rem* should be applied, because *actio pigneraticia* is restricted by privity of contract and is unavailable against third parties.

III. Enforcement

856. Where pledge is in force and debtor defaults, enforced pledge, being *ius preferendi*, quashes any corresponding personal obligation of pledgee to return thing back. Pledge enforcement procedure, in general, is executed by bailiffs or insolvency administrators after the notary issues the enforcement notice according to Law on Notariate Article 49^1. Official procedure with involvement of those bodies, of course, is not necessary where enforcement is carried by the self-help of creditor, permitted by LCC Article 4.219, which states that enforcement from collateral is provided according to the terms of pledge transaction. Creditor, debtor and pledgor (where pledgor is not the debtor) have right to agree on the foreclosure (transfer the ownership of the collateral to the creditor) or any other way of enforcement (private sale, direct collection, public auction, etc.). Agreement on foreclosure in pledge is presumed.

§2. Specific Types of Pledge

I. Financial Collateral Arrangements

857. Financial collateral arrangement is special type of security contract, designed to reduce settlement risk in financial transactions. It is regulated by the Law on Financial Collateral Arrangements, which transposes in Lithuanian law Directive 2002/47/EC of the European Parliament and of the Council of 6 June 2002 on financial collateral arrangements.

858. Financial collateral arrangement means a security financial collateral arrangement, or a title transfer financial collateral arrangement whether or not these are made as separate agreements or are included in the master agreement (on general principles) giving rise to the secured obligation. In any case, the financial collateral arrangement must indicate the secured financial obligation. Secured financial obligations may also consist of or include: (1) present, future or prospective obligations (including such obligations arising under a master arrangement (on general principles) or similar arrangement); (2) obligations owed to the collateral taker by a person other than the collateral provider; and (3) obligations of a specified class or kind arising from time to time. Assets eligible for financial collateral are cashless money and financial instruments that are used to secure performance of financial obligations under a financial collateral arrangement. Financial transaction may be characterised as financial collateral arrangement in sense Law on Financial Collateral Arrangements only where at least one party is domestic or international financial institution, public authority or other qualified body and other is any legal person.

859. Security financial collateral arrangement is an arrangement under which a collateral provider provides financial collateral in favour of, or to, a collateral taker, thus securing the performance of relevant financial obligations to the collateral taker, and where the full ownership of the financial collateral remains with the collateral provider. As security financial collateral arrangement is a security interest, Supreme Court has characterised security financial collateral arrangements as qualified pledge agreements.[436] Later on, this characterisation was reflected directly in LCC Article 4.198(5) by stating that Law on Financial Collateral Arrangements may establish rules other than those in LCC.

860. Subject matter of a financial collateral arrangement is financial collateral. Financial instruments that will pass into the ownership of the collateral provider in the future according to the concluded transactions and money that will be transferred to the account designated by the parties may also be a financial collateral. Financial instruments may be used for the enforcement of obligations only after the title to them has passed to the collateral provider. Unless otherwise established by laws or an arrangement, the financial collateral shall cover income generated by the collateralised financial instruments and money. The collateral provider must be the owner of the provided financial collateral, save where otherwise established by laws. Financial instruments or money that are in common ownership may be provided as financial collateral only upon written consent of all co-owners. In case of a dispute, the provision of financial collateral should be evidenced in writing. Written evidence should identify the financial collateral. The crediting of financial instruments provided as financial collateral into the relevant account (or such collateral forming a credit in the account) or the crediting of money provided as financial collateral into the designated account (or such collateral forming a credit in the account) shall be recognised as written evidence. The parties to an arrangement may agree on the procedure for the valuation of financial instruments. Unless otherwise agreed by the parties to a financial collateral arrangement, the value of financial instruments negotiable on regulated markets is established according to the latest market value of financial instruments in that regulated market.

861. Under the financial collateral arrangement, the collateral taker (creditor) has the right, in case the debtor defaults on his relevant financial obligations secured by financial collateral, to satisfy his claim from the financial collateral or its value prior to other creditors and most importantly outside the insolvency procedure. On the occurrence of an enforcement event, the collateral taker has the right to realise financial collateral provided under the security financial collateral arrangement unilaterally in the following manners, subject to the terms agreed in a security financial collateral arrangement: (1) to sell or appropriate financial instruments or apply their

436. Judgment of the Lithuanian Supreme Court of 6 Oct. 2009 in the civil case No 3K-3-391/2009.

value in discharge of the relevant financial obligations; and (2) in case of money, to set off the amount against or otherwise apply it in discharge of the relevant financial obligations. Appropriation of financial instruments is possible only if the parties have agreed on the appropriation of financial instruments and their valuation in the security financial collateral arrangement. The ways of realising the financial collateral shall, subject to the terms agreed in the security financial collateral arrangement, be without any requirement to the effect that: (1) prior notice of the intention to realise must have been given; (2) the terms of the realisation be approved by a court, other institution or other person; (3) the realisation be conducted by public auction or in any other manner established in the legislation; and (4) any additional time period must have elapsed. Thus, Law on Financial Collateral Arrangements has created separatist regime for recovery of debts in favour of financial institutions.[437]

II. Pledge at Pawnshop

862. Things of personal use may be pledged at pawnshops in order to secure the repayment of short-term credits that are granted to natural persons by pawnshops. When transferring pledged things to a pawnshop, the pledgor gets a pledge ticket (LCC Article 4.227).

863. A pawnshop is responsible for the loss (destruction) and damage in respect of pledged things, if it fails to prove that things have been lost (destroyed) or damaged due to force majeure. A pawnshop has no right to use or dispose of pledged things. However, if within a specified period the amount of credit secured by the pledge of the thing is not returned to a pawnshop, the pawnshop has the right upon the expiration of one month to sell the pledged thing. After the pledged thing is sold, the claim of a pawnshop in respect of the pledgor (debtor) terminates even if the amount received from the sale of the thing is not sufficient to satisfy the requirements of the pawnshop as a creditor (LCC Article 4.228).

437. This superpriority regime was even contested in Lithuanian Constitutional Court on the initiative of Lithuanian Supreme Court, however, unsuccessfully, because Constitutional Court has ruled that transposition of EU financial collateral directive was compliant with Lithuanian Constitution. *See* Judgment of the Lithuanian Republic Constitutional Court of 24 May 2013.

Chapter 10. Loans

864. Under classical civilian reasoning based on Roman law, the loan contract in general is an agreement by which a person, the lender, delivers temporarily to another, the borrower, a thing for the borrower to use, provided that the borrower returns it to the lender at the due date. The object of a loan may be a thing lent for temporary use or a sum of money lent with or without interest. There are various kinds of loans. First, the loan for use is a contract by which the lender undertakes to hand over a non-consumable thing to the borrower, without valuable consideration, for use by the borrower during a specific time or for a specific purpose, and the borrower undertakes to return the thing after having used it. Second, the loan for consumption is a contract under which a lender delivers certain consumable things to a borrower. The borrower is obliged to return things of the same or equivalent quantity, quality, and type within a specified or reasonable period. The lender may or may not charge for the use of the thing loaned. In contrast, a loan for use is always gratuitous: when anything is charged for the use, it becomes a lease. The main differences between those two kinds of loans are that in the loan for use the lender retains the property in the thing lent, and it must be returned *in individuo*, whereas in the loan for consumption the things lent are to be consumed and the property in them is transferred to the borrower, who becomes a debtor to the lender for the same quantity of like articles. Third, the loan of money is a variant of the loan for consumption which concerns money.[438]

865. In my opinion, this classification, especially looking from the perspective of property law, is misleading, wrongly organised and could hardly be employed in modern civil law. First, a loan for use has more in common with lease, than with loan for consumption, because both contracts concern transfer of possession of non-consumable goods for temporary use. The basic difference is that loan for use is gratuitous, while a lease is onerous contract. This tight connection is reflected by LCC Article 6.629 which states that provisions of paragraphs 2 and 3 of LCC Article 6.477, LCC Article 6.478, 6.479, 6.481, paragraphs 1 and 2 of LCC Article 6.489, and LCC Article 6.501 – all of them designed to lease contracts – should apply correspondingly to a contract of loan for use. In contrast, ordinary loan is a legal ground for a transfer of ownership of the fungible property, which at the end of the contract should be returned to the property of the creditor. It means that ordinary loan produces direct *in rem* effect (change of ownership), whereas loan for use is purely obligational contract.

866. Considering the formation of contract, there are two types of loans in Lithuanian law: ordinary loan, which is a real contract, and special type of loan – commercial credit, which is a consensual contract. A real contract means that the formation of the contract takes place by the transfer of the thing or the money. The real loan contract is simultaneously a unilateral contract. Only the borrower should assume one or more obligations, more specifically to pay interest, if foreseen by the

438. Christian Von Bar, Eric Clive, *et al. Principles, Definitions and Model Rules of European Private Law. Draft Common Frame of Reference (DCFR).* Full ed., Sellier, 2009, p. 2456.

contract or by the rules, and to repay the money received. If loan is consensual, it is a bilateral contract, involving an obligation of the creditor to transfer the money for the lender and an obligation to repay for the borrower.[439] Ordinary loan granted to the consumer is called consumer loan. As the rules for ordinary loan are treated as general rules for all loan contracts, *mutatis mutandis* they are also applicable to special types of loans – crediting and consumer loans.

867. From the perspective of financial law, activity of providing monetary loans belongs to the regulated category of lending, which is a financial service also including purchase, advance payment (including factoring and forfeiting) or discounting of a claim arising from an irrevocable payment obligation, with or without the taking of lending risk, irrespective of a person into whose accounting these claims are included and who collects monetary fund's according to the claims. Lending, together with deposit taking, constitutes core commercial banking services, however only crediting and deposit taking are strictly reserved for licensed credit institutions. Doing business in other forms of lending, including provision of ordinary loans, attracts status of regulated financial institution, but per se such form of lending for commercial clients is not licensed in Lithuania. Every financial institution should comply with general requirements set in Law on Financial Institutions, which are quite basic and relatively not burdensome.[440] Only in prescribed cases, where loans are provided for consumers, financial institution should be included in the list of supervised credit providers and comply with specific regulatory requirements.

§1. Ordinary Loan

868. The real character is firmly established in the definition of ordinary loan. Pursuant to LCC Article 6.870 by the loan contract one party (the lender) transfers into the ownership of the other party (the borrower) the money or consumable generic things, and the borrower undertakes to repay the lender the same amount of money (the amount of loan) or return the same amount of things of the same kind and quality, and to pay the interest unless otherwise established in the agreement. The loan contract is formed from the moment of transfer of money or things. Even if contractual documentation is signed, until such transfer there is no contract in legal sense, nonetheless the lender may be liable on the basis of tort law doctrine *culpa in contrahendo* (LCC Article 6.163) for unfair refusal to give loan.

439. *Ibid*, p. 2458, 2461.

440. For instance, according to Law on Financial Institutions Art. 31, prior to taking a decision on the acquisition of the capital or money market instruments, lending or assumption of obligations for a client, a financial institution must ascertain that: (1) the financial assets being acquired, the assets being pledged or other assets wherefrom a claim of the financial institution may be satisfied in the future actually exist and the acquired claim of the financial institution may be satisfied therefrom; (2) the client's financial as well as economic situation and forecasts about it allow to expect that the client will be capable of performing his obligations; and (3) the client performed and performs his financial obligations to financial institutions.

869. According to classical civilian reasoning, based on Roman law, the monetary loan is a priori only a variety of the loan for consumption, because money is a fungible and consumable good.[441] Indeed, as in other civilian jurisdictions, in Lithuania money and consumable generic things fall under the ambit of ordinary loan contract. However, as one could notice in the definition of loan provided by LCC, money is distinguished as category separate from the fungible consumables. In my opinion, this is correct wording. Money should not be classified as consumable property, because after the payment money only changes its owner and is not lost as such. Money is consumed only from the subjective payor's perspective, but property law, which defines and governs legal regime of property, should be guided by objective rather subjective criteria.

870. Although contract of loan creates personal relationship, it also produces *in rem* effect by being *causa traditionis* for property transfer, i.e., the borrower becomes the owner of the things (money) transferred to him. From the moment of transfer of the things the risk of accidental loss or damage of things shall pass to the borrower.

871. As to the requirements of form, LCC Article 6.871 prescribes that the loan contract of natural persons must be made in writing if the amount of loan is in excess of EUR 600. If the lender is a legal person, the loan contract shall be in written form in all occasions notwithstanding the amount of the amount of loan. The requirements of an ordinary written form are satisfied by a loan receipt or any other debt instrument, signed by the borrower, confirming the transfer of the subject matter of the loan contract to the borrower. However, if the amount of loan paid in cash is in excess of EUR 3000, the loan contract must be approved by the notary.

872. Those contracting formalities are important, because according to LCC Article 6.875, the borrower has the right to contest the loan contract if he has not actually received the money or things, or if has received less than specified in the agreement. If the loan contract had to be in written form, it is not be permitted to contest the loan contract subject to the testimony of witnesses, except for the cases stipulated in LCC Article 1.93[442] or if the loan contract is formed by fraud, compulsion or real threat, or by virtue of wilful arrangement of the borrower's agent with the lender, or due to existing grave circumstances. If the loan contract had to be approved by the notary, it is void in case of failure to observe such formal

441. Christian Von Bar, Eric Clive, *et al. Principles, Definitions and Model Rules of European Private Law. Draft Common Frame of Reference (DCFR).* Full ed., Sellier, 2009, p. 2456.

442. According to LCC Art. 1.93(6), prohibition to contest the loan contract subject to the testimony of witnesses may not be applied by a court if they contradict the principles of good faith, justice and reasonableness, in particular where: (1) there exists other written evidence, even though indirect, that proves the forming of the transaction; (2) written evidence to prove the fact of transaction forming has been lost not through the fault of the party; (3) taking into consideration the circumstances in which the transaction was formed, it was objectively impossible to form that transaction in writing; and (4) taking into consideration the interrelations between the parties, the nature of the transaction and other circumstances of importance to the proceedings, prohibition to invoke testimonies of witnesses would contradict to the principles of good faith, justice and reasonableness.

requirement. If it is proved that money or things have actually been not transferred to the borrower, the loan contract shall be deemed not concluded. When the borrower has received less money or things than provided in the agreement, the loan contract is concluded for the actually received money or things. And although LCC states that such circumstances must be proved by the borrower, case law unanimously requires from the lender to prove transfer of loan assets, whereas the borrower bears burden to prove that loan is properly paid back.[443]

873. By agreement of the parties, the debt arising from the purchase–sale, lease or any other agreement may be substituted by the loan obligation according to the rules set forth in LCC Article 6.141–6.144 on novation. LCC also states that in cases provided by laws the loan contract may be concluded by issuing and selling bonds. A bond is defined as a security which confirms its holder's right to receive from the person who has issued such bond, within the term specified in the bond, the amount of the nominal value of the bond or any other property equivalent. A bond also grants its holder the right to receive the interest specified in the bond on the nominal value of the bond or other property rights. The rules designed for loan should be applied to the relations between the person who has issued such bond and the holder of such bond only if the laws do not prescribe otherwise (LCC Article 6.879). Similarly, if the borrower issues a bill of exchange under which he undertakes to repay the received amount of the loan on the term specified in such note, the relations of the parties shall be governed by the LCC chapter on loans to the extent such norms are consistent with the law regulating the bills of exchange (LCC Article 6.878). Although, the purpose of aforementioned rules is clear and correct – to provide the subsidiary application of loan rules for the negotiable debt instruments, the terminology, used there, is conceptually flawed and misleading. First, 'borrowing' by issuance of debt securities is based on the securities sales contract (LCC Article 6.428) and not the loan, therefore the phrase that 'the loan contract may be concluded by issuing and selling bonds' is inherently incorrect. Purchase of debt securities may be labelled as 'loan' only from economic, not legal perspective. Second, a very broad definition of bond presented here does not conform to the MiFID II directive Article 4, which characterises as bonds only those debt securities which circulate in capital markets. Therefore, the notion of bond in LCC Article 6.879 should be replaced by a broader category of debt security, including money market instruments.

874. The payment interest and the procedure of payment thereof may be established by loan contract. If the parties have not agreed on the amount of interest, the interest is determined based on the average interest rate of commercial banks of the place of residence or business of the borrower which existed at the moment of formation of the loan contract. Except when otherwise agreed by the parties, the interest shall be paid on monthly basis until repayment of the amount of loan. It is presumed that the loan contract shall be gratuitous if the subject matter of the loan contract comprises the generic things, unless otherwise established in the loan contract. If the subject matter of the loan contract is money, the loan contract shall be

443. Judgment of the Lithuanian Supreme Court of 26 Mar. 2008 in the civil case No 3K-3-187/2008.

presumed to be onerous. In case of failure by the borrower to timely repay the amount of the loan, the borrower in addition to payment interest shall also pay the default interest from the day when the amount of the loan had to be repaid until the day of its actual repayment, notwithstanding the payment of the procedural interest, unless otherwise established in the loan contract, i.e., LCC for the loans controversially permits capitalisation of default interest. However, according to the case law, in a case of breach of loan contract, payment interest is accruing only until the contract is still in force. After the termination of loan contract, only default interest may be accruing.[444]

875. As an ordinary loan in Lithuania is real and unilateral contract, the only obligation in the contract is duty of the borrower to repay the amount of loan. Pursuant to LCC Article 6.873, the borrower shall repay the received loan to the lender on the term and in the procedure prescribed in the agreement. In cases when the term for repayment of the amount of loan is not set forth in the agreement or the loan must be repaid upon demand, the borrower shall repay the principal within thirty days from the day when the lender stated the demand to perform the agreement, unless otherwise established in such agreement. Except when the loan contract provides otherwise, the borrower shall be entitled to repay the amount of loan of the gratuitous loan prior to the term. The amount of the non-gratuitous loan may be repaid by the borrower prior to the term only upon consent of the lender. Except when otherwise prescribed by the loan contract, the amount of loan shall be deemed repaid from the moment of its transfer to the lender or crediting to the bank account of the lender. When the subject matter of the loan is an amount of money, the borrower shall repay a nominal amount only, notwithstanding the changes of the value of a monetary unit, unless otherwise established in the agreement.

876. LCC also prescribes special rules for loan modalities. Thus, if the loan contract provides for repayment of the amount of the loan in instalments and a regular instalment is not repaid when due, the lender is entitled to demand to repay all the outstanding amount of the amount of loan together with the accrued payable interest (LCC Article 6.874). Where the borrower fails to perform the obligation under the loan contract to provide the security for the performance of his obligations or if the provided security is lost or its conditions become worse due to the circumstances beyond the lender's control, the lender shall be entitled to request the borrower to repay the amount of loan prior to the term as well as to pay the interest, unless otherwise established in the loan contract (LCC Article 6.876). Where the loan contract is formed establishing the provision that the borrower will use the principal for a certain purpose (the purpose loan), the borrower must ensure the lender's possibility to control the usage of the amount of loan by the borrower. If the borrower uses the amount of loan for other than the purpose set forth in the loan contract or if he breaches the condition established in clause 1 of this article, the

444. *See* Judgment of the Lithuania Supreme Court of 25 May 2020 in the civil case No. e3K-7-75-823/2020.

lender shall be entitled to request the borrower to repay the amount of loan prior to the term and pay the interest, unless otherwise established in the agreement (LCC Article 6.877).

§2. Crediting

877. Consensual loan contract in Lithuanian law is called 'crediting'. Acknowledgment of such credit form was, indeed, contemporary move by LCC drafters, since most jurisdictions, including England, Germany and even France, also soft law (DCFR) nowadays provides for this option, at least where lender is credit professional.[445] Consensual character of loan enables to get money from lender by remedy of specific performance, where this remedy is normally permitted (usually only in civil law jurisdictions).

878. LCC Article 6.881 prescribes that by the crediting contract a bank or any other credit institution (creditor) undertakes to grant the debtor the monetary funds (the credit) in the amount and under conditions established in the agreement, and the debtor undertakes to repay the received amount to the creditor and pay the interest. According to Lithuanian financial law, there are only two types of credit institutions – banks and credit unions. Banks are organised as private companies limited by shares, whereas credit unions as cooperatives.[446] Credit institutions in Lithuania are administratively supervised by Lithuanian Bank, who at the same time is supervisory authority and central bank of Lithuania. In addition, the Supreme Court has ruled that bank bears civil liability for behaviour, which clearly deviates from standard of careful banker in cases of credit provision, refusal, continuation or termination.[447]

879. The norms of the ordinary loan contract are applicable to the crediting relations to the extent they do not contradict to the essence and the rules of the crediting contract. One such difference from ordinary loans is that the crediting contract always must be made in writing. Non-observance of this requirement makes the crediting contract void (LCC Article 6.882).

880. Notwithstanding that crediting is a consensual contract, LCC Article 6.883 in some occasions permits refusal to grant or accept the credit. The creditor is entitled to fully or partly refuse to grant to the debtor the credit provided in the agreement upon disclosure of the circumstances expressly evidencing that the credit will not be repaid on due term. If the debtor breaches the obligation to use money only for agreed purpose, the creditor is entitled to refuse to continue crediting the

445. Christian Von Bar, Eric Clive, *et al. Principles, Definitions and Model Rules of European Private Law. Draft Common Frame of Reference (DCFR)*. Full ed., Sellier, 2009, p. 2460.

446. Although, there are about ten times less banks in Lithuania than credit unions, the market is clearly dominated by few banks, who own more than 90% of the lending market. Thus, the lending market is highly concentrated, uncompetitive and oligopolistic. Biggest banks are owned by well-known Scandinavian financial groups, such as DNB, Nordea, Danske, SEB and Swedbank.

447. Judgment of the Lithuanian Supreme Court of 26 Jul. 2013 in the civil case No 3K-3-420/2013.

debtor and demand to repay the granted credit prior to the term. Thus, according to default rules of LCC, refusal is possible only on the basis of subjective situation of debtor, not the creditor or interbank market. However, the parties in sophisticated projects, such as project finance or syndicated credits, normally include market disruption clause, which enables refusal in case of market turmoil. In comparison, the debtor is entitled to fully or partly refuse to accept the credit upon notification to that effect to the creditor until the term set forth in the agreement for granting of the credit unless otherwise established in the agreement.

881. Next to those rules, Lithuanian Court of Appeal in case concerning specific performance of crediting contract has ruled that although statutory law does not expressly provide for exceptions to the specific performance of monetary obligations, it does not preclude exceptions on the basis of reasonableness, justice and fairness (LCC Article 1.5). The court has dismissed the claim of debtor because after the contract formation until the court of first instance order to pay the money more than two years have passed and during this time conditions for crediting could have been changed.[448] This reasoning seems to be wrong because the principle of responsible lending is applicable only before the conclusion of lending contract not after it. After the contract is concluded, it should be performed as agreed and no exceptions on the basis of responsible lending should be available, because it will lead to the violation of contract law rules. Performance of the contract in such cases should be mitigated by the contract law itself, which provides for both general (withholding of performance, LCC Article 6.58) and special grounds (LCC Article 6.883) to refuse to lend money.

882. Next to the monetary crediting used in traditional banking, LCC regulates modalities of consensual lending concerning trade transactions. First modality is crediting with goods. According to LCC Article 6.884, the parties may enter into agreement on crediting with goods establishing an obligation of one party to transfer to the other party the generic things. The amount, assortment, complexity, quality, packing-cases and packaging of goods shall be established in accordance with the rules applicable to sales contracts, unless otherwise determined by agreement of the parties or contradicts the essence of the agreement. Second modality is trade crediting, which is incorrectly called by LCC as commercial crediting. Such wording is wrong because the essence of such form of credit lies not in the commercial nature of contract (B2B), but usage in trade relations. Moreover, trade credit may be perfectly granted in consumer sales (B2C). According to LCC Article 6.885, in the agreement the performance whereof is related to the transfer into the ownership of the other party of money or generic things, the parties may provide for the granting of the credit. The credit may be granted by deferring or apportioning the advance payment, payment for goods, works or services (trade crediting). Both the crediting in goods and trade crediting are subject to the general rules of crediting, unless otherwise determined by agreement of the parties or contradicts the essence of the agreement.

448. Judgment of the Lithuanian Court of Appeal of 6 Dec. 2011 in the civil case No 2A-512/2011.

§3. CONSUMER LOANS

883. The concept and general principles of consumer lending are briefly mentioned in LCC, whereas detailed regulation is found in special laws, implementing EU law. According to LCC Article 6.886, by the credit agreement for consumers a creditor grants or promises to grant to a debtor credit in the form of a deferred payment, loan or other similar financial accommodation, except for agreements for the provision on a continuing basis of services or for the supply of goods of the same kind, where the debtor pays for such services or goods for the duration of their provision or supply by means of instalments. In consumer lending, consumer means a natural person who seeks to conclude or concludes a credit agreement for personal, family or household purposes and who is acting for purposes which are outside his business or profession. A creditor is a person who in accordance with the procedure and in the cases laid down by the law grants or promises to grant consumer credit in the course of his commercial practices.

884. LCC also states that when providing a consumer credit service, a creditor must ensure the adequate application of the principle of responsible lending. This obligation is of crucial importance because is intended to protect consumers against the risks of over-indebtedness and bankruptcy.[449]

885. As it was mentioned above, more detailed regulation of consumer credit is found in special laws implementing EU law, since the development of the EU credit market was accompanied by reinforced consumer rights and harmonisation of national provisions in two consumer protection directives – Consumer Credit Directive (CCD)[450] and MCD.[451] Both those directives are implemented in Lithuanian statutory law: CCD in Law on Consumer Credit and MCD in Law on Credit Related to Immovables. In contrast with both directives, scope of Law on Consumer Credit and Law on Credit Related to Immovables also covers peer-to-peer consumer lending activities and establishes the framework for administrative supervision of lending platforms. Those legal acts are of crucial importance, because in practice consumers are in weak position to negotiate with banks and other credit providers contractual terms. As courts have rigidly enforced such terms,[452] statutory intervention was indispensable to make consumer credit contracts fair.

449. Judgment of the ECJ of 27 Mar. 2014 in the case C-565/12 (*Credit Lyonnais*).

450. Directive 2008/48/EC of the European Parliament and of the Council of 23 Apr. 2008 on credit agreements for consumers and repealing Council Directive 87/102/EEC.

451. Directive 2014/17/EU of the European Parliament and of the Council of 4 Feb. 2014 on credit agreements for consumers relating to residential immovable property and amending Directives 2008/48/EC and 2013/36/EU and Regulation (EU) No 1093/2010.

452. For instance, according to the case law of Supreme Court, banks' right included in standard contract to unilaterally change interest rate (price of the credit) for further period in case where parties failed to agree on new rate of interest at the expiration of initial rate fixation period is valid and fair. It does not seem fair to unilaterally lift the price of contract, especially where the consumer has chosen particular bank due to its attractive interest rate. *See* Judgment of the Lithuanian Supreme Court of 10 Dec. 2014 in the civil case No 3K-3-537/2014.

886. Law on Consumer Credit is mainly applicable to consumer credit agreements up to EUR 75,000, unrelated to acquisition or encumbrance of real estate. Pure leasing contracts, where an obligation to purchase the object of the agreement is not laid down either by the agreement itself or by any separate agreement, as well as some other specific consumer credit types are outside the scope of this regulatory act. Law on Consumer Credit sets the terms of granting of consumer credit and requirements for the provision of information about these terms, the duties and liability of creditors and credit intermediaries in granting consumer credit and assessing the creditworthiness of consumers, the consumers' right of early repayment and the creditors' right to compensation for early repayment of consumer credit. In particular, according to Law on Consumer Credit, in good time sufficient to access the information provided, before the consumer is bound by any credit agreement, the creditor and, where applicable, the credit intermediary shall, on the basis of the credit terms and conditions offered by the creditor and the preferences expressed and information supplied by the consumer, provide the consumer with the information needed to compare different offers in order to take an informed decision on whether to conclude a credit agreement.[453] Before the conclusion of the credit agreement, the creditor must also, following the principle of responsible lending, assess the consumer's creditworthiness on the basis of sufficient information, where appropriate obtained from the consumer and, where necessary, on the basis of a consultation of the relevant database. The assessment of the creditworthiness of consumers on the basis of a consultation of the relevant database shall be performed subject to the consumer's written consent, where such a consent is required by law. Law on Consumer Credit forbids annual interest higher than 75% as well as daily accrual of default penalty higher than 0.05% of non-performed sum.

887. Law on Credit Related to Immovables is applicable to credit agreements under which the borrower duties are secured by hypothec on immovables and credit agreements designed for acquisition or retention of the ownership of the land or other existing real estate or the one being designed. The Law on Credit Related to Immovables in detailed manner sets the conditions for granting a real estate related credit and requirements for giving information on these conditions, obligations, and responsibility of a lender, a credit intermediary, and an operator of a peer-to-peer lending platform within performance of its operations. Among other things, the Law on Credit Related to Immovables establishes precontractual duties of a lender to inform consumer about the financial product and asses her creditworthiness, form and content of the credit agreement, right to withdraw from the credit agreement or terminate it due to default, contractual duty of the lender and the credit intermediary to act in good faith, in a fair, transparent and professional manner, by taking into account the borrowers' rights and interests whenever developing credit products,

453. According to ECJ, CCD does not preclude a Member State from providing, under national law, that, where a credit agreement does not include all the information required under Art. 10(2) of the directive, the agreement is deemed to be interest-free and free of charges, provided that the information covers matters which, if not included, may compromise the ability of the consumer to assess the extent of his liability. *See* Judgment of the ECJ of 9 Nov. 2016 in the Case C42/15 (*Home Credit Slovakia*). However, currently there is no such rule in Lithuanian law, instead administrative penalties are applicable.

operating as a lender or a credit intermediary, providing consultation services related to credit granting and supplementary services, if such supplementary services are provided, or within the course of implementation of the credit agreement, etc.

Chapter 11. Contracts with the Government and Other Public Administrations

888. It should be noted at the beginning of this chapter that contracts with public bodies do not form independent category of respective nominate contract. Those contracts fall under the other categories, such as sale, lease, work and service contracts, but with additional layer of public property and public interest protections.

889. After the period of Soviet dictatorship and its economic utopia, society of Lithuania has done hard work to transform State, its law and economy towards Western-style capitalist democracy.[454] Policy makers of independent Lithuanian wanted to change State internal structure, abandon dictatorship and absorb democratic ideas. Lithuanian independence should have been not only external independence from other nations but also internal independence of private citizens from overwhelmingly powerful State. Important steps were taken, including the adoption of modern and democratic Constitution together with LCC full of economic liberalism. Authority of the State was extremely reduced and balanced by separation of powers, whereas protection of property and freedom of contract were promoted. For instance, LCC Article 2.36 provides that State, municipalities and their institutions are subjects of civil relations subject to the same grounds as other participants thereof. But most importantly, public interest should no longer prevail against private interest, but should be equal to it.

890. From the other hand, for the sake of protection of public order and public interest in the contracts concluded by the public bodies, LCC has provided special protective regime. First, a transaction that is contrary to public order as well as a transaction formed by public legal person that is contrary to the goals of its activities shall be invalid (LCC Article 1.81(1), 1.82(2)). Second, contracts concluded by managing bodies of a public legal person in overstepping their authority shall not impose obligations on a legal person (LCC Article 2.84(1)). Third, LCC Article 6.157(1) prescribes that the parties themselves may not agree on modification, restriction or abrogation of an effect or application of the mandatory rules of law, irrespective of by what law – national or international – these norms are determined. Since rules of Lithuanian public law are deemed to be mandatory by their

454. The same pattern, at least in civil law, was seen also in other post-Soviet states. For instance, the economic philosophy of the post-Soviet civil codes of Russia and Kazakhstan may be reduced to one phrase-free enterprise. The codes exude capitalism. In almost identical language, the provisions of the two civil codes engrave the legal foundations of a capitalist system: the sanctity of private property, freedom of entrepreneurial activity, freedom of contract, equality of all actors in the marketplace, and tort liability of the government for causing harm to private interests. This is a complete reversal of the principles of the Soviet-era civil codes, according to which private property was deemed obscene, freedom of contract was regarded as a fiction of bourgeois law, any form of entrepreneurial activity was condemned, the rules of the game were stacked in favour of the government participants in economic relations, and it was not a tort for the government to misgovern. *See* Christopher Osakwe. *Anatomy of the 1994 Civil Codes of Russia and Kazakhstan: A Biopsy of the Economic Constitutions of Two Post-Soviet Republics.* Notre Dame Law Review, Vol. 73 1998, p. 1420.

nature, civil contract law is in fact flexible and coherent with public law: it lays down basic legal framework for the parties' transactions, without any prejudice to the public order and public interest protected by the mandatory rules of public law.

891. But general civil law protections are proved to be insufficient. From the restoration of independence, Lithuania has immediately struggled with high levels corruption – unfortunate inheritance of Soviet times. This, together with competition policy, was main motive to tighten economic transactions with State and its institutions, adopt protective regime on public property and allow persecutors to defend public interest in civil cases. Thus, first, privatisations of public property[455] (transfer of State property), and public procurement[456] (State spending) both should have been provided according to special procedures, first and foremost by involving general public in tender (auction). Second, public property law has set so-called public law principle, which means that transactions involving state and municipal assets must be concluded only in the cases and by a manner established by legal acts regulating the disposal of state and/or municipal assets. Obviously, freedom of contract was abolished in such cases. Third, procedural law gave to the public persecutor wide locus standi to initiate civil actions for a defence of public interest.

455. Privatisation is a transfer of public property to the ownership of private persons under privatisation transactions concluded in accordance with the prescribed procedure, including transfer of state or municipality control in state or municipality controlled enterprises by floating a new issue of shares financed with additional contributions. According to the Law on the Privatisation of Shares Owned by the State and Municipalities, there are the following methods of privatisation: (1) public subscription for shares; (2) public auction; (3) public tender; (4) direct negotiations; (5) transfer of state or municipal control in an enterprise controlled by the State/municipality; and (6) sale of shares to shareholders of a private limited liability company. The privatisation process is supervised by the Privatisation Commission, which is a special state institution set up for the operating in accordance with laws and the regulations approved by the Government. A privatisation transaction concluded upon privatisation of companies' shares by way of public tender or direct negotiations may include the obligations of the buyer/buyers to preserve the number of jobs, to invest in an enterprise controlled by the State/municipality whose shares are sold or in other branches of the Lithuanian economy.

456. Public procurement contracts in Lithuania are regulated by the LCC and specifically by Law on Public Procurement, which implements EU Directive 2014/24/EU of the European Parliament and of the Council of 26 Feb. 2014 by establishing the procedure of public procurement, the rights, obligations and responsibility of entities of procurement, the procedure for exercising the control of public procurement and settling disputes. The goal of procurement is to award a public contract in compliance with the statutory requirements allowing to acquire for the contracting authority (to perform procurement by the authorising contracting authority) or third persons the necessary supplies, services or works making a rational use of the resources allocated for this purpose. Supplier under this law is any economic entity that may be either a natural person or a private legal person or a public legal person, other organisations and divisions thereof or any group of such persons, which is able to offer or is offering supplies, services or works. The supplies, services or works contracts may be awarded by means of the following procedures: (1) open procedure; (2) restricted procedure; (3) competitive dialogue; and (4) negotiated procedure: with or without publication of a contract notice. The contracting authority shall ensure in the course of performance of procurement procedures and award of contracts, compliance with the principle of equal treatment, the principle of non-discrimination, the principle of mutual recognition, the principle of proportionality and the principle of transparency.

892. Despite those two layers of State protection in LCC and special statutes, LVAT considered that there is a need to push the protection of public interest in contractual matters even more. Accordingly, case law of administrative courts has introduced new concept in Lithuania, having no direct ground in statutory law and without any national doctrinal background, but well known to other civil law jurisdictions – the notion of administrative contract (*administracinė sutartis*).[457] Under the case law such contracts are the contract of general guarantee between the custom and guarantee association,[458] contract for the delegation of right to organise land zoning,[459] tripartite contract between unemployed, employment public agency and private company for the training and employment of unemployed,[460] contract for subsidising the prescribed drugs in drugstores and hospitals from the public funds,[461] contract for the financing from EU structural funds.[462] Other clear candidates for the status of administrative contracts are agreement with tax authority on tax loan, i.e., postponement and allotment of tax obligations (Law on Tax administration Article 2(19)), agreement on exploitation of underground resources, which are exclusive property of State (The Underground Law Article 12), and settlement agreement in administrative litigation (Law on Litigation in Administrative cases Article 51). Public procurement contracts, concession contracts, public–private partnerships and contracts concerning state property are not characterised as administrative by Lithuanian courts, thus falling under the scope of general civil contract law. However, in case of public property contracts, the public law clearly dominates against the private law,[463] and the characterisation of those contracts as civil remains highly debatable. As concern public procurement, most often legislation transposes EU law,[464] but overall, regime became very rigid and tight for private suppliers,[465] leaving doubts about the actual equality of parties to the contract.

---

457. *In a landmark case, decided just several years after the adoption of new LCC, Lithuanian Senior Administrative Court declared that ' the contract of general guarantee between the custom and guarantee association is not civil contract and relationship stemming from it is domain of public, not civil law. This type of relationship between public agency and private person, where public agency concludes contracts with private persons in pursuit of its statutory functions and in a need to satisfy a public interest, in legal practice of European countries and legal doctrine is called administrative contract. As follows from above, the custom in scrutinised relationships acts not as a civil law person, but as public agency, therefore its actions and decision are administrative acts, which can be disputed under the order and time limits established by the administrative law'.* Judgment of the LVAT of *25 Nov. 2005* in the administrative case No. *A-14-1479-05.*
458. *Ibid.*
459. Judgment of the LVAT of 3 Jun. 2013 in the administrative case No. A-492-829-13.
460. Judgment of the LVAT of 15 Sep. 2016 in the administrative case eA-1578-662/2016.
461. Judgment of the LVAT of 6 May 2008 in the administrative case No. A-261-339-08.
462. Judgment of the LVAT of 14 Mar. 2013 in the administrative case No. A-492-118-13.
463. It is even directly set in Law on the Management, Use and Disposal of State and Municipal Assets Art. 9 as the so-called public law principle, which means that transactions involving state and municipal assets must be concluded only in the cases and manner established by legal acts regulating the disposal of state and/or municipal assets. Therefore, freedom of contract is very limited in such cases.
464. First and foremost Directive 2014/24/EU of the European Parliament and of the Council of 26 Feb. 2014 on public procurement.
465. For instance, there are: very short limitations on extinctive prescription of civil actions (Law on Public Procurement Art. 102) and cassatory appeal (CCP Art. 80(4)); prevented from bidding black

893. Summing up, State normally is equal party to the contract in Lithuania, but there are important statutory protections laid down in order to combat corruption and promote competition. One can even notice signs in Lithuanian law of resurrection of public interest dominance over the private one. However, legislators and courts must be very careful here, because self-protectionism of the powerful and interventionist State is alien to the free market economy and democracy, being cultivated in independent Lithuania and protected by its Constitution.

---

list of suppliers, which in practice is quite easy to fall in (Law on Public Procurement Art. 91); much higher stamp burdens on the suppliers (CCP Art. 423^{10}).

Chapter 12. Contract of Partnership

894. Partnership (*societas*) is a form of human cooperation focused on shared business or social goals and functioning within a created organisational framework. In this respect, it exceeds simple exchange of goods and services, characteristic to most other contract types, and may be even a multiparty legal transaction.

895. LCC Article 6.969 provides that by the contract on joint venture (partnership) two or more persons (partners), cooperating their property, work or knowledge, undertake to act jointly for a certain goal or certain activities which do not contravene the law. The concept of partnership *largo sensu* encompasses every organisation of partners, including also partnerships formed as distinct legal entities, such as general partnership, limited partnership, professional partnership of advocates, small partnership and partnership of apartment co-owners. Therefore, the contract on joint venture can also serve as the basis for establishment of partnerships. However, establishment, management, activities, transformation and dissolution of incorporated partnerships are primarily regulated by general rules on legal persons in LCCs' Book Two and specific statutes (Law on Partnerships, Law on Advocacy, Law on Small Partnerships, etc.), not by the LCC contract law rules on the partnership. Important attribute of commercial partnerships is that these are unlimited liability companies (LCC Article 2.50(4)), whereas other partnerships are of more or less limited liability.

896. Partnership *stricto sensu* in Lithuania is called joint venture (*jungtinė veikla*) and means only unincorporated partnership, having legal regime resembling that of a company. This mimicking of a company makes contract of joint venture specific in several critical points. First, although most contracts in practice are formed in the name of partnership, it has no legal personality separate from the partners, thus formally has no property, obligations, procedural capacity, etc. Second, lack of legal personality and need to resemble the model of a company, means that there is a web of partners agreements, and those agreements depending on the number of partners may be either bilateral or multilateral legal transactions. Seeing from this angle, unincorporated partnership is an intermediate step between ordinary contract and a company. However, clear disadvantage of unincorporated partnership, in contrast with a company, is unlimited liability of its partners. Third, assets operated by the partnership conform specific patrimony which jointly belongs to all partners. Accordingly, the property of partnership is the object of common ownership of partners, while debts of partnership also are jointly owned by the partners, some of them even *in solidum*.

897. LCC rules on a contract of partnership (LCC Article 6.969–6.982) are a copy of corresponding Russian ГК rules, with small inclusion from Quebec CC. Contract of partnership (joint venture) formed under Lithuanian law is bilateral, consensual, commutative and onerous contract, as well as multilateral legal transaction, where there are more than two parties. It produces strong *in rem* effects, by creating additional patrimony and common ownership of partners instead of their former individual ownership.

898. There are two main types of unincorporated partnership (joint venture): commercial joint venture and association. The main difference between them is that association is not seeking a profit, whereas commercial joint venture is seeking it. The concept of association, as a non-profit partnership, in LCC is taken from Quebec CC Article 2186. The most important case of association in a case law is partnership in cohabitating couples. Despite significant number of unmarried couples, there are no special rules in Lithuanian family law on unregistered partnership, which could protect weaker party's, usually housewife's, interests. This gap, however, was filled by creative case law of the courts, who did characterise cohabitation of unmarried couples as a type of partnership – association. This legal technique has empowered courts to apply rules of partnership and find proprietary interest of weaker party with respect to the assets formally belonging to another party but created or improved during the period of cohabitation.[466]

899. The contract of joint venture (partnership), according to LCC Article 6.969, should be formed in writing, and in the cases prescribed by the law (e.g., Law on Partnerships Article 3) in notary form. If the requirements set for the form of the contract are not satisfied, the contract is null and void. Next step after the formation of contract is making the contributions of the partners. As joint venture is consensual contract, this step is not a prerequisite for a formation of contract, but is vital for the success of partnership, because contributions by partners create economic basis for the activities of partnership, while the assets themselves become common property. According to LCC Article 6.970, a contribution of a partner shall be deemed everything such partner contributes to the joint venture – money, any other assets, professional or any other knowledge, skills, reputation and business relations. It is presumed that the contributions of the partners are equal unless otherwise established in the contract on joint venture. A contribution shall be assessed in money by contract of all partners. It should be noted, however, that contributions of property for the joint venture, may be blocked in cases prescribed by competition law as a form of prohibited concentration (Law on Competition Article 8–14). Also, the creditors of a partner are entitled to claim the separation of the partner's interest from the common property pursuant to the rules of property law (LCC Article 6.977).

900. The property contributed by the partners, which was previously their ownership, also the production received during joint venture, income and results, shall be common ownership of all the partners unless otherwise established in the law or the contract on joint venture. If the contributed property previously was not the ownership of a partner, and the partner uses such property on any other grounds, this property shall be used in the interests of all the partners and shall also be deemed the property which is jointly used by all the partners, unless otherwise established in the law. One of the partners appointed by joint contract of all the partners shall be in charge of the accounting of the common property. The common

466. *See* Judgments of the Lithuanian Supreme Court of 31 Oct. 2001 in the civil case No 3K-3-1029/2001 and of 14 Mar. 2014 in the civil case No. 3K-3-84/2014.

property shall be used, possessed and disposed of by joint agreement of all the partners. In case of a dispute, at the request of any of the partners the procedure shall be established by the court (LCC Article 6.971). The profit, obtained from the joint venture, should be distributed among the partners in proportion to the value of the contribution of each of them into the joint venture unless otherwise established in the contract on joint venture. The agreement to exclude any of the partners while distributing the profit is null and void (LCC Article 6.976).

901. Partners in joint venture share not only property and profits but also debts and losses. LCC Article 6.974 provides that the distribution of joint expenses and joint losses, related to the joint venture, shall be established in the contract on joint venture. Absent such contract, each partner shall be liable for the joint expenses and joint losses in proportion to the amount of his part of such expenses or damages. The contract which fully releases one of the partners from the coverage of the joint expenses or joint losses is null and void. The exact responsibility of partners under other obligations depends on the type of partnership. In commercial joint venture, all the partners are solidarily liable under the common obligations. In association, responsibility under the contractual obligations is pro rata, whereas under the other shared obligations the partners are solidarily liable (LCC Article 6.975).

902. Specific case is a secret partnership. LCC Article 6.982 prescribes that the contract on joint venture may stipulate that a partner (partners) shall be not disclosed to third persons (the secret partnership). Such secrecy attracts specific legal consequences. For the sake of legal certainty, in case of relations with the third persons, each of the secret partners is liable to the extent of all his property under all the transactions he has concluded in his own name in the interests of all the partners. All the obligations arising among the partners during their joint venture are partial. This is in contrast with legal regime for open partnerships, which is analysed further.

903. Another fundamentally important feature of a contract of partnership is that it creates fiduciary obligations between parties.[467] Structure of partnership consists of multilateral agency relationships, where every partner has power to make legal acts in the name of all partners. This power should be controlled by strict fiduciary standards and remedies, including restitutionary damages (LCC Article 6.249(2)). However, LCC rules on this point are not very elaborated and focus more on transactional procedures than on substantive loyalty aspects, which constitute the content of fiduciary relationships. LCC simply prescribes that while managing joint affairs, each of the partners is entitled to act on behalf of all the partners, unless the contract on joint venture provides that joint affairs shall be managed by one of the partners or all the partners together. If the affairs may be managed only by all the partners together, the conclusion of each transaction shall require the approval of all the partners. In case of relations with the third persons, the right of a partner to conclude the transactions on behalf of all the partners shall be approved by the power of attorney issued by the remaining partners or the contract on joint venture. In case

467. Judgment of the Lithuanian Supreme Court of 18 Nov. 2013 in the civil case No. 3K-3-442/2013.

of relations with the third persons, the partners shall not rely on limitations of the rights of the partner, who has concluded the transaction, to act on behalf of all the partners, except for the cases when they prove that at the time of conclusion of the transaction the third person knew or should have known about such limitations. The partner who has concluded the transaction on behalf of all the partners in excess of the powers granted to him or who has concluded the transaction in his own name in the interests of all the partners is entitled to claim from the other partners the indemnification of the loss incurred if he proves that such transactions were necessary in order to protect the interests of the other partners. The partners who have incurred the damage by virtue of such transactions are entitled to claim compensation from the partner, who has concluded such transactions. The decisions related to the joint affairs of the partners shall be adopted by joint contract of the partners unless otherwise established in the contract on joint venture (LCC Article 6.972). In addition, each partner is entitled to have access to the documents concerning the management of the joint affairs, notwithstanding whether or not he has the right to manage the joint affairs. Any agreements imposing limitations on, or revoking, this right are void (LCC Article 6.973).

904. The contract on joint venture ends: (1) when one of the partners is recognised as legally incapable, of limited legal capacity or untraceable, unless the contract on joint venture or later arrangement of the remaining partners establishes to retain the contract on joint venture among the remaining partners, except for the cases when the contract on joint venture is valid without the above-mentioned partner; (2) when bankruptcy proceedings are instituted against one of the partners; (3) in case of death or liquidation or reorganisation of one of the partners, unless the contract on joint venture or later contract of the remaining partners establishes to retain the contract on joint venture among the remaining partners or substitute the deceased (liquidated or reorganised) partner with his legal successors; (4) when one of the partners refuses to continue as a participant of the termless contract on joint venture; (5) when the fixed-term contract on joint venture is terminated at the initiative of one of the partners; (6) upon expiration of the period of the contract on joint venture; and (7) upon separation of the interest of one of the partners from the common property at the request of his creditors. Upon expiration of the contract on the joint venture, the things assigned for the joint use by all the partners shall be gratuitously returned to the partners who have assigned them, unless otherwise agreed by the parties. From the moment of expiration of the contract on joint venture, its participants shall be solidarily liable against the third persons for the outstanding joint obligations. The property which is the common ownership of the partners after termination of the contract on joint venture shall be distributed in accordance with the rules established in property law. The partner who has contributed a unique thing after expiration of the contract on joint venture shall be entitled to demand to return him the thing unless the interests of other partners and creditors are infringed by such return (LCC Article 6.978).

905. The partner who wishes to waive the termless contract on joint venture shall notify to that effect the other partners at least three months prior to such withdrawal, unless otherwise established in the laws or the contract. One of the partners shall be entitled to terminate event the contract concluded with fixed term or made for a certain goal, if: (1) other partners are in material breach under such contract; and (2) the partner who wishes to terminate the contract cannot perform the contract for important reasons. However, the partner who has terminated the contract shall indemnify to the other partners the direct damages incurred by virtue of such termination. After termination of the contract by one of the partners, the contract remains in force in respect of the other partners. If the contract on joint venture is terminated upon refusal of one of the partners to be a participant of the contract, or at the request of one of the partners, the person who is no longer a participant of the contract on joint venture shall be liable against third persons under the obligations which appeared while he was a participant of the contract on joint venture as if he were a partner (LCC Article 6.979–6.981).

Chapter 13. Quasi-contracts

906. Quasi-contracts are wilful and lawful acts, which give rise to non-contractual obligations of the persons involved when one person without the agreement confers on another a benefit to which he has no right. The absence of voluntary agreement separates quasi-contract from a contract, while the lawful character of quasi-contract separates it from a tort.[468] Moreover, the absence of will to create civil law relations prevents to characterise quasi-contract as a transaction. In the universe of juridical facts, quasi-contracts belong to the operational facts, i.e., lawful acts of person which produce legal consequences as a result of his behaviour and independently from his intention.

907. Quasi-contractual obligations being a legal response to quasi-contracts are the manifestation of corrective justice and fairness in private relations. Lithuanian legal doctrine and case law follows Romanic tradition by accepting a general notion of quasi-contract as an independent source of obligations.[469] Quasi-contracts *par excellence* in Lithuanian law are: performance not due (LCC Article 6.237),[470] unjustified enrichment (LCC Article 6.242) and benevolent intervention in another's affairs (LCC Article 6.229). Lithuanian legal doctrine also adds to this list gaming and wagering (LCC Article 6.243–6.244);[471] however, reasons for this inclusion are unknown since gaming and wagering are capable of creating contractual, delictual (tortious) and unjustified enrichment obligations leaving no space for an additional independent type of quasi-contract.[472]

908. Quasi-contracts usually resemble some kind of real contracts. For instance, benevolent intervention into affairs of another (*negotiorum gestio*) resembles

---

468. As famously pointed out by Stanford Professor Arthur M. Cathcart, 'these obligations occupy a field somewhere between contract and tort'. *See* Arthur M. Cathcart. *Nature and Extent of Quasi-Contractual Obligations. In.* Modern American Law, vol. 7. American Law Blackstone Institute, 1921, p. 2.
469. Valentinas Mikelėnas. *Prievolių teisė. Pirmoji dalis.* Justitia: Vilnius, 2002, p. 63; Judgment of the Lithuanian Supreme Court of 27 May 2011 in the civil case No. 3K-3-256/2011.
470. However, as it will be explained below, the wording 'reception of property not due' is misleading on two points. First, in *condictio indebiti* situations as a quasi-contract (a lawful act in nature) stands not the reception (act of debtor), but transfer (act of creditor) of property. Second, reception of property not due covers not only transfer of property but also performance of services, therefore it is more accurate to name *condictio indebiti* as a 'performance not due'.
471. Valentinas Mikelėnas. *Prievolių teisė. Pirmoji dalis.* Justitia: Vilnius, 2002, p. 63.
472. Possible explanation could be the case law of the French *Cour de Cassation*, which has ruled that certain unfair commercial practices can be counteracted by a recourse to French CC Art. 1371 (the general definition of quasi-contracts). The subject matter of these judgments were ostensible notifications to consumers that they had won lottery prizes. The *Cour de Cassation* has held that such communications may establish a quasi-contract between the sender and the addressee. However, this new type of quasi-contract appears to be a construction sui generis between the law of contract and tort law and seems more closely related to the law of *culpa in contrahendo* (itself often interpreted as a quasi-contractual construction, giving a completely different meaning to the term) than it does to the law of quasi-contracts in the traditional meaning of the concept derived from Roman origin. *See* Christian von Bar, Walter de Gruyter. *Benevolent Intervention in Another's Affairs.* Sellier, 2006, p. 91.

contract of mandate, performance not due (*condictio indebiti*) resembles contract of deposit and unjustified enrichment (*actio de in rem verso*) roughly corresponds to the contract of loan.

909. As in other Romanic jurisdictions, in Lithuanian law quasi-contracts are strictly subsidiary in nature and as such are filling gaps of a contract law. For example, if an insurer pays indemnity to the insured on a mistake, the insured is obliged to return money on the ground of performance not due (*condictio indebiti*), which is quasi-contract. The same result is where the contract is declared null and void – the non-contractual restitution, which is quasi-contractual remedy in nature, should take place (LCC Article 1.80(2)), as normal remedies of contract law are not applicable to extra-contractual situations.

§1. *Negotiorum Gestio*

910. Benevolent intervention into affairs of another (*negotiorum gestio*) as a quasi-contract resembles mandate; hence, it could alternatively and functionally be called *quasi-mandatum*. The element of the mandate or assistance is so important that legal provisions on *negotiorum gestio* do not apply if the management of the affairs of another is performed by a person believing to be managing his own affairs (LCC Article 6.236). In latter cases, rules on unjust enrichment (LCC Article 6.242) instead are applicable. Of course, there should be only the resemblance of the mandate, not real mandate or statutory duty to perform management, because such duty would signal about the contractual or statutory nature of management.[473] For

473. Special and complicated case is a salvage. Maritime law of salvage regulates relationships where crew of one ship helps another ship in danger. Salvage is species of maritime *negotiorum gestio* regulated by the International London Convention on Salvage of 1989 (ratified by the Lithuania in 1999). According to the London Convention Art. 10 every master is bound, so far as he can do so without serious danger to his vessel and persons thereon, to render assistance to any person in danger of being lost at sea. This is not contractual, public or office, but ad hoc duty, which does not erase the voluntary element and does not prevent characterisation of salvage as a species of *negotiorum gestio*. The problem related to maritime salvage is that salvor according to the London Convention Art. 12 is remunerated only in case of success, thus leaving it unremunerated under the Convention in cases where salvage gave no result at all (common law principle 'no cure no pay'). The exception to this is the case of special compensation set in the Art. 14 to the salvor which has carried out salvage operations in respect of a vessel which by itself or its cargo threatened damage to the environment and has failed to earn an ordinary reward. Nevertheless, in cases where London Convention gives no remuneration, a remedy may be given by Lithuanian national law on the basis of general action of *negotiorum gestio*. As to the scope of application, Lithuania by adjoining the London Convention has reserved the right not to apply the Convention when the salvage operation takes place in inland waters and all vessels involved are of inland navigation or no vessel is involved at all. However, Lithuanian Maritime Shipping Law even on salvage in inland waters, where London Convention otherwise should be inapplicable due to adjoining carve-outs made by Lithuania, refers to the London Convention. From the other hand, Lithuanian Maritime Shipping Law applies only for the situations related to the sea, leaving aside internal waters, such as lakes or rivers. It means that neither London Convention nor Lithuanian Maritime Shipping Law are applicable to situations when the salvage operation takes place in inland waters and all vessels involved are of inland navigation or no vessel is involved at all. Instead Inland Waterways Transport Code is applicable, whom Art. 22 prescribes that assistance to a ship in distress and its cargo

example, if a beneficiary knows about the management of her affairs, there is a tacit contract, not quasi-contract.[474] No *negotiorum gestio* exists where person manages affairs altruistically and incurs expenses, which he treats as charity, because this amounts to the contract of gift. And finally, if a beneficiary provokes dangerous situation to secretly profit from benevolent intervention by gestor, the beneficiary makes tort, which prevents quasi-contract to come into existence.

911. Ancient institution of *negotiorum gestio* is a manifestation of moral ideas prevailing in European society. According to the main rule on *negotiorum gestio* set in LCC Article 6.229, where a person voluntarily and without any mandate, instruction or previous assent to act undertakes the management of the affairs of another person, where such management does not fall within his duties, he must manage them in such a way that it conforms to the interests of that other person. The activities of the person managing the affairs of another (manager) shall be governed, *mutatis mutandis*, by the provisions of property law regulating simple administration of another's property. A person who assumes the management of the affairs of another shall be bound to continue the management undertaken until that other person (principal) is in a position to attend to it himself, or until a guardian, curator or an administrator of the property is appointed; if the principal dies, the duty to continue the management shall remain in existence until his heirs take over the management. A person managing the affairs of another person must as soon as reasonably possible inform the principal of everything that has been done; he must also render in writing a comprehensive receipt, expenditure and loss account. A person managing the affairs of another must exercise the necessary concern in his management to the extent that can reasonably be required of him, taking in regard the concrete circumstances in which he acts. The rules on *negotiorum gestio* shall not apply to the activities of state and municipal institutions which act in the interests of other persons if the performance of such activity is within the duties of the institutions concerned.

912. A person who manages the affairs of another person against the latter's will being aware of this is committing a tort, and according to LCC Article 6.230 is liable in damages towards the person against whose will he has acted. The assent or disagreement of a person towards his affairs to be managed by another person shall be of no effect in the instances where an obligation whose performance corresponds to the interests of the society, or the obligation to maintain another person would

---

is provided only if there is a salvage agreement between the masters of ships. However, it would clearly be unreasonable and against good morals to interpret this rule as prohibiting salvage under the general rules of *negotiorum gestio* if no agreement was possible, for example in case where master of the ship was unconscious. Thus, although the institution of salvage is *lex specialis* with respect to general rules of *negotiorum gestio*, it does not prevent application of *lex generalis* in cases unregulated by the law of salvage.

474. This aspect was not properly considered by the Lithuanian Supreme Court who has ruled that in case where municipality after the termination of contract still tacitly used services of rainwater collection provided by the private company (plaintiff), there was management of municipality affairs. *See* Judgment of the Lithuanian Supreme Court of 2 Dec. 2016 in the civil case No. 3K-3-495-313/2016.

not be performed in time without such assent, or where effort is undertaken to avert danger threatening a person's life. Actions performed by the manager of the affairs of another after he became aware of the person's, for the benefit of whom the affairs are conducted, disapproval of such actions shall not create any obligations towards the person concerned, neither towards the person performing the indicated actions nor third persons. However, if a person has undertaken the management of the affairs of another in order to protect the latter against real danger to his person or property, the former shall not be bound to compensate for loss inflicted unless he acted intentionally or with gross negligence. Subsequent ratification of actions of a manager made by the person whose affairs were being managed by the former without a mandate produces the same effects with respect to the management as would have arisen from a contract of mandate or any other contract best corresponding to the nature of the performed actions (LCC Article 6.231–6.232).

913. LCC Article 6.233 provides flexible quantum of recovery, which is focused on the protection of restitutionary interest. Thus, managing the affairs of another gives right to the primary recourse against beneficiary of such actions – the principal who saved at the expense of the gestor time, efforts and probably money. The principal must reimburse the manager for all the useful and necessary expenses incurred and compensate for the damage suffered by reason of the management of his affairs, irrespective of whether the desired result has been attained.[475] Where management of the affairs of another person appears to be profitable, the manager, who has conducted the affairs, shall have the right to be remunerated. In the case of disagreement between the parties, the amount of remuneration shall be established by the court taking in consideration the concrete circumstances of the case and being guided by the principles of justice, reasonableness and good faith.[476] However, the gestor is bound to return to the principal the property received by reason of the management, including the fruits and income therefrom (LCC Article 6.234).

475. The remedial principle underlying *negotiorum gestio* is clear: in order not to discourage the altruistic management of the affairs of others in appropriate circumstances, the gestor is allowed a reimbursement of his expenses if certain strict requirements relating to his conduct are met. Equity and public order will not allow the gestor to be unjustifiedly impoverished in the interest of the dominus, and the law accordingly does not restrict him to the lesser enrichment action but entitles him to an action aimed at eliminating his impoverishment. *See* J.P. Van Niekerk. *Salvage and Negotiorum Gestio: Exploratory Reflections on the Jurisprudential Foundation and Classification of the South African Law of Salvage*. Acta Juridica, 1992, p. 171.

476. In case of maritime salvage special rules set in the London Convention Art. 13 apply. The maritime salvage reward shall be fixed with a view to encouraging salvage operations, taking into account the following criteria without regard to the order in which they are presented below: (a) the salved value of the vessel and other property; (b) the skill and efforts of the salvors in preventing or minimising damage to the environment; (c) the measure of success obtained by the salvor; (d) the nature and degree of the danger; (e) the skill and efforts of the salvors in salving the vessel, other property and life; (f) the time used and expenses and losses incurred by the salvors; (g) the risk of liability and other risks run by the salvors or their equipment; (h) the promptness of the services rendered; (i) the availability and use of vessels or other equipment intended for salvage operations; and (j) the state of readiness and efficiency of the salvor's equipment and the value thereof.

914. Pursuant to LCC Article 6.233, when the management of the affairs of another person has been rightly undertaken and conformed to the principal's interests, the principal shall be bound to perform the obligations assumed by the manager in his name. LCC Article 6.235 similarly prescribes that obligations arising from a transaction formed on behalf and in the interests of another person shall be assumed by the person on whose behalf and in whose interests the said transaction is concluded, providing that the latter ratifies the transaction and the other party to the transaction does not contradict to such assumption, or that this other party on entering into the transaction was aware or should have been aware of the transaction being formed on behalf and in the interests of another person. Where the principal assumes the obligations resulting from a transaction formed in his interests, the rights arising from the said transaction must be likewise transferred to the principal. Where a transaction in the interests of another person is formed by the manager of affairs of that person on his own behalf, the latter shall be liable towards the third persons for obligations resulting from that transaction. Nevertheless, this provision shall have no effect in respect of the realisation of the manager's and the third persons' rights connected with the person whose affairs were being managed.

§2. Unjustified Enrichment

I. General Remarks

915. Unjustified enrichment law is one of the most poorly drafted and most swampy parts within new LCC. For instance, LCC Article 6.237 may seem as establishing single enrichment action (*condictio sine causa generalis*), very similar to the one set in German BGB Article 812. Pursuant to LCC Article 6.237, a person who without any legal ground by his actions or in any other manner intentionally or negligently obtains something that he could not and ought not to have obtained is obliged to return the received benefit to the person on whose account it was received, except in cases provided for by the LCC.

916. However, this would be the wrong insight. Lithuanian law does not provide a single all-encompassing enrichment claim because next to LCC Article 6.237 drafters have added *actio de in rem verso* in LCC Article 6.242. It is clear that in the context of universal enrichment claim, there is no reason (and it would be even weird) to additionally regulate general enrichment situations with subsidiary enrichment claim. Therefore, analysing LCC rules systemically and functionally, the only conclusion which follows is that LCC establishes modern civilian division of enrichment claims into performance based (*condictio indebiti*) and other unjustified enrichment claims (*actio de in rem verso*). Doctrinal works and case law support this conclusion by attributing to LCC Article 6.237 role of *condictio indebiti*, whereas to LCC Article 6.242 role of *actio de in rem verso.*[477]

477. Valentinas Mikelėnas. *Lietuvos Respublikos civilinio kodekso komentaras. Šeštoji knyga. Prievolių teisė.* Justitia, 2003, I t., p. 318, 325. Judgments of the Lithuanian Supreme Court of 10 May 2006 in the civil case No. 3K-3-196/2011 and of 26 Apr. in the civil case No. 3K-3-319/2006.

917. It may be said that binary classification of unjustified enrichment claims in LCC was inherited from Soviet law. However, the demarcation line between general and special enrichment action was changed during the codification. In Soviet law, there were two enrichment situations: (i) acquisition of property at the expense of another without legal ground; and (ii) a saving up of property at the expense of another person without a basis in law or contract. The saving up of property may consist in a transaction whereby the enriched party becomes free of his obligation to the injured party or a third party, or whereby the enriched party is protected from an expenditure which would have otherwise been incurred. It may also consist in the transfer of a right from one person to another, or in the extinction of a right of one whereby another is directly benefited. Expressed in other terms, the saving up of property may result in enrichment only in cases where the property of a given party was legally bound to be reduced but was not in fact so reduced.[478] In this way, Soviet law was very similar to French model, where scope of *'répétition de l'indu'* was understood very narrowly as encompassing only property. Services were the object of *'enrichissement sans cause'*, the famous general enrichment action established by the French Cour de Cassation in 1892 *Boudier* case[479] on the somewhat scanty foundations of the *actio de in rem verso.*[480] LCC today follows slightly different Dutch model, which albeit essentially resembles the French one, presents wider concept of performance in Article 6:203. In contrast with French *'répétition de l'indu'*, Dutch version of *condictio indebiti* is not confined to the transfer of money or things, but it also extends to services or labour rendered or the provision of the enjoyment or use of a thing by the claimant.[481] Contemporary Lithuanian law, in contrast with Soviet law and transitional period Lithuanian doctrine,[482] also attributes provision of services (works) within the scope of LCC Article 6.237, which provides special enrichment action based on the performance.

918. Besides enrichment, another important prerequisite for satisfaction of both types of enrichment claims is a lack for cause for enrichment. For the establishment of the cause, defendant should show not the contractual but proprietary *causa*, for instance, a valid contract or administrative act. Procedural burden to prove cause bears the defendant because it is impossible for the plaintiff to prove the negative fact that the defendant did not do something, i.e., had no cause for the enrichment.[483]

919. Next feature of both enrichment claims, stressed out in Lithuanian legal doctrine and case law, is their subsidiarity to other civil remedies, such as action for

478. G.E. Glos. *The Doctrine of Unjust Enrichment in Soviet Law.* The University of Malaya Law Review, Vol. 3 No. 1, 1961, p. 55.
479. Judgment of the French Supreme Court of 15 Jun. 1892 in the civil case *Patureau v. Boudier*, D. P. 1892, 1, 596.
480. Reinhard Zimmermann. *Unjustified Enrichment: The Modern Civilian Approach.* Oxford Journal of Legal Studies, Vol. 15, 1995, p. 417.
481. H.L.E. Verhagen. *Absence of Basis and Unjustified Enrichment in Dutch Law: The Condictio Indebiti as an Enrichment Action.* Restitution Law Review, Vol. 12, 2004, p. 141.
482. P. Rasimavičius, *et al. Civilinė teisė: vadovėlis.* Kaunas: Vijusta, 1998, p. 362.
483. Judgment of the Lithuanian Supreme Court of 24 May 2013 in the civil case No. 3K-3-310/2013.

specific performance, damages, vindication and even restitution of prestations.[484] However, some qualifications should be made. Since property law in LCC Article 4.97 provides special rules for reversal of unjustified enrichment in case of vindication,[485] there is almost no space left for the application of the general rules of unjustified enrichment. Quasi-contracts are exclusively lawful acts; hence, subsidiary application of unjustified enrichment with respect to damages is possible only where the gain was derived from lawful actions, and it is therefore impossible to strip it with compensatory or restitutionary damages.

920. Subsidiarity of unjustified enrichment to restitution in Lithuanian law may seem mostly confusing because, by definition, restitution is a legal remedy used to avoid or reverse unjustified enrichment,[486] not even mentioning that in comparative works unjustified enrichment law and restitution law are presented as synonyms.[487] However, according to the scheme of LCC based on Quebec law, restitution of prestations is a special self-standing remedial institution of law of obligations, which belongs neither to unjust enrichment nor to contract. Force majeure, avoidance and termination of a contract are special cases involving contractual situations where restitution of prestations is applied as a primary remedy (LCC Article 6.145) and general quasi-contractual rules of *condictio indebiti* (LCC Article 6.237) apply only in a subsidiary (gap-filling) manner. In all other cases of performance not due, such

484. *See* Valentinas Mikelėnas. *Lietuvos Respublikos civilinio kodekso komentaras. Šeštoji knyga. Prievolių teisė.* Justitia, 2003, I t., p. 319, 326; Judgments of the Lithuanian Supreme Court of 3 Dec. 2003 in the civil case No. 3K-3-1163/2003, of 28 Sep. 2009 in the civil case No 3K-3-355/ 2009 and of 10 May 2006 in the civil case No. 3K-3-196/2011.

485. LCC Art. 4.97 provides that the owner in vindicating a thing has the right to demand: from the person who knew or had to know that his possession was illegal (possessor in bad faith), to restitute or recompense all income that such person received or had to receive during the entire period of possession; from an illegal possessor in good faith all income which such possessor received or had to receive since the time when he found out or had to find out about the possession being illegal or found out about the starting of a civil case regarding the restitution of the thing. Illegal possessor in bad faith in his turn shall have the right to claim from the owner the necessary expenses related to the thing since the moment the owner receives income from such thing. Illegal possessor in good faith shall have the right to claim from the owner recompense for all his expenses caused by the thing that have not been covered by income received from the thing. Illegal possessor in good faith shall have the right to keep the parts that have been added to meliorate the thing, provided these can be partitioned without causing damage to the thing. If the parts added as melioration cannot be partitioned or when the thing was meliorated in a different mode, the illegitimate possessor in good faith shall have the right to claim recompense of expenses arising from such melioration, but not greater than the increase in value of the thing.

486. As Lionel Smith has precisely pointed: what is the response to the successful invocation of the cause of action in unjust enrichment? There appears to be only one: restitution. It is very important that we take care to respect the fact that 'unjust enrichment' and 'restitution' are not synonymous. Far from it. Restitution is the response to the cause of action in unjust enrichment. 'Unjust enrichment' is a cause of action, like breach of contract, tort, breach of confidence, breach of trust or crime. 'Restitution' is a response, like 'compensation' or 'punishment'. These are things which the legal system does once it has decided that something must be done. *See* Lionel Smith. *The Province of the Law of Restitution.* Canadian Bar Review, Vol. 71, 1992, p. 681.

487. Jack Beatson, Eltjo Schrage, *et al. Cases, Materials and Text on Unjustified Enrichment.* Hart Publishing, 2003, p. 1; Jeroen M.J. Chorus. *Illegality and Restitution.* European Review of Private Law, Vol. 14, 2006, p. 437; William H. Angus. *Restitution in Canada since the Deglman Case.* Canadian Bar Review, Vol. 42, 1964, pp. 529–531.

as payment by error, which fall into general scope of LCC Article 6.237, the remedy is the same – restitution of prestations – but the rules are applied in the opposite order: first, rules on the performance not due (LCC Article 6.237) and, second, rules on the restitution of prestations (LCC Article 6.145) only in a subsidiary manner. If, for the sake of simplicity, we refer special cases (force majeure, avoidance and termination of a contract) as grounds for primary restitution of prestations and for other cases (payment by error, extinguishment of obligation due to resolutory term, etc.) as grounds for subsidiary restitution of prestations, we will come to the interesting conclusion: so-called subsidiarity of unjustified enrichment claim against performance not due claim is nothing more than the subordination of subsidiary claim for restitution against the primary one. And this is fully justified, having in mind axiomatic prevalence of *lex specialis* over the *lex generalis*.

II. *Actio De In Rem Verso*

921. According to the principles common to the laws of the EU Member States, a person who has suffered a loss which increases the wealth of another person without there being any legal basis for that enrichment has the right, as a general rule, to restitution from the person enriched, up to the amount of the loss.[488] This idea that nobody should be enriched by the expense of another belongs to the jurist of ancient Rome – Pomponius.[489]

922. In Lithuanian law unjustified enrichment principle is set in LCC Article 6.242, according to which a person in bad faith who has enriched himself without any legal cause at the expense of another must indemnify the latter for his damages in the amount of the unjust enrichment. Decrease in the enrichment may be taken into consideration, and the sum subject to repayment may be diminished correspondingly if this decrease results from a cause which cannot be imputed to the unjustifiably enriched person. Enrichment shall not be considered unjust and achieved in bad faith if it results from such performance of an obligation where the party of an obligation who has suffered loss is not able through his own fault to exercise his rights in such a way as to avoid damages, and the other party has been enriched as a result of actions performed by the impoverished party exclusively for his personal interest and at his own risk.

923. LCC Article 6.242 is modelled according to the Dutch BW Article 6.212, however, not perfectly. Obvious shortcoming in the construction of Lithuanian version of *actio de in rem verso* is the element of fault (bad faith), which normally is alien for the characterisation of unjustified enrichment, as a restitutionary obligation. Most probably, the element of fault was Lithuanian way to curb the wide scope of general enrichment remedy (probably the most general remedy in whole private law); however, it immediately clashes with the concept of quasi-contract as lawful

488. Judgment of the ECJ of 16 Dec. 2008 in the Case C47/07 (*Masdar (UK)v. Commission*).
489. *Iure naturae aequum est neminem cum alterius detrimento et iniuria fieri locupletiorem* (Pomponius D.50.17.206).

act and makes no sense why a person, who innocently enriched at the expense of another without any ground, may leave the enrichment for himself. Even the ECJ has ruled that legal redress for undue enrichment, as provided for in the majority of national legal systems, is not necessarily conditional upon unlawfulness or fault with regard to the defendant's conduct. Actions for unjust enrichment differ from actions brought under the rules governing non-contractual liability in that they do not require proof of unlawful conduct – indeed, of any form of conduct at all – on the part of the defendant, but merely proof of enrichment on the part of the defendant for which there is no valid legal basis and of impoverishment on the part of the applicant which is linked to that enrichment.[490] Initially the Supreme Court according to the wording of LCC Article 242 has required to establish the fault of defendant;[491] however, this requirement later on was abandoned in the case law.[492]

According to the Lithuanian case law (which is literally based on the legal doctrine[493]), the conditions for the application of LCC Article 242 are as follows: the defendant is enriched; the plaintiff is impoverished; causal link between enrichment of defendant and impoverishment of plaintiff; absence of justification (cause) for defendant enrichment; the enrichment should exist at the time of suing defendant in court (no change of position); the plaintiff did not take the risk of impoverishment; and no other remedy is available.[494]

924. Analysing functional scope of LCC Article 6.242, according to the notable scheme of German jurist von Caemmerer,[495] several remarks can be made. First, because unjustified enrichment in Lithuanian law is strictly subsidiary to the civil liability law, which covers all wrongs, there is virtually no residual space for the unjustified enrichment as a remedy for restitution of wrongs (*Eingriffskondiktion*), not even mentioning that unjustified enrichment is a quasi-contract and as such cannot be unlawful act. Disgorgement function is carried out by the restitutionary damages (LCC Article 6.249(2)), which is civil liability remedy. Second, although unjustified enrichment is a basic source of a primary recourse (*Ruckgriffskondiktion*), it is subsidiary and capable to create recourse obligations only where subrogation is not applicable. Lithuanian law provides broad array of instances where subrogation is taking effect, therefore leaving tiny space for a primary recourse based on the unjustified enrichment. Examples of such primary recourse is default recourse of the guarantor in the absence of agreement on subrogation (LCC Article

490. Judgment of the ECJ of 16 Dec. 2008 in the Case C47/07 (*Masdar (UK) v. Commission*).
491. *Lietuvos Aukščiausiojo Teismo Civilinių bylų skyriaus teisėjų kolegijos 2010 m. birželio 23 d. nutartis civilinėje byloje Nr. 3K-3-308/2010.*
492. Judgment of the Lithuanian Supreme Court of 10 May 2006 in the civil case No. 3K-3-196/2011.
493. Valentinas Mikelėnas. *Lietuvos Respublikos civilinio kodekso komentaras. Šeštoji knyga. Prievolių teisė.* Justitia, 2003, I t., p. 325–326.
494. Judgment of the Lithuanian Supreme Court of 29 Apr. 2016 in the civil case No e3K-7-89-378/2016.
495. *Von Caemmerer has distinguished* action de in rem verso *as falling into three categories: first, enrichment as a consequence of the commission of a wrong (*Eingriffskondiktion*); second, improvement of the property of another (*Verwendungskondiktion*); and third, cases in which someone extinguished the obligation of another (*Ruckgriffskondiktion*). See Paolo Gallo.* Unjust Enrichment: A Comparative Analysis. *The American Journal of Comparative Law, Vol. 40, p. 442.*

6.90);[496] the cases of vicarious liability of employer or hirer who has paid damages arising from wrongs of its employees or subordinates (LCC Article 6.280); right of social security institutions, which have paid insurance payments, against the person by whom the damage was caused, except in the cases where insurance premiums on behalf of the aggrieved person were paid by the same person who caused the damage (LCC Article 6.290),[497] etc. Third, improvement of the property of another (*Verwendungskondiktion*) is covered by the special rules on vindication (LCC Article 4.97), possessory action (LCC Article 4.34), performance not due (LCC Article 6.240) and lease (LCC Article 6.501), therefore the space for general enrichment action is significantly reduced, but not extinguished. For instance, such enrichment is used by the neighbour of communication constructed by the other neighbour,[498] improvement of property which was used on the basis of void lease contract and left uncompensated by the rules of restitution[499] and road servitude which serves in defendant's interest and which was achieved by the neighbour (plaintiff) during the expensive litigation with land owner. In any case, *actio de in rem verso*, may be efficient remedy to collect indirect enrichment where the *condictio indebiti* claim for a direct enrichment is precluded.[500]

§3. Performance Not Due

925. As was explained before, LCC Article 6.237 establishes general *condictio indebiti* claim, which is a ground for a general restitution of prestations (LCC Article 6.145). It is special claim with respect to general enrichment claim (LCC 6.242) but a general and therefore subsidiary claim with respect to instances for a special restitution of prestations (LCC Articles 1.80, 6.222, etc.). It means that general *condictio indebiti* claim, as ground for a restitution of prestations, occupies an intermediate position within the system of restitutionary remedies.

---

496. Judgment of the Lithuanian Supreme Court of 16 Nov. 2015 in the civil case No 3K-7-301-706/2015.
497. Judgments of the Lithuanian Supreme Court of 1 Oct. 2014 in the civil case No 3K-3-405/2014, of 12 Dec. 2014 in the civil case No 3K-3-552/2014 and of 23 Dec. 2014 in the civil case No 3K-3-564/2014.
498. Judgment of the Lithuanian Supreme Court of 4 Nov. 2002 in the civil case No 3K-3-1318/2002.
499. Judgment of the Lithuanian Supreme Court of 30 Jun. 2016 in the civil case No e3K-3-331-686/2016.
500. One bright example involves case where service contract for the benefit of a third party was declared void. At the time of judgment, the services were already supplied for a third party, but unpaid. The Supreme Court has struggled to apply the restitution, because in view of the Court it should be normally be applicable only where both parties exchange the performances. Instead, the Court has tried to apply the recovery on the basis of performance not due (which is also restitution), however, taking in regard that services were supplied not to the counterparty (customer), but to the third party, recovery from whom was not appropriate on the policy reasons, made conclusion that this remedy is also inapplicable. Finally, the Court has ruled that enrichment is indirect and should be recoverable by the general action on unjustified enrichment (LCC Art. 6.242). *See* Judgment of the Lithuanian Supreme Court of 29 Apr. 2016 in the civil case No e3K-7-89-378/2016. Leaving aside the critique of reasoning related to the restitution, overall, this judgment shows high flexibility and reach of the *actio de in rem verso* under Lithuanian law.

926. One should note that LCC Article 6.237 is labelled 'reception of property not due'. However, this wording is misleading on two points. First, in *condictio indebiti* situations as a quasi-contract (a lawful act in nature) stands not the reception (act of debtor), but the transfer (act of creditor). Reception may be unlawful, for example, where the receiving party is fraudulently silent about the error of paying party, in contrast with the transfer, which is lawful unilateral act made by the party in mistake.[501] If unlawful reception, not the lawful transfer, would be held as a source of restorative obligation, then *condictio indebiti* claim would be impossible at all (because *condictio indebiti* as any other quasi-contracts are lawful acts)[502] or at least subsidiary and restoration of performances would always be carried out by untypical for it damages remedy. This problem is absent where as a source of *condictio indebiti* obligation is an act of creditor, because there is no remedial subsidiarity for the acts of different persons: quasi-contractual act (transfer) of a creditor and a tortious act of a debtor.[503] Second, 'reception of property not due' covers not only transfer of property but also performance of services; therefore it is more accurate to name *condictio indebiti* as a 'performance not due'.

927. According to LCC Article 6.237, a person who without any legal ground by his actions or in any other manner intentionally or negligently, obtains something that he could not and ought not to have obtained is obliged to return the received benefit to the person on whose account it was received, except in cases provided for by the LCC. Accordingly, if a person mistakenly believing himself to be the debtor has paid the debt he was not bound to pay, he shall be entitled to demand the return of the paid sum from the person who received the payment. However, such right becomes extinct where in consequence of the payment the person has destroyed the document proving the debt. In such event the supposed debtor can claim the paid sum from the true debtor (LCC Article 6.238). The obligation to return the received benefit shall also arise where the grounds upon which the property is acquired become subsequently extinct (*condictio causa finita*). LCC Article 6.237 shall likewise apply with respect to the obligations the performance of which is not connected with a transfer of property but only with a supply of appropriate services, as well as in cases where the claim is connected with the recovery of a thing from illegal possession, or the restitution of performance resulting from an

501. Lawful creditor act leading to receipt of his property by the debtor was constantly stressed by the Supreme Court as a prerequisite to apply LCC Art. 6.237, thus supporting its quasi-contractual nature. *See* Judgments of the Lithuanian Supreme Court of 22 Feb. 2006 in the civil case No 3K-3-140/2006, of 26 Mar. 2008 in the civil case No 3K-3-166/2008, of 18 Jun. 2010 in the civil case No 3K-3-276/2010, of 10 Oct. 2011 in the civil case No 3K-3-372/2011, etc.

502. This feature of a performance not due, as a quasi-contract, was affirmed by the court in criminal case, where lawful character of *condictio indebiti* served as successful defence against the incrimination of fraudulent appropriation of mistakenly transferred funds to the bank customer. *See* Judgment of the Kaunas District Court of 18 Jan. 2013 in the civil case No 1A-72-317/2013.

503. Compare LCC Art. 6.237, for example, with Dutch BW Art. 6:203 and Quebec CC Art. 1491, which are much accurate on this point. According to Dutch BW Art. 6:203, a person who has given property to another without legal ground is entitled to reclaim it from the recipient as having been paid while not due. Quebec CC Art. 1491 states that payment made in error, or merely to avoid injury to the person making it while protesting that he owes nothing, obliges the person who receives it to make restitution.

invalid transaction, or the compensation for damage, or the repayments between the parties to an obligation, or with the supply of services to each other. Therefore, the more accurate is to label the object of LCC Article 6.237 claim, not the property, but performance.

928. It can be seen from above that as in case of general enrichment action, the definition of performance not due is poisoned with the element of fault. As it has been stressed in previous chapter, the element of fault for the characterisation of enrichment actions is controversial, because it immediately clashes with the concept of quasi-contract as lawful act and makes no sense why a person, who innocently enriched at the expense of another without any ground, may leave the enrichment for himself. Initially courts have applied fault element, expressly stating that property should be received by intent of negligence;[504] however, after initial application it was finally abandoned by the Supreme Court who ruled that obligation to restore property is not eliminated neither by good faith of defendant nor by the type of his actions (intent or negligence).[505] By such decision Lithuanian case law was aligned with position in the legal doctrine, which, as in case of *actio de in rem verso*, from very beginning has ignored the element of fault.[506] Therefore, according to the currently prevailing view, for the application of LCC Article 6.237 court must establish only three conditions and neither of them is connected with fault: first, the defendant has actually received the property or other performance; second, property or other performance was received without valid legal ground (cause) or such ground has extinguished; and third, property or other performance cannot be claimed by other remedies, such as vindication, possessory action, restitution of prestations, etc. Thus, the cause of *condictio indebiti* action is much easier for the plaintiff to establish than the cause of general enrichment action (*actio de in rem verso*).[507]

---

504. Judgments of the Lithuanian Supreme Court of 16 Dec. 2008 in the civil case No 3K-3-593/2008 and of 16 Mar. 2009 in the civil case No 3K-3-111/2009.
505. Judgment of the Lithuanian Supreme Court of 21 Feb. 2011 in the civil case No 3K-3-68/2011.
506. Valentinas Mikelėnas. *Lietuvos Respublikos civilinio kodekso komentaras. Šeštoji knyga. Prievolių teisė.* Justitia, 2003, I t., p. 317–320.
507. As one Dutch scholar points out, one may wonder why the *condictio indebiti* is present alongside the general enrichment action. An uncomplicated action for reclaiming on payment of the undue should continue to be available in the average case. The payer must have no more to show than his payment to the defendant and the absence of a legal ground for that payment. His claim is valid for restoration of the entire performance *in natura*, or, if restoration *in natura* is not possible, restoration of its value in money. He need not show that he was in fact harmed by the payment. The intricate questions to what extent the payer and the recipient are impoverished or enriched, are largely of no importance here. If, however, the claimant's conduct cannot be seen as payment, the uncomplicated *condictio indebiti* does not lie and he must resort to the more difficult general enrichment action. Under the general enrichment action he can only claim reparation of his damage, so, unlike the claimant in the *condictio indebiti*, he must show that he did in fact suffer damage. Likewise he will have to prove that the defendant was in fact enriched at his expense, and he cannot claim reparation in so far as his damage exceeds the enrichment. There is a further difference in the case that the performance may be restored *in natura*. While the obligee under payment not due has a right to restoration *in natura*, under the enrichment action an award of restoration *in natura* depends on the discretion of the court. *See* Jeroen M.J. Chorus. *Illegality and Restitution.* European Review of Private Law, Vol. 14, 2006, p. 445.

929. Pursuant to LCC Article 6.237, the unjustifiably obtained property must be restituted in kind. Where the unjustifiably received property has been lost or damaged, its true value expressed in terms of money that existed at the moment of the property acquisition, as well as any damages caused by subsequent change of the value of the property, must be compensated. The acquirer of the property shall be liable towards the aggrieved person for any deterioration or shortage, including that of accidental character, of the property acquired that occurred after the acquirer became aware or should have become aware of the unjust enrichment, or the reception of a thing not due. Until the moment indicated above, he shall be liable only for his intent or gross negligence. Where a person in good faith sells the benefit acquired, he shall be bound to return only the amount received for the property sold. Where a person who has received property not due gratuitously transfers the enrichment to a third person, the obligation to return such enrichment passes on to the third person (LCC Article 6.239). Thus, in Lithuanian law although *condictio indebiti* is a personal action, it may nevertheless involve mild proprietary effect – the remedy following the property (*ius persequendi*). In contrast, strictly personal remedy should not depend on the defendant retaining the benefit which he or she had received from the claimant.[508]

930. A person, who has received property without due legal grounds is not only bound to return it, but also reimburse in total the income that he has received or should have received from this property from the time he became aware or should have become aware that the property he received was not due. An interest at the rate of 5% per annum shall be payable for the sum of money received unfoundedly. This interest shall be calculated from the moment when the person became aware or should have become aware of the reception or saving of the money not due. If the recipient in good faith has accepted property not due by mistake, he also has the right to claim for reimbursement of the necessary expenses incurred for the maintenance of the unduly received property during the period indicated above. Such recipient forfeits the right to claim for reimbursement of the expenses if the person who has the right to recover that property relinquishes that right and leaves the property to the person who has received it unjustifiably. The person who has accepted property without any legal grounds and who has not warranted the maintenance of that property to the extent that a reasonable debtor would warrant shall be bound to reimburse for the decrease in the property that took place after the recipient became or ought to have become aware of the existence of his obligation to return the property. Where the nature of the unduly received property is such that it cannot be returned, the value of what was received or performed at the time of the receipt or performance must be reimbursed if the recipient has been enriched, or if he has asked to perform thereof, or if he has consented to perform a counteraction. Where a transaction is acknowledged null and void, and the performance cannot be evaluated in monetary terms, or the received cannot be returned due to its nature, an action for return or compensation may not be satisfied if this would be contrary to

508. Graham Virgo. *The Principles of the Law of Restitution.* 3 ed., Oxford University Press, 2015, p. 4.

the criteria of good faith, reasonableness and justice. If a person mistakenly believing himself to be the debtor has paid the debt he was not bound to pay, he shall be entitled to demand the return of the paid sum from the person who received the payment. The aforesaid right becomes extinct where in consequence of the payment the person has destroyed the document proving the debt. In such event the supposed debtor can claim the paid sum from the true debtor (LCC Article 6.240).

931. The defences against the *condictio indebiti* claim are established in LCC Article 6.241, according to which, the following performance cannot be recovered as received unduly: (1) property transferred for the purposes of performance of an obligation prior to the expiry of the time limit allotted for the performance of that obligation unless the source of the obligation provides for otherwise; (2) property transferred for the purposes of performance of an obligation after the expiry of prescription; (3) property transferred by a person who is aware of the absence of his duty to perform the obligation, or by a person who even though not bound to perform the obligation nevertheless makes the performance and where this conforms to the principles of good morals (case of *obligatio naturalis*); and (4) amounts paid unjustifiably as compensation for damage resulting from bodily damage or death, as well as salary or wages, or other payments equalled to the latter, also pensions and alimony, provided that the receiver did not act in bad faith or there was no mistake in the accountancy. Where a person, without there being a legal ground to do so, accepts a sum of money that is assigned to a third person who has no right to receive it and delivers this sum to that third person, he shall be relieved from his obligation to give the money back if he proves that he did not know and ought not to have known of the existence of the obligation to return the money, and that he could not deliver that sum of money to the third person who had the right to receive it. But apart from this and some other narrow instances, the change of position defence in general is not applicable against the restitution based on LCC Article 6.237.

Selected Bibliography

Agnė Jakaitė. *Civilinė atsakomybė esant ikisutartiniams santykiams.* Doctoral dissertation. Vilnius University, 2012.

Alan W. Mewett. *The Theory of Government Contracts.* McGill Law Journal, Vol. 5, 1959.

Alexandru Mihnea Angheni. *The Legal Nature of the Administration of the Property of Others.* The International Conference Education and Creativity for a Knowledge based Society – LAW, 2012, Titu Maiorescu University.

Andrius Kabišaitis. *Paslaugų sutartis – Lietuvos civilinės teisės naujovė.* Justitia, 2003, Nr. 5(47).

Andrius Smaliukas, Vaida Pacenkaitė. *Ultra vires doktrina naujajame Lietuvos Respublikos civiliniame kodekse. In.* Šiuolaikinės civilinės teisės raidos tendencijos ir perspektyvos. Justitia, 2007.

Andrius Smaliukas. *Property and Trust Law in Lithuania.* Wolters Kluwer, 2017.

Andrius Smaliukas; Gintautas Šulija. Report on Lithuania. *In. Regulating Unfair Banking Practices in Europe – The Case of Personal Suretyships*, Oxford University Press, 2010.

Aristides N. Hatzis *Rights and Obligations of Third Parties. In.* Encyclopedia of Law and Economics, Vol. III. The Regulation of Contracts, Cheltenham, Edward Elgar, 2000.

Arthur M. Cathcart. *Nature and Extent of Quasi-Contractual Obligations. In.* Modern American Law, Vol. 7. American Law Blackstone Institute, 1921.

Asta Dambrauskaitė, Agnė Tikniūtė, *et al. Lyginamoji sutarčių teisė: Lietuva europiniame kontekste.* Justitia, 2013.

Asya Ostroukh. *Russian Society and its Civil Codes*: *A Long Way to Civilian Civil Law.* Journal of Civil Law Studies, Vol. 6, No 1, 2013.

Valentinas Mikelėnas, Vytautas Mizaras, Aurimas Brazdeikis, *et al. Civilinė teisė. Bendroji dalis.* Justitia, 2009.

B.S. Markesinis, Hannes Unberath, Angus Johnston, Lord Bingham, Gunter Hirsch. *The German Law of Contract: A Comparative Treatise.* Hart Publishing, 2006.

B.S. Markesinis, Hannes Unberath, Angus Johnston, Lord Bingham, Gunter Hirsch. *The German Law of Contract: A Comparative Treatise.* Hart Publishing, 2006.

Barry Nicholas. *French Law of Contract.* Butterworths, 1982.

Bénédicte Fauvarque-Cosson, Denis Mazeaud, *et al. European Contract Law: Materials for a Common Frame of Reference: Terminology, Guiding Principles, Model Rules.* Sellier, 2008.

Selected Bibliography

Benedicte Fauvarque-Cosson, Hugh Beale, Jacobien Rutgers, Denis Tallon, Stefan Vogenauer. *Cases, Materials and Text on Contract Law.* 2nd ed., Hart Publishing, 2010.

Bryan A. Garner, *et al. Black's Law Dictionary.* 9th ed., 2009.

Catherine Elliott, Frances Quinn. *Contract Law.* 7th ed., Pearson Longman, 2009.

Charles Wild, Stuart Weinstein. *Smith and Keenans Company Law.* 14th Ed., Longman, 2009.

Christian Von Bar, Eric Clive, *et al. Principles, Definitions and Model Rules of European Private Law. Draft Common Frame of Reference (DCFR).* Full ed., Sellier, 2009.

Christian von Bar, Walter de Gruyter. *Benevolent Intervention in Another's Affairs.* Sellier, 2006.

Christopher Osakwe. *Anatomy of the 1994 Civil Codes of Russia and Kazakhstan: a Biopsy of the Economic Constitutions of Two Post-Soviet Republics.* Notre Dame Law Review, Vol. 73 1998.

Christopher Osakwe. *Modern Russian Law of Contracts: A Functional Analysis.* Loyola of Los Angeles International and Comparative Law Review, Vol. 24, 2002.

Colin C. Turpin. *International Encyclopedia of Comparative Law.* Vol. VII, ch. 4, 1982, Tübingen: Mohr (Siebeck), The Hague: Nijhoff.

Daina Petrauskaitė. *Lietuvos Respublikos civilinio kodekso komentaras. Ketvirtoji knyga. Daiktinė teisė. XII skyrius. Įkeitimas (5).* Justitia, 2004, No. 5 (53).

Dalia Mikelėnienė, Valentinas Mikelėnas. *Lithuanian Contract Law.* International Encyclopedia of Laws. The Hague, Kluwer Law International, 2004.

Dangutė Ambrasienė, *et al. Civilinė teisė. Prievolių teisė.* Mykolo Romerio Universitetas, 2004.

Dangutė Ambrasienė, Indrė Kryžiūtė. *Atsakomybės už preliminariosios sutarties nevykdymą problemos.* Jurisprudencija, Nr. 19(2), 2012.

Daniel Girsberger, Paulius Zapolskis. *Fundamental Alteration of the Contractual Equilibrium under Hardship Exemption.* Jurisprudence. 2012, 19(1).

Deborah DeMott. *Causation in the Fiduciary Realm.* Boston University Law Review, Vol. 91.

E. Allan Farnsworth. *Precontractual Liability and Preliminary Agreements: Fair Dealing and Failed Negotiations.* Columbia Law Review, Vol. 87, No. 2, 1987.

Edita Borevičienė. *Sutartis trečiojo asmens naudai.* Doctoral dissertation. Mykolas Romeris University, 2013.

Ejan Mackaay. *The Civil Law of Contract. In* Contract law and economics. Encyclopedia of Law and Economics. 2 ed. Edward Elgar Publishing, 2011.

Eleonora C. Melato. *Precontractual Liability. In* Contract law and economics. Encyclopedia of Law and Economics. 2 ed. Edward Elgar Publishing, 2011.

Ernst Kramer, Thomas Probst. *International Encyclopedia of Comparative Law.* Vol. 7. *Contracts in general. Defects in the Contracting Process.* Martinus Nijhoff Publishers, 2001.

Francesco Giglio. *The Foundations of Restitution for Wrongs.* Hart Publishing, 2007.

G.E. Glos. *The Doctrine of Unjust Enrichment in Soviet Law.* The University of Malaya Law Review, Vol. 3 No. 1, 1961.

Gediminas Dominas, Valentinas Mikelėnas. *Tarptautinis komercinis arbitražas.* Vilnius: Justitia, 1995.

George M. Cohen. *Implied Terms and Interpretation in Contract Law. In.* Encyclopedia of Law and Economics, Vol. III. The Regulation of Contracts, Cheltenham, Edward Elgar, 2000.

George Triantis. *Unforeseen Contingencies. Risk Allocation in Contracts. Encyclopedia of Law and Economics.* Edward Elgar, 2000.

Graham Stephenson. *Sourcebook on tort law.* 2nd Ed., Cavendish Publishing Limited, 2000.

Graham Virgo. *The Principles of the Law of Restitution.* 3 ed., Oxford University Press, 2015.

Grant Gilmore. *The Death of Contract.* Columbus: Ohio State University Press, 1974.

Gytis Kuncevičius. *The institute of administrative contract and its theoretical grounding.* Summary of Doctoral Dissertation Social Sciences, Law (01 S), Mykolas Romeris University.

H.L.E. Verhagen. *Absence of Basis and Unjustified Enrichment in Dutch Law: The Condictio Indebiti as an Enrichment Action.* Restitution Law Review, Vol. 12, 2004.

Helmut Koziol; *et al. Principles of European Tort Law. Volume 5. Unification of Tort Law: Damages.* Kluwer Law International, 2001.

J. Bell, S. Boyron and S. Whittaker. *Principles of French Law.* 2nd ed., Oxford University Press, 2008.

J.P. Van Niekerk. *Salvage and Negotiorum Gestio: Exploratory Reflections on the Jurisprudential Foundation and Classification of the South African Law of Salvage.* Acta Juridica, 1992.

Jack Beatson, Eltjo Schrage, *et al. Cases, Materials and Text on Unjustified Enrichment.* Hart Publishing, 2003.

Jan Dalhuisen. *Dalhuisen on transnational comparative, commercial, financial, and trade law. Vol. 2: Contract and Movable Property Law.* 4th Ed., Hart Publishing, 2010.

Jan M. Barendrecht; et al. *Service Contracts. Principles of European Law.* Sellier, 2007.

Jan M. Smits. *Contract Law: A Comparative Introduction.* Edward Elgar Publishing, 2014.

Jason P. Bergeron. *Watkins v. Freeway Motors - A Need to Clarify the Principle of Novation.* Louisiana Law Review Vol. 58, 1998.

Jeroen M.J. Chorus. *Illegality and Restitution.* European Review of Private Law, Vol. 14, 2006.

Joel Seligman, Louis Loss, Troy Paredes. *Securities regulation.* 4 ed. Wolters Kluwer Law & Business/Aspen Publishers, 2006.

Johann Andreas Dieckmann. *Normative Basis of Subrogation and Comparative Law: Select Explanations in the Common Law, Civil Law and in Mixed Legal Systems of the Guarantor's Right to Derivative Recourse.* Tulane European and Civil Law Forum, Vol. 27, 2012.

John E.C. Brierley; Roderick A. Macdonal (eds). *Quebec Civil Law: An Introduction to Quebec Private Law.* E. Montgomery Publications, 1993.

Selected Bibliography

Justas Sakavičius. *Turto patikėjimo teisės problematika Lietuvoje.* Doctoral thesis. Social sciences, law (01S), Mykolas Romeris University, 2012.

Konrad Zweigert; Hein Kötz. *An Introduction to Comparative Law.* Clarendon Press, 1998.

Laurynas Didžiulis, Janina Stripeikienė. *Aktualūs finansinės nuomos (lizingo) instituto taikymo klausimai. In.* Privatinės teisės doktrina ir praktika: Liber Amicorum Vytautui Pakalniškiui. Vilnius: Mykolas Romeris University, 2014.

Laurynas Didžiulis. *Fiduciarinių pareigų instituto kilmė, esmė ir recepcija.* Teisė: Mokslo darbai, 2014.

Laurynas Didžiulis. *Finansų tarpininkų profesinė civilinė atsakomybė, kaip investuotojų apsaugos priemonė.* Doctoral thesis. Social sciences, law (01S). Vilnius: Vilnius university, 2014.

Laurynas Didžiulis. *Investicinių pavedimų priėmimo, perdavimo ir vykdymo civilinis teisinis kvalifikavimas.* Teisė: Mokslo darbai. Vol. 100, 2016.

Laurynas Didžiulis. *Numatomo sutarties pažeidimo doktrina: samprata, kvalifikavimo pagrindai ir teisinis poveikis.* Teisės problemos, 2007, Nr. 1.

Laurynas Didžiulis, *EU Digital Content Directive And Evolution Of Lithuanian Contract Law*, 12 Journal of Intellectual Property, Information Technology and E-Commerce Law, 2021.

Leonas V. Papirtis, *et al. Civilinė teisė: bendroji dalis.* Vol. II, Mykolas Romeris University, 2005.

Lina Aleknaitė. *The Prospects of Asset Securitization in Lithuania in the Light of Experiences from the United States of America and Europe.* Vilniaus universiteto leidykla, 2010.

Lina Mikalonienė. *Bendrovės įstatų teisinė prigimtis.* Verslo ir teisės aktualijos. Mokslo darbai. 2011, Nr. 6 (2).

Lionel Smith. *Property, Subsidiarity and Unjust Enrichment. In.* Unjustified Enrichment: Key Issues in Comparative Perspective. Cambridge University Press 2004.

Lionel Smith. *The Province of the Law of Restitution.* Canadian Bar Review, Vol. 71, 1992.

M. Stuart Madden. *Tort Law Through Time and Culture: Themes of Economic Efficiency.* Exploring tort law. Cambridge University Press, 2005.

Marcel C.A. van den Nieuwenhuijzen; *et al. Financial Law in the Netherlands.* Kluwer Law International, 2010.

Marius Kalanta. *Kapitalizmo Lietuvoje tipologinė analizė institucinės kaitos diskurso aspektu.* Doctoral Dissertation. Social sciences, Sociology (05 S). Vytautas Magnus University. Kaunas, 2015.

Martin Boodman. *Third-Party Beneficiaries in Quebec Civil Law.* Canadian Business Law Journal, Vol. 35, 2001.

Matthias Haentjens, Pierre de Gioia-Carabellese. *European Banking and Financial Law.* Routledge, 2015.

Matthias Haentjens. *Harmonisation of Securities Law: Custody and Transfer of Securities in European Private Law.* Doctoral thesis. Amsterdam University, 2007.

Michael Joachim Bonell, Roy Goode, Reinhard Zimmermann, *et al. UNIDROIT Principles of International Commercial Contracts. Text and Official Comment.* International Institute for the Unification of Private Law, Rome, 2016.

Michel Tison. *The Civil Law Effects of MiFID in a Comparative Law Perspective.* Ghent University, Financial Law Institute Working Paper No. WP 2010-05.

Michele Graziadei; Ugo Mattei; Lionel Smith. *Commercial Trusts in European Commercial Trusts in European Private Law. Cambridge University Press, 2005.*

Michelle Cumyn. *Responsibility for Another's Debt: Suretyship, Solidarity, and Imperfect Delegation.* McGill Law Journal, Vol. 55, No 2, 2010.

Mindaugas Maksimaitis, Stasys Vansevičius. *Lietuvos valstybės ir teisės istorija.* Justitia, 1997.

Mindaugas Maksimaitis. *Pabaltijo gubernijų vietinių įstatymų sąvadas.* Teisė: Mokslo darbai, t. 34, 2000.

Olimpiad S. Ioffe. *Soviet civil law.* Kluwer Academic Publishers, 1988.

Olympiad S. Ioffe. *International Encyclopedia of Comparative Law.* Vol. 7, *Contracts in general. Contract in the socialist economy.* Brill Archive, 1981.

P. Garant and J. Garant. *Droit administratif.* 6th ed., 2010.

P. Maggs, *The Civil Codes of Central Eurasia: A Comparison. In Proceedings of the Central Eurasian Studies Society.* Fourth Annual Conference. Cambridge, 2003.

P. Rasimavičius, V. Staskonis, *et al. Civilinė teisė: vadovėlis.* Kaunas: Vijusta, 1998.

P.A. Hall, D. Soskice. *Varieties of Capitalism: The Institutional Foundations of Comparative Advantage.* Oxford: Oxford Scholarship Online, 2003.

Paolo Gallo. *Unjust Enrichment: A Comparative Analysis.* The American Journal of Comparative Law, Vol. 40.

Paul G. Mahoney. *Contract Remedies: General.* Encyclopedia of Law and Economics. Vol. III. The Regulation of Contracts. Cheltenham, Edward Elgar, 2000.

Paulius Miliauskas. *Company Law Aspects of Shareholders' Agreements in Listed Companies.* Doctoral dissertation. Vilnius, 2014.

Pedro A. Malavet. *Counsel for the Situation: The Latin Notary, A Historical and Comparative Model. In.* Hastings International and Comparative Law Review, Vol. 19, 1996.

Phillip Wood. *Principles of International Insolvency.* Sweet & Maxwell, 2007;

Pierre Widmer; *et al. Unification of Tort Law: Fault.* Kluwer Law International, 2005.

R.S. Bevzenko. *Battle for the Law of Real Security: The Third Step in Reforming Russian Pledge Law.* Civil Law Herald, 2015, Vol. 15. Issue 2.

Ralph M. Wrobel. *From Independence to the Euro Introduction: Varieties of Capitalism in the Baltic States. In.* Central and Eastern European Journal of Management and Economics. Vol. 3, No. 1, 2015.

Reinhard Zimmermann. *The Law of Obligations: Roman Foundations of the Civilian Tradition Roman foundations.* Oxford University Press, 1996.

Reinhard Zimmermann. *Unjustified Enrichment: The Modern Civilian Approach.* Oxford Journal of Legal Studies,

Richard Craswell. *Contract Law: General Theories In.* Encyclopedia of Law and Economics, Vol. III. The Regulation of Contracts, Cheltenham, Edward Elgar, 2000.

Richard Stone. *The Modern Law of Contract.* 7th Ed., 2009.

Rūta Lazauskaitė. *Contractual Liability Limitations that Depend on the Will of the*

Parties. Summary of Doctoral Dissertation. Vilnius: Mykolas Romeris University, 2011.
Saul Litvinoff. *Louisiana Civil Law Treatise. Law Of Obligations*. 2d ed., 2017, § 16.20.
Saul Litvinoff. *Subrogation*. Louisiana Law Review, Vol. 50, 1990.
Scott E. Masten. Contractual Choice *In*. Encyclopedia of Law and Economics, Vol. III. The Regulation of Contracts, Cheltenham, Edward Elgar, 2000.
Sjef Van Erp, Bram Akkermans; *et al. Cases, Materials and Text on Property Law*. Hart Publishing, 2012.
Solene Rowan. *The New French Law of Contract. In*. International & Comparative Law Quarterly. British Institute of International and Comparative Law, 2017.
Stasys Drazdauskas. *Bendrosios sutarčių teisės vienodinimo įtaka Lietuvos sutarčių teisei*. Doctoral dissertation (social sciences, law (01 S), Vilnius University, 2011).
Stasys Vansevičius. *Valstybės ir teisės teorija: mokomoji priemonė*. Justitia, 2000
Stefan Grundmann. *Trust and Treuhand at the End of the 20th Century. Key problems and Shift of Interests*. The American Journal of Comparative Law, Vol. 47, 1999.
Stephen_Griffin, Michael Hirst, Peter Walton. *Company Law: Fundamental Principles*. Prentice Hall, 2005.
T. Scott Leo. *The Construction Contract Surety and Some Suretyship Defenses*. William & Mary Law Review, Vol. 34 1993.
Tamar T Frankel. *Fiduciary Law*. Oxford University Press, 2010.
Ulrich Magnus, Hans W. Micklitz. *Comparative Analysis* of *National Liability Systems* for *Remedying Damage Caused* by *Defective Consumer Services*. Final report. Institut für Europäisches Wirtschafts und Verbraucherrecht, 2004.
Valentinas Mikelėnas, Alfonsas Vileita, *et al. Lietuvos Respublikos civilinio kodekso komentaras. Pirmoji knyga. Bendrosios nuostatos*. Justitia, 2001.
Valentinas Mikelėnas, Armanas Abramavičius. *Autotransporto priemonių valdytoju teisinė atsakomybė*. Registrų centras, 2010.
Valentinas Mikelenas, *et al. Civilinė teisė. Bendroji dalis*. Justitia, 2009.
Valentinas Mikelėnas, Vytautas Nekrošius, Egidijus Laužikas. *Civilinio proceso teisė. T. 1*. Justitia, 2003.
Valentinas Mikelėnas. *Civilinės atsakomybės problemos: lyginamieji aspektai*. Justitia, 1995.
Valentinas Mikelėnas. *Lietuvos Respublikos civilinio kodekso komentaras. Šeštoji knyga. Prievolių teisė*. Justitia, 2003.
Valentinas Mikelėnas. *Prievolių teisė. Pirmoji dalis*. Justitia: Vilnius, 2002.
Valentinas Mikelėnas. *Sutarčių teisė. Bendrieji sutarčių teisės klausimai: lyginamoji studija*. Vilnius: Justitia, 1996.
Valentinas Mikelėnas. *The Influence of Instruments of Harmonisation of Private Law upon the Reform of Civil Law in Lithuania*. Juridica International, 2008.
Valentinas Mikelėnas. *The Main Features of the New Lithuanian Contract Law System Based on the Civil Code of 2000*. Juridica International, Vol. 10, 2005.
Valentinas Mikelenas. *Unification and Harmonisation of Law at the Turn of the Millennium: The Lithuanian Experience*. Uniform Law Review, Vol. 5, Issue 2, 2000.

Valerio Forti. *Comparing American Trust and French Fiducie.* The Columbia Journal of European Law, Vol. 17, 2011.

Viktorija Budreckienė. *Teisminės komercinių sutarčių turinio kontrolės ribos.* Doctoral thesis. Mykolas Romeris University, 2016,.

Vincent Karim. *Les obligations.* 4e éd. Montréal: Wilson & Lafleur, 2015.

Vivienne Harpwood. *Modern tort law.* 7th. Ed., Routledge-Cavendish, 2009.

Vytautas Mizaras, Gintautas Bartkus *et al. Lietuvos Respublikos civilinio kodekso komentaras. Antroji knyga. Asmenys.* Justitia, 2002.

Vytautas Mizaras. *Lizingo sutarties sampratos aiškinimas pagal Civilinį kodeksą.* Justitia. 2003.

Vytautas Mizaras. *Pirkimo-pardavimo sutartinių santykių reguliavimas Civiliniame kodekse.* Justitia, 2003.

Vytautas Pakalniškis, *et al. Daiktinė teisė.* Mykolas Romeris University.

Walter Van Gerven, Pierre Larouche; Jeremy Lever. *Cases, Materials and Text on National, Supranational and International Tort Law.* Oxford: Hart Publishing, 2000.

Willem H Van Boom; et al. *On the Intersection Between Tort Law and Regulatory Law – A Comparative Analysis.* Tort and regulatory law. Springer-Verlag/Wien, 2007.

William H. Angus. *Restitution in Canada since the Deglman Case.* Canadian Bar Review, Vol. 42, 1964.

Zenonas Norkus. *Lietuva tarp Estijos ir Slovėnijos: dėl pokomunistinio kapitalizmo tipologinės diferenciacijos. In.* Politologija, Nr. 1 (49).

Selected Bibliography

Index

The numbers here refer to paragraph numbers.

ompliance